BUSINESS
INFORMATION
SYSTEMS

Analysis, Design and Practice

To Julia, Edmund and James

BUSINESS INFORMATION SYSTEMS

Analysis, Design and Practice

THIRD EDITION

GRAHAM CURTIS
University of East London

ADDISON-WESLEY LONGMAN PUBLISHING COMPANY

Harlow, England ● Reading, Massachusetts ● Menlo Park, California

New York ● Don Mills, Ontario ● Amsterdam ● Bonn ● Sydney ● Singapore

Tokyo ● Madrid ● San Juan ● Milan ● Paris ● Mexico City ● Seoul ● Taipei

Acknowledgements

We are grateful to the following copyright holders for permission to reproduce copyright material.

The British Museum for permission to reproduce the web page shown in Figure 5.6 © The British Museum. David Harris for permission to reproduce the Pegasus Mail screen shots shown in Figures 3.13 and 5.3. Digital Equipment Corporation for permission to reproduce the main page of the AltaVista web page shown in Figure 5.7 (http://www. altavista.digital.com). AltaVista and the AltaVista logo and the Digital logo are trademarks of Digital Equipment Corporation. Microsoft Corporation for permission to reprint the screen shots in Figures 3.13 and 5.6. Microsoft and Microsoft Corporation are trademarks and trade names of Microsoft Corporation. Netscape Communications Corporation for permission to reproduce the web page shown in Figure 5.7. Netscape Communication Corporation has not authorized, sponsored, or endorsed, or approved this publication and is not responsible for its content. Netscape and the Netscape Communications Corporation, are trademarks and trade names of Netscape Communications Corporation. All other product names and/or logos are trademarks of their respective owners. United Nations for permission to reproduce their world-wide web home page (http://www.un.org) shown in Figures 5.4 and 5.5

The publisher has made every effort to obtain permission to reproduce material in this book from the appropriate source. If there are any errors or omissions please contact the publisher who will make suitable acknowledgement in the reprint.

Preface

Recent years have witnessed an increase in the use of information technology – so much so that it has rapidly permeated the organization at every level. There is a growing need for those interested in business, management or accountancy to understand the nature of this technology and the way it can best be harnessed to provide information for business functions. This text aims to examine and explain:

- the nature of information and its use in managerial decision making;
- the role of the information system within organizational strategy;
- how recent developments in information technology have been accompanied by the rise of end-user computing in business;
- the way that information is organized, stored and processed by modern information technology as viewed from the interests of a business user;
- how developments in networks and the Internet have made an impact on business;
- the process of analysis and design of a business information system.

Readership

The book is designed as a core text for those undertaking an information systems course as part of a degree or HND in Business Studies or a related field. It is also recommended for second/third-year undergraduate Business Information Systems modules in Computer Science courses. The book will be suitable for professional courses run by the major accountancy bodies and the Institute of Data Processing Management (IDPM). It is also appropriate for conversion courses at the Masters Level or for MBA level modules in information systems. It requires minimal prior knowledge of information technology though an understanding of the basic functions of a business organization is assumed.

Content

It is impossible to appreciate the way that information systems can aid the realization of business objectives unless a basic understanding is obtained both of the information technology, in its broadest sense, and of the way information systems are designed. The level of understanding needed is not to the same depth as that required of a computer specialist. It must be sufficiently comprehensive, however, to enable those in business to assess the opportunities, limitations and major issues surrounding modern business information systems.

Chapter 1 introduces the reader to the idea of information and its relation to management decision making. After covering essential systems concepts an overview of the structure and purpose of a management information system is explained.

Chapter 2 begins by explaining the central ideas behind business strategic planning. The role of the information system is identified in this process. Various strategic uses of information systems, such as their use as a competitive weapon, are explored.

Chapter 3 explains the basic hardware, software and communications components in a business information system. The reader who is familiar with elementary computer science to A-level may omit most of these sections.

Chapter 4 begins by examining the central notions behind distributed computing and its organizational benefits. The latter part of the chapter examines networks and their position within business. Electronic data interchange and its advantages are explored.

Chapter 5 concentrates on recent developments in global networks, especially the Internet. The World Wide Web and its impact on business are examined.

Chapter 6 explains the central ideas behind decision support systems and their development through prototyping. The relation to and role of end-user computing is examined. Human–computer interaction is treated in later sections of the chapter.

Chapter 7 introduces files and file processing, file organization and access in a business system. The chapter highlights the limitations of a file-based approach to data storage and explains the role of databases and database technology in overcoming these. Major data models – hierarchical, network and relational – are compared.

Chapter 8 is a largely self-contained chapter on control in business information systems. It emphasises controls that are not technologically based as well as those implemented through the use of the computer. The need for a risk assessment and control strategy is stressed.

Chapters 9 through to 14 explain, by use of a case study, the stages involved in the development of an information system. The emphasis is on analysis and overall design of the information system rather than detailed design and implementation. The approach taken is in line with many structured methodologies. Both process analysis and modelling and data analysis and modelling are treated extensively.

Chapter 15 provides alternatives to the linear life-cycle approach covered in the previous chapters. Earlier sections include a critique of 'hard' approaches to systems analysis and introduce the 'soft' approaches of Checkland and of the socio-technical school of participative analysis and design. This is covered because it is felt important that the reader should appreciate the scope and limitations of structured methodologies. An introduction to the central concepts of object-oriented methods of analysis and design and of CASE in the development of business systems is also covered. Rapid Applications Development is introduced as an important development approach.

Chapters 16 and 17 provide an explanation of the core ideas behind expert systems and their development. Chapter 16 deals with the storage and use of knowledge in expert systems. The increasing importance of expert systems in business and the involvement of business personnel in their design is reflected in the coverage given in this text. The central ideas and uses of expert systems are first explained. More detailed aspects of knowledge representation and inferencing are covered in later sections of the chapter. Expert systems development is sufficiently different from the design of traditional information systems that it is treated separately. This is achieved in Chapter 17 with prototyping as the development method.

Structure

Although it is intended that the book be treated as a whole and read in sequence, different readers have different interests.

Business perspective: Those interested in information systems and their development from a business perspective might well read Chapters 1, 2, 5, 9 and 15 first.

Development perspective: Chapters 9 through to 15 can be taken as a more or less self-contained section on information systems analysis and design, with the reader being able to dip into previous chapters as it is felt necessary. Similarly Chapters 16 and 17 taken together are a useful introduction to the central ideas lying behind expert systems and their development.

Technical perspective: For those wishing a technical introduction to business information technology, networks, data storage and control, Chapters 3, 4, 6, 7 and 8 can be approached first.

Each chapter contains an initial brief summary of the forthcoming chapter content. This is followed by the main body of the text and, finally, a more extensive summary of topics covered. There are numerous questions at the end of each chapter. These fall into three types. There are straightforward revision questions, which do no more than test the reader's understanding of the text; there are problems that require the reader to apply concepts or techniques covered in the text to a described situation; and there are discussion questions where the reader is expected to apply his or her understanding of the text to a wider business or social context. Also at the end of each chapter are selected references for further reading. Each recommended text or article is generally accompanied by a short description indicating the area it covers and the type of reader for which it is most appropriate.

Third edition changes

This text differs from the second edition in a number of ways. A new chapter on the Internet and business has been added. The chapters on files and on databases have been amalgamated as Chapter 7. In doing this some of the more detailed descriptions of forms of file organization and access have been omitted. The chapter on strategy has been rewritten to provide a more coherent framework for considering approaches to strategy (as outlined in Figure 2.2). Rapid Applications Development has been added to Chapter 15. There have also been numerous minor additions and omissions to bring the book into line with technological developments over the three years since the last edition. Though the book has less pages the content length is about the same – the new format saving forests!

Acknowledgements

I would like to thank colleagues at the University of East London and elsewhere who have provided useful comments on earlier drafts; in particular the comments of anonymous reviewers have been invaluable.

Graham Curtis
March 1998

Trademark notice

Apple Computers™ is a trademark of Apple Computer Incorporated

Apollo™ is a trademark of Apollo Computer Inc

ART™ is a trademark of Inference Corporation

CP/M™ is a trademark of Digital Research

Crystal™ and Data Protection Advisor™ are trademarks of Intelligent Environments Ltd

dBASE™ is a trademark of Ashton-Tate Incorporated

DB2™, IBM 650™, IBM 360™, IBM PC™, IBC PC/AT™, IBM PS/2™, IBM™, IBM Information Management System (IMS)™, IBM Business Systems Planning Methodology™, QBE™ and RDB™ are trademarks of International Business Machines Incorporated

DEC™, DEC 20™, VAX™ and VMS™ and Xcon™ are trademarks of Digital Equipment Corporation

Ethernet™ is a trademark of Dec, Intel and Xerox

Excel™, MS-DOS™, Multiplan™, PC-DOS™ and Windows™ are trademarks of Microsoft Corporation

Expert Edge™ is a trademark of Helix Expert Systems Ltd

Expertech Xi Plus™ is a trademark of Expertech Ltd

EXPRESS™ is a trademark of Management Decision Systems Inc

FOCUS™ is a trademark of Application Builders Inc

Goldworks™ is a trademark of Gold Hill Computers Inc

IDMS™ is a trademark of Cullinet Corporation

IFPS™ is a trademark of Execucom Systems Corporation

Intel™ is a trademark of Intel Corporation

Knowledge Engineering Environment (KEE)™ is a trademark of Intellicorp

Leonardo™ is a trademark of Creative Logic Limited

Lotus® and 1–2–3® are trademarks of Lotus Development Corporation

MACSYMA™ and SYMBOLICS™ are trademarks of Symbolics Incorporated

OPS5™ is a trademark of Verac Inc

ORACLE™ is a trademark of Oracle Corporation Inc

Prestel™ is a trademark of British Telecom

PROSPECTOR™ is a trademark of SRI International

Savoir™ is a trademark of ISI Limited

SUN™ is a trademark of Sun Microsystems Inc

Supercalc™ is a trademark of Computer Associates International Inc

UNIVAC-1™ is a trademark of Unysis

UNIX™ is a trademark of AT&T

VisiCalc™ is a trademark of Visicorp

Information Systems

This chapter covers three interrelated areas – information, systems and information systems. Information is considered in its role of aiding business decisions. By studying the nature of decisions important characteristics of information can be identified. Models of decision making, the cognitive background of decision makers and the levels of managerial activity associated with management decisions are all considered. Properties of business information are developed in terms of the kinds of decision taken and the types of decision taker involved. The provision of information within an organization has an associated cost. To justify this expenditure the information must be of value. The idea of information value, both qualitative and quantitative, is covered.

The framework of a systems approach is used in understanding the information requirements of a complex organization. Characteristics of systems and a systems approach are explained in the second part of the chapter. The ideas of information and a system are put together in developing the concept of a **management information system** (MIS). This is viewed as a collection of information subsystems interacting with a corporate database. Difficulties in the design of these information systems are considered by outlining five distinct approaches towards MIS design. Finally the importance of informal information for decision taking within organizations is stressed.

1.1 Introduction

The pattern of employment has altered radically in the UK over the last two centuries (see Figure 1.1). There was a decline in the importance of agriculture as a source of employment brought on by the industrialization during the early and middle parts of the

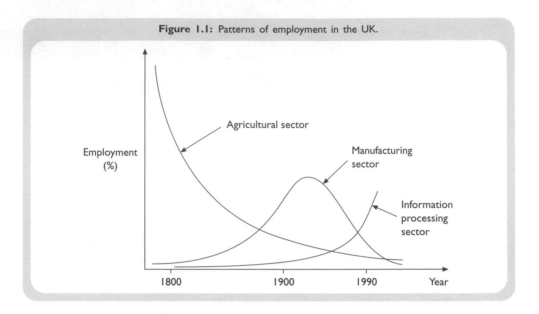

Figure 1.1: Patterns of employment in the UK.

nineteenth century. This was followed by a steady increase in the percentage of the workforce employed in manufacturing, which reached a peak in the early decades of this century. Since the nineteenth century the decline in manufacturing employment has been taken up by two sectors – the service sector and the information sector. By far the fastest-growing of these is the information sector.

Many occupations are now almost exclusively concerned with the handling, processing, provision or transmission of information. Included in these would be jobs in insurance, banking, accountancy, and central and local government. Anyone employed in the postal and telecommunications industries is directly or indirectly involved in the transmission of information. Other areas such as travel, retailing, the police and the armed forces all rely on a greater provision of information than at any time in the past. In manufacturing a declining percentage of the workforce is involved in the production process and an increasing percentage is employed in the processing of information.

What has led to this burgeoning of the information sector? On the supply side the development of faster, cheaper and more flexible technology for information processing (computers) and information transmission (telecommunications) have enabled the information sector to grow. More information can now be provided more quickly and cheaply than before. On the demand side the complexity and volatility of market forces means that businesses require more targeted and more current information to gain a competitive advantage and survive. Externally, they need to be up to date with market preferences, competitors' prices, and the supply and the cost of finance. Internally, pressures to maintain profitability or efficiency require instant information to monitor and control the continuing functioning of the organization.

This book is about information systems for business. The purpose of this chapter is to provide a general understanding of the idea of information, the concept of a system and, putting the two together, to provide an understanding of the nature of an information system for a business.

1.1.1 Data and information

Before we can understand the idea of a business information system it is necessary to look at both the concept of information and the concept of a system. In this section and the subsequent two sections the topic of information and its general characteristics as applied to business are covered.

Many definitions have been proposed for the term **information**. The one that will be used here is that:

- Information is data processed for a purpose.

A business deals with a wide variety of data. Some of this concerns financial transactions. An example of an item of transaction data is the record of the sale of a product to a customer by the business. This fact might be recorded on a piece of paper, such as in a sales day book, or as a series of coded magnetic impressions on a computer disk. However, it is not information until it undergoes some sort of processing and the results of the processing are communicated for a particular purpose. For instance:

1. The record of the amount of the sale may be aggregated with other sales amounts and the result transferred to a debtors' control account. This in turn will form part of a trial balance sheet and a final balance sheet to be presented to shareholders. The purpose of this processing is to provide a summarized snapshot picture of the state of the assets and liabilities of the business.

2. The sales data may also be classified by customer, aggregated with the current balance of the customer and the result compared with a credit limit assigned to the customer. The purpose is to alert the credit control manager that action may be necessary if the credit limit is exceeded.

Data, as given in the example, is the record of an event or a fact. The information derived from this data is used for making decisions, of which planning decision and control decisions are the most important.

1.1.2 Data processes

Data that is formally handled in a business may undergo complex processing prior to presentation and use as information. However complex, though, the total processing can be broken down into simple steps. The types of basic process are:

- classification of data
- rearranging/sorting data
- summarizing/aggregating data
- performing calculations on data
- selection of data.

Examples of each are shown in Table 1.1. In as far as these basic processes are governed by rules they are therefore suitable for a computerized system.

Table 1.1: Examples of types of data process.

Type of data process	Example
Classification of data	Transaction data may be classified as invoice data, payment data, order data
Rearranging/sorting data	Data on employees may be ordered according to ascending employee number
Summarizing/aggregating data	Data on the performance of various departments may be aggregated to arrive at a summary of performance
Performing calculations on data	Data on the total hours worked by an employee may be multiplied by the hourly wage rates to arrive at a gross wage
Selection of data	Total yearly turnover data on customers may be used to select high-spending customers for special treatment by sales personnel

1.2   Decisions

Information is data that has been processed for a purpose. That purpose is to aid some kind of decision. In order to understand more about the different types of information that are provided in business it is necessary to look at the area of decision taking and decision takers and the way that information is used in decisions.

No decision is taken in isolation. Decisions are taken by decision takers who have certain organizational objectives in mind, have a certain background, and have a certain mental way of processing and appreciating information. Moreover, these individuals have personal interests that may affect the decision-taking process. From the corporate point of view information needs to be supplied to these decision takers in order that the decision taken will be the most effective in the light of the organizational objectives.

1.2.1   Cognitive style and background

'Cognitive style' is a term used in psychology that broadly describes the way that individuals absorb information, process it and relate it to their existing knowledge, and use it to make decisions. Cognitive style and personal background act as filters to the information provided to a decision taker. In outline, one approach to cognitive style (Kilmann and Mitroff, 1976) regards individuals as falling into one of two categories in the way that they absorb information. At one extreme some people take in information best if it is highly detailed and specific, often quantitatively based. The various elements of information need not be linked as a whole. The other group absorbs information in an holistic way that is, in a less concrete way, preferring general facts, suppositions and 'soft data' linked as a whole.

After obtaining information the decision must be taken. Once again there appear to be two distinctive styles. One group will involve itself in a high degree of analytic thought

Figure 1.2: Four cognitive styles for absorbing information and taking decisions.

Information absorption style

Decision-making style		Detailed	Holistic
	Analysis	1	2
	Intuition	3	4

in reaching a decision. This group will be capable of providing detailed justifications often involving quantitative reasons in support of final decisions. The other group will rely more on intuition, experience, rules of thumb, and judgement. There will be a concentration on looking at the situation as a whole rather than parts of it independently. This group will often find it difficult to provide justification for recommended decisions. The combination of these information absorption and decision-taking styles is shown in Figure 1.2.

It is not claimed here that one or other of these styles of assimilating information or making decisions is superior. The point is that if information is presented in a way that is not conducive to the cognitive style of the recipient then it will not be fully utilized in a decision. When information systems are designed the designer, if at all possible, should take into account the range of cognitive styles of those for whom the information is provided. This important though obvious point is often overlooked or ignored when information systems are designed for business.

The background of a decision taker is also a powerful influence on the way that information is perceived. Differing subject specializations will lead individuals to judge different aspects of information as being more/less relevant or more/less important for making decisions. For instance accountants will tend to concentrate on numerical information with which they are familiar. They will require the numerical information to be compiled and presented in a standard manner compatible with their expectations and training. They may ignore details of organizational structure and management styles. It is quite possible that they may even fail to perceive the information when it is presented. In contrast the organizational specialist may not understand the importance of numerical, financial and cost aspects of the business organization. This is quite understandable as the specialisms of each only give them a limited model through which to perceive and organize information in a way that is relevant to making decisions.

Personal backgrounds and cognitive styles are not wholly independent of one another. The ability to work best with detailed quantitative information, for example, will not be unconnected with the occupation of an accountant or engineer.

1.2.2 A model of decision making

The process of taking a decision can be described as falling into several stages (Simon, 1965). These stages provide a framework within which decisions can be viewed. To be successfully executed each of the stages will require different types of information. The stages, shown in Figure 1.3, are:

1. **Intelligence:** The decision maker needs to be made aware of the existence of a problem that requires some sort of decision. Information needs to be presented in a manner conducive to this recognition.

future rather than the present. The nature of many of the decisions requires information on the development of market forces, patterns of expenditure, and the economy as a whole. This requires information to be supplied on matters external to the company from sources such as market surveys, trade publications, demographic studies, government reports and commissioned research from specialist suppliers. The fact that the information refers to external areas outside the control of the organization and that it applies to the future means that it is likely to be highly uncertain and will tend to be of a summarized or general nature rather than highly detailed.

Tactical planning and control

This is a managerial activity normally associated with the middle echelons of management. Tactical planning may involve the allocation of resources within departmental budgets, decisions on medium-term work scheduling and forecasting, and planning medium-term cash flows. Examples of control at this middle managerial level are the monitoring of actual production and expenditure against budgets, the analysis of variances and actions taken in response.

Information for decisions at the tactical level will refer to the medium term between now and the next few months or a year. It will be mainly generated internally within the organization though some external information may be necessary. As an example of the latter, it is difficult to set budgets if external raw material prices are the subject of uncertainty or wage rates are set in response to national union negotiations – in both cases external information may be of help. The information will generally be required in an aggregate form – for example, total production for the month of a certain product – though not as consolidated as that for a strategic decision. The internal nature of the information and its time horizon means that it is likely to be subject to less uncertainty than information supplied for strategic decisions.

Operational planning and control

This is concerned with the decisions made in the normal day-to-day operations within a business. Decisions in this area are designed to ensure the effective and efficient use of existing resources to realize budget objectives. These decisions may involve the treatment of personnel (for example, hiring and firing), the control of inventory and production levels, pricing decisions, aspects of credit control over customers and other forms of accounting and cash controls.

Information for operational planning and control is generated almost exclusively within the organization, is highly detailed, certain, and immediately relevant. For instance, the operational decision as to whether to purchase more of an item that has fallen below its reorder stock level will be based on at least some of the following information:

- the number of requisition orders already placed for the item, the quantities ordered and the expected delivery dates;
- the expected future use of the item including any outstanding customer commitments;
- the storage and handling facilities available;
- the range of suppliers of the item, their prices, and their expected delivery dates.

All this information will be held within the organization and once it is recognized as relevant for the decision it can be retrieved and used. Figure 1.4 shows the characteristics

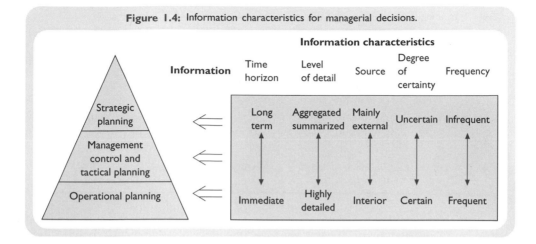

Figure 1.4: Information characteristics for managerial decisions.

Information characteristics

Information	Time horizon	Level of detail	Source	Degree of certainty	Frequency
Strategic planning	Long term	Aggregated summarized	Mainly external	Uncertain	Infrequent
Management control and tactical planning					
Operational planning	Immediate	Highly detailed	Interior	Certain	Frequent

of information supplied for the various levels of managerial activities. These activities need not necessarily be carried out by different people. Indeed, in a very small company decisions at these levels may all be carried out by the same person.

1.2.4 The structure of decisions

Simon (1965, 1977) makes a simple yet important distinction between structured (programmable) and unstructured (non-programmable) decisions. **Structured decisions** are those governed by clear rules. The decision procedure can be expressed as a set of steps to be followed, can be incorporated in a decision table or revealed by a procedural logic flowchart. The information that is needed before a structured decision can be made is clearly specifiable, unambiguous, and once it is obtained, the process of arriving at the decision action is straightforward.

An example of a structured decision would be the granting of credit to a customer where this is done on a points basis. The customer obtains points for: having a job, the salary associated with it, the time the job has been held, whether the customer is married, has children, whether the customer has other credit cards, loans or mortgages. The points are mechanically assigned and totalled. If the total is above a certain threshold the customer is granted credit, otherwise not. Because structured decisions are governed by clear rules they can often be left to low-grade personnel or even be fully automated in some cases.

With **unstructured decisions** it is often unclear what information is needed and how it should be assessed in relation to the decision objectives. These objectives may themselves be unclear or the subject of disagreement. Unlike structured decisions there will be no set procedure or rules for arriving at the decision. The use of rules of thumb (heuristics) and 'experience' is characteristic of unstructured decisions.

An example of an unstructured decision is the hiring of supervisory or senior staff. Here information, such as qualifications and experience, is obviously relevant. But what is not clear is how good qualifications in one candidate are to be measured against experience in a second, and how this is to be offset against the intelligence and adaptability revealed by a third candidate.

Table 1.2: Structure and managerial activity in decision making.

	Strategic planning	*Management control*	*Operational control*
Unstructured	Company reorganization	Personnel management	Dealing with customer enquiries
Semi-structured	Introduction of new product	Analysis of performance	Short-term production scheduling
Structured	Financial structure planning	Allocating budgets	Stock reorder decisions

Gorry and Scott-Morton (1971) have developed the ideas of Anthony (1965) and Simon (1965, 1977) to provide a useful way of categorizing decisions by comparing managerial activities against the *degree* of structure in a decision. This is shown in Table 1.2. The degree of structure corresponds to the extent to which each of the decision-making stages is structured or unstructured. A decision that is highly structured at the stages of intelligence, design and choice would count as a highly structured decision. A lack of structure during each of these three stages would mean the decision was regarded as highly unstructured. Many decisions lie between these two extremes, being structured in some stages but unstructured in others. These are termed **semi-structured**.

As the type of decision will determine the characteristics of the information that is required to make it, the analysis by structure provides a useful guide for the development of management information systems. In general the more highly structured the decision the more likely it is that a computer system can provide useful information. In cases where the intelligence, design, and choice elements are all structured the computer system may not only be used to provide information but also to automate the decision itself. In other cases varying degrees of decision support can be given.

1.3   Value of information

Information produced for business purposes has a cost. The costs are associated with collection, processing and storage. These are present whether the information is produced by a manual or a computer system. In order to justify this cost the information must also have some value. The value is generally to be found in better decision making, whether this be in the area of control, planning or in some other area. How then is information to be valued?

1.3.1   Quantifiable value

Sometimes information provided to an organization or generated within it has measurable benefits in monetary terms. These benefits result from two factors. First, the information may reduce uncertainty surrounding the making of a decision. Second, a decision may be taken more quickly, and therefore be more timely, in the presence of the faster provision of information.

Figure 1.5: An example of the value of information in reducing uncertainty.

Weather

	Dry	Wet
Turnips	40	80
Wheat	100	0

Profit on crops

Probability of dry weather = 0.5
Probability of wet weather = 0.5

$\therefore$ expected pay-off profit for turnips = $0.5 \times 40 + 0.5 \times 80 = 60$
$\therefore$ expected pay-off profit for wheat $= 0.5 \times 100 + 0.5 \times 0 = 50$

If risk neutrality is assumed, optimal expected pay-off profit = 60 for turnips

Assume that perfect weather forecasting information can be provided

If the weather is wet, plant turnips, pay-off profit = 80
If the weather is dry, plant wheat, pay-off profit = 100

$\therefore$ prior to buying information the expected pay-off profit = $0.5 \times 80 + 0.5 \times 100 = 90$

$\therefore$ the value of the information
    = expected pay-off profit with information − expected pay-off profit without information
    = 90 − 60
    = **30**

Figure 1.5 illustrates the way that information can reduce uncertainty and lead to a measurable financial benefit. Assume that a decision faces a farmer. Should turnips or wheat be planted? The matrix indicates the profits for planting turnips and wheat depending on whether the weather is dry or wet. Past records show that it is as likely to be wet as dry (probability = 0.5). The expected pay-off profits for planting turnips and for planting wheat can now be calculated as 60 and 50 arbitrary units respectively. If the farmer is risk neutral the farmer will go for the highest-yield option and plant turnips with an expected pay-off of 60. Let us now suppose that perfect information can be supplied to the farmer on the future state of the weather. Of what financial value is this information? If the information is that it is wet, turnips will be planted and if dry wheat will be planted. The weather forecast will be as likely to show (accurately) that the weather is wet as it will show that it is dry. Therefore the expected pay-off profit for the farmer is 90. The value to the farmer of the information is the difference between the expected pay-offs with and without the information. Any rational farmer would be prepared to pay up to 30 for this weather forecasting information.

Though this example is highly simplified it clearly illustrates the way information can be of aid in a decision. It is necessary to know:

- the range of decision alternatives (plant wheat or turnips);
- the range of factors affecting the results of the decision (dry or wet weather);
- the pay-offs that occur for each decision result (pay-off matrix);
- the probabilities that the factors will be operative (past weather records indicating the probability of wet or dry weather);

- the reduction in uncertainty surrounding these factors as a result of the information (perfect weather forecast leading to elimination of uncertainty).

The calculations involved are much the same if the range of decisions and conditions is increased and we allow that information only reduces, rather than eliminates uncertainty.

Another way that information can prove to be of financial benefit is by being up to date. This enables decisions to be taken more swiftly. Computerized transaction-processing systems and management information systems provide information more quickly than the manual systems that they replace. A computerized system can generate data concerning sales and information on a company's debtors more quickly. This may cut the average time between the sale of a product and the receipt of payment for it. This time is known as the **debtor period**.

Suppose that the average time taken for a customer to pay a debt is six weeks and the amount outstanding from debtors is £6000. If faster processing, such as the immediate generation of an invoice at the time of sale and quicker provision of information on non-payment, can cut the period to four weeks, the average outstanding debt will drop to £4000. This is equivalent to a cash injection of £2000.

Similarly savings in **buffer stock** may be made. Buffer stock is held to prevent a stock-out occurring. Better information can reduce the need to hold such large levels of this safety stock. Often much of this stock is held to counteract the effects of poor and slow stock control. If the levels of stock can be cut from a value equivalent to six weeks' turnover to a value represented by four weeks' turnover then this is equivalent to a cash injection equal to two weeks' turnover at cost prices.

The last two examples illustrate ways in which a computerized information system can lead to quantifiable benefits. However, it is unusual for information to have a total value that is precisely measurable. Generally there will be unquantifiable advantages conferred. In many cases it may be difficult or impossible to place figures on the value of information simply because there may be no quantifiable benefits at all. A decision to obtain and provide the information will be based purely on its non-quantifiable value.

1.3.2 Non-quantifiable value

It is undeniable that information can provide benefits that are not strictly measurable. For example, better information provided to customers on available products and current prices is liable to increase customer confidence, attract new customers, and prevent existing customers from moving elsewhere. It is impossible to put a figure on this value. Why is this? Many other changes are occurring to alter customer preferences: advertising by the company, competitors, responses, changes in consumer expenditure patterns and so on. It is difficult to isolate the effect of the provision of better information from these other factors.

Similar observations apply to information provided for internal decisions. It may be thought that the provision of information improves a type of decision but it is difficult to separate the effect of this information on the decision from all the other influences.

Occasionally, information has other uses than to aid decision making. Performance information on salesmen, for instance, may be used to motivate them to achieve greater levels of sales. Sometimes information is collected without any clear purpose in mind but merely to build up a background understanding of an area. Strictly this should be called

intelligence. In both these cases the information has value or, in the latter case, possible value. In neither is this value quantifiable.

It is a great temptation to restrict attention to the quantifiable benefits associated with the provision of information, especially when taking a decision on whether to undertake an investment in a business information system. However, a limited cost–benefit analysis on this narrow accounting basis would have meant that several information technology projects that have been undeniably successful would not have been given the 'go ahead'. It is important to recognize that even though benefits cannot be quantified this is no reason to ignore them in making investment decisions.

1.4   The idea of a system

We live in a world full of systems. There are central heating systems, telephone systems, computer systems, fuel injection systems, and the human circulatory system to name but a few. As well as these physical systems there are also more abstract systems. Amongst these would be counted systems of logic, and philosophical systems. Social systems containing men and women as social beings constitute a further class which includes, for example, economic systems, social security systems, and legal systems. There are of course business information systems – the subject of this book. The idea of a system provides a useful framework within which to view business information as it flows within an organization, is used for decisions, or is processed by modern information technology. The question that this section is addressed to is 'What is it that such a diverse range of things has in common by virtue of which they are all known as systems?' Before we can study business information systems it is important that we have a clear understanding of the concept of a system.

A **system** can be defined as a collection of interrelated parts which taken together forms a whole such that:

- The collection has some purpose.
- A change in any of the parts leads to or results from a change in some other part(s).

This is a very broad definition. But then the concept of system is itself wide-ranging. The important point in this definition is that a system is a collection of interrelated parts – it cannot be a single thing such as a potato but must be perceived as having an internal structure. Moreover, these parts must be dynamically interrelated through change rather than merely being geographically in close proximity. The system must also have some purpose, goal or objective, and the changes or processes in its parts will normally serve that goal. Most systems, and in particular the systems of interest to this book, have several additional characteristics. An understanding of these characteristics will enrich our concept of a system.

1.4.1   Characteristics of systems

The systems model
Most systems can be illustrated by the model in Figure 1.6. Inputs are accepted into the system and outputs are produced by the processes within the system. In many cases there may be intermediate storage and control over the functioning of the system.

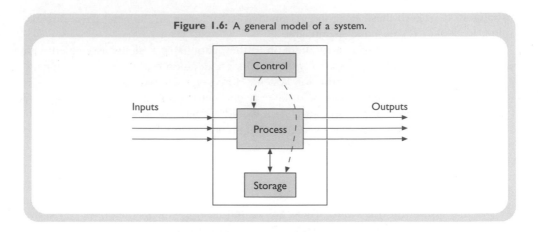

Figure 1.6: A general model of a system.

To see how this model is exemplified by a simple familiar system consider the example of a central heating system. The **input** is gas (energy) at a particular geographical point and electricity (energy) required for the electrical equipment. The **outputs** of the system are heat energy geographically dispersed throughout the house (together with the products of combustion in the boiler such as water vapour). The **process** is the combustion within the boiler, the transfer of the resultant heat energy to the water and the pumping of water through the pipes and radiators. The water within the system provides a temporary **storage** for the heat energy as it becomes geographically dispersed throughout the system. The output heat energy leaves the system and enters the environment by courtesy of Newton's law of cooling. The **control** is provided by the thermostat, which accepts a given standard, say 80 degrees Fahrenheit. The thermostat turns off the input when the sensed temperature rises a given amount above this and turns on the input if it falls below this.

The systems model provides a useful framework within which to view a business organization as it concentrates attention on important aspects of its functioning. Imagine a manual order processing system within a business. Its objective is to process customer orders accurately and quickly. It will help to increase understanding of this system if the inputs, outputs, control, process and storage aspects are clearly distinguished and identified. For instance, suppose for simplicity that the sole input is a customer order. By concentrating on this input we need to determine:

● the data held on a customer order;

● the source of the customer order (for example from salesperson, mail, phone);

● the frequency with which customer orders are received;

● the peaks and troughs in the volume of received orders (and how the processing element of the system deals with these);

● controls and checks existing over acceptance of the order.

These are just a few questions suggested by looking at the inputs of the order processing system. Viewing the manual order processing as a system does not in itself generate these questions but rather directs attention in a way that is helpful in understanding and analysis.

Systems objectives

All systems have **objectives** and in identifying a system the objectives must be specified. This may be easy in the case of a central heating system. The objective is: to convert localized energy (for example, gas energy) into geographically dispersed heat energy in order to maintain the environmental temperature of a building or dwelling within a given range. The objective is clear and there is a straightforward **measure of performance** that can be applied to establish whether the system is meeting its objective. The measure of performance is the temperature as sensed by a thermometer.

Other systems may have objectives that are less clear, or those objectives may be stated in such a way that no easy measure of performance is obvious. Systems that evolve, such as economic systems or business organizations, are less likely to have clear objectives than a system that has been designed. The latter are built to meet objectives specified in advance. In contrast, a national economic system probably has no clear objectives other than the vaguely stated one of satisfying the economic needs of (some of) those participating in it. Measures of performance are often not agreed. Is it gross national product, the rate of growth of national product, the percentage of the workforce employed, the rate of profit, the distribution of product or what? Economists and politicians flourish and differ because these issues are not clearly defined. Business systems lie somewhere between these two extremes.

Inputs and outputs to a system

Although the inputs and outputs to systems can be almost anything, each falls into one of a number of distinct broad categories. They are:

- materials
- energy
- labour power
- information
- decisions
- money.

Business information systems are mainly concerned with information/decision inputs and outputs although they will have others – manual information systems need labour power, computerized information systems need energy.

The inputs and outputs of a system are connected to other systems. This is illustrated in Figure 1.7. The outputs of one system become the inputs to another. It is possible to view the world as being composed of systems. Then there are no outputs that 'disappear'. Of course a person's interest is always restricted to only some of these systems.

Systems environment and boundary

Inputs come from and outputs are transferred to the **environment** of a system. The environment may be defined as whatever lies outside the boundaries of the system but interacts with the system. If something lies outside a system but does not affect the system's behaviour and neither do changes in the state of the system affect it, then that thing would not be in the environment of the system. Environment is not a geographical concept – the central water pumping station is in the immediate environment of a domestic water system though it is located five miles away, whereas the electrical system in the house next door does not lie in the environment of the domestic water system.

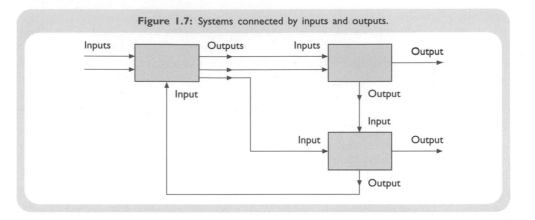

Figure 1.7: Systems connected by inputs and outputs.

The notion of environment has been defined in terms of the concept of **boundary**. The features that delineate the scope of a system form its boundaries. What is perceived as a system with boundaries by one observer will be determined by what that perceiver identifies as the objectives of the system combined with the area over which that perceiver has interest and control. The idea of a system therefore involves not only 'facts' in the world but also the perceptions and interests of the observer.

To see this consider the example of a manager whose objective it is to reorganize the stores within a manufacturing company in order to provide the most efficient service. Viewing the stores as a system, the manager will delineate the scope of the system in terms of the control that that manager has to reorganize the stores. The production of stock and its disposal by selling will be seen as lying outside the system. The manager has little or no control over these areas. However, the organization of the stores, its physical layout, personnel, documentation and procedures will be within the scope of the manager's interest and therefore lie within the system. In contrast, to a member of senior management taking a larger view of the business the stores will only be one part of the system. Others will include production and sales. This manager will see the production and pricing of raw materials, for example, as lying outside the manager's control and so outside the system as perceived.

Closed systems do not have inputs or outputs – they have no environment. Strictly there are no closed systems (except the universe as a whole) but the term is often used of systems that interact only weakly with their environment. For example an economic system is often referred to as closed if it is one that has little or no economic links with the economies of the outside world. Albania is an example. **Open systems** are those systems that are not closed.

1.4.2 Subsystems and systems hierarchies

Systems are composed of subsystems that are interrelated to one another by means of their inputs and outputs. This gives the system an internal structure. Each subsystem is itself a system with objectives, inputs, outputs, and possibly control and storage elements, and so can be further decomposed into its subsystems. In the example above the senior manager regarded the stores as a subsystem.

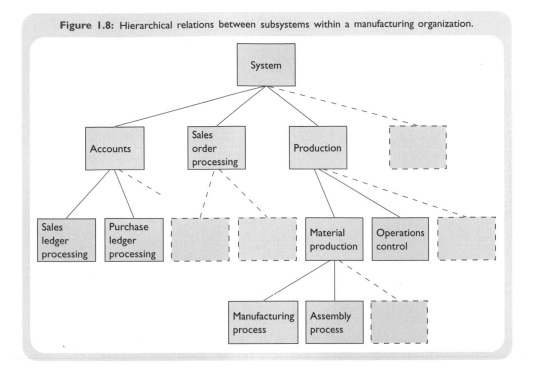

Figure 1.8: Hierarchical relations between subsystems within a manufacturing organization.

The process of decomposition can continue until the most basic elements are reached. Each of these is called a **black box**. A black box has inputs and outputs but its internal structure is ignored. Whether something is a black box is not an objectively given fact. For most people a TV set is a black box with electrical energy and a signal (coded information via the aerial) as inputs, and variegated light (picture) and sound as outputs. For the TV repairer, however, it is a system composed of many interacting subsystems, which themselves may be composed of elements that to the repairer are black boxes. These are the basic electronic devices. A black box is defined entirely in terms of the relationships between its inputs and outputs. Each black box would be checked to establish which one did not produce the required outputs given known inputs. This faulty part would then be replaced. Although it is a black box for the TV repairer it would not be so for the electronics expert.

The decomposition of a system into its subsystems may be shown with a **systems hierarchy chart** as in Figure 1.8. This is a (partial) representation of a manufacturing organization as a hierarchy of subsystems. The subsystems are defined by the functions they perform. The chart gives a clear representation of the hierarchical relations between the various subsystems. At the first level the system can be seen to be composed of accounts, sales order processing and other subsystems. At deeper levels the breakdown of each of their constituents is shown. The purpose of decomposition is to break the larger system into its constituent parts. The process continues until the subsystems obtained are of a manageable size for understanding.

Although the hierarchy chart reveals subsystems relations it does not illustrate the inputs and outputs to the various subsystems nor their interconnection via these inputs

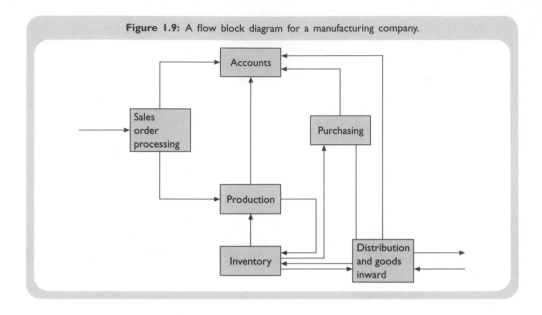

Figure 1.9: A flow block diagram for a manufacturing company.

and outputs. This is shown with a **flow block diagram**. A flow block diagram for the manufacturing company is shown in Figure 1.9. The subsystems are represented by blocks and the flows of inputs and outputs by directed lines (arrows). The diagram shows the subsystems from the level 1 perspective of Figure 1.8.

Each of these subsystems can be decomposed into further subsystems. Figure 1.10 shows the flow block diagram for the production subsystem. There are four subsystems – material production, operations control, production control, and the management subsystems. Each of these is further broken down. For instance, material production contains manufacturing processing, intermediate inventory and product assembly. Two types of input/output flow are distinguished – materials flow and information/data/decisions flow. Apart from the material production the other subsystems correspond to information processing and provision at the three levels of decision making and control – strategic, tactical, and operational – covered earlier in this chapter in Section 1.2.3.

There are no hard-and-fast rules to be followed in systems decomposition into subsystems nor in the diagrammatic techniques used. The only rule is that if their use increases understanding of the system and aids communication of this knowledge then the technique is acceptable; otherwise it is pointless.

1.4.3 Subsystems decoupling

Subsystems can be connected together via their inputs and outputs either directly or through intervening subsystems. The extent of the dependence of the subsystems on one another is known as the **degree of coupling**. Two subsystems are **highly coupled** if a change in the outputs of one causes a substantial change in the state of the other. Two subsystems are **highly decoupled** if changes in the outputs of either have little or no effect on the state of the other. Coupling is a matter of degree.

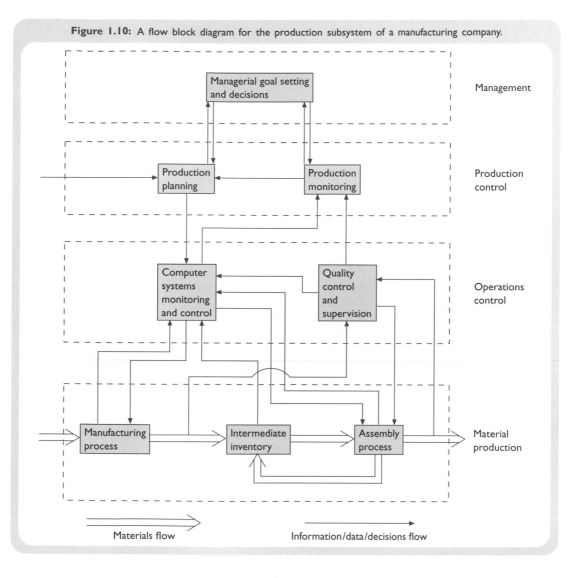

Figure 1.10: A flow block diagram for the production subsystem of a manufacturing company.

Figure 1.11 shows two subsystems that are highly coupled. The output of production is fed directly into sales and distribution and the demands by sales for products are communicated to production. A change in production will have a direct impact on sales and distribution. For such tightly coupled subsystems to work in harmony it is essential that there is close communication between them.

One way to achieve decoupling is by the insertion of a **buffer** or **inventory** between the two subsystems as in Figure 1.11(b). The effect of this is to protect the state of the sales and distribution subsystems from variations in the output of production. For instance, production may come to a halt but sales need not change its activities, at least not in the short term. Goods sold are made up from stock. Another way of achieving decoupling is to ensure that subsystems work with **slack capacity** that can be called upon. In Figure 1.11(c) the production system normally works at less than full capacity and can therefore

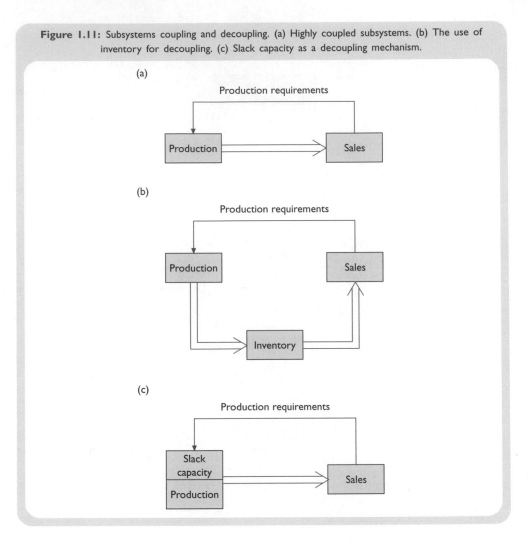

Figure 1.11: Subsystems coupling and decoupling. (a) Highly coupled subsystems. (b) The use of inventory for decoupling. (c) Slack capacity as a decoupling mechanism.

accommodate a variation in the demand for the product from the sales and distribution subsystem. In each of the examples the effect of decoupling leads to a greater stability.

Decoupling generally leads to systems stability. Business systems need internal stability to guarantee continued functioning and survival in the light of a changing economic, market, and financial environment. This is not a free gain as the mechanisms introduce inefficiency or extra cost. In the example the cost was the carrying of buffer stock or the maintenance of slack production capacity. Nevertheless, a certain degree of stability through decoupling is usually thought desirable in any system and is often built in at the design stage.

1.4.4 Total systems approach versus piecemeal approaches

The total systems approach in based on the idea that all subsystems are related to one another and cannot be considered in isolation for:

1. the purpose of understanding the behaviour of the system as a whole;

2. the design of a new system.

In understanding systems, certain characteristics of individual subsystems only make sense in terms of serving overall systems goals. Within a business system this translates into the impossibility of making sense of functional subsystems activities except within the context of corporate objectives. The uncritical concentration on subsystems can lead to overall systems suboptimization even though these parts taken individually appear to be performing optimally.

An example of this may be seen in Figure 1.12. Suppose that it is the corporate objective to minimize the total costs (production costs plus storage costs) of supplying a product to meet an externally given fluctuating sales demand. It seems reasonable to expect that if each subsystem functions at the minimum cost compatible with meeting the sales demand then the system as a whole should be optimized and working at minimum cost. Production minimizes its cost by having a constant run of 100 units per quarter as shown in Figure 1.12(a). This avoids the machine set-up costs of different production runs for different volumes of output. The stock is maintained efficiently at a minimum average cost per unit. However, if the production subsystem can be made to perform suboptimally (with respect to cost minimization) by scheduling a fluctuating production, the extra cost incurred in the change of the production run levels (100 per change) is more than compensated for by the reduced cost of holding stock in the inventory sub-system. This is shown in Figure 1.12(b). Unless a total systems approach were taken it would be difficult to understand why the production subsystem was deliberately avoiding cost minimization in its scheduling.

This is an example that uses simplified figures. However, the general point is that it is not always in an organization's overall interests to adopt a subsystems piecemeal approach and require each subsystem to function efficiently as measured by the same yardstick that is used to measure the system's performance as a whole. The move in organizations towards treating subsystem's as financial cost or profit centres in order to remove internal inefficiency in them is in line with this piecemeal approach.

Another equally compelling reason for adopting the total systems approach is related to issues in systems design. A computerized business information system usually replaces or at least augments a manual information processing system. The formal information in a manual system is conveyed in the form of documents flowing between subsystems. These are demarcated by the traditional functional specializations in the various departments of a business – accounts, purchasing, sales order processing and so on. Concentration on the information inputs, outputs and processes within each of these subsystems independently of each other will generate a computerized information systems design that mirrors this functional decomposition. Given that the processing will all occur within the central resource of the computer there is no reason why this conventional decomposition should not be sacrificed to a more integrated design that takes into account the information system as a whole. In the later chapters on systems analysis and design the approach taken is one that allows the development of integrated information systems.

1.4.5 Control

Systems have objectives. In order to ensure that the system's objectives are met it is important that there is some control operating over the system's functioning. First, this

Figure 1.12: Subsystems optimization versus systems optimization. (a) A case where each subsystem optimizes by minimizing subsystem cost though the system as a whole suboptimizes on cost. (b) A case where the system as a whole optimizes on cost even though the production subsystem is not optimal with respect to cost.

(a)

	Production during period	Stock held at end of period	Sales during period
Period 0		30	
Period 1	100	60	70
Period 2	100	30	130
Period 3	100	60	70
Period 4	100	30	130
	400		400

Cost of production per item   = 100 per unit
Cost of changing production level = 100 per change
Cost of holding stock   = 10 per unit per period

Production costs   = 100 × 400   = 40 000
Cost of changing production level   =   0
Total production cost   = 40 000

$$ 40\ 000$$

Total cost of holding stock   = 10 × (60 + 30 + 60 + 30) = 1 800

Total cost   = 41 800

(b)

	Production during period	Stock held at end of period	Sales during period
Period 0		30	
Period 1	70	30	70
Period 2	130	30	130
Period 3	70	30	70
Period 4	130	30	130
	400		400

Cost of production per item   = 100 per unit
Cost of changing production level = 100 per change
Cost of holding stock   = 10 per unit per period

Production costs   = 100 × 400   = 40 000
Cost of changing production level = 3 × 100   =   300
Total production cost   = 40 300

$$ 40\ 300$$

Total cost of holding stock   = 10 × (30 + 30 + 30 + 30) = 1 200

Total cost   = 41 500

may be needed in order to ensure that a system responds optimally to a change in its inputs or environment. For example, a change in the price of a raw material may lead to its replacement by a cheaper substitute, or a change in a competitor's price may result in a response to ensure a retained market share. Second, the internal functioning of the

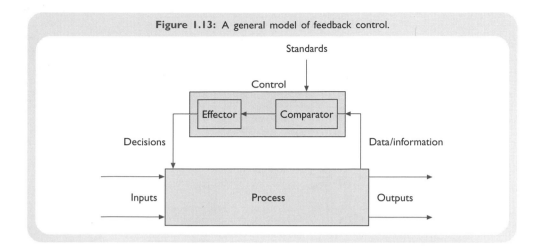

Figure 1.13: A general model of feedback control.

system may require controls to prevent or to remedy the effects of malfunctions or resource degradation. For example, a labour strike or breakdown of equipment requires an internal response to ensure that systems objectives are not jeopardized.

Controls often work by gathering data on the state and outputs of the system, comparing this with the objectives of the system, and taking some corrective measure if necessary. The general model is shown in Figure 1.13. Information on the state of the system or its outputs is collected and compared with some desired standard (**comparator**). The results of this comparison are sent to an element of control, which causes an appropriate decision to be sent to the system (**effector**). This changes the state of the system or its outputs. By continually monitoring the system and changing it in the light of deviations from standards the system can be controlled to meet its objectives. This form of **feedback control** is common in business and industry. For example, in quality control the output of a process is sampled and its quality established. If this does not meet set standards some decision is made to alter the inputs or process involved. Many forms of regular reporting to management are examples of feedback control.

Feedback control may be automated by computerization. This is most widespread in production processes. More commonly, the computer is used to provide information to management, who then perform the control function and make the decisions. Advances in modern information technology and the increasing use of computer systems have cut down the time-lag in the provision of information for control purposes. The subject of control is covered extensively in Chapter 8.

1.5 Management information systems

During the mid-1950s computers were first commercially used to carry out business data processing. These systems were limited to processing transactions. The most common application areas were payroll, high-volume billing (such as in the electricity industry) and simple ledger accounting activities. The results of this processing were stored. It soon became obvious that this wealth of stored transaction data could provide management with useful information. This information first needed to be extracted and processed to

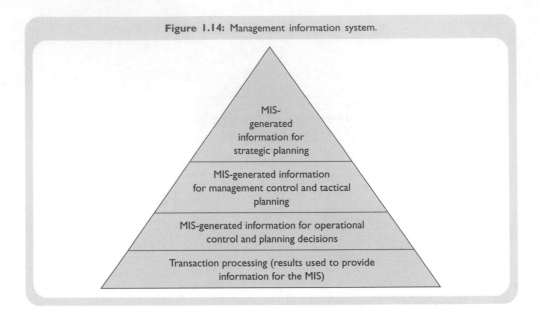

Figure 1.14: Management information system.

be digestible and useful to management. The early management information systems (MIS) were born when programs were written to do just this.

A **management information system** is, as its name suggests, any system that provides information for the management activities carried out within an organization. Nowadays the term is almost exclusively reserved for computerized systems. These consist of hardware and software that accept data and store, process and retrieve information. This information is selected and presented in a form suitable for managerial decision making and for the planning and monitoring of the organization's activities.

Today, no one would design a system for processing transactions without considering the way it could also be used to generate information. Figure 1.14 illustrates the reliance of the provision of information at strategic, managerial and operational levels on the transaction-processing base.

The increase in the power of computing technology witnessed over the last two decades together with its decreasing cost has meant that computers are used more and more by business organizations to carry out routine data processing. Over this period there has also been a change in management thinking to accept the importance of the fast, effective provision of targeted information for management planning and control. The combined effect of these two factors has led to an increased growth in management information systems. Specifically the reasons for this are:

- **Cost:** Once data has been entered for transaction-processing purposes it is within the computer system for the provision of information. The marginal cost of using it to generate information for many different purposes is now low.

- **Speed:** Information can be generated quickly. Even complex reports and statistics on the functioning of a business may take only minutes to prepare if in a standard format. This cuts down the time that management are required to wait for reports once they have been requested. It also means that information provided is up to date and decisions should be more effective.

- **Interaction:** Many modern management information systems provide interactive facilities so that users may request information to be produced online as and when it is needed. This allows end users to be selective about information extracted from the MIS.

- **Flexibility:** As well as being faced with a predictable set of decisions for which information is required, for example budgeting and performance reporting, management are also faced with new problems. A modern MIS will have some in-built flexibility enabling the manager to decide what information is to be produced.

1.5.1 Database

Essential to the idea of a management information system is the ability to retrieve data and use it for the production of targeted information for different purposes. Much data will be stored as the result of transaction-processing operations. It is important that this data is seen as a central resource for the entire management information system and not tied to the application that produced it.

For example, sales transaction data used to update the sales ledger will be stored after the updating process. This data should be available for other purposes. It can be used to provide reports on sales personnel performance as part of the personnel management function. Alternatively, it can be fed into models that use data and information from other sources to forecast cash flows and aid cash management.

In order to achieve the objective of common availability the data needs to be managed as a central resource. The software that creates this database and handles access to it is called a **database management system**. This ensures that data is controlled, consistent and available to provide information.

Figure 1.15 illustrates this position. Within the organization, materials, energy and labour power are accepted as inputs and processed to provide outputs. Accompanying this will be data recording the transactions and movements involved. This will take the form of records of transactions that the company has with its environment. For example the sale of a good, the sending of a purchase order to a supplier, or the supply of a good will all be accompanied by a record of the transactions involved. Also records of transactions between the various departments within the organization will be generated. An example from a manual system is the requisition of a part from stores for production. This is recorded on a requisition form. Resource usage within the organization will also be recorded. Once again, in a manual system the use of individual employee time will be recorded on a worksheet.

The transaction data processing element of Figure 1.15 shows the acceptance of data inputs both from the environment and from internal materials processing within the organization. Transaction outputs are also generated. These may leave the organization, such as an invoice, or be stored on the database, such as the invoice details. This transaction processing is carried out within the computer system.

The database serves as a permanent store for the results of transaction processing, as a temporary store during processing, and as a store for the records of the transactions themselves. Interaction between the programs controlling the data processing and the database is handled by the database management system software. This 'protects' the database from direct contact with the applications programs. These carry out such functions

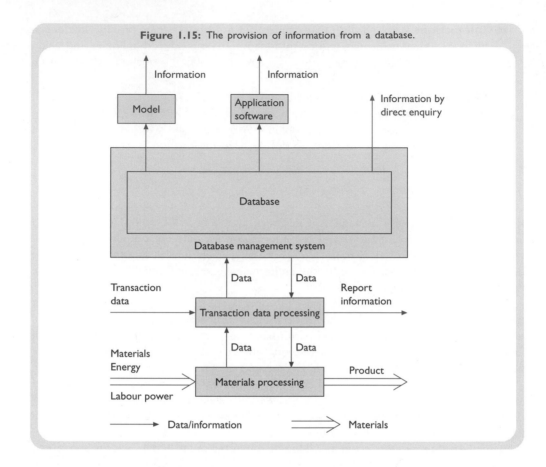

Figure 1.15: The provision of information from a database.

as stock control, payroll processing, sales ledger updating. It also maintains consistency of data within the database.

Once stored, this data is available for the production of information to management in their decision making and control activities. As shown in Figure 1.15 this information may be supplied through a model, may be generated by applications software working on data within the database, or may be obtained by direct enquiry using facilities provided with the database management system. Examples of these methods are now explained.

Models

Transaction data on sales and receipts of payments will be processed and stored on the database. This can be extracted along with data on purchases, payment for purchases, wages, the current bank balance and other data that involves cash flows in or out of the organization. The data is then fed into a model. The model predicts the cash flow position of the company over the next six months on a month-by-month basis. This predictive model will also need data that will not be within the database. Data on inflation rates and growth in market sizes falls into this category. This example illustrates the integrating nature of the database. The original data was used in transaction processing for disparate purposes but has now been brought together and used to predict cash flow. Because the modelling element of the provision of the information is designed to aid decisions, in this case on cash management, it is called a **decision support system**.

Applications software

Applications software will also interrogate the database to produce reports for management decision making and control. For example, from the customer sales accounts it is useful management information to know how the total customer debt is aged. If half of the customer debt has been outstanding for a period of more than 60 days, say, then management will respond differently than if one-tenth of the customer debt is over 60 days old. A report on the ageing of debt provides management with information on how successful it is in its debtor control policy. The ageing information will not be stored on the database but will be derived from data held there. Specifically for each customer account, the date and the amount outstanding on each invoice will be needed to provide a global ageing of debt.

Direct enquiry

Management may also wish to query the database to extract information from it selectively. An example, once again from customer sales accounts, would be to request the names and balances of all customers with an unpaid balance greater than a given figure.

1.5.2 Management information systems as a collection of subsystems

Although Figure 1.15 shows the *ways* in which information may be produced from the corporate database it does not illustrate either the levels of management activity for which the data is provided nor the functional subsystems of the organization served by the MIS. Figure 1.16 superimposes this on the data-processing base. The management information system supplies information for strategic, management (tactical) and operational decision making to all subsystems within the organization. This information provides an essential part of the feedback control mechanism in these areas and is necessary for the realization of subsystem objectives.

In the early days of MIS development it was envisaged that a total systems approach would be taken towards the design of a highly integrated management information system. The reality of MIS development has demonstrated that MIS tend to evolve over time. It is too complex to design the unified system as an initial project. Also, the information needed by different subsystems is markedly disparate and the information required is calculated from differing bases. This has resulted in the development of individual information subsystems that are only loosely connected. The MIS should perhaps better be regarded as a collection of information subsystems, ideally sharing a corporate database. Each subsystem adapts and is tailored to the needs of the functional subsystem that it serves (Dearden, 1972).

1.5.3 Management information systems and decisions

By providing relevant information, management information systems aid the making of decisions. Where these decisions involve planning, current data is used for predictive purposes. This is often associated with using a model to generate future estimates from

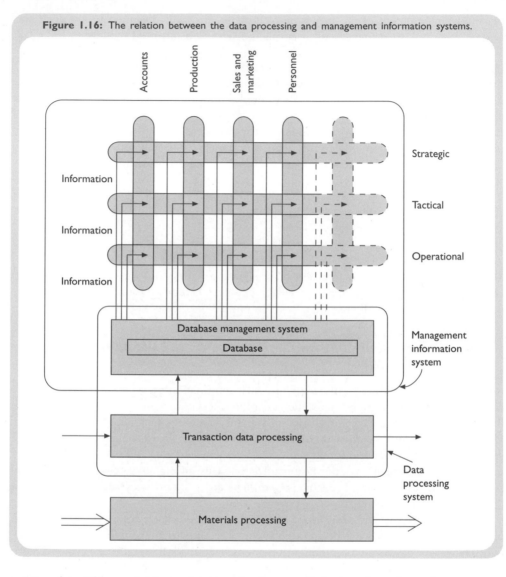

Figure 1.16: The relation between the data processing and management information systems.

existing data. This model is used to test the impact of altering the values of parameters, analysing the effects of alternative plans and testing the sensitivity of predictions to change. Often the model is handled by the user in an interactive way. These decision support systems, as they are known, are an important class of MIS applications, which involve more than just the representation of current information in ways suitable for decisions. In contrast, many control applications require much less – the selection, summary and presentation of information in a manner suitable for exercising control.

Previously (Table 1.2) the structure of decisions was outlined against the different levels of management activities. Those activities of a highly structured operational nature can be replaced by automated computer-based decision making. There is also an area of activities at the strategic unstructured level which require information that is largely external and often subjective. This lies outside the area of relevance for the MIS. However,

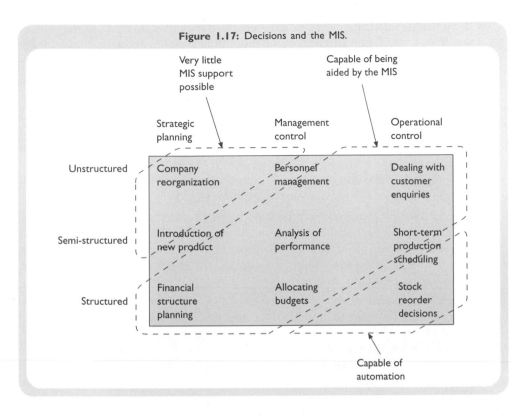

Figure 1.17: Decisions and the MIS.

there is a large band of decisions and activities that can be aided, though not replaced, by the MIS. This is shown in Figure 1.17.

1.5.4 Design of the management information system

The design of the management information system, like the design of any system, needs a methodical approach. A detailed explanation of the stages involved in the analysis and design of information systems is given in subsequent chapters. Here it will be sufficient to note special attributes of information that must be taken into account when designing an information system for management.

- **Relevance:** The information that is generated by the MIS must be relevant for the tasks for which it is provided. The emphasis of the present chapter has been on stressing the importance of information in decision making. An analysis of the decisions taken is required to understand what information is or is not relevant. Information is relevant to a decision if its content potentially affects the decision taken. This is too easily forgotten and information is provided on the grounds that it might be useful. This is often an excuse for not having carried out a proper decision analysis.

- **Accuracy:** Information should be as accurate as is required for the decision to be taken. Inaccuracy within limits may be perfectly acceptable, especially as increasing the accuracy of information will either increase the cost of its provision or slow its generation, or both.

- **Timeliness:** Information must be presented to the user within the time-span within which it is useful. Late information is not useful. Sometimes accuracy must be sacrificed in order to provide information within the optimum time.

- **Target:** The information must be directed to the correct recipient – that is, the person who takes the decisions for which the information is relevant.

- **Format:** The way in which the information is presented to the user will affect its effectiveness. Traditional attention to clear report formats can now be supplemented by the possibility of producing graphical and chart output. The use of colour and more sophisticated graphics opens up further possibilities in designing output formats. The flexibility of presentation opens the possibility of output designed to match the cognitive style of the recipient.

- **Interactive nature:** Some information is best provided on an interactive basis. This is because further information needs to be called up only if shown to be necessary by current information. To provide all information initially that might be relevant to a decision would be to deluge the decision taker and reduce the effectiveness of the decision process.

- **Control:** Some information may be sensitive or may be of value to competitors. Steps should be taken to ensure that secure procedures surround the MIS.

Dos and don'ts in MIS design

Ackoff (1967) in a now legendary article stressed some common myths governing MIS projects. These observations are as relevant today as they were 20 years ago. These myths have a familiar ring to them.

'*If only I had more information I would be able to take better decisions,*' says the manager. The reality is often different. It is not that more information needs to be provided but less and this should be more targeted. Relevant information is being lost in the swamp of large amounts of irrelevant information provided by a poorly designed MIS.

'*The best persons to ask in order to establish what information is needed for decisions are the decision makers themselves.*' This is not necessarily the case. The proper starting point is an analysis of the decision. Decision makers will generally attempt a wide specification of information requirements ('if it might be useful let's ask for it').

'*Management needs to be supplied with accurate, timely, relevant information for their activities – it is unnecessary for them to know how it is produced.*' In many areas, particularly in management accountancy, what appears to be the same information will have different implications depending on how it is compiled. The management accountant needs not only the information but knowledge of the way it is produced.

'*If information is more freely available then departments can coordinate their activities more closely.*' It should be remembered that departments within an organization may also be in competition with one another. This is especially true if they are profit centres or are attempting to gain as large a slice as possible of the organization's finite resources. Information about one another's activities may mean that departments behave in a way that is dysfunctional to the organization as a whole.

Approaches to management information system design

Although most designers for information systems for management would subscribe to these dos and don'ts and take account of the special attributes of information for decision making described above, there still remains much scope for differing approaches in the design of management information systems.

Here five approaches towards the development of a corporate MIS are identified. A brief explanation of each of these approaches and their limitations will indicate the minefield of disagreements that still exist on MIS design (Rockart, 1979).

1. The **by-product** approach to the development of an MIS is perhaps the earliest used. The emphasis is placed on developing a computerized system to deal with all the paperwork that was previously handled within a manual system. Payroll, accounts receivable and accounts payable, stock control, billing and so on are all computerized. Only passing attention is paid to the information needs of management. There is, however, a recognition that information is used by management in their activities and that reports can be provided as a by-product of data-processing activities. Little or no analysis of requirements is undertaken. Information produced by the MIS is generally in the form of voluminous reports from which those that need information find it impossible to disentangle what is relevant.

2. The **null** approach is a reaction against the shortcomings of the by-product approach. As its name suggests the null approach lays little emphasis on the production of formal information for management by means of an MIS. It views the activities undertaken, particularly by top management, as being dynamic and ever-changing. Under these conditions the production of formal information by an MIS according to static requirements is entirely inappropriate. Supporters of this view also find support in the work of Mintzberg (1973), who showed that as much as 80% of a chief executive's time was spent in verbal communication rather than in absorbing information provided in formal reports. While this view has much to recommend it, one should not forget that the needs of lower management are more clearly defined and are more likely to be properly served by an MIS. Secondly, the advent of modern interactive systems with user-friendly query and report generation facilities makes the production of information according to dynamically changing requirements much easier.

3. The **key variable** approach assumes that certain attributes of an organization are crucial for assessing its performance, taking decisions and planning. Examples of such variables might be total cash available, the profit-to-earnings ratio of each plant, or the turnover rate of stock. The key variables in an organization are identified and the MIS is designed to provide reports on the values of these variables.

   A variation to the straight reporting of all variables is **exception reporting**. Here the value of a variable is only reported if it lies outside some predetermined 'normal' range. The idea of variance reporting and analysis is familiar to the accountant. Indeed, the emphasis of such systems always tends to favour financial and accounting data at the expense of other information. This is unsurprising given the accountant's propensity to assess in terms of rates and ratios. The main strength of this approach lies in its recognition that to be effective information must be selectively provided.

4. **Total study** processes concentrate on establishing a comparison between the information requirements of management and the information supply of the current management information system. The IBM business systems planning (BSP) methodology does this by relying on the results of interviewing a large number of managers to determine their key decisions, objectives and information needs. The

results of this fact-gathering are displayed in matrix form for easy handling and visual understandability. An attempt is made at gaining an overall understanding of the organization's information needs and identifying just where the current system is falling down. A plan for filling the gaps is then formulated. The total study process is comprehensive and can be useful at identifying shortcomings. However, in common with many total approaches, it is extremely expensive on manpower and the vast amounts of data collected are not easily amenable to analysis. There is also a significant possibility that in attempts at imposing structure on the network of accumulated facts unacceptable biases may occur.

5. The **critical success factor** (CSF) approach is based on the assumption that an organization has certain goals and that specific factors are crucial in achieving these goals. For instance, the general goals of a company in the automobile industry might be seen in terms of maximizing earnings per share, the market share, and the return on investment as well as the goal of ensuring the success of new product lines. In order to achieve these goals the critical factors for success are automobile styling, tight control of manufacturing cost, and an efficient dealer network.

As well as general goals and critical success factors for a sector, such as the automobile sector, individual companies will have differing additional goals. These in turn will determine critical success factors based on such influences as geographical position, the past history of the company, local competitors and so on. These factors are determined by interviews with relevant top managers. By focusing attention on the critical success factors, management highlights those areas where it is crucial to have good management information. Information subsystems can then be designed to serve these critical factors.

The main applicability of this approach is in the design of systems for the provision of control information to monitor the state of the critical success factors. It is less effective at designing MIS for planning. CSF is an active approach to the design of management information systems rather than the passive acceptance of reported information based on tradition and collected historical data. The CSF approach is therefore genuinely information- rather than data-led. Its chief importance is the recognition that the purpose of providing information is to serve corporate goals.

It should be clear from the foregoing that there is no universally accepted approach to the design of an MIS. Nor should it be believed that the few approaches covered above are exhaustive of those available. There are many different methods, each with strengths, weaknesses and areas of applicability. What is becoming quite clear though is that technical issues in the design of a management information system are of secondary importance. The primary aim in design is to establish information needs and requirements. Without success in this area the MIS will be a failure. This is not a simple task, however. It is an area in which the specialist in organizational behaviour, the management scientist and the psychologist as well as the systems analyst can make valuable contributions.

1.6 Informal and formal information

Decision control and planning within an organization will be based on available information. If this is produced by standard procedures, is objective and is generally regarded as relevant to a decision the information is known as **formal information**. As well

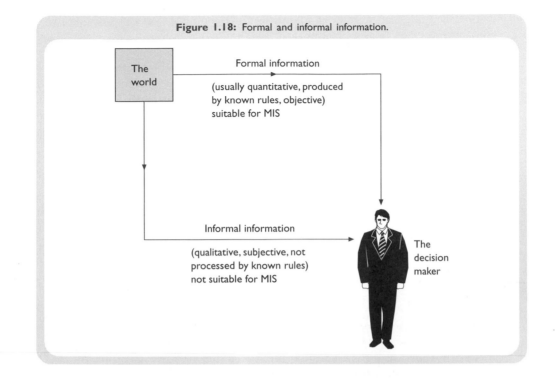

Figure 1.18: Formal and informal information.

as following organizational procedures in its production formal information is generally processed from data by known rules and presented in a standard format (see Figure 1.18). The data from which it is produced is usually quantitative and appears on formal documents within the organization. For example, formal information on actual average material costs of production will be generated from document records containing quantitative details of materials purchased and units produced. Formal information is an important component of the total information available to management. Because of its standard representation and its processing by known rules it is easy to generate using a computer system.

Informal information is also used extensively by management in its activities (Land and Kennedy-McGregor, 1987). This is often subjective, passed by word of mouth, and involves hunches, opinions, guesstimates and rumour. It generally involves explanatory and/or evaluative information. It is most likely to be qualitative in nature. Although an important determinant of decisions it is less likely to be used in their justification. For instance, a decision over job promotion from a junior to a more senior managerial post will be influenced by a variety of information. The candidate's formal qualifications, and the costs and revenues associated with the department over which the candidate has current control, are examples of formal information. The knowledge that the candidate is developing an alcohol-based problem, that the success of the candidate's current department is largely due to an efficient secretary and a competent deputy, are factors that will affect the outcome of the promotion decision. This informal information may be even quite public within the organization. More down-to-earth examples abound. For example, a formal computerized information system will give details of variances from budgets but no explanation as to why these have occurred. This information is precisely what is needed to remedy the situation. Empirical studies suggest that retention of and reliance on a large degree of informal information handling is associated with the more successful organizations (Earl and Hopwood, 1980).

The important point is that although informal information may be subjective, qualitative and not generated by standard procedures or conveyed by usual information channels, it can still be an essential component of effective decision making. Where the managerial activity relies heavily on person-to-person contact, as with top management (Mintzberg, 1973), informal information and its sources are crucial to decisions. By its nature informal information cannot be readily processed or transmitted by a computer system. There is a great danger that in designing a computerized MIS the role of this other component will be ignored. In particular where a computerized management information system is installed and much information retrieval and transmission is now handled through terminals, face-to-face contact between individuals will diminish. As a side-effect this will cut down the informal information flows and may reduce the effectiveness of decision making – just the outcome that the MIS was designed to avoid.

Summary

Information is an essential commodity for the operation and development of a modern business organization. It is distinguished from data in that information has been processed in order to serve some purpose within the business environment. In order to understand the nature of management information it is important to understand the purposes for which it is provided. Information is used in planning, in monitoring and control of business activities and in making decisions. The first two, planning and control, themselves involve decisions, so the primary purpose of information is to aid decision making.

An understanding of the way decisions are taken and the level of managerial activity involved will cast light on general properties of the information used. The categorization of the decision process into four stages – intelligence, design, choice and implementation – provides a useful framework within which to view decisions. The amount of structure implicit in a particular decision can then be analyzed into the degree of structure in each of these stages. Management activity can be seen as falling within three broad bands – operational planning and control, managerial planning and control, and strategic planning. Within each of these there will be a variety of decisions of differing degrees of structure.

Computerized information systems will only be able to provide support for the structured element of a decision because they follow formal rules in their processing. With highly structured decisions, such as in operational control, the computer may replace the decision maker rather than provide information for decision support. As one moves 'up' through the levels of management the types of decision change. At higher levels there is an emphasis on the need for information that is supplied from sources external to the organization, is highly aggregated, uncertain and future-looking, as well as being less rule-bound. The nature of this information makes it unlikely that computerized information systems relying on internally generated information will be of much value.

▷

The estimation of the value of information is a difficult area. In some cases a quantitative measure may be placed on the provision of speedier information, as in debtor control, or in the reduction of uncertainty. There are, however, intangible benefits. It is difficult, if not impossible, to analyze the contribution of more effective information to a better decision, or to isolate the impact of greater information availability to customers on their purchases. It is a great mistake to ignore the intangible, non-measurable benefits in assessing the overall benefit to the firm of a proposed information system.

The provision of information in a business needs to be looked at in a systematic way. A useful perspective from which to operate is to view the organization as a system and apply systems concepts to the design of its information system. The general characteristics of systems were covered in the chapter. It was emphasized that in order to facilitate understanding of the business it is helpful to decompose the total system into its components. These subsystems and their relations to one another can be shown by means of a hierarchy chart. Flow block diagrams provide an alternative method of representation illustrating the flows between subsystems.

Although a system can be understood by analysis into its component subsystems it should not be forgotten that this piecemeal approach to analysis may mask systemic properties that apply to the system as a whole. For example, subsystem optimization may occur at the expense of system suboptimization. The concept of control if viewed from a systems perspective is particularly important in understanding the role of the information system within the organization.

Management information systems are computerized systems that provide information for managerial decision making. These systems rely on extracting and processing data from a commonly shared corporate database that stores the results of transaction processing. Information may be provided via a forecasting model, as the result of the activity of a specially designed applications program or package, or by direct enquiry using powerful database query languages (see Chapter 7).

Designing an integrated, total management information system for an organization is a complex task and one that may lead to a final product that falls short of expectations. Instead, the MIS is better regarded as a grouping of information subsystems that are designed (or evolve) more or less independently to meet the information needs of the subsystems they support. This collection of information subsystems is unified by the shared database. In the design of an MIS the presentation of information, its timeliness, levels of accuracy and the person to whom the information is delivered must be taken into account as well as the information content. No single approach towards the design of an MIS is accepted as standard. The chapter outlined several approaches to illustrate the wide diversity of differences. Finally, informal and formal information were distinguished and the importance of the former to effective decision making stressed. No MIS should block the use of informal information as this will impair the effectiveness of decision making.

The advent of cheap, powerful microcomputers has added a new dimension to the provision of information. Together with versatile packaged software, ▷

designed for use by non-specialists in computing, these have led to the mush-rooming of alternative information centres. They may not rival the sophistication of the traditional MIS that is centrally controlled and developed, but their ability to respond to local information requirements has been both an attraction to their users and a threat to the power and importance of the centralized computing resource.

Exercises

1. Distinguish between *data* and *information*.

2. Give examples of **four** business decisions and specify the information needed for each.

3. What are the differences between strategic, tactical and operational levels of management activities?

4. What are the major differences in the types of information needed for each level of management activity?

5. What influences affect the decision-making process of a decision maker?

6. Outline a model of decision making and illustrate this with a business example.

7. What is the difference between a programmable and a non-programmable business decision? Give two examples of each from business.

8. What problems are there in assessing the value of information for decision making?

9. Outline the main features of a system.

10. Apply the basic systems model to an inventory system, explaining how each of the parts of the model is exemplified in the inventory system.

11. Define *subsystem decoupling*. Give three examples of how this may be achieved in a business system. In each case state the advantages and disadvantages of the decoupling.

12. What is a management information system?

13. What advantages do modern computerized management information systems have compared with their manual predecessors?

14. Outline the ways that information may be processed from a database and presented to management.

15. How is the structure and level of management activity related to the level of support given by a management information system?

16. Give basic guidelines that should be followed in the development of a management information system.

17. Outline **five** approaches to management information system design and explain some of the advantages and disadvantages of each. ▷

18. What are the differences between *formal* and *informal* information? Give examples of each that you encounter in your college or work routines.

19. Information has been defined as 'data processed for a purpose'. Find other definitions for the term *information.*

20. How have technological developments affected the provision of information over the last decade?

21. List **ten** information systems that you encounter in the course of your normal day-to-day activities. What information is provided by each? Can you suggest improvements in the information output which would aid the decisions that they support?

22. By giving examples, explain how there could be more than one interpretation of information. Can this be overcome in the design of the system that provides the information?

23. Could there be a *theory* of information provision?

24. What are the similarities and differences between the field of information systems and the field of management accounting?

25. 'Accountancy restricts itself to a traditional role in the provision of financial information for external bodies and cost information for internal decision making. Its importance is declining and will continue to wither in the face of the growing science of information provision.' Do you agree?

26. 'The information needs of managers are varied and change quickly in today's dynamic business environment. The lack of flexibility in computer systems implies that if managers rely on these for the provision of information then the effectiveness of their decision making will be diminished.' Do you agree?

27. From the perspective of a manager what features of an information system are important to its success?

28. What criteria do you suggest to assess the success or failure of a management information system?

29. It is insufficient (and probably not necessary) to be a skilled programmer in order to design a management information system. What are the desirable skills, areas of knowledge, background disciplines and so on, relevant to be an effective MIS designer?

30. A large company has a well-designed comprehensive management information system. What is the likely impact of this on the following roles:
(a) sales clerk for the receipt of telephone orders?
(b) sales person 'in the field'?
(c) sales manager?
(d) internal accountant?
(e) managing director?

31. You are going to open a chain of fast-food restaurants. What strategic, tactical/managerial and operational information will help ensure an ongoing, successful organization? How can a computer information system help in this enterprise?

32. Double-entry bookkeeping requires that each transaction is recorded twice within an accounting system. This is then used as a form of systems control to ensure that transactions are recorded accurately. Does the reliability of modern computer-based accounting systems make the representation of double entries redundant?

33. How can systems concepts be applied to the following:
(a) the college in which you are studying?
(b) the educational system within the country as a whole?
(c) the railway system?

34. How can systems concepts be applied to the following information systems:
(a) an airline booking/reservation/flight information system?
(b) an on-line home banking system?
(c) a public viewdata system such as Prestel?

35. 'The world is not objectively composed of systems. Systems are imposed by the view of the perceiver. Different individuals will delineate systems differently dependent on their interests and limits of control. Therefore, any approach to the analysis and design of information systems that relies heavily on systems thinking and systems concepts is likely to be subjective, non-scientific and therefore useless.' What is wrong with this point of view?

References

● Ackoff R.L. (1971). Towards a system of system concepts. *Management Science*, 661–70
● Anthony R.N. (1965). *Planning and Control Systems: A Framework for Analysis*. Cambridge MA: Harvard University Press
● Dearden J. (1972). MIS is a mirage. *Harvard Business Review*, Jan/Feb, 90–99
● Earl M. and Hopwood A. (1980). From management information to information management. in *The Information Systems Environment* (Lucas H., Land F., Lincoln T. and Supper K., eds.), Amsterdam: North Holland
● Gorry G.A. and Scott-Morton M.S. (1971). A framework for management information systems. *Sloan Management Review*, **13**(1), 55–70
● Kilman R.H. and Mitroff I.I. (1976). Quantitative versus qualitative analysis for management science: different forms for different psychological types. *TIMS Interfaces*, Feb 1976
● Land F.F. and Kennedy-McGregor M. (1987). Information and information systems: concepts and perspectives. In *Information Analysis: Selected Readings* (Galliers R.D., ed.), Wokingham: Addison-Wesley
● Mintzberg H. (1973). *The Nature of Managerial Work*. New York: Harper and Row
● Rockart J.F. (1979). Chief executives define their own data needs. *Harvard Business Review*, Mar/April 1979
● Simon H.A. (1965). *The Shape of Automation for Men and Management*. New York: Harper and Row
● Simon H.A. (1977). *The New Science of Management Decision*. Englewood Cliffs NJ: Prentice-Hall

Recommended reading

- Ackoff R.L. (1967). Management misinformation systems. *Management Science*, **14**(4), B140–56
  A classic article that covers some of the pitfalls in MIS design as well as containing its own prescriptive methodology.
- Ackoff R.L. (1971). Towards a system of system concepts. *Management Science*, 661–7
  The early pages of this article are useful in that they provide a clear explanation and definition of key systems concepts.
- Chapman J. and Holtham C. ed. (1996) *IT in Marketing*. Oxford: Alfred Waller.
  This book identifies the increasingly important role that IT plays in marketing and explains how to utilize the strength of IT in support of marketing needs. The text consists of 24 articles from different perspectives – academics, marketers, consultants, users. The first section covers an overview of issues. Later chapters specifically cover the ways in which IT can aid marketing. The final section deals with case studies.
- Davis G.B. and Olson M. (1985). *Management Information Systems: Conceptual Foundations, Structure and Development* 2nd edn. New York: McGraw-Hill
  This text covers all the major aspects of information as well as containing a number of sections on systems analysis and design.
- Dearden J. (1972). MIS is a mirage. *Harvard Business Review*, Jan/Feb, 90–99
  Worth reading for an alternative 'pessimistic' approach to the possibility of design of an integrated management information system.
- Forrester T. ed. (1985). *The Information Technology Revolution*. Oxford: Blackwell
  A collection of articles from a variety of disciplines and perspectives on various aspects of information technology and its implications for society.
- Galliers R.D. ed. (1987). *Information Analysis: Selected Readings*. Sydney: Addison-Wesley
  An interesting collection of papers, some previously unpublished, spanning the last 20 years of information systems development. The emphasis is on information and methodologies for developing information systems rather than technical issues.
- Hussain D.S. and Hussain K.M. (1992). *Information Management: Organizations, Management, and Control of Computer Processing*. Hemel Hempstead: Prentice Hall
  This is a straightforward, highly readable text suitable as an introduction for non-specialists at final-level undergraduate or postgraduate levels. The text is divided into four sections dealing with the structure of computing resources within the organization; the control of information processing including quality control, privacy, security, performance evaluation and auditing; the management of processing including standards and resistance to change; and future areas of information systems development including global information management. Each chapter contains a list of exercises.
- Liebenau J. and Backhouse J. (1992). *Understanding Information: An Introduction*. London: Macmillan
  An interesting text for those who wish to enlarge their understanding of the concept of information from a narrow technical definition. The book brings together material from a variety of disciplines including sociology, semiotics, management, philosophy and anthropology.
- Lucas H.C., Jun. (1994). *Information Systems Concepts for Management* 5th edn. McGraw-Hill

A lucid introduction to the central ideas in the field of management information and the impact of computers on the provision of information for organizations.

● Winfield I. (1991). *Organisations and Information Technology: Systems Power and Job Design*. Oxford: Blackwell Scientific Publications

This book examines the impact of IT on organizations – the power structures, the impact of telecommunications on the dispersal of the workforce, career structures and management practices. It is designed for students on a wide range of programmes from business studies to computing. It adopts an organizational perspective.

Chapter 2

Strategy and Information Systems

2.1 The need for a business strategy
2.2 Business strategic planning
2.3 Business information systems strategy

In Chapter 1 the central idea of a business information system was developed by initially exploring the concepts of 'system' and 'business information'. Any introduction or expansion of an information system in a business will require:

- the allocation of large resources;
- a recognition that the firm's activities will change as a result of the information system;
- the intention to improve the organization's services or increase its profits.

Such important decisions should be taken in the light of the business strategy. The subject of this chapter is to expand on the relationship between strategy and information systems. Initially the need for a business strategy is explained together with a suggested overview of the business strategic planning process. The way in which this necessitates an information systems strategy is covered. There are many frameworks within which information systems strategy can be viewed. One framework is outlined in the chapter and its various components are explained. Each emphasizes a different perspective on the issues that a firm may wish to take into account when formulating strategy. They all have one feature in common though – they acknowledge the need for an information systems strategy to be determined by the business needs of the organization, not by the functions of available technology.

2.1 *The need for a business strategy*

A business will function on a day-to-day basis without the obvious need for a business strategy. Orders will be taken from customers, goods despatched, invoices sent and payments from customers acknowledged. Where stock runs low, purchase orders will be drafted and sent, goods will be received, stock stored and inventory records updated, and when the invoices arrive from the suppliers these will be authorized for payment and payment made. Work will be scheduled and products manufactured. Payroll will produce payslips and instruct banks to make automated payment of wages and salaries at the end of the month. Sales reps' cars will be put into garages for maintenance, bills received and so on. This is the day-to-day functioning of business.

A business, or any other organization, may continue to function in this way for some period of time without reference to any strategy. However, a business under these conditions is analogous to a ship under way without a destination or without reference to the environment within which it is voyaging.

There needs to be a strategy and strategic planning for a business for several reasons:

1. As was seen in Chapter 1 the individual departments within an organization (subsystems within a system) may function well in terms of their own objectives but still not serve the objectives of the organization. This is because of a lack of co-ordination between departments, because departments themselves have specific objectives counter to those of the organization, or because subsystems optimization may on occasion lead to total systems suboptimization. It is therefore important that there be an agreed and communicated set of objectives for the organization and a plan on how to achieve these.

2. The organization will on occasion need to make major resource allocations, especially for the purchase and development of new plant, property and machines. Information systems will need expensive hardware and will incur design costs. They will need large resource allocations. These allocations can only be made against an agreed direction for the organization – a strategy for the future.

3. The organization will have responsibilities to a number of different groups. Included amongst these would be the owners, whether it be the shareholders or the public, the employees, the customers, and those that provide finance such as banks. These parties will have a particular interest in the corporate strategy, as their interests will be served or otherwise by the extent to which the strategy takes into account their interests and the success of the organization in meeting these interests.

2.2 Business strategic planning

There is no *one* accepted method that a business should adopt in its strategic planning. There are, however, a number of different steps that would normally be taken in the development of a business strategy (see Figure 2.1).

Most large organizations will already have strategies currently formulated. These strategies are often for a future period of five years. This is a convenient time horizon. If it were longer then future uncertainties would render the planning process for the later stages of little value; if it were shorter then many developments could not be planned through to fruition. (For some organizations the planning horizon will need to be significantly extended – national defence and the nuclear industry are two such examples.)

The business strategy is not frozen into the operations of the business but is evaluated and redrafted from time to time. This often occurs on a yearly basis when the strategy for the next five years will be decided. The business strategic planning process then yields a five-year rolling plan. Unless there are serious problems within the organization or it is undergoing major internal change it is likely that changes to strategy will be incremental. The following sections expand on Figure 2.1.

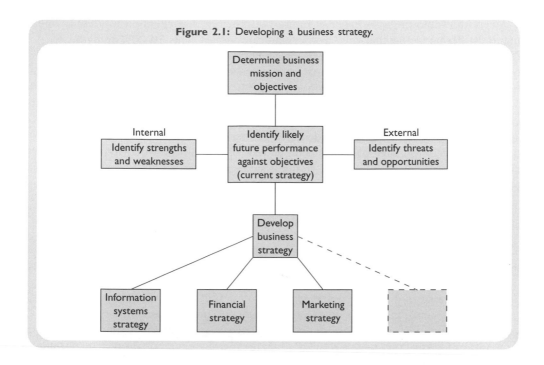

Figure 2.1: Developing a business strategy.

2.2.1   Determine the business mission and objectives

The mission of the organization will be a general statement of its overall purpose and aims. It often consists of a number of individual aims. Examples might be (for a chemical company) 'to become a major supplier of agrochemicals to the farming sector through the research and development of new and more effective fertilizer and pest controls' or (for a chain of hi-fi shops) 'to expand the number of retail outlets and diversify into the sale of all leisure electronic goods'.

The objectives, both medium- and long-term, should support the organization's overall mission. Each objective should have a measurable performance indicator, which can be used to determine the success of the organization in meeting the objective. In the above, an objective could well be 'to increase the number of retail outlets by 35% within three years and the square metres of floor space devoted to sales by 50% within the same period'.

2.2.2   Identify the likely future performance against objectives

The organization should be continuously monitoring and evaluating its performance against its current objectives. Part of this monitoring process will involve forecasts of future sales, cash flows, materials requirements, and profitability, based on the current situation. In other words, when developing business strategy the current operations of the organization will have an implied future scenario, which can be compared with desired objectives.

As an input into the assessment of future performance it is common to identify internal and external factors that will have a significant impact. This **SWOT** (strengths, weaknesses, opportunities, threats) **analysis** will identify internal strengths, such as a highly trained and flexible workforce, and internal weaknesses, such as a poor internal information system, together with external opportunities, such as the opening up of trade through a common European Market, and external threats, such as the absence of low economic entry barriers to the industry.

Given the predictions and the identified strengths, weaknesses, opportunities and threats, it will be possible to estimate the extent of the gap between future objectives and forecast future performance. The business strategy should determine a series of measures and plans that will remove this gap.

2.2.3 Develop the business strategy

The business strategy will be the set of plans that the business will implement in order to achieve its stated objectives. These plans may involve new projects or the continued operation of existing activities.

Most businesses are modelled and managed in a functional way. Human resources, information systems, marketing, financial management, and production are examples of common functions. The business strategy will have as components a human resource strategy, an information systems strategy, a marketing strategy and so on. These strategies will support the business strategy and interact with one another. The information systems strategy is taking on a key role as more businesses rely increasingly heavily on their computerized information systems for all aspects of their business functions.

2.3 Business information systems strategy

The previous section identified, in broad terms, the steps taken in strategic planning. But it provides no insight into what specific factors should be taken into account in business information strategy development. In particular it does not give any framework within which to answer the questions as to which information systems should be developed and why. This section will be directed at these two issues.

First it is important to distinguish between a business information systems strategy and a business information technology strategy.

The **business information systems strategy** is focused on determining what information systems must be provided in order that the objectives of the business strategy are realized. The concentration is therefore on determining information needs and ensuring that the information systems strategy aligns with the business strategy.

The **business information technology strategy** is focused on determining what technology and technological systems development are needed in order that the business information systems strategy can be realized. The concentration is therefore on how to provide the information, not on what information is required. The strategy will also cover how the information resource and information systems development is to be managed.

There is a close interaction between the information systems strategy and the information technology strategy. The importance of distinguishing between them indicates that the emphasis on information systems is that strategy is led by the needs of the business, not by technology.

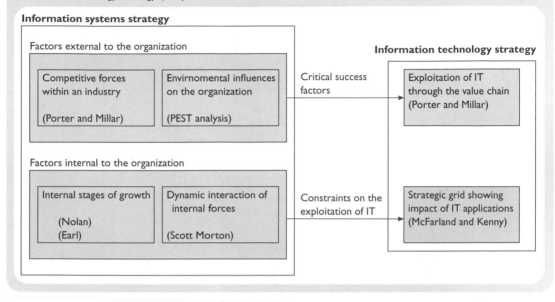

Figure 2.2: A framework for the interrelation of influences on information systems strategy and information technology strategy (Adapted from source material Susan Gasson, Warwick Business School).

There has been a considerable debate as to how best to develop a strategy for information systems/information technology. The urgency of this debate has been fuelled by the speed with which information technology has changed, and by a recognition that information technology is being used less in a support function within the business but is increasingly integral to the business operations and development itself.

Many models have been put forward to guide the strategist in formulation. An important selection is explained in the rest of this section. They have different approaches and objectives, and cover different aspects of the strategy formulation process. The framework in Figure 2.2 indicates that some models address the area of information systems strategy whereas others can be seen as more relevant to information technology strategy. Within the former (information systems strategy) there is a division between those approaches which concentrate on internal aspects of the business as compared to those that focus on areas within the environment of the organization.

2.3.1 Competitive forces within an industry – the five forces model

Modern technology is increasingly being used as part of an information systems strategy which yields competitive advantage for the organization. One way in which a business can gain a **competitive advantage** is by using information technology to change the structure of the industry within which it operates.

The five forces model (Porter and Millar, 1985) views a business, operating within an industry, as being subject to five main competitive forces. The way in which the business responds to these forces will determine its success. These forces are illustrated in Figure 2.3. Information technology can aid a business in using these competitive forces to its advantage. In this way information technology can be seen as a strategic competitive weapon.

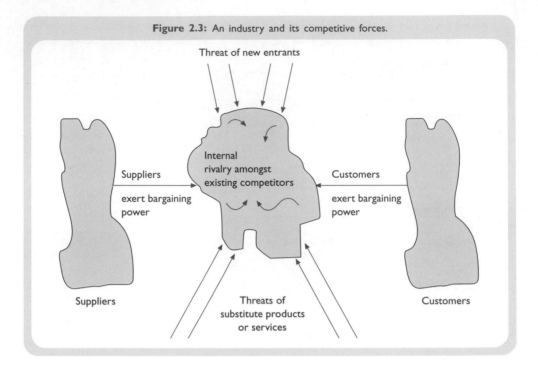

Figure 2.3: An industry and its competitive forces.

Suppliers

The suppliers provide the necessary inputs of raw materials, machinery and manufactured components for the firm's production process. The suppliers to a business can exert their bargaining power on that business by pushing up the prices of inputs supplied using the threat of taking their supply goods elsewhere to a competitor business in the same industry. It is in the interests of the business to make alternative rival businesses who would purchase the supplier's goods seem less attractive to the supplier.

One way of achieving this is by creating good relationships with the supplier by using **electronic data interchange (EDI)**. EDI requires that there is an electronic connection between the business and its suppliers. When supplies are to be ordered this is accomplished by sending structured electronic messages to the supplier firm. The supplier firm's computer decodes these messages and acts appropriately. The advantage of this for both partners is:

- reduced delivery times
- reduced paperwork and associated labour costs
- increased accuracy of information.

For the business that is purchasing supplies, EDI can be part of its just-in-time approach to manufacturing. This yields benefits in terms of reduced warehousing costs.

Creating links with suppliers is becoming increasingly important in the manufacturing sector especially between car manufacturers and the suppliers of component parts.

Customers

Customers can exert power over a business by threatening to purchase the product or service from a competitor. This power is large if there are few customers and many competitors who are able to supply the product or service.

One way in which a business may reduce the ability of a customer to move to another competitor is by introducing switching costs. These are defined as costs, financial or otherwise, that a customer would incur by switching to another supplier. One way of achieving switching costs is to allow the customer to have online ordering facilities for the business's service or product. It is important that the customer gains a benefit from this or there is little incentive for the customer to put itself in a potentially weak bargaining position.

For instance with electronic banking the belief is that once a customer has established a familiarity with one system, gaining advantage from it, there will be a learning disincentive to switch to another. Another example is American Hospital Supplies. It has improved its competitive position by allowing online terminals into customer hospitals. These allowed the swift order/delivery of supplies by using less skilled personnel as compared to more expensive purchase agents. Once established it became very difficult for a hospital to change suppliers.

Substitute products

Substitute products or services are those that are within the industry but are differentiated in some way. There is always the danger that a business may lose a customer to the purchase of a substitute product from a rival business because that product meets the needs of the customer more closely. Information technology can prevent this happening in two ways. Firstly it can be used to introduce switching costs as stated above. Or the technology may be used to provide differentiated products swiftly by the use of computer aided design/computer aided manufacturing (CAD/CAM). In this latter case the business produces the substitute product itself.

New entrants

Within any industry there is always the threat that a new company might enter and attract some of the existing demand for the products of that industry. This will reduce the revenue and profit of the current competitors. The traditional response has been for mature business within an industry to develop barriers to entry. These have been:

- exploiting economies of scale in production
- creating brand loyalty
- creating legal barriers to entry – for example patents
- using effective production methods involving large capital outlays.

Information technology can assist a business in developing these barriers. In as far as information technology makes a firm more productive, for instance by reducing labour costs or speeding up aspects of the production process, any firm attempting to enter the market place will be competitively disadvantaged without a similar investment in capital. If expensive CAD/CAM equipment is common for the production of differentiated products speedily then this will also act as a barrier to entry.

Competitor rivalry

Unless in a monopoly position, any business within an industry is subject to competition from other firms. This is perhaps the greatest competitive threat that the business experiences. Information technology can be used as part of the firm's competitive strategy against its rivals as illustrated in the preceding sections. Close linkages with suppliers and customers produce competitive forces against rivals, as does the investment in technology allowing product differentiation and cost reductions.

In some cases the investment in information technology will be necessary to pre-empt the competitiveness of other businesses. The major investment by the banks in automated teller machines is just one example of this.

2.3.2 Environmental influences on the organization – PEST analysis

Porter's five force model considers the industry sector within which the business operates. However in formulating strategy there are other external factors which the strategist needs to take into account. This is the function of a PEST (Political, Economic, Socio-cultural, Technological) analysis.

The questions to be asked are:

'Which environmental factors are currently affecting and are likely to affect the organization?'

'What is the relevant importance of these now and in the future?'

Examples of the areas to be covered under each heading are given below:

- **Political/legal:** monopolies legislation, tax policy, employment law, environmental protection laws, regulations over international trade, government continuity and stability.

- **Economic:** inflation, unemployment, money supply, cost of parts and energy, economic growth trends, the business cycle – national and international.

- **Socio-cultural:** population changes – age and geographical distribution, lifestyle changes, educational level, income distribution, attitudes to work/leisure/consumerism.

- **Technological:** new innovations and development, obsolescence, technology transfer, public/private investment in research.

At a minimal level the PEST analysis can be regarded as no more than a checklist of items to attend to when drawing-up strategy. However, it can also be used to identify key environmental factors. These are factors that will have a long-term major influence on strategy and need special attention. For instance, included in the key environmental factors for a hospital will be demographic trends (increased percentage of older citizens in the population and decreased percentage of those who are of working age), increases in technological support, government policy on funding and preventative medicine. These key factors are ones that will have significant impact on strategy and must be taken into account.

PEST analysis may also be used to identify long-term drivers of change. For instance, globalization of a business may be driven by globalization of technology, of information, of the market and of the labour force.

In general a PEST analysis is used to focus on a range of environmental influences outside of the organization, and (perhaps) outside of the industry, which are important to longer-term change, and therefore strategy, but may be ignored in the day to day decisions of the business.

As has been seen in Chapter 1 where the characteristics of information needed for decision making were covered, the information needed for strategic decisions partly comes from outside the organization, is future looking, and may be highly uncertain. This is clearly true of some of the areas considered by the PEST analysis. This contributes towards the difficulty of the important task of drawing up strategy.

2.3.3 Internal stages of growth

The preceding two sections explain the way that factors external to the organization will need to be taken into account when developing an information systems strategy. However, factors internal to the organization will also need to be introduced into the strategy. The introduction, development and use of computing information systems cannot be achieved overnight. It requires the organization internally to undergo change and a learning process. This concerns not only the technological factors of information systems but also the planning, control, budgetary and user involvement aspects.

Over the last twenty years several influential approaches have been developed which look at the development of information systems within an organization as proceeding through several stages of growth. In the following sections two of these models will be considered.

The Nolan Stage Model

The earliest of these models, developed by Nolan, explains the extent and type of information systems used within an organization as being determined by the maturity of growth of information systems within that organization.

It was Nolan's original thesis that all organizations went through four stages of growth. This was later refined by adding two intermediate growth stages. The six stage growth model (Nolan, 1979) was used to identify which stage of growth characterised an organization's information systems maturity. This, in turn, had further implications for successful planning to proceed to the next level of growth. The model has been used as the basis in over 200 consultancy studies within the USA and has been incorporated into IBM's information systems planning (Nolan, 1984). Before considering any planning implications of the model the stages will be briefly explained.

The Nolan Stage model purports to explain the evolution of an information system within an organization by consideration of various stages of growth. The model is based on empirical research on information systems in a wide range of organizations in the 1970s. Expenditure on IT increases with the stages (see Figure 2.4).

Within each stage of growth four major growth processes must be planned, managed and co-ordinated:

- **Applications portfolio:** The set of applications which the information systems must support – for example financial planning, order processing, on-line customer enquiries.
- **DP organization:** The orientation of the data processing – for example as centralized technology driven, as management of data as a resource.

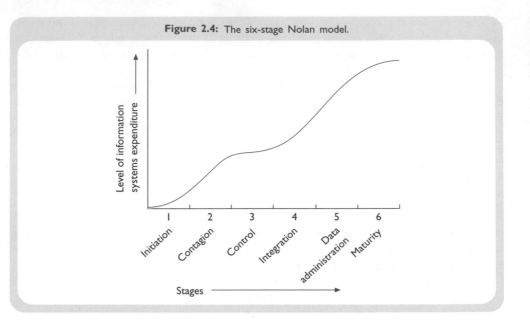

Figure 2.4: The six-stage Nolan model.

- **DP planning and control:** – for example degree of control, formalization of planning process, management of projects, extent of strategic planning.
- **User awareness:** The extent to which users are aware of and involved with the technology.

The stages have different characteristics (see Figure 2.4).

- **Stage 1 Initiation:** The computer system is used for low level transaction processing. Typically high volume data processing of accounting, payroll and billing data characterize the stage. There is little planning of information systems. Users are largely unaware of the technology. New applications are developed using traditional languages (such as COBOL). There is little systematic methodology in systems analysis and design.
- **Stage 2 Contagion:** The awareness of the possibilities of IT increases amongst users, but there is little real understanding of the benefits or limitations. Users become enthusiastic and require more applications development. IT is generally treated as an overhead within the organization and there is little check on user requests for more applications. Budgetary control over IT expenditure and general managerial control over the development of the information system are low. Technical problems with the development of programs appear. An increasing proportion of the programming effort is taken in maintenance of systems. This is a period of unplanned growth.
- **Stage 3 Control:** As continuing problems occur with the unbridled development of projects there is a growing awareness of the need to manage the information systems function. The data processing department is reorganized. The DP manager becomes more accountable having to justify expenditure and activities in the same way as other major departments within the organization. The proliferation

of projects is controlled by imposing charges on user departments for project development and the use of computer services. Users see little progress in the development of information systems. Pent-up demand and frustration occur within user departments.

● **Stage 4 Integration:** Having achieved the consolidation of Stage 3 the organizational data processing function takes on a new direction. It becomes more orientated towards information provision. Concurrent with this and facilitating it, there is the introduction of interactive terminals in user departments, the development of a database and the introduction of data communications technologies. User departments, which have been significantly controlled in Stage 3 by budgetary and organizational controls, are now able to satisfy the pent up demand for information support. There is a significant growth in the demand for applications and a consequent large increase in the supply and expenditure to meet this demand. As the rapid growth occurs the reliance on computer based controls becomes ineffective. In particular redundancy of data and duplication of data become a significant problem.

● **Stage 5 Data Administration:** The response to the problems of Stage 4 is to introduce controls on the proper administration of data. The emphasis shifts from regarding data as the input to a process which produces information as an output, to the view that data is a resource within an organization. As such it must be properly planned and managed. This stage is characterized by the development of an integrated database serving organizational needs. Applications are developed relying on access to the database. Users become more accountable for the integrity and correct use of the information resource.

● **Stage 6 Maturity:** Stage 6 typifies the mature organization. The information system is integral to the functioning of the organization. The applications portfolio closely mirrors organizational activities. The data structure becomes a data model for the organization. There is a recognition of the strategic importance of information. Planning of the information system is coordinated and comprehensive. The manager of the information system takes on the same importance in the organizational hierarchy as the director of finance or the director of human resources.

The Nolan model – implications for strategic planning   The Nolan Stage Model was originally intended to be a descriptive/analytic model which gave an evolutionary explanation for information systems development within an organization. It identified a pattern of growth which an organization needed to go through in order to achieve maturity. Each stage involved a learning process. It was not possible to skip a stage in the growth process. As such the model became widely accepted. On the Nolan analysis most organizations will be at Stage 4 or Stage 5.

However, the model has also become used as part of a planning process. Applied this way the organization identifies the stage it is currently occupying. This has implications for what has to be achieved in order to progress to the next stage. Planning can and should be achieved, it is argued, in the areas of the applications portfolio, the technology used, the planning and control structures and the level of user awareness and involvement. Managers should attend to planning which will speed the process of progression to the next stage and the accompanying organizational learning.

The Nolan model – critique The model is based on empirical research in the 1970s. It cannot, therefore, incorporate recognition of the impact of the new technologies of the 1980s or 1990s. In particular its concentration on database technology ignores the fact that:

- the growth of microcomputers has significantly increased the extent to which users have been able to use information technology and to become autonomous of the computer centre;
- there have been important developments in the area of communications and networks, especially local area networks linking microcomputers and other technologies together;
- new software development tools and decision support tools have shifted the emphasis to the user as development agent.

Despite these limitations the Nolan Stage Model still provides a way of viewing the development of information systems within an organization by recognizing:

- that growth of information systems within an organization must be accompanied by an organizational learning process;
- that there is an important interplay between the stimulation of growth involving the presence of slack resources together with the need for control;
- that there is a shift of emphasis between the users and the computer centre in the process of growth;
- that there is move from concentration on processor technology to data management.

The Earl model

Earl (1989), along with others (e.g. Hirscheim *et al.*, 1988; Galliers and Sutherland, 1991) takes seriously the idea of maturity through stages of growth. For Earl it is of particular importance to note that stages of growth apply to different technologies. The S-curve is still reflected for each technology with the relationship existing between the degree of organizational learning, the technology and time (see Figure 2.5). It is also acknowledged that different parts of the organization may be at different points on the stages of growth.

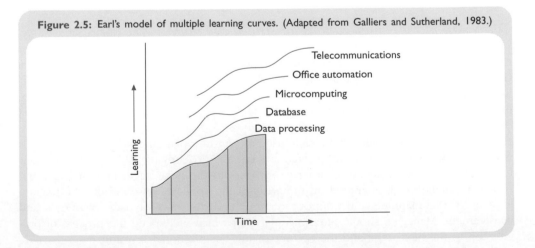

Figure 2.5: Earl's model of multiple learning curves. (Adapted from Galliers and Sutherland, 1983.)

Table 2.1: Earl's stage planning model (Galliers and Sutherland, 1991).

Factor	Stages					
	I	*II*	*III*	*IV*	*V*	*VI*
Task	Meeting demands	IS/IT audit	Business support	Detailed planning	Strategic advantage	Business–IT strategy linkage
Objective	Provide service	Limit demand	Agree priorities	Balance IS portfolio	Pursue opportunities	Integrate strategies
Driving force	IS reaction	IS led	Senior management led	User/IS partnership	IS/executive led: user involvement	Strategic coalitions
Methodological emphasis	*Ad hoc*	Bottom-up survey	Top-down analysis	Two-way prototyping	Environmental scanning	Multiple methods
Context	User/IS inexperience	Inadequate IS resources	Inadequate business/IS plans	Complexity apparent	IS for competitive advantage	Maturity, collaboration
Focus	IS department		Organization-wide			Environment

Earl's model concentrates not on the interplay between expenditure/control but rather on the task and objectives of planning at each stage. The view taken by Earl is that the early focus on information systems development is planned around the extent of IT coverage and the attempt to satisfy user demands. As the organization develops along the learning curve the orientation of planning changes. Senior managers recognize the need for information systems development to link to business objectives and so take a major role in the planning process. During the final stages of growth the planning of information systems takes on a strategic perspective with planning being carried out by teams consisting of senior management, users and information systems staff (see Table 2.1).

2.3.4 Dynamic interaction of internal forces

Nolan and Earl were interested in the various internal stages of growth through which organizations progress in the use of information technology, together with the implications of this for strategic planning. The current section takes a different perspective in that it concentrates on internal organizational forces and how these must be acknowledged in the derivation of a business information systems strategy.

It has long been recognized that there is an internal organizational interaction between people, the tasks they perform, the technology they use to perform these and the structure of the organization in which they work. This derives from organizational psychology and has influenced strategy formulation and, among other areas, approaches to the analysis and design of information systems (see Chapter 15, section 15.2.2 on socio-technical analysis and design).

Following this theme, an organization may be viewed as being subject to five internal forces in a state of dynamic equilibrium (as well as being subject to external influences and forces). This is illustrated in Figure 2.6. It is the central goal of the organization's,

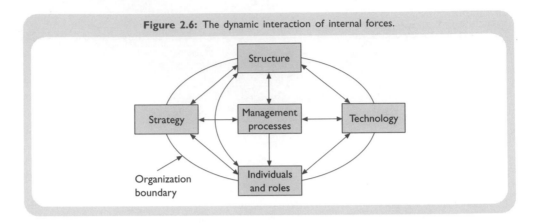

Figure 2.6: The dynamic interaction of internal forces.

management to control these forces and their interaction over time in order that the organization may meet its business objectives and its mission. Scott Morton (1991) takes this model as the basis for research into the likely impacts that changes in IT will have on organizations, and to provide theories of management on how these changes may be steered to the benefit of the organizations concerned.

1. **Technology** will continue to change. The effect of this will be to cut down 'distance' within the organization as geographical separation is rendered less important. This will be aided through the development of telecommunications and will be evidenced by new applications such as e-mail, the intranet, video-conferencing, and shared data resources. The organizational memory and access to it will be improved through more effective classification of data and its storage.

2. **Individuals and their roles** will change as information technology provides support for tasks and increases interconnection within the organization. This will require significant investment in training and the reclassification of roles. The nature of jobs will change as IT facilitates some roles, makes some redundant and has no effect on others.

3. The **structure** of the organization will change as roles vary. The greater interconnection brought about by information technology will lead to integration at the functional level.

4. **Management processes** will be assisted by the provision of easy access to fast, flexible, virtually costless, decision-relevant internal information. This will enable new approaches to operational planning and control within the organization.

5. The key to effective planning and to the benefits of new information systems enabled by information technology, lies in the proper use of **strategy**. This will ensure that information systems/information technology developments are aligned with the business strategy.

2.3.5 Exploitation of IT through the value chain

Continuing developments in information technology, together with decreasing costs, have enabled businesses to exploit new opportunities to change the nature of competition. In

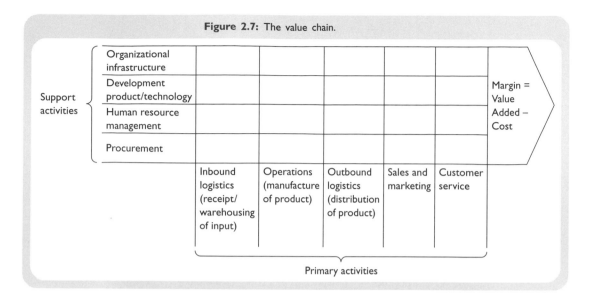

Figure 2.7: The value chain.

a series of publications (Porter, 1980, 1985; Porter and Millar, 1985) Michael Porter has developed a model of a business organization and its associated industry by focusing on the value chain and the competitive forces experienced (five forces model). This allows an understanding of the way competition affects strategy and the way information provision, in its turn, affects competition.

Central to Porter's analysis of the internal aspects of the business and the strategy for its exploitation of IT is the value chain. The **value chain** divides the firm's activities into those that it must carry out in order to function effectively (see Figure 2.7). The value chain consists of nine **value activities**. Each of these activities adds value to the final product. In order to be competitively advantaged the business must carry out these activities at a lower cost than its competitors or must use these activities to create a product that is differentiated from those of its competitors and thereby be able to charge a premium price for the product. The nine activities are divided into two categories – **primary activities** which are concerned with the direct generation of the organization's output to its customers, and **support activities** which contribute to the operation of the primary activities.

● **Primary activities**
- *inbound logistics*: activities which bring inputs into the organization such as receipt of goods, warehousing, inventory control;
- *operations*: activities which transform the product into its final form whether it be physical good or service;
- *outbound logistics*: activities which despatch products and distribute them to clients;
- *marketing and sales*: activities concerned with locating and attracting customers for the purchase of the product – for example advertising;
- *service*: activities which provide service and support to customers – for example maintenance, installation.

Figure 2.8: Information technology in the value chain.

Support activities	Organizational infrastructure	Financial planning models Space optimization		Administrative information Building management systems		Margin = Value Added – Cost
	Development product/ technology	Computer-aided design Market analysis/modelling				
	Human resource management	Optimization of distribution of personnel				
	Procurement	Online ordering of inputs through electronic data interchange (EDI)				
		Automated warehousing	Customization of manufacturing process	Processing orders (through EDI) and automated distribution	Telemarketing	Online monitoring and servicing of equipment. Scheduling servicing
		Inbound logistics (receipt/ warehousing of input)	Operations (manufacture of product)	Outbound logistics (distribution of product)	Sales and marketing	Customer service

Primary activities

● Support activities

- *firm infrastructure*: activities which support the whole value chain – for example general management, financial planning;
- *human resource management*: activities concerned with training, recruitment and personnel resource planning;
- *technology development*: activities which identify and develop ways in which machines and other kinds of technology can assist the firm's activities;
- *procurement*: activities which locate sources of input and purchase these inputs.

As well as having a physical component, every value activity creates and uses information. The competitive advantage of the organization is enhanced by reducing costs in each activity as compared to its competitors. Information technology is used to reduce the cost of the information component of each activity. For instance, inbound logistics activities use information technology to provide information on goods received and use this to update inventory records. Financial planning, an infrastructure activity, will use information technology to collect information provided by many of the firm's activities to generate forecasts on future performance. Information technology may also be used to increase product differentiation for specific customer needs. For instance operations can use information technology to control the production process to generate tailor made output for customers.

Where previously the organization relied on the manual production of information, it is now more common for information technology to permeate its entire value chain (see Figure 2.8). The greater the extent to which this reduces costs or enables product differentiation the greater the competitive advantage conferred on the business.

The organization's value chain is composed of a set of interdependent activities that are linked to one another. These **linkages** need to be coordinated in order to ensure that the activities are carried out in the most effective way. Information is necessary to manage these linkages. One way this may occur is in **just-in-time (JIT) manufacturing**. JIT is an approah to production which requires the output of each stage of the production process to be fed into the following stage without undergoing an intermediate storage stage of indefinite length. The benefits of JIT are that it removes intermediate inventory storage costs for personnel and space, and prevents the organization's working capital being tied up in goods waiting in the production process. JIT can also be extended outside the organization to include the purchase of inputs that are delivered just in time for the manufacturing process which, in turn, produces an output just in time to meet the specific needs of a customer. **Automated billing systems** or **electronic data interchange (EDI)** can be used for the external linkages. For JIT to work the effective management of linkages is imperative and it is here that information technology can provide the necessary information – accurately and on time. Hence cost reductions in the organization's value activities are achieved and the business can gain a competitive advantage.

In summary, information technology is at the basis of information systems within business which increase the competitive advantage of that business over its competitors by:

- reducing the cost of the information component of value activities;
- allowing product differentiation;
- providing information for the effective management of linkages.

The importance of this approach is that it views information not merely as a support for the tasks that a business undertakes but rather as permeating the entire set of business activities. As such its correct provision can give the organization a strategic competitive advantage over its rivals in the industry.

2.3.6 The strategic grid

The strategic grid (McFarlan and McKenny, 1983; McFarlan, 1984) assists the organization in determining within which of four categories an organization finds itself with respect to the impact of IT and its information systems (see Figure 2.9).

The grid plots the extent to which the **existing** applications portfolio has a strategic impact against the likely strategic impact of the **planned** applications development. The four resulting possible positions are:

- **Support:** The role of the information system is to support the transaction processing requirements of the organization. The emphasis on information technology is on cost reduction and information is produced as a by-product of the process.
- **Factory:** The current information systems are an integral part of the strategic plan of the organization. Few strategic developments are planned and the focus of IT activity is on improving existing systems.
- **Turnaround:** This is a transitional phase. Organizations move from the 'support' category to this as a result of internal and external pressures. Internal pressures result from the confidence of management in the support systems together with the recognition of the strategic benefits of information technology as a competitive

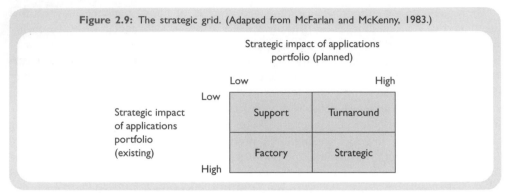

Figure 2.9: The strategic grid. (Adapted from McFarlan and McKenny, 1983.)

weapon. The external pressures come from improving technology acting as an enabler for development together with the increasing use of information technology by competitor firms within the same industry. If the firm continues with strategic innovation it will enter the 'strategic' category, otherwise it will revert to the 'factory' category.

- **Strategic:** This category requires a continuing development of information systems through the exploitation of Information Technology at a strategic level. It can only be accomplished with the commitment of senior management and the recognition of the integral part played by the information system within the entire fabric of the firm's activities.

These categories aid managers in identifying the role and importance of information technology within their business. It plots 'where we are now' rather than 'where we want to go' or 'how we get there'. This is not unimportant since each of the categories implies a strategy for the management of the information system. The 'support' and 'factory' positions are essentially static. They concern the more effective and efficient use of the existing applications portfolio, and as such do not require an extensive senior management involvement. The 'turnaround' and 'strategic' categories imply a dynamic strategy which must, if it is to be successful, involve senior management in an active way in the implementation of strategy. An organization moving from one category to another should be prepared to adopt the appropriate involvement of senior management.

2.3.7 Critical success factors

The Critical Success Factor (CSF) approach was developed initially by John Rockart (Rockart, 1979). Critical success factors are those limited areas of a firm's operations which if satisfactory will ensure that the objectives of the business are achieved. They are thus critical to the competitive performance of the organization. In order to ensure that the critical success factors are satisfactory it is important to have appropriate information identifying their performance. This is a guide to which information systems should be developed viz. those that give information on the critical success factors, and the consequent implications for the information technology strategy.

For example, consider the case of a mail order supplier of clothes:

Objective: To increase market share by 5% per annum.

CSF's: Effective advertising; faster customer order processing; faster distribution service.

Information systems applications: Market research database and analysis; computerized telephone order processing; computerized delivery scheduling.

Each objective taken from the business strategic plan will yield a set of CSF's. In order to identify the CSF's, which will be different for different organizations and different sectors, it is recommended that a consensus is achieved amongst senior managers. This can be achieved in special workshops using an outside facilitator. Not all CSF's will demand information systems support in tracking their performance. However, for those that do the method acts as a valuable way of focusing the development of information systems, particularly the applications portfolio. The strength of using CSF's is that they provide the important link between the business strategy and the information systems strategy with the consequent impact on the information technology strategy.

More recently the CSF approach has been extended (Henderson, Rockart, Sifonis, 1987). The extended approach recognizes that critical success factors determine three distinct areas. Firstly each critical success factor remains critical based only on certain assumptions and information is required on these assumptions. Secondly the performance of each critical success factor must be monitored. This requires information (as explained above). Finally each critical success factor will entail decisions which can be aided by information systems providing decision support. These three areas determine the information systems development.

Summary

There is a general recognition that businesses must strategically plan in order to ensure that individual operating units act in a coordinated way to support the business objectives of the organization, that those objectives are realizable given the internal resources within the business and the external environment, and that current and future resource allocation is directed to the realization of these corporate objectives. Although there is no one accepted method of strategic planning central themes are commonly accepted. Specifically there must be a determination of business objectives, an identification of future performance against these objectives, and the development of a plan to close any identified gap.

Businesses are commonly viewed as being composed of various functions. Each of these will require information in order to plan, operate and monitor performance. The function of the provision of information is thus key to an organization's success. The development of an information systems strategy to support this function recognizes the priority of information systems planning over information technology planning. The latter supports the former.

There are many frameworks within which one can develop an information systems strategy. The one provided in the chapter distinguishes the information systems strategy from the information technology strategy and within the former recognizes both the influence of factors external to the organization and those internal to it.

One of the factors external to the firm is the forces exerted on it depending on the structure of the industry within which it operates. These competitive forces may be exerted by suppliers, customers, existing competitors, new entrants or through differentiated products. An analysis of these forces can provide a guide to information systems strategy. A PEST analysis takes into account other political, economic, socio-cultural and technological influences.

Emphasizing internal factors the work of Nolan suggests that organizations undergo a series of several discrete stages of development in their evolution. By identifying the current stage an organization can plan the most effective and swift route to the next. Although this research was based largely on the evolution of mainframe systems there are striking similarities with the development of microcomputers and local area networks. This approach has been extended by Earl. As well as the internal evolution of the information system within the organization and its connection with technological development, it is important to recognize that the technology will have an impact on the work of individuals and the roles they fulfil. Management control may be significantly effected along with the internal structure of the organization. This must be taken into account in the formulation of strategy.

The work of Porter and Millar views the firm as being composed of a linked value chain consisting of nine primary and supporting activities. If an organization is to be competitive then each of these must function at a cost advantage over similar functions within its competitors, or help to produce a differentiated product. The way in which information technology can be used as a competitive weapon and support these activities and co-ordinate their linkages was examined. The strategic grid of McFarlan and McKenny identifies the strategic impact of existing computer supported applications as compared to planned applications. The firm broadly falls into one of four categories – support, factory, turnaround and strategic. Different information systems strategies are suggested dependent on which category best fits an organization currently and which best fits its likely development.

Critical successful factor approaches view an organization as being crucially dependent on certain factors to meet its objectives. In order to keep the organization on its planned course in reaching these objectives, information on the workings of the factors needs to be supplied by the information system. In this way the strategic information system needs of an organization can be identified and information technology planned to support these.

The chapter looks at a selection of the more influential approaches to information systems strategic planning. Other approaches, for example the Information Engineering approach, attempt to provide a methodology for the complete planning and development process from strategic information systems through to the implementation of designed systems. What has been emphasized in this chapter is that business information needs should determine strategy not the characteristics of the various technologies.

Exercises

1. Consider the business, organization or university within which you work. Does it have:
   (a) a strategic plan?
   (b) a process for developing and reviewing this strategy?
   (c) an information systems strategic plan?
   (d) a process for developing and reviewing the information systems strategy?

2. To what extent and how should the following stakeholders be involved in the setting of information systems strategy:
   (a) users?
   (b) senior management?
   (c) the computer centre?
   (d) customers/suppliers?

3. Several approaches to strategic planning were described in the chapter. Are they all appropriate? Do they complement each other or do they conflict? Which seems the most appropriate?

4. Explain and apply the *five forces* model to:
   (a) a bank
   (b) a motor manufacturer
   (c) a holiday travel company.

5. By considering the business, organization or university within which you work apply the Porter value chain analysis. To what extent is it appropriate? To what extent are information systems used in supporting the activities and linkages? To what extent could information systems be further used?

6. Analyse the applicability of the Nolan stage model to your organization.

7. 'The Nolan stage model was based on empirical research in the 1970s; it therefore predates the microcomputer explosion and cannot be considered in the explanation of current information systems.' Discuss.

8. 'The idea of an organization being directed by the implementation of a strategic plan is misconceived. The power of current procedures within departments and the need to respond quickly means that organizational direction is determined by the myriad of individual decisions taken at lower levels. The best that a strategic plan can do is explain and confirm the path to which the organization is already committed.' Do you agree?

9. Given the Nolan stage model how would you expect the role of the user in the determination of information systems strategy to evolve over time?

10. How does the Nolan stage model differ from the Earl model and what are the likely implications for planning?

11. What are the objectives of the organization within which you work? What are the factors critical to the success of meeting these objectives? To what extent do computerized information systems play a role in the provision of information on these factors?

> **12.** Outline factors along the lines of a PEST analysis specifically related to:
> (a) a bank
> (b) a university
> (c) a motor manufacturer
> (d) a holiday travel company.

References

● Earl M. (1989). *Management Strategies for Information Management.* Hemel Hempstead: Prentice Hall
● Henderson J., Rockart J. and Sifonis J. (1987). Integrating management support systems into strategic information systems planning. *Journal of Management Information Systems*, **4**(1), 5–24
● Hirscheim R., Earl M., Feeny D. and Lockett M. (1988). An exploration into the management of the information systems function. In *Proceedings Information Technology Management for Productivity and Strategic Advantage*, IFIP Conference, March 1988
● McFarlan F.W. (1984). Information technology changes the way you compete. *Harvard Business Review*, May–June, 98–103
● McFarlan F.W. and McKenny J.L. (1983). *Corporate Information Management: The Issues Facing Senior Management.* Homewood, Illinois: Dow-Jones-Irwin
● Nolan R.L. (1979). Managing the crisis in data processing. *Harvard Business Review*, March–April, 115–26
● Nolan R. (1984). Managing the advanced stages of computer technology: key research issues. In *The Information Systems Research Challenge* (McFarlan F.W. ed.), pp. 195–214. Boston: Harvard Business School Press
● Porter M.E. (1980). *Competitive Strategy.* New York: Free Press
● Porter M.E. (1985). *Competitive Advantage.* New York: Free Press
● Porter M.E. and Millar V.E. (1985). How information gives you competitive advantage. *Harvard Business Review*, July–August, 149–60
● Rockart J. (1979). Chief executives define their own data needs. *Harvard Business Review*, March–April, 81–92

Recommended reading

● Edwards C., Ward J. and Bytheway A. (1995). *The Essence of Information Systems* 2nd edn. Hemel Hempstead: Prentice Hall
This text is aimed at the business and particularly the MBA student. It concentrates on information systems and how information systems can be integrated with business strategy. The emphasis is always on information as distinct from the technology which provides it. The book looks at the benefits that accrue from investment in information systems, the management of information systems projects, and the organization of information systems.
● Grindley K. (1995). *Managing IT at Board Level: The Hidden Agenda* 2nd edn. London: Pitman
This is a readable, 'punchy' non-technical coverage of how management is coping/not coping with the problems of IT. It contains references to many practical examples.

● Galliers R.D. and Sutherland A.R. (1991). Information systems management and strategy formulation: the 'stages of growth' model revisited. *Journal of Information Systems*, **1**, 89–114
This article explains the most important stages of growth models together with critiques. It also develops the authors' own variant.

● Gunton T. (1990). *Inside Information Systems: A Practical Guide to Management Issues*. Hemel Hempstead: Prentice Hall
A highly readable text for business students and managers alike, which identifies key issues facing information systems. Though the book adopts a management perspective, technology is explained where necessary.

● Johnson G. and Scholes K. (1997). *Exploring Corporate Strategy* 4th edn. Hemel Hempstead: Prentice Hall
This is a standard text on strategic analysis, choice, and implementation. It is aimed at students on BA Business Studies and MBAs. It covers many of the major themes on strategic choice together with examples, exercises and case studies and has a European orientation although some USA cases are covered. Although it is not specifically aimed at IT there is much of relevance to the strategic use of IT. There is also an accompanying 'text and cases' book.

● McNurlin B.C. and Sprague R.H. Jnr. (1997). *Information Systems Management in Practice* 4th edn. Hemel Hempstead: Prentice Hall
A standard comprehensive text covering the strategy and management of all aspects of information systems. Each chapter has exercises and discussion questions.

● Mintzberg H., Quinn J.B., and Ghoshal S. (1998). *The Strategy Process – Revised European Edition*. Hemel Hempstead: Prentice Hall
Though not particularly directed at information systems or information technology this major text has a very clear explanation of the entire strategy formulation process. It is readable with many well worked case studies. The length of the book, over 1000 pages, makes it a comprehensive reference.

● Peppard J. ed. (1993). *IT Strategy for Business*. London: Pitman
The book contains a structured series of articles designed to cover the major issues in IS/IT. It is aimed at management or business studies students at undergraduate/graduate level. It has a number of articles on such topics as EDI, open systems strategy, and manufacturing systems management.

● Robson W. (1997) *Strategic Management and Information Systems: An Integrated Approach* 2nd edn. London: Pitman
This is a comprehensive text covering all aspects of information systems strategy and the management of information systems. It covers strategic management, management of information systems, and risk management of corporate information systems. It is also useful as a reference text.

● Scott Morton, M.S. ed. (1991). *The Corporation of the 90s: Information Technology and Organizational Transformation*. Oxford: Oxford University Press
This book was written as a result of the 'Management in the 1990s' Research Program which was given the responsibility of identifying the impact of new information technologies on organizations of the 1990s. The book has nine contributions from academics covering such areas as the impact of IT on jobs and skills, IT induced business reconfiguration and the information technology platform. It is written from a management, often strategic, perspective.

● Wysocki R. and Young J. (1990). *Information Systems: Management Principles in Action.* New York: John Wiley

This is a comprehensive readable text aimed at undergraduate and graduate level students of information systems (or computer studies/business studies). It is also of use to corporate management. Its stated purpose is to enable users to deal with information systems issues effectively. It covers and extends much of the material in the current chapter. (See also *Information Systems: Management Practice in Action.* This is an accompanying set of cases.)

Chapter 3

Business Information Technology

3.1 Historical development of computing technology

3.2 Hardware

3.3 Software

In Chapter 1 the areas of information, systems, and business information systems were approached from the perspective of information provision for business needs and in particular for decision support. Little emphasis was placed on the role of technology. In order to understand how computers can be used in the provision of business information, and their scope and limitations, it is important to have a basic understanding of technological concepts. This chapter achieves this by first placing current technology within the historical context of its evolution over the last 40 years. The functional components of a computer are then explained together with the way each function is performed by various types of hardware. The concept of a program is central to understanding the provision of computer-generated information. Various categories of programming languages, including fourth-generation languages and their role in prototyping, are compared. Finally, organizations have a choice between applications packages and specially commissioned software. The advantages of each are outlined.

3.1 Historical development of computing technology

Electronic computers are a comparatively modern invention though their manual predecessors go back several centuries. The mathematicians Pascal and Leibnitz developed some of the first primitive calculating machines in the seventeenth century. It was not until the mid-nineteenth century, however, that Charles Babbage designed his 'analytical engine'. This was to be a mechanical device incorporating a punched card input, memory, calculation section, automatic output and, importantly, a series of instructions that would control its operation. Babbage was helped in this task by Ada Byron, daughter of Lord Byron. She is often referred to as the first programmer and it was after her that the modern powerful programming language, Ada, was named.

3.1.1   The first generation

Progress in electronics allowed the first *electronic* computer to be built in the early 1940s. This was centred around the electronic valve. The valve is a device about the size of a motor car's tailgate bulb or a small domestic electric light bulb. It consists of electrodes enclosed in a glass bulb, which is then evacuated. The valve is responsible for regulating and amplifying flows of electricity. It is usually agreed that the first general-purpose electronic computer was built in the USA. It was called ENIAC. ENIAC was constructed from over 18000 valves and other devices! It worked, by modern standards, at a snail's pace, performing at the rate of 300 multiplications a second. This was, though, considerably faster than any other contemporary device. ENIAC was used for military purposes and was finally taken out of commission in 1955.

Later computers in the 1940s were built around a theoretical design pioneered by the mathematician John Von Neumann. These used the idea of encoding all information in binary numbers (1s and 0s). Information is then easy to represent by means of differing voltages: high voltage equals 1, low voltage equals zero. There is also a store within the machine that holds both the data and the sequence of instructions (program) that controls the operation of the machine. These instructions are then decoded one by one. Even in current computers the Von Neumann model plays a major role in design.

The first computers were seen mainly as pieces of research or military equipment. A Pentagon committee in the late 1940s confidently predicted that the foreseeable worldwide need for computers would be restricted to six machines! By the mid 1950s the possibility of using computers for business data processing was realized. In 1954 the first commercial computers, the UNIVAC-1 and the IBM 650, were produced. The success of the latter gave IBM the lead in large computers – a world dominance it still holds. These earliest computers were purchased only by large organizations. They were used for simple repetitive tasks that, until then, had been labour-intensive. Examples were payroll, billing and simple accounts processing. All the earliest computers were based on the valve. Unfortunately, valves are unreliable, consume a great deal of power, generate much unwanted heat, are large, expensive and slow in operation. In short, the development of the computer was limited by the operating characteristics of the electronics from which it was built.

3.1.2   The second generation

The reason for the increased interest and use of computers in the late 1950s and early 1960s was the development of the **second generation** of computers. These were based around the new technology of the solid-state transistor. Compared with the valve the transistor:

- is faster in operation,
- is more reliable,
- uses less power,
- is smaller in physical size (about the size of the head of a match),
- generates less heat,
- costs less.

These features are interrelated. For instance, the lower consumption of power results in less unwanted heat generation which, in turn, leads to greater reliability. This trend in improvements has characterized every subsequent technological development in computer electronics. Second-generation computers were smaller, cheaper, faster and more powerful than their predecessors. Not only had the hardware technology improved, so had the software. Instead of writing programs using instructions coded in 1s and 0s (or simple mnemonic translations of these instructions) programs were now written in specialized languages such as COBOL. These are known as **high-level languages**. They use instructions that are matched to the kinds of task for which they are needed. For instance, COBOL is particularly suited for writing business applications programs. These source programs are then automatically translated into binary programs consisting of 1s and 0s. This increased the productivity of programmers and enabled them to write more sophisticated software for business data processing.

3.1.3 The third generation

The miniaturization of transistors and their integration on circuit boards ushered in the next generation of computers. The IBM 360 series was introduced in 1964 and became a market leader. During the 1960s and early 1970s the cost of computers dropped. This was accompanied by an increase in their power. Smaller computers were now being built and a number of firms entered the market specializing in these **minicomputers**. One of these, the Digital Equipment Corporation (DEC), now dominates the minicomputer market. Businesses were beginning to use computers for a larger variety of purposes than previously. They were used not only for transaction processing but also for the provision of information for managerial decision making – MIS had been born. Computing equipment was now becoming cheap enough for medium-sized companies to purchase their own computing facilities. The technology of disk storage was also improving, becoming cheaper, more reliable, and providing larger storage capacities and faster access.

3.1.4 The fourth generation

The fourth generation of computers was stimulated by the dramatic developments in microchip technology. A **microchip** is a flake of silicon, smaller than a fingernail, on which millions of transistors have been etched in a mass-production process. Once again, compared to the previous technology the microchip was very much faster, cheaper, more reliable and smaller. As well as carrying out calculations, computers need to have a memory from which data and the program can be quickly retrieved. Microchips could also be used as the hardware for this fast access memory storage. Developed in the 1970s, microchips became used in computers in the middle to late years of the decade. Firms such as Intel and Motorola have established leading positions in the worldwide production of microchips.

   One of the major impacts of the microchip was that it at last became feasible to build small cheap **microcomputers**. This potential was first commercially exploited by Apple Computers – a company that started building microcomputers in a small garage in the late 1970s and had, by the early 1980s, developed into a company with an annual turnover of several hundreds of millions of dollars. Although Apple was the first major producer of microcomputers, IBM entered the market in the early 1980s and rapidly established an industry standard with the IBM PC. This, and its descendants, the IBMPC/AT, the IBM PS/2 and the later IBMs with Pentium microchips, have maintained a dominant control over the market for business microcomputers. The comparatively high price of IBM hardware has allowed cheaper copies (or 'clones' as they are called) of the IBM series to be built using the same types of microchip. These function like the IBM microcomputers and can all use the same software.

A more recent development is the highly portable microcomputer known as a **notebook**. These weigh five or six pounds, are the size of A4 paper and are about an inch thick. The performance of these machines approximates that of their more bulky desktop brothers, though with reduced screen quality and keyboard size. They are intended to be small enough to be carried in a briefcase, and bring genuine portability to business computing.

The development of microcomputers has had a major impact on the way computers are used in organizations. Medium and large organizations will still have a larger computer (minicomputer or mainframe computer) for their major data processing and management information provision. This installation will require a computer centre of trained technical staff to operate the company's information resource. However, the presence of cheap microcomputers has enabled individual departments and sections to purchase their own equipment. They typically use this for word processing, spreadsheet modelling, small database applications, electronic filing and desktop publishing. Because microcomputers are so cheap they can often be purchased using departmental budgets without seeking central approval. This has a number of effects. First, the resulting greater autonomy and control possessed by the department is likely to stimulate computer usage. Second, the power of the central computing resource is diminished. Traditional computer centres often view the mushrooming of microcomputers with alarm. This is not only jealousy but is also based on a real fear of a lack of standardization of hardware and software throughout the organization. Finally, there may also be a duplication of data and applications development effort on the part of staff at separate localities unless coordination is achieved.

The proliferation of local microcomputers in large organizations is one impact of the development of the microchip. Another is the wide variety of businesses that are able to use microcomputers in their day-to-day transaction processing, office work and decision support. A very large number of small businesses can afford to computerize their standard business functions. This has stimulated and been stimulated by the production of cheap software that is easy to use by personnel who have not had a formal technical computer training.

The explosion of microcomputers reflects the breakdown in **Grosch's law**. This law states that the computing power of a computer is proportional to the square of its cost. In other words, it was always more cost-efficient for an organization requiring computing power to purchase a large (and therefore centralized machine) than several smaller microcomputers or minicomputers.

The power of the microcomputer has been further enhanced by the development of **local area networks**. These link various pieces of hardware including microcomputers together in order to communicate with each other and to share scarce resources.

The rapid increase in performance and decrease in price can be seen by consulting Table 3.1. No other form of technology can boast such rapid performance and price developments. If a luxury motor car of the 1940s, for example a Rolls-Royce, had demonstrated changes on the same scale it would cost about a pound sterling, travel at one

Table 3.1: An indicative summary of the effects of technological advance on the performance of computers.

Date	Generation	Technology	Number of instructions executed per second	Storage capacity (number of characters)	Cost (for a typical large computer)	Average time between breakdowns
1950s	1	Valve	1000	10000	£5m	Hours
1960s	2	Transistor	100000	100000	£2m	Hundreds of hours
1970s	3	Integrated transistor circuit board	10000000	10000000	£4m+	Thousands of hours
1980s/90s	4	Micro-integrated circuit (microchip)	1000000000	1000000000	£2m+	Years

thousand million miles per hour at ten million miles to the gallon of fuel. It would also be the size of a matchbox yet, paradoxically, have ten thousand times the luggage capacity of the 1940's Rolls-Royce!

3.2 Hardware

The terms 'hardware', 'software' and 'firmware' occur frequently in any literature concerned with computers. It is important at the outset to have some understanding of their meanings.

- **Hardware** is the physical components within a computer system. Circuits, keyboards, disk drives, disks and printers are all examples of pieces of hardware.

- **Software** is a set of instructions, written in a specialized language, the execution of which controls the operation of the computer. Programs are examples of software.

- **Firmware** is the permanent storage of program instructions within hardware. It is usually used to refer to a set of instructions that is permanently encoded in a microchip. The term 'firmware' is used because it is the inseparable combination of hardware and software.

3.2.1 Functional components of a computer system

A computer system is a system that accepts data as input and produces information as output. Information, as will be recalled from Chapter 1, is data that has been processed to serve some purpose. In producing this the intermediate products of this process may be stored. The process of transformation of inputs into outputs is carried out by electronic circuitry. The process is controlled by a sequence of instructions – the program – which is stored in the computer.

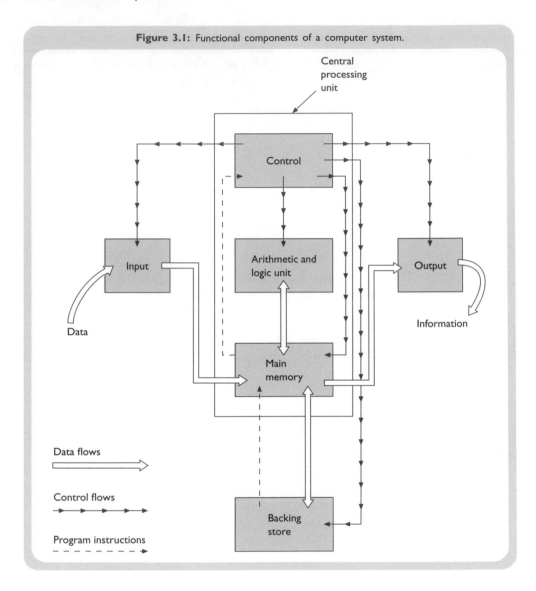

Figure 3.1: Functional components of a computer system.

Computer systems fit the common systems model explained in the Chapter 1. Figure 3.1 illustrates the basic organization of a computer system.

1. **Input:** The purpose of the input component of a computer system is:
   (a) to accept data in the required form;
   (b) to convert this data to a machine-understandable form;
   (c) to transmit this data to the central processing unit.
   Examples of input devices to be explained later are keyboards, magnetic ink character readers, bar-code readers, optical character readers and the mouse.

2. **Central processing unit (CPU):** This is made up of three components: the control unit, the arithmetic and logic unit, and the main memory.

(a) The purpose of the **control unit** is:
  (i) to decode and execute the program instructions one by one;
  (ii) to control and coordinate data movements within the CPU and between the CPU and the other components of the computer system.
(b) The purpose of the **arithmetic and logic unit** (ALU) is:
  (i) to carry out arithmetic operations – for example, to add two numbers together;
  (ii) to carry out logical operations – for example, to compare two numbers to establish which is the larger.
(c) The purpose of the **main memory** (synonyms – fast memory, immediate access memory, core store, and direct access memory) is:
  (i) to store programs during their execution;
  (ii) to store data that is being used by the current program;
  (iii) to store the operating system (this is an important program in the control of the computer; details are covered in a later section of the chapter).
Currently, the main form of hardware for carrying out the functions of the central processing unit is based on the microchip.

3. Secondary storage (backing store): The purpose of secondary storage is:
(a) to maintain a permanent record of data and programs when not being used by the CPU;
(b) to maintain a store for the program and data currently being used if the main memory is not large enough to accommodate the entire program and data;
(c) to maintain a copy for security purposes of data held in the main memory;
(d) to act as a secondary input/output device when the input is in magnetic form or the output is required in magnetic form.
Examples of secondary store hardware to be covered later are magnetic and optical disk devices, magnetic tape machines and tape streamers.

4. Output: The purpose of the output component of a computer system is:
(a) to accept information/data from the CPU;
(b) to convert this information/data into the required output form.
Examples of output devices are printers, monitors, machines for producing computer output on microfilm and voice synthesizers.

In the next sections each of these functional components is treated in some detail. In particular the various ways in which each may be physically realized in a modern computer system are explained and evaluated.

3.2.2 Input devices, media and data capture methods

The purposes of input devices are:

- to accept data in the required form;
- to convert this data to a machine-understandable form;
- to transmit this data to the central processing unit.

Keyboard

The most common keyboard device used is the QWERTY keyboard. It is called a 'QWERTY' keyboard because these are the first six letters on the top left of the keyboard.

The keyboard is derived from the old typewriter standard to which some extra keys have been added for specific computer-based functions. Unfortunately, the typewriter standard layout was not designed to be the most efficient from a data input point of view. Rather, the key layout was organized in the nineteenth century so that old mechanical typewriters were least likely to jam when typing occurred. Modern computers and electric typewriters do not suffer from this deficiency and so the standard is outmoded. Keyboards have been designed that allow a trained typist to input text at the rate of about 180 words per minute. This compares with the QWERTY norm for an input of about 60 words per minute. Why are all standard typewriter keyboards based on this old-fashioned inefficient layout? The answer is partly to do with inertia in the computing industry but also because there is now a huge investment in QWERTY-based equipment and QWERTY-based staff. This does not make it feasible, in the short run at least, for any organization to change.

Keyboards convert the downward contact of a key push into a code for the key selected. The code consists of a string of 1s and 0s. There are a few internationally recognized coding systems for computers. The two most used are the American Standard Code for Information Interchange (ASCII) and the Extended Binary Coded Decimal Interchange Code (EBCDIC). The former code is most commonly used for microcomputers and data communications. The EBCDIC code is used in IBM mainframe computers. Within a coding system each different keyboard character is coded as a separate binary string. For instance, in the ASCII 7-bit code C is coded as 1000011.

Keyboard data entry is almost invariably accompanied by a monitor screen on which the characters input to the keyboard are displayed. The combination is called a **visual display unit** (VDU).

Using a keyboard for data entry is common to a wide range of applications. They fall into three main categories:

1. The entry of data from a source document such as an invoice or an order. Controls must ensure that all the data is copied correctly and completely. Data entry controls are covered in the later chapter on controls.

2. Interactive use of the computer by a user. Here there is no source document but the user is inputting commands or queries into the computer systems.

3. The entry of text data, as in word processing.

Advantages: Keyboard data entry has a number of advantages over other forms of data input:

● There is a low initial cost for purchase of the equipment.

● The method is extremely flexible as it relies heavily on the person entering the data. People are flexible.

Disadvantages: There are also a number of disadvantages:

● For efficient use, training of personnel is needed.

● It is a slow form of data entry. People are slow.

● It is costly in operation as it relies on people. People are expensive to employ compared with the capital cost of equipment.

● Unless there are adequate controls, using a keyboard will lead to high error rates. People are error-prone.

Figure 3.2: Examples of magnetic ink character fonts. (a) E13B. (b) CMC7.

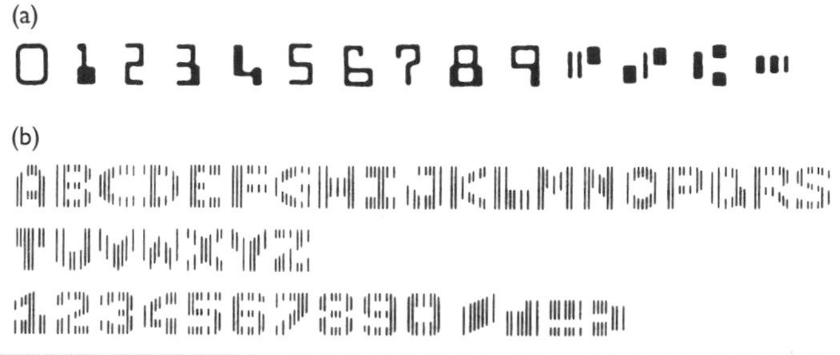

(a)

0 1 2 3 4 5 6 7 8 9 ⑴⑵⑶⑷⑸

(b)

ABCDEFGHIJKLMNOPQRS
TUVWXYZ
1234567890

Magnetic ink character readers

Magnetic ink character recognition (MICR) is a method of data entry widely used in the banking system for customers' cheques. Each cheque has identifying information (cheque number, account code, and bank sort code) printed in magnetic ink in the lower left-hand corner. On depositing a cheque at the bank, the following process takes place. It is passed to an employee, who prints the amount of the cheque using a special machine; this appears on the right-hand side of the cheque. The cheque is then passed under a magnet, which magnetizes the iron oxide particles in the ink. It is finally sent through another machine, which detects the centres of magnetization and converts these into the codes for each character, representing the amount of the cheque.

The style of typeface, called the **font**, used by the British banking system is E13B. Another internationally recognized standard font is CMC7. This has characters as well as numbers and is used by the Post Office in its postal order system. Examples of both fonts are shown in Figure 3.2.

A cheque is an example of a **turnaround document**. This is defined as a document which is:

- machine produced
- machine readable
- readable by human beings.

Because of their machine readability, turnaround documents allow the fast entry of data with low error rates.

Advantages: The advantages of MICR as opposed to keyboard entry are:

- It is cheap in operation for high-volume activities such as cheque processing.
- It has very low error rates. This is of crucial importance in the banking system.
- The magnetic characters are resistant to corruption by the folding of cheques or smudges of dirt.
- It is fast – for example, up to 1000 characters per second can be read.

Disadvantages: There are two main disadvantages:

- The equipment is expensive to purchase.
- The fonts are not easily readable; this limits the use of the method to applications where this is unimportant.

Figure 3.3: Examples of optical character fonts. (a) OCR-A. (b) OCR-B.

(a)

ABCDEFGHIJKLMNOPQRST
UVWXYZ
1234567890 .¬¡:&

(b)

abcdefghijklmnopqrstuvwxyz
ABCDEFGHIJKLMNOPQRSTUVWXYZ
1234567890 .,;:&!?

Optical character readers

Optical character recognition (OCR), though different in technology from magnetic ink character recognition, is similar in concept. Characters are preprinted on documents. These documents can then be passed through an optical character reader at a later stage. This device optically detects the characters on the document and converts them to code, which is sent to the CPU.

Many large public utilities, such as gas, electricity and water, use OCR, as do the major credit card companies. The method is for the billing company to prepare a turnaround document with billing details and an attached counterfoil for payment. The customer returns the counterfoil with their payment. As well as details of the required payment being printed on the counterfoil a special section is reserved for the characters that are to be optically read. This section is generally at the bottom of the counterfoil and appears below a printed warning such as 'do not write or mark below this line'. The characters will give the account number of the bill receiver together with other details. These may include the postal area, the type of customer, the amount of the bill and other management information.

There are a number of standard character fonts capable of being read by commercial optical character readers. OCR-A is a standard American font which is used by about three-quarters of US applications. OCR-B is a standard British font. Examples of these fonts are shown in Figure 3.3.

The characters may be preprinted on the documents using a standard printing technique such as litho. However, it is more usual for the character data to be produced using an electric typewriter or computer-driven printer. Optical character readers have now been produced that will read carefully produced handwritten numbers and letters. This extends the use of OCR beyond the limitations of turnaround documents, as data can be entered by persons between the stages of document production and document reading. However, the technical difficulties encountered in attempting to recognize wide ranges in the way that different individuals produce the same handwritten character result in optical readers that are both very slow and error-prone. OCR for handwritten documentation is expected to improve over the coming years and will then have a greater commercial impact.

OCR has a number of advantages and disadvantages over keyboard entry:

Figure 3.4: A bar-code – EAN standard.

Advantages: The advantages of OCR as opposed to keyboard entry are:

- It is cheap in operation for high-volume activities, such as billing, which can include preprinted characters.
- It has low error rates.
- It is fast. Up to 500 characters per second can be read.
- The fonts are easily readable by people (unlike magnetic character fonts).

Disadvantages: There are two main disadvantages:

- The equipment is expensive to purchase.
- It is easy (unlike MICR) to corrupt the characters; this can often be achieved by small pieces of dirt or smudges.

Both MICR and OCR suffer from the same limitation in that they are inflexible methods of data entry. Keyboard entry allows a large amount of 'intelligent preprocessing' by persons before data entry. This implies flexibility in the interpretation of handwritten data entered on documents between their production and final data entry of their contents.

Bar-code readers

Bar-codes are now familiar as part of the printed packaging on supermarket produce. A bar-code consists of a series of thick and thin black bars divided by thick and thin spaces printed on a light-coloured background. These bars correspond to digits, which are also printed underneath the bar-code.

There are two common systems of bar-codes. The earlier Universal Product Code (UPC) is used in the United States. In Europe the standard is the European Article Number (EAN). EAN consists of 13 digits represented by 26 lines. The digits have a standard interpretation. Two digits indicate the country of origin of the product, five digits indicate the manufacturer, five digits indicate the product, and the remaining digit is used for checking that the other digits have been read correctly by the device reading the bar-code. Figure 3.4 is a bar-code.

The bar-code is machine read either by passing a 'light pen' over it in either direction or by passing the bar-code over a reader machine. The second method is more flexible as the bar-code can be passed over at any angle as long as the code is pointing towards the sensitive screen of the machine. The latter type of machine is common in supermarkets.

Bar-codes are suitable for data input where it is important to maintain a record of the movements of material goods. This occurs at the point of sale in a supermarket, at a library loan desk and in stock control systems.

As mentioned previously, a common use for bar-codes is at checkout points in supermarkets and other retail outlets. The bar-code is read at the point of sale and so such a system is known as a **point of sale** (POS) system. The way these systems typically work is that the code for the product, having been identified by the bar-code reader, is sent to the computer. There, the relevant record for the product is retrieved. The product price and a short description of the product are then sent back electronically to the point of sale, where the details are printed on the till slip. At the same time the computer records of the quantity of the item held are decreased by one unit.

Advantages: The advantages of a bar-code point-of-sales system over the more traditional manually controlled checkout till are:

- Better management information: management has up-to-date information on stock levels and can thus sensibly plan purchases and avoid stockouts. The records of sales are also date- and time-stamped. This enables analysis of sales data to identify fast- and slow-moving items and peaks and troughs in the sales of items. It is also important to be able to have information on consumer patterns of expenditure. It may affect shelving policy if it is discovered that purchases of smoked salmon are often accompanied by white wine whereas peanuts are associated with bottles of beer (or vice versa!).

- Better customer service: there are lower error rates than for manual checkout tills. This is because operators have little scope for incorrect data entry. Itemized bills provide customers with the ability to check their purchases against till slips. Certain types of checkout fraud are also rendered impossible with the system.

- Easier implementation of price changes: because prices are held in computer records a change of price merely requires a single data change in the item record and a replacement of the price card in the shop display. Individual pricing of items is no longer necessary (though see Disadvantages).

- Staff training time to use the systems is minimal.

Disadvantages: The two main disadvantages are:

- The necessary equipment is expensive to purchase and install.

- Unless there is an adequate manual backup system, a breakdown will immediately stop the retail sales of the organization. A typical manual backup is to revert to the old system. This requires that the practice of individually labelling each item is maintained.

Optical mark readers

Optical mark recognition (OMR) is a common form of high-volume data entry method where the application requires the selection of a data item from various alternatives. In its most common form it consists of a printed document on which the various options are displayed together with a box, or field, for each. To select an option the person entering data puts a mark in the relevant box. Part of a typical document is shown in Figure 3.5.

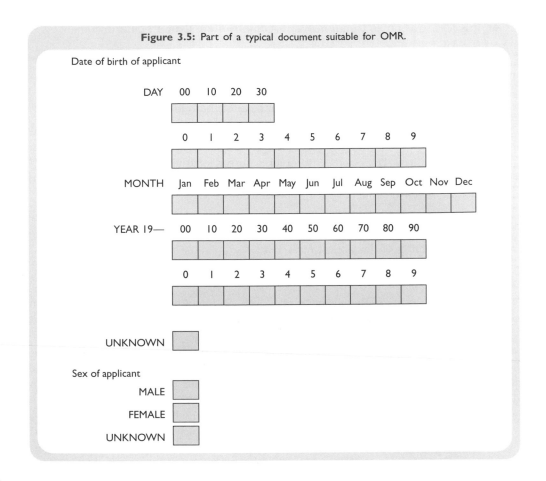

Figure 3.5: Part of a typical document suitable for OMR.

Once marked, the document is passed through an optical mark reader. This machine optically scans the boxes and determines those in which there has been a mark made – a 1 corresponds to a mark and a 0 to the absence of a mark. The computer, which has been preprogrammed with the meanings of the boxes, then interprets the binary code sent from the optical mark reader.

Typical applications are market research surveys, multiple-choice examination questions, time sheets for the entry of start and stop times for employees, and order forms for the selection of stock.

Advantages: OMR has a number of advantages and disadvantages over keyboard entry, MICR and OCR:

- Data can be entered on to a document, not only by data entry personnel at the data entry stage, but also by other people at any stage between the production of the document and its reading. This is a distinct advantage over OCR and MICR, which have a basic 'data out equals data in' limitation.

- No knowledge or skill is necessary to enter data on to the document other than the ability to read and use a ballpoint pen. This is to be compared with skills needed to operate a keyboard.

- It is less susceptible to erroneous machine reading than an OCR document.

- It is cheap and fast in operation as compared to keyboard entry.

Disadvantages: There are also a number of disadvantages:

- There is a high initial cost for the purchase of the equipment.

- Its use is limited to those applications where selection from a few presented alternatives is required. It is therefore not appropriate for applications where character data is required. For instance, to enter a person's surname consisting of up to 15 characters would need 15 rows, each with 26 options for selection. Not only would this use much document space, it would not be easy to enter the data.

- It is not suitable where the printed documents need to be changed frequently as a result of flexible data requirements. Each document change necessitates the reprogramming of the optical mark reader.

Voice data entry

Voice data entry consists of the reception of speech data by a microphone, the conversion of the data into electronic signals, the recognition of the data, and its final conversion into a binary form.

Currently, voice data entry is awaiting technological advances to overcome the limitations of the existing primitive systems. The difficulty is that two people represent the same word verbally in different ways, the same person represents the same word verbally in different ways on different occasions, and two people may speak different words in a similar way. It is the recognition element of current systems that is deficient.

There is, however, massive investment in developing voice recognition facilities. This is because the potential financial rewards are great. These will occur in two main areas. First, the need for typists (as distinct from secretaries) will disappear. Text will be dictated into a microphone and instantly displayed on a screen for voice-controlled editing. There will be no need for a person to be employed to take down shorthand that is then converted into printed text for correction. Hundreds of thousands of typists' jobs will rapidly disappear. Second, voice data input will enable people to interrogate computers remotely via the telephone system or eventually via a small wrist-size transmitter/receiver connected to the public telecommunications network. This will enable the information provision power of computers to become fully portable. Output might be provided by a synthesized voice or connection to a traditional output device.

Currently, voice data entry systems are restricted to applications that require the recognition of no more than a few words. An example is a computerized flight information system, which provides speech-synthesized telephone responses to flight reservation and schedule enquiries.

However software for acceptance of speech which is then turned into text has become more readily available. These programs run on standard PCs and interface with standard word processing packages. In order to work effectively the user must undertake a period of training on the computer – training, that is, of the computer in order to allow it to recognize the particular voice patterns of the user. This typically takes a few hours. Accuracy rates of 95% with speech input at 40 words per minute are claimed as standard at the current level of development.

The main advantage of voice data entry then lies in the possibility of remote interrogation of computers for information and the preparation of text documents by unskilled
personnel rather than in high-volume business data entry.

Other technology and methods for data entry

There are several methods of data entry that have not been covered. They have been
grouped together here for brief explanation because either they are of diminishing importance or are of restricted application.

Badges: These are in the form of plastic cards of the size of a standard credit card. The
card has a magnetic stripe containing identifying information; in fact modern credit cards
also serve as magnetic badges. The magnetic stripe can be read by a machine that converts this into code to be sent to the main body of the computer. They are most commonly used as identification for cash-dispensing machines or point of sales systems for
credit sales. Magnetic stripe badges are easy to copy.

Smart cards: The smart card contains information encoded within a microchip built
into the structure of the card. They are difficult to copy, can contain much information
within them, and can be programmed to self-destruct if incorrect identifying information
is keyed into the machine reading them. The use of smart cards is likely to increase as
a form of identification over the coming years.

Mouse: A mouse is a small hand-held device about the size of a cigarette packet. It contains a ball-bearing on its lower surface and a selection button on its upper surface. As
the mouse is moved over a desk the ball-bearing moves and controls the positioning of
a lighted portion or arrow (cursor) on the screen of a VDU. The cursor can be moved
to a position on the screen to select an item. Alternatively, the movement can be used
to trace out a line. A mouse is used in graphics applications or to replace the movement
of the cursor on a screen normally controlled by special keys on the keyboard.

Touch screen: A touch screen enables the selection of an item from a screen display by
pointing to it with a finger. This breaks a horizontal and a vertical infrared beam, thereby
determining the position of the pointing finger. It is used in some business applications
such as stock dealing.

Kimball tags: These are small punched tags used largely in the retail clothing trade.
Each garment has a tag attached to it with identifying information for stock control purposes. This is removed on sale and later read into a machine. Nowadays, it is common
for the information to be optically or magnetically encoded on the tag.

Magnetic tapes and disks, and optical disks: These are often regarded as input and
output media and the corresponding devices such as disk drives as input and output
devices. In a sense this is true. A name and address file can be purchased on magnetic
disk and read into the computer for use. However, here these media and devices are
regarded as secondary, not because of their importance, but rather because data held on
them must previously have been entered through one of the other entry methods or be
the output of computer processing. They are discussed in the next section.

3.2.3 Factors involved in the selection of data entry devices, media and methods

The data entry methods mentioned previously have different characteristics and therefore will be appropriate for different types of data entry application. The main features that determine the data entry method are as follows:

- **The type of application:** This is perhaps the most important factor. Some applications allow turnaround documents to be used while others do not. Some applications need only allow selections from a limited range of choices, which would suggest OMR, while others require the addition of a wide variety of data. Interrogation generally requires data entry personnel to interact with the computer and so a keyboard is required. It is impossible to specify in advance the range of applications, together with the most suitable data entry method and devices. Each application needs to be matched against the characteristics of the data entry methods before a choice can be made.

- **Costs:** In particular the difference between operating costs and initial costs. Most methods that are low in initial costs, such as keyboard entry, are high in operating costs and vice versa.

- **Speed and volume of input:** Some methods are only applicable to high-volume applications.

- **Error tolerance:** All errors are undesirable but in some applications it is more crucial to prevent them occurring than in others. The banking sector, for instance, is one that places a high priority on preventing error. There are many controls that minimize erroneous data entry. These are covered extensively in Chapter 8 on control. For the purposes of this chapter it is worthy of note that those data entry methods that involve less human skill, such as MICR, are less prone to error than those that do not, such as keyboard.

Over the last two decades the cost of processing hardware has dropped considerably. The costs of producing software are also likely to diminish over the coming years. With the increasing power of computers to process data and the ever-demanding needs of management for information based on this data, the importance of cutting data entry costs will be emphasized. It is likely that automated as compared to manual data entry will increase in the future.

3.2.4 Secondary storage devices

The purpose of secondary storage is:

1. to maintain a permanent record of data and programs when not being used by the CPU;

2. to maintain a store for the program and data currently being used if the main memory is not large enough to accommodate the entire program and data;

3. to maintain a copy for security purposes of data held in the main memory;

4. to act as a secondary input/output device when the input is in magnetic form or the output is required in magnetic form.

All computers need permanent secondary storage facilities. This is because the main memory store within the central processing unit is limited in size, and in the event of a power failure or the machine being switched off the contents of this main memory disappear.

The factors to be looked at when considering secondary storage technology are:

- **Speed of data retrieval:** Given a data retrieval instruction executed within the CPU the quicker the desired data can be loaded into the main memory the better.

- **Storage capacity:** The larger the amount of data stored and accessible to the storage device the better.

- **Cost of storage:** This is usually measured in terms of the cost to store one byte of data (one byte of space is sufficient to store one character).

- **Robustness and portability of the storage medium:** The more secure the data storage medium is against corruption or 'crashes' the better.

Storage devices are often classified according to the type of access to data permitted by them. In general, there are **sequential access storage devices** (SASD) and **direct access storage devices** (DASD). The difference between the two is that with the former, access to data begins at a given point on the storage medium, usually the beginning, and the entire storage medium is searched in sequence until the target data item is found. With direct access storage devices the location of the required data item can be identified. The target data item can then be retrieved from this location or addressed without needing to retrieve data stored physically prior to it; in other words access is direct. Generally, all direct access storage devices also allow sequential retrieval if required.

From a business information and business data processing perspective these differences in access lead to differences in suitability for business applications. In particular, sequential access storage devices are only suitable for those applications that require sequential processing. Here would be included routine data processing operations such as the billing of customers, the production of customer statements, and the production of payroll. Many applications, including all those concerned with the selective retrieval and presentation of information for decision making, require direct access and thus direct access storage media and devices. The increased use of computers for decision support, forward planning and management control has led to the increased use of direct access storage devices as the most important form of secondary storage. Where the store of corporate data is centralized and held for access by many applications then it is imperative to have direct access storage.

This is not a text on the more detailed aspects of hardware. However, it is important to understand the basic principles underlying modern storage devices. Without this knowledge it is difficult to appreciate why the types of business activity impose restrictions on the forms of appropriate storage. The following are common types of storage media.

Magnetic tape

Standard magnetic tape stores data in the form of **records** (Figure 3.6). Several records are collected together and stored in a **block**. Between these blocks of data there are parts of the tape on which no data is stored. These are called **interblock gaps**. The **header label** gives information such as the name of the tape, the name of the program that is used to update it and the last date of update.

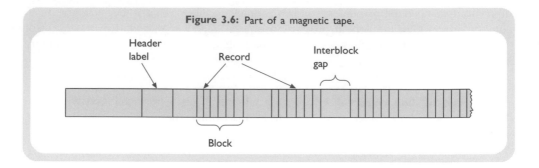

Figure 3.6: Part of a magnetic tape.

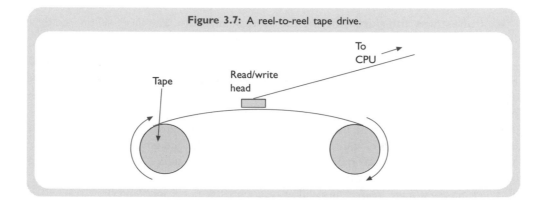

Figure 3.7: A reel-to-reel tape drive.

Data is transferred between the tape and the CPU by means of a tape machine (Figure 3.7). This device passes the tape from reel to reel over a read/write head which either reads the data into the CPU or writes data from the CPU on to the tape. In order to allow the tape-reading device to rest while the computer processes data previously read, the tape machine always stops on an interblock gap. The block is the smallest unit of data that can be read into the machine at one time.

Tape drives are used on larger machines for high-volume transaction processing. To update a payroll file requires at least three tapes and tape drives – one to read the current pay details for each employee, one to read the time-sheet data for the current period and one to write the updated details on to the new tape.

Standard magnetic tape is 4 inches wide. A typical tape might be 2400 feet long. The speed at which the tape can be passed over the read/write head varies from manufacturer to manufacturer but a common speed is about 10 feet per second. Data is packed on the tape and, ignoring interblock gaps, a standard density is 1600 bytes per inch. If one byte is needed to store one character this is slightly less than 20 kilobytes per foot. (One kilobyte is 2^{10} bytes which is just over 1000 bytes. One megabyte is 2^{20} bytes.)

Advantages: There are a number of advantages and disadvantages to using magnetic tapes as a storage medium:

● It is an extremely cheap storage medium – a tape costs about £15.

● Tapes are highly portable and can be easily transferred from place to place.

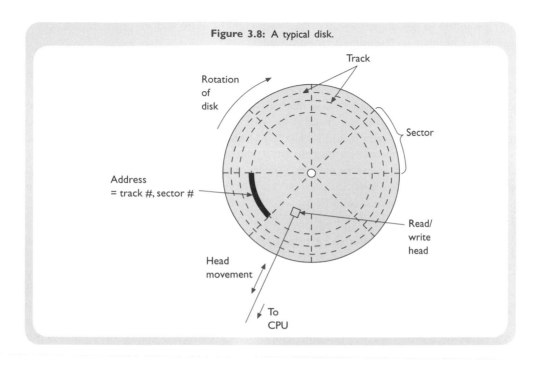

Figure 3.8: A typical disk.

Disadvantages: The disadvantages are:

- No direct access is possible to records; all access is sequential. Using the figures given it is easy to calculate that the average time to search for, and retrieve, an individual record on a fully packed tape is of the order of a minute or two. This implies that tapes are unsuitable for applications that require the selective retrieval of records on a random basis. Tapes are only suitable for those functions where each record on a tape is used in sequence. An example is the preparation of the payroll, where employee records are processed in the order they appear on the tape.

- It is not possible to read and write to the same tape in one operation. It is often necessary to have many tape drives for standard operations.

Although the use of tapes has been diminishing over the last few years they are still employed for standard sequential processes as mentioned earlier. Their cheapness and portability makes them ideal as a security backup medium. Copies of data held on other storage media may be made on tape for transport to a secure location. This is known as **dumping**. Special devices known as **tape streamers** facilitate the fast copying of data onto tape for security reasons.

Magnetic disks

A magnetic disk has a magnetizable surface on which data is stored in concentric rings called **tracks** (Figure 3.8). These tracks are not visible to the eye. Each track is accessed by a movable read/write head. The number of concentric tracks on a disk is determined by the disk-drive manufacturer and the program controlling the movement of the disk head. A disk typically ranges from 40 tracks to over 200. The disk is divided logically into a number of pie-shaped sectors. There are eight or more sectors on each disk. Once again, the number is determined by software.

The combination of a track number (track #) and a sector number (sector #) is called an **address**. The read/write head can be sent directly to an address by rotation of the disk and movement of the read/write head over the radius of the disk. The content of an entire address is the smallest unit that can be transferred between the CPU and the disk in one operation. The fact that (1) the disk is divided into addresses and (2) the read/write head can be sent to a designated address means that provided the address of a piece of data is known or can be calculated, direct access to the data is possible. This characteristic of a disk is the most important in distinguishing it from sequential media such as magnetic tape. Disks can also be read sequentially if required, by first reading one track and then the next and so on.

There are several types of disk:

1. **Floppy disks** or **diskettes.** A floppy disk is, as its name suggests, floppy and is contained within a firm plastic envelope. Floppy disks are 3½ inches in diameter. In most drives both upper and lower surfaces of the disk can be simultaneously employed for storage (double-headed disk drive). As well as having a track and sector the address will then also have a surface number. Floppy disks typically store 1.44 megabytes (Mb) as standard. They can easily be inserted and removed from their drives and are portable. Floppy disks rotate at about five revolutions per second and so access to an address takes less than a second.

2. **Hard disk.** In order to increase the storage capacity of a disk and decrease its access time it is necessary to use different technology. Hard disks (sometimes known as Winchester disks) are single, hard, magnetic disks sealed within their own drives. This provides an environment protected from dust. They can rotate at faster speeds than floppy disks and rather than the read/write head being in contact with the surface of the disk it floats just above it.

   Hard disks have significantly larger storage capacity than floppy disks, with access speeds at least ten times faster. For this reason, it is usual for business microcomputers to have an installed hard disk drive. Two gigabyte (2000 Mb) hard disks are common with the trend being to larger storage sizes. Floppy disks are used for archiving data files, maintaining secure data files (floppy disks can be locked up easily), and for transferring data from one microcomputer to another. Although it is possible to take backup copies of the hard disk on floppy disks, it may take 40 or more floppy disks to back up a complete hard disk. Unless backups of selected parts of the disk are made by using special software (known as archiving software) it is common to use tape streamers.

3. **Exchangeable disk packs**. Larger computers use exchangeable packs of hard disks. These are usually 14 inchcs in diameter and come in packs of up to 10 disks which are double-sided except for the two outer surfaces. The disks are read by means of a movable arm with read/write heads for each surface (see Figure 3.9). Tracks that are directly above and below one another on the disk pack are said to constitute a **cylinder**. A large mainframe system may have many disk drives and so can have many hundreds of megabytes of direct access secondary storage.

The trend in hardware is towards developing disk technology that is cheaper, has greater capacity, faster access times and is more robust.

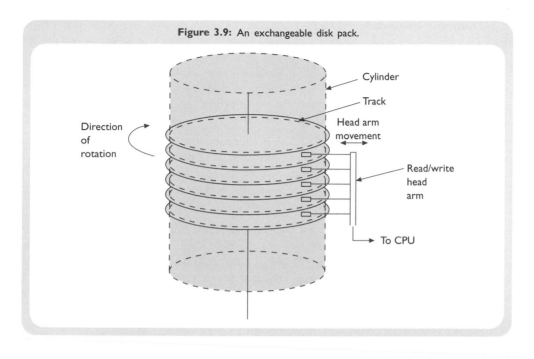

Figure 3.9: An exchangeable disk pack.

Optical disks

Ultimately, the storage efficiency and access speeds for magnetic disk systems are limited by the moving mechanical parts, in particular the read/write head, and by the density with which data can be packed onto the magnetizable medium. In order to progress further, different technology is required. New developments are in the area of direct access optical disk technology.

Optical disk technology consists of encoding data as a series of microscopic pits on the surface of a disk that is covered with a transparent plastic coating. These pits can then be read by means of laser light focused with great accuracy onto the spinning disk. The storage capacity of such disks is huge: for an 8 inch disk it is typically 1000 megabytes (1 gigabyte). The trend is towards increasing this capacity. Because the disks are protected by a transparent plastic cover and there is no danger of the optical head coming into accidental contact (head crash) with the surface of the disk, optical systems are very robust.

There are three main types of optical system. **CD-ROM** was the first to be developed. These disks are capable of read only access but have very large storage capacities. The read rate of CD-ROMs has increased rapidly over the last few years – CD-ROM drives with read in rates of 24 times early read in rates are now common. The initial high costs of production of CD-ROMs have dropped significantly to less than a dollar for large production runs and the cost of CD-ROM drives has dropped from several thousands of dollars to less than two hundred dollars. CD-ROMs have three main uses:

Software provision: Most software is too large to be stored on a single floppy disk and it is now usual that purchased software is provided on CD-ROM. This has paralleled the trend for the inclusion of CD-ROM devices in modern business PCs.

Multimedia provision: Modern PCs have the software and hardware capacity to display graphics, audio and video, as well as text. The storage capacity needed for the data for these is very large. CD-ROMs can meet this requirement. This ability has led to the development of multimedia disks which intersperse text with graphics, audio and visual output. This is particularly common with the multi-billion dollar business of computer games. Businesses are also now producing marketing material that are held on CD-ROM for easy distribution.

Mass storage of reference material: Where reference material seldom changes CD-ROM is ideal for cheap, easy-to-handle storage. Examples are accounting data of UK companies, telephone directories and permanent components details of manufactured products. Text archives of newspapers and academic journals are now provided on CD-ROM for easy access in libraries.

A second type of optical system is the **WORM disk** (write once read many times). This allows data to be written once to any part of the disk. Once written the data cannot be altered although it can be read many times. WORM disk systems are thus more flexible than CD-ROM disks for business purposes. The inability to remove data once encoded opens up the possibility for the permanent archiving of transactions. This is of importance from an accounting perspective in that a complete history of a business transaction's life is permanently held on record. Known as the **audit trail** it can be used to establish the authenticity of accounting balances.

Finally, the full **read/write optical disk** is under current development. This will provide mass, flexible, direct access secondary storage at a low cost per byte of information stored. Unless superseded by new technology it is likely that over time optical disks will rival magnetic media in larger systems as the main form of secondary storage.

3.2.5 Output devices

The purpose of the output component of a computer system is:

- to accept information/data from the CPU;
- to convert this information/data into the required output form.

Broadly speaking there are two important categories of output. **Soft copy** is output that does not persist over time. Examples are the visual output from a VDU or speech from a synthesizer. **Hard copy** output such as printed paper or microfilm persists.

Visual display unit (VDU)

A VDU consists of a cathode-ray tube to display output, together with a keyboard to accept input. The combination allows a dialogue with the computer. VDUs are a common form of output device because they provide a fast output of information that is practically costless and does not yield vast amounts of waste product such as paper. The applications are, of course, limited to those where no permanent record of output is required.

Modern VDU screens are colour and are high resolution, allowing a fine-grain representation of the output. This is not only important for the display of graphics but is essential for operators who may spend many hours each day studying screen output. Screens are designed to be minimally tiring to those using them. As well as being high resolution, modern VDUs provide steady non-flickering images on anti-glare screens.

There is some evidence to suggest that the emissions from VDUs lead to a higher likelihood of miscarriage in pregnancy. There is also evidence to indicate that prolonged work periods on VDUs cause stress and related illnesses.

Liquid crystal display (LCD) output

This screen output does not use a cathode-ray tube. Its quality is inferior to that of the cathode-ray tube VDU but it does have the advantage that the screen is flat. This is particularly important for machines with a high degree of portability, such as notebooks. The development of the flat screen technology of both mono and colour has enabled computer technology to be portable.

Voice output synthesizer

Voice output from computers is currently of limited use. It is chiefly employed where visual output is undesirable – on-board computers in cars, or impossible – blind people. Voice output is also used in building societies in response to enquiries by customers as to their current account status. This works by the customer keying in a request using an electronic keypad placed next to a telephone mouthpiece. The keypad delivers an audible, coded signal which is transmitted via the telephone network to the society's computer. The voice output is then returned to the enquirer.

The future major use for voice output will be in conjunction with developments in voice input when it will provide the output for distant verbal interrogation of computers using telecommunication links such as the public telephone network. The technical problems associated with voice output are minor compared with those of voice input recognition.

Printers

Printed output persists and so is important for permanent records. Printed output is also portable and can, for instance, be posted to customers. The main disadvantage of printed output is its bulk and the expense of paper involved. The benefits of permanent, readable records and portability must be offset against these shortcomings. There are a large range of types of printer all offering a different mix of:

- speed
- quality of output
- range of print fonts
- graphics abilities
- cost of purchase
- cost of operation
- associated noise levels.

The choice of printer will be dependent on how each meets the desired mix of these features.

It is not the purpose here to cover the technology of printers in detail. The interested reader is directed to the references at the end of the chapter. Rather, the main categories are outlined, together with their most general characteristics.

Serial printers: Serial printers produce one character at a time. The two most common types are the inkjet and dot matrix printer.

Inkjet printers eject a stream of special ink through a fine nozzle to form the characters. These are 'painted' onto the paper. Inkjet printers provide good-quality output. They can also provide a variety of fonts and produce diagrams, logos and other graphical output. Modern inkjets can also produce high-quality multi-coloured output. Inkjet printers are quiet in operation. Typical speeds for an inkjet would be about 250 characters per second or three pages a minute. Improvements in technology are ensuring that inkjet printers are becoming a serious rival to personal laser printers for office purposes.

The **dot matrix printer** has a movable print head, which consists of a matrix of pins. For example, a head may contain 252 pins in a matrix of 18 × 14. In printing, the set of pins corresponding to the shape of the character to be printed is impacted onto the ribbon, which then leaves an inked image on the page. Dot matrix printers print at a range of speeds – 250 characters per second would be typical. They are quiet in operation and cost about the same as an inkjet printer. Dot matrix printers are now being developed that are capable of letter-quality printing. Because they are not limited to a particular set of typefaces dot matrix printers can produce a wide variety of type sizes, type fonts, spacings and symbols.

Other less common types of printer include **thermal printers**, which burn away a coating on special paper to leave a visible character.

Line printers: The two most common sorts are **chain printers** and **drum printers**. These are both printers that rely on the impact of a typeface on a ribbon, which then marks paper. Line printers are high speed and can produce between 5 and 30 lines a second depending on the particular type of printer chosen. Line printers are more expensive than serial printers and their speeds mean that they are more suitable for a larger computer, usually a minicomputer or a mainframe computer. The quality of output is low and there is little flexibility in type styles. Line printers are the output workhorses of a large computer system. Because of their low quality output they are generally used for internal reports or high-volume output activities such as printing customer account statements for a large company.

Page printers: Page printers generate a page at a time. The technology can be varied. Page printers based on laser technology are common. The laser page image is directed on to a rotating drum. This leaves an image area, which attracts ink through which the drum is rolled. The image is then transferred to paper. Page printers for large computers cost many tens of thousands of pounds. They can produce output of high quality at up to ten pages a second. Smaller laser printers are now available for microcomputers. These cost less than £500 and produce a page about every 8 to 10 seconds.

Computer output on microfilm/microfiche (COM)

Microfilm is 16 mm or 35 mm film on which several thousand pages of output in sequence can be held. Microfiche is 105 mm film cut up into sheets about 6 inches by 4 inches. A sheet commonly contains 208 pages. In both cases the computer output is recorded directly onto the film rather than, say, being printed and later photographed.

There are many advantages of this output medium as compared to printed output. Printed output is bulky to store in contrast to microfilm or fiche. Connected with this is the ease with which recorded data is retrieved, particularly from fiche. COM is also cheaper and faster per page to produce than print and it is easy and quick to produce multiple copies if needed. The major disadvantage of COM is the need for a special reading machine to understand the output.

COM is suitable for applications that need frequent reference to bulk records. It is important that such data should be stable as any change requires the reprinting of an entire film or set of fiches. Typical applications such as library indexes and stock parts description listings fit these characteristics.

Output to magnetic disk or tape

Rather than producing an output that is directly understandable visually or audibly it is possible to produce output on a magnetic medium such as disk or tape. This is done if the outputs being generated for eventual input into another computer system. Alternatively, it may be used where the disk or tape is employed at a later stage or at a different geographical location to supply output information based on one or other of the other output media.

Output on disk or tape is popular as a persisting medium because it is very cheap and fast to produce. The tape or disk itself is highly portable, requires little storage space, and is even capable of being sent through the post. The obvious drawback of this output method is the need to possess a computer to understand its magnetic contents.

3.2.6 Factors involved in the selection of output device and medium

The following features must be taken into account:

- **The type of application:** This is crucial when considering output. It is important to establish whether permanent copy is required or not, and whether the output is to be distributed or not, and whether receivers have access to special machinery such as microfiche readers or computers.

- **Costs:** Initial costs for the output devices vary enormously. The chief components of running costs will involve sundries such as paper, film ribbons and so on. Depreciation and maintenance must be allowed for those output devices that involve mechanical parts.

- **Speed and volume of output:** Estimates must be made of the requirements under this heading and suitable devices chosen that match them.

- **Quality of output**: Internal documents generally require less high-quality output than external documentation used for clients or marketing purposes.

- **Storage of output:** Bulky output cannot be stored and retrieved easily.

- **Environmental considerations:** This is particularly important for output devices that would normally be located in an office. Many printers produce noise, which causes stress and other complaints. Manufacturers have responded to this need by emphasizing quietness, where applicable, to their advertising and naming of products.

Although aspects of technology have been emphasized in this section it should never be forgotten that the first, and most important, consideration with respect to output is its content and format. Unless attention is paid to the selection of relevant information and its proper presentation at the right time and at the desired level of detail the output will be of little use. This area is covered in the chapters on systems analysis and design.

3.2.7 Central processing unit

The central processing unit (CPU) is made up of three components. These are the main memory, the arithmetic and logic unit, and the control section. A general outline of each is now given (see Figure 3.10).

Main memory
Synonyms are fast memory, immediate access memory, core store, and direct access memory, primary storage. The purpose of the main memory is:

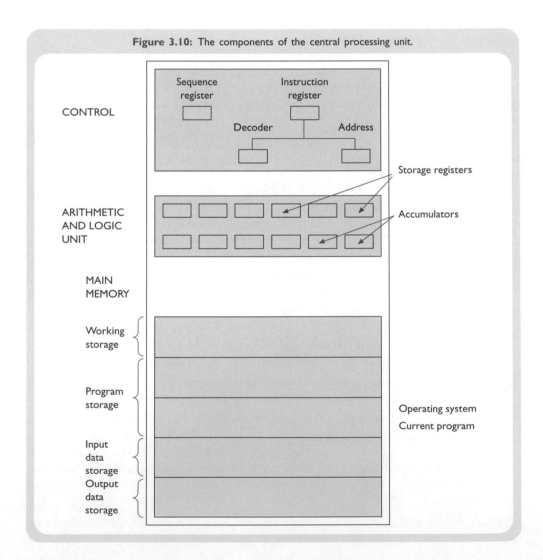

Figure 3.10: The components of the central processing unit.

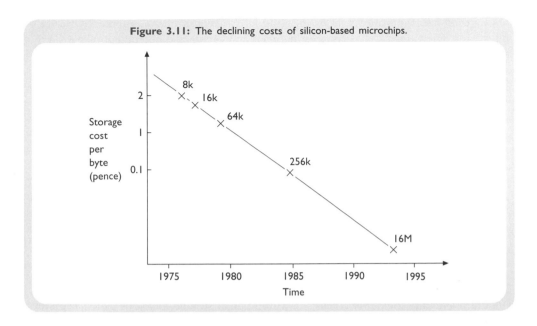

Figure 3.11: The declining costs of silicon-based microchips.

- to store programs during their execution;
- to store data that is being used by the current program;
- to store the operating system.

Main memory nowadays is exclusively based on silicon microchip storage. The unit of storage is the byte, and the declining costs per byte of store can be seen in Figure 3.11. Memory space is divided into separate storage locations. Each storage location is assigned an **address** and holds a certain number of bits of information. It is common for computers to hold one byte (eight bits) at each location. The contents of these locations can be directly recovered using the address of the location. The contents of other addresses do not have to be searched in order to retrieve a piece of data from a given address. Because the time taken to recover the contents of an address is independent of the address, main storage is called **random access memory** or **RAM**.

The contents of RAM disappear when the power supply is disconnected so RAM is said to be **volatile**. Another important feature of RAM is that not only can data be read that is copied from a memory location, but data can also be written to that memory location. In doing this it erases any previous contents.

As shown in Figure 3.10 main memory is divided into several areas depending on the function that is served.

One part of the memory is used to store the current program being executed. In a large computer there may be many 'current' programs, which are programs somewhere between their initiation and completion. The operating system, or a large part of it, is also stored in main memory. The functions of an operating system are covered in a later section in this chapter. Other parts of the primary storage are reserved for holding input data coming from either an input device or secondary storage, for holding output data that is to be transferred to an output device or secondary storage, or for holding working data that is being swapped in and out of the arithmetic and logic unit.

A typical size for main memory in a modern business microcomputer is 32 or 64 megabytes. Each couple of years sees the doubling of average microcomputer RAM. For a mainframe the primary store will run into many megabytes.

Some computers also have **read only memory (ROM)**. ROM, as its name suggests, will not allow the data stored in its memory locations to be written to or changed. The data is permanent even when the electrical power is removed. ROM is sometimes used for the storage of commonly used programs, such as a word processor program, or systems software, such as an operating system. It removes the need to load these from secondary storage when needed. ROM is also used for the storage of **microprograms**. These are series of instructions that carry out commonly used routines.

Arithmetic and logic unit

The purpose of the arithmetic and logic unit (ALU) is:

- to carry out arithmetic operations – for example, to add two numbers together;
- to carry out logical operations – for example, to compare two numbers to establish which is the larger.

The arithmetic and logic unit consists of a number of storage locations called **registers**. These are used for storing data in the ALU before, during and after the execution of a program instruction involving a logical or arithmetic operation. The operation is carried out inside the ALU, its exact nature being governed by the circuitry triggered by the program instruction. Different registers perform different functions. Accumulator and adder registers are examples.

Control

The purpose of the control unit is:

- to decode and execute the program instructions one by one;
- to control and coordinate data movements within the CPU and between the CPU and the other components of the computer system.

Inside the control section are important registers dealing with the execution of a program. One register, called the **sequence register**, contains the address of the current instruction being executed. The **instruction register** contains the current instruction being executed. There are two parts to this instruction. The **operator** stipulates the type of instruction such as **ADD**, **GET**, **MULTIPLY**. This is decoded by circuitry in the decoder. The **operand** contains the address or addresses of the data items on which the instruction must work. Having carried out the program instruction the contents of the instruction register are incremented and this provides the address of the next instruction to be executed.

Data must be moved around the computer. An example is the need to print the output of a program where the output is currently held in main memory. The CPU works by carrying out many millions of instructions every second. In contrast the printer may print only a hundred characters a second. In order to make efficient use of computing resources this speed difference must not be allowed to tie up the fast CPU while waiting for the slow printer to finish its task. What happens is that the CPU instructs the printer to produce output and while it is doing this the CPU can carry out other activities. When the output device has completed its task it **interrupts** the operation of the CPU, which then continues to service the device. Handling these interrupts is a function of the control section.

3.2.8   Current issues involved in central processing unit design

The control section and arithmetic and logic unit are together called the **processor**. These two components are generally held on one silicon micro-integrated circuit (microchip). The immediate access memory is held as several microchips, which are accessible to the processor. Each memory chip may hold 1, 4 or 8 megabytes of memory depending on its type. Technological developments of the CPU are concentrated on two major areas:

- speeding up the operation of the CPU – so that programs run more quickly;
- making larger amounts of cheaper RAM available to the processor – so that a larger number of more complex programs may be held entirely in main memory during execution. This saves the lengthy task of loading parts of programs in and out of secondary storage and main memory during a program run.

In order to achieve these objectives several development strategies are adopted by microchip manufacturers and designers.

1. The speed of the CPU is partly determined by the **clock cycle time**. There is a clock within the CPU and operations can only occur in time with the beat of this clock. If the clock is speeded up then more operations can occur per second. This is one strategy – to design microchips capable of operating with faster clock speeds. Clock speeds are measured in terms of the number of operations per second and are commonly expressed in terms of **megahertz**. One megahertz (MHz) equals one million operations per second. A business microcomputer might be expected to operate at 233 MHz.

2. Increasing clock speed is not the only possibility. All processors are designed to be able to decode and execute a determinate number of types of instructions. This is known as the **instruction set**. It is well known that a majority of these instructions are rarely used. Microchips can be designed to operate more quickly if the set of instructions is reduced to contain those that are most basic and commonly used. If one of the more rarely used instructions is needed it can be carried out by combining some of the more basic instructions. These microchips are known as **RISC** chips (reduced instruction set chip).

3. The ALU and control sections are designed to carry out each operation with a standard size chunk of data. This is known as the **word** length. The earliest microchips worked with a word length of 8 bits or one **byte**. If this is increased then clearly the computer will be able to process more data in each operation. Word sizes of 32 bits are now common in business microcomputers. Mainframe computers use 32-bit and 64-bit words and more. The trend is to develop processors that handle longer words.

4. Data is transferred between main memory and the processor frequently. The processor will be slowed in its functioning if it has to wait for long periods for the transfer of the data needed for an operation. Data is transferred in parallel along data lines. For an 8-bit processor (word length equals 8 bits) there are eight data

lines in and eight data lines out of the processor. Clearly one byte of data can be transferred in one operation. This coincides with the word length. Early 16-bit processors still had only eight data lines in and eight data lines out. Clearly not all the data could be transferred to the processor for the execution of an instruction in one clock cycle.

5. The speeds of operation of processors and memory chips are so fast now that, relatively speaking, a major delay occurs because of the time the electrical signal takes to move from the memory to the processor. One way to shorten this period is to decrease the distance of the processor from the memory. This is achieved by building some memory onto the processor chip.

6. The single processor is based on the Von Neumann model of the computer. In an application, although some of the tasks must be carried out in sequence, many can be performed in parallel with one another provided the results of these tasks are delivered at the right times. There is considerable research and development interest in **parallel processing** using several processors, each working in parallel with the others. This can increase the rate at which the computer can carry out tasks.

7. All the developments mentioned so far are directed at increasing the speed of processing. There is also a need to increase the amount of RAM available to the processor. This cannot be achieved simply by plugging in more RAM microchips. Each RAM location needs to be separately addressable. Memory address lines fulfil this function. If there are 20 memory address lines associated with a processor then a maximum of 2^{20} bytes or one megabyte of memory can be addressed. Modern microcomputers may have 64 Mb of RAM and processors are able to address increasingly large amounts of memory.

8. At the leading edge of developments new technologies based on laser-light switching and chemico/biologically-based processors are being investigated. These are currently in an early stage of research.

Over the last decade and a half chip manufacturers have produced families of processor chips incorporating successive improvements. For instance, Intel, a major international microchip manufacturer, has produced a series of chips that are widely used in business microcomputers. The set consists of the 8086, 80186, 80286, 80386, 80486, Pentium and Pentium II microchips. The later chips are improvements over the earlier ones, having faster clock speeds, larger word sizes, more data lines, and more addressable RAM.

3.3   Software

Software is the general term for instructions that control the operation of the computer. This section deals with the basic sorts of software and the various languages in which it may be written.

3.3.1   The concept of a program

In order to be able to serve any useful purpose the operation of the computer must be controlled by a program. A **program** is a set of instructions, written in a specialized language, the electronic execution of which controls the operation of the computer to serve some purpose.

Software is the general name given to programs or parts of programs. There are two types of software. **Systems software** carries out functions that are generally required in order to ensure the smooth and efficient operation of the computer. Examples are the operating system (explained later), a program for copying the contents of one disk to another or a file reorganization program. **Applications software** performs functions associated with the various needs of the business (as distinct from the needs of the computer). Examples are programs that carry out accounting tasks such as sales, purchase and nominal ledger processing, a modelling program for forecasting sales figures, or a word processing program.

Programs are stored in immediate access memory while being run. The instructions are executed in sequence starting from the first instruction. They are loaded one at a time from immediate access memory into the control section of the CPU where they are decoded and executed. Broadly speaking there are four types of instruction:

1. **Data movement instructions,** when executed cause data to be moved around the computer. The movement may be between the CPU and the input, output, or backing store, or within the CPU itself.

2. **Arithmetic and logic instructions** lead to the transformation of data in the ALU.

3. **Program branching instructions** alter the sequential execution of the program. An unconditional branch instruction leads to the execution of a specified next instruction rather than the instruction immediately after the one being currently executed. This is achieved by putting the address of the desired instruction in the sequence register in the control section. Conditional branch instructions lead to a change in execution order only if a specified logical condition is met: for example, if $x > 19$ then branch to instruction 1200.

4. **Start, stop and declaration** instructions commence the execution of the program, terminate the execution of the program, and make declarations: for example, that a certain area of memory is to be known by a particular name.

3.3.2 Application packages and programs

When faced with the need to obtain software for its business information, decision support or data processing systems, an organization may either commission specially written software or purchase a standard applications package.

An **applications package** is a piece of software designed to carry out a standard business function. It is usually produced by a computer manufacturer or software house intending to sell many copies of the package to different organizations. Purchasers of the package do not own the copyright and will usually have clearly specified limited rights to make copies or alterations. Applications packages are common in the following business areas: all accounting, payroll and stock control functions, word processing, electronic spreadsheets, critical path analysis, financial modelling, statistical analysis, described as being 'off the shelf'.

In contrast, **specially commissioned software** is designed and written for the *specific* business needs of an organization. It may be written 'in house', if the organization is large enough to have a computer centre with a team of programmers, or it may be produced by a third-party software house. In either case, the commissioning organization usually owns the copyright. The software can be written in a high-level language, such as COBOL, though nowadays it is increasingly common to produce programs with fourth-generation languages (see Section 3.3.4). The specification of the business needs of an organization and the translation of these into program specifications is often preceded by a considerable period of analysis and design. Specially commissioned programs are often described as being 'tailor made'.

There are several benefits and limitations associated with purchasing applications packages as compared with commissioned software.

Benefits

In summary the benefits are:

- **Cost:** Applications packages are intended for sale to many purchasers, therefore the research and development costs of the software are spread amongst many organizations. This lowers the cost to purchasers. For instance, a quality accounts package for a microcomputer may cost £2000 and for a mainframe £20,000. This compares favourably with the costs of specially commissioned software, which would be many times greater.

  From the supplier's point of view, when enough packages have been sold to break even with production costs, the profit margin on each additional copy sold is immense. For instance on a £500 microcomputer-based package after subtracting the costs of the disk and manual it is not uncommon for there to be £490 gross profit. However, if there are few sales the software house can suffer a very large loss.

- **Speed of implementation:** A package can generally be purchased and installed on the hardware very quickly as compared to a specially commissioned program, which requires much time to write and debug.

- **Tried and tested:** A successful package has been tried and tested by many previous purchasers. This means not only that various errors that may have occurred in earlier versions will have been remedied, but more importantly that the package will be one that is known to satisfy the general business function for which it was intended. However, a tried and tested package will not be 'state of the art' software but will reflect what was new several years ago.

- **New versions:** New improved versions of a successful package are brought out from time to time. These updated versions are often made available to existing customers at a lower rate. This is one way the customers are assured that their software follows what the market is currently offering. From the supplier's point of view it encourages 'brand loyalty'.

- **Documentation:** Packages often have clear professionally produced documentation. This is a marketing point for the software house. It also prevents customers from encountering difficulties that would otherwise involve the software house in answering time-consuming enquiries. Specially commissioned programs generally do not have such good documentation.

- **Portability:** Packages may be portable from one type of computer to another. As important is the portability of the user interface. For instance, a company that currently uses a particular word processing package on a certain type of hardware may wish to change its hardware. If it can purchase another version of the package on the new hardware that presents the same screens and uses the same files it will not have to retrain its staff or convert files.

Although these reasons are persuasive in opting for packaged software there are some limitations.

Limitations

In summary these are:

- **Lack of satisfaction of user requirements:** This is the most important drawback of purchasing a package. A large business is likely to have specialized information and data-processing requirements. It is common that no package fits these needs correctly. Large businesses can afford to commission software. The situation is different for small organizations. However, their needs are simpler and it is more likely that a package can be found that suits them. Also, they are often not able to afford the extensive costs involved in writing programs.

- **Efficiency:** In order to appeal to as wide a market as possible packages build in flexibility (for example, many report options) and redundancy (for example, the ability to handle many accounts). For the purchaser much of this may not be needed and it will cause the package to run less efficiently on the computer.

- **Compatibility with existing software:** It is unlikely that packages will be compatible with existing specially commissioned software. If interfacing is required it is usually necessary for further software to be commissioned.

The microcomputer market is more heavily package based than the minicomputer or mainframe market. From the demand side this is because there are more microcomputers, and in particular more small businesses with microcomputers, than larger computers. Small organizations are forced for cost reasons to purchase packages to meet their software needs. On the supply side microcomputer-based software can be written and tested as microcomputers themselves are cheap and readily available.

The price of the standard business microcomputer has dropped over the years. This can be explained partly by the decrease in hardware costs and partly by the development of cheaper versions of the IBM PC range by other manufacturers. The numbers of machines has expanded and so, therefore, has the market for software. Many software package producers have sought to undercut their long-established rivals by reducing the price of packages considerably, while at the same time offering much the same facilities.

This initially stimulated the production of 'software clones'. The software clone is a package that to the user appears similar, and produces files similar, to a more expensive package. The program code though is different. From the user's perspective there is little advantage to be gained from purchasing the more expensive and better-established rival. This led to the spawning of many software clones for major microcomputer packages which became the subject of copyright litigation. More recently the software market for mainstream packages (word processing, spreadsheet, database and network software) has witnessed the rise of a few major companies which now dominate the world sales of these products. The packages produced are highly sophisticated and are constantly under upgrade development. In 1995/96 four companies – Microsoft, Computer Associates, Oracle and Novell – each had a worldwide revenue in excess of two billion dollars. The major threat to the revenues of these companies is now coming from 'pirate' copies of software on CD-ROMs emanating from parts of the world that do not properly enforce copyright restrictions.

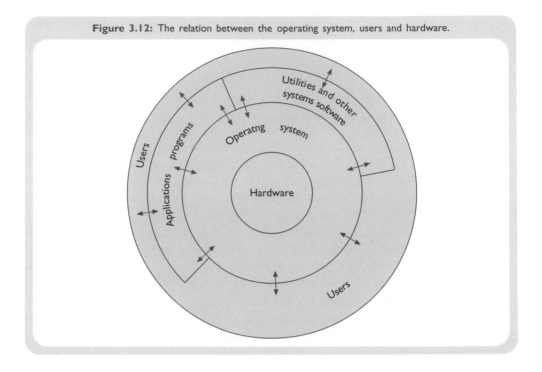

Figure 3.12: The relation between the operating system, users and hardware.

There is also an increasing trend for the suppliers of major packaged software products to ensure that files created by rival packages are capable of being read into their programs. This is particularly the case with word processing, spreadsheet and database software. The intention is to ensure that a potential customer is not prevented from moving from a rival's package by the impossibility of the new package reading old text and data files.

As the number of business microcomputers has increased, package software suppliers have produced more specialized packages. For instance, as well as many standard accounting packages for small businesses, there are now specialist packages for the general professions such as solicitors, insurance brokers and general practitioners, and for more unusual needs of veterinary surgeons, funeral directors and more. As business microcomputers become more powerful in the future and competition between software houses more intense, the packages themselves are likely to become more sophisticated.

3.3.3 Operating systems

An operating system (OPSY) is a piece of systems software that handles some of the housekeeping routines necessary for the smooth and efficient operation of the computer. Its relation to hardware, users and applications programs is shown in Figure 3.12. The operating system is loaded into main memory and run when the power is supplied to the computer. It is usually held initially on disk and is loaded by means of a short ROM-based 'bootstrap' program. The operating system has many functions. The main ones are:

- **Handling input/output:** All applications programs require interchange of data between the CPU and input/output devices. This could be controlled by instructions within the applications program. But as, say, sending output to a printer is common to most programs it makes more sense to produce the controlling instructions once and make the code available as part of the operating system, to be called upon as necessary.

- **Backing store management:** Data and programs need to be loaded into and out of main memory from time to time. It is important that this can be done without overwriting existing files and in such a way that later retrieval is possible.

- **Main memory management:** Similarly, main memory must be allocated to programs and data in such a way that they do not overwrite one another. If the program is too large to fit into main memory then the relevant parts are **paged** into and out of main memory. It 'appears' to the applications program that the computer has an indefinitely large **virtual** memory.

- **Handling job scheduling, multiprogramming, and multiprocessing:** To meet the processing requirements of a business organization needing many 'jobs' performed by its hardware it is necessary to prioritize these jobs and ensure that the CPU acts on them according to this priority. **Job scheduling** is controlled by the operating system. To make more efficient use of the hardware it is often necessary to run more than one program simultaneously so that the fast CPU can carry out operations on one program while waiting for a slow output device to handle the output from another program. The programs are not strictly simultaneous but rather interleaved in their execution. The operating system ensures this efficient **multiprogramming**. In larger computers with more than one central processor the activities of the processors need to be coordinated. The operating system controls this **multiprocessing**.

Operating systems for mainframe computers are considerably more complex than microcomputer operating systems. They need to handle the complexities of multiprogramming, multiprocessing and multi-user access, where there may be several hundreds of terminals connected to a processing function being used for a variety of tasks. Operating systems for mainframes are developed, maintained and updated by the mainframe manufacturers themselves and sold with the computers.

Mainframe manufacturers either produce their own operating systems in house or commission a software company to do this. With microcomputers the main operating systems are produced by Microsoft and Apple. The former produces the set of operating systems for the PC and PC compatibles while the latter produces an operating system for its own Apple computers. Microsoft produced the operating systems MS-DOS and PC-DOS for the early PCs. These are now considered rather primitive in the functions that are provided to the users and have now been superseded by the Windows set of operating systems (Windows 3.1, Windows 95, Windows NT and Windows 98). The Windows set of operating systems require increasingly powerful microcomputers with a large RAM capacity in order that their increased functions can run smoothly.

Developments within the Windows set of operating systems include the ability to hold, run and pass data between many programs simultaneously within the CPU and to display this with sophisticated screen graphics. Windows ensures that the same graphical interface is consistent from one application to the next. It is possible to pass text, data, spreadsheet model output, graphs and images from one application to another. For instance the output of a spreadsheet can be pasted into a word processed document. Essential to this approach is the idea that the interface presented to the human being should be more than

Figure 3.13: An example of a Windows 95 interface.

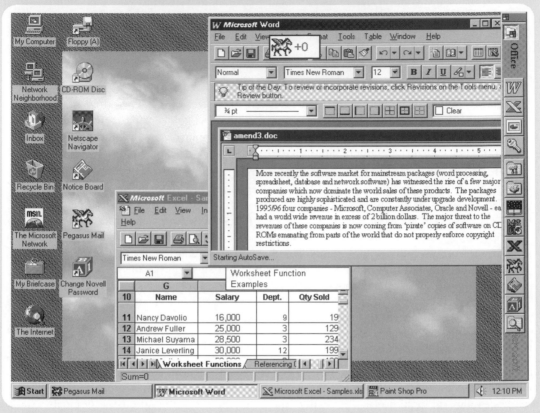

Sources: *Pegasus Mail reproduced with permission. Screenshot reprinted by permission from Microsoft Corporation.*

the ability to type in text commands at a prompt. Rather the use of **windows, icons, mouse and pull-down menus** (WIMPS) increases the ability of the user to interact with the machine (see Figure 3.13). The Windows NT operating system is a network version allowing even greater flexibility. It is clear that the **graphical user interface** (GUI) will become an increasingly common feature in all software applications.

Another development in operating systems is the UNIX range. UNIX is a multi-user operating system containing many features useful for program development. It comes in several versions and runs on a range of microcomputers, minicomputers and main-frame computers. The original intention was that software developed in a UNIX envir-onment on one type of machine would be transportable to another. This is not now as straightforward as the original intention assumed, with different 'dialects' of UNIX being developed for different machines.

3.3.4 Low-level, high-level, object-oriented and the fourth generation of languages

A program is always written in a specialized language. There are a number of categories of language, each exhibiting different characteristics.

Machine code

The only program instructions that can be 'understood' by the CPU are those using the basic set of instructions specific to the type of processor in the CPU. These instructions, known as machine code, consist of strings of 1s and 0s. A typical instruction might be 0110 1010 0110 1011. The first programs were written in machine code in the 1940s. Writing in machine code is extremely difficult. Not only must the programmer think in terms of 1s and 0s when writing code, it is almost impossible to understand code once written. This leads to further difficulties if the program does not perform as intended – that is, has a **bug**. Programs are rarely written in machine code nowadays. Assembly language is used.

Assembly language

Assembly language overcomes some of the difficulties of programming in machine code. The instructions use mnemonics such as **ADD** or **STO** (store) instead of binary. A typical instruction might be **ADD R1,R2,R4** – add the contents of registers 1 and 2 and put the result in register 4, References to memory locations are replaced by reference to named memory areas. The use of binary to represent numbers is replaced by decimal or hexadecimal (a number system having a base of 16). Groups of instructions that are to be repeated many times in a program can be defined and named. These are called **macros**.

These differences mean that programming with assembly language is much easier than with machine code. Assembly languages were developed very early in the history of the electronic computer. Once written, an assembly language program needs to be translated into a machine code program. This is achieved by an **assembler** program. This straightforward program takes the original **source program** and translates it instruction by instruction to become the final machine code **object program** capable of being run on the computer.

Assembly languages are an improvement on machine code in terms of the ease of program production but they do have some drawbacks:

- Each different type of processor has a different set of instructions and a different assembly language. Assembly language programs are therefore not portable from one type of machine to another.

- The assembly language is machine-orientated. Reference is made to registers in the ALU and memory locations. In writing an applications program a programmer would prefer to concentrate on the task to be coded rather than physical aspects of the machine on which the program is to be finally run.

- Because each task must be specified in detail, programming is very time-consuming. There are not instructions suitable for the types of application areas for which programs may be required.

The main advantage of programs written in assembly language, as distinct from programs written in high-level languages covered in the next section, is that operations can be specified in detail, making the most efficient use of the machine. This leads to the production of programs that run quickly on the computer. Assembly language programming is used for systems software where high-speed program execution is required.

High-level languages

High-level languages were developed to increase the productivity of programmers. These languages are task-orientated rather than machine-orientated. This means that instructions within them are more suited to the types of application on which the programmer is employed than to the machines on which the programs will finally run.

Different types of application have spawned different types of high-level language. Well-known languages include:

COBOL (COmmon Business Oriented Language): COBOL was developed in 1960/61 as a general-purpose business data-processing language. It is particularly suitable for processing large numbers of records. COBOL was a widely used commercial language. It conforms to standards set by ANSI (American National Standards Institute) and CODASYL (COnference of DAta SYstems Languages). Although versions do exist for microcomputers, COBOL is used most extensively for business applications running on minicomputers and mainframes.

FORTRAN (FORmula TRANslator): FORTRAN is a language developed in the 1950s specifically for the purposes of scientific and mathematical work. It is rich in its ability to handle formulae.

BASIC (Beginners All Purpose Instruction Code): BASIC was developed in 1963 and 1964 at Dartmouth College as a language that could be understood and learnt very quickly by students. It is now a popular language which is used extensively for programs designed for microcomputers. Despite the existence of an ANSI standard there are a range of different dialects for BASIC each incorporating slightly different features.

Pascal: Pascal, named after Blaise Pascal, the seventeenth century mathematician, was developed in the late 1960s and early 1970s at the Federal Institute of Technology in Switzerland. It was the first programming language designed to encourage **structured programming**. This involves chopping the application up into self-contained **modules**. Each module performs a logically cohesive task. There is a clear specification of what data is allowed to flow between modules. Within each module only certain logical structures are encouraged. The aim is to ensure that programs once written are easily understandable, testable and amendable. Pascal is a general-purpose language used extensively on microcomputer and minicomputer systems. It is very popular with educational institutions as it encourages good programming practice.

Ada: Ada, named after Ada Augusta, daughter of Lord Byron, is a new comprehensive programming language in the Pascal tradition. It is sponsored by the US Department of Defense for use in military applications.

PROLOG: PROLOG is a language specifically designed for writing programs that require reasoning as distinct from record processing, text handling or number crunching. It is therefore used in artificial intelligence applications. Unlike other languages previously covered, which are all based around writing code for procedures to carry out tasks, PROLOG is designed to be able to declare states from which implications are then derived. The language has been chosen by the Japanese for their 'fifth-generation' computer destined to be in production in the late 1990s. PROLOG and another popular artificial intelligence language, LISP, will play a large role in the development of future intelligent business applications.

The languages discussed constitute a selection of some of the more important high-level languages in current use. There are many more. There are several advantages to using high-level languages as compared to low-level assembly languages:

- It should be clear from the descriptions that high-level languages are task-orientated and there are different types of language for different types of programming requirements. This increases programmer productivity.

- High-level languages also increase programmer productivity because each high-level instruction will eventually be relatively straightforward to learn, often using expressions that are near English. Some, such as BASIC, are so straightforward that simple programs may be written after an afternoon's study of the language. Training times for programmers are reduced and programming requires less qualified personnel.

- Programs written in high-level languages should be portable from one type of machine to another. In practice this is unlikely because of differences in dialects. However, changes that are necessary are often minor.

In order for a source program in a high-level language to run on a computer it needs to be translated into a machine code object program. This translation may be by **interpreting** or **compiling**. In either case the translation is carried out by software. When a program is interpreted, as each line is translated into object code it is immediately executed. In contrast, when a program is compiled a compiler program translates the entire source program into object code. The object program can then be executed.

Once compiled object code is produced, it can be used again and again without the need for the source program. Application software producers prefer to release their packages as compiled code. Compiled code is difficult to understand and so is difficult to alter. This prevents unauthorized tampering with programs. In contrast, no permanent object code is produced when a source program is interpreted. Moreover, the interpreted program will run less quickly than the compiled version. This is because of the necessity for the translation as well as the execution of instructions each time the program is run. Interpreting is popular in the writing of programs because there is no need to compile the entire program each time an alteration is made to it.

Compared with assembly language programs high-level language programs, whether interpreted or compiled, always run more slowly. This is partly because inefficiencies occur in the process of compiling or interpreting even though optimization procedures are used. It is also partly because the machine-independent nature of high-level languages prevents programmers from using their knowledge of the internal structure of the CPU to increase run-time efficiency. These shortcomings are not enough to deter the use of high-level languages in business applications where the increases in programmer productivity and the other advantages outweigh the run time considerations.

Object-oriented languages

During the 1980s and 1990s object-oriented approaches have become important within the design of information systems. This has led to the development of object-oriented analysis (OOA) and design methods (OOD), object-oriented databases (OODBs) and object-oriented programming languages (OOPLs). The ideas behind object-oriented analysis are treated later in this book. Given here is a brief summary of the essential ideas behind an object-oriented programming language.

In conventional programming languages primitive procedures are combined by the use of the language to perform complex operations – the more high-level the language the more similar these primitive procedures are to real-world tasks and the more distant from machine structures. However, we study the world not in terms of operations but in terms of objects that have properties, stand in relationships with other objects and take part in operations. If a programming language is used to mirror the world then these features should be deeply embedded in its structure. Object-oriented languages do this by enabling software to be constructed representing objects that have properties and take part in operations.

Three essential ideas lie behind object-oriented languages:

1. Early programming languages usually refer only to a limited number of things, such as integers and strings (a string is a collection of ordered characters). These **data types**, as they are known, are defined in terms of the operations within which they can take part. For instance, integers can take part in the operations of multiplication and addition whereas strings cannot. In later languages, such as Pascal, programmers were able to define their own data types. For example: summer-month = (June, July, August). Relations such as 'earlier than' could then be defined for this data type. **Abstract data types** as used in object-oriented programming languages are an extension of this principle. An abstract data type is a data type, representing a type of object, defined by the programmer in such a way that the data structure is defined along with the named operations within which it can take part. Moreover the exact details of this are kept private from the user. The user has access only to the name of the object, of the abstract data type, and the names of the permitted operations.

2. Object-oriented languages allow for **inheritance**. For example a pig, as well as having various properties characteristic of a pig, also inherits certain properties, such as suckling its young, from the larger type, mammal, of which it is a subtype. Object-oriented programming languages enable this inheritance to be achieved easily and automatically.

3. Once a system has been developed a user has only to specify the name of an object and the name of an operation to be carried out and the system will select the appropriate method for carrying out the operation. **Method selection** is a feature of object-oriented programming languages.

Object-oriented programming languages have borrowed ideas from other languages, particularly Ada, Pascal and Simula. The first genuine object-oriented language to be developed was **Smalltalk** dating back to the 1970s. **C++** is the most commonly used commercial language.

It is claimed that software developed using object-oriented techniques and written using object-oriented programming languages has certain advantages:

- Being similar to the way in which users view the world it is a more natural way of mirroring the world with software.

- Program code, once written, is more likely to be reusable. This is because it relies heavily on the definitions of the object types, which can be reused.

- In terms of measures of program complexity (for example, the number of loops nested within loops) object-oriented software is simpler than programs written in other languages and therefore less likely to contain errors.

Object-oriented techniques are influencing many areas of information technology. CASE (computer-aided software engineering) tools are now likely to be based around object-oriented techniques. In artificial intelligence frame-based approaches (essentially an object-oriented approach) are establishing success as a way of representing knowledge. Object-oriented databases are becoming more popular. It is likely that object-oriented approaches and languages will have a significant long-term impact on the development of information systems.

Fourth-generation languages

Though it is difficult to derive an agreed standard against which programmer productivity can be measured it is generally recognized that there have been significant advances over the last 20 years brought about by the use of high-level languages. It is also generally accepted that with modern, cheap powerful micro, mini, and mainframe computers together with the increasingly sophisticated programs required by business, these productivity increases are insufficient to meet the extra demand placed on software production. There are three separate but interrelated problems:

1. **High costs of software production:** High-level languages have reduced costs by increasing programmer productivity, reducing the training required for programmers and increasing the reliability of programs. However, as hardware costs drop, the cost of software production as a proportion of a company's total expenditure on its information system has been increasing over time. The production of versatile software packages to carry out standard business functions has gone some way to reduce this cost burden. But for an organization that has special needs there is no alternative to commissioning purpose-designed software.

2. **Need to produce systems quickly:** Traditional high-level language programming is still a lengthy business. It cannot be easily speeded up by employing more programmers on the project. The man-month attitude to programming ('if it takes four programmers six months it will take 24 programmers one month') has been shown to be a myth. Project control and communication problems between programmers rapidly increase with the number of programmers. Modern project control and the use of structured techniques in programming have gone some way towards diminishing this problem, especially with larger systems. However, small systems are often needed quickly to meet fast-changing requirements and so some alternative to conventional programming must be found.

Table 3.2: The generations of languages.

Generation	Typical languages	Capabilities
1st	Machine code	Machine orientated, each language specific to a processor type, programs not portable
2nd	Symbolic assembly language	Easier to use than machine code though still machine orientated, each language specific to a processor type, programs not portable
3rd	For example, COBOL, Pascal, BASIC, LISP	Procedurally orientated, task orientated, increase in programmer productivity over 2GL, portable programs
4th	For example, SQL, FOCUS, NOMAD, RAMIS	Designed for fast applications development, some end-user orientated, integrated for interactive applications development around a database, programs generally not portable

3. **Need to produce systems that meet user requirements:** The history of business information systems has many examples of systems that are technically efficient but do not serve the needs of the users and so are underused or misused. Because traditional programming involves a long and expensive development by programming experts much emphasis has gone into methods and techniques that ensure the correct identification of user needs. Another approach is to develop quick, cheap versions or prototypes of systems that users can test for their adequacy before revision and improvement. An extension of this is to develop languages so straightforward and powerful that users themselves can develop their own systems. **End-user computing**, as it is known, requires a different sort of programming language.

Fourth-generation languages (4GLs) attempt to overcome these shortcomings of the previous generations of languages (see Table 3.2). There is no agreed definition of what constitutes a fourth-generation language. It may be a sophisticated language aimed at improving professional programmer productivity by the provision of a range of facilities and routines commonly needed in programming applications. Alternatively, it may be a much more straightforward language designed for end users to construct their own systems. A number of features, though, are common to many fourth-generation languages:

- They are often centred around the storage and retrieval of data in a database, most often a relational database. Although database ideas are covered extensively in the chapter devoted to databases it is sufficient here to understand a database as a centralized, integrated store of commonly shared data for an organization.
- There is an emphasis on instructions to specify what applications are to do rather than how to do them – that is, no **declarative** rather than **procedural** instructions. These instructions often closely resemble their English equivalents.
- There is a powerful interface with the user of the language, enabling interactive dialogue in the development of applications, the specification of input and output screens and reports, the specification of record contents, the use of defaults, and in the use of graphics.

- There are interfaces to conventional programming languages for writing special procedures not covered within the 4GL.

- There are often special facilities for the development of models.

- The use of these very high-level instructions reduces the total number of programming instructions needed in the development of the system as compared with conventional code.

It should be clear from these features that a 4GL is not a conventional language in the sense that say BASIC or COBOL is. The speed, cheapness and ease with which applications can be developed has had impacts in two main areas.

First, the traditional development process for a new system need not be followed. This traditional process involves the progression of a project from its feasibility study through the stages of analysis, detailed specification and implementation. Because the time and costs involved in implementation are great, it is important to ensure that an adequate and final design to meet users' needs is achieved during the specification stage. This linear development process, or rather how a structured analysis and design methodology is appropriate to it, is covered extensively in later chapters. Fourth-generation languages allow the speedy and cheap development of applications software. The importance of this is that a **prototype** version can be developed comparatively quickly and cheaply. This can be tested for its acceptability to users and its appropriateness in the provision of facilities. The prototype can serve either as an integral part of the process of final specification or as a first attempt, which is successively refined over time to make improvements or change to meet evolving user needs. In both cases the ability to deliver a working prototype quickly and cheaply has changed the development strategy to be adopted.

Second, 4GLs have been developed specifically with the intention of **end-user applications development** in mind. One of the problems of the traditional approach to programming to meet user requirements is that these requirements must be translated into a form suitable for a programmer to be able to write a program. It would ease any communication difficulties if users could translate their information requirements directly into the satisfaction of those needs by programs. Fourth-generation languages orientated towards end-user computing allow this and are simpler than the 4GLs aimed at increasing programmer productivity. Some are designed specifically for the development of microcomputer applications. There is a good reason for this. Purchasers of cheap microcomputers often cannot or do not wish to undertake the expenditure of commissioning lengthy programming in conventional high-level languages. If they cannot find an existing package for their application then writing their own software using a 4GL or development tool is often an acceptable middle-ground approach.

In summary, the main advantages of fourth-generation languages are:

- It is possible to develop new applications quickly and cheaply.

- It is possible to maintain and update applications quickly and cheaply.

- Prototyping is therefore facilitated.

- Some fourth-generation languages are designed for end-user applications development and so remove the need for a separate body of experts (programmers) in applications development.

From the foregoing it might be wondered whether fourth-generation languages spell the end of conventional programming for business systems. This is unlikely, not least because there is a large investment in current programs and programming skills involving third-generation languages. These will need continual maintenance and updating. There are, however, other drawbacks and limitations to fourth-generation languages:

● Although 4GLs provide a fast development time for software, the eventual code generated requires more processing power than applications written in third-generation languages such as COBOL. There is a current debate about the trade-off between the costs saved by the short development time in the use of 4GLs and the extra expenditure necessary on hardware to obtain similar performance characteristics in finally developed systems.

● The use of 4GLs particularly by end users can lead to lack of standardization of systems development within an organization because centralized standard-setting and control tends to be diminished.

Currently, many 4GLs are being developed. It is likely that many of these will not stand the test of time but it is equally clear that 4GLs will have a major impact on the development of business information and decision support systems in the future.

Summary

The last four decades have seen the rapid improvement and extensive use of the computer in business data processing and information provision. Successive generations of computers have incorporated technological advances enabling faster, cheaper and more reliable processing. The development of the microchip, as well as improving performance and decreasing the size of computers, has added a new dimension to business computing with the cheap, powerful microcomputer. This has not only extended the types of users to include businesses of all sizes but has also enabled a 'leap to freedom' for users within larger organizations from the control of the centralized computer centre.

As a basis for appreciating the ways in which technology can support business information requirements and decision making it is important to have a background understanding of the hardware and software aspects of technology. Within the chapter the functional components of a computer system and the ways these are implemented with hardware were explained. This was linked in the case of input devices to their suitability for various applications.

Hardware improvements have increased the demand for sophisticated software. Basic software was examined within the chapter. In particular the functions of an operating system were covered. Modern operating systems use graphical interfaces and exchange text, data and images between applications. High-level languages, procedurally based around the types of task for which they were suitable, were designed to increase programmer productivity and program reliability to meet this demand. Structured high-level languages are to be viewed within the context of a structured methodology of systems analysis and design. Object-oriented ▷

languages have been designed in conjunction with object-oriented analysis and design methods to lead to a richer and more natural means of capturing data modelling and processing requirements. The recent development of fourth-generation languages is an alternative to the traditional linear approach to programming through specification, coding, testing and maintenance stages. They are intended to be employed, often by end users, in prototyping. Although having limitations, prototyping is seen as a way of quickly developing systems meeting user requirements that can easily evolve over time. The area of end-user computing and prototyping is investigated extensively in a later chapter. Small organizations, or those with standard business functions, can avoid the cost of specially commissioning software by purchasing applications packages. These have many advantages. The increasing sale of microcomputers has led to a substantial market for packaged software that is particularly user-friendly.

Exercises

1. What specific advantages did advances in electronics provide for the development of computer systems?

2. Why has there been a movement towards the use of microcomputers in large organizations rather than relying wholly on centralized mainframe resources staffed by experienced and highly trained personnel?

3. What are the factors that influence the selection of data capture method, input method, input devices and media for an application?

4. Why is it not feasible to include a code for the price of a product in the barcode associated with its packaging?

5. A large TV rental company has high-street branches throughout the UK. Customers typically sign contracts for TV and video rental. Payment is monthly. The majority of customers pay through direct debit using the banking system. However, a significant minority pay at the high-street branches each month. Customer account records are held on a mainframe computer at the head office and require regular updating with customer payment details. Suggest **two** suitable methods of data capture and input for those customers paying at branch offices. Comment on the advantages and disadvantages of your proposals.

6. Using the data contained within Chapter 3 calculate the cost per byte of storage on magnetic tape.

7. Explain the distinction between *hardware, software* and *firmware.*

8. What characteristics of a business application make it appropriate for computerization?

9. Explain why high-level languages have superseded assembly languages in the production of applications software.

10. It is often claimed that programmer productivity has increased over the years. How would you measure programmer productivity?

11. How do fourth-generation languages differ from earlier generations and what benefits do they offer over traditional languages?

12. What are the advantages of adopting a package approach to the acquisition of software?

13. Give **four** reasons why packaged software is more common for the micro-computer market than for the mainframe market.

14. Outline the functions of an operating system.

Recommended reading

● Bishop P. (1991). *Computing Science* 3rd edn. London: Thomas Nelson and Sons
This is a basic introductory text for computing science. It is intended for those with no previous knowledge of academic computing. It is a useful reference.

● Hirschheim R.A. (1985). *Office Automation: Concepts, Technologies and Issues*. Wokingham: Addison-Wesley
Though advances in office automation are rapid, this book still contains much of current relevance. It is a comprehensive introduction to a range of technologies and surrounding issues.

● Keen P.G.W. (1997). *Multimedia Explained: A Manager's Guide to Key Terms and Concepts*. Harvard Business Schools Press.
This is 'a guidebook to territory as yet unmapped for most business managers'. There is a lengthy and comprehensive introduction which puts multimedia in the context of modern business. The rest of the book is made up of a series of explanations of terms such as authoring, Adobe®, Microsoft®, Web Browsers – arranged in alphabetical order. This is intended as a glossary for business managers who require more than a single line definition of key terms but rather need the concepts explained over several pages.

● Khoshafian F., Brad Baker A., Abnous R. and Shephard K. (1993). *Intelligent Offices: Object-Oriented Multi-Media Information Management in Client–Server Architectures*. John Wiley
This is a useful introduction to optical storage technologies, database management, networks, object-oriented concepts, graphical user interfaces, multimedia and office applications. This can be read as a supplement to this book for a further treatment of selected modern technologies.

● Martin J., Leben J. and Arnold J. *Fourth Generation Languages: Volume II: A Survey of Representative 4GL*. Savant Research Studies
Part 1 of this book gives a clear introduction to the classifications and characteristics of 4GLs. Part 2 gives a detailed overview of some of the most prominent 4GLs.

● Ranade J. and Nash A., eds (1991). *The Best of Byte: Two Decades on the Leading Edge*
A selection of articles from the periodical *Byte* is included in this book. The entries are a diverse range of editorials, product reviews, interviews with gurus and introductory articles.

● Sloane A. (1996). *Multimedia Communication*. London: McGraw-Hill

  This is an academic text about the systems and techniques that can be used to enhance communication through the use of multimedia. At the end of each chapter there are a few exercises. The book is capable of being understood by a student of business and has significant material of importance in the chapter entitled 'Multimedia in Business'.

● Stalling W. (1995). *Computer Organization and Architecture* 4th edn. New York: Macmillan

  This is a detailed text presenting the structure and functions of a computer in much greater depth than the current chapter. It is more than an introductory text.

Chapter 4

Distributed Systems, Networks and the Organization

Major developments over the last 30 years have been achieved in information technology. It is not uncommon to view this purely as the advent and development of computer systems. This, though, ignores the significant impact that improvements and innovations in telecommunications have had as an enabling technology for information systems.

The chapter begins with a consideration of the way in which centralized and distributed systems can be seen as alternatives for handling information provision. The impact of a distributed system on the organization, its benefits and its acceptability are analyzed. In order properly to appreciate issues in networks and distributed computing it is necessary to have at least a basic understanding of the underlying technology. The 'language of networks' is explained, various types of public and local area networks are examined, and the way that issues concerning standards bedevil the full integration of systems is covered. The Internet is important enough to merit a chapter (Chapter 5) on its own, though concepts key to its understanding are covered in this chapter. Finally the impact of electronic data interchange and its effect on the competitive position of the firm within the market is assessed.

4.1   Networks and distributed systems

In the last decade many organizations have adopted the policy of installing several geographically distinct computers within their organizations and linking these with telecommunications. The computers may be microcomputers linked together locally within one site or even one office. Or it might be the linking of minicomputers or mainframe

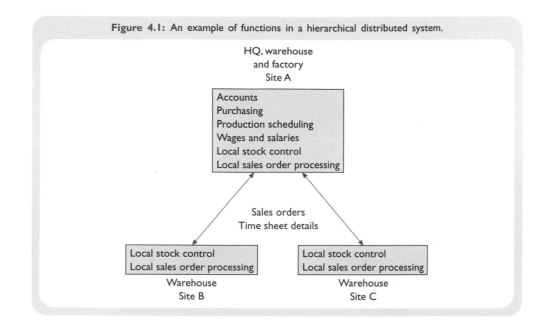

Figure 4.1: An example of functions in a hierarchical distributed system.

HQ, warehouse
and factory
Site A

Accounts
Purchasing
Production scheduling
Wages and salaries
Local stock control
Local sales order processing

Sales orders
Time sheet details

Local stock control
Local sales order processing

Warehouse
Site B

Local stock control
Local sales order processing

Warehouse
Site C

computers across large geographical distances. The issues involved in this distribution of computing power and the linking networks are the subject of this section.

It used to be believed that computing benefited from economies of scale. This is enshrined in **Grosch's law** stating that the computational and data processing power of a computer increases with the square of its cost. It therefore made financial sense for an organization to centralize its computer systems in order to get the most power for its money. Under centralization an organization that is located on several geographically distant sites would then incur a large communication cost. Terminals at each site needed to interchange data constantly with the centralized central processing unit.

With the development of much cheaper computing hardware and, in particular, the development of the microchip, Grosch's law has broken down. There are no longer the same economies of scale to be gained by centralization. Local computers can carry out local processing needs, and the necessity to communicate between different sites in an organization is reduced to those occasions where data held at one location is needed at another. This is called **distributed computing**.

An example of a distributed system is shown in Figure 4.1. A tyre and car battery manufacturer purchases materials and produces goods for sale throughout the country. The headquarters, factory and a warehouse are located at one site. In order to cut distribution costs and satisfy retail outlet orders quickly, the organization maintains two other warehouses in different parts of the country to which the manufactured goods are distributed for storage prior to sale. The headquarters' mainframe computer takes care of centralized accounting, purchasing, production scheduling, wages and salaries, local stock control and local sales order processing. Each of the two warehouses has a small minicomputer to handle its own local stock control and local sales order processing. These two minicomputers are connected to the mainframe computer so that an enquiry can be made to the other warehouses for products not held in the local warehouse that are needed for local retail outlets.

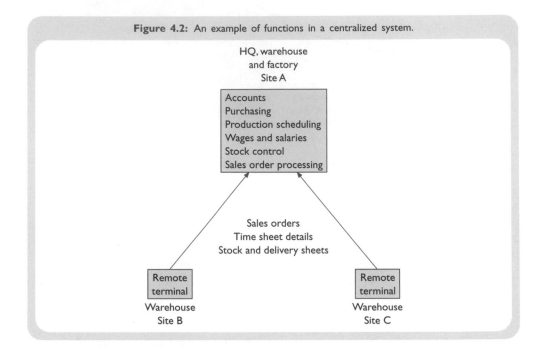

Figure 4.2: An example of functions in a centralized system.

HQ, warehouse
and factory
Site A

Accounts
Purchasing
Production scheduling
Wages and salaries
Stock control
Sales order processing

Sales orders
Time sheet details
Stock and delivery sheets

Remote
terminal
Warehouse
Site B

Remote
terminal
Warehouse
Site C

Most of the stock control enquiries and updates will therefore be on the locally held datastores. On the occasions when the local warehouse cannot satisfy a customer demand interrogation is made of the data held at the other warehouses via the telecommunications links. As the accounting is carried out centrally, although the sales order processing is local, it is necessary to ensure that sales order and delivery details are exchanged between the local computers and the mainframe. As this is not required immediately on a sale then the data can be transferred at the end of each day in one transfer operation. Although accounting, wages and salaries are handled centrally in this organization, an organization with a different structure might grant greater independence to its branches. These functions would then be the responsibility of each site, and headquarters would receive consolidated accounting reports.

Compare this with a centralized system as shown in Figure 4.2. Here all the functions are carried out centrally at headquarters. Each time there is a need to access the data store or carry out any processing the interaction between the local sites and headquarters will involve a telecommunications link – even though the processing of data only concerns stock held at the local site. This involves a heavy telecommunications cost. Moreover unless the links involve high-speed connections the response times in the interaction will be slow. At the headquarters the mainframe will need to be able to accept transactions from many sites and will need to give over some of its processing time to the maintenance and servicing of queues. This problem will be larger the greater the number of sites and the greater the traffic. In this scenario it is unlikely that computer centre personnel will reside at each of the sites. It would be more common to have a centralized team at the headquarters responsible for applications development and the day-to-day running of computer operations. It is easy for users at the local sites to feel isolated – particularly if help is required or difficulties are encountered with the operation of the system. As can be seen from the two treatments of essentially the same set of functions a distributed approach has much to commend it.

It would be simplistic, however, to suggest that there were only two possible approaches – distributed or centralized. In the above case there is a hybrid. In the 'distributed' version of the example certain functions are in fact centralized.

Within the 'distributed' version the distribution of the stock control system, particularly that component dealing with the update of stock data relating to another warehouse held at another site, involves considerable technical complexity as the database itself is distributed. A variation on this is to hold copies centrally of the stock data on each of the sites. Downloading to each site of all the stock data on all of the sites occurs early in the morning. Local processing of data on stock held locally occurs during the day. However, information on stocks at other warehouses is obtained by interrogating the early morning copies received locally. These may be out of date – but only by a maximum of 24 hours. Requests for stock from other sites together with the end-of-day copy of the local stock data are transferred to the centralized mainframe at the end of the day. The central mainframe carries out overnight processing and produces up-to-date stock data for each site, which is downloaded the following morning. This escapes the complexity of requiring a truly distributed database at the expense of forfeiting the immediate update of all stock transactions.

It should be clear from the above that the simple idea of distributed versus centralized does not apply. Rather the question that is addressed nowadays is to what extent and how should the organization decentralize its functions and data?

4.2   The idea of a distributed system

The term **'distributed system'** has been used to cover many varieties of computer system. A computer system is said to be distributed if:

it consists of hardware located at at least two geographically distinct sites, connected electronically by telecommunications, where processing/data storage occurs at more than one site.

In a distributed system there are a number of important features to be considered. These are:

- the locations of processing and the types of interaction between them;
- the location of data storage and the way data is presented to users;
- the nature of the communications links between the various locations;
- the standards governing the nature of the communication.

These are introduced here and covered in more technical detail later in this chapter.

1. **Distributed processing** can occur in several ways. At the simplest level (and hardly justifying the term 'distributed processing') individual computers may carry out their own processing but send messages to one another in an electronic mailing system. A more integrated connection occurs with **cooperative processing** where processing is handled by two cooperating geographically distinct processors. One processor sends the output of its processing to another for completion. The situation becomes more complex if the operating systems of both machines are different. **Cooperative operating systems** are then needed as well.

Figure 4.3: Various network topologies. (a) Hierarchical. (b) Star. (c) Ring. (d) Bus. (e) Hybrid.

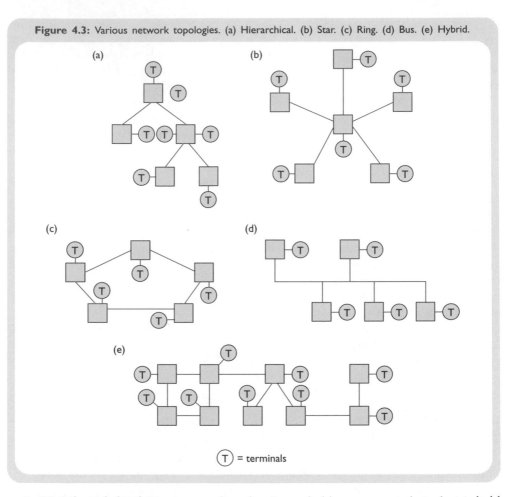

(a)   (b)

(c)   (d)

(e)

Ⓣ = terminals

2. **Distributed databases** occur when data is not held at one central site but is held at various locations. Broadly this can happen in two ways. 'Master' data may be held at a designated site and copies downloaded via telecommunications to other sites to be held locally. When data is needed at a site it consults its own copy of the master data. With such systems it is usually not permissible for a site to change its locally held copy of data relating to another site otherwise the various copies of the data held throughout the organization would become inconsistent. If data changes are to be made, data is uploaded to the master database, which is then updated, possibly overnight. New copies of the database are sent to all sites the following morning.

However, truly distributed databases distribute the data over several sites without duplication. Any user wishing to access the data does so and the data is recovered from the database at the relevant site using database and communications software. As far as the user is concerned it is transparent as to where the data is held. In both cases of distributing data common data definitions and standardization of data operations are crucial.

3. The **nature of the communications links** between the various locations concerns the topology of the network and the technology of its implementation. The ways in which sites may be connected – their topology – are shown in Figure 4.3.

Different topologies serve different purposes. For example the hierarchical topology often characterizes the arrangement in some organizations, which have a centralized mainframe (the top) connected through a **wide area network** to minicomputers at local sites, which in turn have microcomputers connected to them. The ring and bus topologies are common methods of connection for groups of microcomputers that need to communicate with one another and with other devices. These **local area networks** are treated more extensively later in the chapter. Finally many systems may be connected together yielding hybrid topologies. As well as the topology the nature of the hardware – cabling and microchip network cards in machines – and software controlling communications is a major determinant of network characteristics.

4. The **standards** governing the way in which devices 'talk' to one another and the principles governing the way in which users can communicate are currently being specified through internationally agreed standards such as the **Open Systems Interconnection (OSI)** treated later in the chapter.

4.3   Organizational benefits of distributed systems

Distributed systems were first introduced in the 1970s and have become increasingly common in the 1980s and 1990s. This is partly because of technological advances in telecommunications, distributed databases and communications software, and partly because of the recognition of the benefits conferred on an organization by the use of such systems. This is one area in which IT developments have responded to user needs as well as being driven by them.

Organizational benefits are as follows:

- **Increased user satisfaction:** As stated above, users can feel remote from the computer centre, its expert staff, and the development of applications, if geographically separated from the source of the computing power. User needs are often not taken into account and assistance may be slow or at 'arms length' through the computer terminal. Local computer centres serving local needs solve this problem by ensuring that users have greater autonomy. However, from a central organizational perspective, it is important that dispersed sites are connected with one another and the centre. This is not only for reasons of data sharing but also to ensure that, although autonomy may be welcomed, local sites act congruently with corporate goals. Distributed systems ensure that data transfer and connectivity with the centre occur while encouraging local autonomy and user satisfaction.

- **Flexibility of systems development:** An organization that is growing can add to its computer power incrementally in a distributed system by the purchase, installation and connection of new nodes to the network as the needs arise. With a centralized system flexibility is reduced by the inability to grow incrementally. Growth typically involves the overloading of the current system, which is then replaced by a more powerful computer. If further growth is planned this will need to be taken into account by building in redundant computing power in the current system to cope with a future growth in requirements. This is expensive.

- **Lower telecommunications costs:** In a distributed system it is usual for most of the local computing to take place locally. The network is accessed only when data or processing is required elsewhere. Telecommunications costs are reduced as compared to a centralized system which requires transmission of local transactions for central processing.

- **Failsoft:** With a centralized system if a breakdown occurs in the computer all computing functions within the organization come to a halt. This is an unacceptable state of affairs. Backup facilities, such as a duplicated computer or reciprocal agreements with other companies to use their computers in times of breakdown, are expensive and often not satisfactory. However, with a distributed system breakdowns will be limited to one computer at a time. The remaining machines in the network can continue functioning and perhaps also take over some of the work of the failed node. What can be achieved depends on the particular network topology and the communications software.

- **Transborder dataflows:** Many multinational corporations maintain separate computer systems in each country in which they operate. These are connected via networks. Only limited transborder dataflows may be allowed by legislation. Thus it is important to ensure local processing while retaining the possibility of transnational data flows. Data protection legislation on the holding and processing of personal data (data on persons) is often different in different countries and this is particularly restrictive on transnational dataflows.

- **Lower data communications costs:** Processing relating to locally stored data and functions is carried out locally, rather than incurring the cost of data transfer to and from a centralized computer.

- **Response times:** Centralized systems can, at peak loading, give poor response time for users.

Persuasive though these organizational benefits may seem there are potential drawbacks and costs associated with distributed systems. These should be taken into account when assessing the overall systems strategy:

- **Loss of centralized standard-setting and control:** In a distributed system where processing, data storage and computing staff are located at many sites it is common for local practices to evolve, local alterations and 'patches' to software to be carried out to meet specific user needs, and local adjustment to data representation and storage characteristics to occur. All these can lead to non-standardization across the organization and to difficulties in data communications and security.

- **Complex networking software is needed:** This controls data communications.

- **Possibility of replicated common data at several sites:** If the same portion of data is used by all sites it is common for the data to be held as copies at each of the several sites rather than be held once and accessed through the network when needed. This cuts down data communications cost and increases response times. However, it may lead to inconsistencies if the data is updated or changed.

- **Loss of career paths for computer centre personnel:** A large centralized computer centre provides more opportunities for staff development and promotion. Distributing staff leads to smaller numbers of personnel at each site.

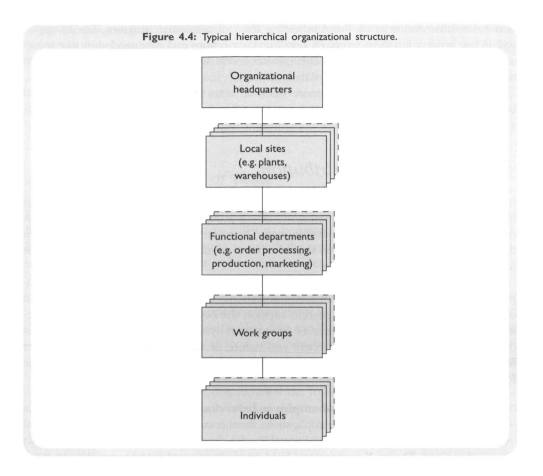

Figure 4.4: Typical hierarchical organizational structure.

4.4   Organizational levels and distributed systems

It is not usual within a distributed system for each node to be directly connected to each other node. Nor is it common, if data is to be distributed, that it is spread over all nodes within the distributed network. It is more likely that the structure for the distributed system reflects the organizational structure it is meant to serve.

A typical organization structure is shown in Figure 4.4. This is a traditional hierarchical structure, which exemplifies many large industrial and service organizations. There is a headquarters for the organization. The organization has several local plants or sites that carry out many of the functions of the organization itself at a local level. Examples are the functional departments of production, stock control and order processing. Within each functional department there are workgroups that reflect groupings of employees that perform much the same function within a department – an example might be customer enquiry handling within a sales order processing department. Then finally there are the individual employees who are the simplest 'processing unit' (i.e. unit that may require a computer for support) within the organization.

Where there are distributed systems within an organization one possible architecture for the distribution is to ensure that where data is distributed and computers are

be used. Each piece of data is stored at one or other of the nodes in the network with no duplication. Distributed database and communications software ensure that when users interrogate or update the data it is transparent to them as to where the data physically resides.

Fully distributed databases are becoming increasingly common. It is likely that this trend will continue although considerable technical problems concerning the database and communications software still need resolving.

4.7 Networks and communications

The development of computer technology and applications software has been accompanied by a corresponding growth in telecommunications and the need to link computers together. Earlier sections have demonstrated the reasons for the distribution of data and computing power and the benefits it confers. The remaining sections investigate the technologies and standards governing the connections.

In the early years of data processing, corporate computing power was concentrated in the organization's mainframe computer. Where remote sites needed access to the computer this was usually achieved through the public telephone network. A link was established between the dumb terminal and the central computer. The nature of the interaction between the two was controlled entirely by the centralized mainframe in a **master–slave** manner. If the amount of data to be exchanged was high and spread throughout the day (as compared to short bursts) it was cheaper to lease a direct line from the relevant telephone company. This also had the advantage that the connection carried a less distorted signal and was subject to less interference. Signal distortion and interference were lower because the connection between the terminal and the computer did not form part of a temporarily connected circuit through a number of telephone switching exchanges. With leased lines data communication speeds were thus able to be higher.

Over time the increased need to provide more extensive computing support for an organization – often at many sites – put a significant burden on the ability of the telecommunications network to carry the volume of data at costs the organization was willing to bear. The advent of local minicomputers for local processing was part of a solution to this problem. These would be linked together via the telecommunications network to form a distributed network. Another part of the solution was the introduction of more effective and cheaper means of transmitting a message from A to B across the public network – the use of digital transmission, packet switching, and new types of physical link (see below).

Even within one site the explosion of the demand by users for computing power, both caused by and enabled by the growth of user-friendly personal computers and applications packages, produced a requirement for communications between them that could not easily be satisfied by channelling all traffic through the site mainframe or minicomputer. Local area networks were designed to provide the necessary communications.

What had been experienced a decade earlier in the 1970s was a drive to distribute computing over many sites in an organization connected by a network of communications. In the 1980s this was repeated in a microcosm and experienced as the need to distribute computing within one site connected by a local network. There were differences, especially the fact that in networking between sites a third party – the telecommunications company or data carrier – was involved, but many of the issues and pressures had a familiar ring to them.

The evolution of distributed computing has been, and still is, bedevilled by the problem of standards. Standards are needed because different types of machine are used to send messages to one another across different types of network. Nowadays this may also involve machines running under different operating systems cooperating with one another to carry out work. Standards problems are particularly noticeable in the area of communications across the public network. The public carriers have often appeared to regard themselves, particularly in the early years, as electronic postal services – their purpose was to ensure that a neatly packaged message was transmitted reliably, swiftly and cheaply between a sender and receiver. The concept was neutral as to whether the package consisted of an electronic message rather than one written on paper. Nowadays the need is for computers not only to connect with one another but to work with one another. This has led to the development of standards to avoid the proliferation of confusion in communication. These standards have only partly been implemented and there is still much progress to be made in this area.

4.7.1 Communications – the basics

Communication involves the transmission of a **message** from a **sender** to a **receiver**. The physical line over which communication is established is known as the **communications channel**.

Where it is possible to send data simultaneously between two devices the type of communication is called **full duplex**. If transmission is possible between both devices, but not simultaneously, then the communication is called **half duplex**. The remaining case, where transmission is possible in one direction only, is known as **simplex** communication.

Transmission signals

Data within a computer is encoded digitally. The two discrete states correspond to 0 or 1 – the two values for the binary digit. This is transmitted within the computer by means of a digital signal where, for instance, 0 corresponds to a low voltage and 1 corresponds to a high voltage (see Figure 4.5(a)).

Transmission through the public telecommunications network has in the past been through communication channels that have been designed for carrying voice (voice-grade channels). This involves the sending and receiving of analog carrier signals (Figure 4.5(b)). In order to ensure that 0s and 1s could be communicated across voice-grade lines the carrier signal needs to be varied. This is achieved by altering either the amplitude of the wave formation – **amplitude** modulation (Figure 4.5(c)) – or by altering the frequency of the wave (increasing the frequency involves decreasing the wavelength and vice versa). This is known as **frequency modulation** (Figure 4.5(d)).

Under these circumstances, to transmit digital signals between one computer and another across the public telephone network required a device to modulate and demodulate the carrier signal at either end. The use of a **modem** (**mo**dulate–**dem**odulate) device is illustrated in Figure 4.6. The modem is a device that is either housed inside the computer's covering or is plugged into the computer.

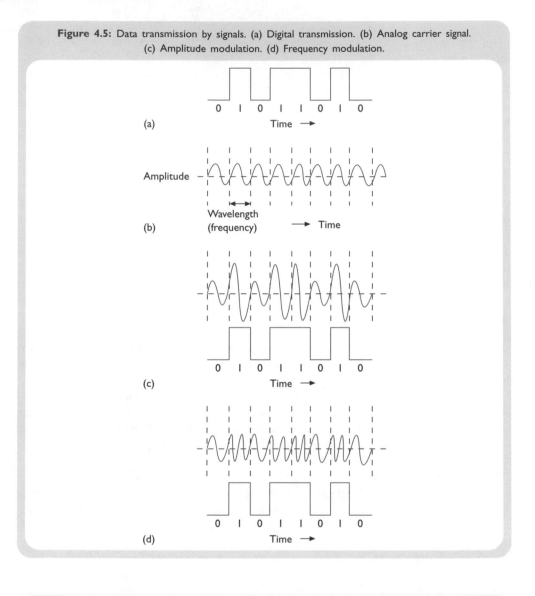

Figure 4.5: Data transmission by signals. (a) Digital transmission. (b) Analog carrier signal. (c) Amplitude modulation. (d) Frequency modulation.

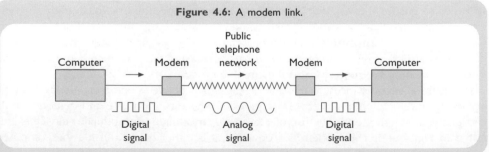

Figure 4.6: A modem link.

Bandwidth

The **bandwidth** of a communications channel is the range of electrical or electromagnetic frequencies that can be used for the signal transmission.

In a **baseband** channel the entire channel is given over to the transmission of a digital signal. Baseband channels may have high transmission speeds – for example, transmission of data at up to 10 megabits per second over a limited range (a few kilometres). With baseband communication only one signal may be transmitted at a time.

A **broadband** channel uses different ranges of frequencies carrying different signals at the same time. Each range of frequencies is modulated to represent the digital signal. In this case the physical link will be carrying many messages simultaneously – the larger the bandwidth the greater the number of signals.

Multiplexing

Most physical communication channels would be underutilized if restricted to conveying one message between a sender and a receiver in a given period. Instead several messages are amalgamated. The amalgamation and subsequent decomposition of all the signals is known as multiplexing (see Figure 4.7 (a)). The device that accomplishes this is a **multiplexer**. A multiplexer enables a single communications channel to carry several messages within the same time period.

Even with a baseband channel it is possible to give the appearance to many senders and receivers that they are simultaneously sending messages to one another down one physical communications link. This is because transmission speeds are high and the transmission time is being divided between the various senders and receivers. In order to do this the signals from the senders must be amalgamated, ensuring that a part of sender A's message is followed by a part of sender B's message, followed by part of sender C's message and so on. An illustration of this **time division multiplexing** is given in Figure 4.7(b).

With broadband channels many messages are sent simultaneously at different frequencies. It is the role of the multiplexer to assemble and decompose these. This is known as **frequency division multiplexing** (see Figure 4.7(c)).

Parallel and serial transmission

Information is transmitted from sender to receiver translated into one of the major bit-coding schemes (usually ASCII). In **serial transmission** the data is sent in a continuous stream with one bit being followed by the next. **Parallel transmission** involves all the bits in a character being transmitted simultaneously along parallel transmission lines. Serial transmission is therefore slower but parallel transmission requires many physical channels. Voice transmission over the public telephone network is usually via a twisted pair of wires and is in serial. High-speed connections between computers and computers, or computers and peripherals such as printers, are nowadays via parallel transmission.

Synchronous and asynchronous transmission

Under **asynchronous transmission** the receiver is alerted to the arrival of an encoded character by a front end signal. This is known as the start bit. A similar signal is placed on the line at the end of transmission of the character. This method is used for the transmission of each character. It is relatively slow, transmission rates rarely being able to exceed 2400 bits per second.

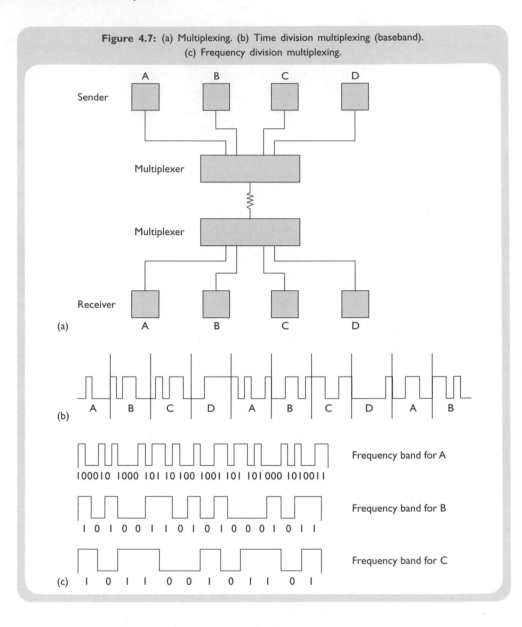

Figure 4.7: (a) Multiplexing. (b) Time division multiplexing (baseband). (c) Frequency division multiplexing.

For faster transmission required in computer-to-computer links both sender and receiver operate at the same rate by synchronization of their clocks. Data is interspersed with synchronization characters which alert the clocks and cause them to synchronize. This is known as **synchronous transmission**.

Transmission media

The physical medium over which signals are transmitted is an important determinant of the speed, reliability and number of messages that can be simultaneously sent.

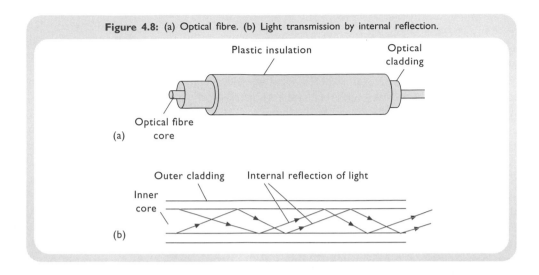

Figure 4.8: (a) Optical fibre. (b) Light transmission by internal reflection.

Twisted pair: A twisted pair consists of two insulated wires twisted around one another. One wire is for the send signal and the other the return. It is common for twisted pairs to be twisted with one another in a spiral configuration and the whole to be shielded by insulation. This is the typical telephone cable where each pair is a dedicated line for a private household. Typical data transfer rates are up to 64 kilobits per second.

Coaxial cable: Coaxial cable is made up of a central wire insulated and surrounded by a further conducting wire. This in turn is surrounded by insulation. Coaxial cable is used also for the transmission of TV signals – either by cable to the home or from the aerial to the set. This type of cabling is common in local area networks such as the Ethernet (see below). The cable can conduct large quantities of data – up to 50 megabits per second with very low error rates.

Fibre optics: A fibre optic cable consists of thin strands of glass, each about the thickness of a human hair. The message is transmitted via a pulsating light beam which is sent down the centre of the fibre optic. The light beam is internally reflected by the outer cladding around the optic (see Figure 4.8). The bandwidth of fibre optic transmission is large – for instance one fibre optic can transmit half a million telephone calls simultaneously. The data transmission rates are several hundred megabits per second. Fibre optic cabling is becoming commonplace for the transmission of public data with common carriers beginning to install fibre optic systems for the transmission of voice, data, text and image. It is also being used for the transmission of data within a single organization in local area networks.

Fibre optics have the following advantages:

- high capacity for message transmission
- insensitive to electrical or electromagnetic interference
- as cheap and easy to install as coaxial cable
- low error rates
- low power consumption

● secure against illicit interception (as this requires physical breaking of the cladding and results in signal breakdown).

Microwaves: Data can be transmitted using waves from the electromagnetic spectrum. Whereas fibre optics use light in the visible wavelengths, microwave transmission uses radio signals of short wavelength. Microwave transmission may be used for satellite transmission or terrestrial links.

With a **satellite link** a microwave beam on which the data has been modulated is transmitted from a ground station to a satellite. The satellite remains in a constant position with respect to the earth (geostationary orbit). The beam is then retransmitted to the destination receiver. Geostationary satellites orbit typically about 22000 miles above the earth's surface. The microwave channel has a very high bandwidth and may handle more than 1000 high-capacity data links. The microwave satellite transmission can relay both analog and digital signals. Unlike a beam of light the microwave beam is not interrupted by cloud or affected by adverse weather conditions. It has a reliable straight-line transmission distance of approximately 30 miles at the earth's surface. As most of the transmission to and from a satellite is through empty space this is sufficient.

Terrestrial microwave links are used when line-of-sight data transmission is needed over short distances (less than 30 miles) and it is inconvenient or impossible to lay cabling. This may occur because of physical difficulties such as ravines or rivers, or because high-bit-rate links are needed between buildings in sight of one another and where cabling cannot easily be laid.

4.7.2   Public transmission links

The transmission between one device and another across common or public places is carried out in each country by one or more organizations licensed by the government of that country to provide these communication services. These are known as **common carriers**. Examples of common carriers are the telecommunications giants AT&T in the USA and British Telecom in the UK.

Leasing

Where a large volume of data traffic is to be exchanged between two sites an organization may decide to lease a line from the common carrier. This is a physical link between the two sites, which is dedicated solely to the leasing organization. Leasing a line has the advantage that the physical link does not require temporary circuit connections to be established between various telephone exchanges. These temporary circuit connections make the signal much more open to distortion and interference and result in generally lower transmission speeds. In cases where there are large amounts of data to be exchanged leasing is also a much cheaper alternative than establishing 'dial-up' links. However, if a large number of nodes need linking over long distances then costs generally prohibit intersite leasing. Because the data travels across a permanent physical channel any network made up of such links is called a **non-switched network**.

Public-switched telephone network

In cases where a channel connection is made for a temporary period during the time of the data exchange but is then discontinued after exchange the connection is known as

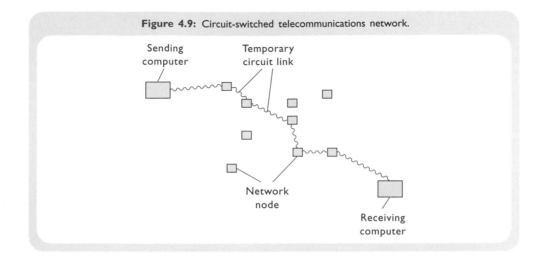

Figure 4.9: Circuit-switched telecommunications network.

switched. Devices that can be connected in this way are said to be part of a **switched network**. In the case of the public-switched telephone network (PSTN) the exchange of data between two sites requires establishing a temporary voice-grade circuit link through the public network of exchanges (see Figure 4.9). As soon as the required data has been exchanged the circuit is broken. This is known as a **circuit-switched network**.

The advantage of this type of connection is that the public switched telephone network allows data exchange between any two points that are connected to the telephone system. This gives great versatility. The disadvantages are that transmission speeds are low, distortion and interference probabilities are high, and costs are high for long periods of connection. Transmission speeds are being increased and the period taken to establish the connection (dial-up time) is being decreased by the introduction of digital networks (see below). Finally with a circuit-switched network the circuit link is dedicated to the sender–receiver connection until broken. It may be the case that during much of this time there is no traffic in either direction and the circuit is 'waiting' for data exchange. The physical links between the exchanges making up the circuit are nevertheless 'tied up' and cannot be used for other purposes. This is an inefficient use of the network.

Packet-switched network

With a **packet-switched network** a message to be sent from a sender to a receiver is split into a number of self-contained packets a few hundred bytes (characters) long by a packet assembler/disassembler (PAD). These packets are routed through the network by being passed from node to node. Each packet may follow a different route through the network. At each node the packet is temporarily stored before being forwarded to the next node in the network. When reaching the destination in the correct order the message is reassembled by a packet assembler/disassembler (see Figure 4.10).

The sender and receiver are oblivious to the assembling/disassembling process and to the routeing. It appears to them that there is a dedicated circuit established between them. Because no actual circuit link exists the connection is known as a **virtual circuit**.

The route for each packet through the network is computer determined to ensure that the network is being used most effectively. Clearly many messages broken into packets

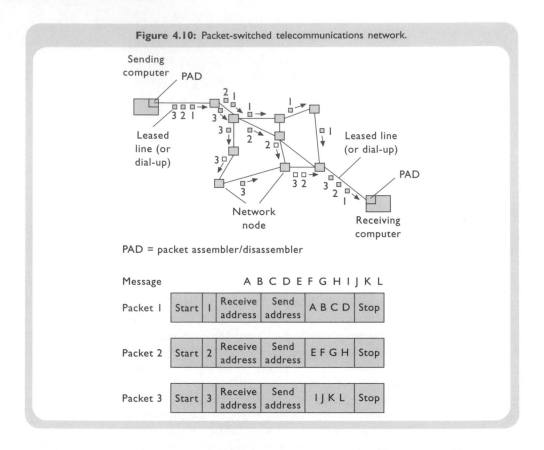

Figure 4.10: Packet-switched telecommunications network.

will be passing through the system simultaneously. Another advantage of packet switching is that data exchanges between two devices along the virtual circuit may involve considerable periods of waiting between a receiver receiving a message and sending out a reply. Because no physical circuit link continuously exists valuable network transmission potential is not being wasted.

Many countries have now installed public packet-switched networks. International packet-switched network data transmission is possible between countries having developed their own systems provided that they follow certain standards in the way they represent data. A commonly used standard is known as **X25**.

Integrated services digital network

Most public telecommunications systems are being upgraded to be integrated services digital networks (ISDN). All switching, networking and transmission is then by means of digitized signals.

In order to ensure that compatibility will exist between different national systems and that equipment can be connected to the system an ISDN standard exists. The basic transmission speed for this system is 64 kilobits per second. A typical domestic user with basic access would have two transmission channels at this speed plus a control channel at 16 kilobits per second. Businesses are offered primary access with 24 channels each running at 64 kilobits per second (one channel being used for control purposes). This is a substantial improvement over typical speeds for voice-grade lines, which are up to 9.6 kilobits per second.

Under an integrated services digital network transmission of voice, data, text, and images will be fully digital. This will allow faster transmission speeds and much faster dial-up times for circuit connection (milliseconds as compared to seconds).

4.7.3 Local transmission links

Local area networks

As well as having minicomputer or mainframe computer facilities most large or medium-sized organizations will also possess a large number of microcomputers, printers and other information technology. The microcomputers can be used for single-station word-processing, spreadsheet modelling, data management or other applications. Frequently, though, it is important for microcomputers to be able to communicate with one another, communicate with the organization's larger computers, share scarce resources such as printers or communicate with the outside world.

In order to achieve this a **local area network** may be used. A local area network (LAN) consists of:

- High-speed cable, such as coaxial cable, connecting the various devices.
- A network card for each device that is connected to the network. This is a micro-chip that manages the transmission of data across the interface between the device and the network cabling.
- Network software such as Novell Netware that manages data transmission around the network cabling.

A local area network is owned by a single organization and does not run outside the confines of that organization. In allows the following types of facilities:

- Downloading of data from the corporate database held on a mainframe computer for local processing – for example, in spreadsheet models.
- Communication of the personal computer with the 'outside world' and other net-works via a **gateway** with the public telephone network.
- Access to the Internet.
- Use of a centralized shared data and program store held on a **file server**. A file server is a high-capacity disk storage device that is attached to the network.
- Sharing of scarce resources by many users connected on the network.
- The use of electronic mail to send messages, memos and electronic letters to other nodes on the network.
- Use of electronic calendar and diary facilities to schedule meetings.

The use of a file server removes the need, and therefore the cost, of a hard disk for each microcomputer. Separate parts of the file server can be allocated for use by each node on the network. Programs for common use are stored on the file server rather than on individual floppy or hard disks. Smaller organizations that do not have a mainframe and

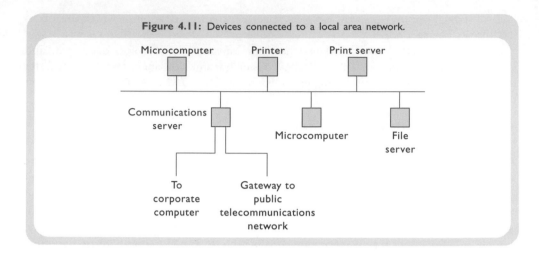

Figure 4.11: Devices connected to a local area network.

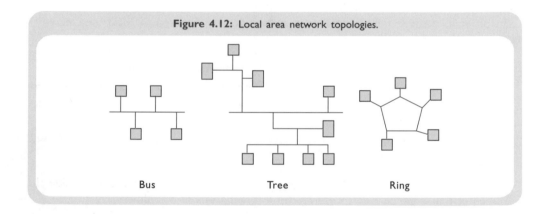

Figure 4.12: Local area network topologies.

which rely entirely on microcomputers can use a file server as a shared database. For instance, most of the major accounting packages for small businesses have a multi-user version to allow this (see Figure 4.11).

The relationship that exists between the various devices within the network exhibits what is known as a **client–server** architecture. With client–server computing the various tasks that need to be performed are distributed over the network. Client devices are those that request services. Server devices are those dedicated to a particular function or task that is called upon by a client. Examples of server functions performed by devices are file servers, print servers and communication servers. A client might be a microcomputer running a spreadsheet model requiring printed output.

Local area networks vary in their topologies and in their transmission speeds. Examples of typical topologies are shown in Figure 4.12. Because LANS are non-switched networks the communication links are shared by all devices. Many devices may wish to transmit on the network simultaneously – the devices are in contention for the services of the network. As it is impossible for two devices to share the network literally at the same time, techniques have been devised to handle the situation. Two are examined here.

Carrier-sense multiple access collision detection (CSMA/CD): This is used on bus and tree networks. When a message is being transmitted from one node to another all nodes read the message and do not transmit while it is on the line. Only when no messages are on the network can a node initiate a transmission. If two nodes attempt to transmit simultaneously the collision is detected, the transmission is blocked and the nodes are forced to wait for a random time interval before retransmitting.

Ethernet is a commonly used type of LAN that employs CSMA/CD. The standard derives from its introduction by the Xerox Corporation. Ethernet systems are tree configurations using coaxial cable. Several hundred devices may be connected in one LAN.

Token passing: This can be used in ring or bus networks. If a device wishes to transmit on the network it removes a transmitted token before sending its message. After transmission the device retransmits the token. If the token is not available it means the network is being used and the device needs to wait until the token is retransmitted.

The **Cambridge Ring** type of network is one using token passing. In it there is a continuously circulating packet of binary digits. If a sender node wishes to transmit, it alters the contents of the packet (takes the token) and puts the message onto the network combined with the address of the node to which the message is to be sent. When it has finished transmitting and has received acknowledgment that the data transfer was successful, the sending node puts the token back in the ring ready for another sender to take. No nodes other than the current token holder can transmit on the ring.

Local area networks have been designed primarily for the transmission of text data. However the increasing use of audio and video presentations, video conferencing, and more general multimedia applications require LANS to support much richer services. These **broadband multiservice networks** can accommodate the high transmission rates associated with data, speech and video. This has involved a new method of transmission and switching known as **asynchronous transfer mode (ATM)**. ATM LANS have now been developed to accommodate this. Also a new generation of ATM wide area networks, known as **metropolitan area networks (MANs)** have been produced to link ATM-based LANs.

Private branch exchanges

Private branch exchanges (PBX) are digital switched networks operating within one organization. Typically they are used for internal voice-switching services for telephone. Because these systems are digitized, though, they can also be used for the transmission of data, text and images within the organization. The switching itself is carried out by means of computer.

4.8 Standards

Users and purchasers of information technology would like to be able to connect different technologies easily. These, once connected, should be able to cooperate in carrying out applications by exchanging information and, where appropriate, by sharing the workload of the application between many devices. Unfortunately too often the following problems arise:

- The technologies cannot physically be connected. The devices just will not 'plug in'.

● Once the devices are connected the information passed from one device to another is packaged and formatted in a way that is not 'recognized' as information by the receiving device.

● Once recognized as information the information cannot be 'understood' with respect to the applications software of the receiver.

4.8.1 The scope of the problem

The problem identified above is not an easy one to solve. There are several reasons for this.

1. The range of the different types of device that handle information and the many media through which the information is channelled would require a significant effort in global standardization to ensure compatibility. There are, for instance, keyboards, processing units, printers, faxes, telephones, monitors, optical scanners, voice recognition devices and bar-code readers. Different media include coaxial cable, fibre optics, twisted pairs of wires, microwave and infrared links.

2. Considering one type of product or transmission medium from the above, there will be many suppliers each of whom may develop their product in what they regard as the most appropriate way. There is no guarantee that each supplier will regard the possibility of substitution of a rival's product as a benefit.

3. Even within one type of product and one supplier it may not always be possible to carry out full interconnection. Products develop over time and respond to the market environment. All companies attempt to standardize interconnections between their products as this encourages brand loyalty. However, advances in technology and the need to respond to competitor developments may on occasion preclude this. The problem is to try and develop the technology so that it looks backwards, forwards and sideways (to competitors) at the same time.

4. As well as competition between suppliers selling the same types of product, there is also rivalry between sectors. In particular there has been rivalry between the suppliers of mainframe computer technology and the suppliers of telecommunications services (the public carriers). This is evidenced in the development of different approaches to communications protocols (agreements over the way information is to be packaged and transmitted). IBM developed its own synchronous transmission protocol **(Synchronous Data Link Control, SDLC)** and its own network standards **(Systems Network Architecture, SNA)**. The two together, SDLC/SNA, defined IBM's product development for the future. The public carriers, acting independently of IBM (and probably as a response to it), identified their own synchronous transmission protocol through their standards-setting body **(Consultative Committee of the International Telegraph and Telephone, CCITT)**. This protocol is called **X25**.

In summary, everyone can realize the usefulness to the user of having the highest possible degree of interconnectedness and interworking between products. However, the independent interests of the suppliers, the need to develop and change to improve technology, and the diversity of the product field place severe difficulties on obtaining agreements on standards. This is most obvious in the area of network communications.

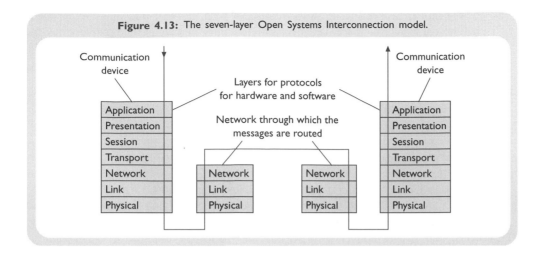

Figure 4.13: The seven-layer Open Systems Interconnection model.

There are several standards-setting bodies that have influence over the development of new technology. The **International Standards Organization (ISO)** has developed a model for standard setting for devices engaged in communication across a network. This is known as the **Open Systems Interconnection (OSI)** reference model.

4.8.2   The Open Systems Interconnection model (OSI)

The OSI model is intended to be a reference model for the development of protocols. It views exchange of information between two devices operating across a network from a number of levels of abstraction. These are known as **layers**. The seven-layer model is shown in Figure 4.13.

The various layers correspond to different functions that must be carried out to ensure smooth and cooperative interconnection:

1. **Physical layer:** Standards for this layer govern the transmission of electrical signals between devices. Specifications would include the physical media, the shape and size of plugs and sockets etc.

2. **Link layer:** This ensures that bits carried across the physical network have an agreed structure. Specification of packet structure and error detection and correction occur in this layer.

3. **Network layer:** This ensures that packets find their way across the network. Specifications for ways of handling address identification and routeing are made here.

4. **Transport layer:** Specification of the way that multiplexing occurs and of the way that packets are assembled and disassembled is handled at the transport layer. The layer is responsible for ensuring that reliable two-way communication is established.

5. **Session layer:** This ensures that the two-way communication, once established, is coordinated between the communicating devices, and that protocols for information exchange are agreed.

6. **Presentation layer:** Specifications here deal with the way that data is encrypted and the way that data is formatted for processing or display in the receiving device.

7. **Applications layer:** This ensures that the information is in the right format for recognition and processing by the receiving application.

It may at first sight seem to be unnecessarily complicated to assume that each of these layers is involved in effective communication and that therefore there need to be standards at each layer. However, if a simple case of postal communication is considered it will be clear how some of these layers are already implemented in a familiar application. It is only a short step to realize that the added complexity of electronic communication yields the need for extra layers.

Imagine that a manager at one organization wishes to order goods from another organization. The manager will need to know the name of the supplying organization and the sorts of information that are required to place an order (item to be ordered, quantity, and so on). This is accepted as standard information for the application of 'making an order' (applications level). The order needs to be presented in a way that can be understood by the receiver. This is written in English, though it need not be for foreign orders (presentation layer). At a lower level, to ensure that the order message is routed through the system properly a recognised address for the carrying network, i.e. postal service, must be added. The standard agreed here is usually the postal code or zipcode (network layer). The order message, just like any other message through the system, has to be packaged in a way that the carrier network can handle. The standards agreed here involve encoding the message on paper, placing it inside an envelope and writing the address on the outside of the envelope (link layer). Finally it is agreed that the letter will be taken to a postbox from which it will be physically picked up and carried through the system. Here the order message is treated just like any other (physical layer). Because the postal example does not require two-way interaction the session and transport layers are missing. There is a certain artificiality in the example but the point should be clear that the placing of an order for goods via the postal service can be viewed from various layers in which standards have to be agreed if communication is to be effective.

The OSI model is a comprehensive one. The problem is that the difficulties outlined in the previous section still make it hard to ensure that standards are laid down and followed. The lack of speed of agreement and implementation has not sat well with the speed of development of the Internet. Consequently different standards and protocols have emerged for much of the transfer of data over the Internet (see Chapter 5). However, there is some success in that standards have been agreed for the lower layers of the OSI model.

4.9   Electronic data interchange

Electronic data interchange (EDI) can be defined as:

> *the transfer of electronic data, from one organization's computer system to another's, the data being structured in a commonly agreed format so that it is directly usable by the receiving organization's computer system.*

What distinguishes EDI from other electronic communications between organizations, such as fax, electronic mail, telephone and telex, is that in these latter cases the information is intended for consumption by a human being who needs to understand it before any action can be taken. With EDI the received electronic data can be immediately processed by the receiver's computer system without the necessity for human interpretation and translation before action.

4.9.1 An example

To see how EDI can be used in the context of significant in-house automation consider the following example. It is important for many manufacturing companies that assemble final products to be assured of the supply of components from their stock. When the stock of a particular kind of component runs low the manufacturer orders replacements from the supplier. The supplier then despatches these and invoices later.

The whole process can take a long time – particularly if the manufacturer's purchasing department needs to draw up a paper order that is posted to the supplier. At the supplier's end this needs to be processed by the accounts and the despatch department. The production of paperwork by the manufacturer and the supplier, together with the transfer of this between organizations can lead to costly delays and errors. It may be necessary for the manufacturing company to maintain larger stocks to take account of the lead time in ordering. This in itself will be a cost. Of course if the supplier is also low on stock of the component it may take several days for this to be notified to the manufacturer. This scenario can occur even if both organizations are fully computerized as far as their own internal transaction processing is concerned.

In the context of full automation and EDI this situation could be handled in the following way. As soon as the manufacturer's component stocks fall below a minimum level a computer-based list of possible suppliers is consulted and the most appropriate chosen. An electronic order is generated on the manufacturer's computer system. This is then transmitted to the supplier's computer system (EDI) where it is electronically matched against stock records of the item held. A stock decrement is effected, and an instruction to despatch the goods with full delivery details is sent to the supplier's despatch department. An electronic acknowledgement of order satisfaction is transmitted to the manufacturer along with an electronic invoice which will await receipt of the goods before payment is made.

In the above EDI automated version there need be no paperwork exchanged at all. Human beings need only limited involvement – for instance, in the loading and distribution of the goods, or in the authorization of the placing of the purchase order by the manufacturer and agreement to satisfy the order by the supplier. These human authorizations can be by entry into the computer system, though it would be quite possible to automate the process of authorization entirely as well. The advantages for both companies are:

- the speed with which the order is satisfied
- the lack of paperwork involved
- the low cost of processing the transaction as the involvement of costly human labour on both sides is minimal
- the lack of human error.

There may be further organizational advantages if the respective trading relationship between the two companies is altered. This point will be fully expanded later in the chapter.

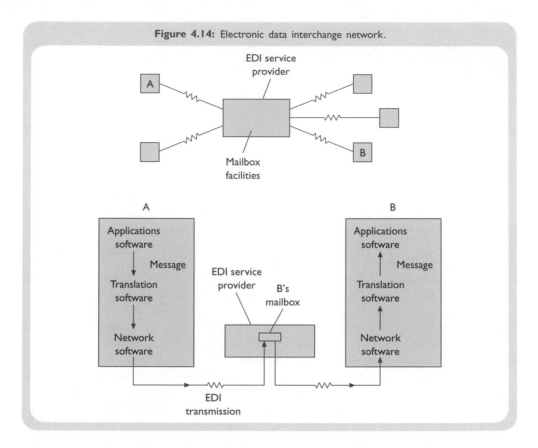

Figure 4.14: Electronic data interchange network.

4.9.2   EDI – the method

EDI may be introduced where a group of organizations wish to ensure that electronic transactions are passed between one another. One of the earliest EDI groups was set up to allow international airlines to process bookings electronically worldwide (IATA). SWIFT (Society for Worldwide International Financial Transfers) is another EDI group. This handles the transmission and processing of international financial transactions between banks.

EDI groups require EDI services in order to effect the data exchanges. These are often provided by a third-party organization. The service provided by the third party is more than merely the transmission of the data. It is customary for added facilities, especially mailbox facilities, to be offered. An electronic mailbox for a client is an electronic storage location for messages or data that are sent to the client by other organizations. The client (addressee) can read the data or messages, which are usually held on an identified area of the service provider's disk space. By providing these services the third party adds value to the data transmission and is thus said to run a **value-added network**.

A typical configuration for EDI transfer is illustrated in Figure 4.14. The message produced by the sender's applications software is translated into the agreed EDI format and placed on the network by the network access software. This electronic data is sent to the mailbox facility of the EDI service provider. Here it is stored until retrieved by the receiver organization using the retriever's network access software. The received electronic data, in the agreed format, is then translated by software into a form directly usable by the receiver's applications programs.

It is clear that a group of organizations needs to agree on standards for message representation and communication in order to take part successfully in EDI. For instance the banks agreed on standards for SWIFT. It is becoming more common though for groups to come together to agree international standards for EDI. This has prompted the United Nations to set up a standards body for the commercial application of EDI. This group – UN/EDIFACT (United Nations/EDI for Administration, Commerce and Transport) – has produced a set of standards, known as EDIFACT, for the electronic transmission of data in relation to commerce in goods and services.

4.9.3 The benefits of EDI

Some of the benefits of EDI are clear from the examples in previous sections. In particular EDI ensures:

● The speed with which an inter-organizational transaction is processed is minimized.

● The paperwork involved in transaction processing is eliminated.

● The costs of transaction processing are reduced, as much of the need for human interpretation and processing is removed.

● Reduced human involvement reduces error.

These are benefits experienced by both sender and receiver in an EDI relationship. Of course there is a cost – the cost of purchase and installation of the technology. However, there are more strategic advantages associated with the introduction of EDI.

First, by increasing the speed of processing of transactions between an organization and its suppliers and between an organization and its customers it enables the supply chain to the customer to provide a faster service. This gives the companies in the supply chain a competitive advantage over other companies in the same sector.

Second, the speed of response to requests for component parts in the manufacturing process enables all participants in the supply chain to reduce their holding of buffer stocks. This reduces the need to tie up a company's assets in unproductive materials and is compatible with the organization of production on 'just-in-time' principles. The whole chain, therefore, gains a competitive advantage within the industry sector.

Finally, it is in the interests of an organization to 'tie in' both many suppliers and many customers through EDI. For example a motor car production manufacturer will gain a significant competitive advantage by linking in many suppliers of substitutable component parts through EDI. While EDI benefits each supplier for the reasons stated above its own position of dominance over the manufacturer in these circumstances is weakened by other suppliers participating in EDI. Similarly it is in the interests of the supplier to link up with as many manufacturers through EDI as possible. The supplier's competitive position is then strengthened because it is no longer dependent on one customer manufacturer.

From the above it can be seen that the presence of EDI in the supply chain increases the competitive advantage of that chain over others in the sector. But, depending on the exact nature of the supplier–customer relationships, individual organizations in the chain may have their competitive advantage weakened or strengthened by EDI.

4.9.4 EDI – a case example

The American pharmaceuticals company, McKesson, began linking in its customer pharmacies in the USA through EDI by the installation of terminals. Pharmacies were then able to input orders for products directly. This saved McKesson the cost of employing sales personnel to take drug orders and reduced the number of paperwork errors. From the customer point of view the system, called ECONOMIST, enabled a speedy and error-free response to ordering stock, especially when late orders were required. McKesson could fill and deliver an order overnight, ensuring that the drugs would be on the shelves the following morning.

Stage two of the involvement occurred when McKesson also offered software through the terminals to assist pharmacists in the preparation of accounts and the improvement of shop layout. This provided an additional source of revenue for McKesson.

Finally McKesson was then able to provide a service to pharmacists in processing the millions of medical insurance prescriptions put through pharmacists each year. This was achieved by electronically passing on the details to the identified medical insurance company. The effect was to save the pharmacist a great deal of time and expense. Once established it was difficult for a competitor pharmaceutical company to compete in the same arena.

Summary

The last decade has witnessed a dramatic increase in the extent use of distributed systems. Distributed computing may be defined as occurring when hardware located at two or more geographically distinct sites is connected electronically by telecommunications so that processing/data storage may occur at more than one location. The network may involve many organizations or the connection of several remote sites within one organization. These wide area networks use transmission services provided by licensed third parties known as common carriers.

The benefits of distributed systems include increased user satisfaction and autonomy – users do not need to rely on a remote computer centre for the satisfaction of their needs. Telecommunications costs are lower as local processing will not involve expensive remote links. Distributed computing also allows for flexible systems development in that computing power can be expanded incrementally to meet demand. Though there are substantial advantages an organization needs to be aware that unbridled distribution may lead to problems of standard setting and loss of control. If data is distributed then duplication of data may lead to inconsistency.

Although technological features will be operative in determining the extent of the use of distributed systems it is important to remember that other features are also significant. In particular the corporate culture and location of decision making need to be compatible with distribution which, by its nature, involves devolution of resources and power. The type of activities undertaken by the organization must also be considered – distribution is more likely to be recommended the less dependent computerized activities are on each other.

There are several ways in which data may be treated in a distributed system. These range from electronic downloading of copies of data to various sites, to the development of a fully distributed database system with minimal duplication of data. Though there are still problems in distributing data, advances in software and telecommunications make this an increasingly attractive option for organizations.

In order to understand issues around distributing computing and the influence of networks a basic understanding of technical issues is required. Transmission of data will be achieved through digital or analog signalling, will involve parallel/serial and synchronous/asynchronous transmission, and may involve the use of high-bandwidth techniques and multiplexing. Media used are likely to be twisted pair or coaxial cable though, increasingly, fibre optics is being employed.

Transmission through the public network has traditionally required the leasing of special lines or the use of the public switched telephone network. Packet-switched networks and integrated services digital network transmission systems are also now in operation. These latter provide faster, more reliable services suitable for the transmission of large quantities of data enabling the integrated transmission of image, data, voice and text.

Local links are usually via local area networks. These optimize the use of scarce resources. They are compatible with the implementation of a client–server approach in the satisfaction of user needs. Local area networks usually exhibit tree, bus or ring structures. They are used to provide commonly shared program and data files, printer services, communications with the corporate mainframe or the public networks, electronic mail, calendaring and other facilities. Different topologies have different approaches to contention handling.

One of the major factors inhibiting the progress of networks and distributed computing is the difficulty in agreeing standards. The reasons for this largely reside in the variety of products and the commercial structure of the supplier market. Early attempts to set standards include SNA from IBM. Currently an important influence on standard setting is the Open Systems Interconnection reference model for standards. This identifies seven layers as requiring standards for full distributed cooperation.

Electronic data interchange (EDI) is one area where developments in telecommunications and networking are having an impact beyond that of merely passing messages between computer systems. EDI is understood as the exchange of formatted data capable of immediate computer processing. Various benefits derive from EDI including cost saving and speedy processing of transactions. In particular, though, EDI affects the nature of the trading relationships between organizations in a sector and, by way of influencing the supply chain, can considerably enhance the competitive advantage of a company.

Exercises

1. What important features need to be taken into account when considering introducing a distributed system?

2. What costs and benefits can an organization expect from using a distributed system for its information provision?

3. What is meant by saying that the 'structure for a distributed system mirrors the organizational structure it is required to serve' – and why should it?

4. Under what circumstances would it be desirable to distribute data and under what circumstances would it be desirable to centralize it?

5. What are the advantages and disadvantages of using a leased line as compared to the public circuit switched telecommunications network? Under what circumstances would it be recommended?

6. How do packet-switched networks differ from circuit-switched networks?

7. Explain the difference between *frequency modulation* and *amplitude modulation*.

8. 'The same features that led to the advent of distributed computing and wide area networks between sites operated a decade later to provide the need for local area networks.' Discuss.

9. What benefits are likely to be gained by an organization if it uses a local area network to connect its separate computing devices?

10. Why has it been so difficult to obtain agreements on standards for interconnecting devices through networks?

11. By consideration of the activities undertaken when making a two-way telephone call to arrange a date with a friend identify the way that the seven-layer OSI model may be applied to each of the functions.

12. What is EDI?

13. How can the effects of EDI be analyzed within the terms of Porter's competitive advantage and competitive strategy approach?

14. Consider a large organization with which you are familiar (e.g. your college, your employer organization, your bank)
    (a) To what extent does the distributed structure of its information systems mirror its organizational structure?
    (b) How important have organizational characteristics such as corporate culture been in determining the extent of distribution?

15. ABC CO is a medium-size company manufacturing and installing office furniture. Manufacturing and installation are located in seven sites spread throughout the UK. Each site also runs its own sales team who promote and sell ABC CO office furniture by providing a concept design service for organizations wishing to refurbish their offices. Currently all computerized information provision and transaction processing is by way of the ABC CO's mainframe computer located in London. Local sites possess terminals connected to the mainframe by public telecommunications. Local site managers are arguing for ▷

more autonomy in responding to the needs of local customers. They claim that the central computer services, for which they are internally charged, provide poor and non-targeted information. As a group, individual site managers have put a case for abandoning the company's central mainframe system – which is due for review with respect to significant upgrading – and replacing this with local minicomputers which would communicate, if necessary, through the public carrier system. All functions appertaining to the local sites would be processed locally. Advise the managing director on this issue.

16. A large regional college is introducing microcomputers to supplement its mainframe provision. Currently the mainframe is used for internal personnel, payroll, accounting, student registration, administrative and financial functions. Academically it is used for student use on computing and engineering courses. It is the long-term intention of the college to ensure that all staff have a PC networked into the college network and that all students have IT skills training, especially the use of word processing and spreadsheet packages. Laboratories are gradually being installed under the direction of the computer centre. For some years the Faculties of Computer Science and Engineering have been unhappy with much of the service provided by the computer centre using its mainframe. These faculties have already implemented laboratories of networked microcomputers for students on their courses. Staff in these faculties have also been networked using a physically separate cabling system as the respective Deans believe that with computing students there is a danger that their knowledge will allow them unauthorized access to staff data traffic. Whereas most of this is not confidential some, particularly examination papers and marks, needs maximum security. The college principal is concerned that there is an absence of strategic planning and control and is unhappy about the current situation. Advise the college principal on a course of action.

Recommended reading

● Ball L. (1992). *Cost-Effective Network Management*. McGraw-Hill
This text is intended to be a technical reference for those involved in operating or managing networks. It is unusual in that it emphasizes cost efficiency aspects of the management of networks and is valuable for those planning or upgrading networks. It is nevertheless accessible reading to those who have completed this chapter.

● Gunton G. (1990). *Inside Information Technology: A Practical Guide to Management Issues*. Hemel Hempstead: Prentice Hall
The scope of this book is much wider than communications though it has two chapters on the area. The text is a highly readable non-specialist account of information technology at a level that a manager would be expected to be acquainted with. Though explaining the technology dealt with, the book's major strength is in providing a historical background to the direction, use and evolution of information technology in business. The text illustrates the effect of the major suppliers of information technology in the area.

● Harasim L.M., ed. (1994). *Global Networks: Computers in International Communications*. Mass.: MIT Press

This is a collection of articles by a range of authors with differing backgrounds, which looks at the global aspects of networks and communications. For example, included are articles on social and cultural aspects of international communication, global education and computer conferencing. The book should be of interest to those who wish for more than a technical treatment of networks and communications.

- Halsall F. (1996). *Data Communications, Computer Networks and OSI* 4th edn. Addison-Wesley
  This is a standard text on communications and networks. Some parts are mathematical/technical in nature. It provides a comprehensive coverage.

- Hodson P. (1993). *Local Area Networks*. DP Publications
  The text is restricted to LANS and interconnections with wide area networks. Although not assuming any initial knowledge the text takes the reader into technical areas of LANS and communications. It is designed for the student and has many exercises and self-help questions.

- Krcmar H., Bjorn-Andrersen N., and O'Callaghan, R. (1995). *EDI in Europe: How It Works In Practice*. Wiley
  This text begins by introducing the basic concepts of EDI together with its benefits and pitfalls. The majority of the book consists of fourteen case studies illustrating lessons to be learned from EDI. There are fourteen contributors, each with an essay on a particular case study.

- Stalling W. (1996). *Local and Metropolitan Area Networks* 5th edn. New York: Macmillan
  This text is aimed at students and professionals in computer science and data communications. It is a comprehensive treatment for those who wish for more than an introduction to the areas involved.

Chapter 5

Business, the World Wide Web, and the Internet

Over the last decade the Internet has developed from a useful facility for the exchange of academic, scientific and military information to become a major force in information exchange globally. This explosion has been driven by the increased use of personal computers in the workplace and at home, and by the involvement of business on the Internet as a way of reaching customers. This chapter sets the foundation for understanding how the Internet can assist businesses in reaching their objectives. It is important that the reader understands the background and basis of the Internet and its facilities. The earlier sections address this. The most important contribution to business activity (along with e-mail) is the World Wide Web. The latter part of the chapter concentrates the contribution to business by the World Wide Web. Example case studies are used and the basics of initiation, design and management of a website are covered. Finally the intranet and its rationale for use by a business organization are outlined.

5.1   The evolution of the Internet

In order to understand the basis of the Internet it is instructive to cover the history of its evolution.

During 1956 the United States set up the Advanced Research Projects Agency (ARPA) to assist the US in gaining increased military competitive advantage and to stimulate advances in science and technology. In the late 1960s the US Department of Defence set up the **ARPANET** group for developing a secure network between computers. This was to develop stable methods by which computers could be connected to one another for military and scientific purposes. It had long been recognized that with the increasing reliance of the US military on computers and computer control of its defence systems it was imperative to ensure that in a 'hostile environment' when parts of a network were not working (or were destroyed) the remaining network should continue to function. Thus from the early days it was assumed that networks were unlikely to be stable but still had to function effectively. The connecting network between such computers became known as the ARPANET. In 1972, ARPANET connection was demonstrated between 40 geographically dispersed machines in the United States. By 1973 the UK had become connected to the ARPANET. During the 1970s various facilities which are used today were initially developed for the ARPANET. These are covered later in the chapter and include e-mail, USENET (an electronic bulletin board) and various methods for transferring electronic files across the network.

For computers to communicate effectively across a network they need to ensure that they transmit and receive information in a standard way. These transmission standards are called protocols. During the 1980s the International Standards Organization (ISO) were in the process of developing a comprehensive layered approach towards all computer communication through the development of the Open Systems Interconnection (OSI). This is covered in Chapter 4. However, progress was not fast enough for ARPANET members and in 1982 the development of the TCP (Transmission Control Protocol) and the IP (Internet Protocol) established the standard for computer network transmission across the ARPANET and became the foundation of the Internet communication standards.

During the 1980s local area networks (LANs) were being installed within businesses and other organizations for internal communication based around PCs. Organizations desired these internal networks to be connected to the ARPANET which now had a much wider function that its original military/scientific objectives. Within the UK **JANET** (Joint Applications Network) was set up in 1984 to provide connections between universities, scientific and other major government organizations. Internal networks within each of these organizations had connections to JANET. JANET itself was linked to ARPANET.

One of the important new US networks commissioned by the National Science Foundation (**NSFNET**) involved the development of five supercomputers located at five major universities. These were to be connected together and each was to be the centre of a regional network with links through the telephone network to local schools and colleges. The philosophy was to provide universal educational connection to the network. This network was to be connected to ARPANET. But as the number of networks had risen so had ARPANET bureaucracy and it had become increasingly difficult to deal with the increased requirements on it. The NSFNET rapidly became more important and connections to it increased rapidly in the United States. The late 1980s saw the serious commercial interest of the telephone companies in the interconnection of computers. MCI took over the management of the telephone connections within NSFNET. In 1989 the electronic mail provider CompuServe linked up with what was now becoming known as the Internet by connection through Ohio State University. By 1990 ARPANET had ceased to exist.

The Internet as it was known by the late 1980s was a collection of networks that could communicate with each other running under the TCP/IP protocol. Its use was still largely confined to educational, government and scientific organizations. Two developments led to the explosive growth of the Internet in the 1990s. The first was the rapid increase in the ownership of PCs, both privately and within businesses. This was most obvious within the United States but was a worldwide phenomenon. PCs were becoming cheaper and much more powerful. Modems, the devices needed to connect the PC through the telephone network, were becoming much faster in operation thus allowing the possibility of graphics and sound being communicated to the PC as well as text. The other major development was the design and development of the **World Wide Web**. This was introduced in 1990. It allows users easily to retrieve information in text and graphic form from the Internet. Extensive use is made of **hypertext** and links to information held on other computers. These links make information readily available and navigation around the Internet is easy. The World Wide Web is covered later in this chapter.

By 1992 over one million users had become connected to the Internet and the World Wide Web via linked networks. In 1993 The White House, The United Kingdom Government, the United Nations and the World Bank all went online with the provision of information on the World Wide Web. Throughout 1993 and 1994 business use of the World Wide Web grew, credit card transactions were established over the Internet and television commercials increasingly made reference to websites. During 1995 sophisticated software **browsers** were developed (Netscape and Internet Explorer (Microsoft)). These enabled advanced use of the World Wide Web to distribute and view video and sound as well as text and graphics. The Microsoft Network was established and easy access made available through the Windows 95 operating system. By 1995, between 40 and 50 million computer users had become connected to the Internet through over 45,000 connected networks spread over 150 countries. The membership and use has continued to grow at an exponential rate. The Internet and the World Wide Web has now become established globally as a major source of information and entertainment to businesses and private individuals.

5.2   How the Internet works

5.2.1   Connection to the Internet

A computer may be connected to the Internet and transmit and receive information from the Internet in a number of ways:

1. If the computer is part of a local area network then it is quite likely that the computer will be connected through the local area network to a gateway which will itself be linked to another network. This is linked to other networks and so on. It is usual for the link to the first network to be a leased (as distinct from a dial-up) line. The links to other networks will be via non-dial-up links also.

2. Another method of connection is via a dial-up line to an **Internet Service Provider** (ISP). An Internet Service Provider is usually a commercial organization which provides access to the Internet for a private user or a small business. The Internet Service Provider has a high speed machine(s) and a fast link into the Internet. The user is usually charged a monthly rental and a per hour connection cost (as well as the cost of the phone call to the Internet Service Provider). The Internet Service Provider as well as providing access to the Internet will usually provide news and other information services, e-mail and the management of a small website for the subscriber. This last is an important service if the subscriber is a small business. See Figure 5.1.

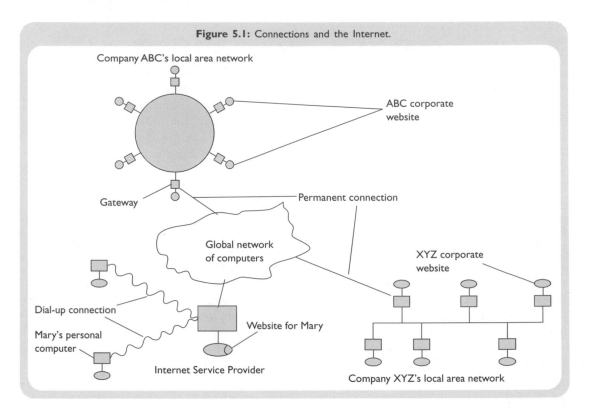

Figure 5.1: Connections and the Internet.

5.2.2 Addresses and domain names

Each computer attached to the Internet is given an address. This consists of a 32 bit number. Conventionally this is expressed as a sequence of four decimal numbers, for example 128.146.16.5. Each number is less than 256. For ease of understanding to humans these host computers are known by more meaningful names. For example, *sunsite.doc.ic.ac.uk*. The name gives information as well as being a formal address. It can be read as the computer identified as *sunsite.doc* located at Imperial College (*ic*) which is an academic site (*ac*) located in the United Kingdom (*uk*). It is convention that each country has an identifier, though it is also convention that the United States omits its identifier.

The host computer names are translated into the relevant 32 bit addresses by means of the Domain Name System (DNS). This is a worldwide hierarchical system of assigning names. Each name is allocated by a name server. This server is responsible for allocating all names within its domain. A domain, for example, might be non-governmental organizations. This authority is derived from the next higher level. There is a set of two letter domains which correspond to the highest domain in each country on the Internet. For example *uk* stands for the United Kingdom and *nl* stands for The Netherlands. Within each country the domains are broken down into lower level domains. For example Table 5.1 illustrates the original high level domains within the United States.

Table 5.1: High level domains within the United States.

Domain	Area
com	commercial organization
edu	educational organization
gov	governmental organization
mil	military organization
org	non-governmental organization
net	network resource

5.2.3 Connection through the Internet

In a previous chapter network connection concepts were introduced and the reader is referred to that chapter for a more extended coverage than here. Connection between one computer on the Internet and another computer on the Internet is not like the connection of one phone to another via a circuit link through the public-switched telephone network. In the case of a phone link a circuit connection is established through the network at dial-up and exists for as long as the telephone call exists.

In the case of an Internet connection the information that passes between one computer and another is divided into packets with different packets taking different routes through the network. There is thus only a virtual circuit connection. In order to ensure that information proceeds from the transmitter computer to the correct receiver computer, and that the information that is received in different packets is assembled in the correct order at the receiving computer, two important standards (protocols) are used.

The **Internet Protocol** (IP) ensures that a packet of data arrives at the correct address (receiver computer) after transfer through the Internet. As the packet passes through the Internet onward transmission from one network to another is handled by computers known as **routers**. The destination address is that explained in the preceding section.

Because a packet of data contains the equivalent of only about 1500 characters it is usual for the information sent between one computer and another to be divided into several packets. Ensuring that these packets arrive at the correct address is the job of the Internet Protocol. However, having arrived:

- the information held in the packets needs to be reassembled in the correct order;
- the receiving computer must determine whether the data has been altered in error during transmission;
- the receiving computer must be able to request the sending computer to resend any packets not received or determined to have been received in an altered state.

All of the information required to do this is inserted into each packet along with the information to be transmitted. The standard protocol which determines how this is done is known as **Transmission Control Protocol** (TCP). The combination of IP and TCP occurs so regularly that it is known as **TCP/IP**. Most operating systems (e.g. Microsoft Windows) contain software to handle these protocols.

If all the data that is being sent can be fitted into one packet an alternative protocol may be used. This is known as the **User Datagram Protocol** (UDP). It has the advantage of being less complex and swifter in operation than TCP.

Some users will be using a telephone connection and modem for the first part of the connection into the Internet. For example, an employee might connect to the Internet from home or whilst travelling on business through the employee's organization's local area network. The first part of the connection will often be made using a protocol known as **Point to Point Protocol** (PPP). This protocol allows a computer to use a modem and telephone line to establish TCP/IP connection to the Internet.

5.3   What the Internet offers

Connection to the Internet makes available a number of facilities that are useful to business and private users (who may also be customers of businesses). Some of these are more important than others. For business, undoubtedly the two most important are **e-mail** and the **World Wide Web**. E-mail has been in existence for a long time (and is used extensively within organizations). The World Wide Web has risen in prominence in terms of usage only over the last two or three years.

In the current section the full range of facilities are covered, though the World Wide Web is only briefly mentioned as it is covered extensively in a later section.

5.3.1   E-mail

Electronic mail (**e-mail**) is the sending of an electronic message or memo from one person to another. The messages are sent and received through the use of e-mail software running on a computer. E-mail has been used for many years.

In Local Area Networks e-mail package software enables users within a company to send and receive messages to one another over the network. These packages work by reserving part of the hard disk of a file server on the network for each person. Each person has an individual address which corresponds to the disk storage location. This is known as the user's **mailbox**. Messages sent to the person are stored electronically prior to (and after) being read in the mailbox. Generally these e-mail packages are user friendly and have a large number of facilities.

E-mail over wide area networks has also been in operation for many years. Users have a mailbox located at a computer which has access to the wide area network. The user reads their e-mail by dialling up to the computer mailbox, or through a terminal if the computer happens to be on-site. Because these e-mail packages have to produce and receive mail which is compatible with other packages over the wide area network the facilities offered in the past were often less than those offered by e-mail packages over local area networks.

Over time both wide area and local area packages have developed to offer the same sort of facilities and easy-to-use interface. The local area packages now also read and produce messages received from or sent to other users over the Internet. Now a person's mailbox is usually held on a file server in a local area network (that of their employer) or on the hard disk of an Internet Service Provider.

An e-mail message typically consists of a header and text (see Figure 5.2). The address consists of both the address of a host machine (the part after @ in the example) and the address of the person's mailbox at the host machine (the part before @ in the example).

Figure 5.2: The format of an e-mail message.

To:	receivername@receiveraddress	*inserted by sender*
From:	g.a.curtis@uel.ac.uk	*inserted automatically by sender's package*
Organization:	University of East London	*inserted automatically by sender's package*
Date:	5th February 1998	*inserted automatically by sender's package*
cc:	copyreceivername@copyreceiveraddress	*inserted by sender*
Reply to:	g.a.curtis@uel.ac.uk	*inserted automatically by sender's package (usually the same as From address)*
The message text is inserted here and can be of any length.		*inserted by sender*

Table 5.2: A comparison of e-mail, post and telephone.

	E-mail	*Post/memo*	*Telephone*
Speed	fast	slow	instant
Security	moderate	high	low
Interactivity	moderate	low	high
Formality	moderate	high	low
As record	moderate	high	low
Multiple recipients	possible (cheap)	possible (costly)	limited

When the message is sent over the Internet it is sent by the **store and forward** method. This means that during its progress from sender to receiver the message is not continuously in electronic transit but may be stored at a computer(s) on the Internet prior to being forwarded on to the next part of its journey. This implies that e-mail transmission over the Internet is not instantaneous. Messages may take a few seconds to several hours.

The use of e-mail provides for several advantages (and disadvantages) over phone or the postal system. These comparisons are outlined in Table 5.2. E-mail is increasingly used within organizations in preference to paper-based memos because:

- it is faster to transmit (almost instantaneous);
- it is more convenient and ecologically friendly (no paper);
- there is an automatic record of when the e-mail is read;
- it is possible to send the same e-mail to a number of recipients for no extra effort.

The use of e-mail over the Internet is also increasing. It is preferred to the postal system because:

- it is faster than post (and unlike telephone messages time differences are unimportant);
- it is more convenient and ecologically friendly (no paper);
- it is possible to send the same e-mail to a number of recipients for no extra effort.

Typically e-mail packages provide several facilities:

1. **Notification of receipt/reading:** On receipt/reading of the e-mail the receiver's package automatically replies with an acknowledgement. It is often useful to know if a recipient has received and (particularly) read a message.

2. **Mailing and distribution lists:** The e-mail package enables a user to build up several lists of e-mail addresses which can be called up and inserted with one key stroke, for example all departmental heads, or all client contact names.

3. **Forward or reply:** A message may be forwarded or replied. Typically this can be accompanied by the reader's comments (editing) and be with or without the original text.

4. **File attachments:** Files, for example word processed document files, or spreadsheets, can be attached to messages and loaded into receiver software.

5. **Folders:** Received messages can be automatically stored in different electronic folders.

6. **Filters:** Filter facilities allow mail to be selectively read and stored depending on whether the messages meet some rule (filter rule) specified by the user. It might be the case that mail from a certain organization is filtered out to a particular folder, or only mail with certain key words in the headings is read.

An example of a typical interface provided by an e-mail package is shown in Figure 5.3.

In order that different e-mail packages can send and receive information other than standard ASCII text e-mail messages to one another it is important that there is a standard way of representing the structure of these messages. This standard is called **MIME** (Multi-purpose Internet Mail Extension). As well as specifying the structure of the messages the MIME standard also specifies how video, graphics, and audio files can be sent as attachments to e-mail messages along with standard ASCII text. The MIME standard ensures that non-text files are converted into text – although the resulting text is not readable. Also, as well as specifying the type of file being sent, the MIME standard specifies the method that needs to be used by the recipient in order to convert the file to its original form. If two different e-mail packages can be used to send and receive non-text files to one another according to the MIME standard these packages are said to be MIME compliant.

It is clear that e-mail is becoming an increasingly important means of communication. This is especially so within a business organization. It is quite feasible that within the next few years e-mail together with the intranet (covered in a later section) may virtually replace paper-based communications within an organization.

5.3.2 The World Wide Web

The **World Wide Web** has increased dramatically the accessibility of information on the Internet and the private and commercial use of the Internet. The World Wide Web together with software that enables a user to browse ensures that text, graphical, video and audio information is globally available in a standard manner. The Web is treated extensively in the following sections (5.4 and onwards) of this chapter.

Figure 5.3: An example of a screen from an e-mail package.

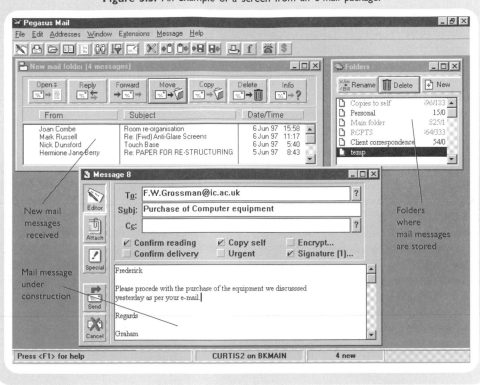

5.3.3 TELNET

Within an organization a PC located on the organization's local area network will be able to run the organization's application programs in one of two ways. The program may be run off the PC's hard disk on the PC, or it may be run over the local area network from a server. The PC is effectively acting as a terminal and as a client to the server. This client–server relationship was explained in Chapter 4. A similar relationship can exist between two computers over the Internet. A client computer can remotely login to a server computer across the Internet. The protocol which governs this remote login is known as **TELNET**, and the process is known as **telnet**. An organization may wish to allow telnet access to (part of) its computer systems for a number of reasons. Chief amongst these is that the organization is providing a public service. For instance it is common for libraries to allow telnet access to their library catalogue. The reader logs on to the library computer and runs the accompanying library software necessary to read the catalogue. Businesses may wish to allow telnet access for specified clients or for its own employees if remotely located (for example the travelling sales person). The telnet access an organization allows to its own computer system is usually the subject of a high level of security restriction and password control.

5.3.4   File transfer protocol (FTP)

Rather than logging on to a remote computer as a telnet session and using that computer's software to access and run applications, it may be desirable to obtain a copy of a file which can then be stored on the client's home computer for later use. In order that this can be achieved over the Internet a protocol – **file transfer protocol** (FTP) – is used. As with telnet there may be security levels allowing access to files only by a login account and a password. Some organizations may allow open access for transfer of files, for example public service or research organizations.

5.3.5   Gopher

One of the main problems about using telnet and FTP is knowing what file and remote computer facilities are available. **Gopher** is a system that assists the user in this area. Computers allowing file transfer and telnet facilities that are within the gopher system will index these in a manner which allows special gopher software to read the index. As well as the names of files available brief descriptions of their contents will also be provided. Having found a gopher site the user will have access through a hierarchical menu driven index. Having found the desired facility this can be selected by 'clicking' on it. Gopher software will automatically set up the telnet session or transfer the files through FTP. The gopher system is particularly useful since reference will be made to other gopher sites allowing the user to move from site to site across the Internet. The system replaces an earlier system, **archie**, which provided more primitive facilities. Gopher facilities are themselves rapidly being replaced by the use of the World Wide Web.

5.3.6   Wide Area Information Service (WAIS)

Wide Area Information Service (WAIS) provides an alternative way of searching for information held on files at remote computers. If a site is a WAIS site all the files on that site are indexed with each significant word that appears in each file having a place in the index (words such as 'and' or 'the' are ignored). A user must first log on to a WAIS client site – i.e. a site running WAIS search software. The user will specify the important terms in the search and the WAIS indexed libraries to be searched. The WAIS software will then provide a list of files and their locations satisfying the user enquiry. The service is superior to gopher in that the user does not need to search through hierarchies of menus and the search will return files with search words in them even if these do not occur in the brief file description. This service is also being used less as the World Wide Web gains prominence.

5.3.7   Newsgroups

The Internet has since its earliest days provided many newsgroups. Newsgroups may be set up to deal with any topic that is of particular interest to a group of people. These can be to do with a hobby, a social issue, a scientific area, a football team, a product, jobs offered – in fact anything. By joining a newsgroup the member has the right to add text that is read by other members of the group and to read text provided by other members of the group. Membership is usually open and free. Members of a newsgroup may be located anywhere in the world and place and read their news through connection with the Internet. They are thus able to take part in a global debate on their area of interest. There are now over 200,000 publicly available newsgroups. The information held by each newsgroup will be administered by a newsgroup administrator. This information will be held on one server (though this may be duplicated). Groups tend to have names which identify themselves – for example *alt.atheism* or *misc.forsale*.

5.3.8 Internet Relay Chat (IRC)

Internet Relay Chat (IRC) was first developed in 1988. It enables a group of users to interact with one another over the Internet in much the same way that a group of people talk to one another in a social situation or at a meeting. At a meeting anyone can talk to anyone else in the group though everyone in the group can hear the conversation of others. Unlike verbal interaction at a meeting all interaction over an IRC is by way of typed text. Each can 'view' the conversations of the others. Internet relay chat groups are called channels. Each channel has one or more operators responsible for managing the channel. These conferencing channels usually concentrate on specific subjects. The main feature that distinguishes IRCs from newsgroups is the immediacy of the interaction between participating members.

5.4 The World Wide Web

In 1989 CERN (the European Laboratory for Particle Physics in Switzerland) proposed the development of the World Wide Web (now commonly known as the Web) in order to enable high energy physicists across the world to collaborate through the easy provision and accessibility of information. Through CERN the National Centre for Supercomputing Applications (NCSA) at the University of Illinois, USA, soon became involved. Certain key features of the Web rapidly became established. Broadly speaking these are:

- a standard way of providing information on web pages stored electronically on a host computer – this would include text, formatting, graphics, audio and video;

- the use of hyperlinks to direct a web page reader to other web pages on the same website or to a different website;

- easy-to-use software that would enable users to transfer quickly between pages on a website or between different websites at the click of a mouse.

In 1993 the NCSA released a web browser program, **Mosaic**, which allowed easy and powerful access to the Web. At the time there were only about 50 websites worldwide. The facilities offered by Mosaic and particularly by its successor software browser, **Netscape**, led to an explosion in the development of websites and the accessing of these by users. (The author of Mosaic, Marc Andreeson, left NCSA to author Netscape). There are now over half a million websites across the world. In order to understand the World Wide Web it is important to understand the basics of hypertext, browsers and the way websites are addressed.

Figure 5.4: An example of a page (on the United Nations) written in HTML.

```
<HTML><HEAD>
<META Name="description" Content="This is the official Web Site of the United Nations Headquarters in
New York.  Here
you will find daily UN News, UN Documents and Publications, UN Overview information, UN Conference
information,
Photos, and other UN information resources.">
<META Name="keywords" Content="United Nations United Nations United Nations United Nations
United Nations United
Nations UN UN UN UN UN UN U.N. UNHQ Secretariat Security Council Security Council Security
Council Security
Council Security Council Security Council Security Council General Assembly General Assembly General Assembly
General Assembly General Assembly General Assembly General Assembly ECOSOC ECOSOC ECOSOC ECOSOC
ECOSOC
ECOSOC ECOSOC">
<TITLE>United Nations Home Page</TITLE>
</HEAD>
<BODY BGCOLOR=#FFFFFF>

<center>
<p>
<A HREF="homepage.map">
<IMG SRC="homepage.gif" BORDER=0 ALT="United Nations Home Page" ISMAP HEIGHT=280 WIDTH=600
ALIGN=BOTTOM USEMAP="#homepage"></A>
<center><FONT SIZE=2>
 <A HREF="http://www.un.org/comments.html">[Feedback]</A>
 <A HREF="http://www.un.org/textindex.htm">[Text-only]</A>
 <A HREF="http://www.un.org/french/">[Fran&#231;ais]</A> <A
HREF="http://www.un.org/spanish/">[Espa&#241;ol]</A>
</FONT></center>
<map name="homepage">
<area shape="rect" coords="17,3,109,35" href="http://www.un.org/aboutun/">
<area shape="rect" coords="18,40,109,70" href="http://www.un.org/events/">
<area shape="rect" coords="18,74,109,106" href="http://www.un.org/geninfo/">
<area shape="rect" coords="18,110,107,140" href="http://www.un.org/reform/">
<area shape="rect" coords="17,144,108,176" href="http://www.un.org/av/">
<area shape="rect" coords="17,179,108,211" href="http://www.un.org/Pubs/">
<area shape="rect" coords="17,214,108,246" href="http://www.un.org/databases/">
<area shape="rect" coords="16,249,108,282" href="http://www.un.org/NewLinks/">
<area shape="rect" coords="140,248,231,283" href="http://www.un.org/News/">
<area shape="rect" coords="238,249,329,282" href="http://www.un.org/Docs/">
<area shape="rect" coords="335,248,425,283" href="http://www.un.org/aroundworld/">
<area shape="rect" coords="432,248,523,282" href="http://www.un.org/search/">
<area shape="rect" coords="137,51,216,96" href="http://www.un.org/peace/">
<area shape="rect" coords="121,143,232,197" href="http://www.un.org/law/">
<area shape="rect" coords="426,52,595,98" href="http://www.un.org/ecosocdev/">
<area shape="rect" coords="435,154,592,188" href="http://www.un.org/rights/">
<area shape="rect" coords="240,211,424,245" href="http://www.un.org/ha/">
<area shape="default" nohref>
</map>
<BR CLEAR=ALL>
</CENTER>
<br>
<HR>
<CENTER><FONT SIZE=-1>
This Home Page is maintained by the UN Department of Public Information with the <BR>
technical expertise of the Information Technology Services Division.<BR>
<ADDRESS>&#169 United Nations 1997</FONT></ADDRESS></CENTER>
</BODY>
</HTML>
```

***Source:** Reproduced by permission of the United Nations*

Figure 5.5: The page on the United Nations (see HTML version, Figure 5.4) as it appears through a web browser.

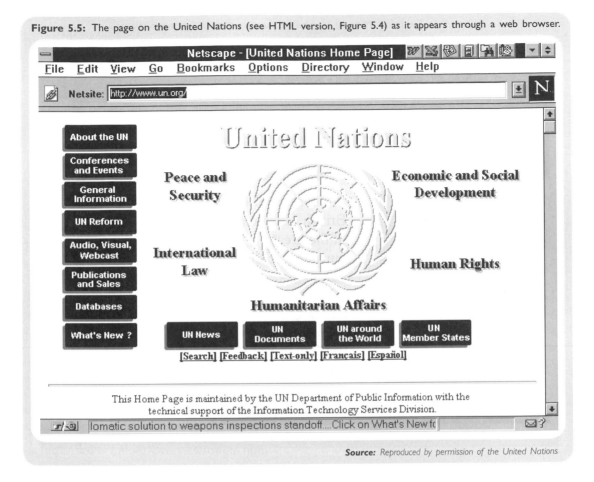

Source: Reproduced by permission of the United Nations

5.4.1 The World Wide Web – basics

Hypertext and Hypertext Markup Language (HTML)

The concept of **hypertext** goes back to the 1940s. The idea is that when reading a piece of text, at certain points terms may need greater explanation, or related information may be helpful to the reader. Where this happens the reader should be able to call up directly the explanation or related information via a link within the text. Of course these explanations are text and may themselves contain terms which need further explanation. These will be linked to other explanations, and so on. This system is known as hypertext.

Pages stored electronically on the Web have these hypertext links within them so that readers of a web page may click on a link and proceed along it to another web page (possibly at another website). In order to do this the structure of the web page and its related links are designed in a special language called **Hypertext Markup Language** (HTML). An example of a page specified in HTML is given as Figure 5.4. It leads to the page (as viewed through a browser) for the United Nations as shown in Figure 5.5.

Later versions of HTML allow for the specification of forms that the viewer of the web page may fill in and send back to the site on which the web is located. This facility is becoming increasingly important as it allows interactivity over the Web. Once interactivity

Figure 5.7: An example of an enquiry in a search engine.

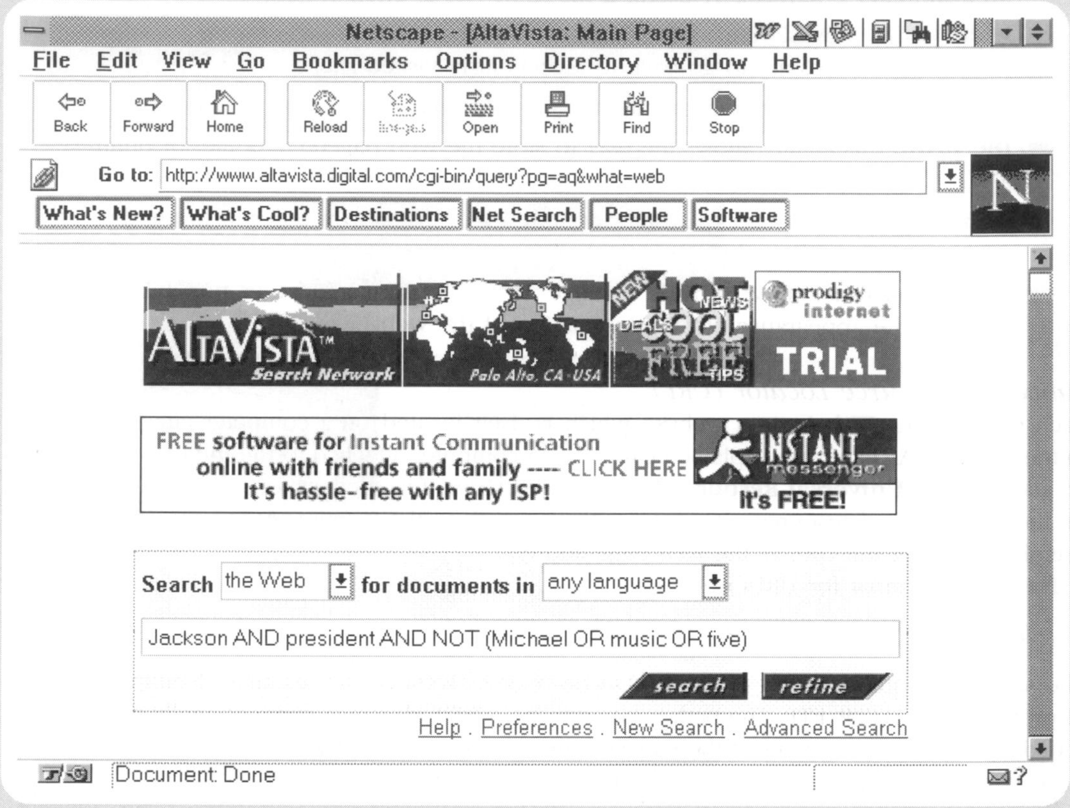

Sources: *Copyright 1996 Netscape Communications Corp. Used with permission. All Rights Reserved. This page may not be reprinted or copied without express written permission of Netscape AltaVista: Main Page reproduced with the permission of Digital Equipment Corporation.*

There are several web search engines. Examples are Alta Vista, WebCrawler and Net-search. The **web search engine** is a program which, when running, makes connection to many thousand of websites a day, retrieving and indexing web pages from these sites. In the course of time a web search engine will have visited and indexed millions of web pages. This index will be stored at the website associated with the search engine. A user accesses the website at which the search engine is located and enters, via a form on the screen, a word or words (known as the search string) of search interest. The web search engine then displays at the user's terminal the URLs of all sites at which the search string is located. The search string may be sophisticated indicating that two or more words must be present (AND), or any of them could be (OR), or some words should not be present (NOT). An example of a search string might be:

Jackson AND president AND NOT (Michael OR music OR five)

A typical search engine page is shown in Figure 5.7.

Plug-ins

Plug-ins are (usually) small programs that are 'loaded into' a larger program in order to add some function. The plug-in may be produced by a (third party) organization different from the publisher of the larger program. Web browsers may have plug-ins associated with them that allow them to carry out extra functions. The following are examples of plug-ins for browsers that extend their functionality:

- **Internet telephone tools:** these allow telephone conversations to be made over the Internet. These usually incorporate facilities such as audio-conferencing, a telephone answering machine and the ability for all participants to view common graphics on the screen as well as participating in discussion.

- **Interactive 3D viewers:** these **virtual reality modelling language** (VRML) viewers allow 3D to be view over the Internet with the possibility of navigation through the scenes depicted.

- **Audio and video viewers:** audio and video viewers are plug-ins that allow the user to view/hear video/audio files transferred over the Internet. Most of these allow viewing to occur before the data transfer has been completed.

- **Streaming audio and video viewers:** these allow the viewer to have on-line viewing of audio or video as it is streamed to the user's browser software through the Internet. Thus live events may be viewed as they occur.

Java

Java is an object-oriented programming language similar to C++. It is used to produce machine-independent portable software. Programs written in Java may be safely downloaded over the Internet and run immediately on the user's computer without the fear of the introduction of viruses. Importantly small Java programs, known as **applets**, may be embedded in HTML in a web page. This may be downloaded across the Internet with the web page and the program executed from within the user's browser program. Security is maintained as the executed program cannot have access to the user's resources such as files, printers and other computers on the same network. An applet loaded over the Internet may only create a link with the host computer from which it was downloaded. The execution of applets allows web browsers to have more interactive areas and thus extends their functions.

5.4.2   Organizational control of the Internet

There is no organizational control over the Internet. However there are a number of organizations with influence. Firstly there are the businesses that are providers of either hardware or major software items used on the Internet. These operate a *de facto* steering direction via the products they produce. Three organizations though are recognized as having authority over coordination of developments on the Internet. The **Internet Engineering Task Force** (IETF) is a large loosely-connected group of designers, researchers and vendors that influence the development of the standards governing the architecture of the Internet. They achieve this through setting up working groups. The IETF is chartered by the **Internet Society** (ISOC) which is a professional member organization of Internet experts that oversees policy and practice. The Internet Society also charters the **World Wide Web Consortium** (W3C) which is a consortium of voluntary member organizations that funds developments on the Web. There is much common membership between the IETF and the W3C.

5.4.3 The World Wide Web and business opportunities

As has been mentioned earlier, the easily accessible World Wide Web together with the rapid increase in personal computers has been responsible for the burgeoning use of the Internet for business.

Businesses and other organizations may develop their own websites for a number of reasons. Amongst these are:

- to advertise services and products;
- to sell services and products;
- to promote the corporate image;
- to provide information (especially public services).

In the case of sales many websites contain web pages that allow the reader to fill in some details – a credit card number, a name and address, for example. In this way organizations can sell products through the Web.

It is possible to identify reasons and advantages an organization might be expected to reap by using a website. These are:

Reduction in cost of advertising: Organizations, particularly those selling products or services, rely on providing information and advertising to a market place in order to attract customers and retain existing ones. The cost of this is considerable, especially if achieved through the media – newspapers, magazines, television, radio, advertising hoardings. Alternatively mailshots may also be used. These are also very expensive unless target mail groups are tightly defined. However, the cost of running a website is comparatively cheap. Computer hardware, design of the site and maintenance seldom takes a start up cost of more than a few thousand pounds or dollars. Once running, the website provides 24 hour access daily across the world. Nowadays the content of advertising on the Web is sophisticated in relation to that provided a few years ago. The move from regarding the design of website material to be the province of the creative rather than the computing media has ensured that the approaches towards advertising commonly seen on television are now becoming more prevalent on the Web.

Cheaper and easier provision of information: Some organizations, particularly public services, provide information. These traditionally have been by way of paper-based publications or through recorded telephone messages. Putting such reports on a website to provide electronic access provides a cheaper way of dispersal of information for the host organization and a faster and more convenient method of access to the public (at least the public with access to the Internet). Government, and non-government organizations which are not commercial, now have extensive information services provided on the Web.

Ease of update: An organization may easily update its product range, list of services, list of prices or any other information if provided on a web page. This compares with the costly resending of catalogues and other paper-based information through the postal system.

Lack of need to maintain a shop front: When viewing an organization's supply of information, or list of products and services, the web user does not need to enter the organization's premises – there is no need therefore for the organization to maintain a costly shop front. Indeed the view of the organization is largely determined by the impression given by its web pages unless the organization is a household name. For a business this is important as it can overcome the limitations of capital investment in the provision of expensive buildings to impress clients. Importantly for the business the web user has little idea whether they are dealing with a large multinational or a small business. In this way the small business can compete with the large. From the perspective of the customer though it is difficult to make judgements about the status of the business behind the web page.

The ease of crossing geographical boundaries: Because the Internet provides global access the business has a worldwide audience through its web pages. If the business is selling a product, provided that postal or shipping services are reliable, even a small business is able to market and sell its products globally. If the product is information this can easily be dispensed electronically.

The absence of the middleman: A business which needs a distributor and a retailer to ensure its goods are sold and delivered to a customer can now dispense with the need for these middlemen. Direct marketing to the customer is possible. It should, however, be pointed out that in many cases retailers provide a service over and above that of merely being point-of-sale seller. Advice and other services may also be provided. But if the customer is in need of no such help then the shop front becomes superfluous.

In the above cases the customer needs to know of the fact that the business or organization in question has a website and that the business is a seller of a product or service which is desired by the customer. This is handled in a number of ways:

- the business will conventionally advertise in the television or press and place the website address on the advertisement;
- the business will ensure that the home page contains key words that makes it easy for a searcher to use a web search index produced by a search engine;
- the organization will attempt to have its link placed on another website so that visitors to this website may click on a hyperlink to the organization's website.

The last method is important and can be achieved in different ways:

reciprocal arrangements: the organization may have a reciprocal arrangement with another so that both websites cross link

web communities: the organization may be part of a group or community that provides a website for a particular interest area (see below on web communities)

commercial advertisement: the organization may pay to have an advertisement and hyperlink on a frequently visited website. For example web search indexes are visited by millions of clients per day. If a company has a corporate logo and link advertised on the web search site then only one tenth of one percent of readers need to click on the hyperlink to ensure that thousands of potential customers are in touch with that company's products or services.

In order to understand the range of ways in which the World Wide Web may be put to the service of business and other sorts of organizations it is instructive to examine a number of case studies.

Case studies illustrating the use of the World Wide Web

For the reasons mentioned above the World Wide Web will come to play an increasing role in the competitive strategy of any company in the modern business environment. The following case studies illustrate areas and opportunities where the Web is currently being used for commercial advantage. In some cases the Web is being used to cut cost in some ways, or reach new markets. In other cases it is quite clearly part of a competitive strategic use of IT in the sense of Porter (see Chapter 2: Strategy and Information Systems).

Case 1: Internet retailing (general)   The growth in Internet retailing has accelerated and is predicted to rise significantly by the first decade of the twenty-first century. This will depend on increased consumer confidence in the security of credit card transactions over the Internet together with the (expected) rise in home computers. Currently products for which the consumer does not have a need to handle or browse prior to purchase are already established on the Web. All sites have 24 hour access. For example:

Computer components and products: Not unsurprisingly, one of the first areas for Internet retailing was in computer products. These tend to be differentiated by specification and by price only. There is nothing to be gained from viewing a hard disk drive or a motherboard prior to purchase. These are also relatively non-bulky items compared to their price.

Books: If the title of a book is known then the only features that will distinguish one retail outlet from another are ease of search and purchase, cost of book and speed of delivery. Provided that the purchaser is prepared to wait a few days for delivery, purchase over the Internet meets the other criteria. Indeed the largest 'bookshop' in the world is currently a warehouse near Seattle with 2.5 million titles on its order list (Amazon Books). However, if the customer wishes to browse through a number of books before selecting then the local bookshop provides a service that cannot be matched by the Internet.

CDs: Similar to books, music CD Internet stores offer a wide range of titles that cannot be matched by any one local store. Unlike books the Internet purchaser can hear a clip from a CD (sent electronically over the Internet) prior to purchase. The largest CD store in the world with over half a million titles (CDNow) sells only through the Internet.

Travel and entertainment: Travel arrangements, flight bookings, theatre bookings can all be made over the Internet.

The features that make a product more likely to be able to be sold over the Internet are:

- browsing over a range of products where touch prior to purchase is not needed;
- no advice is needed from the seller;
- the desired choice is known unambiguously by a title or specification;
- the range of products is large (and difficult to accommodate under one shopfront);
- the products can easily be despatched (ideally non-bulky, high price products);
- there would not be differences in the quality of the product between one seller and another.

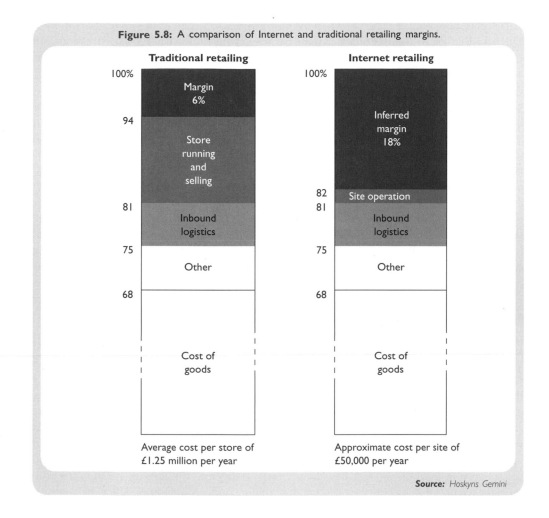

Figure 5.8: A comparison of Internet and traditional retailing margins.

Source: *Hoskyns Gemini*

The economic comparison of retailing through a shopfront and through the Internet are given for a typical outlet in Figure 5.8.

Case 2: Internet retailing (supermarkets) In the UK there is considerable competition between the large supermarkets over the consumable food and drink market. The main competitors are Tesco, Sainsbury, Waitrose, Asda and Safeway. Each has embarked on a number of competitive strategies which seek to extend their markets by the sale of alternative products, for example the sale of clothing (Tesco), or by offering alternative services (both Sainsbury and Tesco offer simple banking services at attractive rates for savers). Each supermarket is also attempting to attract custom away from its competitors. It is known that price and quality of product are features which will attract customers. It is also known that many customers regard the traditional supermarket shopping at weekends less than desirable. There is a target group who would be willing to pay for the extra service of selection, packing and delivery of goods. The Internet is likely to be a key factor in this. The supermarket which can establish the first reliable and user friendly system is likely to attract significant numbers of customers.

Tesco is operating a scheme whereby customers can order goods over the Internet. The user logs on to the Internet shopping centre having previously registered. Goods are provide in a number of categories such as vegetables, bakery, wine. The user navigates a menu system and selects a desired item for a virtual 'shopping basket'. At the end of the session the customer pays by means of a credit card and goods are packed and delivered to the customer's home address within a customer defined time slot of a couple of hours on a customer defined day. In order to speed up proceedings the customer can save the 'shopping list' for the next session and just add or subtract items. Given that there is much commonality between the shopping list from one week to the next this is a considerable saving on time. The cost to the consumer is a flat rate delivery and packaging charge of £5. Tesco report a surge of interest in the scheme and are rapidly expanding it. The scheme itself is not likely to make extra profit on a given Tesco's customer (although reports indicate that customers shopping in this way will tend to order larger 'shopping baskets'). However it is being used to attract customers away from competitors. The main limitation to this approach is the difficulty in delivery. The current supermarket shopping scheme relies heavily on customers driving to and packing their own selections prior to transport. Supermarkets identify the limiting factor to the growth of this method of retailing as the necessary heavy investment in an additional delivery system.

Case 3: Parcel tracking services   The parcel tracking sector of the commercial World Wide Web is the first sector to reach maturity. The four largest courier services in the world now provide tracking facilities for their customers at no customer cost. Each of the companies claims to be saving money as it cuts down the staff needed to answer telephone enquiries on the location of packages. In order to use the facilities customers enter their parcel reference number through a form on the company's web page as viewed through a standard web browser. The carrier's computer system is then searched and the latest information on the parcel is retrieved – when and where it was picked up, its current location, or, if it has already been delivered, the time of delivery and the receiver's name will be displayed. The four main courier companies are now registering hundreds of thousands of 'hits' on their web tracking pages each week. The service is expanding. Companies are placing foreign language interfaces on their sites. It is now possible to arrange pickup of parcels over the Internet with each of these carriers. Quotations of courier rates for transmission of parcels from A to B.

The provision of these services has not increased the demand for courier services and has done nothing to enhance the total courier requirement of the four companies involved. Rather the stimulus has come from the pre-emptive introduction of the first service and the reactive introduction of the others in following it (see Figure 5.9). It is also possible that the service has reduced telephone answering costs.

Case 4: Property services   Support for the purchase and sale of property, particularly residential property, is now becoming widespread on the Internet. Typically, without use of the Internet, a potential purchaser of a property contacts a number of real estate or property agents in the area within which the purchaser wishes to buy. The agent sends details of properties sold by that agent meeting the requirements of the purchaser – for example number of bedrooms, price range, area of garden, etc. This process involves the purchaser in the time consuming process of searching out estate agents and then, within

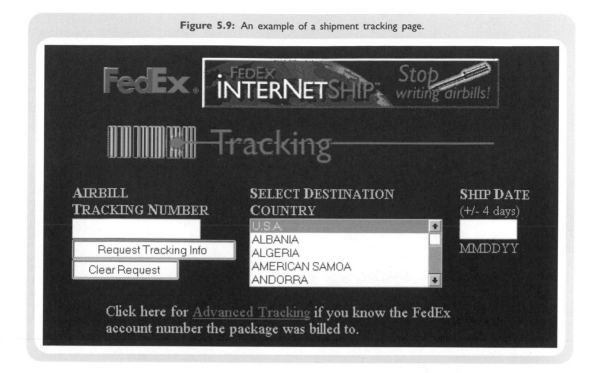

Figure 5.9: An example of a shipment tracking page.

estate agents, finding properties meeting their requirements. This is prior to the filtering of material sent out by agents after a time delay.

The Internet provides search services for purchasers in the following way. A business will set itself up as an Internet Property Agency and will gain the agreement of a large number of agents in a variety of locations within the country to display the details of properties sold through those agents. The potential purchaser accesses the Internet Property Agency website and then 'clicks' through a hierarchical system of maps to identify the desired location – for example UK, London, Hampstead and Highgate. Then, using the website's search facilities, the potential purchaser enters requirements for the desired property (more than five bedrooms, two bathrooms etc.). The website returns brief details of properties meeting these requirements together with 'click' website links to the estate agents supplying those properties. The potential purchaser may then browse through these on the estate agents list for greater detail and photos.

The use of the Internet provides a useful service because:

- the potential purchaser can gain immediate access to details of a range of properties in a particular area meeting their requirements;
- for each agent it ensures a greater market penetration;
- the costs of production and distribution of costly photographic and text details are reduced (for the agent);
- it is possible for the agent to provide sophisticated 3D interactive walkthroughs of properties over the Internet – particularly important for expensive properties where the potential purchaser resides overseas;

- the site provides useful advertising opportunities for the estate agent to advertise the range of other services offered, for example, financial, legal and surveying services.

The Internet will not provide a service that replaces estate agents but will provide a service to ensure that their clients obtain better, faster and more information on desired properties. As such, estate agents entering these schemes are seeking to increase market penetration and as a pre-emptive strike against competitors.

5.4.4 The development and management of a business website

As has been explained earlier a business may choose to develop and maintain a website for a number of reasons. Most commonly these are (some of) the following:

- to advertise services and products;
- to sell services and products;
- to promote the corporate image;
- to provide information (especially public services).

Three main areas must be considered in the development and maintenance of a corporate website. These are **connection**, **publication policy** and **presentation of materials**.

Connection

Strictly speaking a business could develop a website purely for access by its own employees through its own local area network (LAN). It might wish to do this in order to provide a better and more cost-effective internal information service. The remaining sections on publication policy and presentation of materials apply to this although the observations on connection do not.

It is more common, though, for a business to use a website for public access. In order for the website to be publicly accessed over the Internet it must be permanently connected to the Internet. This can be achieved by the organization connecting its own host computer (or local area network) containing its website pages on a permanent connection to the Internet, either through ISDN lines or through connection to one of the established wide area networks. An alternative is to allow a third party organization to handle the provision of the access to the business website by placing the business website pages on that organization's computer systems. This is common for smaller businesses who may wish to use the disk space and web access service provided by Internet Service Providers (such as CompuServe or America On Line). This still requires the business to design and maintain this own web pages which is partly a technical and partly an editorial/creative operation. Nowadays third party organizations are providing services to business which not only involve the provision of public access websites for the business but also the development and maintenance of the content of the website.

A final factor taken into consideration by a business in deciding on the method of connection of its website to the World Wide Web is the security aspect. If the public access website is held by a third party organization then it is impossible for unauthorized access to be made to the business's own computer systems – at least by way of the World Wide

Web. However, update and maintenance of the website contents are not as easy or immediate when the website is under the direct control of the business itself. On the other hand if a business runs its own website on its own host computer/local area network it incurs a risk of unauthorized access and it must take precautions to ensure that security is maintained.

Generally speaking large businesses will prefer to run their own websites and incur the costs of extra computers, permanent connection to the Internet and the need for security. They do this for the convenience of maintaining easy control over the content and update of the website together with the ability to allow a high volume of public access. Small businesses may have neither the finances nor the trained personnel to do this, nor would the volume of public access justify that level of expenditure. These small businesses are likely to opt for a third party provision.

In all cases where possible it is desirable to have a web address that is meaningfully connected to the organization, then those wishing web access will be able to intelligently guess the address. For example, the web address of CNN is *www.cnn.com* not *www.cab net news.com*.

Publication policy

Once an organization has decided to develop its website it will need a policy governing the publication of material. This should cover the following areas:

Objectives of the website: It is usual to state clearly the objectives of the website. This acts as guidance to the overall development.

Responsibility: The policy must specify those with responsibility for the development and maintenance of:

- the pages
- the information
- the computer support.

In a large organization many departments may have the right to provide material for pages governing their activities. The policy must be clear on this matter and the individuals with responsibilities must be identified. The more centralized, hierarchical and authoritarian the organization the less responsibility and authority will be devolved to departments. It is instructive to observe that organizations, such as universities, for which individual autonomy is an important cultural aspect, often allow staff and students the right to develop personal web pages with little or no control over the their content – save the requirement to remain within the confines of the law.

Public relations and consistency of presentation: It is usual for a policy to lay down guidelines for the level of consistency that must be contained within the presentation of each one of its pages. This may cover fonts, the way graphics are presented, layout and the presence of the corporate logo. The pages are what the organization presents to the world and it is imperative that the correct corporate image is conveyed. It is therefore likely that the appearance of the home page (the first page to be accessed at the top of the hierarchy) and subsequent pages may have their style and content closely specified by the corporate public relations department.

Accuracy: The organization will have a view on the need for the maintenance of accuracy of information on its website. It is likely that those with the responsibility for the provision and maintenance of the information will also have the responsibility for accuracy.

Security: As has been mentioned above, security aspects over unauthorized access from outside the organization need to be established. It is also important that within the organization those with rights and responsibilities for page development and maintenance have procedures developed which allow them appropriate access, and those that do not have such rights and responsibilities are denied access.

Audit: It is important that the organization checks whether its publication's policy, as outlined above, is being observed and so will specify the internal audit (procedures for checking) on this.

Presentation of materials

In the early days of the Web the material presented on a website was:

- largely text;
- aimed at the provision of factual information;
- written in source HTML;
- developed by programming/technical personnel.

More recently there has been a shift in orientation. Now material for a website is likely to be:

- a mixture of text, graphics and (possibly) audio/visual using plugins;
- aimed partly at the provision of a corporate image and advertising objective;
- developed using a mixture of high-level web development tools;
- developed by end users or those specifically charged with website development.

The contents of the website of today are more likely to be the province of the advertising and publicity and public relations departments of an organization than of the computing department. This shift in emphasis acknowledges the role of websites in the corporate image and as part of the business interface with the organization's marketplace. The development of high-level tools for the design of web pages has removed the focus of the developer from programming aspects to end presentation issues. These tools will generate HTML code as their output.

Decisions on website development and approach are now considered to be of strategic importance to the organization in the presentation of itself to its market. Once developed it is important that the business website is accessed. This will only be the case if the website address is known. There are a number of ways in which the web address may be publicly available. These are:

- by inclusion of the web address in TV and other media advertising;
- by selection of a web address which is self explanatory – for example *www.ibm.co*;
- by advertising the web address on other websites using hypertext links;
- by inclusion in the catalogues of large indexing websites such as YAHOO or LYCOS.

The business trend is to make more extensive use of websites for the provision of information and the exercise of business operations. This will be fuelled by improvements in telecommunications, the increasing proportion of the population owning PCs, and the economics for the Internet as a medium of information provision and business exchange.

5.5 The Internet and copyright

Copyright law was historically developed to ensure that an author had the exclusive right to copy his or her work and distribute those copies to the public. The author could also assign this right to others. Copyright law was originally designed for the printed world but has been adapted to deal with broadcasting, software and satellite television.

Copyright protects the expression of an idea – not the idea itself. It comes into existence when the expression is fixed on some medium, such as paper or disk. In some countries it may be essential to register the material as copyright. Generally copyright applies to classes of work – for example, literary, sound recordings, films. The **Berne Convention** is an international treaty to which approximately 160 member countries belong. An infringement of copyright, in any one of these countries, of work produced by a foreign national from one of the others, is protected in the country as though the infringement were of locally produced material within the country. In this way the level of protection in each of the countries is standardized for home or foreign publications. In countries not signatory to the Berne Convention the infringement of copyright needs to be enforced in the country of the alleged infringement and is dependent on the law of that country and not of the country in which it originated.

Copyright applies to the Internet. For instance in UK law, copying, even if only temporarily into RAM in order to display on screen, is a potential infringement of copyright. It is not necessary for the material to be printed or stored to disk. Since the only way of accessing material on the Internet involves the temporary storage of material in RAM in the recipient machine it seems to imply that a copyright holder, in placing material on the Internet, authorizes this level of copying. However, the law is at present unclear on this. It is, therefore, advisable for businesses to establish copyright in much the same way as for printed material, by seeking permission, rather than assuming that the presence on the Internet grants copying permission. There is also another important issue. Material on the Internet may already be in infringement of copyright and be held and distributed without the permission of the author. Finally it is common for businesses to hold copies of popular websites on their own servers to prevent excessive employee use of Internet connection. **Mirror sites**, as these are called, are also held in different countries in order to cut down the international Internet traffic. It is quite clear that unless permission has been granted these will infringe copyright.

For any business to copy works from the Internet it is safest to seek permission to copy, to distribute the work, and to authorize others to do so. This applies to text, graphics, video and audio and, in some cases, synchronization of audio and video and graphics.

5.6 The Internet and financial transactions

In the early days of the Web it quickly became clear to businesses that the Internet would be not only a vehicle for dispersing information but also a shop front for the sale of goods and services. This would entail commercial transactions being conducted electronically. As a result 'cybercash' has now become an accepted way of payment over the Internet and particularly over the World Wide Web. It is likely that with increased use of the Web the use of cybercash will become more common. There will be many more transactions. Also, there will be a large increase in the number of small transactions – for example attachment to a news service based on time connected. With a large volume of small transactions the cost of processing the transaction becomes important and needs minimizing.

There are three forms of electronic payment or electronic cash substitutes currently being used.

Electronic credit card transactions: This form of payment has become acceptable prior to the Internet with card swipe and electronic transfer from points of sale. Equally the quotation of a credit card number over the phone will often secure purchase of goods and services. In this respect, the Internet poses little new. The credit card number and other verifying information will be input and the transfer of liability for payment of goods will move from the purchaser to the credit card company who will then take over responsibility for the transfer of funds to seller and recovery of monies at the end of the month as part of a consolidated bill from the purchaser. No real issues arise that are new – although security (see below) will continue to be a concern. The seller will still be able to gain information concerning the purchaser and purchaser's credit card number, and so anonymity of purchasers will not be guaranteed. The transaction costs of processing the transaction are still high relative to the purchase of goods through electronic cash.

Electronic cash or e-cash: With electronic cash a sum of e-cash is purchased from a 'money merchant' and is held electronically in an account. When a purchaser of a good makes a purchase then the merchant is informed electronically and the e-cash is transferred from the purchaser's account to the seller's account at the merchant (or the seller's account at some other merchant who accepts the e-cash). The entire transaction is conducted electronically over the Internet. The anonymity of the purchaser (and of the seller) can be maintained. This is a new form of payment. It requires the acceptance of e-cash which has no intrinsic value by both purchaser and seller. In some ways this mirrors 'paper money'. Paper money has no intrinsic value and only works as a medium of exchange as it is backed by the government and is difficult to reproduce (counterfeit). Governments have no plans to back e-cash in the same way. E-cash will only work if there is confidence in its exchange value and this will be unlikely unless there is confidence in the organization 'backing' it. It is likely that major well-established financial institutions will need to be involved with e-cash before it becomes readily acceptable. There are security issues (see below) but also the need for confidence in the accuracy of the software that handles the accounting aspects. E-cash has one major advantage in that the transaction cost is minimal. Governments will need to take a regulatory interest in e-cash since it is easy to see how repetitive and transnational flows of e-cash could be used for money laundering and tax evasion purposes.

Electronic cash substitutes: Air miles, supermarket points and other forms of non-cash rewards are becoming increasingly prevalent. These may be earned by a purchase on the Internet, recorded electronically, and redeemed electronically for goods, air tickets, etc. These, therefore, become e-cash substitutes.

Electronic payment generates two different types of major security issue. Firstly all transactions over the Internet require the transmission of electronic data. The date is publicly accessible. This may be a credit card number, e-cash, or an electronic cash substitute. The normal way to prevent this information from being identified and copied for fraudulent purposes is to encrypt it. It is also important that no corruption of the information occurs and this will need to be handled with devices such as error checking codes.

The second major security issue surrounds the businesses that operate on the Internet. Businesses may appear to be providing legitimate investment opportunities, for example, but actually deceive the would-be investor into parting with money. There has always been a problem with unscrupulous companies but what renders additional concerns with the Internet are:

- it is largely unregulated;
- it crosses international boundaries;
- the business is not tied to some place the purchaser/investor can visit which is relatively stable such as a building;
- the credibility of the company is largely dependent on the Web page presentation.

These concerns over security are not seen as preventing the use of the Web for commercial transactions but rather viewed as problem areas that should and will be addressed.

5.7 The intranet

The software and technology used to develop website pages by an organization and to access them over the Internet is equally suitable for the development and access of web pages designed purely for consumption by employees and clients of that organization.

This system is known as an **intranet**. It is a privately accessible network using Internet technology and tools. Businesses quickly recognized that the richness of presentation media (text, graphics, audio, video) for presenting information on the Web, and the use of hyperlinks to other Web pages was ideal for the development of an organization-wide information system. This has now been extended to cover direct access from outside of the organization.

Businesses are using intranets for the internal display of:

- company manuals covering employment and other procedures;
- easily updatable internal news and information services;
- company catalogues;
- project noticeboards (to which project participants can add information and comments to be seen by all).

The intranet is replacing historical paper-based information systems because it is both cheaper and more easily updatable. Software specifically aimed at supporting intranet functions is now readily available. For example, the Nissan motor company in the UK has replaced its expensive system for the distribution of company catalogue information to dealers (by fax and the postal service) with an intranet which is accessible by the dealers through dial-in access. This has the benefit of being instantly updatable and immediately accessible.

Summary

The Internet has evolved over the last decade from being a small set of interconnected networks for the exchange of scientific information, to a highly sophisticated set of publicly accessible networks for the global provision of information and services to business and private individuals. The key to this development has been the agreement of protocols for information exchange (TCP/IP) and the exponential growth in the use of technologically advanced microcomputers in business and for personal use. E-mail is now a recognized method of cheap, fast secure information transmission either across a local area network or globally across the Internet. Other facilities provided by the Internet are telnet, enabling remote login to host computers over the Internet and file transfer protocol for the transmission of all forms of files. Newsgroups and Internet Relay Chat allow the development of particular areas of interest globally over the Internet – the latter in interactive real time. Access to stored information held on remote computers has been enabled by the Internet and developments such as gophers and wide area information services have rapidly improved the operation of search and find for this information. However, the most significant development has come in the 1990s with the growth of the World Wide Web.

The World Wide Web allows pages to be written and stored in Hypertext Markup Language (HTML) in such a way that they can be accessed over the Internet using Hypertext Transmission Protocols (HTTP). What is particularly important is the ability to use hypertexts links to other websites or pages for greater amplification of information obtained. The World Wide Web protocols also allow graphics, audio and video information to be stored and retrieved as well as text. The development of web browser software, especially Netscape and Internet Explorer, has enabled inexperienced users to easily retrieve and display information. The ability for users to find information has been increased by the development of web search engines which index millions of web pages. Recently software plug-ins have enhanced the presentation of information.

Business has been swift in realizing the opportunities provided by the Web and has developed websites in order:

- to advertise services and products
- to sell services and products
- to promote corporate images
- to provide information (especially public services).

As various case studies indicated, advantages in using of the Web include a reduction in the cost of advertising, cheaper and easier provision of information, the lack of a need to maintain a shop front, the ease of crossing geographical boundaries and the absence of the middleman. Issues, including copyright and the security of electronic commercial transactions, will need to be tackled before the Internet becomes a stable environment for business operations.

It is likely that the use of the Internet and the Web will continue to grow in importance for business as new applications are exploited and the number of people able to access the Internet increases.

Exercises

1. Explain the difference between the Internet and the intranet.

2. Which factors drive and which factors limit the growth of the use of the Internet for business?

3. By using Porter's 'value chain' and 'five forces' model (Chapter 2) analyze the strategic impact of the use of the World Wide Web for the following business areas
   - food and grocery retail
   - parcel courier tracking
   - property agency
   - banking
   - equity and stock trading
   - news and publishing.

4. Should the Internet be regulated and if so by whom and how?

5. How would a business identify the cost effectiveness of its website?

6. Search the World Wide Web for a range of different business websites and analyze these with a view to answering the following:
   What are the objectives for the business of the website?
   How effective has the business been in meeting these objectives?
   Which features of the website should be added or removed?

7. What information or facilities would you expect to see on a university or college website?

8. 'If the Internet is a lawless frontier, then the service providers are the new marshals in town' (Spar and Bussgang, 1996). Is this the case?

References and recommended reading

- Bickerton P., Bickerton M., and Pardesis U. (1996). *Cybermarketing: How To Use The Superhighway To Market Your Products And Services*. Oxford: Butterworth-Heinemann
  This book is intended for those who wish to use the Internet for marketing their products and services. It is published on behalf of the Chartered Institute of Marketing. It is useful as it emphasizes and develops marketing concepts and techniques in an easily accessible fashion. Intended for practitioners it is practical rather than academic in orientation.
- Cohen F.B. (1995). *Protection And Security On The Information Superhighway*. New York: Wiley
  This book takes as its starting point the assumption that there will be increasing reliance on the Internet and cyberspace for future exchange of information and processing of financial transactions. The more information that flows the harder and the more important it is to protect individuals and organizations from accidents, loss and abuse. The book approaches the subject, not by immediately concentrating on technical issues and solutions, but encourages a perspective which ensures the organization recognizes its dependency on information; recognizes weaknesses in its infrastructure; recognizes the importance

of protection and correctly prioritizes it. Only then is attention directed to the process of protection.

● Frost A. and Norris M. (1997). *Exploiting The Internet*. Chichester: Wiley

This is a good reference book for introduction to the Internet. It avoids much of the technical and practical details which limit the accessibility of some books. It has a broad understandable coverage which will extend the reader's knowledge beyond this brief chapter.

● Hills M. (1997). *Intranet Business Strategies*. New York: Wiley

This is a practical book intended to give readers an understanding of the benefits and effects of an intranet for a business organization. Although aimed at the computing practitioner in an organization the text is readily accessible to students who have a basic understanding of business concepts and of the Internet.

● Porter D. ed. (1997). *Internet Culture*. New York: Routledge

This is a collection of essays which sets out to examine the Internet and its effects on communication between social groups. The perspective taken is to examine a cultural phenomenon from the point of view of psychology, sociology and politics. Although the contributions are not technical (from a computing point of view) they are saturated with the culture of the disciplines from which they emanate. Several are highly interesting, though not recommended for the casual reader.

● Randall N. (1997). *The Soul Of The Internet*. London: International Thomson Computer Press

This is an interesting easy-to-read book that captures the development of the Internet and the people and passions behind its evolution.

● Schulman M.A. and Smith R. (1997). *The Internet Strategic Plan*. Chichester: Wiley

This book is aimed at business managers and personnel who wish to have a step-by-step guide to implementation of access to the Internet and use of its benefits for their company. It adopts a linear approach involving issues to cover in identification of the need for and the requirements for connection to the Internet, education of employees, development and design of policy, and acquisition and installation of the hardware/software to ensure network connectivity. The text is practical in nature and unlike other books in the area, which concentrate either on the technology or the Internet sites, the book looks at organizational issues of development.

● Spar D. and Bussgang J.J. (1996). 'Ruling the Net'. *Harvard Business Review*, May–June, 125–133

Chapter 6

Decision Support and End-user Computing

In Chapter 1 information, decisions and the use of information in decision making were examined. This was achieved without recourse to discussion of any technology involved. Earlier chapters have introduced aspects of technology. This chapter covers how technology supports decisions in systems for planning, control and management. These are known as decision support systems. The chapter analyzes the characteristics and classes of decision support systems including those systems that support group decisions – group decision support systems.

The influence of modern technology and, in particular, the role of fourth-generation languages, spreadsheets, expert systems tools and model generators in their development is emphasized. The role of end users in the specification and development of applications, especially decision support systems, is introduced. The phenomenon of end-user computing, its benefits, and its challenge to management are examined. Prototyping as a method of developing decision support systems within the context of end-user computing is explained. The focus on decision support and end-user computing has emphasized the need for a theory of the role of the user within the total system. Approaches to this area in the context of human–computer interaction are covered.

6.1   Features of decision support systems

Although the term **decision support system** (DSS) is a general one used to cover virtually any computerized system that aids decision making in business, most DSSs share certain features.

DSS support decisions

One of the important characteristics of a decision support system is that it is intended to *support* rather than replace decisions. The Gorry and Scott Morton framework relating the structure of a decision to the level of managerial activity involved in the decision was covered Chapter 1. Computerized systems can replace the human decision maker in structured decisions but are of little help in completely unstructured situations. There is, for instance, a large group of decisions taken by personnel in business organizations that have a structured computational and data transformation element to them as well as an unstructured non-rule-governed component. It is just these decisions that can be aided but not replaced by decision support systems.

Examples of semi-structured decisions are: planning a mix of investments for a port-folio, looking at the financial implications of various ways of financing a short-term cash flow deficit, consideration of alternative production and pricing policies, assessing the impact of potential future changes in exogenous variables such as interest rates, analysis of the credit-worthiness of corporate clients, and assessing the likely impacts of departmental reorganization.

DSSs involve flexible interactive access to data

Decision support systems are designed with an understanding of the requirements of the decision makers and the decision making process in mind. This has implications, two of the most important being:

- The need for **interactive** support: typically many of the semi-structured decisions for which DSSs are relevant involve the decision maker in asking questions that require immediate answers. As a result of this further interrogation is made. Examples are:
  - **what if** – as in 'what would the effects on profits be if we were to be subject to a 5% material cost rise?'
  - **goal seeking** – as in 'what would be the required mix in the liquidation of short-term and medium-term assets to reduce a projected cash deficit to zero over the next six months (the goal)?'
  - **optimization** – as in 'how do we ensure optimum utilization of our machines?'
- Flexible access to data: many semi-structured decisions are only possible if the decision maker has immediate access to *ad hoc* data retrieval and report-generation facilities. For internal decisions this generally means that access by powerful query languages of existing data held in a corporate database is required.

Modern decision support systems meet these requirements by ensuring easy and quick availability of access to decision makers. This can be supplied by terminals placed on the desks of managers. More recently personal computers (PCs), with their local processing power, have been playing a larger role. The use of local area networks between PCs and connected to mainframes has enabled easier data access to decision makers.

The use of spreadsheets and other modelling packages together with database management systems has provided necessary modelling and data retrieval facilities.

DSSs are fragmented

In Chapter 1 we saw that the totally integrated corporate management information system designed as a single project is extremely unlikely to be successful. Information systems are more likely to be loose federations of subsystems evolving separately to serve the information needs of the individual functional subsystems of the organization. This pattern is also exhibited with decision support, where the trend is towards development of models to provide support for individual decisions or types of decision. No attempt is made to develop global comprehensive decision support models for entire organizations.

DSS development involves end users

This is reinforced by the involvement of end-user decision takers in the development of models for computerized support. Nowhere is this more pronounced than in the use of local PCs and spreadsheet modelling. The purchase of PCs and the development of models are often carried out independent of any knowledge or aid from the centralized computer centre. The use of fourth-generation languages in general has increased the influence of end users over decision support design.

In summary, the trend in modern decision support systems is towards end-user involvement in the development of fragmented simple models targeted to aid, rather than replace, the kinds of decision to be made. Easy and flexible interactive access to data and modelling facilities is as likely to be provided by PCs and networks as by the more traditional centralized larger computers.

6.2   Types of decision support system

Decision support systems can be divided into a number of categories depending on the types of processing of data and information involved and the types of decision made.

1. **Data retrieval and analysis for decision support:** These systems rely on interaction with an existing database:
   (a) **Simple entry and enquiry systems:** These support decisions by providing immediate interrogation of a database for specific enquiries. Examples are stock enquiry systems, airline booking systems and account enquiry systems. They are used to aid operational decisions – for instance, whether to reorder stock.
   (b) **Data analysis systems:** These provide summaries and selected reports of data held on the database. An example is a system to provide information on the rate at which sales orders are being satisfied.
   (c) **Accounting information systems:** These are very similar to the last category as accounting information is provided as an analysis of accounting transaction data. However, because accountants commonly need the same types of report – for example, aged analysis of debtors, summary balance sheets, cash reports, profit and loss reports – and such information is prepared according to professional accounting standards, much of this information is supplied by accounting applications packages.

2. **Computational support for structured decisions:** These involve using existing general data held on a database and computation together with details of individual cases to arrive at information for a decision. An example would be a motor insurance quotation system. This accepts data on an individual, searches a database of insurance companies' terms, and computes a set of calculated premiums, which optimize on some group of variables such as low cost, maximum protected bonus or minimum excess.

3. **Decision support involving modelling:** These systems rely on the use of existing data from a database or user input data, which might be hypothetical. Using

this data its consequences are calculated using a model. The model reflects relationships that the decision taker believes to hold between the variables relevant for a decision.

(a) Spreadsheet models are used to represent accounting relationships between numerical accounting data. They are used to take the tedium out of budget preparation and forecasting. The sensitivity of the organization to changes in the values of accounting data are then easy to estimate by hypothetical 'what if' changes.

(b) Probabilistic models incorporate elements of probabilistic reasoning and risk analysis in their modelling calculations.

(c) Optimization modelling involves mathematical computation of optimization or goal seeking based on constraints.

Many decision support systems in this category exhibit all three characteristics.

6.3 The development of decision support systems

The development of a decision support system is determined by the types of information and the facilities needed for taking the decision. In this sense DSS development is decision led. Because an intimate knowledge of the decision-taking process is needed it is important that the end users – that is, the decision takers – are involved in the process of design. They may carry out the development and design themselves, as is common with spreadsheet modelling, or it may be undertaken by analysts and programmers.

Decision support systems are developed using programming languages or produced by packages specifically incorporating decision support development tools. These methods will now be considered. In all approaches it is generally considered advisable to develop prototypes initially.

6.3.1 The use of very high-level languages

Conventional high-level languages such as C++ and BASIC can be used to develop decision support systems. They are extremely flexible. However, decision support systems using these languages involve a lengthy analysis and design phase. They are not suitable for prototyping. It is now not common to use them, especially as technical efficiency considerations, which may be important with transaction processing systems, are not so important for decision support.

Fourth-generation or very high-level languages are more appropriate. They are particularly useful as they are generally database orientated. This is important for those systems that rely on data retrieval and analysis for decision support. An example of a prominent fourth-generation language is SQL, which can be used on many relational database systems such as IBM's DB2 and ORACLE. The advantages of using them are that:

● Applications development is speedy.
● Many are end-user orientated.
● They are more likely to be declarative rather than procedural.

Fourth-generation languages are more extensively covered in Chapter 3.

6.3.2　The use of spreadsheets

Of all the computerized productivity tools made available to the decision maker in business organizations over the last decade the electronic spreadsheet is among the most powerful, widely employed and user friendly.

Spreadsheets are a particularly suitable tool for the accountant, though they may be used for many general business-modelling tasks. A popular area is the development of cash flow forecasts. A firm's cash flow position can be crucially affected by changes in average debtor or creditor periods, in the pattern of expected future costs and sales, and the charge incurred in remaining in overdraft, which are particularly sensitive to interest rate changess. Model building and 'what if' analysis enables the accountant to keep an up-to-date and changing view of the firm's current and future cash flow position without the laborious need to recalculate in the light of unexpected changes.

To understand the idea of a spreadsheet imagine a large sheet of paper divided into 9999 rows and 256 columns. This is a common spreadsheet size. Through the keyboard the user may enter text, a number or a formula into each cell (row/column intersection). Spreadsheet software running on a microcomputer provides a computerized equivalent of this grid-like worksheet. The entry in each cell is made by moving a highlighted box, called a cursor, to the required cell. This is achieved by means of cursor control keys on the keyboard or the use of a mouse. The cell entry is displayed on the screen. For example, in row 35 column 19 the text '**SALES**', or the number **100.23** might be entered. Or again the formula **(ROW 23 COLUMN 2 + ROW 14 COLUMN 3) * 2** might be added. In the last case the resulting number calculated from the formula would be displayed on the screen in the cell position. Any cells referred to in a formula may themselves contain numbers or other formulae. In this way cells may be linked together.

The example in Figure 6.1 concerns the projected sales, sales income and costs for two types of compact disc player, CD-A and CD-B. Figure 6.1 would be displayed on the microcomputer screen. Figure 6.2 shows the logic behind the model from rows 4–30 and columns 1–3 as it would be entered at the keyboard. Text is clearly shown as enclosed by quotation marks. Note that **R29C4** means 'row 29 column 4' and **R(–6)C** means '6 rows prior to the current row same column'. The separation of data in rows 29 and 30 from the logic of the model makes it easy to carry out 'what if' analysis. Suppose the managing director of the company wanted to know the impact of an increase in material cost of components for CD-A compact discs. After the estimated figure has been entered in row 29 column 6 the spreadsheet program will automatically recalculate all cells that are affected by the change. The managing director can carry out as many 'what ifs' as required.

As well as standard arithmetic functions most spreadsheets have the ability to calculate financial ratios such as internal rates of return and net present value, along with common statistical functions such as standard deviation.

A feature of many spreadsheet packages is that the individual spreadsheet models may be linked together so that figures in one spreadsheet may be fed into another. For instance, the cost side of the production of compact disc players would be modelled by the production department. The responsibility for developing the sales forecasting part of the model in Figure 6.1 might lie with the sales department. Selected parts of each of these separate spreadsheets, saved on disk, can then be linked to a third spreadsheet, which produces the projected profit/loss forecast for the next six months. Changes, or

Figure 6.1: The output of a spreadsheet for profit forecasting.

	1	2	3	4	5	6	7
1	Compact disc players TYPES CD-A and CD-B						
2	6 months projections from January						
3							
4	SALES	Jan	Feb	March	April	May	June
5	units CD-A	43	43	44	44	45	45
6	units CD-B	121	109	98	88	79	71
7							
8	price CD-A	123	121	118	116	113	111
9	price CD-B	278	306	336	370	407	448
10							
11	income CD-A	5289	5235	5182	5129	5076	5025
12	income CD-B	33638	33302	32969	32639	32313	31989
13		--------	--------	--------	--------	--------	--------
14	TOTAL	38927	38537	38150	37768	37389	37014
15							
16	COSTS						
17	labour CD-A	1075	1086	1097	1108	1119	1130
18	labour CD-B	5203	4683	4214	3793	3414	3072
19							
20	materials CD-A	2795	2823	2851	2880	2908	2938
21	materials CD-B	21296	19166	17250	15525	13972	12575
22		--------	--------	--------	--------	--------	--------
23	TOTAL	30369	27758	25412	23305	21413	19715
24							
25	PROFIT	8558	10779	12738	14463	15976	17299
26							
27	TABLES	Jan price	Price	January	Sales	Material	Labour
28		per unit	growth	sales	growth	cost per unit	cost per unit
29	CD-A	123	0.98	43	1.01	65	25
30	CD-B	278	1.1	121	0.9	176	43

'what ifs', in the subsidiary spreadsheets feed through to the main spreadsheet by way of the linking.

Because spreadsheet packages represent information to the user in rows and columns they are particularly suitable for tasks that require report production.

They can therefore be used to produce profit and loss, balance sheets and other reports. However, most modern spreadsheets provide the facility to present information in other forms such as charts, diagrams and graphs.

Spreadsheets packages also enable the development of models that interact and extract data stored in a database. This is important where future rolling projections based on current rolling figures are needed.

Modern spreadsheet packages incorporate their own very high-level programming languages. Though limited, these enable the user to write various application programs that interact with the spreadsheet model or which control the interaction of the spreadsheet with the user.

The use of spreadsheets as an interactive modelling tool is limited by the matrix nature of the model representation and data input. Only applications that are high in number handling as distinct from text handling are suitable for spreadsheet applications.

Figure 6.2 The logic part of the model in Figure 6.1.

	1	2	3
4	"SALES"	" Jan"	" Feb"
5	" units CD-A"	R29C4	RC(−1)*R29C5
6	" units CD-B"	R30C4	RC(−1)*R30C5
7			
8	"price CD-A"	R29C2	RC(−1)*R29C3
9	"price CD-B"	R30C2	RC(−1)*R30C3
10			
11	"income CD-A"	R(−6)C*R(−3)C	R(−6)C*R(−3)C
12	"income CD-B"	R(−6)C*R(−3)C	R(−6)C*R(−3)C
13		"------------------"	"------------------"
14	"TOTAL"	R(−3)C+R(−2)C	R(−3)C+R(−2)C
15			
16	"COSTS"		
17	"labour CD-A"	R29C7*R(−12)C	R29C7*R(−12)C
18	"labour CD-B"	R30C7*R(−12)c	R30C7*R(−12)C
19			
20	"materials CD-A"	R29C6*R(−15)C	R29C6*R(−15)C
21	"materials CD-B"	R30C6*R(−15)C	R30C6*R(−15)C
22		"------------------"	"------------------"
23	"TOTAL"	SUM(R(−6)C:R(−2)C)	SUM(R(−6)C:R(−2)C)
24			
25	"PROFIT"	R(−11)C−R(−2)C	R(−11)C−R(−2)C
26			
27	"TABLES"	"Jan price"	" Price"
28		" per unit"	" Growth"
29	" CD-A"	123	0.98
30	" CD-B"	278	1.1

There are other drawbacks to the use of spreadsheets. Spreadsheet model design, though capable of being carried out by end users, is time-consuming. Unless much 'what if' investigation is to be carried out or the same relationships used again and again it is often quicker and more flexible to use pen and paper. Spreadsheet package manufacturers are conscious of this limitation and are constantly adding new facilities to speed up complex model building. It is also now becoming obvious that spreadsheet model development cannot be carried out in an *ad hoc* manner if reliable, testable, and amendable models are to be built. It is necessary to follow good modelling practice.

Another limitation of spreadsheets is in their ability to display only a small part of the spreadsheet at a time on the screen. Package manufacturers have attempted to overcome this by the provision of **windows**. Windows show several selected rectangular sections of the spreadsheet simultaneously on different parts of the screen.

Despite these limitations spreadsheet packages will continue to be used widely within business, especially accounting and decision making, not least because models can be built using them by those without technical computing skills. The trend in the future is to make these packages more user friendly and able to interact more with other standard commercial packages. Although these packages will have other facilities, such as built in word processing and database facilities, they will continue to be based on the same philosophy of the electronic matrix worksheet.

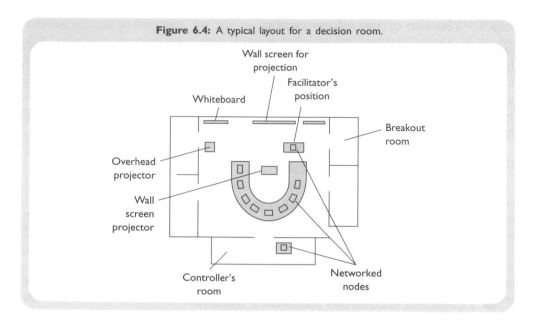

Figure 6.4: A typical layout for a decision room.

computerized support within a fixed period of time using a facilitator. Specific computer-based tools are provided (see below).

3. **Tele/computer conferencing:** If groups are composed of members or subgroups that are geographically dispersed, tele/computer conferencing provides for interactive connection between two or more decision rooms. This interaction will involve transmission of computerized and audiovisual information.

Whereas decision networks can be viewed as the use of local area networks, for decision making involving groups the decision room is an entirely new development.

The decision room is used by an organization to create an environment in which groups may enhance their decisions. The decision-making process is guided by a **facilitator**. The facilitator is usually not from within the organization but a trained professional in group dynamics brought in for the decision-making sessions. There will also usually be a computer controller whose responsibility it is to maintain computer communications and software support within the room.

The decision room (an example of which can be seen in Figure 6.4) consists of a table with networked workstations for the participants and workstations for the facilitator and controller. The screen of any node of the network can be projected onto the wall screen. The facilitator can also ensure that, if required, any participant's screen can replace some or all of the other nodes for demonstration or interactive purposes. Breakout rooms, used for smaller discussions, are also equipped with similar networked machines. A combination of overhead projector, flipchart, photocopier and other presentation devices are provided as well.

The software may take many forms but will always consist of tools that aid group decision making, are easy to use and are interactive. Examples of software (as well as spreadsheet and statistical/graphical packages) are:

- **Brainstorming:** Brainstorming software may be used at any stage of the proceedings but is particularly valuable at early stages when members of the group
need to think and converse freely on issues. A problem or statement can be entered
for comment. This will appear on all screens. Each individual may then produce
comments, which are anonymously consolidated and displayed. The tool increases
creativity and lateral thinking.

- **Voting:** It is frequently important to obtain a swift view on the acceptability of
proposals from a group perspective before proceeding. Voting software enables
this to happen. It is not merely restricted to yes/no but will also enable different
formats for expressing preferences including multiple choice and 1–5 scales.

- **Policy formation:** Software can aid policy formation by allowing decision makers
to identify connections and relations between issues and communicate this to all
present for comment.

The software will be used as part of a methodology followed by the facilitator in arriving at decisions. Much work is still to be done in the area of development of tools to
support decision rooms.

Decision rooms are expensive to equip and all but the largest organizations would
find it difficult to justify the expenditure – particularly so as the use of the decision room
is not regarded as an everyday occurrence. It is becoming more common for establish-
ments, especially academic institutions, to hire out these facilities to organizations when
needed.

It is difficult to analyze the effectiveness of these group decision support systems
although it appears that they are most likely to be beneficial (and to be regarded as
beneficial by participants) for larger group sizes (size eight and above). Participants are
aware of the need to impose some structure on groups this size and welcome the direction given by the decision room and the facilitator.

6.5   End-user computing

End-user computing generally refers to a situation in which the target users of an information and decision support system are involved extensively in the specification, development and use of the system and its applications.

This is to be contrasted with the more traditional approach where analysis, design and
development of computer systems are carried out by a team of analysts and programmers
affiliated to a centralized computer centre. In this case the final users of the system are
likely to be involved only at two stages. First, they may be required at the early stages
of specification for interview to establish the nature of the activity to be computerized
together with the information required. Their next involvement is likely to be at the stage
where the system is tested.

In end-user computing those that use the system will be expected to play a leading
role in most, if not all, of the following:

- the identification of the need for a system or application
- the specification of the type of system and/or software to satisfy that need
- the purchase/resourcing of the hardware/software

- the development of the application according to corporate standards
- the use of the application for business purposes
- the management of security/backup for the application.

6.5.1   The rise of end-user computing

The growth of end-user computing began in the late 1970s, continued through the 1980s, and is now, in the late 1990s, seen as an important component of the approach of most organizations to their information and decision support provision. The trend was stimulated by demand considerations and facilitated by supply developments.

First, the backlog of computer applications developments that accumulated in many organizations meant that users were becoming increasingly frustrated with the computer centre. When applications were finally delivered they were often over budget and disappointing in that they did not meet user expectations. Although end-user computing was not the only response to this situation (another was the design of more appropriate methodologies for systems analysis and design) it can be seen as one of the resultant reactions to problems with the traditional approach to information systems development and management – problems that had been building up throughout the previous decade.

Second, the introduction of microcomputers placed computing power within the reaches of departmental budget holders and users of information systems. The rapid increase in the power of microcomputers together with the decrease in costs was supplemented by the production of software specifically designed for the end user. This situation continued throughout the 1980s. End users wanted the autonomy provided by PCs. Software suppliers responded to this by designing programs serving end-user requirements. This in turn stimulated the growth of end-user computing.

Third, there was a general increase in computer literacy amongst business users. This was an essential prerequisite for the full growth of end-user computing. The improvement in computer literacy can be partly put down to the stimulus of the reasons mentioned above – the demand for more independence from the computer centre and the availability of the means of establishing that independence. However, it should be remembered that the growth in computing at universities and colleges was also turning out computer-literate graduates who were able to utilize computer support in their work.

6.5.2   Types of end-user computing

End-user computing as a category involves a range of individuals with differing types of skills, access to and relationships with the computer system. End-user computing may be at varying stages of maturity of development in different organizations. If end-user computing is going to be managed well within the organization then an understanding of the types of end user is essential so that proper training, control, resourcing and applications development can be undertaken, and an understanding of the stage of development will determine appropriate strategies for management of the process.

Categorization by skills of end users

One categorization, by Rockart and Flannery (1983), distinguishes end users in terms of the type of computer skills they possess and the way this interacts with the types of information the end user requires. There are six categories, and end users may 'progress' from one category to another. Each is distinguished by a different type of skill and information requirement. Recognition of this will aid end-user management.

1. **Non-programming end-user:** This is the 'traditional' end user. In this category the user is not involved in the systems development process. The non-programming end user responds to prompts and menus on screens, inputs or extracts data. Typically the user will have little understanding of the way the application is built. The data entry clerk, the shop assistant using computer-based checkout facilities, or the airline reservation clerk are examples in this category.

2. **Command-level end user:** Users in this category have a greater understanding of the way the application is handled. Typically individuals will be able to form database query commands or interact with the operating system using commands. This level of user is generally responsive to training if their systems level knowledge is in need of upgrading.

3. **Programming-level end user:** This category refers, not to the traditional programmer in the computer centre, but to personnel usually working within one of the functional business departments, such as accounting, who have a deep understanding of the use of 4GLs or development tools in building applications. An example would be the management accountant who, with a thorough understanding of both spreadsheet software and management accounting, can develop spreadsheet models to support management accounting decisions.

4. **Functional support personnel:** Users in this category are technically skilled information systems developers located within functional departments within the organization. The difference between this category and the previous category is one of perception. For example, accountants who develop models for decision support would primarily view themselves as accountants (programming end user), whereas computer-trained systems developers in an accounting department will need to know about accounting in order to develop systems. These latter personnel would nevertheless regard themselves as information systems professionals (functional support personnel).

5. **End-user support personnel:** End-user support personnel usually reside in the computer centre. They will be specialists in the technicalities of a range of applications development software packages. Their understanding, though, will be limited to the software aspects, not to an understanding of the business nature of the applications developed. They will provide support on development, from a technical point of view, choice of software and installation services.

6. **Data-processing programmers:** Though the term is slightly archaic now this category of users is composed of highly trained computer centre personnel. The data processing programmer is likely to be computer trained (not business trained) and to take creative decisions using the full power of the array of software available. This breadth and depth distinguishes the data-processing programmer from the programming-level end user.

As can be seen by examination of the different categories there is a wide range of skills and approaches associated with end users. All categories represent end users in the sense of persons who use the computer system for business purposes or take part in the applications development process. However, the term 'end-user computing', as introduced at the start of this section, is restricted and generally understood to involve only categories 3 and 4 – programming-level end users and functional support personnel. The different categories in the Rockart and Flannery typology provide insights into what activities are appropriate for what types of personnel, what training must be provided in order to develop end users from one category to another, and how an organization might decide to spread its approach to applications development using 4GLs between different types of user. As with any categorization its chief purpose is to enhance understanding and to differentiate what was previously undifferentiated.

Categorization by maturity of end-user computing

A previous chapter dealt with the Nolan stage model for the evolution of information systems within an organization. Huff *et al.* (1988) have adapted this approach to consider the development of end-user computing specifically. As with the Nolan model the importance lies in identifying the stage of growth associated with the organization. This provides a guide to obtain the most effective management strategy for the process of growth to the next stage of maturity. The model has five stages in which the degree of integration of the applications is taken as the measure of maturity:

1. **Isolation:** Applications are developed in an individually uncoordinated way. There is no exchange of data between applications. The developments are more associated with learning than with enhancing productivity.

2. **Standalone:** Applications development takes place at a greater rate. These are still 'standalone' applications developed and used generally on personal microcomputers. There is no exchange of data between applications. Individuals come to depend on their own applications development support for enhancing their productivity. Data, if shared with other applications, is rekeyed in.

3. **Manual integration:** The next stage is where the need for significant exchanges of data is recognized. This may occur through the physical exchange of disks or through the downloading of files over a local area network. Issues of standards in hardware, software and communications become more important.

4. **Automated integration:** This stage differs from the previous one chiefly in that the focus towards automation of data exchange increases. Integration and the need to exchange data are now considered in applications development and design. End-user exchange of data still requires substantial knowledge of the location of data, and exchange is only effected by transfer commands.

5. **Distributed integration:** Here the physical location of data becomes transparent to the user. Network or other software handles the data supply. The application serving the end user may use data distributed fully across a network.

If organizations are to proceed in their growth towards maturity in end-user computing, then management must plan to move smoothly from one stage to the next. It is particularly important to emphasize standardization issues in order to achieve the integration necessary in the later stages.

6.5.3 The benefits of end-user computing

End-user computing confers many benefits on an organization. Amongst those most commonly identified are the following:

- End users are now able to satisfy their own requirements in many cases. This cuts down the wait period resulting from the backlog of applications awaiting development in the computer centre.
- Innovation and control over one's own information provision stimulated by end-user computing encourages autonomy and responsibility in users.
- End users are able to translate their information requirements into applications without the need to transfer these via an analyst/programmer, who will not in general be an expert in the application area. This reduces one of the main difficulties in systems development – that of designing a system that meets user requirements.
- End users are able to release analyst/programming staff for other uses. In particular, centralized resources such as the corporate database will not be developed or controlled by end users.
- End users are able to adapt their systems to their needs as they evolve.

6.5.4 The risks of end-user computing

Its liberating impact has undoubtedly been a major force in the growth of end-user computing. There are, however, risks and pitfalls that can easily remove corporate advantages or create corporate problems. These may occur even if the benefits to the performance of the individual are realized. Many risks concern proliferation without standardization. Amongst these the following are the most important:

1. Quality assurance may be diminished in end-user applications development as compared with centralized systems analysis and design. The centralized control of a computer centre, combined with the knowledge that a lack of quality control would revisit the programmers and analysts at a later date, meant that quality issues have always been accorded a high priority within traditional computing centres. The potential anarchism, especially at the earlier stages of the growth to maturity of an organization's end-user computing, can yield problems. This may be revealed in a number of ways:
   (a) poor development methodologies, which yield error-prone applications;
   (b) incomplete testing;
   (c) inadequate or non-existent development documentation and user manuals – both may make it difficult for anyone but the developer to use the system;
   (d) inadequate access control, backup and archiving.

2. Computer centre analysts are used to making complete systems specifications. The end-user developer is far more likely to be interested in a swift development without the need for producing a complete specification. The familiarity that users have with their own requirements can be a drawback. The systems analysts may be able to provide insights with a more general questioning approach.

3. At later stages of mature growth, when end-user applications involve the manipulation of shared data, the absence of controls on data may yield data integrity problems.

4. Unless there are mechanisms in place for directed growth, unrelated applications in different areas of the organization may be created that duplicate each other. Although this can create waste it must be borne in mind that other benefits, such as the creation of user autonomy and responsibility, must be offset against this.

5. Costs of hardware and software need to be monitored. If the growth of end-user computing does not proceed in parallel with central policies on purchase standardization and bulk purchase discounts then the benefits will be jeopardized.

6. End-user applications are likely to service local needs and objectives. This is only beneficial to the organization if these are congruent with and support global corporate objectives.

7. There is a risk that users produce private and informal information systems that run counter to company policy or against the law. Compliance with data protection legislation is one known area of difficulty.

6.5.5 End-user applications development and management

If the corporate benefits from end-user computing are to be realized then ultimately the organization must proceed to the final stages of the Huff model – that is, to distributed integration. This requires a responsible role to be taken both by the computer centre and by the end users themselves.

The role of the computer centre

- **Standard setting:** Standards need to be set, monitored and maintained for end-user computing. These will apply to hardware, software, systems analysis and design, documentation, data structure definition, data communications, access, security and the privacy of personal data. It is not an easy task for the computer centre to ensure that these standards are adhered to and at the same time create the necessary climate of autonomy within which end-user computing can flourish.

- **Communications and networks:** As well as maintaining standards for communications and networks it is likely that the computer centre will be responsible for the provision and maintenance of a cross-organizational local area network. This is key to successful integrated end-user computing as well as bringing benefits such as electronic mail and the sharing of scarce resources.

- **Training:** The computer centre is usually responsible for training end users in the use of development packages. As well as providing end users with the necessary skills this is also an important mechanism for developing a culture of standards following.

- **Data administration:** The computer centre will also be responsible for defining the corporate data structure so that it meets the needs of the organization including, of course, those of the end users.

- **Research:** End users will rely on the computer centre to be continuously aware of developments in the software and hardware market. The mature computer centre is providing a research service to ensure that the needs of end users are satisfied.

The role of end users

- **Applications portfolio identification:** One of the benefits conferred by end-user computing is the autonomy granted to the development of applications meeting user requirements. However, this should not be done independently of corporate

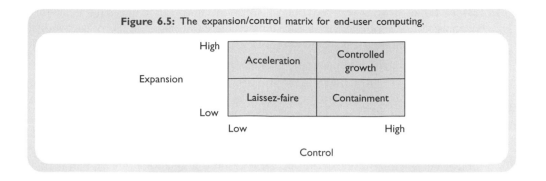

Figure 6.5: The expansion/control matrix for end-user computing.

objectives, nor should it be done in isolation from similar or complementary developments in other departments. It may be the case that cross-departmental applications are implemented. This coordination facility is not easily established.

- **Applications development and implementation:** End-user departments are responsible for applications development. This must be in accordance with policies and standards set out by the computer centre.
- **Applications operation:** As the end user is responsible for the application the end user is also responsible for security. This includes following procedures for secure access, backup and recovery. Once again it is usual that standards in these areas will be set by the computer centre.

Influences on end-user computing development

Managerial approaches to end-user computing should be designed to create effects in accordance with the information systems strategy of the organization. The aims will always attempt to maximize the benefits and minimize the disadvantages of end-user computing. Two important influences on end-user computing need to be managed (Munro *et al.*, 1987):

- the rate of expansion of end-user computing
- the level of control over end-user computing activities.

The rate of expansion is managed by: (a) making hardware and software easier/more difficult to obtain; (b) making information easier/more difficult to obtain; (c) imposing/relieving the end-user departments of the costs of end-user computing. The level of control over activities is managed by: (1) more or less restrictive standards over the purchase of hardware/software; (2) the level of requirement of mainframe use as compared to microcomputer use for applications; (3) restrictions on access to data.

In general the organization may manage the rate of expansion to yield a high or low rate of growth of end-user computing. Similarly by use of the above levers the organization may ensure a high or low level of control over end-user activities. The matrix of possibilities that this yields is shown in Figure 6.5. High expansion strategies are associated with forcing the growth of end-user computing in order to obtain its benefits. High control strategies are aimed at limiting the disadvantages of end-user computing, particularly those associated with lack of standards, duplication and waste. As can be seen there are four broad possible mixes of strategy:

1. **Laissez-faire:** This is the 'no policy' situation. End-user computing is neither encouraged nor controlled. This state typifies the early stages of the organizational growth path – either the isolation or the standalone stage in the Huff growth model.

2. **Containment:** Here the organization concentrates its strategies on channelling any end-user activities. The growth of end-user computing is not organizationally encouraged by its policies yet it is recognized that where such activities occur they must be controlled lest organizational disadvantages result.

3. **Acceleration:** The policies taken by an organization wishing to 'kick start' end-user computing will stimulate growth of activity without emphasis being placed on control. An organization adopting policies within this quadrant will be risk taking. This is unusual as it is consonant with a planned diminution of computer centre control.

4. **Controlled growth:** Policies are in place both to encourage expansion and at the same time to ensure a directed effort at the organizational level. This is a characteristic of a mature level of organizational end-computer development and activity. It corresponds to a situation in which the roles of the end users and of the computer centre as identified in the previous two sections are fully realized.

In summary, the essence of the analysis of Munro *et al.* is that there are just two dimensions to manage with respect to end-user computing: the rate of expansion and the level of control over activities. Depending on how these are managed the organization will have end-user computing broadly falling into one of the four categories (though in reality these categories shade into one another).

Generic management strategies for end-user computing

Gerrity and Rockart (1986) defined four generic management strategies for end-user computing. These offer a different perspective on the management of end-user computing from that of Huff *et al.* in the previous section, though one that is not necessarily in conflict with it. The four generic strategies are examined below.

1. With the **monopolistic approach** the computer centre attempts to block the development of end-user computing. This is not so much a strategy for management as a strategy for prevention. It can only succeed for a short time. The pressures, mentioned earlier, fuelling the growth of end-user computing eventually make this policy untenable. In particular the combination of the backlog of applications waiting for development, the increasing computer literacy of end users and the decreasing cost/increasing power of microcomputers and software ensure that this policy ultimately fails.

2. The **laissez-faire** approach involves doing nothing to stimulate, prevent or interfere with the growth or control of end-user computing. Once again this is not so much a policy for the management of end-user computing as the absence of one. With *laissez-faire*, end-user computing may initially flourish but soon the problems associated with the lack of control start arising. In particular the inevitable lack of standards causes difficulties. In addition the duplication of end-user effort, poor selection of inappropriate (and often expensive) hardware and software, and the lack of training make this an untenable generic policy in the long run.

3. The **information centre approach** offers both support and control. The computer centre designates specific groups of staff who are assigned to respond to the needs of end-user computing. These needs could be for training, package support and installation, analysis of needs, production of user support documentation, and applications development. The emphasis is on creating an organizational culture of support for end-user computing. The identified support groups are decentralized from the computer centre. However, because these groups are organizationally linked to the computer centre and are themselves computing professionals they will ensure that proper standards are maintained over the development and use of end-user applications. This is a common approach in many organizations. However, its very strength – the presence of computer professionals in a support role thus ensuring standards – is also a weakness. The support personnel will still not have the requisite knowledge of the business activities they support.

4. In the **management of the free economy approach** the relationship between the computer centre and the end users is altered. This approach recognizes the importance both of providing the end users with freedom to define their own needs and yet at the same time of providing the end user with the skilled support needed to guide development and ensure standards. The balance is achieved by following a number of guidelines:

    (a) A clear statement of the strategy for end-user computing is needed. This should be a senior management function, which must identify the role of end-user computing within the information systems strategy and the business strategy.

    (b) Balance between the responsibilities of the computer centre and of the end users must be clearly articulated.

    (c) The provision of end-user support should be by an information centre independent of the computer centre. In this way end users will be assured of their autonomy.

    (d) Identification of a range of critical end-user applications must be made. These are then given a high organizational priority.

    (e) There is a continuing emphasis on improvement, growth and autonomy for end-user computing through the use of education.

The management of end-user computing is regarded as important yet there is no received wisdom on the most appropriate strategy. For other views see Galletta and Hufnagel (1992) and Clark (1992).

End-user applications development – prototyping

One method of developing an application is to carry out the process of development through a series of linear stages. In this approach the computer centre is heavily involved at all times. The process can be summarized in the following way:

A user department identifies a need satisfiable by a computerized system. The computer centre will investigate and provide a feasibility study and report. If this report and its cost implications are accepted by management then computer centre personnel carry out a detailed analysis of the data and activities and specify a systems design that will satisfy these. Upon acceptance of the design, the computer centre develops software, purchases and installs hardware, tests the system and finally hands it to the end users for ongoing use.

The previous paragraph summarizes a linear approach to systems development. Each stage of the project is completed before proceeding to the next. Clear specifications and reports are provided at each stage. The computer centre is responsible for managing and working on what may be a very large project, involving many staff, with a large budget, to be developed over a lengthy period. This approach is at odds with the type of end-user development examined in the preceding sections. In the linear approach end users have no involvement at most stages in the development process. The linear approach has had numerous significant successes (and some failures!) in the design and delivery of large well-defined systems. The approach is covered extensively in later chapters on structured process and data analysis, design and implementation. However it may not be the best way forward for the development of decision support systems, where end-user knowledge and involvement is important and there exist applications development tools and 4GLs. In this case **prototyping**, involving end users, may be the most appropriate development method.

Prototyping: Prototyping is the approach where systems are developed swiftly, without having undergone a complete analysis and specification. The system that is developed is known as the **prototype**. The process relies on the prototype system itself being an aid to the specification – by consideration of the prototype and identification of its weaknesses an improved version can be developed. Prototyping also relies on the presence of software tools to produce prototypes quickly. Typically, users take part in the prototyping process either with or without the aid of the computer centre. The process is thus heavily user-orientated. There are two types of prototype:

- **Discardable prototypes:** In this situation the prototype is produced and assessed as to its suitability in meeting user needs. An operational version of the system is then written in a third-generation language and is used for ongoing work. Discardable prototypes are developed when there is a need to produce a final version that is technically efficient in the way it uses computing power. This is most common if a large volume of data needs manipulation. The discardable prototype written in the 4GL may have been produced quickly, but is unlikely to use code that is efficient. Other features, such as error-checking routines and security, will need to be added to the final operational system.

- **Operational prototypes:** In the development of a system using prototyping it is not uncommon for a first prototype written in a 4GL to be refined and replaced by a second. This in turn may undergo successive alterations until a final version that satisfies the user is good enough to become a working version. At the various stages of development and use the prototype is always thought of as being the current version open to change as needs arise. The approach is only possible through the use of fast systems-building tools and 4GLs. The process of development is one of iteration.

Advantages of prototyping:

1. By using prototyping it is possible to obtain working versions of a system very quickly, often within days. This is particularly important where decision support systems are involved. With these systems, as dictated by the varying information needs of management in making decisions, the type of computer-based support needed may vary within a short period of time. It is not easy for linear methods, with their long lead times, to be so responsive.

2. Often it is difficult to provide clear detailed specifications for the requirements of a system. This may be because these requirements are not readily understood. With a linear approach it is assumed that there is a clear understanding both of the current set of operations and of those that need to be computerized. Unless this condition is met developers may be forced into some type of prototyping which can, amongst other advantages, be viewed as a systems specification method.

3. Prototyping is end-user driven. It should therefore meet the requirements of end users. Involvement in the development of a system is one of the ways in which a user gains confidence and understanding of the system. This in turn increases the likelihood of a system's being successful. Many of the benefits of end-user computing are realized with the prototyping approach to development.

4. A system developed through operational prototyping is capable of easy adaptation.

Disadvantages of prototyping:

1. Because of prototyping's iterative nature, there is no clearly defined deliverable or completion deadline. This may give rise to considerable management concern. One of the guidelines of project management is to specify deliverables, deadlines and budgets. None of these clearly fits the prototyping approach.

2. As has been stated above the prototyping approach is aimed at obtaining speedily working systems meeting user requirements in terms of functionality. Code inefficiencies may be a drawback.

Prototyping is most appropriate in the following situations:

- The user finds it difficult to define the requirements of the system clearly.
- It is important to develop a system quickly – this is often the case with systems needed for decision support.
- User satisfaction, understanding and confidence are important considerations.
- Appropriate development tools are available.
- Users are committed to being involved with applications development.
- End-user autonomy is regarded as important.
- Low-volume transaction processing is involved.

Prototyping is least likely to be appropriate when:

- Appropriate development tools are not available and not understood by the users/computer centre.
- End users are unwilling to commit the necessary development time to prototype development.
- High-volume transaction processing is required.
- Technical efficiency in the use of computer-processing resources is a high priority.

Because of the nature of decision support systems and their relation to end-user computing, prototyping is an important approach to applications development. Expert systems are one class of decision support system. They are often developed by prototyping methods. An example of how prototyping is applied to expert system development is given extensive treatment in Chapter 17. Prototyping is also an important component of approaches such as Rapid Applications Development (RAD) using CASE tools. These are covered in Chapter 15.

6.6 Human–computer interaction

Early in the development of business information systems it was realized that the way the screen or printed output was designed influenced the ease and accuracy with which users understood the information supplied by the computer. It was also recognized that input screen design was also crucial to input performance and accuracy.

Attention was given to the design of the **man–machine interface** (MMI), as it was called, in order to ensure maximum effectiveness of the information system. Concerns concentrated on presenting information that was necessary and sufficient to user needs and to present that information in the most uncluttered way. Determination of what information was necessary and sufficient was achieved through a careful analysis of the task for which the user needed the information. (The reader's attention is drawn to the section on input/output design in Chapter 14 for further coverage of related issues.)

It is now recognized that this approach is no longer sufficient for the following reasons:

● The development of decision support systems has brought with it a recognition of the change of emphasis from information supplied in order to perform a task to information supplied in order to support a decision. As has been stressed earlier in the chapter the use of the computer for decision support involves not only an analysis of the decision but also the decision maker's cognitive style, the objectives of the decision, and the organizational setting within which the decision is taken. The focus on screen design is no longer sufficient.

● The increase in end-user computing, particularly the involvement of end users in applications development, has meant that designers of development tools are required to take into account the background, skills and objectives of these end users. Without attention to this point, development tools could well turn out to be technically powerful but unusable.

● Developments in computing power and the sophistication of software, particularly dealing with graphics, have led to a range of pictorial screen possibilities. This has made possible a much richer set of methods of communication with the user. It is easier to take into account the vastly increased range of people using computers and the purposes for which they use them.

● Failure of computers to achieve the business objectives for which they were designed has often been put down to user resistance and a failure to take into account user needs (as distinct from the information a user requires to perform a task). Several studies on the introduction of new technologies, including information technology, suggest that designers need to extend their focus beyond the narrow technical system to be designed. They should also take into account the interrelationship between the technical system, the tasks to be performed, the people involved in these and the organizational setting.

All of the above has shifted the emphasis from the man–machine interface as the focus of design to a consideration of the interaction of the human with the computer systems in an organizational setting. This is the study of **human–computer interaction (HCI)**.

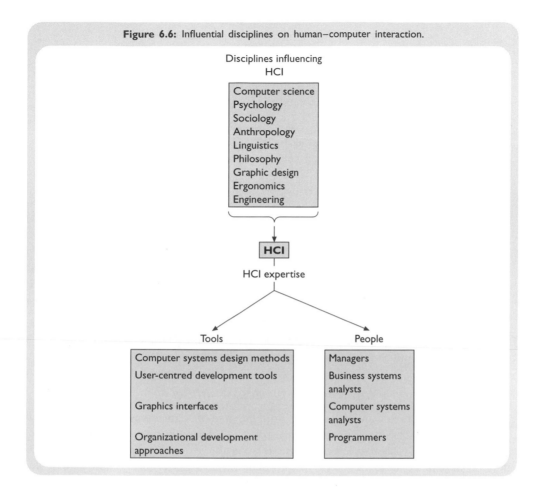

Figure 6.6: Influential disciplines on human–computer interaction.

Disciplines influencing
HCI

Computer science
Psychology
Sociology
Anthropology
Linguistics
Philosophy
Graphic design
Ergonomics
Engineering

HCI

HCI expertise

Tools

Computer systems design methods

User-centred development tools

Graphics interfaces

Organizational development approaches

People

Managers

Business systems analysts

Computer systems analysts

Programmers

The phrase 'human–computer interaction' appeared in the mid-1980s. There are many definitions. The following gives a picture of the scope of the term:

Human–computer interaction is a discipline concerned with the design, evaluation and implementation of interactive computing systems for human use and with the study of the major phenomena surrounding them. (ACM SIGCHI, 1992, p. 6)

It is important to realize that what distinguishes human–computer interaction is the last phrase – the study of the major phenomena surrounding them. This goes far beyond the scope of input/output screen design.

The major features of human–computer interaction design for computerized information systems are:

1. The approach is user centred. End users are involved as much as possible in the design process. Involvement may occur though users' building systems with user-orientated development tools, or by participation in the analysis and design process.

2. The approach integrates knowledge from a wide range of disciplines. The major influential disciplines in the area of human–computer interaction are shown in Figure 6.6.

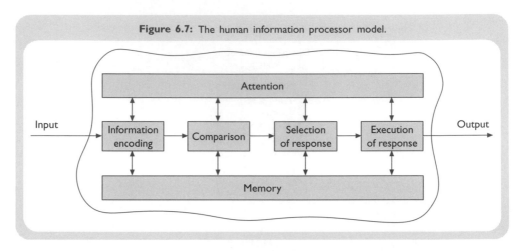

Figure 6.7: The human information processor model.

3. Rather than the development of a system occurring in a linear fashion (analysis through design to implementation), the process of design involves iteration of various stages. Often this involves the building of prototypes, which can be used to test the efficacy of the human–computer interaction.

In order to account properly for the human in human–computer interaction design it has been necessary to utilize a model of the human within the process.

6.6.1 The human information processor model

One of the most influential models derives from the area of cognitive psychology, in which the human is treated as an information processor. The human information processor model starts out from the basis that information enters via the senses through the processes of attention and perception. Decoding of information takes place and comparison of the internal representation of the information is made with the internal representations within the memory. A response is selected, executed and output. Within the model information is processed in a linear manner (see Figure 6.7). By concentrating on the sequence of operations and their timing a proper account can be taken of the human in human–computer interaction. Areas of general interest, amongst others, would be on:

- how information is perceived and encoded
- how information/knowledge is represented in memory
- how comparisons are made
- how information is stored and retrieved from memory

and specifically on:

- how humans represent models of familiar objects to themselves
- how users learn to use computer systems.

The human information processor model has been profoundly influenced by the development of computing itself. More sophisticated versions of the simplified model outlined here have included, for example, analogs of serial and parallel processing, and of buffer stores.

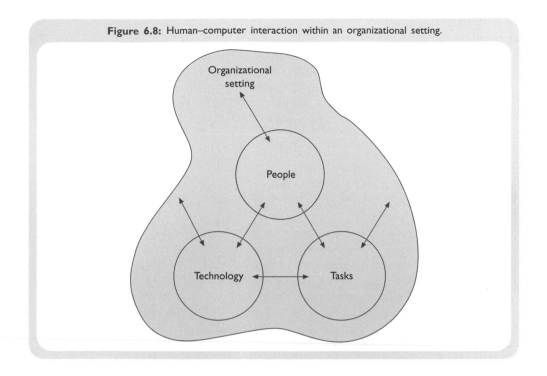

Figure 6.8: Human–computer interaction within an organizational setting.

6.6.2 The distributed cognition approach

The human information processor model has recognized that the human is more than merely the provider of information to, and receiver of information from, the interface with a computer system. The user has a task to perform and will process information internally for the execution of this task. The basis of the approach assumes that an understanding of the internal processing within the mind of the user will enable the design of a better interactive system.

Later approaches to human–computer interaction recognize that the human information processor model is too limited. Its concentration on the individual, the computer and the task leaves out important dimensions of human–computer interaction. Specifically:

● Users do not carry out individual information-processing tasks in theoretical settings. Rather the user performs part of a complex function involving many interrelated tasks for a purpose.

● This function occurs in a real organizational setting.

● Users interact with one another, particularly in teams.

Distributed cognition is an evolving theoretical framework for human–computer interaction that takes account of these points. The approach goes beyond the individual to viewing activities as involving the interaction of people, technology and tasks in an organizational setting (see Figure 6.8). The emphasis is on the study and design of functional systems that concentrate on the way information is transmitted and processed through the various components of the system in order to perform a function such as accounting control. The components will include computers and humans. This and similar approaches have influenced the development of systems design methodologies. See, for example, the socio-technical approach and soft systems analysis – both covered later in Chapter 15.

Human–computer interaction involves concepts that pervade many aspects of analysis, design and the use of information systems. The reader is referred to other parts of this text, particularly input/output design, Windows interfaces, sociotechnical design, soft systems analysis, knowledge representation techniques, group decision support and prototyping.

Summary

The last four decades have seen the rapid improvement and extensive use of the computer in business data processing and information provision.

Decision support systems make use of many of these aspects of modern technology. They aid, rather than replace, decision making. They may involve the selection and analysis of data from a corporate database, the use of models for predicting outcomes, optimization techniques, or the application of details of particular cases to general rules in order to support decisions. Decision support systems allow flexible access to data and the interactive use of models. These systems supply information to managers for semi-structured problems. In the design of decision support systems the emphasis is on standalone systems rather than the grand design of the total integrated decision support system. Because the development of a decision support system is driven by the type of decision-making process and the information needs of the decision, end users play a prominent role in design. Fourth-generation languages, spreadsheets, expert systems shells and tools, and model generators are all used in decision support system (DSS) design.

Group decision support systems are a more recent development that take account of the fact that many decisions are taken in group situations. The group decision support system involves not only standard technology for decision support, but also specific software to aid group activities such as brainstorming, voting and policy formation. Group decision support takes place in carefully constructed environments with an experienced facilitator to enhance the decision process.

End-user computing has been fuelled by the need to develop systems, particularly decision support systems, that speedily meet the needs of users. This has been facilitated by the presence of easy-to-use enabling software. 'End users' is a term covering a wide range of individuals, involving different types of skill and different information requirements. The growth of end-user computing progresses through several stages in an organization depending on the level of integration of applications. At all stages to be successful it is necessary to manage the process. The computer centre is expected to set standards and also to take on the role of the provision of training, education and technical support to end users in the development of their own systems. There are several different approaches to the management of end-user computing. One emphasizes the importance of managing the balance between control and expansion. Another concentrates on the role of the end-user support and examines the information centre concept.

▷

The traditional linear development process for systems, where progression is through a number of stages culminating in the final implementation of the system, may not be appropriate for the production of decision support systems. Prototyping is an alternative that is compatible with the need to develop systems quickly in situations where a clear specification is not available, when there is a need to involve users in development, and there is a desire to create adaptable responsive systems. Discardable prototyping is the approach that views the role of the prototype as the specification of the functionality of the desired system. The final version is written to ensure greater technical efficiency in computer processing. In operational prototyping the prototype is successively and interactively refined until it becomes the final version. Prototyping has been made possible by the design of 4GLs and applications development tools.

Developments within decision support systems, the rise of end-user computing and prototyping have emphasized the need for a theory on the way in which the user interacts with computer systems. The study of human–computer interaction provides for this. Approaches that look merely at input/output screen design have been superseded by those that regard the user as an information processor in performing a task (human information processor model). Later approaches have attempted to remedy the limitations of this approach by concentrating on the functions performed by users and technology within a real organizational setting.

Exercises

1. Why has there been a movement towards the use of microcomputers in large organizations rather than relying wholly on centralized mainframe resources staffed by experienced and highly trained personnel?

2. Identify characteristics of a decision support system and explain how these distinguish decision support systems from the more general notion of an information system.

3. What classes of decision support system are there? Give examples of each.

4. In Chapter 1 decision making was divided into four stages. The first three were intelligence, design and choice. By selecting an appropriate example illustrate how decision support systems can be used in each of these stages.

5. Why are there many different types of aid and approach to the development of decision support systems?

6. What special advantages do spreadsheets confer over the use of pen and paper in accounting modelling?

7. Why is it important to have a facilitator in group decision making using a decision room?

8. What characteristics of group decision making distinguish it from individual decision making? How could these be supported by a GDSS? ▷

9. What are the risks associated with end-user computing? How can they be reduced?

10. By considering the classification of types of end user identify the types of training and support needed for each.

11. As a senior manager working in an organization that can best be described as adopting the monopolistic approach to end-user computing, what policies would you wish to see adopted in order to transform the management of end-user computing to a managed free-economy model?

12. What is the difference between a *computer centre* and an *information centre*?

13. What are the main features and benefits of prototyping?

14. You have been commissioned to conduct a third-party investigation into decision support systems as used in ABC CO. This has revealed that many departments are developing their own applications independently and without the knowledge of the computer centre. The computer centre has traditionally taken a very strong line against end-user computing and has been unwilling to provide support for end-user applications development. In the current situation the proliferation of end-user decision support systems involves duplication of resources, data and applications. The management culture of senior management is one of centralized control. How would you advise the company to proceed?

15. Distinguish between *input/output design* and *human–computer interaction design*.

16. For each of the disciplines mentioned in Figure 6.6 discuss how these may be of use in HCI design.

17. Outline the main differences in approach between the human information processor model and the distributed cognition model to understanding human–computer interaction.

References

● ACM SIGCHI (1992). *Curriculum for Human–Computer Interaction*. ACM Special Interest Group on Computer–Human Interaction Curriculum Development Group, New York
● Clark T. (1992). Corporate systems management: an overview and research perspective. *Communications of the ACM* February, 60–75
● Galletta D.F. and Hufnagel E.M. (1992). A model of end-user computing policy. *Information and Management*, **22**(1), 1–18
● Gerrity T.P. and Rockart J.F. (1986). End-user computing: are you a leader or a laggard? *Sloan Management Review*, **27**(4), 25–34
● Huff S.L., Munro M.C. and Martin B.H. (1988). Growth stages of end-user computing. *Communications of the ACM*, **31**(5), 542–50
● Munro M.C., Huff S.L. and Moore G. (1987). Expansion and control of end-user computing. *Journal of Management Information Systems*, **4**(3), 5–27

- Rockart J. and Flannery L. (1983). The management of end-user computing. *Communications of the ACM*, **26**(10), 776–84.

Recommended reading

- Alter S. (1980). *Decision Support Systems: Current Practice and Continuing Challenges.* Workingham: Addison-Wesley

  This is one of the early classic texts on decision support systems. It is based on empirical research into a large number of systems and contains several well-developed cases.
- Carr H.H. (1988). *Managing End-User Computing.* Englewood Cliffs NJ: Prentice-Hall

  A comprehensive introduction to end-user computing and information centres from the point of view of management. The book concentrates on organizational development issues.
- Edwards J.S. and Finaly, P.A. (1997). *Decision Making with Computers: the Spreadsheet and Beyond.* London: Pitman

  Aimed at the reader with existing knowledge of the use of computers and spreadsheets, the intention of the book is to explain new decision-making techniques which will enable the most effective use to be made of the spreadsheet facilities. It also contains chapters on the methodology of good spreadsheet design. It is aimed at the business person rather than the computer scientist.
- Grey P., ed. (1994). *Decision Support and Executive Information Systems.* Englewood Cliffs NJ: Prentice-Hall

  This is a series of articles on areas such as the concept of decision support, DSS case studies, group decision support systems, executive information systems and case studies, and expert systems. The book is suitable as a core text on a decision support systems course.
- Hobuss J.J. (1991). *Applications Development Center: Implementation and Management.* New York: Van Nostrand Reinhold

  This book explores the notion of the applications development centre and its relation to applications prototyping and CASE. This is a readable text investigating the practical issues involved in application development centres. It is suitable for business and management students as well as those studying computer science.
- Maude H.E. and Willis G. (1991). *Rapid Prototyping: The Management of Software Risk.* London: Pitman

  The book is intended primarily for software engineers though students will find it a useful supplement to software engineering courses. The book outlines the main purposes of rapid prototyping and its associated project management. It has a comprehensive coverage of all major techniques of rapid prototyping, linking this to risk management.
- Meyer J. (1992). *Quattro Pro for Windows: Self Teaching Guide.* John Wiley

  An example of a standard introductory support text for spreadsheet modelling.
- Preece J. (1994). *Human–Computer Interaction.* Wokingham: Addison-Wesley

  This is an excellent text, which goes from introductory to an advanced level in the coverage of all the main issues in human–computer interaction. It combines theoretical frameworks and practical examples in a clear manner. Recommended as essential reading for a first text in HCI.
- Sprague R.H. Jnr and Watson H.J., eds (1993). *Decision Support Systems: Putting Theory into Practice* 3rd edn. Englewood Cliffs NJ: Prentice-Hall

This is designed as a core text for a decision support systems course (or as a supplement for an MIS course). It consists of 25 articles grouped into topics such as DSS – its conceptual foundations, its development, its environment, executive information systems, group decision support systems, and expert systems.

- Turban E. (1994). *Decision Support and Expert Systems* 4th edn. New York: Macmillan
  This is a comprehensive textbook covering all aspects of DSS and expert systems from the perspective of a manager wishing to know about management support technologies. It is has several case studies and chapter-end questions.

Chapter 7

File Organization and Databases for Business Information Systems

This chapter covers the organization, storage and access to business data held in files and databases. The chapter introduces key concepts in the representation of data at both a logical and a physical level. The central ideas behind files and file access are explained. Files and file-based approaches to data storage are important but they suffer from limitations. Database systems were developed as a response to these shortcomings. File-based and database approaches to data storage are compared. The central ideas underlying databases and database management systems are explained. As well as highlighting the facilities offered by database systems, the importance of data models is stressed. Three main types of database model are covered – network, hierarchical and relational. The analysis of an organization's data requirements, the development of a data model for that organization and database design techniques are left to the chapter on data analysis and modelling within the chapters on systems analysis and design.

7.1   Files and file structures

The survival and successful growth of a business organization depends crucially on the data it keeps. Whether the business is computerized or not, much of this data will be held in files. A manufacturing company will keep files on its employees, customers, stock

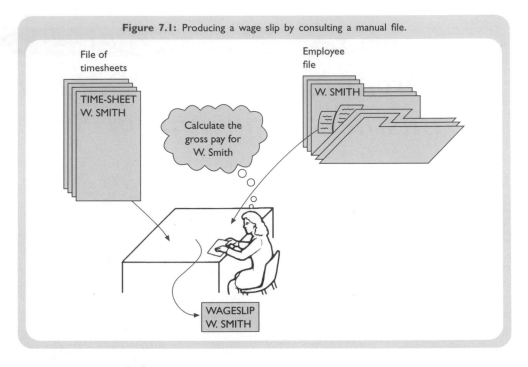

Figure 7.1: Producing a wage slip by consulting a manual file.

supplies, plant and many other items. These files will be updated by data on employee hours worked, customer sales and payments, and stock transactions. The files will be searched and sometimes sorted.

Simple concepts used in the operation of manual files are often a good guide to computerized data processing. Figure 7.1 is an illustration of the process of producing a wage slip. Time-sheet data on an employee is taken from a file. The relevant employee record is then found in the employee file. Data from this record is used to produce a wage slip and the employee record is updated. In a computer-based system exactly the same description could be applied. The only difference is that the files would be held on tape or disk and the process of producing a wage slip would be handled by a computer program.

Document files in manual systems contain records. For instance, an employee file will contain records on employees. These records are often collections of employee data prepared on preprinted company documentation. Other documents, old references and the like are kept in an individual employee's record. A cursory glance through document files may indicate that there is little organization in them.

By contrast, a **computer file** is more structured. It contains records of the same **record type** rather than a mixed collection of data held in different formats. An example of a simple employee file is shown in Figure 7.2(a). For each employee, data such as the employee# (# is the symbol that commonly abbreviates number), name, date of appointment, salary and sex are held. This data will be used in a number of activities such as preparing the payroll, establishing the length of service of employees and so on.

Each record is a collection of **data items** on each employee. These data items are also sometimes known as **field values**. For instance, in Figure 7.2(a) the field values are 1234, Smith, Jones, 14500. . . .

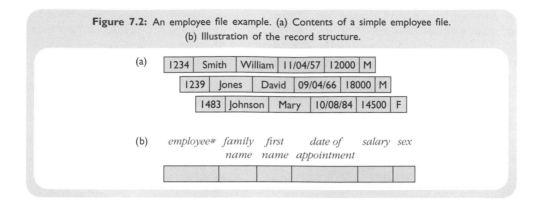

Figure 7.2: An employee file example. (a) Contents of a simple employee file. (b) Illustration of the record structure.

(a)

| 1234 | Smith | William | 11/04/57 | 12000 | M |

| 1239 | Jones | David | 09/04/66 | 18000 | M |

| 1483 | Johnson | Mary | 10/08/84 | 14500 | F |

(b) *employee# family first date of salary sex*
name name appointment

Figure 7.3: The relation between the world and data.

	World		**Data**		
Example		**Corresponds to**		**Example**	
Bill Smith	Object	⟶	Record	1234	Smith	William...
Employee	Object type	⟶	Record type	*(employee#, family name ...)*	
Sex	Attribute	⟶	Field	*sex*	
Male	Value of attribute	⟶	Field value or data item	M	

The **fields** themselves correspond to the types of data held on the employee and are *employee#, family name, first name, date of appointment, salary* and *sex*.

The record type (or structure as it is often called) is shown in Figure 7.2(b). Saying that a file contains records of the same record type means that all records in the employee file exhibit that structure. It is important to realize that we know that Smith is the family name of the employee and William is the first name *not* because of our knowledge of typical family and first names but rather because of the positions of the data items in the record structure.

The distinction between data and the objects in the world on which the data is kept is important. It is necessary to keep this distinction in mind in order to understand some of the modelling ideas covered in Chapter 12 on data analysis and modelling. This is summarized in Figure 7.3.

The **key field** of a record type is an important concept. It is the field that uniquely identifies a record. The key field in the employee record would be *employee#* because a value such as 1234 will only occur in *one* record. This is the reason that employers are given employee numbers – to identify them and their records. If there are two key fields in a record type one is called the **primary key**. This is the one that is most likely to be used to pick out the record. For instance, in an employee record the National Insurance number of the employee would also be a key but the *employee#* would be the primary key.

Obviously, the record structure in Figure 7.1(b) has too few fields to be realistic for an employee file. It is left as an exercise for the reader to list the fields that he or she would expect to find on an employee record type. Think of the processes for which a business might wish to use an employee record. The data needed for these will give a clear indication of which fields should exist.

7.2 Records and record structure

A simple record structure consists of a fixed number of fields of a fixed length. The record structure in Figure 7.2(a) is an example of this. There are shortcomings associated with these restrictions. An important problem arises with the desire to have many occurrences of the same field in a record. For example, in an employee file it may be useful to hold, not only the **current position**, **date of appointment** and **salary**, but also the history of the employee with the organization. One way to achieve this is to have a fixed number of fields for the past history. This may not be satisfactory. An employee may have held only one position with the firm, in which case several fields will be blank, or may have had more positions than can be accommodated by the number of repeated fields. In the latter case only the most recent history of the employee can be held. The solution is to allow a field or group of fields to be repeated. Figure 7.4(a) gives an example of this. Note that the key is underlined and that the repeating group of fields

Figure 7.4: (a) A two-dimensional record structure. (b) A three-dimensional record structure.

(a)

employee#	family name	first name	date of appointment	job description	salary	sex
1234	Smith	William	11/04/82	machinist	9200	M
			09/11/83	senior machinist	9800	
			04/01/85	foreman	10300	
			02/12/86	supervisor	12000	

Record structure

(*employee#, family name, first name, [date of appointment, job description, salary]* sex*)

(b)

Record structure

(*part#, part description, quantity held [component#, quantity used, [supplier*]*]*)

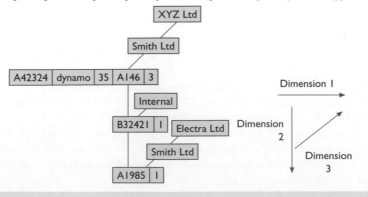

is indicated by **[field1, field2, . . .]***. The star symbol indicates repetition. The employee record shown is regarded as two-dimensional.

A record structure can have repeating fields within repeating fields. For instance, a record of stock held by a manufacturing company may contain a variable number of fields for the components and for each component a variable number of fields for the suppliers. This is shown in Figure 7.4(b). It is called a three-dimensional record structure.

Record structures can be multi-dimensional but details of the number of repeating groups and groups within groups must be held somewhere in the record. When programs are written to obtain information from these files the programmers' task is made considerably more complex. They now need to pay particular attention to the structure of the record as well as to the task for which the obtained data is to be used.

7.3   Physical and logical views of data

An important concept in data processing and systems analysis and design is the difference between a physical and a logical view of data. Broadly speaking, a **logical view** is concerned with the nature of the data or information as viewed independently from the physical details of storage or presentation. In contrast, a **physical view** involves physical aspects of the storage and presentation. The difference is important. A business computer systems analyst will be interested in the nature of the data stored and in what forms it needs to be retrieved. Exactly how this data is stored will be of less interest. Technical details on, say, disk sector division and blocking factors are not needed. The analyst is concerned with the use made of data in the functioning of the business. The technical systems analyst and the programmer, though, must pay attention to physical detail in order to design technically efficient storage and write programs that access data in stored files.

In the present context the difference between a logical and a physical view of files and record structures can be summarized as follows:

7.3.1   Records

A **logical** view of a record structure consists of the names of the record fields including repeating groups. A logical view of a record (logical record) is the set of data items filling that structure.

A **physical** view of a record structure shows how the logical view of the structure is implemented. The following, from Figure 7.2, illustrates physical details:

- The **employee#** consists of up to six characters preceded by leading blanks.
- The *family name* and the *first name* consist of characters, the two fields being divided by a*.
- The *salary* consists of a binary number 16 bits long.
- The *date* consists of six characters representing the year/month/date in that order – for example, 6 February 1996 is represented as 960206.

A **physical record** is the minimum chunk of data that is transferred between the storage medium and the CPU in the course of data processing. It is sometimes called a block. The physical record may contain many logical records or, if the logical records are large, several physical records may be spanned by one logical record.

7.3.2 Files

A **logical** view of a file is the representation of the logical records together with the order in which they are represented for storage and retrieval purposes. For instance, an employee file might have its records arranged in ascending order of *employee#* as they were in Figure 7.2.

A **physical** view of a file consists in the way that the physical records are stored. For example, an employee file can be stored on several disks with an index stored on a different disk from the disks on which the records are stored. The records can be stored physically adjacent to one another in ascending order of *employee#*. Once one track is filled, the next track inwards contains the next record. When records are deleted they may not be removed from the disk but merely marked with an *X* in the delete field of each physical record. These are all physical details of a file.

When programs are written, the programmer will need to be aware of some of the physical structure of the records and the way that the files may be spread across tracks. The analyst who is designing the file structure for a system, however, need initially only concentrate on the logical aspects of the files to ensure that the data held is sufficient for the task for which it is required. Later, the analyst will decide on how the file is to be physically arranged. The distinction between logical and physical views is never as clear cut in practice as has been suggested. Rather, there is a spectrum ranging from logical to physical on which a particular view will lie. As will be demonstrated in Chapters 9–14 on systems analysis and design, the distinction between logical and physical views of data, though difficult to grasp at first, is important because it runs right through the process of analysis and design.

7.4 Data storage – files, records and lists

There are many ways of categorizing files. In data processing there is an important division of files in terms of their usage. Files may be master, transaction or backup files.

1. A **master file** consists of records that contain standing data on entities that are of a permanent nature and are of importance for the successful operation of the business. For example, an employee master file holds the employee name, address and date of birth, all of which need little or no change, together with data on gross pay to date, tax paid to date which would be regularly updated. Master files can be logically organized in a number of ways. For example, an employee master file may be in employee number sequence or with an index on employee name or both.

2. A **transaction file** contains records, each of which relates to a single, usually dated, event or fact. These files are source data and are used to amend or update master files. For example a timesheet transaction file contains records, each of which has data on the number of hours worked by a particular employee.

3. **Backup files** are copies of transaction files and master files held for security purposes.

Files may be physically stored on disk in the following ways:

sequentially: records are physically ordered by some field such as employee number;

randomly: records are stored at a physical address computed by an algorithm working on a field value such as the employee number;

indexed: records are physically stored randomly with a sequentially ordered index field (e.g. by customer name) and a pointer to the physical location of each record;

indexed-sequential: records are physically stored sequentially ordered by some field together with an index which provides access by some, possibly other, field.

If files need only be processed sequentially, then they may be stored sequentially. The sequential update of an employee master file by timesheet data is an example. However, if individual records need to be accessed from time to time by some field, for example employee name, then one of the other storage methods must be used.

In the files considered so far, the individual records have not been connected to one another in any way. With a simple **list structure** each record has one field within it which points to (has the address of) another record in the structure. Thus a list could be linked by pointer fields that point from one record to another in ascending order of customer name alphabetically. Insertion and deletion of records merely involves re-adjustment of pointers. Sequential processing involves passing along the list. List structures may be extremely complex with many pointer fields in each record so that records can be accessed sequentially in many ways. Also indexes may be attached to list structures to allow maximum flexibility in data access. If all the fields of a record which can take values have indexes the file is said to be **fully inverted**.

Because pointer organizations allow data to be retrieved in flexible ways, list structures are amongst those used in databases. Access to the database and the insertion and deletion of records is controlled by specialized software called a database management system. This is covered extensively in later sections of this chapter.

7.5 File-based and database approaches to data storage

A central feature of a database approach is the recognition that data is an important resource of an organization. Data is not regarded merely as the input and output of the data-processing department but as a valuable asset that requires careful planning and management.

The database is a store of data, which may be used for many applications within the organization. It must be designed to service these and future needs. In particular, it must allow extraction of information for management information requirements in as flexible a manner as is needed for management decision making. For this reason the database is at the heart of a comprehensive and evolving management information system.

The main characteristics of a modern database are:

- It is an integrated store of shared data for servicing the requirements of many users and applications.
- It is structured in a manner that is logically meaningful to the organization. For example, if data were held both on employees and on the company projects on which they work, then in the database there would be a link between the data on each employee and the data on the projects on which they work.
- There is minimal redundancy of data; this means that as far as possible the same item of data will not be repeated in the database.

Modern databases are usually held online on disk. Databases require careful design because they hold information that is structured for the organization. An important aspect

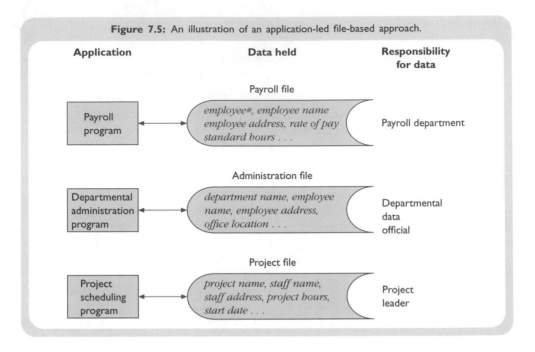

Figure 7.5: An illustration of an application-led file-based approach.

of management is the use of software to handle all data access to the database. This software, the **database management system**, interfaces between users and user applications and the database itself, so enabling centralized control over the data. The main characteristics of a modern database management system (DBMS) are:

● It is software that handles all read and write access by users and application programs to the database.

● It is capable of presenting users with a view of that part of the database that is relevant to their needs.

● It presents a logical view of data to users – details of how this data is stored and retrieved by the database management systems software are hidden.

● It ensures that the database is consistent.

● It allows authorization of different users to access different parts of the database.

● It allows the person in control of the database to define its structure.

● It provides various facilities for monitoring and control of the database.

The differences between a file-based and database approach towards data can be seen in Figures 7.5 and 7.6. There are three application programs considered in this example. In Figure 7.5, the company runs a payroll program that uses a payroll master file for employee details. The data on this payroll file is the responsibility of the payroll department. The company also runs a program for handling various departmental administration routines to do with staffing and staff locations. This was developed later and has its associated file, the administration file. Each department has an official who is responsible for forwarding data changes for this file. The company also has a program for aiding the scheduling of staff to the various projects on which they work. Ensuring that project

Figure 7.6: An illustration of a database management system interfacing user programs and a database.

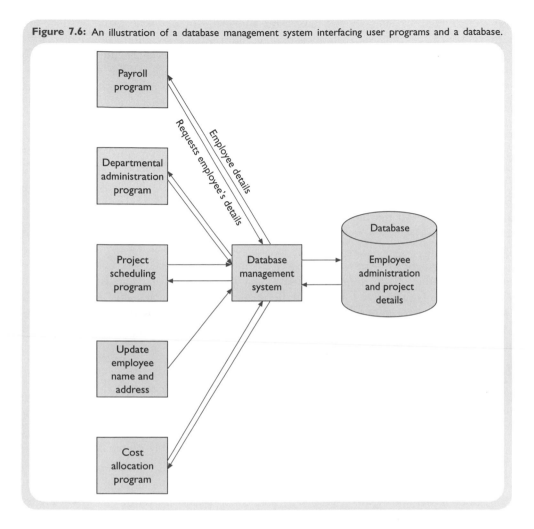

details are up to date is the responsibility of each project leader. This example typifies characteristics of the file-based approach:

- Files are developed in a piecemeal fashion to service the data needs of an application and are associated with that application.
- The same data may be repeated on many files – for example, *employee address*.
- The same data may be held under different names – for example, *employee name* and *staff name*.
- The physical characteristics of storage of the same data on different files may be different.
- The responsibility for data is dispersed.

Two main problems arise with this approach. First, amendment of data is likely to lead to inconsistent data being held by the organization. In the example, if an employee changes his address, unless this is notified to all persons responsible for files on which this data is held, updates will be haphazard and inconsistency will result. Second, the retrieval of data for new applications is difficult. Suppose it is required to develop a program that allocates costs against projects (for pricing purposes) and allocates costs against departments (for internal budgeting and management accounting). All this data is present but is spread over three files and is not easily accessible. It may be difficult to retrieve as it is not stored in a manner convenient for this new application.

The central weakness of the application-led approach is that files are tied to applications, not to the objects or entities to which those files refer. Another way of viewing the position of the data needs of the organization in the example is to recognize that there are three types of entities involved – **EMPLOYEES**, **DEPARTMENTS**, and **PROJECTS**. Not only may details be held on these entities but there are also relations between them. **EMPLOYEES** *work* on **PROJECTS** and are *members* of **DEPARTMENTS**. These relationships are ignored in the file-based approach only being recognized when needed for an application. Databases and database management systems manage to encode these relationships.

In Figure 7.6 the database approach overcomes the difficulties experienced by the applications-led file-based approach by storing all the organizational data in an integrated manner, which is accessible to all applications. Access to this database is always through the database management system. This ensures that consistency is maintained if data is altered, such as an employee address. The DBMS also provides data in the form required for new applications – for example, a cost allocation program.

7.5.1   The advantages of using a database approach

1. **Data redundancy is reduced:** In the application-led file-based approach data, such as *employee name*, may be unnecessarily duplicated in various files. This is a waste of storage space and can be reduced, if not entirely eliminated, in a database system.

2. **Data consistency can be maintained:** A corollary of the elimination of redundancy is that update inconsistency is reduced. Some inconsistency may result unless care is taken in database design because some duplication of data is not eliminated.

3. **Independence of data and programs is possible:** In the file-based approach considered earlier in this chapter the application programs are closely interdependent with the file structure. For example, the payroll programs will need to 'know' how the employee file is organized in order to access records. It makes a great deal of difference if the file is organized sequentially by *employee#* or organized with an *employee#* index. At the level of the record, the order of the fields and the length of each will probably need to be 'known' by the program. It is not possible to change the file organization or change the record structure without changing the program or programs that access it. The program is dependent on the data.

   In a database system many programs will share the same data. It is not desirable to require each program to be changed when there is a change in the physical form of storage of data. (Changes in physical storage can be made for reasons of technical efficiency.) The database management system maintains the same view of the data to the accessing program no matter how the data may be physically reorganized on the disk.

4. **A logical view is presented to the user or user programs:** Following from point (3) it is clear that the view of data presented to users or user programs must be independent of the physical storage details – it must be logical. Many database management systems allow different logical views of the same data to be presented to different users or programs. This is important as it frees programmers from a need to pay attention to the physical details of storage and allows them to concentrate on the applications to be coded. In the example covered earlier in this chapter it is much easier for programmers to develop the cost allocation program if it is not necessary to consider the physical details of data retrieval. Programmers can concentrate on *how* to do a task not on how to obtain the data to do it.

5. **Applications development is enhanced as data sharing is possible:** The ability to use the database management system to retrieve data across the database in any required form once it is stored opens up the range of applications for which the existing data can be used.

6. **Standards may be enforced:** The fact that all access to data occurs via the database management systems allows the individual responsible for this, the database administrator (DBA), to ensure that applications standards are followed in the representation of data.

7. **Security is more easily implemented:** The database administrator will control access to the database. The DBA can ensure that authorization codes for users are set restricting their access to only those parts of the database and for only the functions (read, write, copy) that are legitimate to their data purposes. Databases allow more effective control over access than the dispersal of responsibility associated with file-based systems. However, a breach of security may lead to a greater risk, as more data is accessible than with a traditional file-based system.

The advantages of a database approach can be summarized in that it leads to a system where:

- Data management and control is more effective.
- The ability to share data is increased.

7.5.2 Disadvantages of a database approach

Databases have become more common in recent years but they still have limitations and there are circumstances that might suggest a file-based environment is more appropriate.

1. **Database design involves time and cost:** When an organization opts for a database approach it is necessary to pay considerable attention at the outset to the design of the database structure. This involves a study of the entities on which the organization wishes to hold data, the types of data to be held on these entities and the relationships and links between them. In comparison, a file-based approach leads to a piecemeal design of files for applications as they are required. This both simplifies design and spreads the cost over time as applications arise.

2. **Database hardware and software costs need to be taken into account:** The database management system for a mainframe computer system is a complex piece of software costing many thousands of pounds. It is usual to use a standard package

such as IDMS or ORACLE. As the entire database must be online all the time it is also essential to purchase large amounts of disk storage.

3. **Database access is slower than direct file access:** Recovery of data from a database using a DBMS involves another layer of software over and above an application program directly reading a file. The database may be physically implemented using large numbers of pointers, which will slow up access. These two considerations imply that database access is considerably slower than reading files.

Over time, disk technology has become cheaper and faster, which diminishes the importance of some of the disadvantages and partially explains why there is a drift towards business databases. In general, a file-based approach will seem more appropriate (as compared to a database) if:

- Different applications require different data.
- Fast, repetitive transaction processing in high volumes is to be undertaken.
- The application needs of the organization are unlikely to change over time.
- Information production is according to standard formats – little flexibility is required.

For these reasons it is common to use file-based systems for accounting purposes, particularly financial accounting and bookkeeping, where heavy transaction processing occurs. The flexible requirements of internal management accounting and the provision of information for tactical and operational management decisions are best served by database systems supplying data through management information systems.

7.5.3 Database users

The corporate database is an important resource and may be needed by several types of user. These generally fall into one of three categories. Each has differing levels of understanding of the database and differing requirements.

The database administrator

The database administrator (DBA) is an experienced and senior member of the computer centre staff. The post requires involvement with different categories of user as well as extensive technical knowledge. The dependence of the organization on the smooth and effective management of its data resource ensures that the DBA's post is one of considerable responsibility. The DBA is typically involved in:

- assisting the development of the database during the analysis and design life cycle of the information system;
- achieving and maintaining an acceptable level of technical performance of the database;
- attaining a satisfactory level of security including:
  - ensuring that authorization codes for database access are implemented according to the rules of the organization;
  - ensuring that backup and recovery facilities in case of database failure are adequate;
  - establishing integrity constraints within the database;

- monitoring usage of the database from the point of view of accounting and the efficient utilization of the data resource;
- reorganizing the physical structure of the database when necessary;
- setting standards for documentation and data representation within the database;
- liaising with users of the database to ensure that their data requirements are satisfied;
- educating the organization on the use and availability of the database.

Applications programmers

Applications programmers are responsible for developing and maintaining programs for the functions required by the organization. Many of these programs will involve manipulation of data held in the database. Major programming languages contain instructions that enable calls to be made on the database via the database management system. This **data manipulation language** (DML) typically contains instructions governing the handling of data such as **STORE**, **RETRIEVE**, **MODIFY**, **DELETE** and **INSERT**. The programmer needs to know enough of the structure of the database in order to provide correct data-handling instructions in the host language.

Casual users

These are management and clerical personnel who make specific data enquiries of the database. This is an important group of users who are able to make *ad hoc* requests for information reports in a flexible way. They use simple query languages (see Section 7.5.4) for framing their requests. This group of users has been greatly liberated by the presence of online database systems. Previously, reports they required needed to be extracted in standard form and often produced at standard times. By being able to target their requests for information to what is relevant and obtaining speedy online responses their decision-making ability has become more effective.

7.5.4   Database utilities

In order to aid the DBA and other users in their tasks concerning the database utility programs or modules are commonly used.

Query languages

Query languages are designed for casual users making enquiries of the database. Unlike data manipulation language commands embedded in a host programming language such as COBOL, these languages can be used for *ad hoc* queries of the database. They are easy to understand and use and generally consist of near-English expressions. An example might be:

DISPLAY ALL EMPLOYEE.*employee-name* **FOR** EMPLOYEE.*employee-age* $\rangle$ 60

meaning 'display on the screen a list of employee names for all employees who are over 60 years old'.

It is easy to combine conditions in data enquiries. In the case of the employee/project/department example used earlier in this chapter, a typical request might be 'display all employee numbers and names for employees from any department located in London and working on more than two projects'. Such a request is easy to frame using a query language. It would be virtually impossible to extract such information from the file-based system. Examples of simple enquiries using actual query languages on databases are given in Sections 7.9 and 7.10.

Data dictionaries

A data dictionary may be defined as a store of data about data. The data dictionary will keep information on the record types, field names and types, and other information on the structure of the database. Data dictionaries are useful for the development and maintenance of the database structure. Nowadays data dictionaries are often part of the database itself.

Accounting and monitoring utilities

These are used by the DBA to determine the extent of use of the database by individuals, departments and other cost and use centres. This is useful information for charging the database to the various user departments.

Report generators

It is sometimes necessary to produce output data in a special format. This may be desirable for reasons of clarity or standardization in the company. Alternatively, there may be accepted and required formats for certain types of report. Common examples are balance sheets and profit and loss statements. Output data from a database is printed or displayed on the screen in a standard form. This is generally just a list of the data items produced by the database management system. Report generators are utilities that allow different formats to be defined for the data. They are generally powerful and easy to use.

Backup and recovery

In order to make sure that data is not lost irretrievably after a database failure it is common practice (from time to time) to dump or store the database on a secure medium. Between these dumps a record is automatically kept of every transaction that affects the database (insertion, deletion and modifications). This combination of the saved database plus the log file of these transactions allows the state of the database before failure to be recovered.

Concurrency control

Database contain data that may be shared between many users or user applications. Sometimes there may be demands for concurrent sharing. An example is the simultaneous access to inventory data in a multi-access system by two different users. No problem arises if each demand is to read a record but difficulties occur if both users attempt to modify the record at the same time. The database utility responsible for concurrent usage then 'locks' one user out until the modification by the other has been effected.

Physical reorganization

These aid the DBA with the efficient restructuring of the physical database when necessary. This restructuring is necessary as data modification, addition and deletion of records change the physical characteristics of the stored data resulting in slow access times or inefficient storage of data across many disks.

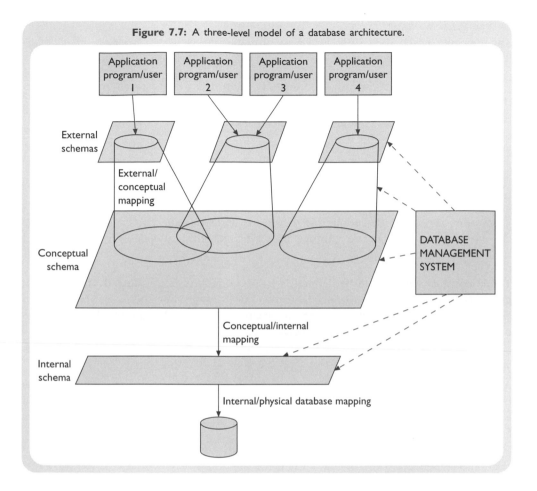

Figure 7.7: A three-level model of a database architecture.

7.6 A three-level architecture for databases

Some of the key reasons for the use of a database have been illustrated in terms of:

- the separation of the data from the applications that use it;
- the presentation of a logical view of the data independent of the physical details of storage;
- the restriction and presentation of only relevant data to users and application programs.

Central to the understanding of the way a database and DBMS works in achieving these aims is the concept of schemas and views. This is shown in Figure 7.7 (derived from the ANSI/SPARC Study Group's report in 1978).

In overview, the conceptual schema provides the logical view of the entire database, the external schemas provide 'tailored' views of the database for each application or user, and the internal schema provides information on the detailed aspects of data storage which have little to do with the logical content of the data.

Conceptual schema

The conceptual schema is the logical view of the entire database. Amongst other details it will contain a specification of:

- The types of data held on each entity of interest to the organization. For example, the following might be held on a supplier:

    supplier#:numeric(6) *supplier-name*:character(15)
    supplier-address:character(30). . . .

    This is similar to the specification of a record type.

- Any relationship between the entities. For example, suppliers PROVIDE products.

- Any restrictions on data – for example, *item-quantity* > 0.

- Authorization codes applicable to various items of data. For example, employee salary data may only be read by a user with authorization codes 5,6,9 and modified by a user with code 9.

The conceptual schema will be defined in a special language, the **data definition language** (DDL). This language is specific to the DBMS used. The schema can be regarded as derived from a model of the organization and should be designed with care as it is usual for its structure to remain relatively unchanged.

External schemas

An application program or user is uninterested in large sections of the database and is best presented with a view of the relevant sections. This is the external schema and it exists in a subset of the conceptual schema. There may be a different external schema for each user of the database.

For instance, it is usual for a user to require only certain types of record and logical relationships between these. Within these records the user may need access to only a few selected fields in order to perform the specified user tasks. The external schema supplies just this window on the conceptual schema.

Internal schema

This describes how the database is implemented in terms of pointers, hashing functions, indexes, stored record sizes and so on. It is concerned with storage details that are not part of a logical view of the database.

Mappings between schemas

As well as maintaining these views the DBMS needs to keep a record of how each view is connected to (that is, maps to) each other. For instance, components of the internal schema will be represented at a logical level by components of the conceptual schema. It must be possible to reorganize the physical database without altering the logical content of the database (conceptual schema) or to alter the conceptual schema without altering the existing external schemas. The presence of mappings enables this.

For instance, it may be necessary to add extra fields to hold details on an employee's health where health details were not held before. This alteration to the conceptual (and internal) schema should not affect existing external schemas that have no need of this data. Again, it may be decided to reorganize the storage characteristics of the database for efficiency reasons. Although this may affect the internal schema it should not affect either the conceptual or external schemas.

7.7 Models and schemas

It was stated in Section 7.6 that the conceptual schema was derived from a model of the organization. It is important to be clear that a conceptual schema is defined in a data definition language that is particular to the DBMS used. Each DBMS imposes different restrictions on what can and cannot be defined. Some database management systems severely limit what can be specified within the conceptual schema for the benefit of providing fast data access times. Others are very flexible at the expense of slow access speeds.

Most database management systems fall into one of three types depending on what restrictions are imposed. These types correspond to three distinct models of data structures – network, relational and hierarchical data models. The data model, then, is the type of data structure that is most appropriate for a DBMS. A conceptual schema is the definition of that model within the DBMS data definition language.

The three main types of data model surveyed here are important as they have influenced the development of commercial database software. Many other types of data model exist though they have not had the same impact on the industry. For each type of model, what constitutes the basis of an external, conceptual and (particularly) internal schema cannot be properly explained without reference to general or specific characteristics of database management systems exemplifying the model.

7.3.1 Data structures and occurrences

One of the main differences between a file and a database is that the former is simply a collection of records of the same type whereas the latter consists of:

- different types of records
- collections of records of each of these types
- links between the records depending on whether there are relationships in the world between the entities for which the records stand.

The database has structure that is absent from files. The most important structure from the point of view of the data models is the allowable links or relationships that exist between records of different types.

1:n relationships (one-to-many relationships)
Figure 7.8(a) shows the 1:n relationship existing between departments and the employees attached to them. The relationship is 1:n because each department may have many employees but each employee can only be attached to *at most* one department. The arrowhead is attached to the n side of the relationship. Occurrences of this structure are shown in Figure 7.8(b).

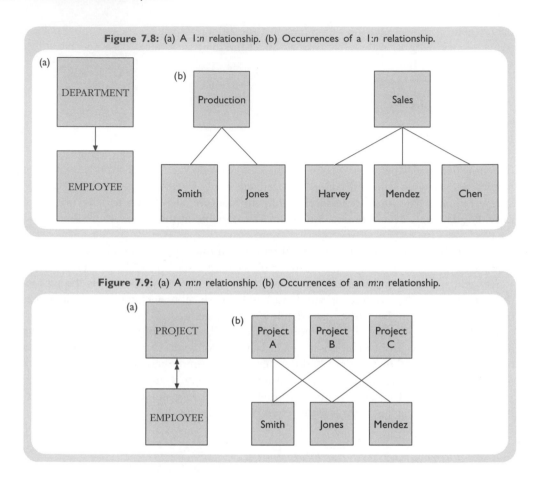

Figure 7.8: (a) A 1:*n* relationship. (b) Occurrences of a 1:*n* relationship.

Figure 7.9: (a) A *m:n* relationship. (b) Occurrences of an *m:n* relationship.

m:n relationships (many-to-many relationships)

Figure 7.9(a) shows the *m:n* relationship existing between employees and the projects on which they work. The relationship is *m:n*, or many to many, because each employee may work on many projects and each project may be worked on by many employees. Occurrences of this structure are shown in Figure 7.9(b).

The three main data models for databases are covered in the subsequent sections. The simple example model in Figure 7.10 is used to illustrate the restrictions of each of the data models.

7.8 Network models

The network model allows the representation of all 1:*n* relationships existing between records. The treatment here is in line with the recommendations of the Database Task Group (DBTG) report on the Conference on Data Systems Languages (CODASYL) in 1971 and following years. It is often referred to as the CODASYL model. The treatment follows the spirit of the approach, although CODASYL terminology is avoided where possible.

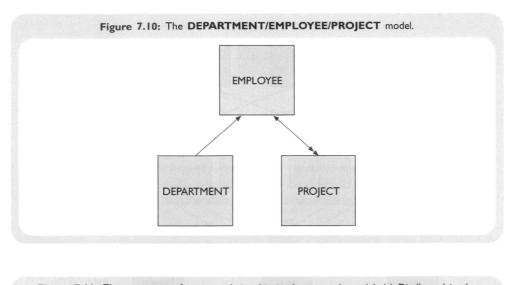

Figure 7.10: The **DEPARTMENT/EMPLOYEE/PROJECT** model.

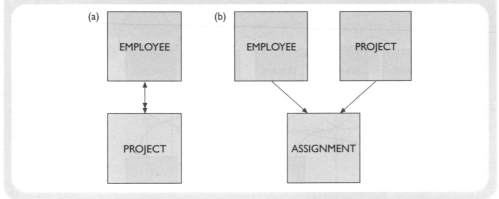

Figure 7.11: The treatment of an *m:n* relationship in the network model. (a) Disallowed in the network model. (b) Representation of an *m:n* relationship using link records.

7.8.1 The model structure

A major restriction on databases following the network model is that no many-to-many relationships are allowed. To see why this is limiting consider the projects/departments/ employees example used earlier. As well as having employees attached to departments, the organization also runs projects on which employees work. Each employee may work on many projects and each project has many employees working on it. This cannot be directly represented in the network model. Instead a dummy or **link** record type is used translating the many-to-many relationship into two one-to-many relationships. This is shown in Figure 7.11(a) and 7.11(b). Each employee works on many assignments and each project is served by many assignments. The link records need not contain any data and may represent nothing meaningful to the organization. It is just a trick to stay within the constraints of the network model. In (b) there might be data inside each **ASSIGNMENT** occurrence recording the amount of hours each employee works on each project.

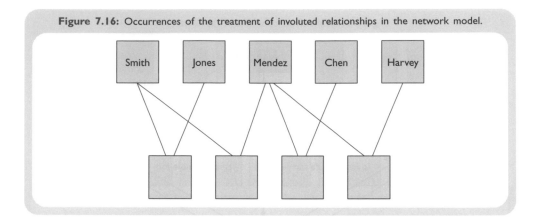

Figure 7.16: Occurrences of the treatment of involuted relationships in the network model.

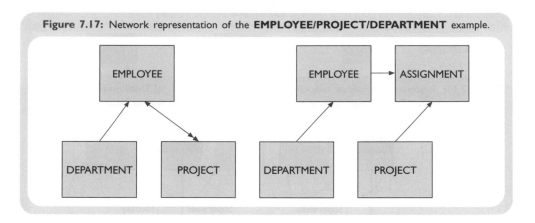

Figure 7.17: Network representation of the **EMPLOYEE/PROJECT/DEPARTMENT** example.

- For each record type – its name and a list of fields within the record.
- For each relationship – the name of the relationship, the record types at both the 1 and the n ends of the 1:n relationship (**set**, **owner**, and **member** in the CODASYL terminology).
- The logical order in which records on the n side of a 1:n relationship can be retrieved – this amounts to a statement of how the pointers are organized.
- Certain restrictions on whether records are obliged to be within relationships.

7.8.2 Data manipulation

Data can be inserted into and retrieved from databases exhibiting a network structure in very flexible ways. Resetting the pointers if a record is inserted or deleted is complicated, but this is automatically handled by the database management system. However, commercial systems, while allowing flexible record retrieval, require the user to have an understanding of the pointer organization in order to navigate around the database. This implies that the user is not presented with a truly logical view of the data. This is one of the main weaknesses of databases based on the network model.

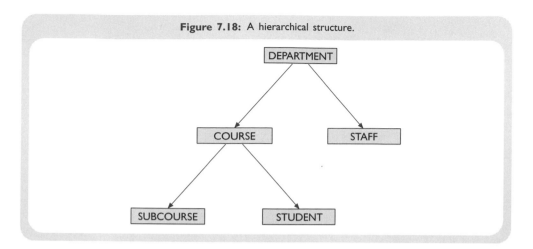

Figure 7.18: A hierarchical structure.

7.9 Hierarchical models

Databases and database management system software based on hierarchical data structures were the first to be developed. IBM's Information Management System (IMS) is one of the most commonly used systems.

7.9.1 The model structure

Hierarchical data models in common with network models do not allow direct representation of many-to-many relationships. They also have a further restriction that distinguishes them. The allowable structures are in the form of trees.

Figure 7.18 shows a hierarchy for part of a college database. The top record type, **DEPARTMENT**, is known as the **root**. The links between the various record types (or **nodes** as they are sometimes known) represent the relationships.

Each department may run many courses but each course is run by only one department. This relationship is represented by the one-to-many downward-pointing link between the **DEPARTMENT** and **COURSE** record types. Each **COURSE** consists of many **SUBCOURSES** and each **COURSE** has many **STUDENTS** registered on it. **COURSE** is a **parent** record type and **SUBCOURSE** and **STUDENT** are dependent record types at lower levels. They are all the **children** of **COURSE**. The tree consists only of one-to-many downward-pointing links.

Figure 7.19 illustrates three structures that are disallowed within the limitations of the hierarchical model but which would be representable within a network structure. Structure (a) is not a tree structure but is a network. If there is more than one path between any two record types then the structure is a network. Structure (b) contravenes the requirement that all relationships should be downward pointing. Structure (c) has more than one relationship between two record types and so is not a tree structure.

An instance of the hierarchical model shown in Figure 7.18 is given in Figure 7.20. Each record occurrence, apart from **Business**, is connected to only one record occurrence at a higher level. The record occurrences of **Marketing** and **Business/Economics** are known as **twins**. If a record is deleted then all records connected to it at a lower level are deleted. For instance, if the **Accounting** record is deleted (perhaps because the course is

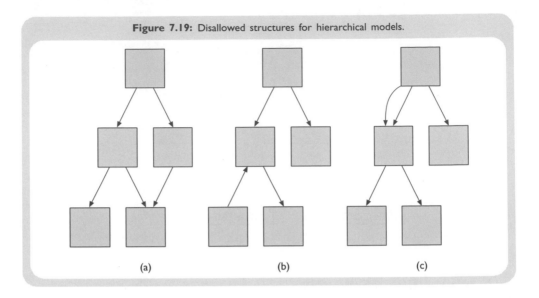

Figure 7.19: Disallowed structures for hierarchical models.

(a)   (b)   (c)

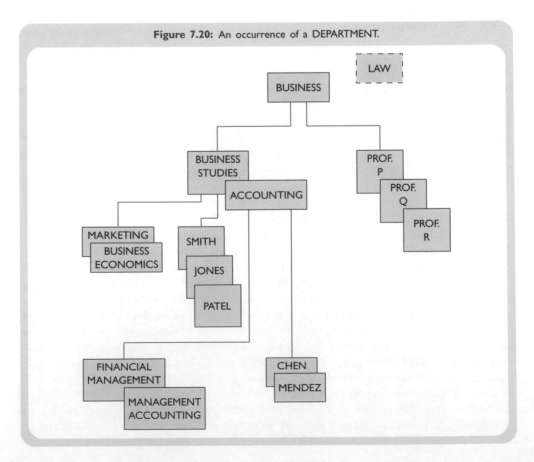

Figure 7.20: An occurrence of a DEPARTMENT.

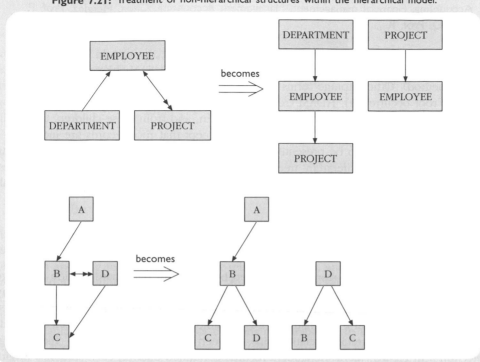

Figure 7.21: Treatment of non-hierarchical structures within the hierarchical model.

no longer offered) then the records **Financial Management, Management Accounting, Chen** and **Mendez** are also lost from the database.

The problem of many-to-many relationships and network structures is handled by the development of independent hierarchical structures. In Figure 7.21 the **PROJECT/EMPLOYEE/ DEPARTMENT** structure is represented by two simple hierarchies. The diagram also shows a representation of another network structure. More complex structures may require several hierarchy trees.

7.9.2 Conceptual, internal and external schemas

The conceptual schema of a hierarchical database may be taken as the set of hierarchy trees defining the structure. The conceptual schema will also specify the fields within each record type within the hierarchy. This gives a logical view of the way the database is organized.

It is difficult to equate much else in the way of external and internal schemas with hierarchical databases without consideration of specific commercial products. For instance, IMS stores each hierarchy tree as a separate single file. This file will contain record occurrences of many types. The internal schema can be thought of as a collection of specifications of the data organization of these files. The file can be stored in many ways. The occurrence in Figure 7.20 can be stored as a sequential file with the records adjacent to one another in the following order:

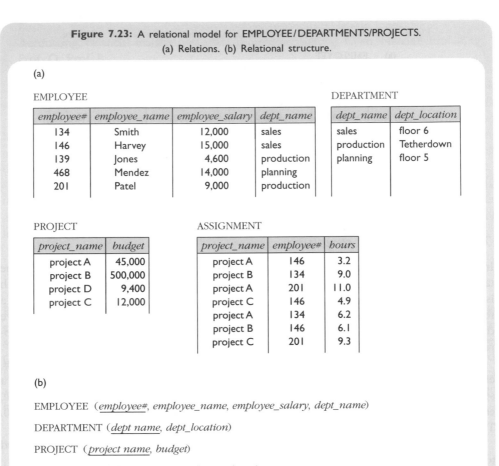

Figure 7.23: A relational model for EMPLOYEE/DEPARTMENTS/PROJECTS.
(a) Relations. (b) Relational structure.

(a)

EMPLOYEE

employee#	employee_name	employee_salary	dept_name
134	Smith	12,000	sales
146	Harvey	15,000	sales
139	Jones	4,600	production
468	Mendez	14,000	planning
201	Patel	9,000	production

DEPARTMENT

dept_name	dept_location
sales	floor 6
production	Tetherdown
planning	floor 5

PROJECT

project_name	budget
project A	45,000
project B	500,000
project D	9,400
project C	12,000

ASSIGNMENT

project_name	employee#	hours
project A	146	3.2
project B	134	9.0
project A	201	11.0
project C	146	4.9
project A	134	6.2
project B	146	6.1
project C	201	9.3

(b)

EMPLOYEE (*employee#*, employee_name, employee_salary, dept_name)

DEPARTMENT (*dept name*, dept_location)

PROJECT (*project name*, budget)

ASSIGNMENT (*project name, employee#*, hours)

Second, as the set is an ordered n-tuple the column ordering *is* significant. In the *EMPLOYEE* table if *employee_salary* occurs between *employee#* and *employee_name* then it is a different relation. In practice, both of these pure conditions may not be followed in commercial relational database management systems. Different attribute order is often allowed, as users generally do not access a value in a row by its relative position but by the column name under which it falls. Some systems also allow an ordering amongst rows to be expressed, for example according to ascending *employee#*. Rows can then be retrieved in order.

The theoretical system, though, allows access to a tuple only by value and there is no implied index or ordering. The physical implementation in terms of indexes and pointers is unseen by the user.

The network model and hierarchical models represent relationships by links. The relational model represents a relationship by a relation or table. This is shown in Figure 7.23. The model in (b), together with the specification of the domain of each attribute, corresponds to a conceptual schema.

Remember that each employee belongs to just one department, whereas each department may have several employees. The key to the **DEPARTMENT** relation is *dept_name* and if this is added to the **EMPLOYEE** relation we can represent the fact that an employee is a member of a department. Loosely speaking, given an *employee#*, 139, the relevant **EMPLOYEE** tuple can be identified and the fact that the employee is in the production department established. Then from the **DEPARTMENT** table the relevant **DEPARTMENT** tuple containing the information on the department of production may be identified.

Many employees are able to work on one project and each project might have many employees assigned to it. This is shown by capturing the many-to-many relationship in a new relation, **ASSIGNMENT**. This has as its key the group key consisting of the key of **PROJECT**, *project_name*, and the key of **EMPLOYEE**, *employee#*. In order to be able to identify a row uniquely it is necessary to specify both the *project_name* and the **employee#**. The field, *hours*, allows data on the number of hours that each employee works on each project to be stored.

In general, a $1:n$ relationship is represented in the relational model by inserting the key attribute of the entity on the n side of the relationship into the relation representing the entity on the 1 side of the relationship. A many-to-many relationship is represented by creating a new relation, which has as its group key the key attributes of each of the entities in the relationship.

It is important to be clear about the way the relational and network data models are data models of the world. The world can be viewed as being constructed of three types of component. There are entity types (types of objects), there are attributes of these objects, and there are relationships between the objects. The relational model represents an entity type by a relation or table and the attributes by columns of the table. An individual object with values of its attributes corresponds to a row in the table. A relationship between two objects is not modelled as a third type of component. Rather, the key attributes of each entity type are associated in a table that acts as proxy for the relationship. Relationships are not distinguished from entity types in the relational model. We only see the distinction because the table representing a relationship has a composite key, its components being the keys of the tables representing the entities in the relationship. There are only two distinct kinds of components in the relational model – tables (or relations) and values of attributes. In contrast, the network model straightforwardly represents entity types by record types, entities themselves by occurrences of these record types, relationships by links between the record types (CODASYL sets), and values of attributes of objects by data items in record occurrences.

Some of the advantages of relational systems are:

- Relational database models involve no non-logical concepts such as indexing, storage details, or ordering that occur in the network and hierarchical models.

- They require no non-logical access paths (via pointers, CODASYL sets or the like) to data items. These items are retrieved purely on the basis of the rules and conditions.

- The relational model is therefore a logical data model independent of storage considerations. It can be thought of as falling neatly into conceptual schema level.

- Relational database systems allows large chunks of data to be processed in a single operation.

7.10.2 Conceptual, external and internal schemas

The relational equivalent of a conceptual schema is the set of relations defined in the relational model, together with specification of the domains of each attribute. In relational database management systems these **base tables** have an independent existence.

At the internal schema level each base table will probably correspond to a stored file and each row in the table to a record in the file. There may be many indexes associated with a given file. The conceptual view should not reveal these indexes (or if it does data access should not be specifiable via them).

The equivalent of an external schema for a relational model is sometimes called a **view**. A particular view consists of presenting those attributes and tables needed for the specific purpose of a user. The contents of the view will be equivalent to a set of relations generated from the relations stored within the database. These relations may be either base table or relations capable of being generated from these by the relational operations described in Section 7.10.3.

7.10.3 Data manipulation

As well as independently existing relations (known as primary or base relations) which are stored, it may be necessary to generate new and temporary relations (known as **derived** relations) to answer user enquiries. The operations that may be legitimately performed on relations can be described using either the relational algebra or the relational calculus. The workings of both the algebra and the calculus have been extensively investigated from a mathematical perspective and their properties are fully understood. All data manipulation is based on these, rather than the traversal of hierarchies or networks between records.

Three relational algebra operations **SELECT**, **PROJECT** and **JOIN** are illustrated. Each takes a relation (or number of relations) as its argument and produces a relation as its value.

1. **SELECT:** This produces a new relation consisting of a number of selected rows (tuples) from an existing relation. For example:

   SELECT EMPLOYEE **WHERE** *employee_salary* > 13,000

   gives the relation in Figure 7.24(a).

2. **PROJECT:** This produces a new relation consisting of a number of selected columns (attributes) from an existing relation. For example:

   PROJECT EMPLOYEE **OVER** *employee_name*, *dept_name*

   gives the relation in Figure 7.24(b).

3. **JOIN:** This produces a new relation from two existing relations joined over a common domain. It is best described algorithmically. First, take the first row from the first relation and compare the attribute value from the common domain with each value of the attribute from the common domain in the second relation. Wherever the two values are identical, form a row by concatenating the first row with the row from the second relation (striking out the repeat of the common attribute). Do this for each row in the first relation. For example:

   JOIN EMPLOYEE **AND** ASSIGNMENT **OVER** *employee#*

   gives the relation in Figure 7.24(c).

Figure 7.24: Examples of relational operators. (a) Use of **SELECT**. (b) Use of **PROJECT**. (c) Use of **JOIN**. (d) Use of nested operators.

(a)

employee#	employee_name	employee_salary	dept_name
146	Harvey	15,000	sales
468	Mendez	14,000	planning

SELECT EMPLOYEE **WHERE** employee_salary > 13,000

(b)

employee_name	dept_name
Smith	sales
Harvey	sales
Jones	production
Mendez	planning
Patel	production

PROJECT EMPLOYEE **OVER** employee_name, dept_name

(c)

employee#	employee_name	employee_salary	dept_name	project_name	hours
134	Smith	12,000	sales	project B	9.0
134	Smith	12,000	sales	project A	6.2
146	Harvey	15,000	sales	project A	3.2
146	Harvey	15,000	sales	project C	4.9
146	Harvey	15,000	sales	project B	6.1
201	Patel	9,000	production	project A	11.0
201	Patel	9,000	production	project C	9.3

JOIN EMPLOYEE **AND** ASSIGNMENT **OVER** employee#

(d)

employee_name	project_name	hours
Smith	project B	9.0
Smith	project A	6.2
Harvey	project A	3.2
Harvey	project C	4.9
Harvey	project B	6.1

PROJECT (**SELECT** (**JOIN** EMPLOYEE **AND** ASSIGNMENT **OVER** employee#)
WHERE dept_name = sales) **OVER** employee_name, project_name, hours

It is possible to nest the operations. Suppose that a user wishes to establish the names, projects worked on, and hours worked on these projects by staff within the sales department. This could be achieved by the following nested operations:

PROJECT (**SELECT**(**JOIN** EMPLOYEE **AND** ASSIGNMENT **OVER** employee#)
WHERE dept_name = sales) **OVER** employee_name, project_name, hours

By working from the innermost nesting outwards the resulting relation can be constructed. See Figure 7.24(d).

Relational algebra also uses other operations. There is a **DIVIDE** operation as well as the set theoretic operations corresponding to **UNION**, **INTERSECTION** and **DIFFERENCE**.

Relational algebra involves a procedural specification of how the final relation is to be constructed by defining intermediate relations to be produced. The relational calculus in contrast, defines a relation in the form of a predicate. The calculus is a version of the predicate calculus applied to relational databases.

The relational algebra provides a formally precise way of extracting data. However, it is difficult to use to specify complex enquiries. It is not used itself to query a relational database nor as a set of data manipulation procedures. Query languages and data manipulation languages derived from the algebra have been developed. These are straightforward to use and provide the ease and flexibility of enquiry that make relational databases powerful in the provision of information. IBM's SQL (Structured Query Language) and QBE (Query By Example) are examples.

7.10.4 SQL

SQL is a relational data manipulation language developed by IBM initially for use with its relational database management system DB2. The language can be used for stand-alone queries or embedded in programs written in various languages. The language is simple enough that substantial parts may be employed by casual users for queries on the relational database. SQL has become the standard relational data manipulation language. Basic operations are covered below.

Projection
The project operation is implemented in SQL by the construction:

> **SELECT** ⟨attribute 1, attribute 2 . . . ⟩
> **FROM** ⟨relation⟩

The projection in Figure 7.24(b) would be framed as follows:

> **SELECT** employee_name, dept_name
> **FROM** EMPLOYEE

This produces the result in the table in Figure 7.24(b). With SQL it is possible to specify any desired order amongst the columns. A different command would have produced dept_name followed by employee_name. SQL projection differs from the logical projection operation in that duplicate tuples resulting from the projection would not be removed; in other words, the result of SQL projection is not strictly a relation.

Selection
Selection is achieved by adding a qualification to the **SELECT** command. Its construction is:

> **SELECT** ⟨attribute 1 . . . ⟩
> **FROM** ⟨relation⟩
> **WHERE** ⟨qualification⟩

Figure 7.25: The result of the SQL **JOIN** command on **EMPLOYEE** and **ASSIGNMENT**.

Smith	project B	9.0
Smith	project A	6.2
Harvey	project A	3.2
Harvey	project C	4.9
Harvey	project B	6.1
Patel	project A	11.0
Patel	project C	9.3

SELECT EMPLOYEE. *employee_name*, ASSIGNMENT. *project_name*, ASSIGNMENT.*hours*
 FROM EMPLOYEE, ASSIGNMENT
 WHERE EMPLOYEE. *employee#* = ASSIGNMENT. *employee#*

The qualification is a Boolean construction using **AND**, **OR** or **NOT**. Using the **EMPLOYEE** relation in Figure 7.23 the following selection:

SELECT *employee_name*, *employee#*
 FROM EMPLOYEE
 WHERE *employee_salary* > 8,000
 AND (*dept_name* = Sales **OR** *dept_name* = Production)

would yield

SMITH	134
HARVEY	146
PATEL	201

Join

Join is achieved by specifying the two attributes (with common domain) over which the join is to be made. The construction is:

SELECT ⟨attribute 1 . . . ⟩
 FROM
 WHERE ⟨attribute from relation 1 = attribute from relation 2⟩

If it is wished to select the names, project and hours worked on the projects by staff as shown in the **EMPLOYEE** and **ASSIGNMENT** relations in Figure 7.19 the join operation with the selection would be:

ASSIGNMENT.*project_name*, ASSIGNMENT.*hours*
SELECT EMPLOYEE.*employee_name*,
 FROM EMPLOYEE, ASSIGNMENT
 WHERE EMPLOYEE.*employee#* = ASSIGNMENT.*employee#*

This command gives the display in Figure 7.25. SQL commands may be nested and several relations may be 'searched' by using join qualifications with more than two relations. The following command lists employee names, the projects on which they work and the budgets of these projects using the relations in Figure 7.23:

Figure 7.26: A QBE query on EMPLOYEE.

Query

EMPLOYEE	employee#	employee_name	employee_salary	dept_name
		P. Fred	> 13,000	P. Stores

Response

employee_name	dept_name
Harvey	sales
Mendez	planning

ASSIGNMENT.*project_name*, PROJECT.*budget*
SELECT EMPLOYEE.*employee_name*,
   FROM EMPLOYEE, ASSIGNMENT, PROJECT
      WHERE EMPLOYEE.*employee#* = ASSIGNMENT.*employee#*
         AND ASSIGNMENT.*project_name* = PROJECT.*project_name*

SQL allows nesting of the **SELECT-FROM-WHERE** construction and it is often easier to conceptualize a query this way. For instance, the following query selects the names of employees working on a project for more than 4 hours.

   SELECT *employee-name*
     FROM EMPLOYEE
      WHERE *employee#* = **ANY** (**SELECT** *employee#* **FROM** ASSIGNMENT
                      WHERE *hours* > 4.0)

(Note: As it stands this will lead to repeats of some employee names.)

As well as searching, SQL allows deletion and insertion of rows using the **DELETE** and **INSERT** commands. These work using the same underlying principles as the constructions that apply to **SELECT**.

7.10.5   Query By Example (QBE)

Query By Example (QBE) developed at IBM, is a query language for relational database systems that uses the idea of a table (relation) with which to frame the query. The language is very simple to use and casual database enquirers can be trained quickly to be proficient in QBE. Figure 7.26 illustrates a typical QBE query and response. The language is designed to be used interactively with a VDU. Upon pressing a designated function key, the user is presented with a skeleton table. The name of the relation is then entered. From the various fields shown the user may select the fields to be displayed in response to the query by entering ⟨P.dummy⟩. P indicates print and the underlined dummy is an example of the field. This example need not necessarily be in the database. Conditions are entered in the other fields as desired. Figure 7.26 is an example involving selection and projection from one relation. It specifies the retrieval of all **employee_name**s together

Table 7.1: Databases compared.

	Chronological development	*Processing speed*	*Ease of physical implementation*	*Flexibility of representation*	*Flexibility of data retrieval*	*Ease of understanding*
Network	second	2	2	2	2	3
Hierarchical	first	1	1	3	3	2
Relational	third	3	3	1	1	1

Key 1 = best, 3 = worst

with their *dept_name*s where the employee earns more than £13,000 per year. More complex queries may involve several relations. The power of QBE to represent queries is approximately equal to that of SQL.

7.10.6 Assessment of Relational Database Models

The relational model, relational database management system and relational languages have had a large impact on the development of sophisticated data resources. Their advantages over database systems based on other models are summarized below and in Table 7.1.

Advantages

- They provide a clear and conceptually straightforward representation of complex data relations.
- They allow powerful data manipulation and query languages to operate on them.
- The database is maintained in a table form, which is a 'natural' representation of data to business-orientated users.
- Query languages (such as QBE) can be developed exploiting this tabular form.
- Data is accessed by value and conditions and the database can be accessed from any point (relation).
- Access paths are not seen (or usable) by the database users.
- The representation of the data is entirely logical, once again reinforcing the simplicity of representation from the point of view of users and application programmers.

Disadvantages

- The indexes used in implementation are often large and require heavy storage overheads.
- The operational speed of current commercial relational database systems is slower than their hierarchical or network counterparts. This makes them unsuitable for high-volume processing activities.

As disk storage capacities and disk access speeds rise combined with the diminishing cost of disk storage, the flexible features of relational databases will ensure their long term superiority in the marketplace.

7.11 Microcomputer databases

There are many database software packages designed for microcomputers currently on the market. The majority of these call themselves 'relational databases'. In general, these are not fully relational database systems as described in this chapter. Most produce tables of records with indexes on chosen fields. The tables are held as indexed files on disk. The user can perform, project, select and join operations on the tables. Most packages come with their own programming language in which the commands for these operations are embedded. Simple applications can be developed easily and quickly by staff who have had little training. However, the user is aware of the physical structure of the database unless special programs have been written to provide a protected user interface. The majority of packages do not allow different users to be presented with different views of the database, do not allow concurrent usage by several users (through a local area network), and cannot be seen as falling easily within the ANSI/SPARC three-level model of a database system. Most of the security and monitoring features of mainframe database systems are absent. This is not to denigrate the usefulness of micro-database packages. Such packages have been extremely effective as sophisticated record keepers and selective data retrievers – especially when user-friendly interfaces have been written using their accompanying programming languages. However, generally it would be a mistake to think, when a micro and a mainframe database system are being discussed, that each provides much the same facilities.

The increasing power of business microcomputers is allowing the possibility of rewriting large mainframe database packages such as ORACLE so that they run on these powerful microcomputers. Much the same facilities are present on both the microcomputer and mainframe versions of the systems (although the speed and capacity of the former are less than that of the latter). SQL has gained acceptance as a standard for a relational database query language. Indeed, ORACLE and other database systems now use this. The future trend in medium and large businesses is likely to be towards this new breed of microcomputer database system for local databases. These will have links to mainframe databases for other enquiries. The advantage of a standard, such as SQL, with a package such as ORACLE, is that the same SQL commands can be used to access the local database associated with the microcomputer as can be used to access IBM mainframe relational databases, for example – and all from the same microcomputer. This will increase the availability of access to an extended database to microcomputer users.

Summary

Business organizations need to keep and process data for their survival. Data are held in master files about ongoing entities of interest to the business. Examples are customer, debtor, employee and stock files. Data used to update master files are stored in transaction files. Examples are sales, payments, receipts, time-sheet returns, credit notes and sales order files. The storage and access strategies for disk files go hand in hand. List structures offer the capability of sequential access whilst providing for fast record insertion and deletion. Inverted list ▷

structures place attribute values in indexes and pointer fields are transferred from the records to the index. This opens the way to retrieval of records based on properties of record fields other than the key field.

The database approach recognizes data as an important resource of the organization that is shared by many applications and so requires careful planning, management and control. Databases and database management systems have been developed to replace file-based systems of data storage. This is because, firstly, sophisticated file interrogation techniques have led to the need for automated data management and, secondly, business has demanded more flexible data retrieval and reporting facilities to meet the needs of managerial decision making.

File-based, application-led approaches to data storage often lead to problems. The duplication of data over many files, each being the responsibility of a different person or department, can lead to update difficulties and the presence of inconsistent data within the organization. The same data may also be represented in different storage formats in different files and the files themselves may have different organization and access characteristics. The dependence of application programs on the files that serve them increases the difficulty of changing data storage structures without having to change the programs that access them.

The database approach, on the other hand, recognizes the importance of developing an integrated store of data structured in a meaningful manner for the organization. The database contains data stored with minimal redundancy and organized in a manner which is a logical reflection of the relationships between the entities on which data is held.

Database management systems are sophisticated software packages that maintain the database and present an interface to users and user programs which is independent of physical storage details. This logical presentation of the data facilitates user enquiries and applications program development – programmers need be concerned only with what data is required for an application, not on the physical aspects of how to retrieve it. The independence of the logical representation also allows physical reorganization of the database without the necessity of application program changes. Commercial database systems define the logical structure of the database using a data definition language (DDL) and allow data alterations through a data manipulation language (DML). Other facilities provided are data dictionaries, accounting utilities, concurrency control, backup, recovery and security features.

In understanding database systems it is useful to identify three separate levels at which data may be represented:

- the conceptual schema (an overall logical view of the database).
- the external schema (a logical presentation of part of the database in the way most suitable to meet a user's requirements).
- the internal schema (the representation of storage and access characteristics for the data).

Three data models have had significant impact on the development of commercial database management systems software. They are, chronologically, the hierarchical, network and relational models.

Both the hierarchical and the network models impose restrictions on the way relationships can be represented and data accessed. The hierarchical is more limiting, restricting data to tree structures using downward pointing $1{:}n$ relationships. Network structures do not allow the direct representation of $m{:}n$ relationships. Relational database management systems are table-based logical representations of data structures which allow simple and powerful data manipulation. The advantages of relational systems in terms of their representation and retrieval characteristics are to be set against their slow speed of operation. This makes them unsuitable for high-volume transaction-based data processing.

The way that a data model is developed for an organization and the design of a database to incorporate this model is reserved for the chapter on data analysis and modelling within the chapters on systems analysis and design. The entity-relationship modelling approach will be used and the techniques of normalization (often associated with the design of effective relational databases) will be explained there.

Exercises

1. Explain the following terms:

file	variable-length record
backup file	transaction file
record type	inverted list
file update	fully-inverted file
record	master file
field	

2. Explain the difference between logical and physical files.

3. Explain the advantages and disadvantages of using a flat file as against a multi-dimensional file.

4. By considering a stock record give an example of an entity, attribute, record, field, data item, key and a repeating group.

5. Figure 7.27 shows an order form for the ABC company.
    (a) Suggest a record structure suitable for keeping data on orders. Show any repeating fields and specify field sizes and types.
    (b) The order file is to be kept as a permanent record so that customers can make enquiries concerning the status of their order and its contents by giving the order. The status possibilities for the order are 'received', 'awaiting stock', 'being processed', 'finished'. The file is also used in end of week batch processing of orders. Suggest a suitable file organization and provide a justification for your answer.

Figure 7.27: Order form for the ABC company.

```
ABC COMPANY _____        Delivery address _____
Order#          _____                         _____
Date            _____                         _____
Customer#       _____                         _____
Customer name   _____
Invoice address _____
                _____


Item#   Item description              Quantity    Price       Total
___     _____        _____      _____      _____
___     _____        _____      _____      _____
___     _____        _____      _____      _____
___     _____        _____      _____      _____
                                                          Subtotal ____
          Discount ___% Discount _____
                       Sales tax _____
                                                          Total ____
```

6. Using your knowledge of the way a typical business functions, suggest typical record structures for each of the following:
   (a) employee record
   (b) stock record
   (c) sales-ledger customer record
   (d) salesman commission record.

7. Using your own experience suggest data files and records that might be used in the following types of organization (ignore standard files such as employee, sales ledger and so on):
   (a) a computer dating service
   (b) a library
   (c) a video cassette hire club
   (d) a hospital
   (e) a motor insurance broker.
   For each file suggest the likely process for which the file will be used.

8. A theatre accepts postal and telephone bookings for its forthcoming performances up to a period of six months in advance. About half of the bookings are directly from the public. The remainder are from agencies who need to be invoiced on a regular basis. Specify a set of files sufficient to support the processes involved in booking and the satisfaction of queries on seat availability. For the files you should define the record layouts.

9. A road transport freight company is to introduce a computer-based system for handling customer bookings for the transfer of customer freight from ▷

one town to another. Each lorry will make a special journey from one town to another if the customer's freight consignment is sufficient to count as a full lorry load. Otherwise, different consignments are accumulated and transferred from the source town to the destination town on one of the freight company's standard journeys. It has been decided to implement the system as a series of files. The following have been suggested:

(a) customer file
(b) consignment file
(c) journey file
(d) special-journey file
(e) lorry file.

The application must be able to accept and record consignment bookings, assign these consignments to journeys, ensure that invoicing for completed transport of consignments occurs and answer random queries from customers on expected delivery dates. You are required to specify record layouts for the various files.

10. 'There is no reason for an accountant, financier or any other business person involved with a computerized file-based information system to know about the storage organization of data in files and access methods to that data, only about the nature of the data'. Do you agree?

11. Define the following terms:

database	relation	relational join operation
database management system	attribute	database query language
data independence	domain of an attribute	data dictionary
database administrator	key	report generator
data redundancy	relational selection operation	internal schema
data sharing	relational projection operation	conceptual schema
concurrent use of data		external schema

12. Explain the difference between a *data definition language* (DDL) and a *data manipulation language* (DML).

13. What limitations are there for the application-led file-based approach and how does the database approach overcome these?

14. What is the distinction between a *conceptual schema* and a *data model*?

15. Describe three types of database user. How do the facilities offered by a DBMS assist each in their interaction with the database?

16. Explain the terms *internal schema*, *external schema* and *conceptual schema*. Illustrate your answer by reference to the **PROJECT/EMPLOYEE/DEPARTMENT** example in Section 7.5.

17. What DBMS utilities aid the DBA in the performance of his/her responsibilities?

18. State the rules governing the types of links allowable between records in a network structure.

19. Under what conditions would a network structure also qualify as a hierarchical structure?

20. Give an example of two relations and the result of applying a **JOIN** operation over a different attribute from each (with the same common domain).

21. In the relational algebra the use of the **PROJECT** operation on a table may produce a table with less rows than the original. Why?

22. Discuss the advantages for an applications programmer in separating the physical storage details of the database from the view of it presented to the programmer.

23. 'Designing a database is no more nor less complex than designing a series of files.' Why is this incorrect?

24. 'A database that meets all the future organizational needs is a myth. Applications change. It is more efficient to design piecemeal to meet current requirements than to embark on the grand design.' Discuss.

25. An accountant may value a resource or asset in a number of ways – the cost of acquiring the asset, the cost of replacing the asset if lost, the saleable (realizable) value of the asset, and the value of the asset in use, are four methods. Data is often regarded as an asset of an organization. What are the problems in valuing data with the above methods?

26. For what reasons would an accountant be interested in the range of views or external schemas available to users?

27. What are the advantages and disadvantages of taking dispersed data within an organization and integrating it into a centralized database?

28. 'It is a difficult task and a significant cost to determine each individual's external schema which, together with the extra run time cost in displaying records within this schema (particularly for relational database systems) makes it desirable to allow users access to the conceptual schema. Anyway, this gives them maximum flexibility.' What is to be said for and against this view?

29. By considering the advantages and disadvantages of the file-based and database approaches suggest **five** characteristics of an organization's information provision requirements that would indicate that a file-based approach is appropriate and suggest **five** characteristics that would indicate that a database approach is suitable.

30. Define a schema illustrating the network approach to the **PROJECT/EMPLOYEE/ DEPARTMENT** example used in the text.

31. The following outline schema was developed for a customer company database for a large organization manufacturing and wholesaling a wide range of chemicals for agricultural pest control, land fertilization, domestic cleaning, paints, corrosion prevention and medical disinfectant purposes.

customer#	contact telephone number	credit terms
customer name	customer type	invoice date
customer address	[major product category]*	discount
invoice address	standard delivery day	turnover this year
[delivery address]*	[account salesman]*	turnover last year
contact name	credit limit	current balance

▷

Identify **four** potential users of this data and specify suitable external schemas for each. (The star symbol * indicates repeated attributes.)

32. Construct a network model to represent the structure shown in Figure 7.28.

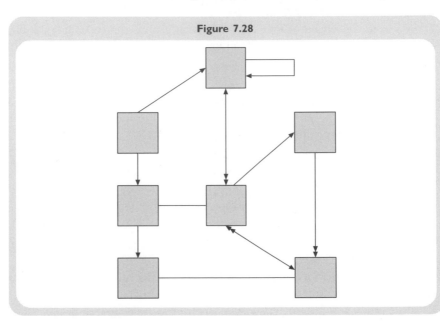

Figure 7.28

33. Represent the structure in Figure 7.28 as a hierarchical model, using hierarchy trees.

34. Using the information in Figure 7.29:

   (a) What records would be displayed in response to the following queries?

      (i)   **SELECT** *supplier_name*
          FROM SUPPLIER
          WHERE *supplier_city* = London

      (ii) **SELECT** *warehouse#*
          FROM STORAGE
          WHERE *part#* = P2 **AND** *quantity_held* > 40

      (iii) **SELECT** SUPPLIER.*supplier_name*, CONTRACT.*part#*
          FROM SUPPLIER, CONTRACT
          WHERE SUPPLIER.*supplier#* = CONTRACT.*supplier#*
                  AND CONTRACT.*quantity_supplied* > 30

      (iv) **SELECT** FIRST.*supplier#*, SECOND.*supplier#*
          FROM SUPPLIER_FIRST, SUPPLIER_SECOND
          WHERE FIRST.*supplier_city* = SECOND.*supplier_city*

      (v) **SELECT** *supplier_name*
          FROM SUPPLIER
          WHERE *supplier#* = **ANY** (**SELECT** *supplier#*
                                FROM CONTRACT
                                WHERE *part#* = P1)

Figure 7.29

SUPPLIER

supplier#	supplier_name	supplier_city
S1	Smith	London
S2	Jones	London
S3	Smith	Derby
S4	Patel	Kentucky
S6	Mendez	Bristol

PART

part#	part_name	price
P1	dynamo	20
P2	alternator	30
P3	carburretor	30
P7	dynamo	27

WAREHOUSE

warehouse#	w_city
W1	London
W2	London
W3	London
W4	Leeds

CONTACT

part#	supplier#	quantity_supplied
P1	S1	43
P1	S2	49
P1	S3	58
P1	S6	14
P2	S1	5
P2	S6	134
P3	S1	19
P3	S2	19
P3	S3	14
P3	S4	21
P3	S6	31
P7	S6	34

STORAGE

part#	warehouse#	quantity_held
P1	W1	482
P1	W2	394
P1	W3	201
P2	W1	43
P2	W2	41
P2	W3	31
P2	W4	41
P3	W1	95
P3	W2	0
P3	W4	91
P7	W1	6
P7	W2	5
P7	W2	1
P7	W4	4

(vi) **SELECT** supplier_name
   FROM SUPPLIER
   WHERE supplier# = **ANY** (**SELECT** supplier#
                     FROM CONTRACT
                     WHERE part# = **ANY** (**SELECT** part#
                               FROM STORAGE
                               WHERE warehouse# = 3))

(b) Design relational database enquiries in an SQL-like language to:
   (i) Determine the *part#*s of dynamos.
   (ii) Determine all *supplier#*s of suppliers who supply more than 40 units of *part#* P1.
   (iii) Determine all *part#*s and *part_name*s stored in either warehouse 1 or warehouse 2.
   (iv) Select all suppliers located in the same city as any warehouse.
   (v) Select all *supplier_name*s who supply parts in any warehouse not located in the same city as the supplier.
(c) In (a)(iv) above how can the query be altered to avoid unnecessary repeats? ▷

35. For the relations:

BOOK (_book#_, title, author, stack address)

BORROWER (_borrower#_, borrower name, borrower address, borrower status)

LOAN (_loan#_, _borrower#_, date, loan status)

Specify SQL or relational algebra expressions to represent the following queries:

(a) What are the titles of all books by Tolstoy?

(b) What book titles were loaned on or before 1 April 1988?

(c) List the borrower names and book titles for staff users (**borrower status** = staff) that have been borrowed since 11 November 1987 and are still on loan (**loan status** = on loan).

36. In a college the following records are kept:

student records – **student#, student name, student address, course#**,

course record – **course#, course name, course level, course tutor**,

subject record – **subject#, subject name, main text**,

staff record – **staff#, staff name, staff office#**,

Make any plausible assumptions about the nature of the relationships between student, course, subject and staff.

(a) (i) Design a network model for the college records.

(ii) Design an external view suitable for an application that produces a list of textbooks to be purchased by each student.

(b) (i) Design a relational model for the college records.

(ii) By means of selection, projection and join, design an external view revealing for each student their student#, name and a list of textbooks.

Recommended reading

● Burch J.G. and Grudnitski G. (1989). *Information Systems: Theory and Practice* 5th edn. New York: Wiley

This provides a chapter that introduces the three main types of data model. It is non-technical and concentrates on logical aspects of the data.

● Date C.J. (1994). *An Introduction to Database Systems: Vol 1* 6th edn. Reading MA: Addison-Wesley

A classic comprehensive textbook in this area. Although largely technical and written for the computer scientist, this provides a clear introduction to databases and data models.

● Date C.J. (1986). *Relational Database: Selected Writings*. Reading MA: Addison-Wesley

● Gessford J.E. (1991). *Business-Wide Database Planning*. John Wiley

This text explains a business-wide information structuring/MIS approach to top-down data modelling. The methodology involves the development of entity relationship models for various business functions such as marketing and engineering through to database design. There is also an introduction to distributed databases. The book is accessible to those who have covered the chapters on databases and on data analysis.

● McFadden F.R. and Hoffer J.A. (1995). *Database Management* 4th edn. Benjamin Cummings

This is a standard student text governing all aspects of database design and database management. Each chapter has review questions, problems and exercises.

- Nolan R. (1973). Computer databases: the future is now. *Harvard Business Review*, Sept/ Oct, 98–110
  One of the earlier articles emphasizing the importance of a database.
- Pratt P.J. and Adamski J.J. (1994). *Database Systems Management and Design* 3rd edn. International Thomson Publishing
  This is a detailed student text on databases. Also included are chapters on SQL, micro-computer database management, and fourth-generation environments.
- Smith P.D. and Barnes G.M. (1987). *Files and Databases: An Introduction.* Addison-Wesley
  A modern technical introduction to files and databases. This book provides more advanced reading for those interested in following up material in this area.

Chapter 8

Control in Information Systems

This chapter introduces general principles behind control and security in systems. These are then applied to computerized information systems. The increasing dependence of business on the reliable, complete and accurate processing of data by computers, often without manual checks, indicates that controls must be planned and designed. This occurs before the development of computer systems and their surrounding manual procedures. Security and control are therefore considered prior to systems design, not as afterthoughts. The increasing use of computers in the processing and transmission of confidential data and funds has also made computer systems attractive targets for fraud. The need to take steps to guard against this possibility has been a powerful stimulus to an emphasis on security in the process of systems analysis and design.

In the early part of this chapter the basic concepts of control systems are developed by considering the general ideas behind feedback, feedforward and preventive controls. These are explained and applied to manual business systems. Controls over computerized information systems are introduced by identifying the various goals and levels of control that are applicable. Controls over data movement into, through, and out of the computer system are covered, together with controls over the transmission of data between computers or through the public telecommunications network. Some of the ways that fraud may be prevented are by restricting access to the computer system, to the data within it, or by scrambling the data prior to storage or transmission so that it is useless to unauthorized persons. The methods of achieving these ends are also explained.

Computer systems always lie within and interface with a surrounding manual system. Not only should computer aspects of this combined socio-technical system be the subject of control but also the organizational and personnel elements. To aid security it is important that the system is structured in a way that facilitates this. The way that functions are separated as a means of control is developed in later sections of this chapter. The reliability of controls and security procedures operating over a working transaction and information-processing system can ▷

be established by means of an audit. Although auditing is a large area in itself, the overall strategy adopted and the aid given by computer-assisted tools in the auditing of computer-based systems is outlined. Data on persons is the subject of data protection legislation. This has implications both for security and for the design of systems holding data on persons. The reasons for the rise of this legislation and the general principles behind the Data Protection Act in the UK are explained together with the effects of the legislation on personal data security and access. Finally, the need for a methodology for the identification of risk and the design of controls is stressed. Controls are an integral part of systems design, which is covered in Chapter 13 on systems design and Chapter 14 on detailed design.

8.1 Control systems

Controls, if they are to be effective, must operate in a systematic way. This section considers the general principles behind control systems before applying these to business systems. Some controls work by sensing or predicting the state of a system, comparing that state with a desired standard, and then carrying out some correcting action if the state does not meet favourably with the standard. Other controls prevent (or attempt to prevent) a system from moving away from a desired state. They do this by preventing abnormal but possible occurrences that would have this effect.

Feedback and feedforward are examples of the first type of control. Preventive controls are examples of the second. Feedback and feedforward controls involve the collection and processing of data and so operate within the business information system. Preventive controls prevent inaccurate and unreliable data processing, damage to data processing equipment and unauthorized access to data, and so too are within this environment.

It is one of the responsibilities of management to ensure that adequate and effective controls are present at all levels within a business organization. There is always a cost–benefit dimension to the existence of any control – it is insufficient to consider the control outside this context. All controls have some cost associated with their installation and also a probability/possibility that they will fail in their control function. On the benefit side there is the prevention or correction of the undesired state of affairs. It may be possible to assign a money value to this benefit, but it is important to bear in mind that this undesired state of affairs might not have happened in the absence of the control (this is particularly true with preventive controls), so probability factors also have to be taken into account here. Cost–benefit considerations surrounding a strategy for control within a business are covered in a later section of this chapter but it should be made clear from the outset that the major question surrounding a control is not 'does it work?' but 'is it cost–benefit effective?'.

8.1.1 Feedback control systems

The general nature of a feedback control system is shown in Figure 8.1. It consists of:

- A **process** that accepts inputs and converts these into outputs.
- A **sensor**, which monitors the state of the process.

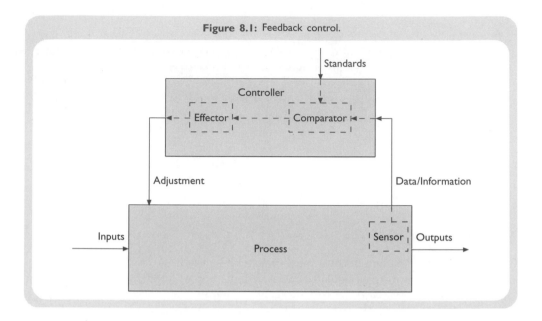

Figure 8.1: Feedback control.

- A **controller**, which accepts data from the sensor and accepts standards given externally. The controller then generates adjustments or decisions, which are fed into and affect the process.

- A **comparator** within the controller, which compares the sensed data with the standard and passes an indication of the deviation of the standard from the monitored data to the effector.

- An **effector** within the controller, which on the basis of the output of the comparator makes an adjustment to the output from the controller.

The example often given of a controller within a feedback control system is a thermostat. It accepts data about temperature from a sensor, compares it with a standard that is set by the householder and if the temperature is below or above this standard (by a certain amount) makes an adjustment to the boiler, turning it either on or off.

Feedback control enables a dynamic self-regulating system to function. Movements of the system from equilibrium lead to a self-correcting adjustment, implying that the combination of process and controller can be left over long periods of time and will continue to produce a guaranteed output that meets standards. Automated controller–process pairs are seldom encountered in business (though they often are in production engineering). It is common, however, for a person to be the controller. That is, an individual will monitor a process, compare it against given standards and take the necessary action in adjustment. This is one of the roles of management.

In an organization it is usual for control to be applied at several levels. The controller of a process at level 1 supplies information on the process and adjustments to a higher-level controller (who also receives information from other level 1 controllers). The information supplied may be an exceptional deviation of the process from the standard (exception reporting) or perhaps a summary (summary reporting). The higher-level controller can make adjustments to the functioning and structure of the system containing the level 1 controllers with their processes. The higher-level controller will also be given standards and will supply information to an even higher-level controller. The nesting of control may be many levels deep. At the highest level the controllers are given standards externally or they set their own. These levels of control correspond to levels of management. Above the lowest levels of control are the various layers of middle management. Top management responds to standards expected of it by external bodies, such as shareholders, as well as setting its own standards.

The study of feedback control is called **cybernetics**. Cybernetics ideas and principles have been applied to the study of management control of organizations (see for example Beer, 1981). Although real organizations are never so simple and clear cut that they fit neatly into the feedback model, the idea of feedback provides a useful perspective on modelling management decision making and control.

In order to be useful, feedback controls, as well as satisfying the cost–benefit constraint, should also be designed in accordance with the following principles:

1. Data and information fed to the controller should be simple and straightforward to understand. It must be designed to fit in with the intellectual capabilities of the controller, require no longer to digest than the time allowed for an adjustment to be made, and be directed to the task set for the controller. It is a common mistake for computerized systems that are responsible for generating this data to generate pages of reports that are quickly consigned to the rubbish bin.

   For example, a person in charge of debtor control (where the process is one of debtor-account bookkeeping) may only need information on debtor accounts that have amounts outstanding over a set number of days, not information on all accounts. On these debtor accounts the controller probably initially needs only summary information, such as the amount of debt, its age profile, and the average turnover with the debtor, but not the delivery address or a complete list of past invoices.

2. Data and information fed to the controller should be timely. Two possibilities are regular reports on deviations from standards or immediate reports where corrective action must be taken quickly.

3. Each controller (manager) will have a sphere of responsibility and a scope for authority (ideally these should cover much the same area). It is important that the standards set and the data provided to the controller are restricted within these limitations. The manager is in the best position in the organization to understand the workings of the process and may often be expected to take some responsibility for the setting of realistic standards.

Standard cost systems – an example of feedback control

In management accounting the term **standard cost** refers to the budgeted cost incurred in the production of a unit of output. It will be made up of various components such as material, labour and power as well as overheads such as machine maintenance. During the production process the various costs of production are monitored and the **actual cost** per unit is established. This is compared with the standard cost and variances of the actual cost from the standard are calculated. There may be some labour variances attributable to the cost of labour or the amount of labour per unit of production. There may be variances on material or overheads or some combination of both. On the basis

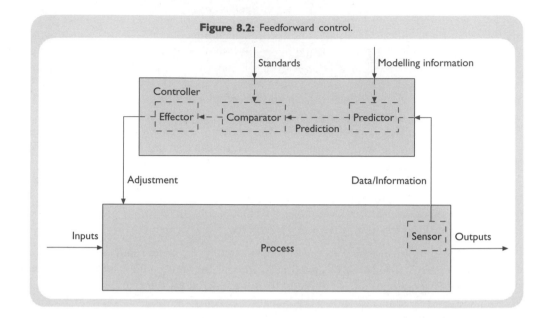

Figure 8.2: Feedforward control.

of the variance analysis, various adjustments to the production process may be recommended. For instance, an adverse labour variance analysis might be adjusted by speeding up a production assembly line or increasing piece-rate benefits.

8.1.2 Feedforward control system

The general nature of a feedforward control system is shown in Figure 8.2. The chief difference from a feedback control system is that the monitored data on the current performance of the system is not used to compare this performance with a standard but is used to predict the future state of the system, which is then compared with the future standard set. To do this, a further component called a **predictor** is added to the controller. The predictor takes current data and uses a predictive model of the process to estimate the future state of the system. In carrying out the prediction it is likely that future estimates of variables occurring outside the process, but affecting it, will need to be input into the predictor. The prediction is then fed into the comparator and effector, which will make any necessary adjustment to ensure that the system meets future objectives. The success of feedforward control depends on the suitability of the model and modelling information.

Cash flow planning – an example of feedforward control

Most organizations like to keep their cash balances within certain limits. To stray outside these limits leads to excess funds that could be profitably employed, or to diminished funds making the company vulnerable to a cash crisis.

The cash inflows and outflows of a company result from a number of factors. Inflows will generally be receipts from customers, investments and sales of assets. Amongst outflows will be payments to suppliers for purchases, wages and salaries, payments for overheads, payments of interest on loans, capital expenditures, tax payments and dividends.

Inflows and outflows will be spread over periods of time, and the amounts and exact timing will be subject to uncertainty.

It is important that predictions (accurate within limits) are made so that adjustments can be implemented to ensure that the cash balances remain at the desired level. For instance, a predicted cash drop may be financed by a sale of securities held by the organization rather than incurring a heavy bank overdraft with a punitive interest rate.

Feedforward systems are needed because time is required to implement the necessary adjustments, which need to be active rather than reactive. In this cash management example it is common nowadays to use computer-aided prediction either with spreadsheets or with financial logic-modelling packages. The predictions are passed to a senior manager or financial director, who takes the decision on the adjusting action.

8.1.3   Preventive control systems

Feedback and feedforward control work by a controller 'standing' outside a process and evaluating current or predicted deviations from a norm as a basis for taking adjusting action. Preventive controls, by contrast, reside within a process, their function being to prevent an undesired state of affairs from occurring. Just as with the other types of control mechanism, preventive controls are an integral part of manual and computerized information systems. Within business information systems these controls are broadly aimed at protecting assets, often by ensuring that incorrect recording of assets does not occur, and by preventing inaccurate processing of information. Preventive controls fall into a number of categories.

Documentation

Careful design of documentation will aid the prevention of unintentional errors in recording and processing. Several points need to be taken into account for the preparation of document formats:

- Source documentation requires enough data entry spaces on it to collect all the types of data required for the purposes for which the document is to be used.

- Transfer of data from one document to another should be minimized, as transcription errors are common. It is usual to use multipart documentation, which transfers the contents of the top copy through several layers by the pressure of the pen.

- Documents should be clearly headed with a document type and document description.

- Documents should be sequentially prenumbered. Provided that any 'waste' documents are retained, this allows a check on the completeness of document processing. It is aimed at preventing the accidental misplacing of documents and ensures that documents used for the generation of fraudulent transactions are retained for inspection.

- A document generally represents the recording of some transaction, such as an order for a set of items, and will undergo several processes in the course of carrying out the transaction requirements. It is important that wherever authorization for a step is required, the document has space for the authorization code or signature.

● The documentation needs to be stored in a manner that allows retrieval of the steps through which a transaction has passed. This may require storing copies of the document in different places accessed by different reference numbers, customer account numbers and dates. This is called an **audit trail**.

Procedures manual

As well as clearly designed forms the accurate processing of a transaction document requires those responsible to carry out the organization's procedures correctly. These should be specified in a procedures manual. This will contain a written statement of the functions to be carried out by the various personnel in the execution of data processing. Document flowcharts (covered in Chapter 11 on process analysis and modelling) are an important aid to unambiguous specification. They indicate the path that is taken through the various departments and operations by a document and its copies until the document finally leaves the business organization, or is stored.

The procedures manual, if followed, prevents inconsistent practices from arising that govern the processing of transactions and other operations. Inconsistency leads to inaccurate or incomplete processing. The manual can also be used for staff training, further encouraging consistent practice within the organization.

Separation of functions

It is sound practice to separate the various functions that need to be performed in processing data. These different functions are the responsibility of different personnel within the organization. The separation is aimed at preventing fraud.

If a single member of staff were to be in charge of carrying out all the procedures connected with a transaction then it would be possible, and might be tempting, for that person to create fraudulent transactions. For instance, if a person were responsible for authorizing a cash payment, recording the payment and making the payment then it would be easy to carry out theft. When these functions are separated and placed in the hands of different individuals fraud may still be tempting but less possible as collusion between several persons is required. It is usual to separate the following functions:

● the custody of assets, such as cash, cheques and inventory;
● the recording function, such as preparing source documents, carrying out book-keeping functions and preparing reconciliations;
● the authorization of operations and transactions, such as the authorization of cash payments, purchase orders and new customer credit limits.

These functions may also be carried out in different geographical locations (in different offices or even different sites). If documentation is passed from one department to another the physical isolation of personnel provides further barriers to collusion.

Both functional and geographical separation are difficult to implement in a small business organization as there may be so few staff that separation becomes impossible.

Personnel controls

A business relies on its personnel. Personnel must be selected and trained effectively to ensure that they are competent to carry out the tasks required of them.

Selection procedures should establish the qualification, experience and special talents required for the post being offered. Tests, interviews, the taking up of a reference and the checking of qualifications held will determine whether a candidate meets these requirements. The prevention of incompetent personnel being selected for tasks is an important control because once they are hired, the employment legislation in many countries makes it difficult to remove a member of staff even if that person's unsuitability for the job is discovered.

Training needs to be planned carefully to ensure that it delivers the necessary skills to staff, given their initial abilities and the tasks that they are to perform.

Supervision of staff at the workplace, as well as preventing fraud, also aids staff who are learning a new process by giving them the confidence that experience and authority are available to assist them with any difficulties that may arise.

Finally, it should never be forgotten that the personnel in an organization are people in their own right, with a wide range of interests, abilities, limitations, objectives and personality styles. If they are to work together successfully and happily, considerable ability needs to be displayed by management in preventing interpersonal differences and difficulties from escalating and leading to disputes that affect the smooth running of the organization.

Physical controls

One way of avoiding illegal loss of assets such as cash is to exclude staff from unnecessary access to these assets. A range of physical controls may be used to prevent access – locks, safes, fences and stout doors are obvious methods. It may be equally important to prevent records from being unnecessarily available to staff. Once again, physical controls may be used as a preventive measure. There are a range of natural hazards that affect a manual information system, hazards which can be guarded against. Fire controls, for instance, are an essential and often legally required feature of a business.

8.2   Controls over computerized information systems

If terminal operators never keyed in inaccurate data, if hardware never malfunctioned or disks never became corrupted, if there were no fires or floods, if computer operators never loaded incorrect tapes, if software always achieved what was intended, if people had no desires to embezzle or steal information, if employees harboured no grudges, if these or many other events never occurred there would be no need for controls. However, they do happen and happen regularly, sometimes with devastating results.

The three types of control – feedforward, feedback and preventive – covered in Section 8.1 are applicable to manual information systems. The presence of a computer-based information system requires different controls. These fall within the same three-fold categorization, although in computer-based systems there is an emphasis on preventive controls.

Controls are present over many aspects of the computer system and its surrounding social (or non-technical) environment. They operate over data movement into, through and out of the computer to ensure correct, complete and reliable processing and storage. There are other controls present over staff, staff involvement with the computer, staff procedures, access to the computer and access to data. Further controls are effective at preventing deterioration or collapse of the entire computing function. This section starts by considering the aims and goals of control over computer systems and then covers these various areas of control.

8.2.1 Goals of control

Each control that operates over a computer system, its surrounding manual procedures and staffing has a specific goal or set of goals. These goals may be divided into categories. There are primary goals, which involve the prevention of undesired states of affairs from occurring, and there are secondary goals directed at some aspect of loss. If the primary goals are not achieved other controls take over and provide some support. The various levels of control are:

1. **Deterrence and prevention:** At this level the goal is to prevent erroneous data processing or to deter potential fraud. Many controls are designed to operate at this level.

2. **Detection:** If fraud or accidental error has occurred (that is, the primary goal has not been achieved) it is important that the fraud or error is detected so that matters may be corrected if possible. Indeed, the existence of detection often acts as a deterrent to fraud. Detection controls are particularly important in data communications where noise on the communications channel can easily corrupt data.

3. **Minimization of loss:** Some controls are designed to minimize the extent of loss, financial or otherwise, occurring as a result of accident or intention. A backup file, for example, will ensure that master file failure only involves a loss from the time the backup was made.

4. **Recovery:** Recovery controls seek to establish the state of the system prior to the breach of control or mishap. For instance, a reciprocal arrangement with another company using a similar computer will ensure that the crucial data processing of a company can be carried out in the case of massive computer failure.

5. **Investigation:** Investigation is a form of control. An example is an internal audit. Nowadays the facilitation of investigation is one of the design criteria generally applied to information systems development in business.

Controls are directed at:

1. **Malfunctions:** Hardware and software occasionally malfunction, but the most common cause is 'people malfunction'. People are always the weak link in any person–machine system as far the performance of specified tasks is concerned. They may be ill, underperform, be negligent, misread data and so on. Unintentional errors are common unless prevented by a system of controls.

2. **Fraud:** Fraud occurs when the organization suffers an intentional financial loss as a result of illegitimate actions within the company. (Fraud might be regarded as the result of a moral malfunction!). Fraud may be of a number of types:

   (a) Intentionally inaccurate data processing and record-keeping for the purpose of embezzlement is the most well-known kind of fraud. The advent of the computer means that all data processing (including fraudulent data processing) is carried out faster, more efficiently and in large volumes. Embezzlement may take the form of a 'one-off' illegitimate transfer of funds or may use the massive processing power of the computer repeatedly to carry out transactions each involving a small sum of money.

   There is a now-legendary fraud perpetrated by a bank's computer programmer who patched a program subroutine for calculating the interest payments to customer accounts, so that odd halfpenny interest payments (which are not recorded in accounts) were transferred to his own account. A halfpenny is not a fortune except when transferred thousands of times a day, every day.

(b) The computer is used for processing transactions that are not part of the organization's activities. It is not uncommon for staff to use the mainframe or microcomputer facilities to word process private documents occasionally or to play adventure games when the time is available. At the other end of the scale, and more seriously, computer centre personnel have been known to run their own independent computer bureau from within the organization using large chunks of mainframe processing time, company software and their own time paid for by the organization.

(c) Illegitimate copying of data or program files for use outside the organization's activities may be considered a fraud. For instance, the transfer of company customer data to a competitor may cause financial loss.

3. **Intentional damage:** Computer centres have been the target for sabotage and vandalism. The angry employee who pours honey into the printer or plants a logic bomb within the software is an internal enemy. Increasingly, computer centres are aware of the possibility of external attack from pressure groups that step outside the law.

4. **Unauthorized access:** Unauthorized access is generally a prelude to fraud or intentional damage and therefore needs to be prevented. It occurs when persons who are not entitled have access to the computer system or its communication facilities 'break in'. Hackers generally do this for fun but there may be more sinister motives. Many internal company personnel as well as the public at large are in the category of those not entitled to use the computer system. Alternatively, unauthorized access may occur when a person who is entitled to access does so, but at illegitimate times or to part of the computer for which he or she is not entitled. For instance, company employees may access parts of the database for which they have no authorization.

5. **Natural disasters:** Included in this category are fires, earthquake, floods, lightning, and other disasters that may befall a computer installation. Each of these may be unlikely but their effects are serious and imply a large financial loss to the company. Power failures are rare nowadays in developed countries but if there is a power cut and the temporary non-functioning of the computer is a serious loss then backup power supplies need to be provided. The same is true for communications facilities. There are a large number of rather special circumstances that might need to be taken into account. For instance, a large computer installation located near a naval radar and communication base had to be rebuilt inside a Faraday cage (a large, meshed-metal surround) to avoid interference.

6. **Viruses:** Computer viruses have become prevalent in the 1990s. A virus is computer code that has been inserted (unauthorized) into a piece of software. Upon execution of the software the virus is also executed. Its function may be innocuous, e.g. to flash a 'HELLO', or harmful, such as destroying files or corrupting disks. The virus may be resident in the software for a long period of time before being activated by an event, such as a specific electronic date within the computer. Copying and distributing software (containing viruses but not known to do so) on floppy disks can spread viruses quickly.

8.2.2   Controls over data movement through the computer system

Erroneous data processing by a computer system is likely to be the result of incorrect data input. This is the major point at which the human interfaces with the machine and it is here where important controls are placed.

Input controls

Many of the controls over data input require some processing power to implement. They could be classed as processing controls but given that interactive data input with real-time correction is becoming very common it is convenient to lump these together as controls over input.

Accuracy controls:

1. **Format checks:** On entry, the item of data is checked against an expected picture or format. For instance, a product code may always consist of three letters, followed by an oblique, followed by two digits and then three letters. The picture is AAA/99AAA.

2. **Limit checks:** A data item may be expected to fall within set limits. An employee's work hours for the week will lie between 0 and 100 hours, for example, or account numbers of customers lie between 1000 and 3000.

3. **Reasonableness checks:** These are sophisticated forms of limit checks. An example might be a check on an electricity meter reading. The check might consist of subtracting the last reading recorded from the current reading and comparing this with the average usage for that quarter. If the reading differs by a given percentage then it is investigated before processing.

4. **Check-digit verification:** Account reference codes consisting of large numbers of digits are prone to transcription errors. Types of errors include:
   (a) Single-digit errors: where a single digit is transcribed incorrectly, for example, 4968214 for 4966214. These account for approximately 86% of errors.
   (b) Transposition errors and where two digits are exchanged, for example, 4968214 for 4986214. These amount to approximately 8% of errors.
   (c) Other errors: such as double-digit errors and multiple transpositions. These comprise about 6% of errors.

   In order to detect such errors a check digit is added to the (account) code. The digit is calculated in such a way that the majority of transcription errors can be detected by comparing the check digit with the remainder of the (account) code. In principle there is no limit to the percentage of errors that can be detected by the use of more and more check digits but at some point the increasing cost of extra digits exceeds the diminishing marginal benefit of the error detection.

   The modulus-11 check-digit system is simple and is in common use. The principle is as follows:

   First, take the code for which a check digit is required and form the weighted total of the digits. The weight for the least significant digit is 2, the next least significant is 3. . . . If the number is 49628 then:

   $$(4 \times 6) + (9 \times 5) + (6 \times 4) + (2 \times 3) + (8 \times 2) = 116.$$

   Second, subtract the total from the smallest number divisible by 11 which is equal to or higher than the total. The remainder is the check digit. In the example:

$$121 - 115 = 6 \ (= \text{check digit})$$

(If the remainder is 10 it is common to use X as the check digit.) Thus the account number with the check digit is 496286.

Suppose that an error is made in transcribing this number during the course of manual data processing or on input into the computer. A quick calculation shows that the check digit does not match the rest of the (account) code. For example, the erroneous 492686 is checked as follows:

$$(4 \times 6) + (9 \times 5) + (2 \times 4) + (6 \times 3) + (8 \times 2) + (6 \times 1) = 117.$$

117 should be divisible by 11. It is not, so the error has been detected.

The modulus-11 method will detect most errors. Because of its arithmetic nature computers can carry out these checks quickly.

5. **Master-file checks:** With online real-time systems where interactive data entry is available, the master file associated with a transaction may be searched for confirming data. For example, a source document order form that is printed with both the customer code number and customer name may be handled by input of the customer number at the keyboard. The master file is searched (perhaps it is indexed on account reference number) and the name of the customer is displayed on the screen. This can be checked with the name on the source document. This type of check is very common in microcomputer-based accounting packages. Obviously it is not possible with batch systems.

6. **Form design:** General principles of good form design were covered earlier in Section 8.1.3. With respect to data input, the layout of source documentation from which data is taken should match the screen layout presented to the keyboard operator. This not only minimizes errors but also speeds data input. Data fields on source documents should be highlighted if they are to be input.

Completeness totals: To input data erroneously is one type of error. To leave out or lose data completely is another type of error against which controls are provided.

1. **Batch control totals:** The transactions are collected together in batches of say 50 transactions. A total of all the data values of some important field is made. For example, if a batch of invoices is to be input, a total of all the invoice amounts might be calculated manually. This control total is then compared with a computer-generated control total after input of the batch of transactions. A difference indicates either a lost transaction or the input of an incorrect invoice total. The method is not foolproof as compensating errors are possible.

2. **Batch hash totals:** The idea is similar to control totals except that hash totals are a meaningless total prepared purely for control purposes. The total of all customer account numbers in a batch is meaningless but may be used for control by comparing it with the computer-generated hash total.

3. **Batch record totals:** A count is taken of the number of transactions and this is compared with the record count produced by the computer at the end of the batch.

4. **Sequence checks:** Documents may be prenumbered sequentially before entry and at a later stage the computer will perform a sequence check and display any missing numbers.

duplicate computations. The outputs of each set of circuits are compared for discrepancy. This reduces the probability of processing errors.

Hardware should be designed to incorporate fault detection, avoidance and tolerance features. Duplicating central processing units, input/output channels and disk drives for comparing the results of data processing is one option. Another is to maintain redundant components, which are brought in when hardware failure occurs or during maintenance. A third option is to increase the tolerance of the system to hardware failure by having a common pool of resources such as CPUs and disk drives which meet the needs of tasks as required. If one of these fails operations can still continue, though somewhat degraded in performance, in the remainder.

Output controls

Output controls ensure that the results of data processing are accurate, complete and are directed to authorized recipients:

1. **Control totals:** As in input and processing control, totals are used to detect data loss or addition.

2. **Prenumbering:** Cheques, passbooks, stock certificates and other documentation of value on which output is produced should be prenumbered and accounted for.

3. **Authorization:** Negotiable documents will require authorization, and steps must be taken to ensure their safe transport from the computer centre to the relevant user department.

4. **Sensitive output:** Output that is regarded as confidential should be automatically directed to secure output devices in a location that is protected from personnel not entitled to view the output.

Data transmission controls

Data transmission occurs between the various local peripheral components of a computer system and the CPU and may, on a wider scale, also involve telecommunications links between a number of computers or peripherals and the central computing resource. These latter links are vulnerable to unauthorized access, giving rise to data loss, data alteration and eavesdropping. All communication is subject to data transmission errors resulting from electronic 'noise' interfering with the reliable transmission of 1s and 0s.

1. **Parity bit control:** Characters will be encoded as strings of bits according to some standard or other such as ASCII. A parity bit is added to the end of the bits representing a character. 'Odd parity' ('even parity') means that the resulting total (that is, the coded character plus the added 1 or 0) must consist of an odd number (even number) of 1s. The set of bits is tested by hardware, and any failure to meet the control standard requires retransmission. For its success as a detection control it relies on the corruption of data affecting an odd (usually 1) number of bits, otherwise the errors may be compensating.

2. **Echo checks:** The message transmitted by the sender to the receiver is retransmitted by the receiver back to the sender. The echoed transmission is then compared with the first transmission. Any discrepancy indicates a data transmission error somewhere. Echo checks are common between the CPU and VDUs or printers.

3. Control total: At the end of a transmitted message a set of control totals is placed that give information such as the total number of blocks or records sent. This is checked on receipt of the message.

8.2.3 Access controls

Access controls are usually aimed at preventing unauthorized (as distinct from accidental) access. The controls may seek to prevent persons who are authorized for access from having unauthorized access to restricted data and programs, as well as preventing unauthorized persons from gaining access to the system as a whole.

Controls over access to the computer system

Before a user is granted access to the system that user needs to be identified, and that identification authenticated in order to establish authorization. It is common for users to be given login codes or user identification codes. These are not regarded as particularly secret. The authentication of the identity is established by:

- a unique characteristic of the person, such as a voice print or fingerprint;
- a security device unique to that person, such as an identity card;
- a password.

Unique personal characteristics are currently infrequently used but will be employed with greater frequency in the future. Developments await technological advancement, particularly in voice recognition.

Security devices are commonly used where physical access control is important, such as entry into the various rooms of a computer centre.

Passwords are the most common form of authentication or identification. A password scheme requires the user to enter a string of characters, which the computer checks against its internal record of passwords associated with user identification. Generally, there is a facility for the user to change his or her password once logged into the system. The use of passwords appears a simple and effective access control but there are limitations.

User-selected passwords are often easy to guess. The number of people who choose 'PASS', 'FRED', the name of their husband, wife, child or dog is notorious. A recent report on computer security indicated that for a number of years the chairman of a large organization used 'CHAIRMAN' as his password. It is easy to see why these passwords are selected. Users are not interested in computer security but in the easiest legitimate access to the system, in order to perform the tasks for which they require the computer. They may view passwords as a necessary hindrance to carrying out their tasks rather than an essential component of the organization's security system.

System-generated passwords appear to be a possible solution but these are difficult to remember and therefore likely to be written down, which provides further security problems. An alternative is to require individuals to change their passwords regularly. This makes them less vulnerable (whether user selected or system generated) but more difficult to remember.

It is generally recognized that good password security depends on better education of users for the need for security, rather than on more technologically sophisticated techniques.

Password details are encrypted within the computer, and are never displayed on the screen. They should not be accessible even to senior computer centre personnel. Loss of a password should require a new user identification code to be issued, as well as a new password.

Although password controls are common they are not infallible, even with the most conscientious user. Short programs have been written that repeatedly attempt to log into a computer system. The program may be set to increment the tried password in a methodical fashion until a password fitting the login code is achieved. It is easy to prevent such clumsy attempts by automatic testing of the number of password trials associated with the login code. When a given number of unsuccessful attempts have been made in a period of time no further login is possible under that code.

It is harder to prevent other equally simple but more elegant methods of password evasion. A simple terminal emulation program may be written and run. To the user sitting in front of the screen it appears that a perfectly normal request for a login code and password is presented. On entering these details they are recorded on a file for future consideration by the person attempting to gain unauthorized access. The user will not realize that this has been done as the terminal emulation program will then display a simple error message or abort and pass the login code and password to the control of the legitimate procedure for handling login access.

Control over access to data

Once legitimate (or unauthorized) access has been gained to the computer system the user should then be faced with other restrictions. Obviously any system of control should not allow all users access to all files and programs. Generally users are restricted to:

- The execution of a limited number of programs.
- Access to a limited set of files or part of the corporate database.
- Access to only certain items within these files or database.
- Performing only limited operations on these areas of access. For instance, one user may be entitled to read and write to various records, another may be restricted to read only, and a third to read and copy.

In deciding on data access two issues arise:

1. the policy to be adopted;
2. the mechanisms by which the policy is implemented.

Under 1 certain principles should be followed for a sound policy on security.

- Each user should be entitled to access data and perform operations within the computer system only to the extent needed to carry out that user's legitimate tasks. Put another way, access is restricted to the minimum compatible with the user's needs. For instance, a management accountant might be entitled to read stock records but not to write to them and neither to read nor write to employee records. Once again, a member of the department dealing with weekly wages may only be entitled to read the employee records of those who are waged (not salaried). For this policy to be carried out it is necessary to spend considerable time and effort determining for each user the nature of tasks that they perform and the

Figure 8.3: Examples of access matrices. (a) Operating system access matrix.
(b) Database access matrix.

(a) **Subject/**
user   **Object**

	File 1	File 2	File 3	File 4	Device 1	Device 2
A43801	Read		Execute			
A43802		Read/Write		Execute	Use	
A43803	Read	Read			Use	Use
A43804	Read		Execute		Use	

(b) **Subject**
user   **Stock details**

	Stock ID	Description	Quantity held	Cost price	Sale price	Reorder level	Reorder placed
Management accountant	Read	Read	Read	Read	Read	Read	Read
Inventory control	Read	Read	Read/Write		Read	Read	Read
Purchasing	Read	Read		Read	Read	Write	Write

range of data needed for these. As well as restricting authorized users, limitation also minimizes the damage that can be achieved through unauthorized access via the route taken by an authorized user.

● The simpler the control mechanism the more effective it is likely to be. Complex mechanisms are more difficult to maintain and less easily understood.

● It is often claimed that the design of the security mechanisms (though not of course their specific content) should not rely on secrecy for part of their effectiveness.

● Every data access request should be checked for authorization.

Under 2 the mechanisms by which the policy is implemented are known as **access control mechanisms**. They come into force both at the level of the operating system and also independently through the database management system. They may be represented in an access matrix where the rows of the matrix are users or user groups and the columns are the objects over which access is controlled. The cell entries indicate the type of access allowed for the user–object combination. Figure 8.3 is an illustration of the ideas behind an access matrix for operating system controls and database control over records.

Operating system access controls: may be organized in the form of hierarchies where superior users have all the access of inferior users plus extra rights. Another approach is to associate with each object, such as a file, a list of users that are authorized to use it and the type of operation they may perform. The access control list for a file then corresponds to the non-emptying cell entries for a column in the matrix in Figure 8.3(a).

Operating systems may store files in tree structures where a user 'owns' a tree or part of a tree as that user's file space. It is common for that owner to have maximum rights over the tree or subtree whereas non-owners have restricted rights as specified by the owner. A facility may also be available to set passwords over trees or subtrees, so further enhancing security.

Database management system access controls: are more fine-grained in their selectivity than operating system access controls. They will restrict access not only to records but also to specified logical relationships between these records and individual fields within the records. The nature of the allowed operations will also be defined. Read, update, insert and delete are common. Unlike operating system access controls, database management system access controls may be data dependent as well as data independent. In some database environments data items are selected by value; therefore access can be allowed on the basis of the values satisfying some condition. For example, a user may only be allowed to read an employee salary field if that employee salary is less than a specified amount. Database controls are selective, so they require a detailed study of each user's data requirements if the access is not to be too slack (ineffective controls) or too tight (impeding user tasks).

Cryptographic controls

Preventing unauthorized access to the computer system and then restricting access of legitimate users to subsets of the file base or database may be regarded as insufficient control in the case of very confidential data. If a breach of security leads to data access then it is a further control to store the data in an encoded form so that the data will be meaningless and worthless to the intruder. Cryptography is the science of coding and decoding for security purposes.

Encoding data, or encrypting it, is not only used as a secure storage form but is particularly important in data transmission where communication channels are vulnerable to eavesdropping. Cryptography has always been important for military communications but has only recently been of commercial significance. This is a result of electronic funds transfer and the increasing use of networked computers in transference of confidential business data.

The security process involves the conversion of the plain text message or data into cipher text by the use of an encryption algorithm and an encryption key. The opposite process, decryption, involves deciphering the cipher text by the use of an algorithm and decryption key to reproduce the plain text data or message. If the encryption and decryption keys are identical the entire procedure is known as a **symmetric cryptoprocess**. Otherwise it is known as **asymmetric**.

A simple cryptotransformation of the kind used in schoolboy secret messages is shown in Figure 8.4. This is called a **substitute transformation**. In the case of encryption used for communication the key is transmitted over a highly secure data link from the message sender to the receiver. The cipher text can then be sent through a less secure channel, often at a much faster speed. If encrypted data is stored then the key is kept separate from the cipher text. The application of the key with the decryption algorithm (which can be public) enables decryption to produce the original plain text. Simple encryption algorithms and keys, such as those shown in Figure 8.4, which associate a unique character on a one-to-one basis with each character of the alphabet are easy to 'crack'. A

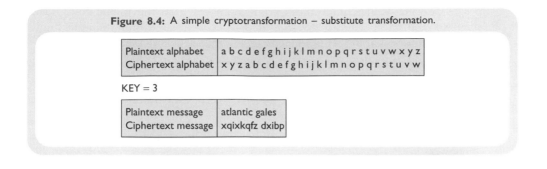

Figure 8.4: A simple cryptotransformation – substitute transformation.

| Plaintext alphabet | a b c d e f g h i j k l m n o p q r s t u v w x y z |
| Ciphertext alphabet | x y z a b c d e f g h i j k l m n o p q r s t u v w |

KEY = 3

| Plaintext message | atlantic gales |
| Ciphertext message | xqixkqfz dxibp |

common method is to take the most commonly occurring cipher text character and associate it with 'e', which is the most commonly used letter in the alphabet in English prose. The next most common are then paired and so on. More complex algorithms and keys ensure that plain text characters are differently coded depending on their position in the plain text.

The Data Encryption Standard: A Data Encryption Standard (DES) was agreed in the USA in 1977. This standard is for non-military data. The standard requires splitting the plain text into 64-bit blocks. The encrypting algorithm requires the iteration of a certain transformation 16 times to produce a 64-bit cipher text block. This is performed on each 64 bit plain text block. The key used in the algorithm for both encryption and decryption consists of 64 bits (8 of which are parity bits). Once the key is possessed both encryption and decryption are straightforward algorithmic processes, which may be carried out effectively and quickly by a computer.

The security of the system (datastored or message transmitted) now relies on the security of storage or the security of transmission of the key. This is an improvement, as security control now has to be maintained over a piece of data of 64 bits (the key) rather than several megabytes of stored or transmitted data. Obviously the key itself should be made unpredictable, say, by randomly generating the 64 bits.

Doubt has recently been cast on the DES. Using very fast computers, a large enough piece of cipher text and its corresponding plain text, all 2^{56} possible keys can be used to decrypt the cipher text. The result of each decryption can be compared with the given plain text and the correct key established. The time taken to carry out the exhaustive search would be a matter of hours rather than weeks, and if computing power continues to increase both the cost and time taken for such an analysis will drop considerably. It has been argued, though, that the principle behind the DES is sound and can be guaranteed against plausible advances in computing power by increasing the key to 128 bits (16 of which are parity bits). This would require an exhaustive search of 2^{112} keys.

Public key cryptography: While the DES uses asymmetric cryptoprocess public key cryptography is an asymmetric cryptosystem. It works as follows:

- The encryption and decryption algorithms are straightforward and public.
- A receiver has a code number, which may be public. This number is the product of two very large prime numbers (each in excess of 100 digits), which are known to the receiver but to no one else. It is impossible, because of the computational

power needed, to determine these prime numbers from the public code. (The standard method of dividing the code by successively large prime numbers until a perfect divisor is found is too lengthy even with a high-powered computer.)

● The transmitter of a message selects an encryption key determined by the public receiver code number satisfying certain conditions, which are publicly known.

● As well as the cipher message, the receiver code and the encryption key are transmitted.

● It is impossible to 'back encrypt' the cipher text to reach the plain text using the encryption key.

● The decryption key can only be found by calculation using the encryption key together with the prime numbers whose product is the public code of the receiver. The system relies on the impossibility of discovering these primes from the public receiver code.

The system is very attractive as different receivers can have different public codes and transmitters can change encryption keys as often as is liked for security. The cipher text, the encryption keys and the receiver keys can be transmitted without jeopardizing public security. The strength of the system relies on the impossibility of determining the decryption key without the two large prime numbers. Recent research by mathematicians has come up with more efficient algorithms for determining whether a number is prime than the traditional sieve of Eratosthenes (to determine if a number is prime divide it by each whole number less than or equal to its square root). It remains to be seen whether this will affect the security of the product of primes method of cryptography.

As data communication traffic increases in volume and the need for maintaining secure data storage and transmission becomes more important it is likely that cryptosystems will become an integral part of data handling. Trends in data protection legislation, where data holders are legally obliged to take reasonable steps to ensure the privacy of personal data against unauthorized access, can only increase this movement.

Physical access controls
The access controls considered earlier in this section all assume that physical access to some aspect of the computer system, such as a terminal or data transmission channel, has been achieved and the task is to prevent the unauthorized intruder from gaining further access. Physical access controls aim to prevent this initial state from arising. They are particularly effective when the computer system is geographically centralized. The greater the dispersion of equipment and distribution of connected computing power the less effective they become. (It is easier to maintain control over equipment that is located in one big box (the computer centre) than when it is geographically dispersed in smaller boxes all connected by communication lines.) Currently the trend is towards networks and decentralized computing; therefore physical access controls play a less important role than previously in the prevention of unauthorized access. The following are some of the most common types of these controls.

Magnetic cards: Plastic cards with user identification encoded on magnetic stripes on the card are a popular form of access control to equipment and to the rooms containing the equipment. The user runs the card through a magnetic stripe reader and the details are checked for authenticity. In some systems the user is also required to input a personal identification number. These systems are popular because they are cheap and also provide computer-based monitoring of access if the magnetic stripe-reading equipment is connected to a computer. For instance, a computer centre may have a magnetic card reader on each door within the building. At any moment the computer has a record of who is where in the building and how long they have been there. Moreover, the records of personnel movement may be retained on a file for future analysis if required.

Smart cards: Smart cards are the same size as magnetic cards (that is, credit-card size) but contain information encoded on microchips built into the cards. They store more information and are harder to counterfeit than magnetic cards but their cost of production is higher. They are used in a similar way to magnetic cards in access control.

Closed-circuit video monitoring: As for many other installations that require security controls, closed-circuit video can be used. It is expensive if manned operation is required but may be used as an unattended video record of computer centre occupants.

Signature access: Traditional sign in/sign out procedures can now be made more secure as computer-based signature checking is possible. As well as determining the authenticity of the shape of the signature (which is fairly easy to forge) checks can now be made of pressure and the way that the pen moves in forming a signature when it is not directly in contact with the paper. These latter two properties are difficult to copy.

Guards and escorts: Guards may be placed at entry points to the computer facility and act as administrators over other entry procedures and escorts for unfamiliar personnel or sensitive material.

Data transmission controls: Data transmission lines throughout the computer centre should be securely embedded. It is particularly important if the lines pass out of the building, as they may with a local area network, that attention should be paid to preventing unauthorized tapping.

8.2.4 Organizational control

Up to now in this chapter controls over data movement through the computer system and access to the system and the data within it have been considered. Many of these controls are technical and clear cut in the sense that they require some kind of physical or electronic mechanism (for instance a computer) to implement, or they are straightforward procedures connected with these (such as the batching of transactions and calculation of a control total prior to data input). Other controls are more general and are best thought of as principles rather than clearly defined procedures or mechanisms. In particular, the way the information systems function is organized and managed and the way the work is allocated between different personnel will affect the overall accuracy and reliability of information processing. Also, if certain principles are followed in systems project development then the resulting information systems are less prone to failure – however failure may be interpreted. These areas are outlined in this section.

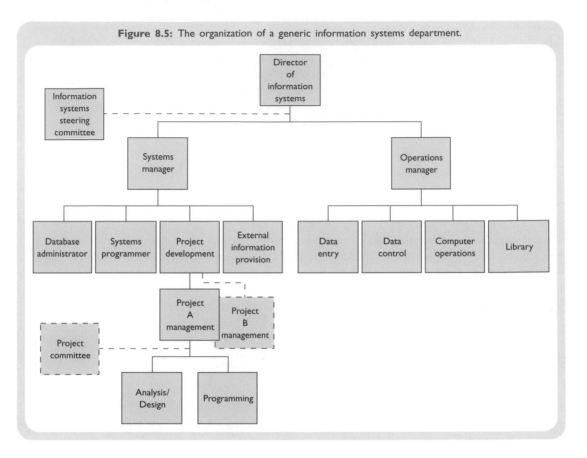

Figure 8.5: The organization of a generic information systems department.

Organization of the information systems function

Over recent years the emphasis in business computer systems has shifted from the processing of data on a batch basis to the provision of information, often interactively within an integrated total information system consisting of the computer, computer centre personnel, users and tasks for which the information is provided. This move towards the information-based approach has, in some organizations, been accompanied by the partial decentralization of equipment and application processing as a result of the proliferation of microcomputers and microcomputer-based networks. It is difficult to maintain the same degree of control over microcomputer-based systems. Their easy access, their simple-to-use operating systems and their floppy disks are both an attraction to users and a problem for the exercise of control. This section concentrates only on those information systems functions carried out centrally in what was, and still often is, called the computer centre.

Figure 8.5 is a hierarchy chart of the typical divisions of responsibility in a generic information systems department. The functions are divided into the day-to-day data entry and processing and the other activities such as the administration of the database and systems project development. The chart illustrates a project-centred approach where programmers and analysts are assigned to development projects as they become current.

Director of information systems: This person fulfils two roles. Externally to the computer centre, but within the organization, the director represents the information system at a senior managerial level (vice-president or director). He or she will be expected to play a part in deciding the overall goals and plans of the organization and in ensuring that the information system contributes to them. Internally, the director is responsible for the establishment of a structure and personnel base that will lead to a reliable and cost-efficient provision of information, not only currently but throughout the changing future of the organization. As well as a thorough understanding of technical issues concerning information systems the director needs considerable managerial and administrative skills.

Operations manager: This person is responsible for the day-to-day execution of the organization's data and information processing. The operations manager reports directly to the director and administers the subordinate functions as shown in Figure 8.5.

Data entry: Personnel in this role prepare and verify source data for entry and processing. They are also responsible for input of prepared data via the input devices such as keyboards or optical character readers.

Data control: Data control staff record and chart the progress of data-processing jobs. They also ensure that input control procedures are followed and are responsible for the preparation and checking of control totals for establishing the completeness of input and processing.

Computer operators: The computer operators load tapes and other storage media such as exchangeable disk packs, monitor and respond to console messages during processing, load printers with paper and remove the output hard copy and generally service the day-to-day processing activities.

File librarian: The librarian is responsible for storing offline files held on tape and disk. It is important that the librarian maintains a record of files and programs checked out to other personnel for use.

Systems manager: This management responsibility is for the development of new projects and the maintenance of existing software and the database. Within project development the systems manager is responsible for setting standards for systems design, programming and documentation, for overall planning and coordinating new applications, and for the allocation of staff resources (analysts and programmers) to projects.

Database administrator: The database administrator ensures that the database is maintained in a secure manner and functions efficiently to the satisfaction of data requests from users and application programs. He or she will be involved in amending the database conceptual schema and defining external schema in the course of new project developments. The role of the database administrator was covered more extensively in the chapter on databases.

Systems programmers: This group ensures the effective functioning of the operating system and its associated utilities, compilers, database management system and software.

Table 8.1: Perpetrators of computer fraud (%).

	UK	USA	S. Africa
Executives and supervisors	38	14	22
Programmers	10	21	11
Other non-supervisory staff	–	14	14
Clerks/other non-supervisory staff	35	13	30
Others/external	17	38	23

Sources: UK: Audit Commission *Computer Fraud Survey 1985.*
USA: *American Bar Association Report on Computer Crime* 1984.
S. Africa: KMG Acken and Carter *Computer Crime in South Africa.*

They will give technical support to applications programmers on programs that require special interfacing with the operating system. The system programmers will carry out operating system enhancements as supplied by the computer manufacturers.

Project managers: Each project will have a manager whose task it is to ensure that adequate detailed planning and administration of the project is carried out. This will involve setting points at which various 'deliverables' such as documentation (according to standards) or programs will be completed. The manager is also responsible for ensuring that development standards are adhered to, especially in program development and testing.

Systems analysts: The analyst determines the information needs of the users and produces a system design in accordance with these. The process of systems analysis and design and the role of the analyst is considered extensively in the following chapters.

Programmers: The programmers convert the process design by the analyst into programming code in a specified language.

External information provision: Although much documentation within a computer centre is for internal consumption there are requirements externally within the organization for details on aspects of information provision. These may take the form of newsletters, user manuals for applications programs and presentations to other department of services offered by the centre.

Separation of functions and control of personnel

The separation of functions and control of personnel was considered from a general standpoint in the coverage of preventive controls presented earlier in this chapter in Section 8.1.3. Applied to the computer centre, functional separation is accomplished between four separate areas: computer operations, project development, the file and program library, and data entry and control. The importance of computer centre staff in perpetrating fraud can be seen in Table 8.1. These figures should be treated with caution as, first, the categories produced in the various reports are not identical and, second, much computer fraud goes undetected or unreported.

The separation of analyst/programmer functions from those of day-to-day computer operations prevents programmers who make unauthorized changes to programs from having the power to put those programs into operation. Conversely, access to programs and program documentation is restricted for operations staff to prevent a computer operator from making unauthorized program changes then activating that program.

Programmers should have written instructions specifying program changes and these changes should be fully documented. During systems development the program specifications supplied by analysts provide such documentation. At all times it is inadvisable to allow programmers access to live data or current master files.

Computer operations staff should be closely supervised. Rotation of personnel in shifts and ensuring that at least two members of staff are always present in the computer room are steps that can be taken in centres with large numbers of staff.

A separate file library in which all access to program and data files requires authorization is a further control. Details of loans should be kept.

The separation of data entry from the function of data control provides a measure of security against fraudulent transactions generated on data input. There should, anyway, be independent controls (such as batch totals) created by departments originating transactions. These should be administered by data-control personnel as well as those controls emanating from within the computer centre. Within data entry it is common to separate the functions of master-file amendments (such as insertion of a new customer) from transaction entry to prevent the creation of a fictitious customer and subsequent processing of fraudulent transactions.

Systems programmers are in a particularly powerful position and it is important that they do not have unrestricted access to live data files and are not able to execute applications programs. One further safeguard is to ensure that applications programs documentation is not made available to them.

These separations of duties are more difficult to maintain in a small organization, where it is common for one member of staff to fulfil several functions. Microcomputer-based systems are perhaps the extreme case where integration of functions is commonplace.

8.2.5 Contingency planning

In spite of all the controls that may be devised to support the reliable workings of the computer centre, hazards may arise that lead to breakdowns. Some, such as a lengthy power cut, can be safeguarded against and overcome by a backup power generator. Others, such as fires, floods, riot, earthquake or sabotage, are more devastating. Many organizations have moved away from a decentralized manual approach to data processing with pieces of paper, to using a centralized electronic computer. Although their activities now depend on computer support, the organization cannot afford to come to an immediate standstill in the face of computer failure.

The recent increase in distributed systems has diminished the consequences of failure. Even if one computer site suffers a disaster the others may take over much of its important activities in the short term. This assumes that network links have not been severed and that copies of the files and database at the breakdown site are maintained elsewhere so that they may be loaded into the network. It is uncommon to opt for distributed systems purely on the basis of this graceful degradation in their function (except perhaps for military systems operating in hostile environments). Rather, it should be seen as a useful feature of distributed data storage and processing.

Some form of contingency planning is needed in order to take care of the unexpected computer failure (even in the case of distributed systems). These plans should involve several areas:

- Copies of files and databases should be regularly made and stored at a distant location, so that when computer operations are restored the original position of the organization may be recovered.

- Personnel need to be appointed (beforehand) to take managerial responsibility in the case of a disaster. They will need to be acquainted with procedures to be followed and with activities that are judged to be essential to the organization (as distinct from those that can be suspended). It is impossible to plan completely for all the unlikely disruptions that may arise, and the success of the contingency plan will depend on how these personnel adapt to the changed working conditions.

- Standby procedures and operations for the period of disruption will need to be arranged.

With respect to the standby plans there are a number of approaches that may be taken. Generally, those that cost more give a faster and higher level of support in the case of failure. They can be broken down into the following categories:

1. **Manual backup:** This is a short-term stopgap, which may be used before other standby assistance is brought in. If stock lists and accounts (particularly sales ledger) are printed at regular intervals then the trading of the organization may be maintained for several days. There will need to be special stationery for data entry that will enable input of transactions, occurring during the disrupted period, after computer support has been re-established.

2. **Hot-line support:** A company may offer hot-line support as a service on the basis of an annual fee. Usually it works in the following manner. The company has a set of popular minicomputers or a mainframe and also has contracts with user organizations having similar equipment to take over their data-processing activities in the case of disaster. Generally, the servicing company will guarantee immediate support in the case of computer failure in the serviced organization and the level of support will depend on prior arrangement (and the fee). In some cases almost total support can be guaranteed and the computer users in the serviced organization will hardly notice the switch-over to operations at another site. Problems may arise in the unlikely event of a computer failure simultaneously occurring in more than one serviced organization. There may also be reservations about processing confidential data off-site.

3. **Company-owned backup facility:** This is a low-risk high-cost way of meeting a computer failure. The entire system is duplicated at another site.

4. **Reciprocal agreement:** Two companies with the same equipment may agree to carry out each other's essential data processing in the case of failure. As well as possible security problems arising it is unlikely that each of the organizations will have much spare computer capacity.

Survey reports have indicated that major accounting firms are concerned about the lack of computer contingency planning in British companies. Of computer disasters occurring over the five-year period surveyed two-thirds were judged by the accountants to have been preventable and of these an inadequate backup facility was given as the major reason in over half the cases. Half of the accountants surveyed carried out checks and reported on disaster recovery procedures during the audit but little interest was shown by clients. Of companies surveyed, four-fifths were inadequately protected against fire and nearly all had no flood precautions and little or no protection against sabotage. All the current evidence points to little change having occurred in the 1990s. The combination of inadequate protection against unlikely computer failures together with poor or absent backup and recovery procedures is likely to turn a crisis into a disaster for most UK companies and underlines the need for adequate contingency planning.

8.2.6 Audits

The primary objectives of an **external audit** are to express an expert and independent opinion on the truth and fairness of the information contained in financial statements, and to ascertain and evaluate the reliability of the systems that produced this information. Secondary objectives include the investigation of fraud, errors and irregularities and the provision of advice on these and other matters to clients.

The primary objective of the **internal audit** is to evaluate controls against fraud and to maintain surveillance over the organization in order to detect fraudulent activity.

Both internal and external audits are a form of control. As well as improving preventive controls against unreliable processing they also serve to deter fraud and detect errors once they have occurred.

An extensive coverage of auditing is beyond the scope of this book – only the basic strategies are covered and then applied to a computer-based system.

The approach to an internal audit

1. First, the auditor needs to establish an understanding of the way the system functions. This will be achieved by consulting document flowcharts, procedures manuals and examples of documentation, by interviewing personnel and by observing the way that transactions are processed.

2. The next step is to document and evaluate the internal control that operates over the procedures and functioning of the system. Controls are divided into two categories. First, there are actual controls such as the provision of a check digit associated with an account code number or the preparation of a control total. The purpose of an actual control is to ensure that data is recorded and processed accurately. Second, there are higher-level controls designed to ensure that the actual controls work properly. These higher-level controls tend to conform to principles covered earlier in Section 8.1. Examples are the separation of the custody of an asset from its recording, the supervision of personnel and the authorization of a transaction by a second person.

   The controls are evaluated to decide whether 'in theory' they are adequate to meet the standards required of the system. The auditor may have a checklist against which the controls will be evaluated. For instance, the evaluation checklist dealing with company purchase orders might have the following questions:
   (a) Can goods be purchased without authority?
   (b) Can liabilities be incurred even though goods have not been received?
   (c) Can invoices be wrongly allocated?

Each of these would be subdivided. For example:

(a)(i)   What are the limits to a buyer's authority?

(a)(ii) Are unissued orders safeguarded against loss?

(a)(iii) Are purchase requisitions tied to their associated orders?

(a)(iv) Is purchasing segregated from receipt of goods, stock records and accounts payable?

3. The next stage is compliance testing. The performance of compliance tests is designed to provide the auditor with reasonable assurance that the controls established under 2 were functioning effectively throughout the period to which the audit is applied. For example, the auditor may check on compliance with the control over purchasing by:

(a) testing for evidence of a sequence check on purchase orders;

(b) testing for evidence of purchase order approval;

(c) testing for evidence of a sequence check on goods received documentation;

(d) testing for evidence of authorization of changes to purchase ledger balances.

The evidence may be provided by examination of existing documentation and records, or re-performance of the way a transaction is handled, or again by interview and enquiry as to whether and how the controls are operated. The auditor may use statistical sampling techniques in research and these lead to statistical confidence factors.

The auditor attempts, at this stage, to identify those areas of weakness in the system over which controls are ineffective or are not properly administered throughout the period.

4. The fourth stage is substantive testing. If empirical evidence established under 3 indicates that the controls may be relied on, little substantive testing is required. However, where the controls are weak it is necessary independently to verify that transactions have been properly processed and that account balances are correct. This is a lengthy and expensive process and as the cost of the auditors is borne by the company it is in their interests to ensure that internal controls can be relied upon.

5. Finally, the auditor will produce an audit report, which may be qualified if material weaknesses have been discovered in the organization's system of control.

Auditing computer-based systems

The advent of the computer has meant that transaction recording and processing happen in part within the confines of a computer system. In order to testify to the satisfactory treatment of transactions the auditor needs to take account of this new development. There are two approaches:

Auditing around the computer: The computer is treated as a 'black box'. The auditor examines the inputs and outputs and verifies that the outputs correspond to correct procedures operating on the inputs. However, the auditor does not attempt to check the processes carried out on the data within the computer. This approach can only be adopted when relatively simple computer processing occurs. The greater the complexity of the system the more serious is the omission of being able to examine the intermediate steps in the processing of transactions.

Auditing through the computer: Not only are the processes and controls surrounding the computer subject to the audit but also the computer processing controls operating over this processing are investigated. In order to gain access to these, computer audit software will aid the task of the auditor. These packages typically contain:

- interactive enquiry facilities to interrogate files;
- facilities to analyze computer security logs for 'unusual' usage of the computer system;
- the ability to compare source and object (compiled) program codes in order to detect dissimilarities;
- the facility to execute and observe the computer treatment of 'live transactions' by stepping through the processing as it occurs;
- the generation of test data;
- the generation of aids showing the logic of applications programs.

The general strategy adopted in a computer-based audit will be similar to that outlined earlier in this section. The actual controls and the higher-level controls will be evaluated and then subjected to compliance testing and, if necessary, substantive testing before an audit report is produced.

The area covered in an audit will concentrate exactly on those controls covered in Section 8.3 of this chapter. Specifically, the auditor will need to establish the completeness and accuracy of transaction processing by considering:

- input control
- storage control
- processing controls
- output controls
- data transmission controls.

The auditor will also need to be satisfied that there are adequate controls over the prevention of unauthorized access to the computer and the data within it. The auditor's task will further involve a consideration of the separation of functions between staff involved in transaction processing and the computer system and that adequate supervision of personnel is administered.

As more and more firms become computerized the importance of computer-based audits and the pressure to audit through the computer grows. Auditing is not a straightforward task that can be completed by satisfying a checklist of questions. Rather, it involves experience and the ability to apply that knowledge to differing circumstances. No two information systems are the same. From the point of view of analysis and design of computer systems audit considerations are becoming increasingly important. Nowadays, the design of an information system not only needs to take the information provision requirements and computer security into account but also the need to design the system so that auditing is facilitated.

8.3 Data protection legislation

Data protection legislation has been enacted in many countries in the last 20 years in the wake of increased concern over data held on persons using powerful computer-based storage and processing technology. It is a generally recognized right that on the one hand individuals should have some protection surrounding the holding and use of data on them, but on the other that individuals and organizations, including the state, also have rights to possess and use personal data to serve their purposes. Data protection legislation attempts to define this balance and to reconcile competing needs. The essence of the problem is to ensure privacy for individuals yet not restrict the legitimate workings of the state and other aspects of society.

Concern over data protection has increased as a result of the power of modern computers to process, store and transmit vast amounts of data cheaply and quickly. This sets them apart from their manual predecessors. Specifically:

- Large files of personal data can be interrogated easily, often using indexes on names, addresses, account numbers and so on. Manual file access is more difficult.

- The speed of response to an interrogation is extremely fast in computer-based systems as compared with their manual counterparts.

- Computer-based files can be interrogated from any part of the world (if telecommunications and outside access are provided).

- The presence of networking facilities means that entire files can be transmitted and duplicated anywhere in the world in a matter of seconds or at the most in minutes.

- It is technically possible to cross-reference and link disparate files to obtain 'personal profiles' on individuals.

- Individual records can be selected easily on the basis of sophisticated searches: for example, find all names and addresses of individuals owning a black Ford, living in the Greater Manchester area and with a criminal record.

In themselves these characteristics of modern data storage and processing are not undesirable. However, they have certain implications. First, inaccurate (as well as accurate) data can be transmitted and duplicated quickly and efficiently. Second, remote data access, targeted data retrieval and the linking of files mean that data access ability in the wrong hands can lead to a severe misuse of power. Finally, there is a danger that data on private aspects of a person's life held for legitimate purposes may be spread and become widely accessible, intruding on that person's right to privacy.

These concerns have led to data protection legislation in many countries – Sweden (1973), USA (1974), West Germany (1977), Canada (1977), France (1978) and Norway (1978). However, it was not until 1984 that data protection laws were enacted in the UK.

The Younger Report (Cmnd 5012, 1972) initially carried out an investigation into the idea of privacy in general and identified a need for attention to computer-based systems. The Lindop Report (Cmnd 6353, 1975) dealt specifically with the storage and processing of personal information in computer systems in the public and private sectors and provided outline recommendations on a data protection act. However, it was not until 1984 that the first stages of the Act became effective. The government's support for the legislation was more to do with the Council of Europe Convention on Data Protection, with which it was obliged to comply, rather than a deep adherence to data protection principles.

8.3.1   Data protection principles

The Data Protection Act in the UK contains eight principles governing data protection:

1. Personal information shall be obtained and processed fully and lawfully.
2. Personal data shall be held and used only for specified purposes.
3. Personal data shall not be used or disclosed in a manner incompatible with those specified purposes.
4. Personal data shall be adequate, relevant and not excessive in relation to those specified purposes.
5. Personal data shall be accurate and kept up to date.
6. Personal data shall not be kept longer than is necessary for the specified purposes (except in the case of archive and historical records).
7. A **data subject** (that is, a person on whom data is held) shall be entitled:
   (a) to have access at reasonable intervals and without undue delay or expense to personal data;
   (b) to have personal data corrected or erased where appropriate.
8. A **data user** (that is, a person who holds data) or computer bureau is required to ensure that appropriate precautions are taken against unauthorized access to, or alteration, disclosure or destruction of personal data and also against accidental loss.

All users holding personal data (or computer bureaux handling personal data) are required to register with the Data Protection Registrar (an office created by the Act) and to supply:

- the name and address of the data user or computer bureau;
- a description of the data to be held and the purpose for which it is held;
- a description of the intended source of the data;
- identification of persons to whom the data is to be disclosed;
- names of non-UK countries to which the data is to be transferred;
- the name and address of the person responsible for dealing with data subject enquiries and access.

The Registrar then has the power to ensure that data is used in accordance with the data protection principles. Failure to register as a data user is a criminal offence under the Act. Data subjects are also entitled to compensation for damages incurred through inaccuracy or loss of personal data or unauthorized access to the data. The compensation though is awarded as a result of a civil action brought by the data subject.

8.3.2   Entitlement to access

An individual is entitled to be informed by any data user if that user holds personal data on the individual. The data subject is entitled to a copy of this data, after payment of a small fee, provided the user is satisfied as to the authenticity of the identity of the data subject.

There are certain circumstances in which the data subject is not entitled to access. These occur when:

- data is held for law enforcement and revenue purposes when access may jeopardize these purposes;
- data is held purely for statistical and research purposes;
- data is held by bodies responsible for regulating the provision of financial services (already covered in the UK by the Consumer Credit Act 1974);
- legally privileged data is held;
- backup data is held for security purposes;
- certain data is held for social work and medical health purposes.

8.3.3   Exemptions from the Act

There are a number of exemption classes that do not require registration under the Act.

1. All data processed and stored manually is exempt from the Act.

2. Data held purely for purposes that present no threat to the data subject is not covered by the Act. This includes data held for payroll and pension, for accounting, for text preparation, for domestic purposes and for mailing lists. The restrictions are very tight. For instance, it would not be possible to use a person's payroll records to establish the number of days that an individual had been away sick (except if it was needed for preparation of payroll) without coming within the scope of the Act.

3. Data that is crucial to the interests of the state and public agencies, such as crime, tax and national security, is not within the scope of the Act.

8.3.4   Implication for management

Management concerns fall into two main areas. First, it is necessary to ensure that information systems that hold personal data are designed so that it is possible to meet the requirements of the Act. Second, the operation of these systems must not contravene the law. The following areas are of particular concern:

- Controls governing unauthorized access and administered disclosure of data are necessary.
- The system (file structure or database structure) should be designed so that random retrieval of personal data for data subject enquiries is possible, and that the cost of doing so is minimized.
- Personal records should have additional fields indicating the source of personal data and dates of file updates, so that personal enquiries concerning the accuracy of data may be handled effectively.
- Data that is in dispute will need to be flagged as such and the dispute status notified to data recipients.
- The database and files need to be regularly maintained to ensure that personal data that is no longer relevant, such as that rendered redundant by changes in the law, for example tax law, or no longer applicable as it is out of date for the specified purpose for which it was held (see data protection principle 6), is purged and that current data is used to update the records.

- Secure data-disposal techniques need to be established. For instance, out-of-date data files held on magnetic media must be degaussed rather than merely written over with new data.

- The authenticity of the identity of data subjects needs to be verified before personal data can be released. Procedures for this must be carefully planned.

- The presence of microcomputers within the organization has increased the difficulty of maintaining personal data in accordance with the principles of the Act. By their nature, microcomputers encourage distributed responsibility and administration of data files (including personal data) but it is the organization that is responsible for registration under the Act.

In order to ensure that the corporate information system complies with the data protection legislation it is not uncommon to appoint a data protection officer with this responsibility.

8.3.5 Criticisms of the Act

The Act has been severely criticized from several quarters for different reasons.

It is often claimed that it is a weakness of the Act that only 'automatic' processing and storage are covered and the maintenance of manual records is ignored. It is pointed out that to escape the Act personal data merely needs to be transferred to a manual system. Though this can be regarded as a failing of the Act from the perspective of those concerned with the misuse of personal data (no matter how stored and processed) it misses one of the main aims of data protection legislation. This is to ensure that the new computer technology with its massive power to misuse data is in some way controlled.

A second, and more telling, criticism is that the Act is weakest in those areas of most concern – that is the maintenance (and possible misuse) of data (possibly inaccurate) by state and other public agencies where this will have significant and uncheckable consequences on the citizen. These organizations often gain exemption under the Act.

Third, special interest groups have claimed the right to exemption from the Act on various grounds. Many of these claims have not been upheld and, as with most legislation, there are aggrieved parties.

Finally, the lack of adequate resources for the Data Protection Registrar's Office has meant that it would have been unable to handle the applications for registration by all those required to register within the time period as laid down in the Act. This shortcoming has been lightened somewhat since it has been estimated that only a minority of those data users obliged to register under the Act did so by the legally required date. (This follows the pattern experienced by other countries introducing data protection legislation.)

The need for data protection legislation is generally acknowledged in most advanced countries. To date legislation has not been standardized. In other areas this lack of uniformity is not an important drawback, but in data protection different laws applying in different countries opens up the possibility that countries with 'weak' legislation will become data havens, where datastores are interrogated internationally using sophisticated telecommunications. Within the UK there is a long way to go before legislation as comprehensive as that of her European neighbours is introduced, and data users need to become aware of the importance (and sometimes even existence) of current legislation.

8.4 Risk identification and controls

In Section 8.2 it was stressed that controls cannot be viewed in isolation from cost–benefit considerations. The decision to implement a certain control will have initial and operating costs and these have to be set against the likely benefit. These benefits will include the expected saving resulting from the prevention of loss that would have occurred in the absence of the control. The possibility that the control, on occasion, may be insufficient to prevent the loss from occurring must also be taken into account.

Two approaches to risk analysis can be identified. These are quantitative approaches, many of which use sophisticated modelling techniques to arrive at cost–benefit optimal mixes of controls, and **heuristic approaches**, which are more concerned with situations in which controls and failures of control are not easily structured or quantifiable.

8.4.1 A quantified approach to risk and controls

The method explained in this section (covered in Burch and Grudnitski, 1986) involves deriving a matrix in which the columns are types of hazard and the rows are types of control. A type of control might be effective against several different types of hazard. For instance, input controls are effective against inaccurate data input, incomplete data input (loss of documents) and fraud. Similarly, a type of hazard such as fraud may be prevented by different types of control – personnel controls, computer access controls, data access controls and the separation of organizational functions. Part of a hazard–control matrix is shown in Figure 8.6.

Having established the type of hazard that each type of control is effective against it is necessary to assign numerical values to the following:

- the loss value associated with each type of hazard;
- the probability over a given period of time that the hazard will occur.

The expected loss associated with the hazard can be computed by multiplying the loss value by the probability that the hazard will occur. For instance, if fire has an expected loss of £1,000,000 and the probability of its occurrence is 0.01 per year then the expected loss is £10,000 per year. This calculation is repeated for each type of hazard and the total expected losses found. Suppose that they are equal to £55,000 in each year. Then this figure may be used to justify the expenditure of £55,000 per annum on controls.

Of course it will be pointed out that there are different types of fire, which are associated with different loss values and different probabilities. In essence this does not affect the calculation as the expected losses for each type of fire may be calculated and the sum total for fire found. The further criticism that there may be a range of loss values occurring with differing probabilities associated with each type of fire can also be accommodated. There is a great danger though that too much emphasis is placed on the numerical sophistication of the model when in reality accuracy is swamped by the guesswork accompanying estimation of the loss values and probabilities. It is often better to restrict the calculation to the average loss and the probability that it will occur. Even this may involve very rough estimations.

It is now necessary to establish the effect of the controls. For each control numerical values are assigned to:

Figure 8.6: Part of a hazard-control matrix.

	Errors and omissions	Lost data and documents	Computer failure	Unauthorized access	Fire	Fraud
Input controls	✓	✓		✓		✓
Processing controls	✓					✓
Output controls	✓	✓		✓		✓
Storage controls		✓				✓
Operating system controls				✓		✓
Records management	✓	✓			✓	
Accounting controls	✓	✓				✓
Contingency plan			✓		✓	
Physical security			✓	✓	✓	

- the installation cost of the control
- the operating cost of the control
- the probability over a given period of time that the control will fail.

Each control will be effective against a number of hazards and the total cost of the control per annum is equal to the sum of the following three costs:

1. the installation cost (divided by the number of years over which this is to be spread);

2. the operating cost per annum;

3. the total of all expected losses associated with each hazard over which the control is applied, multiplied by the probability that the control will fail to prevent the respective hazard from occurring.

This gives some measure of the net cost of the control, and as a rule of thumb if this is less than the expected loss associated with the hazards to which the control is applied, then the control is justified.

The total impact of a range of controls can be found by summing net costs of each control, together with the expected losses associated with hazards over which the set of controls is not applied. This assumes that the controls are mutually exclusive in the sense that no two controls apply to one type of hazard. The range of controls with the smallest cost value is the one that is most cost–benefit efficient and this value gives a financial measure of the advantage of the range over the 'no control' situation where the cost is £55,000.

Where the controls are not mutually exclusive this needs to be taken into account as the loss associated with a failure of one control may be prevented by the action of another. The techniques are standard but the computation can become quite lengthy and it is often possible to profit from computer-aided support.

Having determined and implemented the optimum mix of controls these should be reviewed periodically as costs and probabilities change.

In determining expenditure on these controls management would also take into account the time–cost of money (by discounting or payback techniques) and also weigh the implementation of controls against alternative projects that are competing for the scarce resources of the organization.

Criticisms of the quantified approach

The method illustrated is an example of just one type of quantified approach to risk analysis. Others differ but all concentrate on a mathematical modelling of losses costs and probabilities. Certain common criticisms are directed at all these types of approach.

First, it is agreed that the approaches do not help to determine which types of threat exist for an organization and which types of control would be effective. The quantified methods are useful only once this initial investigation has been carried out.

Second, quantitative approaches assume that figures can be assigned to expected losses and probabilities, whereas in practice this is not possible.

Both of these points have merit but should not be seen as invalidating quantitative approaches; rather they indicate that they should be limited in scope. The first criticism shows they are incomplete and are best regarded as part of a total approach.

The second criticism varies in strength depending on which hazards and which controls are considered straightforwardly quantifiable. For instance, research can determine the average number of errors and the resulting loss occurring in every 1000 account numbers entered on a VDU. This can be used in the cost–benefit analysis. Other hazards such as fire may be estimated by consulting actuarial records (after all, insurance companies have to base their premiums on some cost–benefit analysis) or the local fire station may be able to identify particular fire hazards in a computer installation, enabling figures to be put on losses.

However, figures for some hazards, such as fraud, are notoriously difficult to estimate because they are specific to industry/company computer systems. Once important hazards and controls become impossible to quantify the chance of a cost–benefit analysis applied to an overall system of controls vanishes and controls are justified on a piecemeal basis.

It is perhaps best to view quantitative risk analysis modelling as providing one channel of information amongst others relevant to managerial decisions on the nature and extent of controls.

8.4.2   Heuristic approaches

Strategies that attempt to access risk based on experience and partial information using rules of thumb are known as 'heuristic'.

Perhaps the simplest heuristic technique is the checklist of areas that should be considered in reviewing a system of controls. This may be compiled from the experience of many practitioners and will incorporate what might be described as 'group knowledge'. The checklist may serve no more than to direct attention to the areas of possible weakness and indicate types of control that are effective.

Other approaches recognize that the major sources of computer-associated loss are caused by accidental or deliberate actions of persons. It is important to clarify and assess the strength and weakness of personnel at all levels of the organization associated with computer use. For instance, employees are known to work with greater accuracy and effectiveness in certain working conditions rather than others; motivation and career prospects have effects on the likelihood of an employee perpetrating damage and fraud.

Previous incidents may also be a guide to future losses. Various scenarios can be sketched and discussed with computer personnel to assess the impact of these. Controls can then be identified and added to the scenarios, which are then reconsidered. This iterative process may be repeated many times. This type of approach can be extremely valuable in promoting communication and cooperation between those involved in considering the scenarios, and so is regarded as part of an education process in the importance of controls.

Heuristic approaches are of assistance in those areas where quantitative techniques are weakest. It is becoming clear that risk identification and analysis, together with taking appropriate measures in control, are an increasingly important feature both in the operation of computerized information systems and in their design. As a result methodologies are gradually evolving to aid this process.

Summary

The design, application and administration of controls is an integral part of the analysis and design of any information system. There are three main systems of control that may be applied to both manual and computerized information systems.

First, feedback control mechanisms monitor the state of a system and its output, compare these with a desired standard and make appropriate adjustments in the case of deviation. Feedforward control mechanisms use the current state of a system together with a model of the system to predict future states. If these do not meet systems objectives then appropriate action is taken to alter the state of the current system. Finally, preventive controls operate continuously preventing an undesirable state of affairs from arising.

Controls operate at various levels. They may deter or prevent errors from occurring, detect errors that have occurred, minimize the loss associated with a failure, enable recovery or facilitate investigation. In a computerized system they are directed at malfunctions in hardware and software, poor performance by personnel, fraud and various types of physical hazard.   ▷

Controls over data movement through the computer are particularly important in respect of transaction areas. The controls operate at key points over input, storage, processing, output and transmission of data.

Other controls, mainly aimed at fraud, prevent unauthorized access to the computer system and restrict access to files and parts of the database within it. Encryption is a way of encoding data so that in the case of a breach of security the data is meaningless.

The organizational structure of staff functions supporting the information system ensures not only that proper administration occurs, but also that the separation and compartmentalization of functions lead to added security.

An important aspect of information systems development is to develop a contingency plan that is called into operation during massive computer failure. This will make provision for new staff functions to deal with the emergency, the arrangement of standby or backup facilities and the eventual recovery of the information system.

Legal requirements to audit the financial accounting aspects of a computer system, as well as ongoing audits, act as a further control. There will not only identify the effectiveness of existing controls but may have a deterrent effect on fraud. Modern computer-based audits use software tools to aid the audit procedures. These enable auditing through the computer rather than limiting the audit to events around it and allow the examination of input and output documentation.

Recent data protection legislation implies that steps must be taken to ensure that the design of an information system enables it to function in accordance with data protection principles. These include the necessity to take reasonable precautions over the security and accuracy of personal data as well as the facility to allow individuals to obtain personal data held on them by the system.

Managerial strategy on the implementation of a system of controls will always take into account cost–benefit considerations – the cost and effectiveness of controls versus the expected loss in their absence. Quantitative models may aid the process of risk analysis but are complementary to other approaches.

Exercises

1. Explain the ideas behind feedback control.

2. Explain the ideas behind feedforward control.

3. How do feedback and feedforward control differ?

4. Give an illustration of feedforward control in:
   (a) inventory planning
   (b) budgeting.
   What features of your example correspond to each of the components in the general feedforward model? ▷

5. Give an illustration of feedback control in:

(a) production

(b) internal auditing

(c) credit control.

What features of your example correspond to each of the components in the general feedback model?

6. What is preventive control and how does it differ from feedback and feed-forward control?

7. (a) What categories of preventive control are there?

(b) Give an illustration of each of these categories in the following areas of a business:

(i) payroll

(ii) cash receipts

(iii) stores.

8. How is functional separation used as a control in accounting systems? Illustrate your answer with several examples.

9. List and explain **five** levels of control.

10. Is there a clear distinction between input controls and processing controls?

11. Which of the following account codes (containing a check digit modulus-11 in the least significant position) is a legitimate account code?

(a) 459364   (c) 27

(b) 36821   (d) 19843.

12. Is there a clear distinction between accuracy controls and completeness controls?

13. Explain the following checks and controls:

control total	format check	concurrency control
hash total	reasonableness check	run-to-run control
sequence check	limit check	parity bit
field filling check	error log	echo check
check digit	transaction log	
master file check		

14. Explain the difference between *fault detection*, *fault avoidance* and *fault tolerance*.

15. Explain the difference between *identification* and *authentication of identification*.

16. Why is it necessary that computer users need both a login code and a secret password rather than just a secret password, which could serve as both identification and, because it was secret, authentication of identification as well?

17. Give four conditions that password authentication of identification should satisfy in order to ensure maximum security.

18. What characteristics should a secure access control policy exhibit?   ▷

19. Explain the difference between a *symmetric* and an *asymmetric* cryptoprocess.

20. Describe the responsibilities of the various members of staff supporting a large computerized information system. What aspects of the functions performed by each are control functions?

21. How is functional separation achieved in a modern computer centre?

22. List **five** physical hazards that may affect a computer system and state physical controls that would prevent these or aid recovery in the case they occurred.

23. Explain the difference between *substantive* and *compliance testing*.

24. What questions should an auditor be asking in order to evaluate controls over a sales ledger system?

25. 'It is insufficient to consider whether a control is justified purely on monetary cost–benefit grounds; it is equally important that it works.' What confusion is involved here?

26. (a) Calculate check characters (modulus-23) and add to the least significant positions in the following codes:
NUT23A
NUT45BS/23
QWER.
(b) Why is 23 a natural divisor for check-letter systems?
(c) Why is a check-letter system modulus-23 more secure than a check-digit system modulus-11?

27. Draft a clear policy for user guidance on the practice of secure password procedures.

28. 'It is better to surround the access control procedures with secrecy as this builds yet another barrier that the person attempting to gain unauthorized access needs to penetrate.' What is to be said for and against this view?

29. 'We ensure that personal data held on the database is accessible only to authorized personnel by preventing other database users from accessing personal data records by their key fields or other identifying fields such as name or address and preventing display of these fields.' Is this a secure personal data protection policy in the light of powerful query languages?

30. What effects has the move towards microcomputers and local area networks had on achieving security against fraud for such systems?

31. What errors, deliberate or accidental, are:
(a) more likely to occur in a computer-based information system than a manual system?
(b) more likely to occur in a manual information system than a computer-based system?

32. A bank has a centralized computer system with online terminal connections at each of its 300 branches. These terminals are operated by counter tellers. Each branch also has an automated online 'card point', which can be used by customers to directly withdraw cash, make deposits, request statements ▷

and pay bills to accounts. The bill account details must be notified in writing to the bank in advance. There is a personal identity number (PIN) code associated with each customer's card. For security purposes this is known to the customer and no one else. The PIN needs to be entered for each 'card point' transaction. The card may also be used over the counter at branch offices to carry out the same transactions as offered by the 'card point' machine, though the tellers key in all the details.

Identify preventive controls that should be present in such a system and specify the purpose of each control.

33. 'The computer-based audit cannot be regarded as independent as:
(a) the auditor is paid by the client,
(b) the auditor relies on the client to supply information on the workings of the computer system. What steps can be taken to ensure auditor independence?

34. What special factors need to be taken into account in deciding whether to change from a manual system holding *personal* data to a computer-based system?

35. What problems would a large organization with a centralized computer system holding personal data on thousands of subjects experience in providing data subjects with adequate access to records?

36. You have been appointed data protection officer for your company. It has a large number of microcomputers holding personal data used by many users. At present no attempt has been made to satisfy the requirements of data protection legislation. Outline the steps that you would take in order to ensure that your organization complies with legislation.

37. 'Personal data held in manual systems poses a threat just as real as that in computerized systems so should be covered by data protection legislation.' Do you agree?

38. One of the supply stores associated with a large company has been becoming steadily dissatisfied with the organization's centralized management information system. Stores personnel fill out documentation on each item supplied from stores. These documents are batched and sent to the computer centre at the end of the day for batch data input. A stocklist is printed each night and sent back the following day with any errors discovered in the previous day's batch of transactions. A list of items to be reordered is also prepared and sent to the purchasing department, a copy being sent to stores. The computer centre is having staffing difficulties and transaction data input is falling behind. The daily printout of stock holdings now gives little guide to the true stock position as the majority of stock is fast moving. Purchase order processing has also fallen behind, leading to frequent stock depletions. This is not through failure in the purchasing department, but rather it is the result of the late notification by the management information system of items for purchase.

Joe Smith in stores is well known for his microcomputer enthusiasm and he has devised and created a stock control program for the stores ▷

which is now running on a small micro purchased by the manager from the stores budget. Joe has designed a simple user interface so that all members of staff can use the system. Only he understands the way the program works and accesses the records. There is no possibility therefore of anyone else tampering with code. This is regarded as a security asset by the manager as they often have temporary staff. Everyone in the stores is more than pleased with the system. Every time an item is supplied from stores details are first entered in the microcomputer system and then the stock records are updated. The stock supply form is then filled out for batch input by the computer centre as before. The microcomputer-based system also provides immediate response to enquiries on the stock position of any item. This saves many fruitless journeys to attempt to retrieve stock that is out but is not yet recorded as such on the computer centre records. In fact little importance is now attached to the data sent to the computer centre or received from it.

An informal order system has also been developed. When stocks drop below their reorder level indicated on the microcomputer-based system, a printout is sent to the purchasing department where a purchase order is drawn up and despatched. This is 'authorized' in retrospect when the official notification of items to be purchased comes through on the computer centre printout. This may occur days later indicating the extent of the backlog that can arise.

You have been called in to assess the system from the point of view of security and control. Identify security and other weaknesses in the system and suggest a range of controls and changes that should operate given that the microcomputer system and the management information system are to be retrieved.

References and recommended reading

- Baskerville R. (1988). *Designing Information System Security*. Wiley
  This covers the detail of the design of secure systems. The book uses a structured approach to analysis and design – an approach used later in this text. The early chapters are particularly helpful for the non-specialist.
- Beer S. (1981). *Brain of the Firm: The Managerial Cybernetics of Organizations* 2nd edn. Wiley
  This is an interesting, highly readable text, which applies cybernetic principles and control mechanisms as evolved in the human being, by analogy, to the management of an organization.
- Burch J.G. and Grudnitski G. (1986). *Information Systems: Theory and Practice* 5th edn. New York: Wiley
  As well as containing a chapter on the general treatment of control this book stresses and develops a method of risk and hazard assessment.
- Chambers A.D. (1991). *Computer Auditing* 3rd edn. Pitman
  A reliable text, which covers the major issues in computer auditing.
- Cushing B.E. and Romney M.E. (1996). *Accounting Information Systems and Business Organizations* 6th edn. Reading MA: Addison-Wesley

This book gives extensive coverage of control as applied to accounting systems for the non-technical reader.

● Fites P., Johnston P. and Kratz M. (1992). *The Computer Virus Crisis* 2nd edn. New York: Van Nostrand Reinhold
This book is an excellent introduction to computer viruses – what they are, how they work and how to avoid them. It also provides a list of known viruses at the time of publication and an analysis of their effects.
● Lane V.P. (1985). *Security of Computer Based Information Systems*. London: Macmillan
This is a comprehensive text covering the major areas of security of computer systems. Although technical in approach the reading matter is accessible to the non-specialist. The book contains useful references for further extended reading.
● Norman A.R.D. (1983). *Computer Insecurity*. London: Chapman and Hall
Interesting for its extensive compilation, explanation and analysis of computer crimes.
● Schweitzer J.A. (1987). *Computer Business and Security: The New Role for Security*. Butterworth
This provides a practical task-based approach to integrating computing and information provision into the security functions of a modern business organization. The book is management orientated.
● Warman A.R. (1993). *Computer Security within Organizations*. Basingstoke: Macmillan
This is a non-technical introduction to all aspects of computer security. It deals with basic concepts and the hazards that information technology can bring including chapters on legislation and standards for development. The book approaches the subject from an organizational and management perspective.
● Wong K.K. (1984). Data protection law. *Data Processing*, **26**(1), 34–7.
Though slightly superseded by events this provides an excellent highly summarized introduction to the principles behind data protection legislation and its implications for systems analysis and design.

Chapter 9

Information Systems Development: An Overview

9.1   The need for systems analysis and design
9.2   The need for a structured approach to analysis and design
9.3   The life cycle of a system
9.4   The structured approach and the life cycle

The purpose of this chapter is to introduce and give an overview of the process of systems analysis and design. The first section identifies the need for analysis and design. It is recognized that systems developments do not occur in isolation and an overall systems strategy for the organization is required. The way that steering committees provide for this is explained. Various participants are involved in the process of analysis and design. The role of the analyst is highlighted in the earlier part of this chapter. The remainder of this chapter is given over to justifying the need for a methodology – in this case a structured approach – and explaining in general terms how this is applied to the life cycle. Details of the stages involved are explained in Chapters 10–14. Chapter 15 deals with approaches to systems understanding, analysis and design that are alternatives to the structured approach.

9.1   The need for systems analysis and design

At first, the following might seem a plausible course of action by an organization when purchasing and installing a computer system. The first step is to identify the application areas. For instance, these might be accounting, budgeting and word processing. A search is then made of the computer users' literature in order to establish the names and reviews of accounting, spreadsheet and word processing packages. A small group of likely candidates for each application is selected. These are then demonstrated by the dealers selling them and the package that best meets the needs of the users for each application is chosen. Compatible hardware is then purchased, often recommended by the dealer, and the equipment is installed. The software and the existing business data is loaded up and, hey presto!, the organization has a working information system that meets the requirements of the users and delivers all the benefits associated with computerization.

   This approach may work when a small business is in need of computer-assisted support for its standard procedures and when those needs are clearly identified. It is unlikely that it will be satisfactory for the development of a more complex system for a medium-sized or large organization. As a rule, the larger the organization the more complex and individual are the data processing and information needs of that organization, and the greater is the potential amount of funding available for a computer project. These organizations are most likely to develop their own system or pay specialist firms to do this for them. Their needs are individual and often initially unidentified. Tailor-designed systems are required.

For larger systems the requirements of users must be identified and a suitable system designed and specified meeting those needs. This must take account of the hardware, the software and the data storage structure. The design must incorporate control and security features. It must also take account of predictable future needs. The hardware will be purchased and installed, the programs written and tested and existing data loaded into the data structure. The system will be tested and necessary amendments made. Staff training will be organized. Finally, after the system is up and running, continued maintenance will be necessary. All of this requires many people with differing areas of expertise. The sums of money involved may be large; the time taken for completion many months or even years. It is essential that the project is planned and coordinated properly.

9.1.1 The need for an information systems strategy

During the past 30 years computerized data processing and information provision have changed vastly. Developments in technology have included the microprocessor, sophisticated telecommunications systems, networking, new office automation equipment and the development of cheap, user-friendly packaged software. These changes have allowed cheap and powerful processing facilities to be open to all parts of an organization. Within the organization the needs of users have evolved rapidly. In order to prevent anarchic chaos through the development of many internal independent information systems it is necessary to provide some kind of control by way of a well-worked-out information systems strategy.

This strategy will aim to identify those business activities within the organization that are appropriate to computerized systems development. It will map out, in broad terms, a plan for the development of projects. The strategy will look closely at the size of the investment and consider which of the returns are appropriate and where they will come from. It will incorporate new developments in technology and future needs wherever possible. This strategy will also decide between a policy of centrally controlled development of projects and a strategy of local developments to meet local needs. This latter approach is likely to be applicable to large organizations that already have a philosophy of dispersed management control. A policy on internal charging for computer services needs to be established. For instance, is the running of the computer centre (or information centre) to be an organizational overhead or is it to be charged to user departments? If charging is agreed then on what basis? All these issues need to be incorporated in a systems strategy if the information systems development is to have any coherence.

A large organization will not have just one computer systems project running at any one time. Rather, several projects will be under way simultaneously. Each will have a different starting point in time, a different projected completion date, and will probably be within a different area. These areas will not be completely independent – there will be some overlap and interaction. For instance a project to develop computer support for cost-efficient planning of production may be tied into a separate project dealing with stock control. These projects need to be coordinated with one another as well as ensuring that each is internally well organized. Moreover, as a project may take a number of years

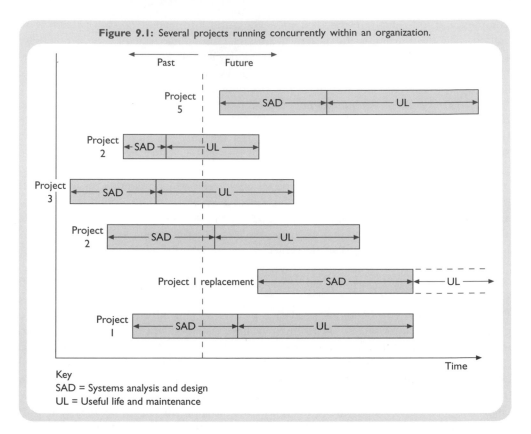

Figure 9.1: Several projects running concurrently within an organization.

before it comes online and its lifetime may be short, it is often necessary to start planning and designing its replacement before it finally becomes outdated or fails to meet the changing requirements made of it (see Figure 9.1). All of this indicates some need for overall project control and coordination as well as an information systems strategy.

9.1.2   Information systems steering committees

The responsibility for overall strategic planning and control of computer systems development will usually reside in a standing steering committee. This will not be a committee required to take detailed technical decisions. In fact many of its members will have little technical knowledge or experience. It will be required to frame overall development strategies and allocate resources. Its aim is to ensure that the information systems within the organization deliver an effective service compatible with cost efficiency. The purposes of the committee may lie within the following areas:

● *To recommend an overall policy for information and data-processing systems development*: This will include such issues as whether or not to standardize on the computer equipment of one company, whether to go for a centralized or decentralized system, the method of charging for development and use of computer systems within the company, the policy on data protection legislation, and the resources available for information systems projects.

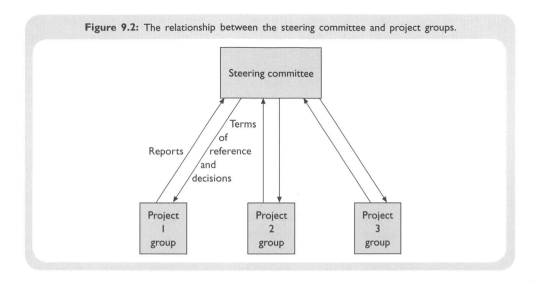

Figure 9.2: The relationship between the steering committee and project groups.

- *To ensure that individual user-department needs are being satisfied*: The information system should service the needs of the organization. The presence of individual user-department managers or representatives ensures that user views are articulated.

- *To initiate and monitor individual projects*: This will include: specification of budgets, scope and objectives of each project; setting up a project team for each project and determining its terms of reference; receiving progress reports and taking major decisions – for example, stop/go on a project (see Figure 9.2).

- *To coordinate individual projects*: Individual projects that will affect one another must be made aware of this in order to ensure harmonious development. It is also important that projects are not viewed independently but taken together as a strategy.

- *To report 'upwards' to top management*: Management will need summary reports on project development and present and future costs.

- *To be responsible for the appointment of senior personnel in the computer centre*: Job specifications and appointments will be decided at this managerial level.

Typically, the steering committee will meet regularly. It will be composed of managers of the departments that use the information systems, the head of the computer centre or its equivalent and other senior members of the computer centre, such as the chief analyst, and any other person that senior management judges necessary. One of the most important functions of the steering committee is to initiate and set the terms of reference for new projects.

9.1.3 Reasons for project initiation

Projects are initiated by the steering committee but where does the idea for a new development come from? What causes a recognition of the need for computer systems development? There are a number of reasons. The following are amongst the most common.

1. *The current system cannot cope*: Many systems projects replace old systems. The previous system may have been a manual system or be based on a computer. Either way it may not have been able to cope with the demands on it. For instance, increases in the volume of transactions processed may have made the system so slow that it ceases to be efficient. Backlogs in orders may build up. Staff may be bogged down with excessive paperwork of a routine nature. Or a merger may lead to a change in organizational structure that renders the current system inappropriate.

2. *Cost savings*: One of the most common reasons for the earliest computerization projects was the replacement of time-consuming, and therefore expensive, manual, rule-governed, repetitive procedures by quick, cheap computer substitutes. This was most notable in the area of payroll and mass billing for the nationalized industries where computer systems quickly and cheaply carried out the tasks of entire rooms of clerical workers. Nowadays most savings in these areas have been made and this is rarely a reason for computerization.

3. *The provision of better internal information for decision making*: Management has recognized the ability of computers to supply fast, accurate, targeted information. If management decisions are analyzed for their information requirements information systems can be designed to enable more effective decisions to be taken.

4. *The provision of competitive customer services*: This may range from fast enquiry services and clear, itemized bills to customer-operated input/output equipment. Automatic cashpoint systems are in the latter category. Once one bank supplies this service they all must or else lose their customers.

5. *The opportunities provided by new technology*: Unlike cars, old computer systems are rarely scrapped because they wear out. It is possible though that outdated technology does not offer the same range of facilities as that currently being produced. Networks, improvements in storage devices and processing power, and the development of micros with their cheap and end-user-orientated packages have in themselves opened new doors for the exploitation of the benefits of computerization.

6. *High-technology image*: Some companies feel that their image suffers unless they are seen to be using computers in their operations. These companies always display the technology in prominent areas such as reception.

7. *Changes in legislation*: Changes in legislation such as data protection legislation may act as the trigger for new systems development. Other examples include significant alterations to taxation or changes to National Insurance legislation in the UK, or the basis for the preparation of company accounts.

9.1.4 The participants in analysis and design

It is common for a computer systems project to be initiated because someone has recognized that a problem exists with the way that things are currently done. Alternatively, an opportunity is perceived that will lead to an improvement on the present system. In either case the **users** of the existing system will play an important role. They can provide information on the current system. They will also be able to specify, in their own terms, the requirements of the new system.

Programmers are responsible for turning those requirements into programs. When executed these will control the operation of the computer, making it perform to serve

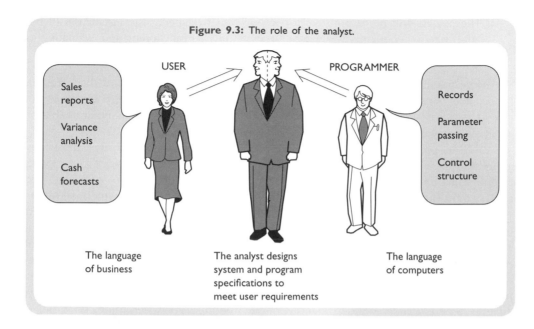

Figure 9.3: The role of the analyst.

USER   PROGRAMMER

Sales reports

Variance analysis

Cash forecasts

Records

Parameter passing

Control structure

The language of business

The analyst designs system and program specifications to meet user requirements

The language of computers

the needs of users. However, the programmer will be a computer specialist and will see the problem in computer terms. He or she will be talking a different language from the users. There is a communications gap.

This gap is filled by the **systems analyst**. This person is able to understand and communicate with users to establish their requirements. The analyst will also have an expert knowledge of computers. He or she will reframe those requirements in terms that programmers can understand. Code can then be written. It is important that the analyst is a good communicator and can think in terms of the user's point of view as well as that of the programmer (see Figure 9.3).

This translation of requirements is not a straightforward process. It is not, for instance, like translation from German into English. It is more helpful to think of it along the lines of architecture and building. The client (user) states his or her understanding of what the building should look like and what functions it should perform (user statement of the requirements of the system). The architect (analyst) then takes these intentions and provides a general sketch of the building that will satisfy them (logical model of the intended system). Having agreed this with the client (user) the architect (analyst) then draws up a detailed blueprint of the design (detailed program specification) from which the builders (programmers) can work. Just as the architect's task is a skilled one requiring a knowledge of building materials so the analyst needs a knowledge of computers.

The analyst's task is not restricted to providing specifications for the programmers. The analyst has a range of responsibilities:

1. The analyst is responsible for investigating and analyzing the existing system as to its information use and requirements.

2. The analyst judges whether it is feasible to develop a computer system for the area.

3. The analyst designs the new system, specifying programs, hardware, data, structures and control and other procedures.

4. The analyst will be responsible for testing and overseeing the installation of the new system, generating documentation governing its functioning and evaluating its performance.

The analyst is likely to come from either a computer science or a business background. He or she will usually possess a degree and/or be professionally qualified. Sometimes an analyst may have risen 'through the ranks' from programmer to programmer/analyst to a full systems analyst.

As well as possessing significant technical skills in computing, the analyst must fully appreciate the environment and work practices of the area within which the computer system will be used. Knowledge and experience are necessary but not sufficient. The analyst must, above all, be a good communicator with business personnel as well as with the technical staff. He or she must be able diplomatically to handle conflicts of interest that inevitably arise in the course of a project. Managerial, particularly project management, skills are another essential asset as a project involves a complex interaction of many people from different backgrounds working on tasks that all have to be coordinated to produce an end product. The design process is not mechanical and the analyst must demonstrate both considerable creativity and the ability to think laterally. Finally, analysts need to exude confidence and controlled enthusiasm. When things go wrong it will be the analyst to whom people look as the person to sort out the problems and smooth the way forward.

9.2 The need for a structured approach to analysis and design

Suppose for a moment that information has been collected on the workings of an existing manual system, for example a payroll system (Figure 9.4). This is a simple system that accepts as inputs:

- transaction time-sheet data (such as **employee#**, *number of hours worked*, *date*);
- standing data on each employee (such as **employee#**, *hourly wage rate*, *tax code*);
- standard tax and National Insurance tables that give deductions for various levels of gross pay.

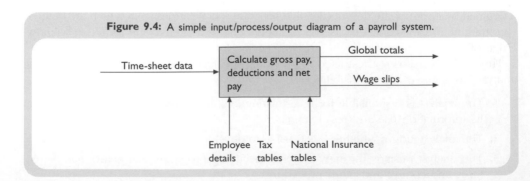

Figure 9.4: A simple input/process/output diagram of a payroll system.

The time-sheet data is compiled on each employee by the manager of the department in which that employee works. The employee data is supplied by the personnel department and is held in the wages department on an employee master file.

Each week the wages clerk works out the gross wages and deductions applicable to each employee by using the time-sheet details and performing calculations after consulting the employee master file and the two tables. Some global totals for management, the Inland Revenue and others are also calculated.

The systems analyst has a relatively straightforward task in analyzing and designing a computer system that entirely mimics the workings of this manual system in terms of the data accepted, the processes occurring and the output produced. The computer system will have certain advantages over the manual system in terms of speed, reliability and operating costs, but the data processes, data inputs and outputs will all be similar. The analyst designs a computer master file for the employee record. This contains fields for storing exactly the same data as the manual master file. The analyst designs a VDU screen to look like the old time sheet. A program is specified that accepts time-sheet data as input at the keyboard, reads the master file details on the employee, reads the two tables (now stored as files), computes the gross wage and the various deductions, writes this to a file for later printing of the wage slip, and if required updates the employee master file with new information such as the gross pay to date.

Of course, things will not be quite this simple as the program will need to handle enquiries, produce end-of-year summaries of employees' pay and carry out a range of other tasks. However, given estimates of the average numbers of transactions processed and records maintained, standard documentation forms to record the manual system (document description forms would be an example), and standard forms to define the computer system (so that programmers have a clear specification of requirements to work from), analysis and design becomes a straightforward task. The technical expertise will lie in the selection and sizing of hardware.

The following points emerge from the example as described:

1. The computer system was expected to be a copy of the existing manual system. No evaluation or redesign of the system was expected. This enabled the analyst to proceed immediately from a *physical* description of the existing system to a *physical* design of the computer system. The physical description of the existing system involved the description of input and output documents used and their contents, together with the records held on employees and the types of data held within those records, and a description of the manual processes undertaken to prepare a payroll. The physical design included a specification of the computer file and record structure, the VDU screen format and the program specifications.

2. The system was not expected to change much over time. The data needed for payroll does not change in form and the procedures for calculation are constant.

3. The existing system was clearly understood by those working with it. It was easily defined as data needed for calculation and the calculations themselves are precise.

4. The processes did not need to have data made available to them from outside the payroll subsystem, and data within the subsystem was not used by processes elsewhere. In other words the system is not a small part of a larger integrated system involving shared data.

5. Although simplicity is a relative term, as can be seen from the example, producing a payroll is not a complex process. One would not expect to have large teams of analysts and programmers used in devising the new system.

It is easy to understand how things can be more complicated by dropping some of the assumptions implicit in the example.

1. If it is assumed that a subsystem is to be designed that is an integrated part of a much larger system with which it shares data and processes, a straightforward piecemeal *physical* description of the existing system will not lead to an integrated new system. This is because the existing geographical and departmental boundaries between subsystems will be translated into the new system. No attempt is made to 'step back' and view the system as a whole. Although individual subsystems will be designed optimally, the system as a whole may function suboptimally (see Figure 9.5).

2. The existing area may be a part of a much larger intended system, which does not currently exist in its entirety. Redesign may be required because of new features that are added with computerization or simply because a new system provides the chance to evaluate and change an existing manual system that is not running efficiently.

3. The requirements made on the system may also change over time and the structure of the data and processes may need amending. This adds further difficulty as in designing the system not only do current practices need to be catered for but the design must also allow for change.

4. The added complexity may mean that large teams of analysts and programmers will be involved. This in itself brings problems as these teams need organizing, monitoring and coordination. Communication can easily break down between and within teams.

5. Users and management need to understand what the new system is offering before major investment in hardware and software is undertaken. It is important that communication tools are developed that aid this understanding. A physical specification of a system in terms of file structures and access methods, computing processing power in instructions per second, RAM size and so on will not be appropriate.

These considerations have led analysts to develop what is now called a structured approach to the analysis and design of information systems.

9.2.1 A structured approach

The main features (see Figure 9.6) of this approach are:

1. (a) Once a physical description of the existing system has been obtained the analyst's attention is turned to building a logical model of that system. This involves abstracting away from physical details to leave the bare-boned logic of the system. For instance:

    (i) The media on which data are stored are ignored. It is irrelevant to the logical model whether data is stored on manual record cards, scraps of paper, magnetic tape or anything else. Only the type of data is recorded in the logical model.

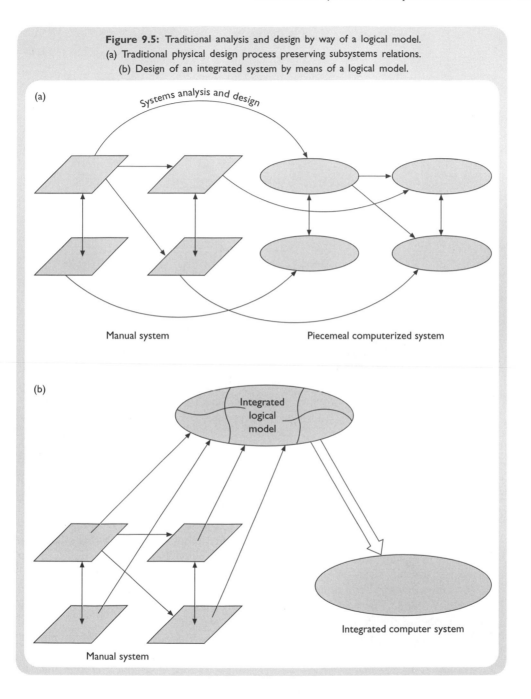

Figure 9.5: Traditional analysis and design by way of a logical model.
(a) Traditional physical design process preserving subsystems relations.
(b) Design of an integrated system by means of a logical model.

(a)

Systems analysis and design

Manual system   Piecemeal computerized system

(b)

Integrated logical model

Integrated computer system

Manual system

(ii) The organization of the data stores is ignored. For instance, it is irrelevant that the data stored on the manual record cards is stored in employee order with a side index based on name. Only the type of data held is found in the model.

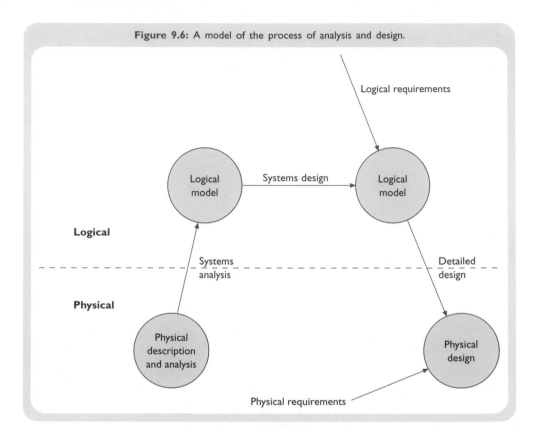

Figure 9.6: A model of the process of analysis and design.

(iii) Who or what carries out the data processes, or where they are carried out, is not relevant to the logical model. The fact that the employee John Smith consults a price catalogue before pricing a customer order in the sales department is translated in the logical model as a process for pricing order details using price data from a data store. Geographical and physical boundaries are not shown in the logical model. Document flows between operations in departments become data flows between the processes that use the data.

(b) Once this has been done extra logical constraints and requirements are added as needed. A new system may now be designed at the logical level. The logical model of the designed system will aid in the physical design.

(c) The new physical system is now defined and incorporates any further physical constraints. It is only at this stage that the analyst is concerned with file sizes, storage media, processor types, allocation of disk space, construction of program code and so on.

2. (a) Complex problems and functions are partitioned and then decomposed into their parts, which themselves are further partitioned and decomposed (process analysis). For instance, a complex process such as 'establish future product availability' can be broken down into the three subprocesses 'establish current

stock', 'establish future production' and 'establish existing commitment to allocate future product'.

(b) The basic entities in an organization are ascertained and the relations between
them charted before looking in detail at the fine-grain level of what information is to be held on each (data analysis).

(c) This is a 'top-down' approach. In contrast a 'bottom-up' approach starts by
considering in detail the individual tasks and the data items needed for these.
The system is then built up from this basis. The latter approach is only effective in the case of relatively simple systems in which little redesign or alteration
is needed.

3. Emphasis is placed on rigorous documentation and charting. This mirrors the *physical* → *logical* → *logical* → *physical* development discussed in this section. The
documentation:

(a) aids communication between analysts and users by concentrating on the logical
aspects of a system rather than technical, physical features which may confuse
the user;

(b) encourages the design of (structured) programs that are straightforward to
code, easy to test and are (through their modular make-up) amenable to future
alteration;

(c) aids the organization and scheduling of teams of analysts and programmers for
large projects;

(d) enables effective design and representation of the database;

(e) acts as permanent documentation of the system.

This section provided a rationale for adopting a structured approach and outlined some
of its main features. Section 9.3 traces an overview of the development process. Chapters
10–14 apply the structured approach in detail to these stages.

9.3 The life cycle of a system

In order to develop a computerized information system it is necessary for the process of
development to pass through a number of distinct stages. The various stages in the systems life cycle are shown in Figure 9.7. These stages are completed in sequence. The
project cannot progress from one stage to the next until it has completed all the required
work of that stage. In order to ensure that a stage is satisfactorily completed some 'deliverable' is produced at the stage end. Generally this is a piece of documentary evidence
on the work carried out. Successful completion of the stage is judged by the documentation. This is known as the 'exit criterion' for the stage.

It is common for some of the tasks carried out during a stage of the process to be initially unsatisfactory. This should come to light when the exit criteria are considered. The
relevant tasks will need to be redone before exit from the stage can be made. Although
'looping' within a stage is commonplace, once a stage has been left it should not be
necessary to return to it from a later stage. This structure – a linear development by
stages, with deliverables and exit criteria – enables the project to be controlled and managed. The benefits of this staged approach are:

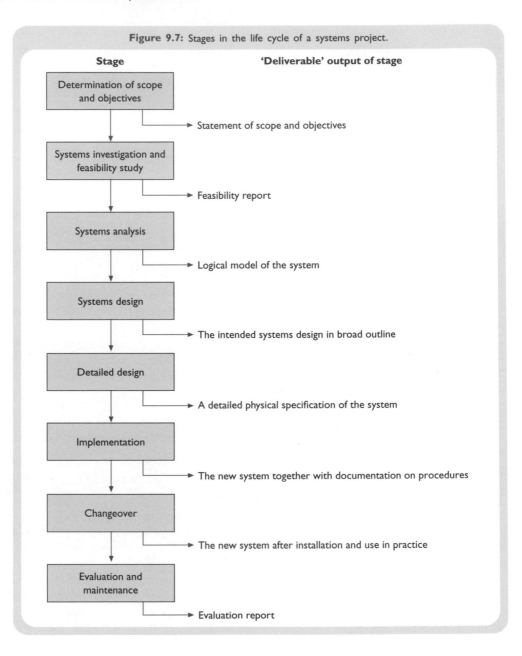

Figure 9.7: Stages in the life cycle of a systems project.

Stage	'Deliverable' output of stage
Determination of scope and objectives	→ Statement of scope and objectives
Systems investigation and feasibility study	→ Feasibility report
Systems analysis	→ Logical model of the system
Systems design	→ The intended systems design in broad outline
Detailed design	→ A detailed physical specification of the system
Implementation	→ The new system together with documentation on procedures
Changeover	→ The new system after installation and use in practice
Evaluation and maintenance	→ Evaluation report

- Subdivision of a complex, lengthy project into discrete chunks of time, makes the project more manageable and thereby promotes better project control.
- Although different parts of a project may develop independently during a stage, the parts of the project are forced to reach the same point of development at the end of the stage. This promotes coordination between the various components of large projects.

- The deliverables, being documentation, provide a historical trace of the development of the project. At the end of each stage the output documentation provides an initial input into the subsequent stage.

- The document deliverables are designed to be communication tools between analysts, programmers, users and management. This promotes easy assessment of the nature of the work completed during the stage.

- The stages are designed to be 'natural' division points in the development of the project.

- The stages allow a creeping commitment to expenditure during the project. There is no need to spend large sums of money until the previous stages have been satisfactorily completed (see Figure 9.8).

The approach progresses from the physical aspects of the existing system (systems investigation) through logical analysis (systems analysis) and logical design (systems design) on to the physical aspects of the new system (detailed design, implementation and evaluation).

Stage 1   Determination of scope and objectives

Before an analyst can attempt to undertake a reasonable systems investigation, analysis and design there must be some indication given of the agreed overall scope of the project. The documentation provided on this acts as the analyst's initial terms of reference. This may be provided by the steering committee or written by the analyst and agreed by the committee. Either way it delimits the analyst's task.

The statement of scope and objectives will indicate an area to be investigated, such as sales order processing. It will also specify a problem or opportunity that the analyst should have in mind when investigating this area. For instance, sales order processing might be perceived to be too slow and the company fears that it is losing customers. The document should also specify a date by which the feasibility report (see Stage 2) is to be produced and the budgeted cost allowable for this.

Stage 2   Systems investigation and feasibility study

The output of this stage is a report on the feasibility of a technical solution to the problems or opportunities mentioned in the statement of scope and objectives in Stage 1. More than one solution may be suggested. The solution(s) will be presented in broad outline. An estimate of the costs, benefits and feasibility associated with each will be included. The purpose of the report is to provide evidence for the steering committee to decide on whether it is worth going ahead with any of the suggestions. If the whole project is dropped at this stage there will have been very little cost to date (sunk cost) (see Figure 9.8).

In order to establish the feasibility of a future technical system it will be necessary for the analyst to investigate the current system and its work practices. This will provide evidence for the functions that the new system must perform even in the case of substantial redesign. The analyst will need to interview users and view existing documentation. The information collected during this stage will be useful for the next stage of the life cycle as well.

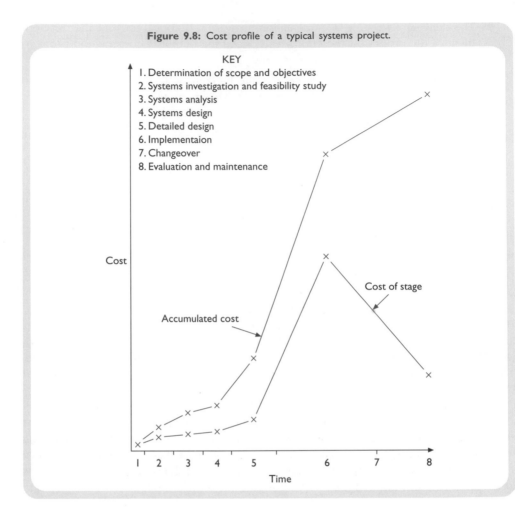

Figure 9.8: Cost profile of a typical systems project.

KEY
1. Determination of scope and objectives
2. Systems investigation and feasibility study
3. Systems analysis
4. Systems design
5. Detailed design
6. Implementaion
7. Changeover
8. Evaluation and maintenance

Stage 3   Systems analysis

Provided that the project has been given the 'go ahead' as a result of the feasibility study the next task for the analyst is to build a logical model of the existing system. This will be based partly on information collected during the stage of systems investigation and partly on new information gathered from the existing system.

The purpose of this stage is to establish what has to be done in order to carry out the functioning of the existing system. This 'what has to be done' is not to be confused with what actually happens in the existing physical system. That is, it is not to be confused with who does what to which document before transferring it from one department to another, or who provides what information for whom on whose authorization. Rather, the central question to be asked is 'what, logically speaking, must be done in order to satisfy the objectives and functions of the system under investigation?' This will involve a decomposition of the functions of the system into their logical constituents and the production of a logical model of the processes and data flows necessary to perform these. This is called **process analysis**. The logical model will be illustrated by data flow diagrams and structured techniques for specifying algorithms. Incorporated into this model will be any additional logical requirements to be made of the new system. No decisions on the way the system will be physically realized should be apparent from this model.

The processes will be fed by data. This data will relate to entities of interest to the organization. These entities will stand in relation to one another. For instance, data will be held on **EMPLOYEES** and the **DEPARTMENTS** in which they work. Thus **WORK** is a relationship between **EMPLOYEES** and **DEPARTMENTS**. These entities and relationships are combined in a data model of the organization. This procedure is called **data analysis**.

The output of this stage will be a logical process model as revealed by data flow diagrams, together with the specification of the process algorithms, data dictionary and a data model. This output is reviewed by management and users. Agreement needs to be established as to whether the model is a reflection of the logic of the problem area.

Stage 4   Systems design

Once the analysis is complete the analyst has a good idea of what is logically required of the new system. There will be a number of ways that this logical model can be incorporated into a physical design. For instance, are the datastores to be implemented as a series of files or is there to be a database? If a database is the chosen route should this be centralized or distributed? The data flow diagrams will reveal the processes and the data flows between them. How many of the processes are to be incorporated into a computer system and how many are to remain manual? Of those to be computerized which are to be run under batch processes and which interactively online? Is the computerized system to be centralized or distributed?

There will not be one correct answer to these questions. Rather, there will be a range of alternative designs. Each of these will have different cost and efficiency implications. Some will yield more computerized facilities than others. Structured tools, such as data flow diagrams, enable these design alternatives to be clearly identified. They also allow the various options to be presented in a manner that requires little technical expertise in order to understand them.

The analyst will suggest two or three design alternatives to management together with their implications. Management will then decide amongst them. Often these alternatives will reflect a low-, a medium-, and a high-cost solution to the problem. The first will provide a system that is very basic. The second alternative will incorporate more facilities while the third may go beyond this to illustrate the full potential of extensive computerization.

By the end of this stage the attention of the analyst is turning away from purely logical considerations to the various ways, in general terms, that the logical model can be physically implemented. This stage ends with a choice between the alternatives presented to management.

Stage 5   Detailed design

The stage has passed beyond that when the analyst can only look at the logical requirements of a system or at broad-outline design solutions. Detailed physical specifications need to be made so that the system can be purchased/built and installed. There are a number of distinct areas that must be considered:

1. Programs will need to be written so that the computer can perform the various functions required of it. These programs will be coded by programmers, who need a clear statement of the task to be programmed. Structured tools make possible clear specifications from which the program is written. They also enable the programs to be easily testable and amendable if necessary.

2. Hardware requirements must be specified that, together with the programs, will allow the computer system to perform its tasks efficiently. These requirements for terminals, disk drives, central processing units, cables and so on must be detailed enough to allow the purchasing department to obtain the items.

3. The structure of the database or system of files will also be specified.

4. A schedule for the implementation of the system will be derived at this stage. This will ensure that during implementation all the various activities are coordinated and come together at the right time.

These areas can be summarized as software, hardware, data storage and the schedule for implementation. Two other threads will run through consideration of these areas. The first is security. The system must be designed to ensure maximum reliability in secure, complete, accurate and continuous processing. The second is the user–machine interface. Unless this is designed with the characteristics of the tasks and the users in mind it is unlikely that the system will be fully effective in meeting its objectives.

The systems specification is a highly detailed set of documents covering every aspect of the system. From this it is possible to estimate costs accurately. The specification is finally ratified by senior management or the steering committee. Once it is agreed, large sums of the project budget can be spent on major purchases and programmers' time.

Stage 6   Implementation

During implementation the system as specified is physically created. The hardware is purchased and installed. The programs are written and tested individually. As programs often interact they will also be tested together.

The database or file structure is created and historic data from the old system (manual or computer) is loaded. Staff are trained to use the new system. The procedures that will govern the operation of the new system are designed and documentation detailing these is then drafted. Particular attention will be paid to security features surrounding the conversion of existing files, whether manual or computer-based, to the new system.

The system is formally tested and accepted before changeover.

Stage 7   Changeover

Changeover is that time during which the old system is replaced by the newly designed computer system. This period may be short if, at the time the new system starts running, the old system is immediately discarded.

Alternative methods of changeover exist. The old system can be run in parallel with the new. Although expensive in labour costs this method does have the advantage that if the new system fails there is a backup system to rely on. The old and the new systems can also be compared with one another for discrepancies in their performance and output. Another approach is to run a pilot scheme. This involves running a small version of the system before the full systems implementation is carried out. The way that the pilot system functions allows identification of any errors and shortcomings that will be encountered in the full system. These will be involved in the life cycle of a project. No matter how extensive the planning has been, no matter how rigorous the systems testing, there are always unexpected problems during the first few days or weeks of use of the new system. The problems should be minor if the preceding stages of the project have been carried out according to correct standards. These teething troubles may be technical or they may result from the use of the system for the first time by inexperienced (though trained) company personnel. After the system has 'settled down' the next phase of the life cycle is entered.

Stage 8 Evaluation and maintenance

By now the system is running and in continual use. It should be delivering the benefits for which it was designed and installed. Any initial problems in running will have been rectified. Throughout the remainder of the useful life of the system it will have to be maintained if it is to provide a proper service.

The maintenance will involve hardware and software. It is customary to transfer the maintenance of the hardware to the manufacturer of the equipment or some specialist third-party organization. A maintenance contract stipulating conditions and charges for maintenance is usual. The software will need to be maintained as well. This will involve correcting errors in programs that become apparent after an extended period of use. Programs may also be altered to enable the machine to run with greater technical efficiency. But by far the greatest demand on programmers' time will be to amend and develop existing programs in the light of changes in the requirements of users. Structured techniques of design and programming allow these changes to be made easily.

It is customary to produce an evaluation report on the system after it has been functioning for some time. This will be drawn up after the system has settled into its normal daily functioning. The report will compare the actual system with the aims and objectives that it was designed to meet. Shortcomings are identified. If these are easily rectified then changes will be made during normal maintenance. More major changes may require more serious surgery. Substantial redesign of parts of the system may be necessary. Alternatively, the changes can be incorporated into a future system.

9.4 The structured approach and the life cycle

Structured systems analysis and design both define various stages that should be undertaken in the development of a systems project. In the life cycle the structured techniques and tools are used in analysis and design. Their benefits are realized throughout the project in terms of better project control and communication, and during the working life of the system in terms of its meeting user requirements and the ease with which it can be modified to take into account changes in these requirements.

The philosophy of the approach distinguishes it from more traditional methods used in analysis and design. Central to this is the idea that a logical model of the system needs to be derived in order to be able to redesign and integrate complex systems. This is evident in the stages of systems analysis and design. The detailed tools are explained in Chapters 10–14 but they all follow from and through this central idea. Table 9.1 summarizes these as applied to the stages of the life cycle.

Table 9.1: Stages of the life cycle.

Stages	Purpose	Comments
Determination of scope and objectives	To establish the nature of the problem, estimate its scope and plan feasibility study	
Systems investigation and feasibility study	To provide a report for management on the feasibility of a technical solution	Involves the analyst in investigation of the existing system and its documentation. Interviews used
Systems analysis	To provide a logical model of the data and processes of the system	Use of data flow diagrams, entity relationship models, structured English, logic flowcharts, data dictionaries
System design	To provide outline solutions to the problem	Automation boundaries indicated on data flow diagrams, suggestions offered on type of systems for example, centralized v distributed, file v database. Cost estimates provided
Detailed design	To provide a detailed specification of the system from which it can be built	Programs specified using hierarchical input process output (HIPO) and pseudocode, hardware and file/database structures defined, cost estimates, systems test plan and implementation schedule designed
Implementation	To provide a system built and tested according to specification	Code programs, obtain and install hardware, design operating procedures and documentation, security/audit considerations test system, train staff, load existing data
Changeover	To provide a working system that has adequately replaced the old system	Direct, parallel, pilot or phased changeover
Evaluation and maintenance	To provide an evaluation of the extent to which the systems meets its objectives. Provide continuing support	Report provided. Ongoing adaptation of software/hardware to rectify errors and meet changing user requirements.

Summary

Organizations can best utilize the benefits from changing and improving modern information technology by designing a corporate information systems strategy. This will outline the areas and approach taken towards information systems within the organization. It will decide on the overall development plan, the resources available and the likely benefits. The information systems steering committee initiates and takes major decisions on individual projects. This committee is also responsible for coordinating project developments and monitoring their progress.

All but the smallest and simplest projects require a series of stages to be undertaken to develop them successfully. This set of stages is known as the systems project life cycle. It consists of defining the scope of the area of the project and arriving at a decision on its feasibility. A logical model of the existing system is developed taking into account the extra requirements of the new system. Various physical solutions to the task of computerization are outlined in broad detail, together with their costs and implications during systems design. The design of the chosen solution is then developed and specified in greater physical detail. This specification acts as a blueprint from which the system is implemented. After implementation and changeover, benefits accrue to the organization during the system's working life. A post-implementation review of the success of the system in meeting its objectives provides useful information for maintenance and design of its eventual replacement.

In order to ensure that a successful development takes place, a structured approach to analysis and design is recommended. This involves the use of techniques and tools that reinforce the central idea of taking account of the logical requirements of a system before attending to the physical design. This avoids premature physical commitment to systems that would not satisfy user needs. Structured methods also facilitate the management of the project and the coordination of programmer teams and others involved in the development. Documentation ensures that communications between analyst, users and programmers are clear. The final system is likely to be one that is easily adaptable to the changing user requirements associated with any modern, evolving organization.

Exercises

1. Why is systems analysis and design essential for large systems whereas it may not be appropriate for a small system for a small organization?
2. Why is a systems analyst needed?
3. Outline the stages involved in a systems project. What is the purpose of each stage?
4. What role does the information systems steering committee fulfil?
5. Why have an information systems strategy rather than developing new systems as and when they become needed?

6. Why is it important that the life cycle be divided into stages with deliverables to mark the exit from each stage?

7. Under what circumstances is a piecemeal approach to developing a computer system appropriate and under what circumstances is it inappropriate?

8. What is the purpose of a feasibility study?

9. What benefits are expected from adopting a structured approach to analysis and design?

10. What is wrong with taking early physical design decisions? Surely this would aid in an accurate early estimation of cost?

11. Outline a profile of a suitable person to appoint as a systems analyst.

12. Explain what the main cost components are in each stage of the life cycle.

13. In what ways does the move towards the local use of microcomputers in user departments threaten a centralized policy of control on the development of information systems?

14. 'One of the major problems with developing an information system is the difficulty of communication between users on the one hand and programmers and hardware manufacturers on the other. The latter supply systems to satisfy the requirements of the former. The analyst, far from facilitating this communication, will make it less effective – it is just one more person involved in the chain of communication. The use of a suitable structured methodology with its emphasis on communication tools and the logic of requirements, analysis and design, rather than technical detail, makes systems analysts ultimately redundant.' Do you agree?

15. 'It is important that a systems analyst has a strong technical background in computers rather than a background in general business practices.' What is to be said for and against this view?

16. 'User needs are often hard to identify prior to gaining experience from the running of a system. It is therefore a mistake to adopt the philosophy of designing *the* system to meet user needs. It is better to design and implement a "rough and ready" version of a system to see how users take to it. This can then be systematically amended to remove its shortcomings. The process of design becomes iterative rather than linear.' What is to be said for and against this view?

17. 'Steering committees are just one further level of bureaucracy preventing the swift development of computer systems that meet user needs. It would be better if user needs were communicated directly to the computer centre, who could then develop the relevant systems.' Why is this not a workable procedure?

18. 'If the people who were going to use the computerized information systems were involved in decisions as to what kind of system was needed and how to design it then better information systems would be produced.' Do you think this is a desirable and realistic policy?

Recommended reading

- Avison D.E. (1998). *Information Systems Development: A Database Approach* 3rd edn. UK: Alfred Waller
  This book provides a multidisciplinary approach to database design and information systems development including business objectives, organizational structure and management culture through to data and logic modelling. The book links with the multiview approach.
- Brooks F.P. Jnr (1995). *The Mythical Man-Month: Essays on Software Engineering – Anniversary Issue.* Harlow: Addison-Wesley
  This is a twentieth anniversary publication of the important text published 1975 – *The Mythical Man-Month.* This is a highly readable essay on software project management and how it can go wrong. The essays are based on the author's experience of project management for the IBM series 360 and the development of the massive operating system, OS/360, for this. From it the author draws many morals on pitfalls to be avoided. Historically the author was writing at the time that structured approaches to systems analysis and design were being developed to overcome such problems.
- Davis G.B. and Olson M.H. (1985). *Management Information Systems: Conceptual Foundations, Structure and Development* 2nd edn. Maidenhead: McGraw-Hill
  Although not specifically dealing with a structured approach to systems analysis and design, this book covers aspects of different approaches to the life cycle. It also contains material on information systems planning for organizations.
- Downs E., Clare P. and Coe I. (1992). *Structured Systems Analysis and Design Method: Application and Context* 2nd edn. Hemel Hempstead: Prentice Hall
  This is a description of SSADM, which is a formal methodology adopted by the UK government for the systems analysis and design stages of information technology. It provides the reader with an understanding of the detail that surrounds a commercial methodology based on structured methods.
- Gane C. and Sarson T. (1979). *Structured Systems Analysis: Tools and Techniques.* Englewood Cliffs, NJ: Prentice-Hall
  This is one of the classic early texts in the area of structured systems analysis and design. It is highly readable with a large number of examples.
- Shelley G., Cashman T. and Adamski J. (1991). *Systems Analysis and Design.* Boyd and Frazer
  This is a standard clear and comprehensive text on systems analysis and design. It includes case studies, discussion and review questions. The book does not promote any specific methodology but gives a good explanation of basic concepts.
- Warner T. (1996). *Communication Skills for Information Systems.* London: Pitman
  This is specifically aimed at the explanation and development of the necessary communication skills required by those involved in the development of information systems in order to communicate effectively with IT personnel, managers and end users. It has sections of group dynamics, presentations, interviews, writing reports, user documentation and training. The text is very practical in orientation.
- Wood-Harper T. (1992). *Rapid Information Systems Development.* London: McGraw-Hill
  This is a practical guide to non-experts who intend to develop and plan their own information systems. No one methodology is advocated though the book borrows techniques from several. It includes an explanation of soft systems methods (especially problem identification), information modelling and socio-technical modelling. There is a short summary of major methodologies. This could be read in conjunction with this chapter or the one on alternative methodologies.

Chapter 10

The Systems Project: Early Stages

10.1   Initial stages
10.2   Statement of scope and objectives
10.3   Systems investigation
10.4   The feasibility study and report

This chapter deals with the early stages in the development of a computerized information system. The main channels of information open to the analyst for information gathering during systems investigation are explained, together with their weaknesses in the accurate provision of information. It is important that the analyst has a frame of reference through which to conduct the systems investigation. Here the systems model is used. During investigation the feasibility of a proposed system is assessed. The central ideas behind the economic, technical and operational feasibility of a system are explained, together with the difficulties encountered in arriving at an overall economic assessment of the project. The feasibility report and its role in project control and decision making are covered. During this chapter a case study is introduced. This is developed in Chapters 11–14 as the life cycle of the system unfolds.

10.1   Initial stages

The impetus to develop a computerized information system arises because someone somewhere has perceived a need or opportunity that can be satisfied by the introduction of modern information technology. In a large organization with an information systems strategy and existing technology the impetus will be generated through the information systems steering committee. In a smaller organization the idea will be introduced by, or at least channelled through, a senior member of management.

The reason for initiation of a computer systems project, as explained in the previous chapter, is likely to be a combination of a number of the following reasons:

- The current information system, whether manual or computer-based, cannot cope with the demands placed upon it.
- There are significant cost savings realizable by the cheap processing power of a computer.

- Management perceive a need for better internal information for decision making.
- Computerization will provide better services for the organization's customers.
- The advent of new types of technology opens up a range of available facilities that the organization wishes to exploit.
- The organization wishes to promote a high-technology image, possibly as part of a much wider-ranging marketing strategy.
- Changes in legislation require systems redesign.

10.1.1 The case study

Throughout this, and the subsequent chapters on the systems life cycle (Chapters 11–14) it is helpful in understanding the stages, tools and techniques if they are explained by way of a case study. The case study used here concerns a company called Kismet Ltd. Kismet purchases electrical goods from a range of suppliers and manufacturers and distributes these goods to retail trade outlets.

Case studies are a useful vehicle for understanding the process of systems analysis and design but they will never be a substitute for learning through the actual *practice* of analysis and design. The most important respect in which any case study is limited is that it preselects information to be presented to the reader and presents this in a neatly summarized and organized way. In reality the analyst would be subject to a large amount of (often unconnected) information collected from various interviews, existing works standards manuals, samples of transaction documents, auditor's reports and so on.

Only a part of the Kismet organization is covered here. In Chapter 1 it was seen that it is often convenient to view a business as being made up of several subsystems. Each of these is determined by the function it fulfils. Examples are the sales, manufacturing, storage, purchasing, accounting, planning and control subsystems. This study provides a slice through three of these. It deals with the basic processing of orders from customers, the generation of invoices, and the provision of some management information.

Kismet Ltd

Kismet Ltd supplies a range of hi-fi, TV, radio and video goods to retail outlets throughout the country. The goods are supplied by manufacturers who each supply a variety of types of equipment. Currently Kismet has over 40 suppliers who supply a total of over 500 different item types. The number of suppliers is expected to remain fairly constant during the foreseeable future though the range of types of equipment may alter considerably. Kismet has approximately 1200 live customers and receives on average about 300 orders per day, each one averaging 10 items requested.

Kismet employs about 150 people in a number of departments:

- Sales order department: accepts and processes customer orders.
- Credit control department: responsible for customer credit checks.
- Stores department: responsible for stock control.
- Invoicing department: responsible for customer invoicing.
- Accounts department: handles general accounting requirements and the provision of reports.

- Packing and despatch department: responsible for goods inward and goods outward.
- Purchase department: responsible for placing orders with suppliers.
- Sales and marketing department: deals with advertising and establishing new outlets.
- Payroll department: prepares Kismet's payroll.
- Maintenance department: responsible for general maintenance and also maintenance of Kismet's fleet of vans.
- General administration: handles administration not specifically covered elsewhere.

Kismet was started 30 years ago by Mr Kismet (senior) and has grown rapidly in the last five years with the increased consumer use of video recorders, compact disc players and the whole range of modern electronic leisure equipment. Mr Kismet (junior) has pioneered this development with a subsequent 300% increase in trade in the last three years. However, problems are beginning to emerge. Kismet's domination of the north-east of the country and its expansion into the north-west is being threatened by a serious rival, Hardy Ltd. This company was set up nine months previously with a large injection of capital. Hardy Ltd provides a direct public customer link for telephoned credit card orders for the purchase of electronic leisure equipment. Also, and this is most serious for Kismet, Hardy is now moving into the area of supplying retail outlets, in direct competition with Kismet.

The management of Kismet has been conscious for some time of slowness in satisfying the orders received from retail outlets. These orders are taking an increasing time to process. This has been further exacerbated by the expansion of Kismet over the last three years. The entirely manual system that Kismet uses has not been able to cope adequately with the increase of trade, even though more staff have been employed. Hardy is able to offer a superior service because of its modern computerized data processing and information systems, which give it a significant edge over Kismet.

Mr Kismet (senior) has long resisted his son's representations to computerize the business. This is partly because of loyalty to his older employees, who have been with Kismet since its foundation. He fears that they, like him, would be unable to make the transition to computerization. Also he is conscious of the demise of his best friend's business, which rapidly moved from being a flourishing enterprise to bankruptcy as the result of a completely mismanaged and inappropriate introduction of a computer system.

The recent rise of Hardy and his own impending retirement have forced Mr Kismet (senior) to reconsider the possibility of computerization. He has subsequently given responsibility for the project to his son. Although knowing little about computers the son realizes the potential and sees this as a necessary requirement if Kismet is to stave off the threat from Hardy and to expand further (satellite TV and personal computers).

Mr Kismet (junior) has called in a systems analyst with whom he wishes to discuss the problems and opportunities.

10.2 Statement of scope and objectives

It is important to 'get the project off the ground' in the right way. It would be a mistake to call in the systems analyst, provide a verbal indication of what is needed and let the analyst 'get on with it'. Very often it is not clear at the outset what the task of the analyst is to be – it is clear neither to the analyst, nor to the steering committee nor to management.

A common approach that avoids this pitfall is that the analyst is required to provide a written statement of the scope and objectives of the project. It works like this. The analyst is given a rough indication, often verbally, of the problem or opportunity as perceived by the project initiator. The analyst then looks into the problem and the system within which it is located. The purpose is to come up with a written statement of what the analyst perceives as the problems to which the systems project is addressed, its scope and objectives and some very rough estimate of the costs. This document will act as a starting point from which the analyst will investigate further and eventually produce a feasibility report.

The statement will not be the result of much investigation on the part of the analyst. Indeed, it is important that only a small amount of time, and therefore cost, is incurred before the analyst and management have an agreed understanding, however broadly specified, of the project. The investigation may only take a day or two.

With respect to Kismet the analyst spends some time with the new managing director Mr Kismet (junior) and then tours the company for the remainder of the day where he talks to a number of personnel. After this the analyst produces the statement of scope and objectives (see Figure 10.1).

This is to be taken as the initially agreed scope of the project. At this stage the analyst will not feel tied to any of the figures except the requirement to provide a feasibility report within the two weeks at a cost of £1,500 or less.

10.3 Systems investigation

The analyst now must become thoroughly familiar with the existing system. In particular the analyst has to determine:

- the objectives of the existing system;
- how the existing system works;
- any legal, government, or other regulations that might affect the operation of the system – for example, the Data Protection Act in the UK;
- the economic and organizational environment within which the system lies and in particular any changes that are likely to occur.

Why should the analyst pay much attention to the workings of the existing system because, after all, is this system not deficient? Or else why would there be a need to replace it? There are a number of observations to make. First, although it is assumed that the problem is one that is amenable to a computerized solution this has not, as yet, been established. It may turn out that a change in existing manual procedures or organizational structure is the best way of solving the problem. This will only come to light after investigation of the existing system. Of course analysts may be blind to such alternatives. Analysts are trained to look for technical solutions. They may also have a vested commercial interest in a computerized solution so that it is easy for them to miss alternative solutions. There is, though, a second reason for extensively studying the existing system. This will give the analyst a thorough understanding of the nature of the activities to be incorporated in the final computerized system. No matter how weak the existing system is, it must function at some level of effectiveness. This will provide a rich source of information from which the analyst can work.

Figure 10.1: A statement of scope and objectives.

Statement of scope and objectives

Project name: Sales order processing – Kismet Ltd date: dd/mm/yy

Current problems:

  The following problems have been identified:

1. The sales catalogue of prices and products used to price customer orders is often out of date. In particular, new items are not catalogued immediately and items that are now no longer stocked still appear. The problem is located in the time-consuming nature of the manual preparation of the catalogue from the inventory records.

2. Customer enquiries are sometimes difficult to deal with as records of orders are not stored in a form that is easily accessible.

3. Orders that cannot be immediately satisfied from current stock – that is, back orders – are not processed consistently.

4. Owing to the large number of documents flowing through the system the time taken to process an order may be days, even if all the goods are held in the warehouse.

5. Data within the system is generally stored in a way that makes it difficult for management to retrieve useful information. For instance, regular reports are time-consuming to produce and are often late, rendering them ineffective for control purposes or to aid medium-term strategies.

Objectives:
  To investigate initially the feasibility for computerization of the sales order processing, invoicing and stock systems.

Constraints:
  The entire project is to be budgeted for completion within six months at a cost of approximately £100,000.

Plan of action:
  Investigate fully the existing sales order processing, stock and invoicing systems. Investigate the feasibility of a computerized system as a solution to the current problems.
  Outline in general terms the recommended system(s) with costs.
  Produce a report on this feasibility within two weeks with a budget of £1,500.

10.3.1 The analyst's channels of information

The analyst needs to obtain information about the existing system and its environment. There are five main sources that the analyst can use:

1. interviews

2. documentation

3. observation

4. questionnaires

5. measuring.

Interviews

This is the most important way in which an analyst will obtain information. Setting up interviews with key personnel at all levels in the organization ensures a rich and complete view of what is happening. Interviewing is more of an art than a mechanical technique. It improves with experience. There are, however, several guidelines that are recognized as being essential to successful interviewing.

First of all the analyst must have a clear purpose for each interview undertaken. This should be specified by the analyst as part of the preparation for the interview. It is not enough to define the purpose as 'attempting to find out more about such-and-such an area'. This will lead to a rambling interview. Rather, the analyst should establish the missing information that the interview is meant to supply. The analyst should prepare thoroughly for the interview by becoming familiar with technical terms that are likely to be used by the interviewees and with their positions and general responsibilities. The analyst should also outline a list of questions to be asked during the interview.

During the interview the analyst should:

- Explain at the beginning the purpose of the interview. This gives the interviewee a framework of reference for answering questions.
- Attempt to put the interviewee at ease.
- Go through the questions that were prepared. General questions should be asked first followed by more specific questions on each topic area. The analyst should always listen carefully to replies and be able to follow up answers with questions that were not in the original list. The analyst must always bear in mind the purpose of the interview and discourage time-wasting digressions.
- Never criticize the interviewee. The analyst is merely seeking information.
- Not enter into a discussion of the various merits or weaknesses of other personnel in the organization.
- Summarize points made by the interviewee at suitable stages in the interview.
- Explain the purpose of note taking or a tape recorder if used.
- Keep the interview short; generally 20 minutes or half an hour is sufficient.
- Summarize the main points of the interview at the end.
- Book a following interview, if required, with the interviewee at the end of the interview.

No checklist of guidelines is adequate to become a good interviewer. The list given should enable any serious pitfalls to be avoided.

Problems with the interview as a channel of information: The interview, though the most valuable tool for information gathering for the analyst, is limited in that:

1. The interviewee may refuse to cooperate with the interviewer through fear of job de-skilling, redundancy, or the inability to cope with the new technology as a result of computerization. This may take the form of a direct refusal to take part (unlikely), being vague in replies, or, by omission, continuing to let the analyst believe what the interviewee knows to be false.

2. The interviewee may feel that they should tell the analyst how the tasks that they carry out *should* be performed rather than how they actually *are* performed. It is common for people to cut corners, not follow works procedures, adopt alternative practices. All of these may be more efficient than the officially recommended practice but it is difficult for the interviewee to be honest in this area.

3. Clerical workers do tasks. They generally do not have to describe them and may not be articulate in doing so.

4. The analyst cannot avoid filtering all that the interviewee says through the analyst's model of the world. The analyst's background and preconceptions may interfere with the process of communication. One of the distinguishing marks of good interviewers is the ability to think themselves quickly into the interviewee's frame of mind. This almost therapeutic skill is not one that is usually developed through a training in computing.

Documentation

Most business organizations, particularly large ones, have documentation that is of help to the analyst in understanding the way they work:

- Instruction manuals and procedures manuals provide a statement of the way that tasks are to be performed.
- Document blanks that are filled in by personnel within the organization and then passed between departments or stored for reference give the analyst an indication of the formal data flows and data stores.
- Job descriptions define the responsibilities of personnel.
- Statements of company policy provide information on overall objectives and likely changes.
- Publicity and information booklets for external bodies provide a useful overview of the way that a company works.

The problem with using documentation is that there is often a great deal of it, particularly in large organizations. The analyst has to read extensively in order to gather a small amount of useful information. Unlike interviews, where the analyst can direct the information that is provided by targeted questions, documents cannot be so easily probed. Finally, documentation may be out of date and the analyst has little way of knowing this. The last thing to be changed when a clerical procedure is altered is usually the documentation governing it. Despite these weaknesses documentation is a useful channel for information gathering.

Observation

Observation of employees performing activities within the area of investigation is another source of information for the analyst. Observation has the edge over the other methods of information gathering in that it is direct. The analyst wishes to understand the way that the existing system functions. Interviews provide reports from people of what they do, subject to all the distorting influences stated. Documents are an indication of what employees should be doing, which is not necessarily what they are doing. Only by observation does the analyst see directly how activities are performed.

However there are some notable drawbacks:

- It is extremely time-consuming for the analyst.
- When observed people tend to behave differently as compared to their behaviour unobserved – the 'Hawthorn effect' – thus devaluing the information obtained.
- Observation, unlike interviewing, does not reveal the beliefs and attitudes of the people involved.

Observation is, however, an important source for the analyst on informal information flows between individuals. These are often essential for the efficient execution of activities. They may not be obvious from interviews and would not appear in documentation.

Questionnaires

Questionnaires are of only limited use in obtaining information for the purposes of investigating an existing system (as opposed to market research where they are essential). This is because:

- It is difficult to avoid misunderstandings on the part of respondents as they cannot gain clarification of a question on the questionnaire if it is judged to be vague or confusing.
- Questionnaires that are simple provide little information; questionnaires that are more ambitious are likely to be misunderstood.
- Response rates to questionnaires are often low.
- To set a good questionnaire the analyst often has to have more information about the system under investigation than the questionnaire could hope to provide in the first place.

Certain limited situations may make a questionnaire suitable. These usually occur when the number of people involved makes interviewing prohibitively expensive, the questions are generally simple, a low response rate is satisfactory, and the questionnaire is used to confirm evidence collected elsewhere.

In designing questionnaires it is important to:

- Keep questions simple, unambiguous and unbiased.
- Use multiple-choice questions rather than ask for comments. This makes the questionnaire both easier to answer and easier to analyze.
- Have a clear idea of the information that is required from the questionnaire.
- Make sure that the questions are aimed at the level of intellect and particular interests of the respondents.
- Avoid branching: for example, 'if your answer to question 8 was "yes" then go to question 23 otherwise go to question 19'.
- Make clear the deadline date by which the questionnaire is to be returned and enclose an addressed and prepaid envelope.

Measuring

Sometimes it is important to have statistical information about the workings of the existing system. The total number of sales ledger accounts and the activity of each will be of interest to the analyst who is looking at the possible computerization of an accounting system. The statistical spread as well as the gross figures may be relevant. For instance, with a sales order processing system not only may the average number of sales orders processed a day be of use to the analyst, but the pattern of these orders throughout the day and through-out the week may be of significance. Are there peaks and troughs or is it a constant flow?

10.3.2 Approaching the investigation

Although the foregoing channels provide the analyst with information it is necessary to have some plan or some framework within which to study the existing system.

Flow block diagrams

A flow block diagram may be developed at an early stage in the investigation to repres-ent the system. Flow block diagrams show the important subsystems in an organization and the flows between them. They provide a good overview of a system within which more detailed investigation can occur. It is common for flow block diagrams to be based around the traditional functions of a business – sales, purchasing, manufacturing, stores, accounting, planning, control, and so on. These diagrams were treated in detail in Chapter 1. A flow block diagram of Kismet is given in Figure 10.2.

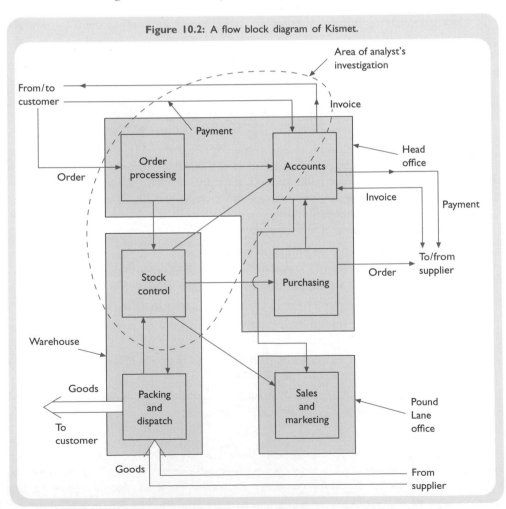

Figure 10.2: A flow block diagram of Kismet.

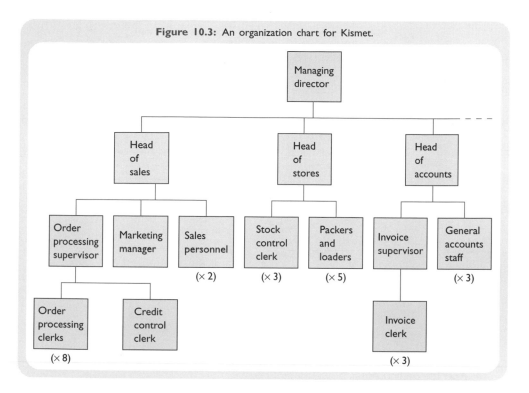

Figure 10.3: An organization chart for Kismet.

Organization charts

Organization charts show the various roles and their relationships within an organization. They are usually hierarchical in nature, reflecting relationships of control, decision flow and levels of managerial activity between the various elements of the hierarchy. The chart enables the analyst to establish key personnel for interview. An organization chart for Kismet is given in Figure 10.3.

Task identification

Within each subsystem the analyst will identify key tasks. A useful model to adopt is the system model (see Figure 10.4), where the task is regarded as a process for converting an input into an output. There may be intermediate storage requirements and there will be some control over the operation of the task. This gives the analyst a template by which a task can be investigated. Key questions that should be satisfied are:

- What different types of input are there into the task?
- And for each input:
  - What is the structure of the input?
  - Where does it come from?
  - What is the rate of input (how many per hour)?
  - Is it regular or are there peaks and troughs?
- What different types of output are there to the task?

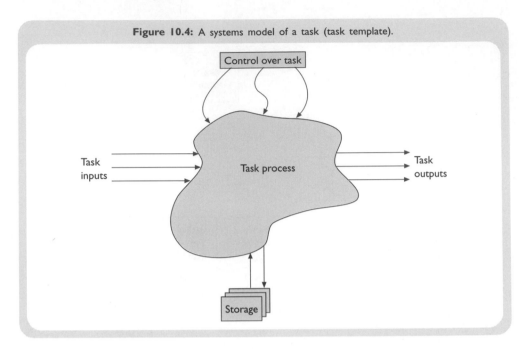

Figure 10.4: A systems model of a task (task template).

- And for each output:
  - What is the structure of the output?
  - Where does it go to?
  - What is the rate of output (how many per hour) required?
  - Is it regular or are there peaks and troughs?
  - What is the purpose of the output?
- What is the logic of the process?
- Does it require discretion or is it rule-governed?
- What is the purpose of the process?
- What experience or training is necessary to become competent at it?
- What level of accuracy is required?
- What stores, files or records are consulted in performing the task?
- How often are these consulted?
- What indexes or keys are used for selecting the correct record?
- How many records are in the available record store?
- What types of control are exerted over the task?
- Who is responsible for each control?

After investigation the analyst should have a good understanding of:

- Who does what.
- When it is done.
- Where it is done.
- How it is done.
- Why it is done.

Figure 10.5: Examples of questions to be asked of the Kismet sales order processing supervisor during a systems investigation.

Inputs

What is the content of a customer sales order?
Does the company transcribe customer orders to company documentation?
How many sales orders are received per day
Are there heavy/light times of the week/year?
What do you do if a sales order is incomplete in its specification?

Process

What is done with the sales orders?
How are they divided amongst the sales order processing personnel?
At what stage is it established that stock exists?
What is done if stock is not currently held?
How are the orders priced?
What happens to an order for an item of stock not held by the company?

Outputs

What is produced by the process?
Where does it go?
Are reports, summaries or totals provided?
How quickly are the priced sales orders produced from the customer orders?

Control

What accuracy controls operate over the transcription of the orders to company documentation?
What controls operate to ensure that all customer orders received are processed?
How is it established that customers have not exceeded credit limits?

Storage

What catalogues, records, files are consulted?
What information is obtained from them?
Whose responsibility is it for ensuring the accuracy of the information?

Staffing

How many staff are involved?
What are their roles?
How do the controls operate over staff?

Costs

What is the budgeted cost for processing an order?
What is the actual cost of processing an order?
How are costs split between variable and fixed costs?

Growth

Is it envisaged that there will be growth in demand for sales order processing?

This framework provides a useful outline on which the analyst can base questions during an interview. Figure 10.5 gives an example of some of the questions to be asked of the sales order processing supervisor at Kismet. These are based on this framework.

10.4   The feasibility study and report

One of the purposes for carrying out a systems investigation, perhaps *the* main purpose, is to establish the feasibility of introducing a computer system. Amongst other things this will provide some estimate of the likely costs and benefits of a proposed system. The

These are all issues in the area of organizational behaviour and 'people problems'. Analysts often have a training in programming or other technical areas and it is easy for them to ignore this vital component of feasibility.

10.4.4 Feasibility report

A feasibility report will be written by the analyst and considered by management prior to allowing the project to continue further. It will go to the steering committee in the case of a large organization. In a smaller organization without a steering committee structure the report will be assessed by senior managers as part of their normal activities.

As well as providing information on the feasibility of the project the systems investigation will have provided much information that will also be incorporated in the feasibility report. In particular:

● The principal work areas for the project will have been identified.

● Any needs for specialist staff to be involved in the later stages of the project will have been noted.

● Possible improvement or potential for savings may have become apparent during the investigation.

Outline headings for a typical feasibility report are given in Figure 10.7.

Figure 10.7: The contents of a typical feasibility report.

Title page: Name of project, report name, version number, author, date.

Terms of reference: These will be taken from the statement of scope and objectives.

Summary: This gives a clear concise statement of the feasibility study and its recommendations.

Background: Statement of the reasons for initiation of the project, the background of the current system, how it features within the organization, how it figures in the organization's development plans, what problems it encounters.

Method of study: Detailed description of the systems investigation including personnel interviewed and documents searched, together with any other channels of information. Assumptions made and limitations imposed.

Present system: Statement of the main features of the current system including its major tasks, its staffing, its storage, its equipment, its control procedures, and the way it relates to other systems within the organization.

Proposed system(s): Each proposed system, if there is more than one, is outlined. This will include a statement of the facilities provided. (Data flow diagrams, explained in Chapter 11, and other charting techniques may be used as a pictorial representation of the proposal.) For each proposal its economic, technical and organizational feasibility will be assessed. Major control features will be included.

Recommendation: The recommended system will be clearly indicated with reasons why it is preferred.

Development plan: A development plan for the recommended system is given in some detail; this will include projected costs for future stages in the life cycle with estimates of the time schedule for each.

Appendix: This will provide supporting material to the main report. It will include references to documents, summaries of interviews, charts and graphs showing details of transaction processing, estimates of hardware costs and so on. In fact, anything that is likely to be of use to those reading the report that will enable them to make a more informed decision will be included.

Once the feasibility report has been accepted the project can proceed to the next stage. This is to provide an analysis from which a new system can be designed and implemented. Chapters 11 and 12 cover the two main aspects of analysis – analysis of processes and analysis of data. Various tools and techniques will be explained; although these are normally used in analysis, there is nothing to stop the analyst using them in the stages of systems investigation. The various charts and diagrams can then be included in the feasibility report. This is tantamount to carrying out broad aspects of *systems* analysis and *systems* design (as opposed to *detailed* design) prior to the provision of the feasibility report. This makes possible a more comprehensive development of a proposal or range of proposals. It also allows better communication of these proposals within the feasibility report as the techniques used are designed for facilitating communication.

Summary

After senior management or the steering committee have recognized the need for the development of an information system it is necessary to carry out a formal feasibility study. This will involve an analyst. The analyst will need to have an understanding of the scope and objectives of the proposed systems project. It is customary for a written statement in this area to be agreed between the analyst and those that are commissioning the project. Although this will only give the broadest indication of the scope of the intended system it will provide the analyst with a direction in which to proceed in systems investigation. Also, importantly, it will give the analyst a budget and time schedule within which to provide a feasibility report.

During systems investigation the analyst will obtain information by interviewing key personnel, searching current documentation and reports, observing the existing system, measuring various key variables such as the number of transactions processed and the time taken for each transaction, and possibly using questionnaires for response from large groups. All of these channels of information suffer from distorting influences that devalue the accuracy and use of the information gathered through them.

In order to organize the way that the information is obtained it is helpful for the analyst to have a framework of reference. This is provided by the systems model. At the highest level, flow block diagrams will aid the analyst in representing the major components within the organization and the flows between them. At the more detailed level, when key tasks are considered, it is appropriate to view them as processes for converting inputs into outputs using storage while being subject to control. Organization charts give the relationships between the various roles within the organization.

A feasibility report is provided by the analyst for the systems project. As well as giving a description of the present and proposed systems it contains an assessment of the feasibility of the proposal(s). This will not only take account of the economic feasibility – the economic costs and benefits – but will also look at the technical and organizational feasibility. The feasibility study and report is essential for proper project control. It enables senior management, who are ▷

responsible for major resource decisions, to take a decision on the continuation of the project with a minimum of sunk cost. The more unusual the requirements of the proposed system or the greater the sums involved in its development, the more extensive will be the systems investigation prior to the feasibility report. Various charting and diagrammatically based techniques such as data flow diagrams and entity–relationship models, explained in Chapters 11 and 12, may also be used. After acceptance of the feasibility study the analyst, together with a project group in the case of larger systems, will proceed to full scale analysis and design.

Exercises

1. What is the purpose of a statement of scope and objectives?
2. During systems investigation what channels are open to the analyst in gathering information about a system? What are the strengths and weaknesses of each?
3. What is the purpose of a feasibility study?
4. Explain the terms *economic feasibility, technical feasibility* and *organizational feasibility.*
5. Why is it difficult to undertake an economic assessment of a project at an early stage in its development?
6. What features of a task (or group of tasks) are likely to make it technically non-feasible?
7. 'In the feasibility report it is common for the analyst to outline more than one proposal and recommend just one of these.' Surely the analyst should either give only the recommended option or, alternatively, outline several proposals with their implications and let management decide the most suitable?
8. What benefits are likely to result from:
   (a) computerizing the records system in a library?
   (b) computerizing a sales order and invoicing system (as in Kismet)?
   (c) providing a computerized point of sales system in a supermarket?

Recommended reading

● Buss M.D.J. (1987). How to rank computer projects. *Harvard Business Review*, January/ February 1983. Reprinted in *Information Analysis: Selected Readings* (Galliers R.D., ed.), Sydney: Addison-Wesley
Provides a procedure by which competing computer projects can be assessed when faced with managerial decision takers who have conflicting objectives.
● Couger J.D. (1987). Techniques for estimating systems benefits. In *Information Analysis: Selected Readings* (Galliers R.D., ed.), Sydney: Addison-Wesley
This paper covers in detail some of the techniques for estimating and computing economic benefits.

- Davis W.S. (1983). *Systems Analysis and Design: A Structured Approach*. Reading MA: Addison-Wesley

  This book provides a good straightforward coverage of feasibility studies, the content of a feasibility report and interviewing. Three case studies are used to illustrate the general points.

Chapter 11

Process Analysis and Modelling

In Chapter 10 the first stages of the life cycle for a systems project were described, namely the feasibility study and the collection of information. The analyst now has a large amount of documentation on the existing system. However, to be of use this information must be organized and analyzed before a new design, probably involving computerization, can be developed.

The purpose of this chapter is to illustrate the method to be adopted by the analyst in analyzing and modelling the processes that handle the data and information within the organization. The approach taken is to move from a description and analysis of the existing physical system and to derive a logical model of the processes involved. Physical analysis is illustrated using manual systems flowcharts, which picture the formal document flows within departments and processes in an organization. The logical model is derived in the first instance using data flow diagrams, which show the relationships between logical data flows and processes. The content of each data flow together with other useful information on it is contained within a data dictionary. The logical content of the processes can be described using structured English, decision tables, and logic flowcharts. These are all covered in this chapter. In order to be of use in systems design the process model of the system must be supplemented with a data model. The production of this is considered in Chapter 12 on data analysis and modelling.

11.1   Systems analysis

The purpose of systems analysis is to ascertain what must be done in order to carry out the functions of the system. This will involve a decomposition of the functions of

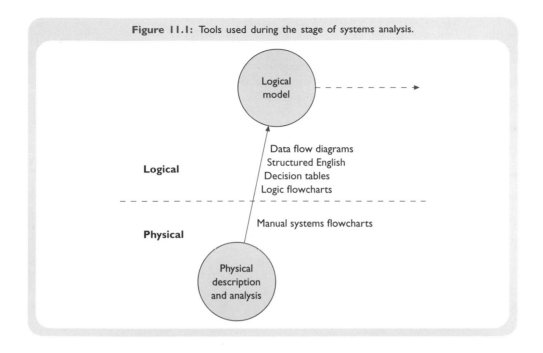

Figure 11.1: Tools used during the stage of systems analysis.

Logical model

Data flow diagrams
Structured English
Decision tables
Logic flowcharts

Logical

Manual systems flowcharts

Physical

Physical description and analysis

the system into their logical constituents and the production of a logical model of the processes and of the data flows necessary to perform these. The logical model will be illustrated by data flow diagrams at the various levels of process decomposition. The algorithms will be revealed by structured process specification techniques such as structured English, decision tables and logic flowcharts. The importance of concentration on the logical features of a system (what logically needs to be done in order to carry out the functions) as distinct from the physical features (who does what, where, with which file and so on) is to avoid making premature commitments to physical design. The rationale for adopting this approach was covered in Chapter 9, which outlined the need for an information systems development methodology.

Prior to production of the logical analysis it is often helpful to carry out a physical analysis of the document flows between processes and departments within the existing system. As well as enabling the analyst to identify key tasks these charts can be used to evaluate control and efficiency aspects of the current system.

The output of the stage of systems analysis will be a logical model of the functioning of the system. This will consist of diagrams, charts and dictionaries, which are the product of the techniques used in the analysis. An important feature of a structured approach to systems analysis and design is the generation of clear and helpful documentation that can assist communication not only between the programmer and analyst but also between management and users and the analyst. The fact that a logical model is produced in systems analysis removes complicating and distracting physical elements that would hamper communication. The movement from the physical to the logical model and the techniques used are illustrated in Figure 11.1.

11.2 Manual systems flowcharts

After investigation the analyst may have collected an unwieldy batch of interview notes, details of observations, questionnaire responses and sundry documents. In the initial stages of analysis it is important to arrive at a methodical description of the existing manual system and to carry out some analysis at a physical level, prior to developing a logical model of the system. The flow of *formal* information within a system often occurs through documents that pass from one department to another. A traditional tool of systems analysis is the manual systems (document) flowchart.

The basic idea is that certain tasks performed on documents are common to many applications – filing, preparing multiple copies, collating, sorting. These are given special agreed symbols (Figure 11.2). The life history of a document from origination (entry from outside the system or preparation within) to destination (exit from the system or filing) is recorded on the flowchart. The passage of the document from department to department is also shown.

The best way to understand a manual systems flowchart, sometimes called a document flowchart, is to study one. Here the Kismet case study is developed giving a detailed description of the processes occurring during order processing. A manual systems flowchart covering these is shown in Figure 11.3.

11.2.1 Procedures adopted during order processing

The customers mail their orders to Kismet HQ. On receipt of an order in the sales order department a five-part company order form is filled out giving (amongst other information) the order#, order date, customer#, customer name, item 1 code#, item 1 quantity number, item 2 code#, item 2 quantity number *and so on. The top copy of this form is temporarily filed in* customer# *sequence for customer enquiry purposes (rather than* order# *sequence, as customers enquire about a recently placed order they will not be in possession of the* order#*). Each item is provisionally priced on the remaining copies of the form from a sales catalogue held in the order department. The priced copies are sent to the credit control section.*

The credit control section provisionally calculates the order value. Brief details of the customer account are then consulted to establish that the customer exists, is correctly named, and that the total value of the order, when added to the current balance, does not exceed the credit limit of the customer. If all these conditions are met then the order copies are stamped 'approved', signed, and returned to the sales order department, one copy of the order being retained in the credit control department filed by customer#*. If the above conditions are not met the order copies are temporarily filed to be dealt with later by the credit control manager.*

On receipt of the approved order copies in the sales order department, the top copy is extracted from the temporary file and sent to the customer as an acknowledgment. One of the 'approved' copies is filed in the order department in the 'approved order' file under order#*. This is to enable staff to retrieve details of the order in the case of further customer queries. The remaining two copies are sent to the stores department and the invoicing department. The invoicing department files the copy under* order#*.*

Figure 11.2: Basic symbols used in the preparation of manual systems flowcharts.

Flowline
Gives direction and sequence of flow

Manual operation
For example, the preparation of a batch total

Document
For example, a company order form

Generalized offline storage
This is storage not directly connected of the central processing unit of the computer. It therefore covers all manual storage, for example a manual file of invoices

Generalized input/output
The place or activity at which a document enters or leaves the system as it is covered in the chart

On page connector

Off page connector

Collate activity

Sort activity

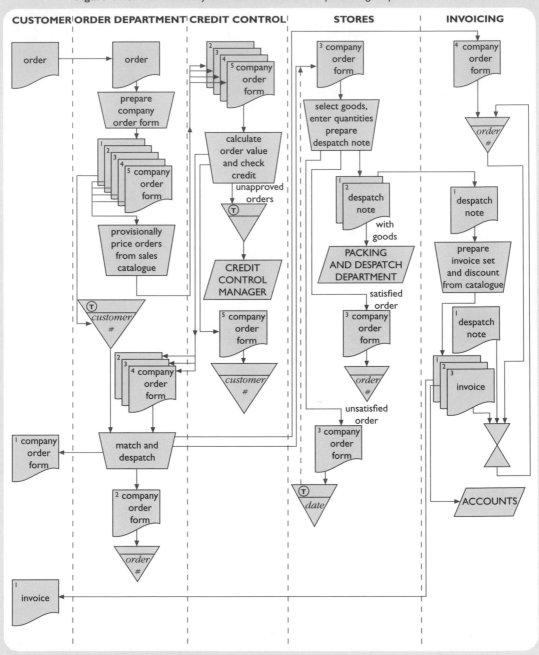

Figure 11.3: The manual system flowchart for order processing/despatch in Kismet.

The stores department selects the goods as ordered and enters the quantities supplied on the order form. A two-part despatch note is made out giving the goods supplied together with their quantities. One copy of this is sent to the invoicing department and the other is sent with the goods to packing and despatch. If the entire order is supplied then the order form is filed in the stores department under **order#***, otherwise the goods supplied are noted on the form and it is filed in* **date** *sequence. Periodically the stores department goes through the unsatisfied back orders and attempts to supply the goods ordered. The stores department also updates the inventory records.*

On receipt of the despatch note the invoicing department prepares a three-part invoice using the sales price of the goods from the catalogue. The discount applicable to a customer is calculated. This is based on the customer's geographical location, total purchases during the last 12 months and the total value of the order. Sales tax is added and totals formed. One copy of the invoice is sent to the customer and one is sent to accounts for updating the customer accounts and other ledgers. The remaining copy is filed in the invoicing department with the order copy and despatch note under **order#***.*

The flowchart for the order processing and despatch in Kismet is given in Figure 11.3. Note that the flow lines indicate flows of *documents*. The following practical points will assist in the drawing of flowcharts:

- The chart is divided into vertical sections representing different locations for operations.
- Though not shown, a far-left section may be used for additional (brief) narrative.
- The chart proceeds as far as possible from left to right and top to bottom.
- Documents are shown at origination, on entry into a section and then again only as required to avoid confusion with other documents.
- Ensure that all documents are accounted for by being permanently filed, being destroyed, leaving the system as charted (for example to the credit control manager in Kismet), or transferring to another flowchart.

There are a number of advantages and disadvantages in the use of manual systems flowcharts.

Advantages

- Flowcharts are easier to understand and assimilate than narrative. This becomes more pronounced with increasing complexity of the system.
- The preparation of a chart necessitates the full understanding by the analyst of the procedures and sequences of operations on documents.
- Incompleteness in tracing the destination of a document is easily discovered, indicating the need for further investigation on the part of the analyst (in Kismet, where does the customer's original order go?).
- Little technical knowledge is required to appreciate the document and so it can be used as a communication tool between the user of the system and the analyst in order to check and correct the latter's understanding.

- Weaknesses within the system, such as preparation of unnecessary documents, lack of control, unnecessary duplication of work and bottlenecks are easily located.

Disadvantages

- With heavily integrated systems flowcharts may become difficult to manage (large sheets of paper!). The use of off-page connectors and continuation is sometimes necessary but tends to reduce the visual impact and clarity of the chart.
- They are difficult to amend.
- It must be realized that when analyzing an existing system informal information is an important part. The flowchart does not incorporate any recognition of this.

The systems flowchart is not only of use to the analyst when carrying out the stages of analysis and design of a computerized information system. Management may use the flowchart to impose uniformity on groups of systems as the structure of the processes surrounding document handling are revealed. This may be necessary to ensure that, say, one branch of an organization handles order processing in the same way as another. The flowchart may be used as an aid in the preparation of internal audit and procedures manuals. In the former case it is possible to ensure that essential information is provided to management at the correct stage. Auditors may use the flowchart in a review of internal control as a guide to determining auditing procedures in the annual audit.

The task of evaluation of the system is often considered as part of analysis. As has been pointed out, flowcharts assist in this task. A typical approach to evaluation of the order and despatch system of Kismet would use the chart to answer a number of questions. Note how easy it is to answer the following typical list of questions by using the flowchart:

1. Can goods be despatched but not invoiced?
2. Can orders be received and not (completely) dealt with?
3. Can customers be invoiced for goods that are not despatched because of low stocks?
4. Can goods be despatched to customers who are not credit-worthy?
5. Can invoicing errors occur?
6. Can sales be invoiced but not recorded?

11.3   Data flow diagrams

Although systems flowcharts provide a useful tool for analyzing a physical description they may impede the design process. This is because they draw attention to physical detail. It is important to realize that the systems analyst will be designing a system to *do* something. This 'something' can be specified by describing its logic and the actions on data. To concentrate on existing physical detail will obscure the functions of the system, will restrict the designer's creativity, and will cause premature commitments to physical design in the early stages of the project.

For instance, it is of little importance to a computer design that one copy of a Kismet company order form is temporarily filed in the order department, while four copies go to credit control where, after approval, one is filed, the remaining copies being returned to the order department, after which the first copy is sent to the customer.

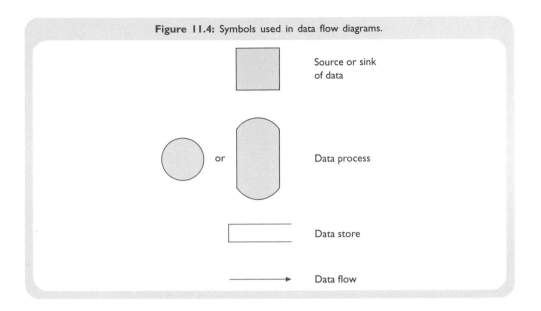

Figure 11.4: Symbols used in data flow diagrams.

Source or sink of data

or

Data process

Data store

Data flow

If the whole procedure is to be computerized, including the order approval, the process will occur within the computer as an exchange of data between files or a database and programs. But again, to assume total computerization is to make a possibly premature physical design decision. It may be more effective to retain parts of the old manual system.

The point to realize is that the processes, the exchanges of data and the stores of data are important, not their particular physical representation, whether it be, for instance, a sequential file on tape, an indexed file on disk or a composition of two manual files in two separate locations.

Data flow diagrams assist in building a logical model of the system independent of physical commitments. They show the various flows of data between the processes that transform it. Data stores and the points at which data enters and leaves a system are also shown. The basic symbols used in drawing data flow diagrams are shown in Figure 11.4.

- **Data source** or **data sink:** The square indicates a source or sink for data and is a reflection of the ignorance as to what happens to the data prior to its emergence from the source or after its disappearance into the sink.

- **Data process:** The circle or rounded rectangle indicates a data process. In this, a brief meaningful identifier of the process is written. It is important to realize that only *data* processes occur in a data flow diagram. Physical processes are not mentioned. For instance, the fact that goods are selected from their stock locations to satisfy an order is not a data process but a material task. A data process is one that transforms only data. It may be that this process will be carried out by a computer program, a part of a computer program, a set of computer programs or manually. The data flow diagram is neutral on this point.

  The identifier used in the data process symbol should, ideally, be both meaningful and succinct. It is good practice to restrict identifiers to a concatenation of imperative verb and object. For example *process stock transaction* or *check credit status* are both acceptable. It is bad practice to try to describe the process. For

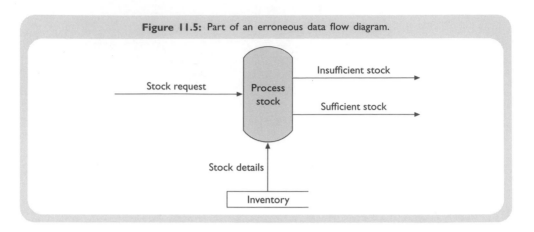

Figure 11.5: Part of an erroneous data flow diagram.

example, it is a great temptation for the novice to 'name' a data process as *check the application for the account against the credit point list to establish the credit-worthiness and the credit limit of the customer.* This is not acceptable.

● **Data store:** A data store is represented by an open-ended rectangle with a suitable identifier. This is distinguished from a data sink by the fact that the data is stored and it (or some part of it) will be retrieved. A sink indicates ignorance, as far as the diagram is concerned, of the fate of the data. No particular storage medium is implied by the data store symbol. It could be a magnetic tape or disk, a document or even some person's memory. Once again it is a great temptation for the newcomer to represent material stores. This is a mistake.

● **Data flow:** The line represents a data flow. The nature of the data is indicated by a name (or names). Wherever that piece of data flows within the diagram it should be tagged with the same name. Once again it is important to realize that these are flows of *data* and not material flows. If a data flow diagram is drawn representing part of a system in which goods accompanied by a despatch note are moved, it is the despatch note, or to be more exact the despatch note details, that appear on the data flow diagram. There is no mention of the goods.

It is also a common error to confuse data flows with flows of control. This is illustrated in Figure 11.5. Obviously what the designer of the diagram intended is that the exit data flow travels one way if there is sufficient stock, and the other way if there is not sufficient. It is not usual to indicate the conditions under which data flows on a data flow diagram. This would tempt the analyst to think of the system from the point of view of control rather than data flows.

The difference between a data store and a data flow often confuses the beginner. It is helpful to think of an analogy with water. Water flowing down a pipe is analogous to a data flow whereas water in a reservoir is the analogy for a data store.

11.3.1 Data flow diagrams: an example from Kismet

In systems investigation the analyst will have collected a great deal of information on tasks performed on document flows within the system. These tasks will be involved with

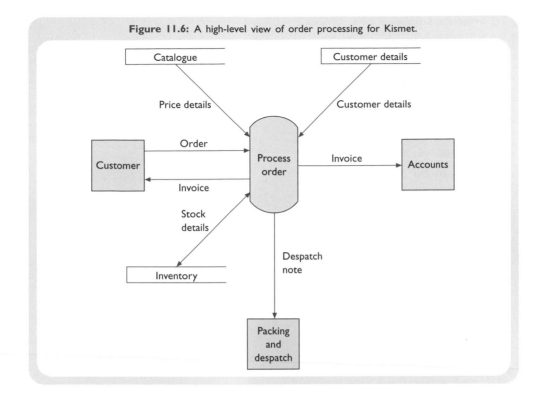

Figure 11.6: A high-level view of order processing for Kismet.

the processing of business transactions and the generation of management information. The document processing will probably have been charted in a manual systems flowchart. In drawing data flow diagrams a logical approach is taken. It is important to ignore the location of processes in the manual system, the documents involved and who is responsible for the tasks. The designer should concentrate on the functions that are carried out.

If Kismet is considered, as described in Section 11.2, it can be seen that one very general course of action is taken. Orders from customers are processed to generate despatch notes (which eventually accompany goods sent to the customer) and to make up invoices (sent to the customer and to the accounts department). In doing this a price catalogue and customer account details are consulted and inventory records are updated.

This is indicated in Figure 11.6. In itself it is not very informative although, even at this level, in a more comprehensive analysis of all Kismet's functions there would be other interfacing subsystems such as purchasing, payroll, and accounting. If the analyst had seriously misunderstood the structure of the system this would be obvious at a glance.

Further progression can be made by decomposing this order processing function into its component parts. There are three different types of task that occur when Kismet Ltd processes a customer order. First, the company order is generated and approved. Second, stock is selected, inventory updated and a despatch note prepared. Finally, invoices are made up and sent to the customer and to accounts. Involved in this are various data flows, stores, processes, sources and sinks.

Read the case study and note where the sources, sinks, processes, stores and flows occur. These are:

1. **Sources/sinks:**
   (a) customer
   (b) credit control manager
   (c) packing and despatch department
   (d) accounting.

2. **Processes:**
   (a) generate approved company order
   (b) process stock transaction
   (c) make up invoice.

3. **Data stores:**
   (a) inventory
   (b) catalogue
   (c) customer details
   (d) company order store
   (e) company order/invoice/despatch note.

4. **Data flows:**
   (a) customer order
   (b) company order
   (c) price details
   (d) stock details
   (e) customer credit details
   (f) invoice
   (g) customer invoice details
   (h) despatch note.

The data flow diagram at the first level can now be drawn (Figure 11.7). The following points should be noted:

1. The diagram can be thought of as starting at the top left and moving downwards and to the right. This gives some idea of the sequence of tasks performed, though it is not a rigid rule.

2. Each data flow, source/sink, process and store is labelled. It is a convention that where source/sinks or stores are repeated they are given a diagonal line at the corner of the symbol (see the CUSTOMER source/sink). A data flow that is repeated is given the same name.

3. Certain tasks are left out of a data flow diagram. Any error-handling routine is usually omitted. For instance, although not stated, there would be a procedure for handling an incorrectly prepared company order form when the *customer name* and *customer#* were found not to correspond.

4. Departments and physical locations are ignored in the data flow diagram except where they appear as sources or sinks. For instance, although the processing of the stock transaction occurs in the stores and the generation of the approved company order occurs in the order department this information does not appear in the diagram.

5. Although the goods would accompany the despatch note to PACKING AND DESPATCH this is not shown on the data flow diagram as it is not a data flow.

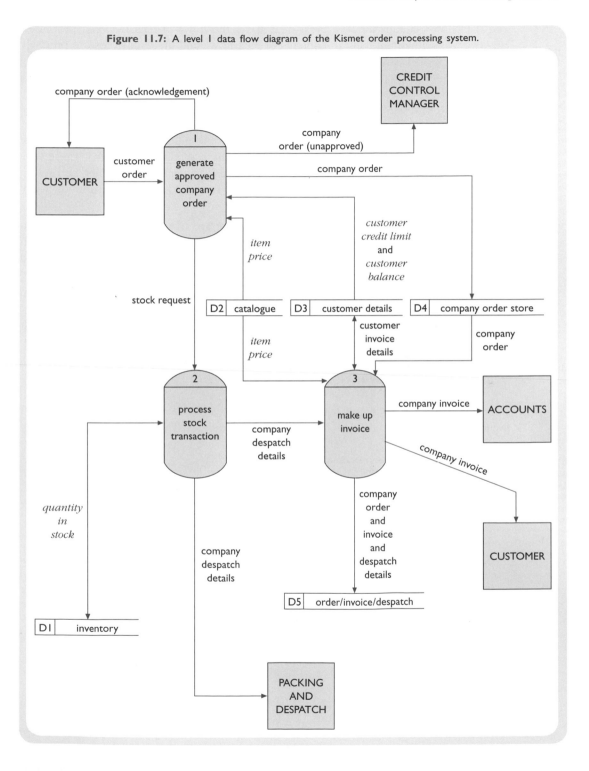

Figure 11.7: A level 1 data flow diagram of the Kismet order processing system.

The data flow diagram shows a great deal about the flows of data between processes. However, it is important that the contents of data flows and the data stores are precisely specified as well. This will be of use when designing files or a database and when writing programs. A tabular representation of the contents of the various data elements appearing in the data flow diagram is shown in Figure 11.8.

The following points arising from this diagram should be noted:

1. The description in the case study does not go into much detail on the contents of each document or file (except in the case of the company order form). These contents are either implied by the nature of the task (*customer address* must be present to despatch the invoice) or should be found on the 'document description form' prepared by the analyst during investigation.

2. Extra detail will be stored for other tasks that are not part of the case as documented. For instance, under inventory there would be reorder levels. This omission does not matter as it would be remedied when the procedures for purchase and reorder of goods were incorporated in a data flow diagram.

3. The exact content of the data stores and flows will be recorded in a **data dictionary**. This is often described as a store of data about data. The dictionary is of considerable importance in analysis and design and is covered in Section 11.4 of this chapter.

4. The meaning of [. . . .]* is that the contents of the brackets may be repeated an indeterminate number of times.

Data flow diagrams for simple systems are relatively straightforward to design. However for larger systems it is useful to follow a set of guidelines. These are:

1. Identify the major processes.
2. Identify the major data sources, sinks and stores.
3. Identify the major data flows.
4. Name the data flows, processes, sources, sinks and stores.
5. Draw the diagram.
6. Review the diagram, particularly checking that similar data flows, stores, sources and sinks have the same name and that different data flows and so on have different names.

11.3.2 Data flow diagrams at various levels

Two interconnected questions arise concerning data flow diagrams. These are:

1. What level of discrimination of processes should be shown on the data flow diagram? For instance, in Figure 11.7 the data process *generate approved company order* could be regarded as consisting of a number of subprocesses such as *accept order*, *check credit limit*, and *price order*. Should these be shown as processes?

2. What is the maximum number of processes that should be shown on a data flow diagram?

Figure 11.8: Table of descriptions of the data flow diagram elements for Kismet.

Source/sink
Customer
Credit control manager
Packing and despatch
Accounting

Process
(1) Generate approved company order
(2) Process stock transaction
(3) Make up invoice

Data flow

Customer order
  customer#
  customer name
  [item#
  item quantity]*
  delivery address

Company order
  order#
  order date
  customer#
  customer name
  customer address
  delivery address
  [item#
  item quantity
  item price]*
  total

Company despatch details
  despatch#
  order#
  customer#
  customer name
  delivery address
  despatch date
  [item#
  item quantity]*

Company invoice
  invoice#
  invoice date
  customer#
  customer name
  customer address
  order#
  [item#
  item price
  item quantity]*
  subtotal
  sales tax
  discount%
  total payable

Stock request
  order#
  customer#
  customer name
  delivery address
  [item#
  item quantity]*

Customer invoice details
  customer#
  customer name
  customer address
  turnover year to date

Data store

D1 Inventory
  item#
  quantity in stock
  .
  .
  .
  .
  .
  .

D2 Catalogue
  item#
  item price
  .
  .
  .
  .
  .

D3 Customer details
  customer#
  customer name
  customer address
  [delivery address]
  customer balance
  customer credit limit
  turnover year to date
  registration date
  .
  .
  .

D4 Company order store
  see Company order

D5 Order/invoice/despatch
  see Company order
  and invoice
  and despatch details

A major objective of a data flow diagram is its use in communication of the logical process model of the organization. It is difficult to understand a data flow diagram when it has more than seven to nine processes. This is the practical upper limit. If there is a tendency to overstep this then the data flow diagram should be redrawn, with processes that

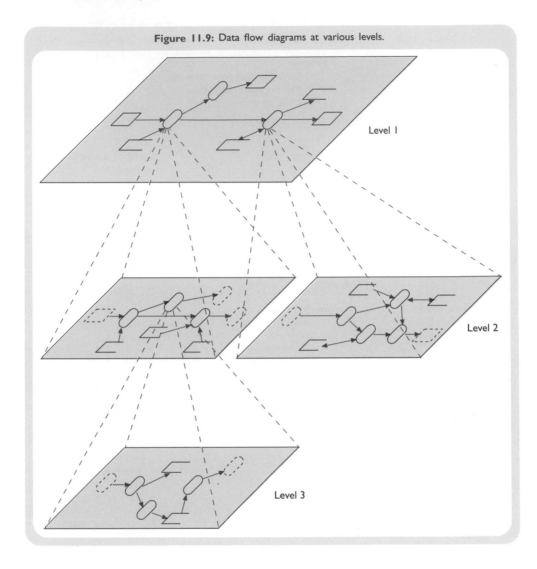

Figure 11.9: Data flow diagrams at various levels.

are logically grouped together being replaced by a single process that encompasses them all. The processes are not 'lost' from the model. They should appear on another data flow diagram that shows how this combined process can be exploded into its constituents. These constituents themselves may be complex and can be broken down into linked data processes shown on a data flow diagram at a lower level. This should be repeated until the processes are logically simple: that is until they cannot be broken down any further. This is illustrated in Figure 11.9.

The generation of levels in data flow diagrams has two other advantages. First, it naturally falls into line with the analyst's approach to top-down decomposition. That is, the analyst considers the major functions and processes first. These are then decomposed into their constituents. The analyst can therefore concentrate on the higher-level data flow diagrams before designing the others. Second, the various levels correspond to the various degrees of detail by which the system is represented. This is useful for the analyst when discussing the results of the analysis with members of the organization. Senior management are more likely to be interested in a global view as given in a high-level data flow diagram. Other personnel will be concerned with more localized areas but in greater detail. For example, the person responsible for supervising the generation of approved company orders in Kismet will be interested in a lower-level, more detailed explosion of the *generate approved company order* process.

The processes in the data flow diagram for Kismet (Figure 11.7) can be further decomposed. The generation of an approved company order is really a number of tasks:

1. Accept the order.
2. Prepare the company order form.
3. Price the goods.
4. Provisionally calculate the value of the order.
5. Check the credit-worthiness of the customer.

This is shown on a level 2 data flow diagram (Figure 11.10). The number 1 task in level 1 is exploded into seven tasks, 1.1–1.7. The inputs and outputs of this exploded chart must match those of the *parent* for which it is the functional decomposition.

There are two exceptions to this. First, certain local files need not be shown on the parent. In Figure 11.10 the *unapproved orders* store is such a file. It is only used as a temporary repository for the unapproved orders and does not feature in the rest of the system. Second, for the sake of clarity it may be necessary to amalgamate a number of data flows at the parent level. If functional analysis were carried out on function number 2, **process stock transaction**, the input/output data flow would be composed of an input flow with **item#** and **quantity in stock** as the data elements and an output with **item#**, **transaction type** and **item quantity** as elements.

If necessary, further analysis of the level 2 diagram could be undertaken by exploding chosen processes to a level 3 diagram.

11.3.3 Design commitments of the data flow diagram approach

It is important to separate the process of analysis from that of design. This may be difficult. The process of analysis goes beyond description as every case of model building is partly a process of design. Another aspect of design is that the choice of data flows, stores, processes, sources and sinks is just one way of characterizing what is important in an organization's information system. To use these to build a model already commits the analyst to a certain design strategy: that of top-down, reductionist design.

However, within the design implications inherited through the use of structured techniques such as data flow diagrams, there is some separation of analysis from design. In the case of Kismet the generation of an approved company order follows a certain (unnecessarily repetitive) procedure, which is illustrated in the data flow diagram (Figure 11.10). In an ideal design it is unlikely that the company order emanating from task 1.2 would be stored in the company order file waiting for the trigger from the successful order-vetting (task 1.5) before despatch of the acknowledgment. Rather, a copy of the approved company order form would be sent to the customer as part of the output of task 1.5. In analysis the analyst considers what, logically, *is* done in order to carry out the functions of the organization. In design the analyst states what, logically, *should* be done for the organization to carry out its functions efficiently and effectively. The

Figure 11.10: A level 2 data flow diagram of the Kismet *generate approved company order* process.

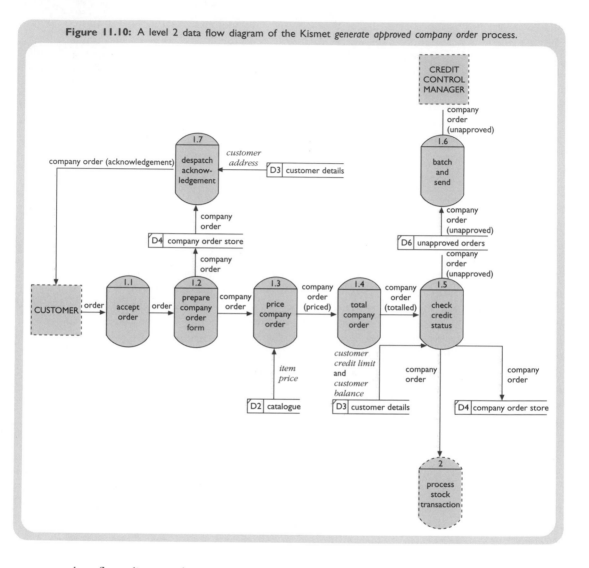

data flow diagram, by stripping away the physical aspects of a system and revealing its logic at the appropriate level of detail, makes it easy to see improvements that can be made.

11.3.4 Summary so far

The data flow diagram is an important tool of structured analysis and design. It ensures that a top-down approach is taken. This promotes a logical, as opposed to physical, view of data stores, flows and processes. In this way no premature commitment to physical aspects of design is made. Eventually the data stores *may* form part of the file structure or database of the system and the data processes *may* become the programs or subroutines. The flows will then correspond to the data passed in and out of programs and to and from the file structure or database. This though can be decided at a later stage.

The levels of data flow diagram correspond to the levels of top-down decomposition and the various levels of detail that management and users will need in order to discuss sensibly the analyst's understanding of processes.

The diagram may also be part of the agreed document provided at the end of analysis. Its non-technical nature means that it can be easily understood by users and agreed upon as a correct analysis of the system. This makes it a powerful communication tool, bridging the gap between analysts and users.

Finally, it makes it easy to sketch out different design alternatives for a future computerized system. How this is done will be covered in Chapter 13 on systems design.

11.4 Data dictionaries

A data dictionary is a store of data about data. It provides information on the structure and use of data within an organization. It is therefore closely connected with the data flow diagram and, as covered in Chapter 12, with the data model. The contents of a typical entry in a data dictionary are given in Figure 11.11.

Figure 11.11: Typical contents of a data dictionary entry.

Name:
Included here are all the names by which this data element is known. If there is more than one then these are termed 'aliases'.

Type of data
For example: data flow, data store, data item.

Structure
In the case of a data flow or data store this gives the list of data items including repeats. If the type of data is a data item its 'picture' may be given – for example. 'AA9999' – together with the range of permissible values.

Usage characteristics:
This details the list of processes that the data flows/data stores interact with. In the case of a data item this list will give the data aggregates which use the item. Information on the data such as the frequency, volume and security issues surrounding the data is often given, as this will aid the designer in deciding on the physical characteristics of the proposed system.

Name:　　　　　　　　　**Type:**
　　Invoice　　　　　　　　　Data flow

　　　aliases:
　　　　customer invoice
　　　　client invoice

Structure:
　　Aggregate: (*invoice#, invoice date, customer#, customer name, order#, [item#, item price,*
　　　　　　　　item quantity]*, subtotal, sales tax, discount%, total payable)

Usage characteristics:
　　Output process 3 – *make up invoice*
　　input to sink – *accounts*
　　input to sink – *customer*

The data dictionary provides a precise and unambiguous specification of the data elements within the system. It may be kept as a card index or nowadays on a computer. Cross-referencing between data elements is then easy. The data element *order#* referred to in the entry under invoice can easily be cross-referenced to discover that its structure is, for instance, followed by five digits.

It is important that data descriptions held in a data dictionary are not duplicated in several places. This is done so that if a change is made to some aspect of a data element the alteration is only made in one place in the dictionary, thus ensuring the maintenance of consistency.

The data dictionary is used right through the process of analysis to detailed design and into programming, as the reference point to which any questions on the structure of data can be directed. Nowadays computerized data dictionaries, sometimes called **data encyclopedias**, enable a considerable amount of extra information to be held on data, thus increasing the reliance of analysis and design on an adequate data dictionary.

If a table is made out when a data flow diagram is first drawn (as in Figure 11.8), this will provide much of the information for the data dictionary.

Along with the data flow diagrams and process specifications (covered in Sections 11.5–11.7) the data dictionary constitutes the logical model of the system.

11.5 Decision tables

The data flow diagram demonstrates the decomposition of the functions performed in an organization into simpler data processes and flows. Some of these processes may be complex in themselves but are not suitable for further decomposition in the data flow diagram. An example of this might be Kismet Ltd's procedure for calculating discounts. Although not given previously in the case study the firm's policy was summarized by the invoice manager to the systems analyst as follows:

> *Three factors determine the percentage of discount. The first is the total value of the order (we like to encourage our customers to place single large orders rather than smaller multiple orders as it makes delivery and van scheduling easier). The discount is 3% for orders over £4000. If the delivery is within 50 miles of the warehouse delivery costs are cheaper and a 2% discount is given except if the 3% discount for large orders has been granted. In this latter case only a 1% discount is given if the delivery is within 50 miles. Customers who have made purchases of more than £100,000 over the past 12 months are granted a further 2% discount. These measures are designed to encourage large purchases from local high-turnover retailers. We would like to offer a more targeted discount policy, though this would be more difficult to administer. We hope that one aspect of computerization is that automated discount calculation will help us to give a more personalized encouragement to our customers.*

The decision table for this policy is shown in Figure 11.12. The conditions that are important for determining the discount are shown in the top left-hand quadrant. In the top right-hand quadrant are the range of entries for these conditions. In this case a condition applies (Y = yes) or it does not (N = no). Note the pattern of the entries. It makes it easy to see that all eight entries have been included. Each column can be thought of as representing a type of order. For instance, column 3 represents a large order (> £4000),

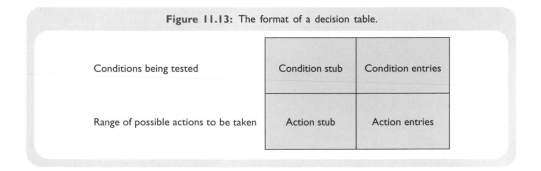

Figure 11.12: A decision table for Kismet's discount policy.

Order > £4,000	Y	Y	Y	Y	N	N	N	N
Delivery < 50 miles	Y	Y	N	N	Y	Y	N	N
Turnover > £100,000	Y	N	Y	N	Y	N	Y	N

Discount									
0%									X
1%									
2%							X	X	
3%					X				
4%			X			X			
5%				X					
6%	X								

Figure 11.13: The format of a decision table.

Conditions being tested	Condition stub	Condition entries
Range of possible actions to be taken	Action stub	Action entries

not delivered within 50 miles, from a customer with a turnover of more than £100,000. The action to be taken can be found by following the column down to discover that a discount of 5% (X = action) is to be allowed. This is an example of the general format for decision tables. This format is given in Figure 11.13.

Figure 11.12 is a simple decision table. There are only two possible entries for each condition, Y or N. This is called a **limited-entry decision table**. With three conditions there are $2^3 = 8$ columns, with four conditions there are $2^4 = 16$ columns. If there are n conditions there will be 2^n columns. With a large number of conditions the decision table becomes very wide: for example, seven conditions leads to $2^7 = 128$ columns. Fortunately it is often possible to collapse the columns. Wherever two columns differ only to the extent of one entry, and the action(s) associated with each column are identical, the effect of the Y or N entry is nil. The two columns can be replaced by one column, which has the Y and the N replaced with a single '–' but is otherwise identical to the columns it replaces. The decision table can be collapsed until no two columns satisfy the pairwise condition stated.

As well as limited entry tables there are **mixed** or **extended entry tables**. These are used when there is not a simple value yes or no (true or false) associated with a condition. For instance, there might have been three possible ways of differentiating the size

Figure 11.14: Decision tables illustrating Hardy's discount policy.

Table A

Retail store chain	Y	Y	Y	Y	Y	Y	Y	Y	N
Order size	<£2,000	<£2,000	£2,000 to less than £5,000	£2,000 to less than £5,000	£5,000 to less than £10,000	£5,000 to less than £10,000	>£10,000	>£10,000	–
One delivery	Y	N	Y	N	Y	N	Y	N	–
Discount 4%		X							
6%			X						
9%	X								
10%						X		X	
11%		X							
15%					X		X		
Note to manager							X	X	
GO TO table B									X

Table B

Order > £3,000	Y	Y	Y	Y	N	N	N
Order > £5,000	Y	Y	N	N	N	N	N
Delivery < 50 miles	Y	N	Y	N	Y	N	N
Turnover > £100,000	–	–	–	–	–	Y	N
Discount 0%							X
3%						X	
4%					X		
5%		X		X			
9%	X		X				
Send note to manager	X	X					

of the order as far as discounting was concerned − < £2000, ⩾ £2000 but > £5000 and ⩾ £5000. These three entries would appear in the condition entry, and the condition 'order size' would appear in the condition stub.

Finally, there are a range of special actions that may be present in the decision table. These concern the way that the user of the decision table moves around the table or to another table. Perhaps the most useful is the GOTO action, which causes the execution of another decision table. This is used when the types of action and conditions applicable to a case divide neatly into exclusive classes depending on the value of some condition. Care should be taken when using this action as a number of tables interconnected by GOTOs can give the appearance of logical spaghetti.

These variations on the basic table are illustrated in Figure 11.14. This is the revealed discount policy of Kismet's competitor, Hardy Ltd.

In the case of an order from a retail electrical store chain a discount of 4% is allowed if the order is less than £2000, 6% if the order is between £2000 and £5000 and 10% if the order is £5000 or more. There is a further discount of 5% if there is only one delivery address. A note of the invoice is sent to the manager if the total amount invoiced is greater than £10,000. With all other types of customer a 4% discount is given if the order is more than £3000. A 5% discount is also allowed if the delivery is within 50 miles. 3% is allowed if no other discounts have been made and the customer has an annual turnover with Hardy of more than £100,000. A note of any invoice in excess of £5000 is sent to the manager.

Decision tables are a valuable tool in analysis. Within the general format of the table, conditions are unambiguously specified and separated from actions, which are clearly stated. The declarative style of the table accords well with the way that certain processes are considered as the implementation of a set of conditions.

The straightforward non-technical character of the tables makes them a valuable communication tool between analysts and users in checking the analyst's understanding of a process. In design the tables can be used to specify the requirements of a program. They facilitate analyst–programmer communication.

Although it takes intelligence to construct a decision table it requires a very limited repertoire of mental abilities in order to use one. They are therefore in a form suitable for incorporation into a computer program. There are programs that accept a decision table as input and produce program code to implement the table as output. The program runs interactively with users by requiring answers to basic questions. These questions correspond to the conditions.

Finally, decision tables cover in a methodical way the totality of possible combinations of conditions that might apply in a particular case, and so can be used to check on the completeness and consistency of a policy that involves the taking of different actions when different conditions are satisfied. In order to see this consider the following example:

Kismet's management have decided that computerization offers them the opportunity to offer a more complex and targeted discount policy. It has decided to offer its customers a differential discount depending on whether the order is large (over £5000), whether the year-to-date turnover of the customer is large (over £100,000), whether the order is to be delivered to one address only and whether the delivery, or deliveries, are within 50 miles. After many hours of discussion the management have arrived at the following policy:

1. *A high-priority order is defined to be one from a high-turnover customer who requires a large order or who is using only one delivery address.*

2. *A low-priority order is defined to be one which is neither large nor from a customer with a high turnover.*

3. *If the order is large and to be delivered to only one address a discount of 10% is allowed, with an additional discount of 5% if that address is within 50 miles.*

4. *No order that is to be delivered to multiple addresses may receive more than 5% discount.*

Figure 11.15: The use of a decision table to illustrate inconsistency.

		H	H	H	H					H	H			L	L	L	L
Large order		Y	Y	Y	Y	Y	Y	Y	Y	N	N	N	N	N	N	N	N
Large turnover		Y	Y	Y	Y	N	N	N	N	Y	Y	Y	Y	N	N	N	N
One address		Y	Y	N	N	Y	Y	N	N	Y	Y	N	N	Y	Y	N	N
Within 50 miles		Y	N	Y	N	Y	N	Y	N	Y	N	Y	N	Y	N	Y	N
Actions																	
Give	Rule 3	15	10			15	10										
	Rule 4			≤5	≤5			≤5	≤5			≤5	≤5			≤5	≤5
percent	Rule 5									10	10	5	5				
	Rule 6	≥5	≥5	≥5	≥5					≥5	≥5						
discount	Rule 7													3	3		
	Rule 8							5	5								
	Rule 9	≥10		≥10		≥10		≥10									
TOTAL		15	10	(a)	5	15	10	(b)	5	10	10	5	5	3	3	(c)	(c)

Notes

H = High-priority order (Rule 1)

L = Low-priority order (Rule 2)

(a) Rules 4, 6 and 9 are inconsistent

(b) Rules 4, 8 and 9 are inconsistent

(c) There is insufficient information to assign a discount.

5. However, an order that is not large from a customer with a turnover of more than £100,000 should receive a 10% discount except in as far as this conflicts with rule 4, in which case they will obtain the maximum discount applicable under that rule.

6. High-priority orders are to be given at least 5% discount.

7. Low-priority orders are to be given a 3% discount if there is only one delivery address.

8. Orders from customers with a turnover of less than £100,000 to be delivered to multiple addresses shall receive a discount of 5% if the order is large, irrespective of whether the delivery is within 50 miles or not.

9. All large orders that are to be delivered within a 50 mile radius are to receive at least 10% discount.

10. All applicable discounts are to be totalled.

This policy has been analyzed in Figure 11.15. Although this does not exactly follow the format of Figure 11.13 it is, in principle, a decision table separating conditions and actions. The effects of each of the rules on each of the types of order (each type of order corresponds to one column in the condition entry quadrant) are shown in the action entry quadrant. The total effect of all rules on a type of order is shown, where possible, in the TOTAL row. For example, column 2 corresponds to a large order from a customer with a turnover in excess of £100,000. The order has one delivery address, which is not within the 50 mile zone surrounding the Kismet warehouse. It is judged to be a high-priority order (rule 1) and so is to be accorded at least 5% discount (rule 6). The order satisfies rule 2 and so is given a 10% discount.

It is clear that the policy is inconsistent. Notes (a) and (b) of Figure 11.15 indicate where the inconsistency arises. This could be eliminated by removing rule 9. It would be the analyst's responsibility to point out to management the inconsistency and advise on possible ways of eliminating it. An inconsistent policy cannot be incorporated into a program. It is ultimately the responsibility of Kismet to decide on the policy. It is a business decision. Normally all the analyst would do is to comment on the formal properties of the policy.

In summary there are a number of advantages and disadvantages in the use of decision tables to represent the links between conditions and actions.

Advantages

- They provide a clear tabular representation linking conditions with actions and so act as a communication tool.
- The declarative style corresponds to the way that many processes are understood as conditions that determine actions.
- They ensure an exhaustive coverage of all possible cases.
- They can be used to investigate inconsistency and redundancy in a set of rules.
- They are easy to follow in operation.
- They can be incorporated into program specifications.

Disadvantages

- They can become very large and unwieldy with large numbers of conditions.
- They are only suitable for representing processes where there is little interleaving between the evaluation of conditions and the execution of actions.

11.6 Logic flowcharts

Decision tables are one way of clearly representing the logic of a process and are most suitable when only few actions need to be undertaken as a result of the evaluation of a (possibly complex) set of conditions. If, though, the process is one that involves inter-mingling the evaluation of conditions with the execution of various actions then the proliferation of GOTO statements to subsidiary decision tables makes it difficult to follow the logic of the process. Logic flowcharts overcome this difficulty.

The symbols used in logic flowcharts are shown in Figure 11.16. Their use can be illustrated by the representation of the following example in flowchart form. It concerns the approval of orders in the credit control section of Kismet. The procedure, stated here, can be regarded as a fuller version of the summary that appeared previously in the case study in Section 11.2. The additions mainly concern the procedure to be followed in the case of error discovery and the maintenance of a running total of the value of approved orders. The order set has been priced and valued. Now is the time for credit approval.

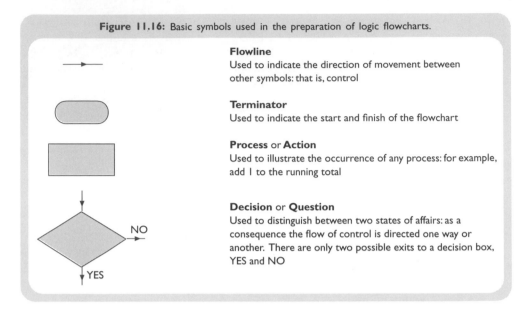

Figure 11.16: Basic symbols used in the preparation of logic flowcharts.

Flowline
Used to indicate the direction of movement between other symbols: that is, control

Terminator
Used to indicate the start and finish of the flowchart

Process or **Action**
Used to illustrate the occurrence of any process: for example, add 1 to the running total

Decision or **Question**
Used to distinguish between two states of affairs: as a consequence the flow of control is directed one way or another. There are only two possible exits to a decision box, YES and NO

The credit control clerk processes a stack of order sets for which provisional values have been calculated and inserted. The presence of the **customer#** *and* **customer name** *are first checked. If either is absent then the customer file is consulted and the missing entry inserted. If there is no reference to the customer in the file the order set is sent to the credit control manager. If the number and name are found not to match then the order 4 set is sent back to the order processing section together with an internal company P22 form for investigation. In all other cases the* **order value** *is added to the* **current balance** *and compared with the* **credit limit**. *If this has been exceeded the order set is sent to the credit control manager along with the customer records. If the order has passed these tests the order set is stamped 'OK approved' and put in the out-tray. At the end of the stack the contents of the out-tray are returned to the order processing section and the total value of all the approved orders is entered on the daily totals sheet.*

The flowchart is shown in Figure 11.17. The flow lines indicate flows of control *not* flows of data or documents. When it is said that there is a flow of control between points A and B all this means is that after the operation at A has been carried out the operation at B is carried out. Nothing passes between points A and B.

The following conditions apply to flowcharts:

- Each question or decision box has exactly two exits: one corresponding to Yes or True and the other to No or False.
- All flows of control must end in a decision box, action box or terminator and must always ensure that the process eventually stops.
- Generally the flowchart is designed so that the flow of control goes from the top of the page downwards.

The flowchart in Figure 11.17 follows these principles. The repetitive nature of the processing of one order after another is accomplished by means of directing the flow of

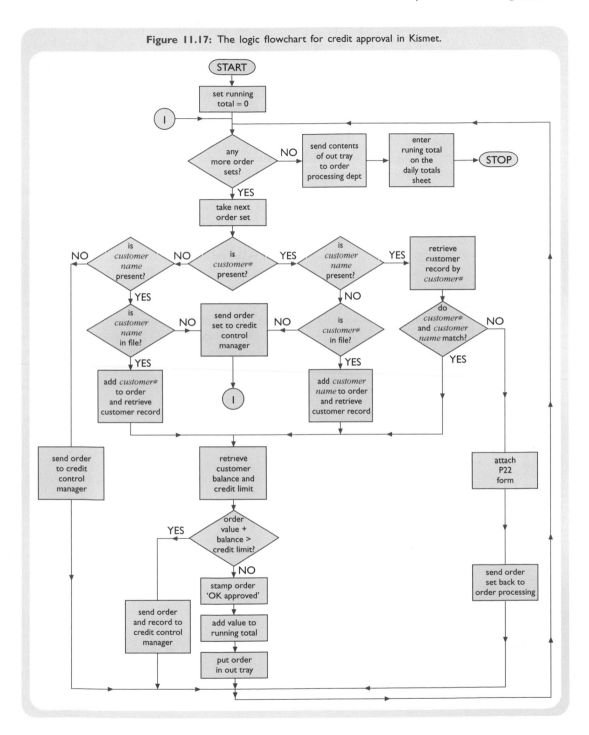

Figure 11.17: The logic flowchart for credit approval in Kismet.

control from the end of the approval process, as applied to one order, back to the top of the chart. There, a test is performed to establish whether there are any more orders in the stack before proceeding. A running total is maintained.

Flowcharts have several advantages. Their pictorial representation makes them easy to follow and understand – the different paths through the process are obvious at a glance. They can therefore be used as a basis for agreement between the analyst and the user on the correctness of the analyst's understanding. They may also form part of the firm's procedures manual.

Flowcharts can be given for high or low levels of analysis. For instance, to answer the simple question 'is the customer name in the file?' requires the execution of a number of actions and the consideration of further questions. If the records in the file are ordered by *customer#* it implies the following type of procedure for the clerk. Go to the filing cabinet, start at the first record, compare the *customer name* with the target *name*, if identical, stop – the *customer name* is in the file, else carry out the procedure on the next record and so on. The level of the chart is generally high at the analysis stage and such low-level specifications are ignored.

Logic flowcharts can also be used in the design stage as a way of specifying a procedure precisely. If it is intended that a program be written from this specification it is called a **program logic flowchart**. The flowchart will be presented generally at a much more detailed level. Variable names will be included, procedures for establishing counts will be outlined and so on. The presence of the decision box encourages the use of the GOTO programming structure and so program flowcharts may lead to programming techniques that result in non-structured programs. This may be a reason to discourage their use at the design stage.

In summary the main advantages and disadvantages in the use of logic flowcharts are:

Advantages

- They provide a pictorial representation of a series of actions and are therefore easy to understand and natural to follow.
- They are used in procedures manuals to indicate the sequences of actions that are to be followed in carrying out a task – for example, an audit.
- They are very good at representing cases where there is an interleaving of actions and the evaluation of conditions (compare this with decision tables).
- They may be used to specify programs to programmers.

Disadvantages

- They encourage the use of GOTO statements if used in program specifications in design. This may lead to programs that have a logic that is difficult to unravel.
- They are difficult and time-consuming to alter once drawn.

11.7   Structured English

As well as using decision tables or logic flowcharts, procedures can be represented through the use of structured English. This also has the effect of imposing a structure on the specification, which encourages the use of structured programming. Structured English is a precise, highly restricted subset of the natural English language. There is no accepted standard for structured English but all usages have a number of features in common. The vocabulary of the language is restricted to:

- Precise verbs phrased in the imperative mood. All adjectives, adverbs, words with vague or ambiguous meanings are avoided. Complex sentence structures involving subordinate clauses are broken down into their atomic constituents. Irrelevant phrases are dropped. For instance, the sentence 'The large document containing the particular details on the customer should now be edited carefully by the clerk making sure that all entries are made clearly with an indelible pen' would probably be reduced to 'edit document containing customer details'.

- References to items of data should use the same terms as applied in the data flow diagram and the data dictionary.

- Certain reserved words are used for revealing the logical structure of processes.

The logic of any process can be described by using three structures (Figure 11.18):

1. **A sequential block of statements:** The statements should be concise and contain a verb and object. For example:
   (a) Compute total.
   (b) Set sales tax equal to total multiplied by sales tax rate.
   (c) Set total equal to total plus sales tax.
   (d) Compute discount.
   (e) Set net total equal to total minus discount.
   (f) Write net total on invoice.

2. **Decision structures:** These are used when it is required that one sequence of operations be carried out if a condition is satisfied and another set if it is not satisfied. The structure takes two forms:
   (a) The two-way decision

   IF ⟨condition⟩
      THEN ⟨block-1⟩
      ELSE ⟨block-2⟩

   where the **ELSE** is not compulsory. For example:

   IF total > credit limit **THEN** refer to credit control manager
                     ELSE stamp 'OK approved'

   (b) The multi-way decision
      CASE ⟨variable⟩
      CASE I ⟨value-1⟩
         do block-1
      CASE 2 ⟨value-2⟩
              do block-2
      CASE 3 ⟨value-3⟩
              do block-3

Figure 11.18: The logical form of structured English.

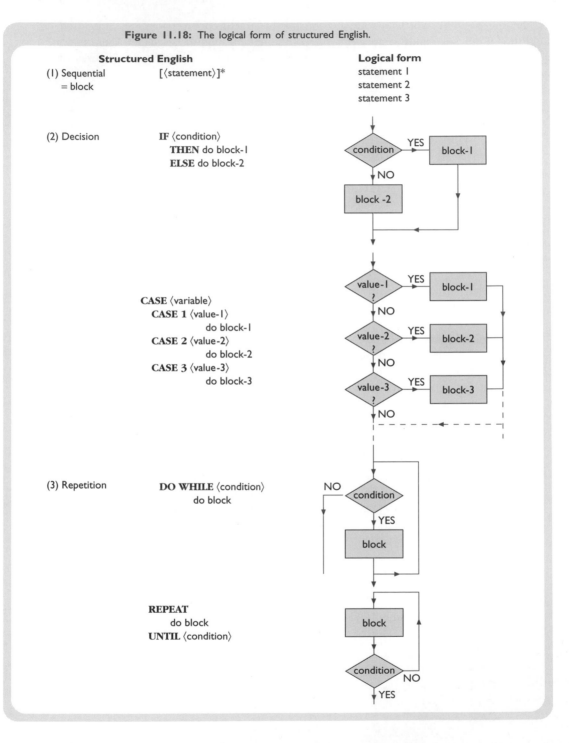

For example:

CASE invoice value
  CASE 1 invoice value < £2,000
      add 1% to discount percent
  CASE 2 £2,000 ≤ invoice value < £5,000
       add 3% to discount percent
  CASE 3 invoice value ≥ £5,000
      add 6% to discount percent

3. **Repetition structures:** These are used where a process is repeated until some condition is met. There are two forms of repetition statement:

DO WHILE ⟨condition⟩
  do block

and

REPEAT
  do block
UNTIL ⟨condition⟩

In the former, the test as to whether the condition is satisfied occurs before the loop is entered (and so the loop will not be traversed at all if the condition fails first time). In the latter the test occurs after the loop has been traversed implying that the loop is traversed, at least once.

For example:

DO WHILE stack of invoices is not empty
  get next invoice
  add invoice total to running total

The example now discussed illustrates the use of structured English for specifying a process. It concerns the task of pricing the Kismet company order sets and is taken from a statement supplied by the clerk responsible for pricing the orders. It covers error cases not given in the case study.

> *I get the stack of orders to price from the supervisor. I first of all tidy the pile and then go through the orders one by one until I have finished. After this I put the stack of priced orders in the credit control section's in-tray. I carefully price each item in turn by consulting the sales catalogue. Sometimes I cannot find the item because it is a new product and I then have to look at the supplement. If I have no luck there I just put a big query mark by it on the form. After I have finished I put the order in the out-tray.*

The structured English version is given in Figure 11.19(a). Note how the rambling description of the process, as given by the order pricing clerk, is transformed into a set of precise statements.

The indenting is important as it gives a clear indication of the structure of the logic governing the process. Statements may also be nested as shown in the example.

To illustrate the scope of an **IF** statement or a **DO** statement it is sometimes clearer to use **ENDDO**, **ENDIF** and **ENDCASE** statements. These fill a role analogous to brackets in elementary arithmetic. The expression $6 - 3 \times 7 + 3$ can be made much clearer by

Figure 11.19: The structured English representation of the pricing process for Kismet. (a) Structured English without ENDIF and ENDDO. (b) Structured English with ENDIF and ENDDO.

```
(a)  get stack of orders
     DO WHILE there are more orders in the stack
          get the top order
          DO WHILE there are more unpriced items on the order
               get next unpriced item#
               IF item# is in the catalogue
                 THEN write item price on the order
                 ELSE IF item price is in the supplement
                         THEN write item price on the order
                         ELSE write ? on the order
          put the order in the out tray
     get the stack of orders from the out tray
     put the stack of orders in the credit control section's in tray

(b)  get stack of orders
     DO WHILE there are more orders in the stack
          get the top order
          DO WHILE there are more unpriced items on the order
               get next unpriced item#
               IF item# is in the catalogue
                 THEN write item price on the order
                 ELSE IF item price is in the supplement
                         THEN write item price on the order
                         ELSE write ? on the order
                       ENDIF
                 ENDIF
          ENDDO
          put the order in the out tray
     ENDDO
     get the stack of orders from the out tray
     put the stack of orders in the credit control section's in tray
```

the insertion of brackets: $(6 - (3 \times (7 + 3)))$. In fact in many cases it is necessary to bracket in order to indicate the precise meaning of the formula. Similarly **ENDDO**, **ENDIF** and **ENDCASE** fulfil the role analogous to the right-hand bracket.

The structured English version of the Kismet pricing clerk's routine using **ENDDO** and **ENDIF** statements is shown in Figure 11.19(b).

Structured English representations of processes may be a little difficult to follow for the uninitiated, particularly if there is a high degree of internal nesting. However, as mentioned at the beginning of this section they do have the attraction of encouraging structured coding of programs.

Whether decision tables, a logic flowchart or structured English is chosen as the representation of a process depends on its nature. Complex sets of conditions determining few actions with little iteration suggest a decision table representation. Otherwise a logic flowchart or structured English representation will be suitable, the choice being the result of the trade-off between diagrammatic clarity and the wish to encourage structured code in the design stage.

Summary

The purpose of systems analysis is to arrive at an understanding of a system that is sufficient to design a computerized replacement. This replacement may involve substantial redesign and the integration of physically disparate manual systems. In order to achieve this a structured approach is taken to systems analysis. This chapter was concerned with structured process analysis and modelling. Its main features are:

- a commitment to a 'top-down' decomposition in which data and processes are analyzed into their constituent parts;
- an emphasis on the development of a model of the system as a prerequisite for successful design;
- an assumption that developing an information system is largely a technical exercise.

The main tool used is the data flow diagram which models the data flows between data processes, stores and sinks. This diagram reveals the logical model at various levels of detail depending on the degree of decomposition and the intended recipient of the diagram. The nature of the processes is specified via decision tables, logic flowcharts or structured English, all of which have their relative strengths and limitations. The data dictionary maintains information on the nature of the data itself. The entire repertoire of techniques is aimed at deriving a logical model, independent of physical commitments, and at producing documentation which is precise, thus facilitating communication between users, management, programmers and the analyst.

Much attention has been given to the analysis of the organization into its functional components, the further breakdown of these into individual processes, the charting of the data flows between them and their representation by various tools. What has been lacking from the analysis is the treatment of the data stores and the nature of the data itself. Some would regard this as perhaps the most important feature of analysis and it is to this that the next chapter is devoted.

Exercises

1. What are the scope and objectives of systems analysis?
2. When considering a complex integrated system why is it important to use a methodical approach to systems analysis and design?
3. What benefits are to be obtained in analysis by initially focusing on processes and functions at a general, rather than a detailed level?
4. What are the advantages and limitations of:
   (a) decision tables
   (b) logic flowcharts
   (c) structured English
   as representation tools for processes?

5. Can a situation represented by a logic flowchart, decision table or structured English always be represented without loss of information by all three? What determines the choice of method of process specification?

6. What are the advantages and limitations of manual systems flowcharts?

7. Explain the purpose of a data dictionary.

8. 'There is little difference between data flow diagrams and document flowcharts – they both represent the flow of data between processes.' Do you agree?

9. 'At the stage of analysis an understanding of the existing system is more important than technical computer expertise, and as the tools of analysis are relatively easy to understand it is more effective if existing users carry out the analysis and computer experts are brought in only at the design stage.' Do you agree?

10. 'Only the outputs of a system are of interest to an organization. Therefore an analyst needs to analyze the outputs required, specify the inputs necessary to produce these and then design the new system to transform these inputs 'By concentrating on formal data and processes the analyst ignores the fact that much useful information within an organization is of an informal nature – opinions, hunches and qualitative approximations. The analyst is therefore bound to produce an inadequate analysis and design of a computerized information system.' What is to be said for and against this view?

12. 'By concentrating on formal data and processes the analyst ignores the fact that human beings, with personal limitations and preferences, will operate the system within an organization. The analyst is therefore bound to produce an inadequate analysis and design of a computerized information system.' Do you agree?

13. 'Rather than adopt the "grand" overall approach to systems analysis and design it is better to develop a computer system piecemeal. Mistakes are then small ones and can be easily rectified.' Do you agree?

14. A large lending library handles book issues and returns, enquiries and sends out notices regarding overdue books to borrowers. All procedures are currently manual. The library deals with a large number of postal and telephone transactions. The majority of its books are stored in underground stacks. The library thus needs a fast response information system and to this end has purchased a database management system.

Initial analysis indicates that the following information has been stored on books, borrowers and loans in the current manual system:

For each book: book number, author, title.
For each borrower: ID number, name, address.
For each loan of a book to a borrower: date due for return.
A record of books reserved for potential borrowers is also maintained.

The database is to be designed to support the following functions currently carried out manually:

● *Book issue processing*: On receipt of a request for a loan the librarian makes an enqaniry to establish whether the book is held by the library and is available (that is, not on loan). If the book is not held then that information is given to the potential borrower by a note.

   If the book is held but is on loan the potential borrower is also informed, a note that the book is to be reserved on return is made, and it is established by enquiry whether the book is overdue or not. If it is overdue a note is sent to the current borrower pointing out the overdue status of the loan and that a request for the book has been made. If the book is directly available then it is issued to the potential borrower and details of this loan, including the date due for return, are stored.

● *Book return processing*: On receipt of a returned book the librarian cancels the loan and makes an enquiry to establish whether the book is reserved. If it is reserved then it is issued to the reserver and the reserve note is cancelled. Otherwise the book is returned to the stack.

● *Enquiry processing*: There are two types of enquiry:
   (a) Given the name of borrower establish what books he/she has on loan and when they are due for return.
   (b) Given the name of book establish which borrower, if any, has the book and the date due for return.

● *Overdue processing*: When books become two weeks overdue a notice is sent out requesting their return. A similar note is sent every two weeks until return.
   (a) Draw a high-level combined data flow diagram for the processes.
   (b) Draw an exploded data flow diagram for each of the processes.

15. The daily invoicing routine for an invoice clerk is as follows. At the beginning of the day the stack of sales orders with their associated despatch notes is taken from the in-tray and processed. The details of each order are checked against the details of the relevant customer account and a discount is calculated. A customer within the trade is allowed 15% off the list price. There is also a special 5% discount for any customer who has been ordering regularly for 2 years provided that the customer has not received the trade discount. Any order over £1000 is allowed a bulk discount of 10% off of the list price in addition to any other discounts. If the total to be invoiced exceeds the customer's credit limit a note is sent to the manager prior to despatch of the invoice. When all invoices have been despatched a note of the total invoiced is sent to the manager.
   (a) Draw a logic flowchart illustrating the day's procedure.
   (b) Represent the above by using structured English.

16. Design a manual systems flowchart to illustrate a procedure that Kismet Ltd might use to handle return of goods. This flowchart should be compatible with Figure 11.3.

17. A theatre accepts postal and telephone bookings for its forthcoming performances up to a period of six months in advance. About half of the bookings are directly from the public, the remainder being from agencies. ▷

When a member of the public makes a booking by telephone either a credit card number is taken and the booking is firmly made, or a reservation for the seat is taken. In the latter case the member of the public must collect and pay for the ticket at least half-an-hour before the performance.

In the case of agencies, on receipt of a block-booking request by phone or mail, the theatre runs a credit check on the agency account and makes out a confirmation note for those requested seats that are still available. This is sent to the agency as both a confirmation of booking and an invoice. At the end of each month the theatre sends a statement of account to each agency.

Half an hour before the performance starts all those seats that have been reserved by the public but have not been collected are released for general sale.

The theatre also receives enquiries on seat availability from both agencies and the public.

(a) Draw a data flow diagram illustrating the data flows, processes and stores necessary to carry out the invoicing, enquiry and booking facilities of the theatre.

(b) For each data flow and data store illustrate the structure of the data concerned.

18. The following is an account of the manual operations that occur at the head office of a chain of supermarkets:

Each supermarket submits a daily cash report plus supporting documentation to the head office by post. This is passed from the mail room to the area manager. The area manager's staff carry out checks on the arithmetic of the cash reports and on submitted bank deposit slips and petty cash vouchers. All of these documents are then passed to the cashier's department after any queries have been reconciled.

Each day's cash report is summarized and entered into a cash analysis book in the cashier's department. This cash analysis book forms part of the main cash-book into which weekly totals are entered. At the end of each week the cashier's department reconciles the cash-book with the bank pass sheets. The cash reports are then sent to the accounts department.

Every week each supermarket also submits, by post, records of deliveries made by suppliers together with other stock movement details. These are sent to the area manager's office, where the unit costs and sales prices are entered on the document and delivery records. The complete set of documents is then passed to the accounts department. The area manager's office also receives delivery sheets sent from the company's own warehouses. These are for goods supplied to the supermarkets. These sheets are priced at cost and at selling prices before being submitted to the accounts department.

The accounts department receives the stock movement forms, the direct and internal delivery sheets and the cash reports. The department then prepares a monthly report for each supermarket at cost and selling prices.

Draw a document systems flowchart with any necessary narrative showing the various document flows. (Note that many temporary and permanent files are implied in the description without being explicitly stated.) ▷

19. When a library first receives a book from a publisher it is sent, together with the accompanying delivery note, to the library desk. Here the delivery note is checked against a file of books ordered. If no order can be found to match the note, a letter of enquiry is sent to the publishers. If a matching order is found, a catalogue note is prepared from the details on the validated delivery note. The catalogue note, together with the book, is sent to the registration department. The validated delivery note is sent to the accounts department, where it is stored. On receipt of an invoice from the publisher, the accounts department checks its store of delivery notes. If the corresponding delivery note is found then an instruction to pay the publisher is made, and subsequently a cheque is sent. If no corresponding delivery note is found, the invoice is stored in a pending file.

Draw a data flow diagram for this information.

20. As a systems analyst you have been commissioned by the ABC Company to computerize their sales order processing. It is believed by the Board of ABC that the attractiveness of their product to customers can be increased by ensuring that all customers receive a discount off the list price of ABC's products. It is further intended that a maximum discount of 25% on any transaction should not be exceeded. To this end they have isolated the following customer/transaction features:

regular customers
cash transactions
bulk order
trade customers.

The board suggests the following policy where (all discounts are off the list price and are to be added together):

(a) Those customers who are trade receive 15% discount provided that the transaction is a bulk order; otherwise the discount is 12%.
(b) Non-trade customers are allowed 5% discount provided that the order is bulk.
(c) Cash transactions receive 13% discount if trade; if not a 10% discount.
(d) All regular customers are allowed 10% discount unless the total discount allowable under rules (a), (b) and (c) is greater than 10%, in which case the greater discount will apply.

By means of a decision table advise the board as to the suitability of its discount policy in the light of its stated aims.

21. A stack of student records, ordered by *student#*, contains up to five records on each student covering the student's exam results in one or more of the following – accounting, economics, law, maths, systems analysis. A clerk is required to process these records and must produce an average for each student, which is then entered on a summary sheet. Not all students take all five subjects. The clerk also computes an average mark for each exam for each of the five subjects and enters it on the summary sheet.

(a) Produce a structured English specification of a suitable process to achieve these aims.
(b) Represent this process by a logic flowchart. ▷

22. A firm pursues the following discount policy on its products (all discount being offered as a percentage of advertised price).

(a) Those customers ordering more than ten items receive at least a 1% discount.

(b) Those customers who are not regular customers receive at most a 2% discount.

(c) All those regular customers who order more than 10 items receive a 2% discount plus an additional 1% discount if they pay by cash.

(d) Any person paying cash and who is either a regular customer or orders more than ten items (but not both) is to receive a 2% discount.

(e) All customers who satisfy just one of the following conditions – ordering more than ten items, paying cash or being a regular customer – receives a 1% discount in as far as this does not conflict with rules (a)–(d).

(f) Any customer not covered by the preceding rules receives no discount.

By using decision tables, evaluate the above rules as to their consistency, comprehensiveness and redundancy. Can the rules be replaced by a simpler set?

Recommended reading

● Aktas Z.A. (1987). *Structured Analysis and Design of Information Systems*. Prentice-Hall
This is a comprehensive collection of structured tools and techniques as applied to analysis and design.

● Cutts J. (1997). *Structured Systems Analysis and Design Methodology* 3rd edn. Oxford: Blackwell Scientific Publications
This is a standard text on structured systems analysis and design. It is comprehensive, clear and suitable for a detailed understanding of structured methods.

● De Marco T. (1980). *Structured Analysis: Systems Specifications*. (Yourdon) Prentice-Hall

● Gane C. and Sarson T. (1979). *Structured Systems Analysis: Tools and Techniques*. Prentice-Hall
The books both by De Marco and by Gane and Sarson are classics in the application of structured techniques to systems analysis and design. Both are designed for the professional analyst yet are readable by those without an extensive computer science background.

● Wood-Harper, A.T., Antill L. and Avison D.E. (1985). *Information Systems Definition: The Multiview Approach*. Oxford: Blackwell Scientific Publications
This book applies the structured techniques covered in this chapter to a case study. The approach is integrated with other approaches, particularly data analysis as covered in Chapter 12.

Data Analysis and Modelling

The data flow diagram shows the data processes and the flows of data between them but does little to represent the contents of the data store. The trend towards the use of integrated databases in business information systems means that the analysis and design of the database is an important stage in the systems life cycle. In this chapter entity–relationship modelling is introduced to derive a data model of the organization. The resulting data model is 'fine tuned' through normalization. Finally, the adequacy of this model is tested against the functions that it will be required to service. The aim is to provide a data model that leads to an effective database design, that is sufficient to satisfy the organization's data processing and information needs. The latter part of the chapter deals with the interrelationship between data modelling and process modelling.

12.1   Top-down versus bottom-up approaches to data modelling

A bottom-up approach to designing the data store involves extracting data fields as indicated on the document description forms. These are the forms that the analyst uses to specify the data content of existing documents within the system. Any extra data elements that might be required as inputs to processes that are new to the system are then added. These data elements are then grouped into records. It is quite likely that each of the original documents within the manual system gives rise to a record. For instance, a company order form might give rise to a record the fields of which are *order#*, *order date*, *customer#*, *customer name*, *[item1#**, *[item1 quantity]**. . . . These records form the basis of files. There is a record for each order and the collection of these is the order file. Decisions are then made on the medium for each file, on the way the file is to be organized and on the indexes needed to retrieve the information for an application. This approach to analysis and design is called **bottom-up** because the system is developed from the basic building blocks – the data fields – upwards through the records and files.

This approach is adequate if small systems that require little or no internal integration are to be designed. However, if there are a large number of fields, which are shared between many applications, it becomes increasingly difficult to design the system without repeating the same data fields unnecessarily. This point can be made by using an example from Kismet. A bottom-up approach leads to the design of a stock file that contains stock records having as fields *item#*, *item description*, *quantity held*. . . . This is the responsibility of the stores department. There is also a catalogue file of records containing fields such as *item#*, *item description*, *price*. . . . This is the responsibility of the sales department. Each time a new item is entered on the stock file it needs to be entered on the catalogue file and each time a description is altered on one it needs to be altered on the other. Of course this can be done by designing a program that will take the contents of one file and reconcile them with the other. However, this is a piecemeal solution to a problem that has been created by designing the data store in a piecemeal fashion to satisfy each of the applications separately.

A deeper problem with this approach occurs if substantial redesign of the system is required. Here, the existing documentation is not a good guide to the final data store contents. It is difficult to decide on the fields required at the outset and the extent to which they are to be shared between applications.

What is needed is a way of developing the data store for the organization so that it does not suffer from the limitations of the bottom-up approach. Data analysis using **top-down** data modelling achieves this. This approach leaves physical design considerations until the last available opportunity in the analysis and design cycle. If the logical rather than physical structure of the data is considered the analyst is not likely to be sidetracked by details on sequencing of records or indexes on files. In the spirit of decomposition associated with structured techniques a top-down approach to data analysis first considers the types of objects on which the organization would wish to keep data and the relationships between them. This is followed by a consideration of the kinds of data to be kept on these objects and only at a later stage how this is to be physically stored within the computer system.

There are other reasons for taking this approach to data analysis. The functions for which data are used in an organization are likely to change over time, though the structure of the data itself may remain constant. For instance, different types of report may need to be drawn from the data from one year to the next. The data structure can be seen to be the fixed element and the functions as dependent on it. If this is assumed then it becomes clear that to design a data store that satisfies the temporary functional contingencies of the time will be unsatisfactory when these change. It seems more sensible to design the data store in such a way that it mirrors or models the structure of the objects and relationships within the organization and also the data held on these.

Integrated databases and the programs that interact with them (database management systems) have been explained fully in Chapter 7 on databases. It is important to realize that many commercial database systems allow the database to be defined by providing a high-level logical model of the data structure. The storage structure details are (largely) controlled by the database management system. The outcome of top-down entity–relationship data modelling provides such a suitable model.

12.2   Entity–relationship modelling

The fundamental assumption behind entity–relationship modelling is that an organization's data structure can be modelled with the use of just three distinct sorts of object. These are as follows:

12.2.1   Entity type

An entity type is a type of thing that is capable of an independent existence and on which the organization may wish to hold data. This is the key characteristic of an entity type. For instance, the entity type **EMPLOYEE** is the type of thing on which a payroll department may wish to keep data such as *employee#* and *date of birth*. The entity type is an abstract concept of which there are particular entity occurrences. It is on these occurrences, strictly, that data is held. An example of the entity type **EMPLOYEE** is the man called 'Bill Smith' by his work colleagues and 'father' by his daughter. Entity types may also have as their occurrences documents, such as the entity type **ORDER**, or more abstract occurrences, such as the entity type **ACADEMIC COURSE** (it is not possible to see, touch or feel a BA in Business Studies). To reiterate, if an organization wishes to keep data on a type of thing that has an independent existence then it should be regarded as an entity type.

12.2.2   Relationship

The entity types applicable to an organization may bear some relationship to one another. For example, the entity type **EMPLOYEE** will bear some relationship to the entity type **DEPARTMENT** because the structure of the organization requires each employee to be a member of a department. Not all entity types will bear relationships to other entity types – the entity type **ORDER** will not have any special relationship with **EMPLOYEE** for instance. The relationship between an employee and the department of which he/she is a member will be called the 'membership' relationship – any other meaningful name could have been used. Such relationships exist (in reality), and therefore questions are often asked concerning them – 'Which department does Bill Smith belong to?', 'Who belongs to the stores department?'. This suggests that relationships between entity types form an important feature of an organization, one that is worth modelling.

12.2.3   Attribute

The entity types that are deemed applicable to an organization also have attributes. These can be thought of as properties. The entity type **EMPLOYEE** has the attributes *name*, *employee#*, *date of birth*, *sex* and so on. For a particular occurrence of the type **EMPLOYEE**, say the man Bill Smith, these attributes have the values *William John Smith, 3123, 21 April 1954, male*. The man, Bill Smith, will of course have other properties, such as an inside leg measurement, a colour of eyes and a National Insurance number, but only some of these will be relevant to the entity type **EMPLOYEE** and so be attributes of that entity type. Each entity occurrence of an entity type must be separately identifiable by some attribute. This attribute is called the **key attribute**. The key attribute of **EMPLOYEE** would be *employee#*. This is because each *employee#* will identify one and only one employee. Two employees could not have the same *employee#*. If they could, then *employee#* would not be a key attribute.

The use of the categories of entity, relationship and attribute is one way of viewing the world or in this case the organization. Although these terms carry no physical implications about the way that data will be physically represented in the computer it is often the case that a direct correspondence will eventually be set up. The entity type will be represented by a record type. The attributes will be represented by fields of the record type. An individual occurrence of an entity will then correspond to a particular record with certain values for the fields. So the entity type, **EMPLOYEE**, and the entity occurrence, Bill Smith, can be represented by the record type and record:

record structure:
name employee# date of birth sex
record occurrence:
William John Smith 3123 21/04/54 male

The relationships between the entity types can be represented in different ways. One way is by the use of a pointer from one record standing for one entity to another record corresponding to the second entity involved.

12.2.4 Types of relationship

There are a number of useful distinctions between various types of relationship. These distinctions are determined by the number of occurrences of the respective entity types that play a part in the relationship.

1:n relationships

Figure 12.1(a) shows a 1:*n* relationship. This can be understood as stating that each department has *n* employees as members and each employee is a member of one department. A representation of occurrences exhibiting this is shown in (b). Note that the relationship is still 1:*n* even though **Stores** has only one member, Salvador Mendez. The restriction on the relationship is that each employee can be a member of *at most* one department. If departments can exist without having any employees as members (a possible, though unlikely occurrence) then this may be shown as in (c). The dotted line indicates that an occurrence of a department need not be attached to any employee. Similarly (d) indicates that it is possible for an employee to exist who is not a member of any department.

m:n relationships

Suppose that each item that exists in the stores department may be supplied by many suppliers and each supplier may supply many items. This is said to be an *m:n* relationship. Figure 12.1(e) and (f) indicate *m:n* relationships.

1:1 relationships

There are also 1:1 relationships. In Western society each man is allowed to be married to at most one woman and each woman may be married to at most one man. This is shown in diagrams (g) and (h).

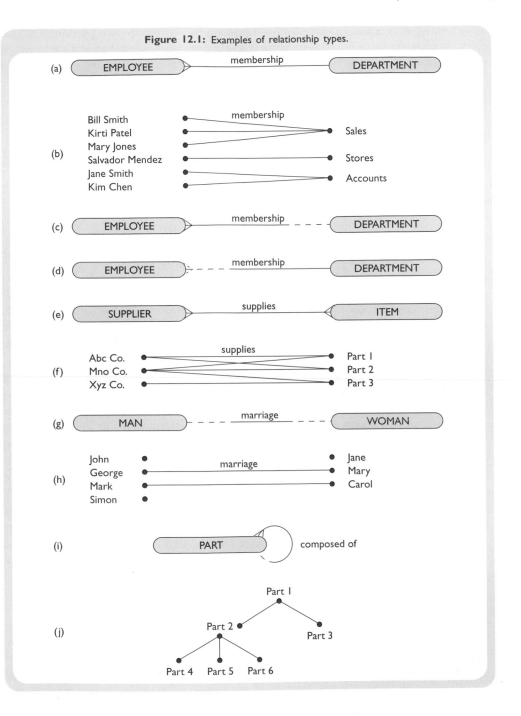

Figure 12.1: Examples of relationship types.

Involuted relationships

Relationships occasionally may be involuted. This means that an example of an entity type is related to another example of the same entity type. For instance, it is common for a part used in a later stage in a production process to be composed of parts that are manufactured at an earlier stage. Thus components are made up of components which are themselves made up of components and so on. This is shown in Figure 12.1(i), which implies that the parts and composition follow the tree-like structure in (j). The dotted line is necessary because there must be some parts that will be basic: that is, not composed themselves of parts.

12.3   Data analysis and modelling – an overview of the method

In top-down data analysis using entity–relationship modelling the analyst follows the steps outlined in Figure 12.2. As an example, this method is later applied in Section 12.4 to the Kismet case study. First an overview of the method is given.

1. **The analyst defines the major data areas to be covered by the model.** These major data areas will usually be determined by the major functions of the organization. Sales order processing, marketing, accounts, purchasing, manufacturing, inventory and administration are all examples of major functional areas. The analyst will then concentrate on each of these areas in turn and develop a data model for each area. Later, the models will be amalgamated. This division into functional areas is only carried out if the organization is complex. With a simpler organization the development of a data model will be attempted without division.

2. **The analyst selects all the important entity types for the chosen data area in the organization.** There is no mechanical rule that can be applied to determine the selection of entity types. However, a good rule of thumb to determine whether something is an entity type is to ask the question 'Is this the sort of thing that the organization is going to wish to keep information on for any reason?'. The analyst will obviously be guided by the results of the systems investigation phase. It is clear that an organization like Kismet holds information on orders, items, invoices and so on. The analyst lists these entity types. At this stage the analyst should specify the key attribute for each entity.

3. **The analyst determines what relationships exist between the entity types.** At this stage the analyst determines what relationships within the organization hold between the entity types previously identified. In deciding what relationships exist the analyst must look not merely at what actually is the case but also at what could be the case. Suppose that **PART** and **SUPPLIER** have been isolated as entity types and that they stand to one another in the relationship 'supplies' – **SUPPLIERS** supply **PARTS**. Suppose further that *as a matter of fact* each supplier supplies many parts and each part is supplied by only one supplier. The relationship would not be regarded as $1:n$ if it *might be* the case that a part could be supplied to the organization by more than one supplier. It would properly be regarded as $m:n$. The analyst has to determine not just the factual position concerning entity occurrences but also the semantics of the relationships themselves.

4. **The analyst builds the entity model and draws an entity diagram.** The entity model is the aggregation of all entities and the relationships that exist between them. The entity diagram is the representation on paper of the model, using the symbols and conventions displayed in Figure 12.1. It has been developed as a high-level

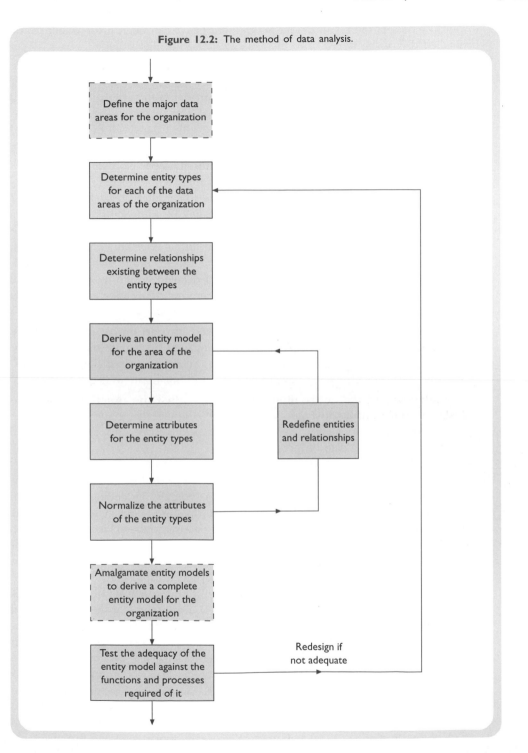

Figure 12.2: The method of data analysis.

logical model of the organization. No thought has as yet been given either to the detailed data to be stored or to the physical details of that storage.

5. **The analyst determines the attributes of each entity.** Having decided on the overall structure of the model the analyst will begin to fill in the detail by listing attributes of each of the entities. These will correspond to data that will be stored on each entity. Although it is a good idea to make these attributes as comprehensive as possible – it assists later stages – it is likely that there will be additions and deletions to the attribute list attaching to each entity as the design continues.

6. **The attributes on the entity model are normalized.** Normalization ensures that the entity model consists of entity types in their simplest form. This is important for the design of a data model that will lead to an efficient database as an end product of design. The effect of normalization will be to decompose entity types into their constituent simpler parts. These parts are themselves entity types. The process of normalization continues until certain formal constraints have been met. Normalization is explained in its application to the Kismet case in Section 12.4. Normalization is also used at the later stage of detailed design to ensure that the final database exemplifies a structure that minimizes duplication of data and so avoids inconsistencies and other anomalies in the database.

7. **The separate entity models are amalgamated into an entity model for the organization as a whole.** This step is relevant only if separate data areas were previously defined for the functions within the organization. In a simple organization the entity model initially developed is for the organization as a whole.

8. **The adequacy of the entity model is tested against the functions and processes required of it.** How can the analyst be sure that the entity model that has been developed is adequate? There are two questions to be answered:
   (a) Will the required data be present?
   (b) Can the data be accessed?
   A clear idea of the data that is required for the functions and processes of the organization has been established during process analysis and modelling (Chapter 11). The data flow diagrams and the specification via structured English, logic flowcharts and decision tables give a clear picture of what data is required. The analyst should check that all the data required is present in the data model. This will mean establishing that data required for processes is contained as attributes. It will also mean that the paths through the model to extract the data are present.

   To see this consider the following example. Suppose that a process for automatic reordering of an item in stock is triggered every time that the quantity held falls below its reorder level. In order to carry out the application a list of suppliers that supply the item must be available to the process. In other words, given an item it needs to be ascertained that the set of suppliers for the item can be retrieved. The most obvious way for this to happen is if the entity type **ITEM** is connected to the entity type **SUPPLIER** through the relationship 'supplies'. Given the value for the identifying attribute of **ITEM**, in this case *item#*, it is possible to retrieve all **SUPPLIERS** connected through the relation (see Figure 12.3). The top part of the diagram is the relevant part of the entity model showing that the **ITEM** entity is accessed (illustrated by the double-ruled arrow) and retrieved. Then the **SUPPLIER** entity is accessed through the relationship 'supplies' (illustrated by the

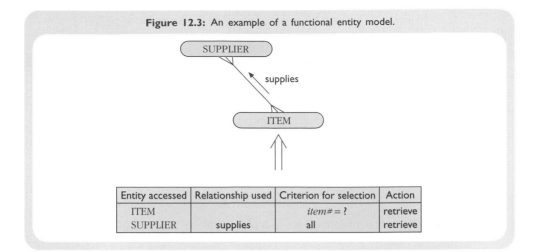

Figure 12.3: An example of a functional entity model.

Entity accessed	Relationship used	Criterion for selection	Action
ITEM		*item# = ?*	retrieve
SUPPLIER	supplies	all	retrieve

single-ruled arrow). All occurrences of the entity type attached to the selected **ITEM** entity are then also retrieved. If analysis and modelling must take place. This will add or redefine entities, insert relationships that were omitted or add new attributes.

Once all these steps have been carried out the analyst will have poduced a data model of the organization sufficient for the provision of data for the various functions and processes that the information system will need to fulfil.

The foregoing is portrayed as a clear-cut, straightforward process but in practice development of the entity and functional entity models may be messy. One problem is that it is not always clear whether something should be treated as an attribute, an entity or a relationship. To see this for a simple example consider the treatment of marriage.

1. *Relationship*: 'Marriage' can be regarded as a relationship between two entity types – **MAN** and **WOMAN**. This is a one-to-one relationship as shown in Figure 12.4(a).

2. *Attribute*: Marriage, or rather **married status**, can be regarded as an attribute of a man, woman or employee. Married status is shown in Figure 12.4(b) as an attribute.

3. *Entity type*: **MARRIAGE** can also be regarded as an entity type. After all marriage is an event and data on it can be stored – its date, the church or registry office where officiated, the name of the bride and so on. The entity type **MARRIAGE** is illustrated in Figure 12.4(c).

There is no single answer as to the correct way to treat marriage. It all depends on the circumstances. If the marital status of an employee is to be recorded for tax calculation purposes then marriage, or more accurately **married status**, will be an attribute. If, when given details of a person, details of the spouse need to be established then marriage will be represented as a relationship between entity types. However, the public records office will wish to keep information on marriages and for them marriage is appropriately modelled as an entity type.

Part of the skill in conceptual data modelling is deciding on these categories. It is not uncommon for an analyst to revise a decision and redesign an entity model treating a former attribute as a relationship.

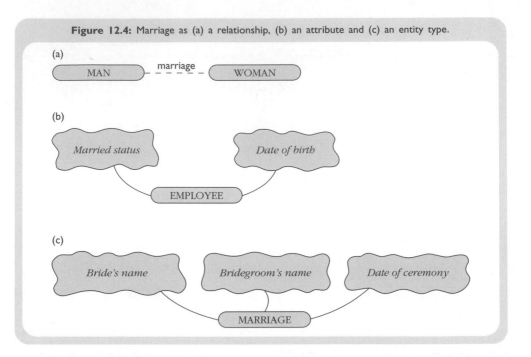

Figure 12.4: Marriage as (a) a relationship, (b) an attribute and (c) an entity type.

12.4   Data analysis and modelling as applied to Kismet Ltd

(1) The analyst defines the major data areas to be covered by the model
Within Kismet, the case study is restricted to the sales order processing subsystem. In a complete system to Kismet other areas would also be involved. The major data areas correspond to the major functional areas of the system. Examples of these would be purchase order processing, stock control and despatch scheduling.

(2) The analyst selects all the important entity types for the chosen data area in the organization
If the Kismet case study given in Section 11.2 of Chapter 11 is consulted, it is seen that the following are good candidates for entity types for the order processing function area. It is important to remember that the crucial question to ask is 'Is this the type of thing that the organization would want to keep information on?'.

CUSTOMER   MAIL ORDER   COMPANY ORDER   ITEM
SALES CATALOGUE   GOODS   DESPATCH NOTE   INVOICE

On further consideration it is clear that some deletions can probably be made from this list.

The mail order from the customer is probably a document that is filed for future reference. All of the information on the order is transferred to the company order form. The company order is therefore the obvious entity type and the mail order can be removed.

The company order entity type will be referred to now as the **ORDER**. This could only be realistically checked by the analyst by asking such questions as 'Is all the information on the mail order transferred to the company order form?'.

The terms item and goods refer to the same type of thing. So this would be one entity type – **ITEM**.

The sales catalogue might be an entity type in itself with such attributes as *date of preparation* and *person responsible for preparation*. Conversely, it may be no more than a selection from the set of data that is already held on the items, such as *item#*, *item description*, *selling price*. If the latter is true then it should be removed from the list of entity types and is viewed as the output of a process that selects certain attributes of **ITEM**.

No reference has be made to an entity type **DEPARTMENT**. This would obviously be an entity type in a complete data analysis of Kismet but has been left out here for simplicity.

The list of entity types is **CUSTOMER, ORDER, ITEM, DESPATCH NOTE, INVOICE**.

The analyst determines that the key attributes, that is the attributes by which the entities are to be identified, are:

customer#, *order#*, *item#*, *despatch#* and *invoice#*.

(3) The analyst determines what relationships exist between the entity types

The various relationships in which the entity types are involved can be obtained by consulting the case study in Chapter 11. The analyst may be tempted here to use his/her general knowledge of the semantics of business entity types but it can be dangerous to assume that what is true in most business organizations is true in all. The analyst should be relying heavily on interviews. For the purposes of Kismet it is assumed that the details of relationships have been established or checked by the analyst. Most will be obvious. Here two examples are considered:

Each **CUSTOMER** may place many **ORDERS** but each **ORDER** can be placed by only one **CUSTOMER**. The relationship is therefore $1:n$.

Each **ORDER** requests many **ITEMS** and each **ITEM** can appear in many **ORDERS**. The relationship is therefore $m:n$.

In the latter case it is important to be clear that an occurrence of the entity type **ITEM** is itself an abstract object. An example of an occurrence is the Glauckman 20 watt hi-fi speaker (of which there may be many physical examples in stock). An attribute of the Glauckman 20 watt hi-fi speaker is *quantity held*, the value of which might be six. Individual examples of the Glauckman 20 watt hi-fi speaker have not been referred to. (This is very different from the example **EMPLOYEE** used in Section 12.2, which has as an occurrence, the physical object Bill Smith.)

The relationships between the entities are a listed in Table 12.1.

Wherever possible each relationship is given a name that is meaningful. Customers place orders. An obvious name for the relationship between **CUSTOMER** and **ORDER** is 'places'. Other names are more artificial. Difficulties arise when the relationships do not have natural names or where the same name would normally be used for different relationships. Apart from clarity, the reason for naming is that there may be more than one relationship between two entity types and it is necessary to distinguish them.

Figure 12.6: Entity type ORDER showing repeating groups of attributes.

ORDER

ORDER (*order#*, *order date, customer#, customer name,* [*item#, item quantity, item price*]*)

ORDER

order#	order date	customer#	customer name	item#	item quantity	item price
123	11/12/97	101	Smith's	12	19	23.78
				14	2	145.99
				15	5	200.00
				23	1	96.00
126	11/12/97	102	HI-FI Ltd	11	2	67.89
				14	3	145.99
127	12/12/97	101	Smith's	13	1	99.99
				14	2	145.99

their constituents. Initially first normal form (1NF) is achieved, then second normal form (2NF) and finally third normal form (3NF). Normalization for the entity type **ORDER** is carried out as an example. This is illustrated in Figures 12.6–12.9.

Figure 12.6 shows the entity type **ORDER**, the attributes of order with the key attribute underlined, and a set of example data on three orders.

First normal form: An entity is in first normal form (1NF) if there are no repeating groups of attributes.

It is clear that for each **ORDER**, *item#*, *item quantity*, *item price* are repeated for each item ordered. These repeating groups can be removed by recognizing that each order contains a number of order details. Thus **ORDER DETAIL** is an entity type. Each **ORDER** is made up of many **ORDER DETAILS**. So the relationship is 1:n. This is shown in Figure 12.7. Note that the entity type **ORDER DETAIL** contains the *order#* of the **ORDER** to which it relates. This ensures that the order details are always linked to the relevant order where the non-repeating attributes, such as the *order date* and *customer#*, appear. The key for **ORDER DETAIL** is the set of attributes consisting of *order#*, *item#*. Each on its own will not identify a unique occurrence of **ORDER DETAIL** but together they guarantee this.

Socond normal form: An entity is in second normal form if it is in 1NF and every attribute that is not part of the key depends on the whole key.

In Figure 12.7 the entity type **ORDER** has only one attribute as its key so all the other attributes depend on this attribute. Considering **ORDER DETAIL**, the *item quantity* depends on the whole key. This is because the amount of an item ordered in an order depends not only on the item (the item is ordered in other orders) nor only on the order (there are other items ordered in the order). However, the combination of *order#* and *item#* fixes the *item quantity*. The same is not true of *item price*. This depends only on the *item#*. When it is realized that order details are about items ordered it becomes clear that ITEM is an entity type.

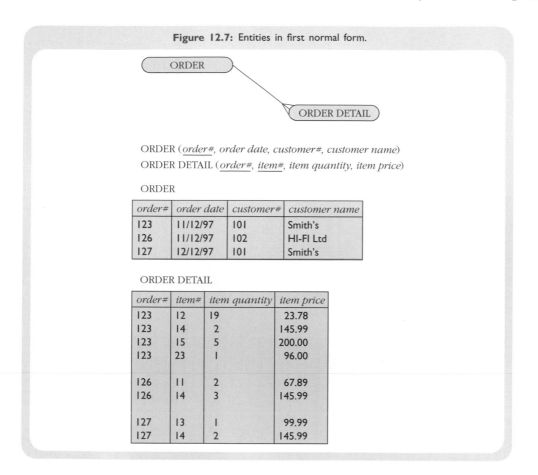

Figure 12.7: Entities in first normal form.

ORDER (*order#*, *order date, customer#, customer name*)
ORDER DETAIL (*order#*, *item#*, *item quantity, item price*)

ORDER

order#	order date	customer#	customer name
123	11/12/97	101	Smith's
126	11/12/97	102	HI-FI Ltd
127	12/12/97	101	Smith's

ORDER DETAIL

order#	item#	item quantity	item price
123	12	19	23.78
123	14	2	145.99
123	15	5	200.00
123	23	1	96.00
126	11	2	67.89
126	14	3	145.99
127	13	1	99.99
127	14	2	145.99

This is shown in Figure 12.8. Each **ORDER DETAIL** is about only one **ITEM**. But each **ITEM** may be referred to by many examples of **ORDER DETAIL** from different orders. The relationship is 1:*n* as shown. The advantage of second normal form is that data on an item such as its price only occurs once. This contrasts with the repeated prices for items with *item#* 1 and 2 in Figure 12.7. The data model will be used to design an effective database. A good database design minimizes the duplication of data.

Third normal form: An entity is in third normal form if it is in 2NF and each attribute or (set of attributes) that is not part of the key depends on nothing but the key.

In Figure 12.8 both **ORDER DETAIL** and **ITEM** contain only one non-key attribute each. So each of these attributes can depend, by definition, only on the key. However, the entity type **ORDER** has an attribute *customer name* that depends on the *customer#*. Customer name is a fact about the customer. Customers place orders.

This is shown in Figure 12.9. A new entity type **CUSTOMER** is introduced. This has a key, *customer#*, and one non-key attribute, *customer name*. Each **CUSTOMER** may place many **ORDERS** but each **ORDER** is placed by only one **CUSTOMER**. The relationship is 1:*n*. Note once again that the new model avoids repeating data. The customer name, Smith's, appears only once.

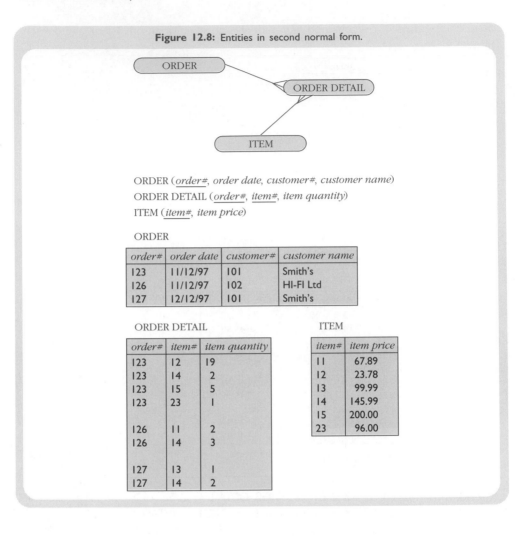

Figure 12.8: Entities in second normal form.

ORDER (*order#*, *order date, customer#, customer name*)
ORDER DETAIL (*order#*, *item#*, *item quantity*)
ITEM (*item#*, *item price*)

ORDER

order#	order date	customer#	customer name
123	11/12/97	101	Smith's
126	11/12/97	102	HI-FI Ltd
127	12/12/97	101	Smith's

ORDER DETAIL

order#	item#	item quantity
123	12	19
123	14	2
123	15	5
123	23	1
126	11	2
126	14	3
127	13	1
127	14	2

ITEM

item#	item price
11	67.89
12	23.78
13	99.99
14	145.99
15	200.00
23	96.00

Another important feature of normalization is that a fully normalized set of entities and attributes ensures that data on entities is not dependent on the existence of other entities. Returning to Figure 12.6 it is clear that if there had been no order with **order#** = 126 then data on customer 102, such as the customer's name, HI-FI Ltd, and data on item 11, such as the item price, £67.89, would not appear. The normalized form of the entity–relationship model allows maintenance of this data because it is in its 'proper' place connected with the entity to which it relates.

In summary, normalization of entity types leads to a data model that will form the basis of a good database design because it:

● decomposes entity types into their simple atomic constituents;

● ensures that data is not unnecessarily repeated;

● allows data on entities to be independent of the existence of other entities.

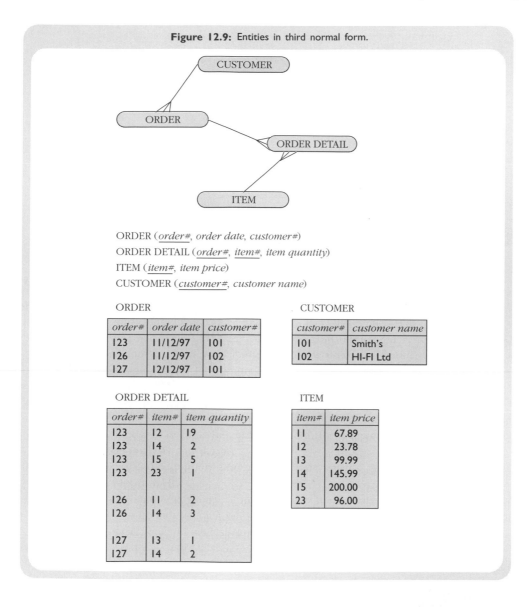

Figure 12.9: Entities in third normal form.

ORDER (*order#*, *order date*, *customer#*)
ORDER DETAIL (*order#*, *item#*, *item quantity*)
ITEM (*item#*, *item price*)
CUSTOMER (*customer#*, *customer name*)

ORDER

order#	order date	customer#
123	11/12/97	101
126	11/12/97	102
127	12/12/97	101

CUSTOMER

customer#	customer name
101	Smith's
102	HI-FI Ltd

ORDER DETAIL

order#	item#	item quantity
123	12	19
123	14	2
123	15	5
123	23	1
126	11	2
126	14	3
127	13	1
127	14	2

ITEM

item#	item price
11	67.89
12	23.78
13	99.99
14	145.99
15	200.00
23	96.00

It is also important to realize that the data that was associated with the original unnormalized entity is still recoverable. All the data in Figure 12.6 on individual **ORDERS** can be reconstructed from the entities and attributes in Figure 12.9. The entities are connected at the table level by their key attributes.

Having normalized each of the entity types in the model it is possible to amalgamate them to provide a new comprehensive entity model for the data area under analysis. This is shown in Figure 12.10. The decomposition of the entity type **ORDER** has given rise to only one new entity type, **ORDER DETAIL**. Both **CUSTOMER** and **ITEM** already appeared in the model and their attributes were already in the attribute list.

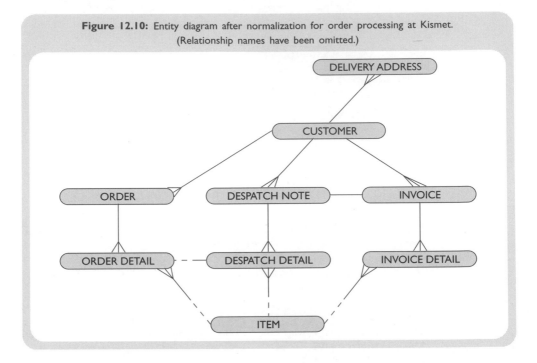

Figure 12.10: Entity diagram after normalization for order processing at Kismet. (Relationship names have been omitted.)

(7) The separate entity models are amalgamated into an entity model for the organization as a whole

If the system for which the data model was being derived was relatively simple then the result of Stage 6 will be the entity model for the organization, or rather that part of the organization that is the subject of investigation. If, though, division into separate data areas was carried out these must now be amalgamated to provide a comprehensive data model. In doing so it will be discovered that entity types appearing in one area also appear in others. Obviously the resulting attributes of the entity type will be the combined set of attributes appearing in every data area in which the entity type occurs.

A combined entity diagram for Kismet dealing with stock control and purchase order processing, as well as sales order processing, is given in Figure 12.11.

(8) The adequacy of the entity model is tested against the functions and processes required of it

Top-down data analysis produces an entity model that is a representation of the entities on which the organization may wish to hold information and of the important relationships between them. The model will form the basis for design of a computerized data store and is derived independently of any analysis of the functions or processes that will require access to the data. Although the functions and processes that use the store may change over time it is important to establish that the current needs can be met. Functional analysis is concerned with the way that functions and processes map onto the data model. It acts as a test of adequacy of the model.

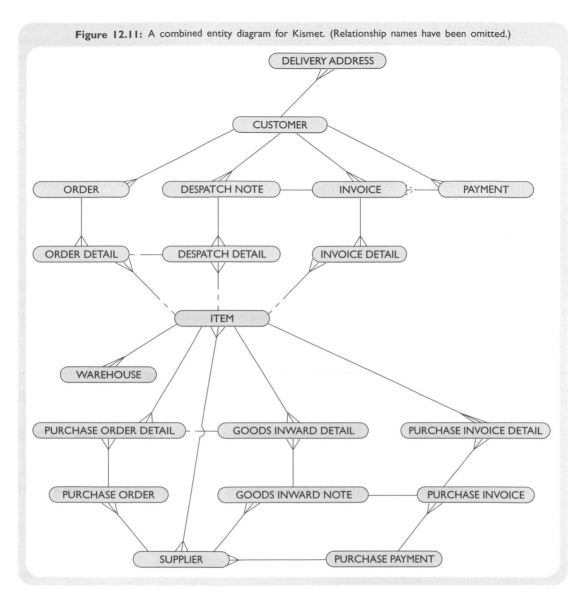

Figure 12.11: A combined entity diagram for Kismet. (Relationship names have been omitted.)

The processes that are going to need data from the data store have been established in the course of process analysis and modelling. This was covered in Chapter 11. For each of these processes functional analysis applied to the data model provides:

- a list of entity types that need to be accessed to provide the data for the process;
- the order in which the entities are accessed;
- the criteria used to select the entities – for example, an **ORDER** might be selected by a given *order#* or all **ORDERS** connected via a relationship to a **CUSTOMER** might be selected;
- the nature of the access to the entity (retrieve, update, delete and create).

12.5 Process modelling and data modelling – the links

It would be wrong to think that process analysis and modelling as described in Chapter 11, and data analysis and modelling as described in this chapter, are rival approaches to systems analysis. Rather, each has evolved in response to particular problems and conditions.

Structured process analysis was developed in an attempt to overcome the difficulties of designing large integrated systems. Such systems cannot be designed by individuals by themselves. The task is too complex and time-consuming. Instead, teams of programmers and analysts are assigned to a project. A large project will require several teams, each dealing with a particular aspect or subsystem of the total system considered. In the development of an integrated system the interests of each individual and each team overlap and it is necessary to establish effective communication. The problem is that agreements between parties on some aspect of analysis or design are likely to impact on the work of others. Multi-way communication is necessary. It is all too easy to develop a tower of Babel where communication and project control, rather than the system under investigation, become the problem. It was common for projects to drift over budget and fail to meet time deadlines. An initial response to a project that was slipping behind its schedule was often to add more manpower in the form of extra analysts or programmers. This often aggravated, rather than alleviated, the problem by increasing communication difficulties.

One of the aims of structured process analysis and design is to respond to these software engineering problems by providing an approach that makes effective project control easier. This is achieved by concentrating initially on the logic and not the physical detail of the processes in an organization. These processes are systematically decomposed into manageable chunks or modules. At the program development stage the individual modular specifications can be coded separately in a form that is easy to test. Various standards for documentation go with this approach, which at the early stages emphasize features important to the eventual users.

In contrast, top-down data analysis was developed in order to take account of the fact that processes often share the same data and that the data stores need to be designed in an integrated manner that allows this. To do this an effective data model of the organization is developed. With the realization that the data structure of the organization is unlikely to change much over time, although the processes that use the data might alter, came the emphasis on the importance of data analysis and even on the priority of data analysis over process analysis.

It is impossible for an analyst to concentrate on either process or data analysis to the exclusion of the other. The degree of attention paid to each will depend on the nature of the system under investigation. A system in which there is a high degree of integration and shared data, and for which it is intended to design a database that can service not only the present but the future needs of an organization, will require a heavy initial input of data analysis in conjunction with process analysis. By contrast, complex processes using simple data structures will require only cursory attention to data analysis.

The way that data and process analysis and design interact is shown in Figure 12.14. Here the approach taken has been that structured process analysis and modelling is complementary to data modelling.

One point of contact is in the development of the functional entity model where the entity model, as derived from a 'snapshot' picture of the entity–relationship structure of the organization, is tested against the requirements of the existing processes, as analyzed and revealed through data flow diagrams, structured English descriptions, decision tables

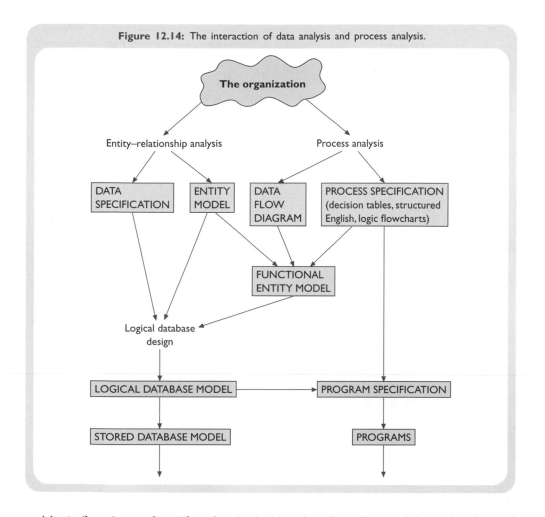

Figure 12.14: The interaction of data analysis and process analysis.

and logic flowcharts. If it is found to be lacking then the entity model may be changed at this stage.

Another point of contact is via the data dictionary (not shown). Lists of attributes on each entity type, arrived at during data specification, are reconciled with the data needs of processes as revealed in the data flows in the data flow diagram.

The logical model of the database is designed from the entity model and data specifications. This will incorporate any constraints imposed by the limitations of the chosen model type: for example, hierarchical database model. Eventually this gives rise to the stored database model and the database itself. Process specifications lead to the program specifications. From these the programs are written that carry out the required data and information processing for the organization. These will require stored data and so will make calls on the database.

The approach to analysis taken in this chapter and in Chapter 11 can be considered 'scientific' in that it is based on some of the fundamental assumptions of natural science and engineering. The approach has the following characteristics:

● Reductionist – progress is achieved by the decomposition and analysis of problems and processes into their constituents.

- Importance of technical considerations – data and processes are the subjects of analysis and design; people are seen as important only in as far as they interface with the system.

- Technology orientated – it is expected that the end result of analysis and design is to provide a computerized system that overcomes the shortcomings of the existing system.

- Realist – the system being analyzed, its objectives, its structure and processes are taken as having an existence and form independent of any subjectivity of the analyst.

This approach has a great deal to recommend it but, as will be seen in Chapter 15, there are limitations and alternatives.

Summary

The aim of analysis is to summarize and model key elements of a system in a way that facilitates understanding, enables evaluation and aids design. Data analysis is concerned with the development of an abstract data model of an organization appropriate for the design of an effective database.

The importance of data analysis has been increased by:

- the increase in the use of integrated databases;
- the treatment of data as a resource of an organization rather than an input/output product;
- the recognition that although processes change over time the structure of the data held by an organization is relatively stable.

Data modelling is specifically aimed at creating a structure for the store of data that meets organizational requirements. This is achieved by identifying the basic entities and relationships in an organization. Attributes are determined and a normalized set of entity types derived. The entity model is then designed. Its adequacy is established by testing it against the data requirements of the processes that it will serve. This leads to the construction of functional entity models, which indicate the order and selection criteria for data access during a process. The entity–relationship model and its associated data specification of entity attributes is the basis from which the logical database model is designed.

Data analysis and process anaysis are complementary activities in the analysis of a system. Although the first concentrates on deriving a data model of the organization while the second concentrates on modelling processes, the adequacy of the data model is dependent on its ability to serve the processes with the required data. The links are established through the functional entity model and the data dictionary.

The approach to analysis in this chapter and in Chapter 11 is often regarded as 'scientific'. It has all the hallmarks of an engineering philosophy. The approach is reductionist; it concentrates on data and processes by restricting the scope of analysis to technical rather than social aspects of a system; it views the problem solution in terms of computerization; and finally it assumes a realist philosophy with respect to the systems, their functioning and their objectives.

Exercises

1. Explain the difference between *bottom-up* and *top-down* data modelling. Why is top-down data modelling generally preferable? Under what circumstances is bottom-up modelling appropriate?

2. Explain the difference between an *entity type*, a *relationship* and an *attribute*. Give examples of each.

3. Give examples of 1:*n, m:n* and 1:1 relationships.

4. What is a *key attribute*?

5. What is the purpose of normalization?

6. Explain the differences between 1NF, 2NF and 3NF.

7. What is the purpose of deriving a functional entity model?

8. What reasons might an analyst give for carrying out data analysis prior to attempting process analysis?

9. Given that William Smith is both an employee in an organization and also a project leader then he is an entity occurrence of both the entity types **EMPLOYEE** and **PROJECT LEADER**. Is this a weakness of entity–relationship modelling, as the same data (values of attributes) may need to be kept on William Smith at two occurrences?

10. Entities have attributes and stand in relationships to one another. However, relationships also may have attributes. For example an employee (entity) works (relationship) on a project (entity). Not only do both the employee and the project have attributes but so does the relationship – works. Mary Jones works on Project A from February to April. This period of work is not an attribute of Mary Jones or of Project A but of the relationship of Mary Jones to Project A. Can entity–relationship modelling handle this difficulty?

11. An object may fall under two distinct entity types. This is particularly true of people who play different roles in an organization. For instance, John Black is both a lecturer to students and a course director of a course. Can the entity–relationship model deal with this adequately or does it need a new category – that of role?

12. Using the data given in Question 14, Chapter 11:
    (a) Identify entities, attributes and relationships for the library.
    (b) Design a suitable entity model and functional entity models for the system.

13. Each department in an organization consists of a manager and several departmental staff. Each manager is in charge of only one department and departmental staff are assigned to a single department. Attached to each department are several projects. All departmental staff are assigned to projects, with some staff being assigned to several projects, not necessarily in the same department. Each project is run by a management group consisting of the manager of the department together with a selection of staff working on the project. No departmental staff member is ever required to sit on more than one management group. ▷

(a) Draw an entity diagram for this information.

(b) Draw a functional diagram for the function: determine which departmental staff working on a given project are not attached to the department responsible for that project.

14. A local hospital consists of many wards, each of which is assigned many patients. Each patient is assigned to one doctor, who has overall responsibility for the patients in his or her care. Other doctors are assigned on an advisory basis. Each patient is prescribed drugs by the doctor responsible for that patient. Each nurse is assigned to a ward and nurses all patients on the ward, though is given special responsibility for some patients. Each patient is assigned one nurse in this position of responsibility. One of the doctors is attached to each ward as an overall medical advisor.

(a) Draw an entity diagram representing these relationships.

(b) Draw a functional diagram representing:
   (i) Function 1: Determine which nurses are responsible for those patients that are the responsibility of a given doctor.
   (ii) Function 2: Determine the drug usage prescribed by a doctor.
   (iii) Function 3: Determine the range of wards covered by a doctor in any of his/her roles.

15. Lift Express is an nationwide organization concerned with the servicing and repair of lifts supplied and installed by its parent company. Lift Express divides the UK into five regions and all service and repair operations within a region are handled by the regional headquarters. At present all operations are based on a manual system.

On discovery of a lift fault or of the need for it to be serviced, a customer telephones or writes to the regional headquarters. Details of the request for service/repairs are made on standard company documentation by clerical staff at the HQ. Service engineers are all home-based and details of the customer's requirements are phoned (fault) or posted (service request) to a selected engineer who is based within the same region as the customer. (In the case of faults, documentation detailing the fault is posted later to the engineer.) After visiting the customer, the engineer produces a charge sheet for the job, a copy of which is sent back to the regional HQ, where it is stapled to the original request details. An invoice for the customer is generated and then posted.

Currently, Lift Express is losing work to a rival company. The reason has been located as an inadequate customer request and information processing system. Specifically, there are significant delays in paperwork, leading to an unacceptable time period occurring between a customer request and an instruction to the engineer, and between a job being completed and an invoice generated. There are difficulties in scheduling engineers' roads – some are overworked while others are not fully employed. Management is finding it difficult to extract decision-making information from the system, for instance given a customer – the number of calls booked not as yet completed, or an individual engineer – the amount of income generated per month by the engineer. ▷

In order to remedy these faults it has been decided to implement a computerized information system.

(a) Explain the principles of data analysis and suggest how these can be applied in designing the information system for Lift Express.

(b) Define entity types and relationships important to the functioning of the system and then design an entity model.

(c) Design a functional model and data access table for the following: determine the number of calls handled by a given engineer for a given customer.

16. Titanic plc is a shipping company dealing with the transport of container freight worldwide using its own fleet of vessels. Consignments are moved to and from their source and destination ports by local rail networks. Titanic is concerned with the port-to-port transfer. Each of Titanic's ships makes various journeys throughout the year (a journey is considered as a voyage from one port to the next with actual or estimated depature and arrival dates). Each ship may carry many consignments at once depending on its capacity and the weight and size of the consignments. The transfer of a consignment from its source to its destination may take many journeys. A consignment may also be unloaded at one port and later picked up by another of Titanic's ships in travelling from its source port to its final destination.

Amongst other functions the shipping clerks perform the following:

1. On receipt of a request to move cargo from a source to a destination port the clerk checks possible sets of journeys that will accomplish this and ascertains whether the ships involved have enough capacity and facilities, given their existing consignments, to transport the goods.

2. If the transfer investigated under 1 is possible then the relevant bookings are made, otherwise the order is transferred to the departmental manager who will take further action.

3. The shipping clerk also has to answer occasional enquiries as to the location of a specific consignment: that is, at which port is it located, or between which two ports is it travelling. Titanic plc is about to introduce a computerized system dealing with its cargo scheduling.

(a) Identify entities, attributes and relationships relevant to Titanic.

(b) Ensure that attributes are suitable for carrying out Titanic's functions.

(c) Design functional models suitable for Titanic's functions.

17. In the UK investors in a building society may hold several investment accounts, where each account is associated with one of the society's high street branches. The investor may make withdrawals from the account or payments into it at any of the society's branches. Details of the transaction, such as the date, amount and so on are recorded. As well as investment accounts for borrowers, mortgage accounts are also associated with the branch that grants the mortgage. Payments into the mortgage accounts may be made at any branch office. It is also possible to transfer funds directly from an investment account to a mortgage account. ▷

> (a) Identify entity types, relationships and attributes for this information. Hence design an entity model.
>
> (b) Indicate entities accessed, their order, the selection criteria and purpose in order to perform the following functions. Draw a functional diagram for each.
>
>   (i) Determine how many withdrawals a given investor makes on a certain day.
>
>   (ii) Determine the percentage of an investor's transactions made at the branch holding the account.
>
>   (iii) Set up a new investment account for an existing investor together with a first deposit and a transfer to a mortgage account.

Recommended reading

● Avison D.E. (1998). *Information Systems Development: A Database Approach* 3rd edn. UK: Alfred Waller

This book provides a multidisciplinary approach to database design and information systems development including business objectives, organizational structure and management culture through to data and logic modelling. The book links with the multiview approach.

● Benyon D. (1995). *Information Management and Modelling* 2nd edn. Oxford: Blackwell Scientific Publications

This covers in detail methods of information analysis and modelling. Aimed at students of management and business studies this is a clear text extending the contents of the current chapter.

● Chen P. (1976). The entity–relationship model – toward a unified view of data. *ACM Transactions on Database Systems*, **1** (1), 9–36

A comprehensive coverage of the entity–relationship approach involving rigorous specification of terms.

● Gessford J.E. (1991). *Business-Wide Database Planning*. John Wiley

This text explains a business-wide information structuring/MIS approach to top-down data modelling. The methodology involves the development of entity–relationship models for various business functions such as marketing and engineering through to database design. There is also an introduction to distributed databases. The book is accessible to those who have covered the chapters on both databases and on data analysis.

● Kent W. (1983). A simple guide to five normal forms in relational database theory. *Communications of the ACM*, **26** (2)

By using a simple worked example this article covers the three normal forms covered in this chapter together with 4NF and 5NF.

● Rock-Evans R. (1988). *Analysis Within the Systems Life Cycle: 2 Data Analysis – The Method*. Pergamon Infotech

A practical guide to all aspects of data analysis and modelling.

● Veryard R. (1992). *Information Modelling: Practical Guidance*. Hemel Hempstead: Prentice Hall

Though this book is aimed at systems analysts and designers it is a clear introduction for readers who wish to carry the role of information modelling in information systems development to a more detailed level than in this chapter. The book contains many case studies and some comprehensive exercises.

● Wood-Harper A.T., Antill L. and Avison D.E. (1985). *Information Systems Definition: The Multiview Approach*. Oxford: Blackwell Scientific Publications

This book applies data analysis to a case study. The approach is integrated with other approaches including structured process modelling as covered in Chapter 9.

Chapter 13

Systems Design

13.1   The transition from analysis to design
13.2   Suggesting alternative designs
13.3   Automation boundaries
13.4   Walkthroughs and formal reviews

In Chapters 10, 11 and 12 it was seen how the analyst proceeds from the collection of descriptive material on the functioning of the existing physical system through to the analysis and development of a logical model of that system. Data flows between processes were represented and analyzed using data flow diagrams at various levels, data processes were specified using decision tables, structured English and logic flow-charts, and a conceptual data model for the system was derived.

This chapter deals with the transition from analysis to design. This initially involves the recasting of the high-level models to eliminate any remaining physical aspects and to take account of any additional requirements that a new system must satisfy. These models can be used to design, in outline, various proposals for the new system. At this stage the extent of computerization will be decided, together with which processes are to be carried out in batch as distinct from online mode. Decisions will also be taken on whether to centralize or distribute the system and on whether to opt for a file-based or database system. Design considerations for these alternatives are outlined in this chapter. Two or three alternative designs are submitted and assessed through a formal review. As soon as one of these outline proposals has been accepted then detailed design work can commence. Detailed design is covered in Chapter 14.

13.1   The transition from analysis to design

The aim of analysis is to derive a logical model of the way that the existing system works. This is on the assumption that the existing system provides a good guide to *what* is required of a new system (as distinct from *how* the new system is to achieve these requirements). Certain limitations should be obvious:

- There may be requirements of the new system that are not being satisfied by the current system – these need to be taken into account.

- Inefficiencies in the existing system may become translated into the logical model; ideally the model should reveal the logic of an efficient system and so should be amended.

- It is often the case that physical aspects creep into the logical analysis – these should be removed.

These three points are now dealt with.

13.1.1 Treatment of new requirements

It is desirable to review the requirements to be made of an information system when it undergoes a major change, such as computerization of a manual system or replacement of an existing computer system by another. This review may throw up new requirements. These will be established by interviews with management and users. By definition, the logical model of the existing system cannot contain these. It is important, then, that the logical model is amended to reflect these new requirements.

These additions are likely to lead to new processes, which will be added to the higher-level data flow diagrams. They will interact via data flows with existing data stores and/or processes. Added processes are decomposed into their exploded functional constituents on lower-level data flow diagrams. If their operation is governed by sophisticated logic then this must be specified using one of the tools of specificaion, such as structured English.

Often, new requirements concern the extraction of new types of management informa-tion from data stores rather than the alteration of the existing pattern of transaction pro-cessing. This can be simply accomplished at the data flow diagram level by inserting a process that accepts as input the data flows from the relevant data stores and produces as output the required data. It will also be necessary to establish that the entity model, as revealed by the entity diagram, is sufficient to provide the data for the function. In other words, the access path through the model must be checked by drawing a func-tional entity diagram.

Kismet

With the Kismet case study one of the problems that management listed with the exist-ing document-handling system was the difficulty of deriving useful management informa-tion. For example, management needed a regular report on the total value of goods sold, analyzed by each item type within customer types. This is vital information to establish which sectors of their market are growing and which are declining with respect to their sales. Examples of customer types might be retail specialist chains (chain stores dealing with electrical goods only), retail non-specialist chains, single specialist shops (the local hi-fi shop) and single non-specialist shops. Examples of item types are compact disc, turntable, mini rack system, graphic equalizer. An example of a partial report is given in Figure 13.1.

It is a notable weakness of the existing system that such reports are difficult to extract. The documents are stored in a manner that makes it time consuming and costly to obtain this information. One of the benefits of computerized information systems is that informa-tion for use in decision making can be extracted quickly and cheaply from the results of transaction processing.

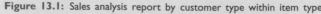

Figure 13.1: Sales analysis report by customer type within item type.

Start date 12/12/97	Stop date 12/01/98	
Stock analysis code	Customer analysis code	Value
A1	1	45,123
	2	100,876
	3	1,122
	4	0
A2	1	107,879
	2	232,112
:	:	:
:	:	:

Figure 13.2: A data flow diagram for the production of the sales analysis.

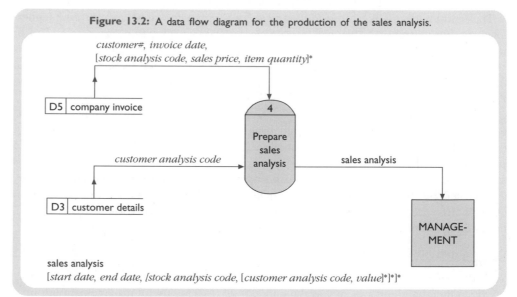

The process for generating this report can be incorporated in a straight-foraward way in a data flow diagram (see Figure 13.2). In order to produce this report for any selected invoice, it is necessary to extract the invoice details (and hence the stock analysis codes of the items sold), and the customer for whom the invoice is generated. The analysis code of the customer can then be obtained.

This may be established by reference to the entity diagram developed in Chapter 12 and shown in Figure 12.10. The new functional entity diagram governing this process is shown in Figure 13.3. For any selected **INVOICE** it is possible to retrieve the **CUSTOMER** receiving the invoice through the customer/invoice relationship and hence determine the *customer analysis code*. For the invoice it is also possible to retrieve the **INVOICE DETAILS** through the customer/invoice details relationship. This gives the *item#*, *sale price*, and *item quantity* for each item sold under the invoice. The value of that item sold can then be

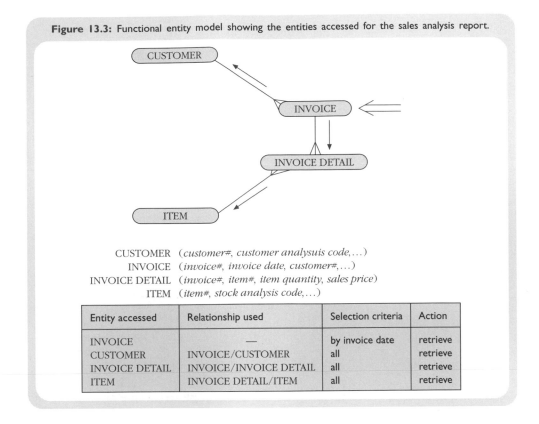

Figure 13.3: Functional entity model showing the entities accessed for the sales analysis report.

CUSTOMER (*customer#, customer analysuis code,...*)
INVOICE (*invoice#, invoice date, customer#,...*)
INVOICE DETAIL (*invoice#, item#, item quantity, sales price*)
ITEM (*item#, stock analysis code,...*)

Entity accessed	Relationship used	Selection criteria	Action
INVOICE	—	by invoice date	retrieve
CUSTOMER	INVOICE/CUSTOMER	all	retrieve
INVOICE DETAIL	INVOICE/INVOICE DETAIL	all	retrieve
ITEM	INVOICE DETAIL/ITEM	all	retrieve

calculated. The **ITEM** can then be retrieved via the invoice detail/item relationship and hence the *stock analysis code* obtained. There is now sufficient data to derive the analysis of all invoices between specified dates by customer analysis code within stock analysis code and so provide the report.

13.1.2   Treatment of inefficiencies

The data flow diagram has been developed using top-down decomposition of the major processes occurring in the Kismet order processing system. Inevitably the decomposition as revealed by lower-level data flow diagrams is not purely a result of a logical analysis of the nature of the major processes. Rather, the lower-level structure tends to be determined partly by what is done in the existing system to fulfil a function as well as by what needs to be done as determined by the logic of the function. If what is done is unnecessary or inefficient this may have unfortunate repercussions on the logical model. It is at this transition stage that the model should be adjusted.

Kismet

An example of this occurs in the Kismet case study. From Figure 11.10 in Chapter 11, process 1.2 and the surrounding processes have been extracted and are shown in Figure 13.4. The copy of the company order is temporarily stored in the company order store D4. Another copy is priced and then a credit check is performed on the customer. If

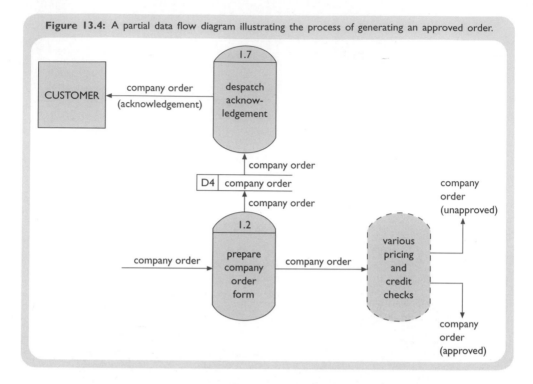

Figure 13.4: A partial data flow diagram illustrating the process of generating an approved order.

successful, the credit check triggers the despatch of the stored company order to the customer as an acknowledgement of receipt of the order. This is clearly unnecessary. Why not send the acknowledgement company order as an output of process 1.5, the credit check? Historically, of course, the reason for the temporary store is to maintain a record of the order in the sales department while the company order is sent to the credit control section and back. This would take time and the sales department might need to answer a query on the customer order while it is in transit (the enquiry process is not shown). If the entire system is to be computerized (perhaps a premature judgement) then this time-lag may not occur. In fact in an online system the aim is to eliminate this time-lag completely. The logical model of the system has inherited the inefficiency of the physical system on which it is based.

The important point to be made here is not to reach a definite answer on the peculiarities of the Kismet case but rather to reinforce the observation that there is nothing sacrosanct about a logical model derived from the study of an existing system – it can be changed as seen fit. Nor is there any clear-cut set of rules as to how to modify the model before design can start. Indeed, any modification could be considered to be part of design, although here these changes are referred to as a transition from analysis to design.

13.1.3   Treatment of physical aspects

Certain physical considerations may have crept into the logical model. For instance, data store D5 in Figure 11.7 contains the order/invoice/despatch note trio. These are disallowed as bedfellows in the logical model and should be indicated on the data flow

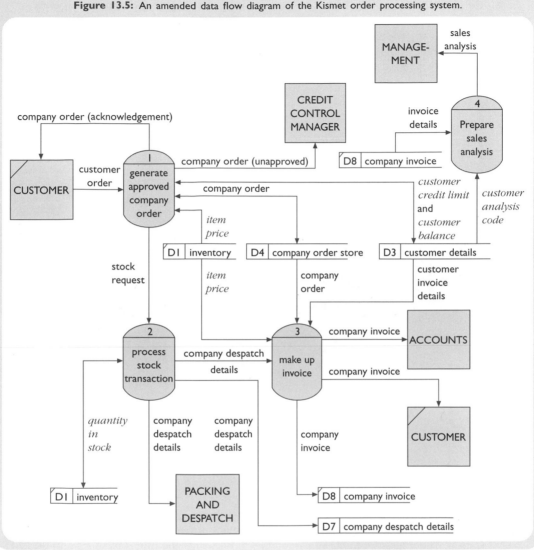

Figure 13.5: An amended data flow diagram of the Kismet order processing system.

diagram as separate stores. They have been thrown together purely for convenience in the physical manual files. There is no fear that by separating these the connection between them is lost. The links remain at an attribute level, as each of the trio contains the attribute *order#*. Also, each order is linked to its relevant invoice(s) and despatch note(s) through relationships in the entity model.

Amended data flow diagrams are shown in Figures 13.5 and 13.6. These incorporate the addition of the sales analysis generation process and the other comments given in this section. Notice also that the catalogue has disappeared as a separate store. The information on item sale prices is held in the inventory store (the **ITEM** entity) and this is accessed for prices during the generation of a company order and invoice.

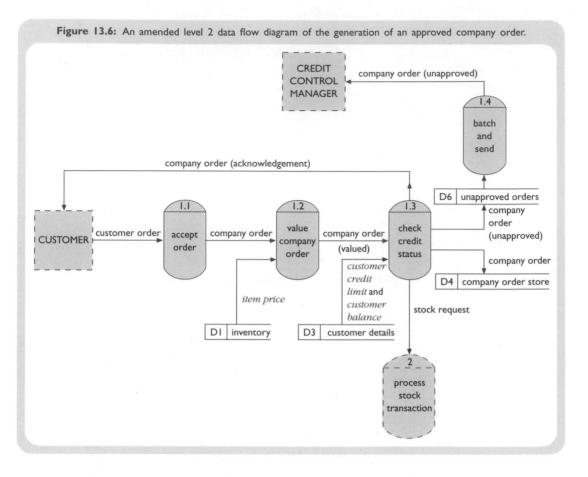

Figure 13.6: An amended level 2 data flow diagram of the generation of an approved company order.

13.2   Suggesting alternative designs

Up to this point the analyst has concentrated on the question of *what* is to be done in order to satisfy the data processing and information provision requirements of the organization. The analyst's attention is now directed towards the question of *how* to do it. This is a two-step process. First, the analyst suggests, in outline, two or three different alternatives. This is termed **systems design**. One of these is selected by management. Second, the detailed design of the chosen system is carried out. Detailed design is covered in Chapter 14.

Why should the analyst be presenting general alternative systems when there has already been a costed proposal in the feasibility study? The analyst now has a much greater understanding of the system than earlier on in the investigation. There may be new opportunities for a different extent or type of computerization from what was previously envisaged. Having developed a logical model it is also easy to sketch and present these alternatives to management.

In preparing a design the analyst will need to make various choices. There will be decisions on the extent of computerization – which processes in the process model will be computerized and which will be manual – and decisions on the type of system for those processes that are computerized. In the latter case choices are involved over:

- centralized and distributed systems
- file-based and database systems
- batch and online systems
- input methods
- applications packages and specially designed programs
- hardware.

General design considerations on each of these are summarized here and then applied to Kismet.

13.2.1 Centralized and distributed systems

A distributed computer system is one where:

- There are two or more geographically separated computers.
- These are linked by telecommunications.
- The network of computers serves a single organization.

A centralized computer system is one with a single computer servicing the needs of the organization. There may be remote terminals connected by telecommunications.

A large organization on many different sites may decide to have a distributed system because most of the data processing and information provision is localized to each site. Local data storage and processing is then feasible. The need for distributed computing (as distinct from several standalone computers) comes from the requirement that data and the results of processing at one site are available to computers at other sites.

A single-site organization may also decide to have a collection of micro/minicomputers and connect these via a Local Area Network. This is possible if no large centralized processing power is needed. It has the advantage that each node on the network can be devoted to local needs such as decision support using spreadsheet modelling or word processing, and nodes can be added to the network when needed.

Advantages of distributed computing

- Telecommunications costs between several sites are reduced provided that most of the processing is locally based.
- There is greater flexibility, as additional computers can be added to the networks as needed.
- The organization is not reliant on a single computer, which might break down.

Disadvantages of distributed computing

- Commonly used data is often replicated at many sites – changes in this data, unless happening to all occurrences, can lead to an inconsistent organizational datastore.
- With several computers at dispersed sites lack of standardization of equipment, software and data storage is possible.
- Control is more difficult.

The main advantage of keyboard entry is that it is very flexible on the kinds of data that can be input.

- **Preprinted character recognition:** The main examples are optical character recognition (OCR) and magnetic ink character recognition (MICR). The input equipment 'reads' the input document and converts the characters to a machine-understandable form. There is a high initial cost for the purchase of the equipment but very low operating costs, as little labour is used for input. This means that this method is suitable for high-volume input. Low error rates are also a feature. The method is limited to those applications where known identifying data can be pre-printed on documents – for example the cheque and account number together with the bank sort code on a cheque, or the account code and amount on an electricity bill. The method is inflexible on the kinds of data to be input.

- **Optical mark recognition:** This is used where a preprinted document is produced that contains selection boxes. These are marked indicating choices and can be 'read' by special equipment, which is preprogrammed as to the location of the boxes. The presence or absence of a mark is converted to a machine-understandable form. Once again there are high initial costs, low operating costs, and low error rates. This method is suitable for high-volume applications where selection amongst alternatives is required. Typical applications are market research surveys, automated marking of multiple-choice examination questions and stock selection.

- **Bar-code reading:** Bar-codes that identify items are preprinted and attached to the items. The bar-codes are read in by special readers, often using laser light. Bar-codes need to be attached to items, so the method is associated with data input over the movement of material goods. Examples are the sale of goods in supermarkets, library loans and stock movements. The input of the data is simple to achieve, needs no skills and is error-free. The applications to which it is put are limited.

- **Punched cards:** Before cheap computer-processing power was available punched cards were a popular form of input. Once produced, punched cards can be quickly and efficiently input into the computer system. They have been superseded by keyboard input.

- **Voice input:** There are many technical problems to be overcome before speech input is widely available. Once achieved, speech input will revolutionize the use of computers. Typists will no longer be needed, as direct speech input into word processors will be possible. Remote data input via telecommunications combined with speech or some other form of output will mean that no skills or equipment other than the telephone will be needed for computer use. Currently, voice input is limited to simple voice-activated enquiries such as flight availability enquiry systems. It is not used in mainstream information systems.

13.2.5 Applications packages and specially designed programs

It may be possible to purchase an applications package rather than writing special programs for the system. Packages are written by a third party and sold to many customers, so the cost of this alternative is considerably cheaper than designing, coding and testing programs from scratch. Packages also have the advantage that they are quick to implement, can be demonstrated in action prior to purchase, and generally have good documentation. They will also have been tried and tested by many previous purchasers. These can be consulted on the quality of the package and the support given by the software house or dealer selling it.

However, packages will not integrate with existing software that has been specially written for the organization. The package may also not suit precisely the data processing and information needs. The software house selling the package will attempt to introduce as much flexibility as possible into it thus accommodating as wide a market as possible. However, this may introduce unwanted inefficiency into the program.

The analyst is more likely to recommend a package if:

- Cost is a major consideration.
- The system needs to be implemented quickly.
- The data processing and information requirements are standard ones for the type of business function to be computerized.
- The organization does not have a mature computer centre that can write and maintain software.
- Well-established packages from reputable companies exist.

Some business functions are more amenable to packages than others. For instance, all businesses have standard accounting activities – sales, general and purchase-ledger processing, and payroll. It is common to buy packages for these. Even quite large companies will purchase mainframe software in these areas.

13.2.6 Hardware

Different designs will have different hardware requirements. Some of these factors have been taken into account in the choice of input method and equipment. The analyst will need to take decisions on suitable processing, output, communications and storage hardware. This will depend largely on the amount of processing required by the system, the complexity of the software and the number of users attached to the system. Choices on whether to develop a centralized or distributed system will obviously have hardware implications. The amount of data to be stored and decisions over adopting a file-based approach as opposed to a database with a database management system will affect storage hardware needs.

The analyst suggests two or three alternative systems to management. All the factors discussed in this section will be taken into account in each design. Management will need not only an explanation of the alternative designs but also estimates of the costs and the time schedules associated with each alternative. The data flow diagrams will provide a valuable tool for the analyst in developing alternative high-level designs as they can be used to indicate which features of a system are to be computerized and how this is to be achieved. The way that data flow diagrams do this is treated in the next section.

13.3 Automation boundaries

As well as revealing the logic of data flows between processes in process modelling, the data flow diagram can be the basis of design in selecting and communicating which

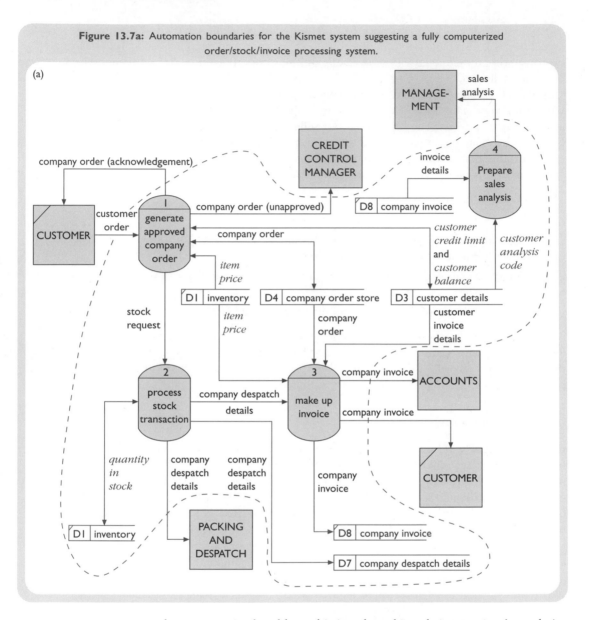

Figure 13.7a: Automation boundaries for the Kismet system suggesting a fully computerized order/stock/invoice processing system.

processes are to be computerized and how this is to be achieved. Automation boundaries are used. The data flow diagram as a design aid can be best understood by a consideration of a few examples.

In Figure 13.7(a) the automation boundaries suggest that the entire order processing system for Kismet is to be computerized. Customer orders flow into the system and company invoices, despatch notes, and approved and unapproved company orders flow out.

In contrast, Figure 13.7(b) shows the automation boundaries as encompassing the production of the company order (approved as a customer acknowledgement or unapproved and sent to the credit control manager) together with the company invoice. The stock processing and generation of the despatch details are carried out manually. The computer

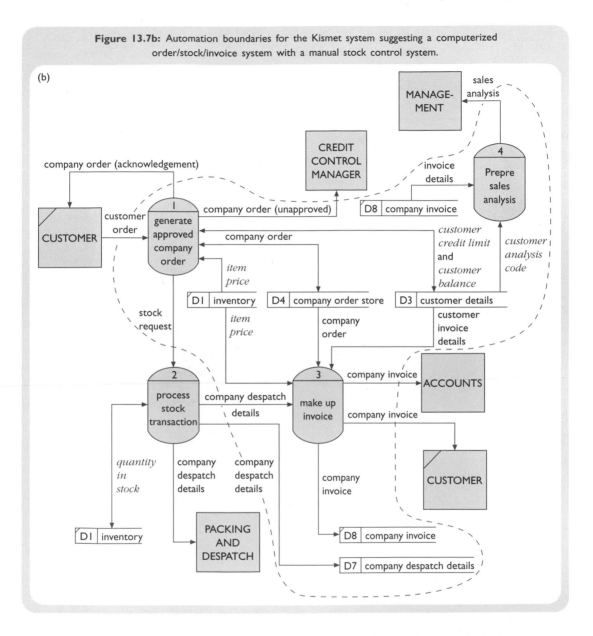

Figure 13.7b: Automation boundaries for the Kismet system suggesting a computerized order/stock/invoice system with a manual stock control system.

system produces a stock request which is (presumably) sent to the warehouse, where the goods are picked and a despatch note manually generated and sent with the goods to packing and despatch. The despatch note details are then input into the computer system, which retrieves a copy of the order from the company order store and generates a company invoice. These two alternative approaches can be clearly presented and discussed with the aid of the data flow diagram.

Figure 13.8 provides two alternatives for process 1 – that of generating an approved company order. The diagrams show the difference between the representation of a batch-processing system and an online real-time system.

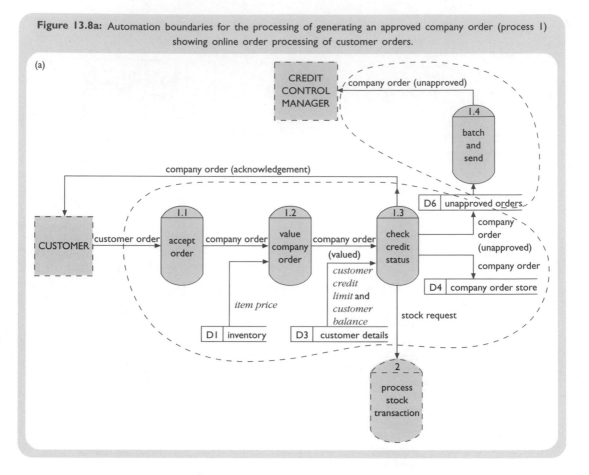

Figure 13.8a: Automation boundaries for the processing of generating an approved company order (process 1) showing online order processing of customer orders.

Figure 13.8(a) illustrates an online system for the processing of approved orders. The customer order details when input are immediately subject to pricing and credit checking and if successful a stock request is output to process 2 – process stock transaction. The unapproved orders are temporarily stored in D6 where they are output in a batch for the credit control manager.

In Figure 13.8(b) the orders are input and temporarily stored prior to pricing and credit checking. The automation boundaries suggest that the input of the orders is distinct from the processes that follow. In the data flow diagram it is also easy to see that the unapproved orders are stored and then output in a batch for consideration by the credit control manager. Likewise, the stock requests from the approved orders are stored and later used as input to the stock process.

At this stage the analyst should present two or three alternative designs as suggestions for the way in which the new computer system can be developed to meet the needs of the organization. More alternatives will just confuse management. These designs may be different ways of physically providing much the same facilities – the choice between online and batch processing or between centralized and distributed systems can be regarded as falling under this heading. Or they may be different designs providing different levels of facilities. In the latter case the suggestions might be:

Figure 13.8b: Automation boundaries for the processing of generating an approved company order (process 1) showing batch processing of customer orders.

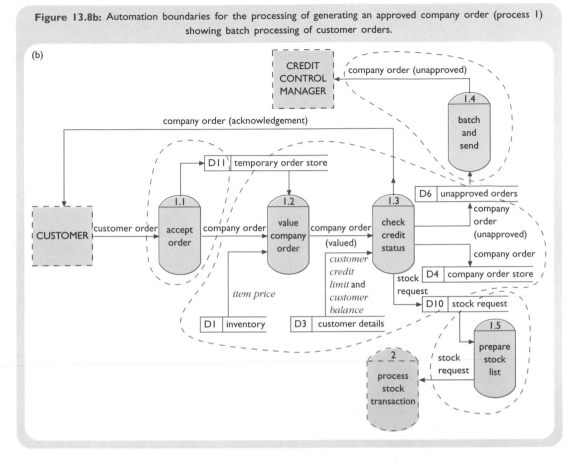

- a minimal low-cost system that meets the basic needs for which the systems project was initiated;
- a medium-cost solution that will indicate extra opportunities that can be realized by computerization at moderate cost;
- a grander system that illustrates how the organization can exploit the full benefits of computerization in the area of the system under consideration.

For instance, a basic design for Kismet would cover just the order processing and invoicing as in Figure 13.7(b). A medium-cost solution (Figure 13.7(a)) will handle stock control as well. This can include an automatic reordering system that produces purchase orders for suppliers when stocks of an item fall below a certain level. In other words, the analyst may provide a basic design and also one that provides extra facilities (at extra cost). A more extensive computerization would involve the integration of the accounting system with the order processing system and stock control systems, would have facilities for accepting credit card purchases by phone direct from the public, and would have programs that optimally schedule van deliveries.

In presenting the various alternative designs the analyst will have made decisions on all the features listed in Section 13.2 – online and batch, centralized versus distributed systems, file-based versus database systems, packages and specially written programs, hardware, and input methods. For each design the analyst will be required to submit cost estimates and also a schedule for the time to be taken to complete the project. It is crucial in systems design that the analyst always maintains a clear idea of the management constraints and organizational objectives under which the project is being developed.

The suggested systems designs will be presented to management at a structured formal review. At this stage management will select one system and will give the 'go ahead' to the analyst to start the work of deriving a detailed design for this system. Walkthroughs and formal reviews occur at several stages during a project's life cycle. Section 13.4 covers these.

13.4 Walkthroughs and formal reviews

At various stages the analyst may wish to present aspects of his or her work to others. This is achieved through walkthroughs and reviews. The difference between them is that a walkthrough is an interactive presentation of some part of the system by the analyst. The aim is for the analyst to present ideas or problems and receive useful feedback provided by the participants. In contrast, the formal review is a public presentation of some aspects of analysis and design and is used as a milestone in the computer project. Formal reviews are often used as exit criteria from one stage in the analysis and design process so that progress may be made into the following stages.

13.4.1 Walkthroughs

A walkthrough consists of perhaps three or four people, including the analyst, who will present some aspect of the system in the stages of analysis or design. Data flow diagrams, entity–relationship models and flowcharts may be used to illustrate points. Each walkthrough should last for no more than 20 to 30 minutes – much longer and the participants' attention will wander. The participants, other than the analyst making the presentation, may be other analysts or programmers, users or management.

The purpose of the walkthrough is to communicate some particular aspect of systems analysis or design to the group so that useful feedback may be provided for the analyst.

The walkthrough is often used when analysts run into particular problems or wish to check out their understanding of a part of a system with users. They are informal semi-structured meetings that occur on an *ad hoc* basis throughout analysis and design. Communication is of the essence in a walkthrough so structured tools, with their emphasis on logic rather than physical details, are indispensable aids.

13.4.2 Formal reviews

Formal reviews may occur at many points during the systems analysis and design of a project and are used as a formal recognition that some major point has been reached in the process. A successful formal review implies that the next stage may be started, an unsuccessful one that some failure in analysis or design has been noted and needs to be reworked.

At formal reviews (sometimes called **inspections**) the analyst or team of analysts make a formal presentation. This will be backed up by documentation, which will have been previously circulated to participants. It is the purpose of the review to find errors or shortcomings in the stage of analysis or design presented.

The participants in a formal review are generally as follows:

1. **The moderator or review leader:** This individual is responsible for organizing the review after being notified by the analysts that the required stage has been achieved. The review leader circulates the documentation, schedules the meeting and ensures that all relevant and interested parties are invited as inspectors.

   During the inspection the review leader ensures that all the relevant points are covered in a proper manner. Given that the nature of the inspection process is fault-finding, it is important all participants in the project realize that finding faults at this stage is beneficial to the project as a whole. To discover these later will need redesign, which will undoubtedly be both expensive and troublesome. Equally, it is important for the inspectors to realize that an overcritical stance may be counterproductive. Either analysts will be induced to cover up or minimize the importance of errors or they may not wish to make a presentation until everything is 110% perfect. Political considerations may also influence the review session. Participants may have a vested interest in delaying, blocking or changing the course of development of a project. It is the responsibility of the review leader to ensure that the review is conducted in the most unbiased constructive way possible.

2. **Inspectors:** The inspection group consists of:
   (a) technical people who may be brought into the review for their experience in the area;
   (b) representatives of those who will use and be affected by the new system;
   (c) specialists who will have an interest in the system once it is working.
   Auditors are the most important examples of this last group.

   The role of the inspectors is to assess the proposed stage with a view to locating errors or shortcomings. They will base their examination mainly on documentation provided beforehand by analysts.

3. **Systems analysts:** The systems analyst provides beforehand the documentation on which the presentation will be based. During the presentation the analyst may provide a brief overview of the contents of the documentation. The main part of the presentation, though, will revolve around questions on the documentation raised by the inspectors and answered by the analyst.

After the formal review (at which a secretary may take notes on the major points raised) it is the responsibility of the analyst to rework areas that have been found to be lacking and to satisfy the review leader that this has been done. In the case of serious shortcomings another review will be required.

Formal reviews may occur at a number of points during the development of a project. Major reviews will probably occur at the following:

1. Systems design: to consider alternative designs.
2. Detailed design: to consider the systems specification consisting of:
   (a) hardware specifications
   (b) database or file specifications
   (c) program specifications
   (d) input/output specifications
   (e) identification of procedures surrounding the system
   (f) implementation schedules.
3. Implementation: to consider the results of a formal systems test.

Reviews are one of the important controls that may be exercised over the development of the project.

Summary

The purpose of systems design is to present alternative solutions to the problem situation. High-level logical models have been developed for the system, involving no prior physical design considerations, so it is easy to illustrate and communicate different approaches in outline for new systems.

The logical model of the system needs to be amended to incorporate any new requirements. At this stage inefficiencies in the model and any physical aspects are removed. Both of these are legacies of having used an existing physical system as the basis for analysis and design. Alternative designs are illustrated using automation boundaries on the data flow diagrams. In deriving these designs the analyst must pay attention to physical design features. The most important of these concern decisions over centralized and distributed processing, file-based and database systems, online and batch processing, packages and programs, input methods and hardware. The analyst will restrict the number of suggested designs to two or three. For each, a cost estimate and implementation schedule will be given. The presentation of these suggestions will be made during a formal review. Management will decide on which, if any, of the presented systems is to be undertaken. The analyst will carry out a detailed design of the chosen system. This work is covered in Chapter 14.

Exercises

1. What are the objectives of systems design?

2. How is *systems analysis* distinguished from *systems design*?

3. In providing alternative systems designs what considerations should a systems analyst employ?

4. How do automation boundaries help in the design process?

5. How is the difference between online and batch processing shown with the use of data flow diagrams and automation boundaries?

6. What is the difference in purpose between a *walkthrough* and a *formal review*?

7. What roles do the participants in a formal review play?

8. What are the specific advantages and disadvantages for Kismet in adopting a batch system as distinct from an online system for order approval as shown in Figure 13.8?

9. What are the specific advantages and disadvantages for Kismet in adopting a more highly automated system as indicated in Figure 13.7(a) as compared to that shown in Figure 13.7(b)?

10. Go over your answers to the data flow diagram question number 14 (the library system) and number 17 (the theatre booking system) in Chapter 11. For each:
    (a) Eliminate reference to any physical aspects that have entered the model.
    (b) Suggest additional processes/functions that would be useful to a library and also to a theatre booking system and incorporate them in the data flow diagrams.
    (c) Derive two alternative designs for each and illustrate these by automation boundaries in the data flow diagrams.

11. 'A proposed system was given in the feasibility study along with its associated costs and benefits. It is a waste of time and money to present alternatives at this stage when a system has already been agreed.' How would you answer this criticism?

Recommended reading

- Downes E., Clare P. and Coe I. (1992). *Structured Systems Analysis and Design Method: Applications and Context* 2nd edn. Englewood Cliffs NJ: Prentice-Hall
  This is a clear comprehensive explanation of SSADM (structured systems analysis and design method) with numerous examples. It can be used as a standard text on systems analysis and design courses for computing students.
- Layzell P.J. and Loucopoulos P. (1989). *Systems Analysis and Development* 3rd edn. Bromley: Chartwell-Bratt
  This is a text designed for students that clearly explains and develops the life cycle using structured methods. As well as being applicable to this chapter it is also relevant for all the chapters on analysis and design.
- Flynn D.J. (1997). 2nd edn. *Information Systems Requirements: Determination and Analysis.* Maidenhead: McGraw Hill
  This is a comprehensive coverage of information systems analysis and design suitable for the student of computing studies who wishes to become acquainted with management and non-technical issues in analysis and design.
- Skidmore S., Farmer R. and Mills G. (1992). *SSADM version 4: Models and Methods.* NCC Blackwell
  A clear straightforward text suitable for reference on SSADM.
- Yourdon Inc. (1993). *Yourdon Systems Method: Model Driven Systems Development.* Englewood Cliffs NJ: Prentice-Hall
  This is useful as a statement of a systems development methodology by one of the founding father companies of structured systems analysis and design. It is suitable as an example reference of a commercial methodology.

Chapter 14

Detailed Design, Implementation and Review

14.1   Detailed design

14.2   Systems specification

14.3   Implementation

14.4   Systems changeover

14.5   Evaluation and maintenance

In Chapter 13 it was seen how the analyst uses the logical model of the system to suggest design alternatives for the new physical system. Broad decisions were taken over the extent of computerization and the types of system that could be developed for this. Having obtained agreement from the relevant management authority on the choice of system the analyst must now carry out detailed design of the new system. This chapter covers this and subsequent stages in the systems life cycle.

The detailed design of the system includes specification of the hardware, software, database, user interface and time schedule for implementation. The detailed specification is analogous to an architect's or engineer's blueprint – it is the document from which the system will be built. Once agreement has been obtained on the detailed design, steps will be taken to acquire and install the hardware, write or purchase and test the software, train staff, develop the database and convert and load the contents of existing files. The system is then ready to take over from the current one. Various methods of changeover are discussed. After changeover a post-implementation review considers the effectiveness of the system and its relation to its specification and original objectives. Finally, ongoing maintenance and development will be needed during the useful life of the system.

14.1   Detailed design

Data flow diagrams were used to develop a high-level logical model of the processes and the data flows between them in the system. They were particularly helpful in sketching design alternatives using automation boundaries. The logic of the processes themselves has been captured in structured tools such as decision tables, structured English, or logic flow-charts. The data model of the organization has been produced using entity–relationship modelling.

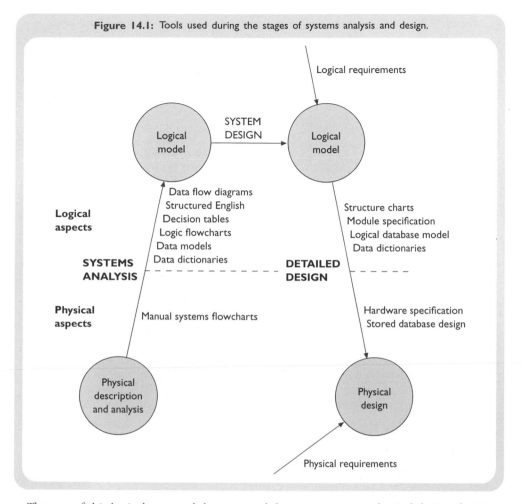

Figure 14.1: Tools used during the stages of systems analysis and design.

The use of this logical approach has ensured that no premature physical design decisions have been taken. The concentration has always been on the question 'What logically is required of the system and what logically must be achieved in order to do this?' not 'How are we physically going to accomplish this?' However, the time has come to move away from these logical models towards the detailed physical design of the computerized system (see Figure 14.1). The data flow diagrams and logic representations developed so far will be invaluable in producing program specifications. The entity model will be essential in designing a database model.

Any system can be considered as being composed of input, output, storage and processing elements. This approach is used in looking at the various tasks to be covered in detailed systems design. Control in systems has been covered extensively in Chapter 8. Control features figure prominently in the design of all the other elements.

14.1.1 Process design

Process design covers the need to design and specify the processing hardware, and to design and specify the software for running in the central processing unit.

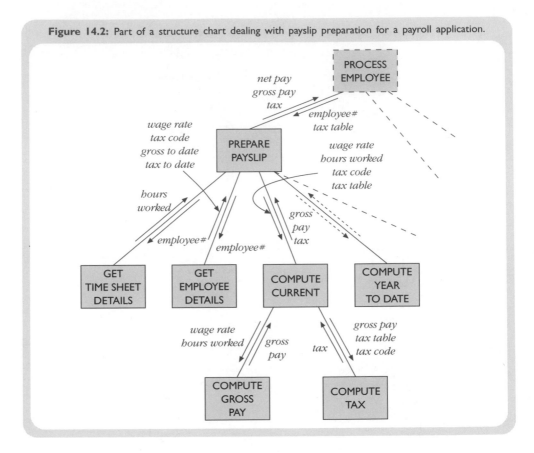

Figure 14.2: Part of a structure chart dealing with payslip preparation for a payroll application.

The specification of processor hardware is a technical skill beyond the scope of this text. The analyst will need to consider the demands to be made on the processor. In particular, the volumes of transactions to be processed per day and the processing requirement for each, the speed of response needed for interactive enquiries, the number of simultaneous users and the types of peripheral devices required, the amount of RAM, the complexity of programs and the extent to which the system should be able to cope with future increases in demand are all determinants of the processing power required. Decisions taken on whether to centralize or distribute computing and the mix between batch and online processing will all affect the decision.

The development of program specifications is facilitated by the structured tools used so far. Programs are regarded as being composed of various modules. These program modules should be constructed so that each performs a single independent function, is independently testable and leads to code that is easy to understand and amend at a later date if necessary. The modular design should also facilitate the addition of extra modules if needed later and so aid the flexibility of the system. Connections between **modules** can be illustrated with a **structure chart**. These terms will now be explained. An example of part of a structure chart and a module specification can be seen in Figures 14.2 and 14.3.

Figure 14.3: A module specification for the input/process/output for the PREPARE PAYSLIP process.

SYSTEM	PAYROLL PROCESS
MODULE NAME	PREPARE PAYSLIP
AUTHOR	J. SMITH
DATE	3/3/98
MODULE CALLS	GET TIME SHEET DETAILS
	GET EMPLOYEE DETAILS
	COMPUTE CURRENT PAY
	COMPUTE YEAR TO DATE
	: : : :
	: : : :
MODULE IS CALLED BY	PROCESS EMPLOYEE
MODULE INPUTS	*employee#*
	tax table
MODULE OUTPUTS	*gross pay*
	tax
	net pay
PROCESS	**DO** GET TIME SHEET DETAILS
	DO GET EMPLOYEE DETAILS
	DO COMPUTE CURRENT
	SET *net pay = gross pay – tax*
	DO COMPUTE YEAR TO DATE
	: : : :
	: : : :

Modules

A module contains a set of executable instructions for performing some process. At the design stage these instructions may be specified using structured English or decision tables. At a later stage this specification will be converted into program instructions in the chosen programming language.

Data may be passed from one module to another. This is akin to being passed from one data process to another in a data flow diagram. In Figure 14.2 part of a set of interconnected modules handling a payroll process is shown. Each module is named and the data flows between modules are illustrated.

The chart shows that the module PREPARE PAYSLIP requires that four other modules be executed. These are GET TIME SHEET DETAILS, GET EMPLOYEE DETAILS, COMPUTE CURRENT PAY and COMPUTE YEAR TO DATE. The module COMPUTE CURRENT PAY is said to be called by the module PREPARE PAYSLIP. COMPUTE CURRENT PAY itself calls COMPUTE GROSS PAY and COMPUTE TAX. The inputs and outputs from any module are shown entering or leaving the module box. Needless to say, all the data inputs and outputs will be in the data dictionary.

A module is independently specified in a module specification as illustrated in Figure 14.3. This is sometimes called an **input/process/output (IPO) chart**.

The module specification, together with the data dictionary entries, is sufficient on its own for the programmer to write code. It is not necessary when coding a module to have any understanding of the other modules in the system or to have them fitting together.

This is very different from traditional programming methods where monolithic code would be produced. The integration between functions then allowed programmers to produce a code that was very efficient in its use of central processor time. However, programs were difficult to understand and bugs were frequently time-consuming to find and correct. Alteration of the code at a later stage, for example to introduce an additional function, might lead to unpredicted effects elsewhere in the program. It soon came to be the case that over 50% of the cost of a project over its life cycle was concerned with debugging, amending and generally maintaining software.

Central processing power is now cheap. It is not necessary to produce monolithic code designed to be efficient in its use of computing power. Rather, the aims have been to maximize flexibility so that programs are easy to alter, to enable programmers to produce code that is readily understandable once written and to ensure that addition of new functions is straightforward. The programming task as a consequence becomes more predictable. This is one of the advantages of the structured approach – the programming task is more easily controlled (and incidentally, more easily costed). As will be seen in Section 14.1.2, data flow diagrams can be directly translated to produce interconnected modules.

Structure charts

The structure chart, part of an example of which is shown in Figure 14.2, is a diagrammatic representation of the way that modules are connected. For each module it shows what data is input and output and what other modules call it or are called by it. There is no more information (in fact considerably less) in a structure chart than in the set of module specifications. The structure chart does, however, give a picture of the system that is easy to understand. Frequently, the data flows between modules are omitted for the sake of clarity. The structure chart is hierarchical. The use of hierarchical charts together with input/process/output specifications is called the **HIPO (hierarchical input/process/ output) technique**.

Looking at Figure 14.3 it can be seen that the module PREPARE PAYSLIP calls up the four modules GET TIME SHEET DETAILS, GET EMPLOYEE DETAILS, COMPUTE CURRENT PAY and COMPUTE YEAR TO DATE in that order. These will each be independently specified. Figure 14.2 shows these as occurring in order from left to right. This is the implied sequence of execution of modules.

Corresponding to the three basic structures of structured English:

sequential (DO A, DO B . . .)

decision (IF ⟨condition⟩
        THEN DO A
        ELSE DO B)

repetition (REPEAT A
        UNTIL ⟨condition⟩)

Figure 14.4: The relation between structure charts and structured English.
(a) Sequence. (b) Decision. (c) Repetition.

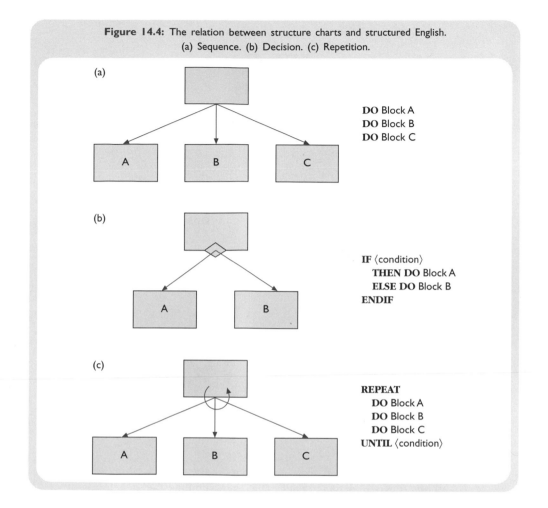

(a)

DO Block A
DO Block B
DO Block C

(b)

IF ⟨condition⟩
    THEN DO Block A
    ELSE DO Block B
ENDIF

(c)

REPEAT
    DO Block A
    DO Block B
    DO Block C
UNTIL ⟨condition⟩

there are notational variants in the structure chart. These are illustrated in Figure 14.4.

Each module is normally considered to call its submodules and execute or perform them from left to right as shown in Figure 14.4(a). Each submodule may itself call submodules and is not considered to have been executed until all its submodules have been executed. This order is shown in Figure 14.5.

Wherever a decision has to be made to execute one module rather than another this is indicated by a diamond placed at the connection point as in Figure 14.4(b). For instance, a part of a module dealing with processing a stock transaction will carry out different procedures if the transaction is an increment to stock (receipt of a delivery corresponding to a purchase order) than if it is a decrement (despatch corresponding to a sales order). The parent module will test the transaction to determine its type.

A module may be executed repeatedly. This will be the case with batch transaction processing where each one of a batch is treated in the same way. For instance, in preparing payslips the process of computing pay is repeated for each employee. This iteration is shown by means of the circular arrow as in Figure 14.4(c).

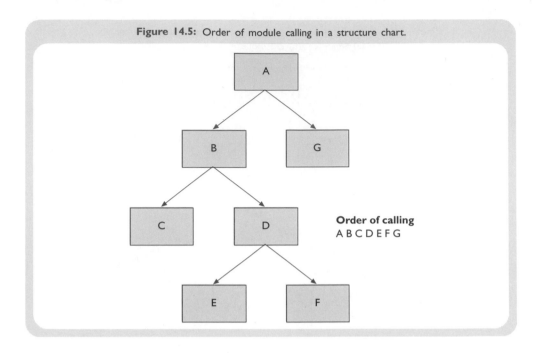

Figure 14.5: Order of module calling in a structure chart.

Order of calling
A B C D E F G

14.1.2   Modular design

The advantages of modular design as represented using hierarchical structure charts and module specifications are:

- Easier design of programs: analysts can specify major tasks at a high level and later break these down into their detail. This complements the development of the analysis stage, in which top-down decomposition was stressed.

- The structure developed through modular design consists of manageable chunks. This means that the parts of the system and their interrelations are represented in a way that can be understood as a whole.

- Individual programmers and designers can be given different modules and can work relatively independently of one another.

- Project management, scheduling of design, costing and allocation of manpower are made easier.

- The separate modules may be individually tested so that errors can be precisely located and are easily corrected.

- The final system will be modular. Individual modules can be 'lifted out', altered or inserted easily with the confidence that their effect on other modules is specified by input and output data and the processes that occur.

In order that design may achieve these ends it is crucial that modules are loosely coupled and cohesive.

Coupling

The idea of coupling has been introduced in Chapter 1 where the degree of subsystem coupling was defined in terms of the extent to which a change in the state of one subsystem led to a change in the state of another. Modular decoupling is similar in concept. As data is what passes between modules it is data connections that are important.

Two modules are less coupled:

- the fewer the number of types of data item passed from one to the other;
- the less they share the same data from a data store.

A module that is only loosely coupled to other modules has a simple interface and is therefore easy to design, code, change and test independently.

Cohesion

Modules as well as being loosely coupled should be cohesive. This is harder to define. A module is more cohesive if:

- It consists of one single function such as COMPUTE GROSS PAY.
- It consists of more than one function but each is executed in sequence: for example, PREPARE PAYSLIP consists of four sequentially executed modules.
- It performs a set of independent actions that are linked by being performed at the same time. Examples of this are initialization and termination routines concerned with data structures used by a set of processes.

The advantages of modular design as stated can only be fully realized with modules that are loosely coupled to one another yet highly cohesive internally.

14.1.3 Development of the structure chart and module specification for Kismet

The level 1 data flow diagram for the Kismet order processing system is given again in Figure 14.6(a) and the level 2 breakdown in Figure 14.7(a). These will be used to generate a (partial) structure chart for the Kismet system.

The main part of the level 1 data flow diagram suggests that there are three separate functions. The first deals with the generation of approved orders. The second processes stock transactions to update stock records and produce despatch notes. Finally, invoices are made up and despatched. This can be seen in the simple structure chart of Figure 14.6(b).

The structure chart dealing with the generation of the approved orders is shown in Figure 14.7(b). As is common in the production of hierarchical structure charts the data flows between the various modules are omitted. This is usually done to simplify the chart. There is, however, another reason. The structure is prepared before the individual module specification and it is at that point that the analyst's attention is devoted to the precise description of the data flows. Structure charts are then first derived without all the data flows.

Consideration of the data flow diagram in Figure 14.7(a) indicates that the process of generating an approved order includes three important parts: preparing the priced company order, checking the credit status of the customer for the order and, depending on the result of the credit check, handling the order in one way or another. This is shown by the second-level decomposition of the tasks in the structure chart (Figure 14.7(b)).

Figure 14.6: (a) A data flow diagram of Kismet's order processing system.
(b) Part of a structure chart for the Kismet order processing system.

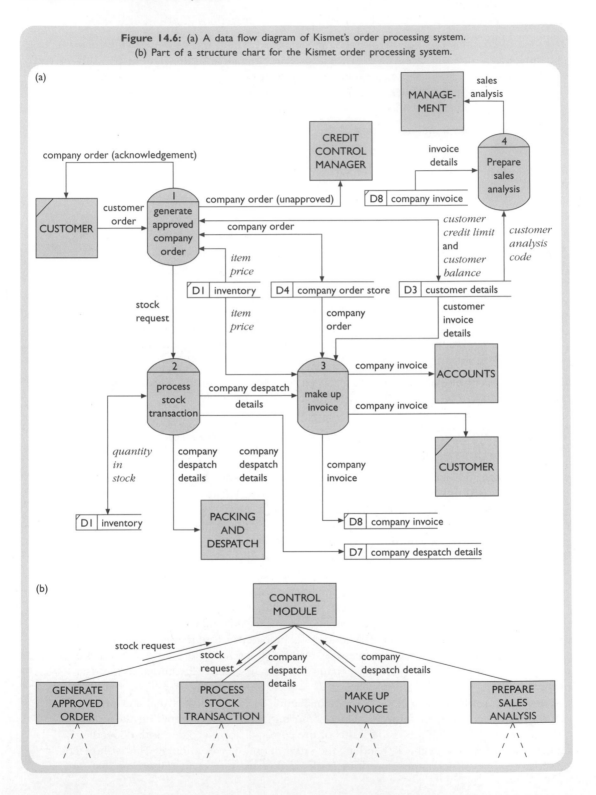

Figure 14.7: (a) The data flow diagram for the generation of an approved order.
(b) A structure chart for the generation of an approved order.

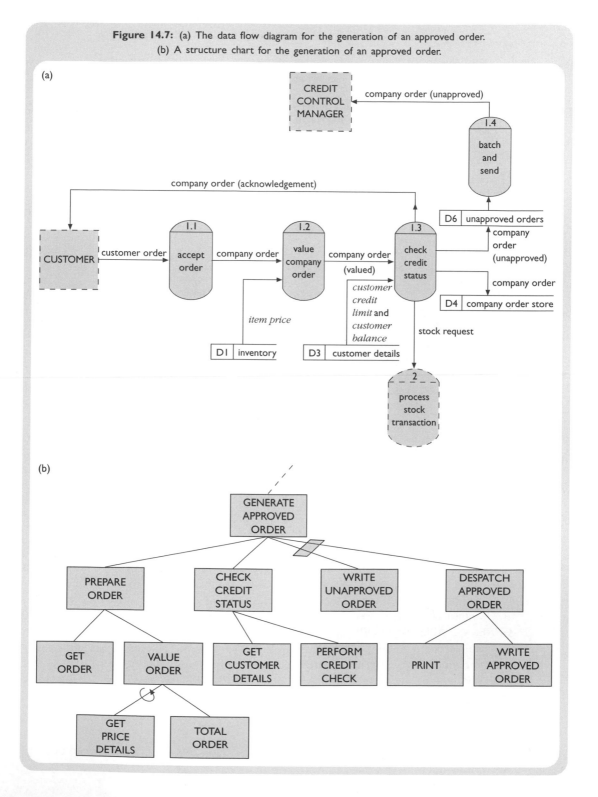

Figure 14.8: A module specification for CHECK CREDIT DETAIL.

SYSTEM	ORDER PROCESSING
MODULE NAME	CHECK CREDIT STATUS
AUTHOR	J. SMITH
DATE	3/3/98
MODULE CALLS	GET CUSTOMER DETAILS
	PERFORM CREDIT CHECK
MODULE IS CALLED BY	GENERATE APPROVED ORDER
MODULE INPUTS	*order total*
	customer#
MODULE OUTPUTS	*company order approval flag*
PROCESS	**DO** GET CUSTOMER DETAILS
	DO PERFORM CREDIT CHECK

Preparing the priced order consists of two tasks. First, the order details are obtained through keyboard entry. This is shown by the module GET ORDER. Second, the order details are then used to value the order (VALUE ORDER). This itself consists of two tasks. The first is to obtain the price details for each item ordered and the second is to calculate the total value of the order. Note that preparing the order involves the two processes GET ORDER and VALUE ORDER in that sequence. This is just the sequence of the two corresponding data processes in the data flow diagram – process 1.1 and process 1.2 (Figure 14.7 (a)).

The next process in the chain, process 1.3, is performed by the next module to be executed – CHECK CREDIT STATUS.

Finally, depending on the outcome of the credit check, the order is stored (unapproved) in the store D.6 or printed for despatch to the customer and stored (approved) in the store D.4. This corresponds to the alternatives shown on the structure chart (Figure 14.7(b)).

The approved order is also needed by the module concerned with processing the stock transaction. It is passed, minus its price details, as the output 'stock request' of the GENERATE APPROVED ORDER module via the control module.

A sample of a module specification is given in Figure 14.8. The data inputs and outputs will be defined in the data dictionary. Note that the modules called and the module that calls it determine the position of the module CHECK CREDIT STATUS in the hierarchy chart.

Summary so far

The way a data flow diagram is used for the preparation of a structure chart can be summarized as follows:

1. View the diagram to establish whether the data processes fall into groups each associated with a type of process. View the resulting grouped collections of data processes to establish the key functions in each group. If each group has only a single data process within it this is straightforward.

2. Decompose these functions to obtain modules that are highly cohesive and loosely coupled. Note that the sequence of data processes will indicate the left-to-right ordering of modules. Data flows that are conditional on a test performed in a data process will correspond to alternative module selections. This can be indicated using the diamond symbol. Lower-level data flow diagrams are to be used in this decomposition.

3. Now specify each module separately ensuring that named data items and data collections are entered in the data dictionary and that the data produced by major modules corresponds to the data being passed between processes in the data flow diagrams.

This gives a general idea of the development of a hierarchical structure chart and module specification. Do not form the impression that once the data flow diagrams have been developed the production of the modular structure chart is a mechanical task. It is not. The analysis of the high-level diagrams can often be difficult. Most important is the realization that to discover key functions and to decompose these into their constituents, each of which performs a single logical function that is translatable into a cohesive module, requires more than an uncritical reading of a data flow diagram. It is necessary for the analyst to obtain a deep appreciation of the system and the functions it performs. Although structured methods attempt to replace the art of design by the science of engineering there is still a place for creative understanding.

14.1.4 Data store design

During systems analysis and design a conceptual data model of the organization was developed. This was based on modelling entities and their relationships. Later, attributes of the entities were established. A normalized entity model was then developed to third normal form. The resulting normalized entities have been checked by deriving functional entity models to ensure that the various processes can be served with the data that they need. During systems design a decision will have been made as to whether to service the future data needs of the organization via a database approach using a database management system or via an application-led file-based approach. The considerations involved in this choice were covered in Chapter 13. Either way, detailed design of the data store will be required and this will be aided by the normalized data model.

File-based systems

In general, a file-based approach will have been chosen if there is little or no common data usage between applications and there is a need for fast transaction processing. The analyst will need to design record layouts. This involves specifying the names of the fields in each record, their type (for example, text or numeric) and their length. Records may be fixed or variable length. In the latter case this is either because fields are allowed to vary in length or because some fields are repeated. Record structures can become quite complicated if groups of fields are repeated within already repeating groups of fields.

As well as record design the storage organization and access for each file must be decided. This will determine the speed of access to individual records and the ease with which records can be added and deleted within the file. The most common types of storage organization are sequential, indexed, indexed-sequential, random storage with hashing, lists and inverted files. Different file organizations have different characteristics with respect to ease and speed of data storage and retrieval. Depending on the type of application the most appropriate organization is chosen. The topic of files, file organization and file design was covered extensively in Chapter 6 and the reader is referred there for further information.

The analyst will need to specify suitable backing-store hardware. This may involve tapes and tape read/write devices but nowadays is more likely to be disk-based. In order to select appropriate hardware the analyst must take into account the number of files and within each file the number of records and the storage required for each, the file organization chosen, the response time required, and the likely future developments, especially in terms of increases in size. These characteristics will allow the analyst to calculate the total storage requirements and to specify appropriate hardware.

Database systems

It is likely that a database approach will have been selected if the same data is shared between many applications, if there is a large degree of integration of data and if flexible reporting and enquiry facilities are needed.

The analyst will use the conceptual data model as a guide for selecting the appropriate database model. If the conceptual data model is hierarchical in nature, the applications for which it is to be used generally require hierarchical access, and if fast access to records is required, it is likely that a database management system operating with a hierarchical model will be chosen. Relational and network database management systems give greater scope in the representation of data structures. Relational database systems, in particular, allow great flexibility in the storage and retrieval of data. Although their relatively slow access times and high storage overheads can be a disadvantage the current development of cheap and fast-access disk-based hardware is diminishing these drawbacks.

Relational databases appear to be establishing themselves as *the* databases for the future. It is becoming common for relational database management software to be accompanied by sophisticated query/fourth-generation languages, interfaces with spreadsheet models, and networking facilities with other relational databases. Prewritten template software produced by fourth-generation languages for standard business functions, especially accounting, can also be purchased and tailored to the needs of the organization. An example is ORACLE, a relational database system, with SQL. Databases, database management systems and data models were covered extensively in Chapter 7 on database systems. The reader is referred to this chapter for a fuller account of the terms and concepts used in this section.

Provided that the database management system intended for purchase is known, the analyst can begin designing the **conceptual schema**. This is an overall logical view of the data model cast in terms of the data definition language of the database management system. It will contain integrity and authorization rules. In the case of a relational model this will be a relatively straightforward translation of the normalized entity model. Each entity and each relationship will become a table. Each attribute of an entity will become a column in the table corresponding to the entity. The derivation of a conceptual model for hierarchical and network systems is less straightforward. This is partly because the notion of a genuine conceptual schema does not strictly apply.

For each user of the database an external schema is defined. This is part of the database that a user is entitled to access in order to carry out a function. The analyst will have determined the data needs of the users for their various tasks during systems analysis. This can now be accommodated within the database design. The access will correspond to certain entities, attributes of those entities, and paths through the database via relationships.

The analyst must also design the internal schema. This describes how the database is physically stored. It will make reference to record ordering, pointers, indexes, block sizes and access paths. Good internal schema design will ensure an efficient database. Unlike conceptual and external schemas, an internal schema makes reference to physical aspects of the database. The way that external schemas relate to the conceptual schema, and the way this in turn relates to the storage schema, is specified in terms of external/conceptual and conceptual/internal mappings.

The design of the database must proceed in tandem with the module design as the programs specified need access to the database. There are therefore intimate relationships between the data flow diagrams, data models, structure charts, module specifications, database schemas and data dictionaries. For a large organization there will be many data flow diagrams. The entity model may have several *hundred* entity types. It is a complicated task coordinating the interrelations between the various elements in analysis and design. **Computer-aided systems engineering** (CASE) software packages help in this. They also semi-automate the design process. See Chapter 15.

As in the case of file-based systems the analyst will need to estimate sizes and types of hardware required.

Data store design for Kismet

The analyst has decided to develop a relational database system for Kismet. Although the organization carries out transaction processing, one of the major requirements of the new system is that it will be able to provide flexible enquiry and reporting facilities. This, together with the stable and integrated nature of the model, suggests that a relational database is appropriate.

The analyst will convert the fully normalized conceptual data model to produce the relational conceptual schema. Part of this schema is shown in Figure 14.9(a). It is defined within a typical relational data definition language (DDL). This definition should be compared with the corresponding normalized entity model for Kismet developed in Chapter 12, which covered data analysis and modelling. As can be seen, the derivation is straightforward. The fields *order#* and *item#* are character fields each composed of six characters. The fields are not allowed to be empty for any row of the table. The *item quantity* is an integer.

One of the functions required by Kismet is online enquiry of the status of any customer order. Given a customer *order#* it is required that the contents of the order and the items and quantities despatched against this order should be accessible. This is defined as a view or external schema in Figure 14.9(b). The fields selected and tables accessible are specified. The relational join ensures that an *order#* is followed through the three tables. Once again, the reader should compare this with the conceptual schema and the entity model developed in Chapter 12.

though not as bad as 'ERROR 243 @45'. A helpful error message should not only analyze the error but also provide help to the user in recovery – for example 'NUMERIC ACCOUNT CODE NOT EXPECTED. ALL ACCOUNT CODES BEGIN WITH A CHARACTER. PLEASE TRY AGAIN (FOR LIST OF ACCEPTABLE ACCOUNT CODES PRESS FUNCTION KEY 1)'.

Response time: Generally, response times to commands should be short. Lengthy response times, particularly for regular users, lead to irritation, errors and non-acceptance of the system. For complicated tasks and requests though, especially with inexperienced users, rapid response times may increase errors and prevent learning.

Given all these considerations the analyst will design the user interface with a model of the user in mind. Users can be categorized in several ways that affect the design. Three important categories are:

1. *Casual v. regular users*: Regular users become more knowledgeable about the system through use. They are also more likely to be provided with training if interaction with the computer system occupies much of their job. For such users fast response times, interactive commands and defaults are important.

2. *Passive v. interactive users*: Interactive users are those that either develop systems or build decision support models. They are liable to have or want to have the facility to navigate around the system. Those responsible for using the system to answer online enquiries also often fall within the category of interactive user. These users rely heavily on a systematic knowledge of command structures. Passive users are best served with menus and form-filling that restrict their area of choice. Data input personnel fall into this category.

3. *Novice v. expert users*: This category is not the same as casual v. regular users. For instance, it is possible for both a novice and an expert to be a casual user of the system. Expert casual users are likely to require targeted but unobtrusive help facilities whereas novices will need a complete step-by-step set of screen instructions.

The design of the user interface is one aspect of the design of the total system involving the user. **Human–computer interaction**, covered in a previous chapter, locates issues in user interface design within the much broader framework of the function of the system and the place of technology and people within this.

Reports and input documents

The analyst will also be responsible for designing documents that are used for input and for reports produced as output by the system. Many of the same considerations apply as for user interface design. Input documents should match screens as far as possible. Printed reports should always be designed with the aim of logical presentation and clarity in mind.

Kismet: input/output design

Kismet users fall into a number of categories. There are data input personnel such as those concerned with order entry, payments received, purchase orders and so on. These will be regular users passively responding to forms as presented on the screen. There will also be staff dealing with and tracing particular orders, dealing with customer enquiries and the like. These may be the same people as the order entry staff though they need different and more flexible skills.

Figure 14.10: A screen layout design for Kismet customer order entry.

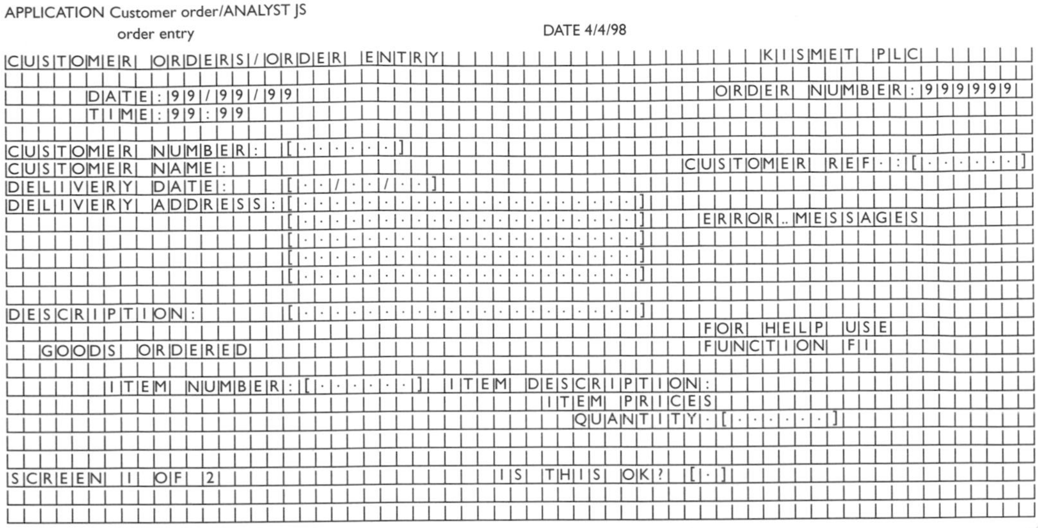

APPLICATION Customer order/ANALYST JS
order entry   DATE 4/4/98

```
CUSTOMER ORDERS/ORDER ENTRY                              KISMET PLC
        DATE: 99/99/99                         ORDER NUMBER: 999999
        TIME: 99:99
CUSTOMER NUMBER: [[·|·|·|·|·|·]]
CUSTOMER NAME:                                 CUSTOMER REF: [[·|·|·|·|·|·]]
DELIVERY DATE:     [[··/··/··/··]]
DELIVERY ADDRESS: [[·|·|·|·|·|·|·|·|·|·|·|·|·|·|·]]
                  [[·|·|·|·|·|·|·|·|·|·|·|·|·|·|·]]   ERROR..MESSAGES
                  [[·|·|·|·|·|·|·|·|·|·|·|·|·|·|·]]
                  [[·|·|·|·|·|·|·|·|·|·|·|·|·|·|·]]
                  [[·|·|·|·|·|·|·|·|·|·|·|·|·|·|·]]
DESCRIPTION:      [[·|·|·|·|·|·|·|·|·|·|·|·|·|·|·]]
                                                FOR HELP USE
   GOODS ORDERED                                FUNCTION F1
        ITEM NUMBER:[[·|·|·|·|·|·]] ITEM DESCRIPTION:
                                       ITEM PRICES
                                       QUANTITY·[[·|·|·|·|·]]

SCREEN 1 OF 2              IS THIS OK? [[·]]
```

Middle management will use the system for monitoring and predicting the performance of the company. For example, the sales manager will wish to draw off reports of sales by customer type, by geographical area, by type of item, by date and by other parameters. This user is not likely to be a regular user of the computer system. Other members of the sales and accounts departments involved with sales and profit forecasting will interactively use and develop spreadsheet models fed by actual data. These will become expert interactive users.

An example of a specification of a form to appear on a screen is given in Figure 14.10. The customer order entry is carried out by a regular user of the system. A number of points should be noted and would be included along with the specification. The system generates the date, time and order number. This not only saves time but is done for reasons of security and control. The data entry clerk is presented with a customer number data entry field. The customer name is then displayed as an error control. The delivery address is extracted from the customer account details and displayed on screen but the operator has the ability to overwrite this. The items ordered are entered by item number with a flashback description check. This screen is one of two. The second screen would allow more items to be ordered. The data entry clerk has the option to accept or reject the entered data as displayed on the screen. Various other checks would be performed. For example, the data would be validated as being possible: for example, not 31 June. The user is a regular user so no on-screen help is given. If help is required, particularly as a result of error messages, this can be called up as described using keyboard function F1.

There will be a large number of such layout designs specifying the complete user interface for Kismet. The analyst will have designed these with the different types of user in mind.

14.2   Systems specification

Detailed design results in a **systems specification**. This is a comprehensive document describing the system as it is to be produced. There is no agreed format for this specification but it is likely to include the following:

- An executive summary: this provides a quick summary of the major points in the specification.
- A description of the proposed system and especially its objectives. Flow block diagrams and data flow diagrams can be used. The work to be carried out by the system and the various user functions should be covered.
- A complete specification of:
  - Programs: these will include module specifications and structure charts, together with test data.
  - Input: this will include specimen source documents, screen layouts, menu structures, control procedures.
  - Output: this will include specimen output reports, contents of listings, and so on.
  - Data storage: this is the specification of file and database structure.
- A detailed specification of controls operating over procedures within the system.
- A specification of all hardware requirements and performance characteristics to be satisfied.
- A specification of clerical procedures and responsibilities surrounding the system.
- A detailed schedule for the implementation of the system.
- Cost estimates and constraints.

The systems specification fulfils a number of roles. First, it is used as the exit criterion from the stage of detailed design prior to the stage of implementation. The systems specification is agreed by senior management, often the steering committee. Once accepted, large amounts of money are allocated to the project. This is necessary to purchase hardware, to code software, and to carry out physical installation. Second, the specification acts as source documentation from which programs are written and hardware tenders are arranged. Third, the document acts as a historical record of the system for future users and developers. Finally, it is used in the assessment of the system once the system is being used. Does the system meet its response times? Is it built according to design? These are examples of questions that can only be answered in consultation with the systems specification.

14.3   Implementation

Once the systems specification has been agreed its implementation can begin. This is the stage when things are done rather than analyzed or designed. There are various separate but related tasks to be accomplished. Programs are written and tested, hardware is acquired and installed, staff are trained, the system is tested, and historic data from the old manual system or computer system is loaded into the files or database. Many of these tasks are carried out simultaneously. It is important that they are all completed before changeover to the new system is effected.

14.3.1 *Program development and testing*

One of the outputs of the detailed physical design stage was a set of program specifications. These are used by programmers as the blueprint from which to write the software. Program development and testing is one of the most costly phases in the systems life cycle. Historically, it was also the phase most likely to be over budget and completed late. Early programming techniques compounded these difficulties. The software produced was often unreliable and costly to debug and maintain.

Structured techniques, though, have produced a set of specifications for cohesive decoupled modules. These reduce programming complexity and ensure reliability and easy maintenance of software. Each module can be coded and separately tested. Structured analysis and design facilitates structured programming.

Structured programming allows only a small number of logical coding structures. In particular the **GOTO** command, so popular with novice programmers using BASIC, is disallowed. The use of **GOTO** commands, which direct a change in the order of program statement execution, leads to logical spaghetti in program execution. It becomes extremely difficult to understand and debug programs once written. The coding structures allowed correspond to those in structured English. It is common for programming languages to use instructions such as **CASE** and **IF THEN ELSE** statements. Blocks of code are nested within these logical structures in the program. Internally, the blocks themselves will of course exhibit the same allowable logical structure (see Figure 14.11). The other main feature of structured program code is that although variables (containing data) are passed in and out of a module all other variables used within that module have no meaning outside it. In structured programming the variables are declared in the code. This corresponds to structured module specifications and structure charts, where data flows are explicitly stated.

Program testing is of critical importance in the development of software. It is one of the tasks of the analyst to specify test plans for the software. Individual modules are tested as they are written. This ensures that they separately perform to specification. Modules are tested grouped together. This enables an assessment of their successful integration to be made. Finally, the entire set of programs is tested.

It is difficult to state what constitutes an adequately tested program. For instance, a program may perform perfectly well with standard data input but how does it perform with erroneous data – a negative-value sale for instance? How will the program react to an unusual set of key punches? Much program code is devised to deal with these situations. It has been estimated that from 50% to 80% of program code is devoted to error handling of one sort or another. There are a number of types of testing.

- **Random test data** can be generated, processed and the accuracy of processing checked.
- **Logical test data** may be developed using the logical limits for acceptable and unacceptable data.
- **Typical test data** assesses the performance of the software using past actual data.

It has been assumed that programs are to be developed specially for the system using conventional high-level languages and structured techniques. There are other approaches. For example, it may have been decided at the systems design stage to opt for applications packages for some or all of the data-processing and information provision. The benefits

Figure 14.11: Allowable coding structures and their relation to structured English.

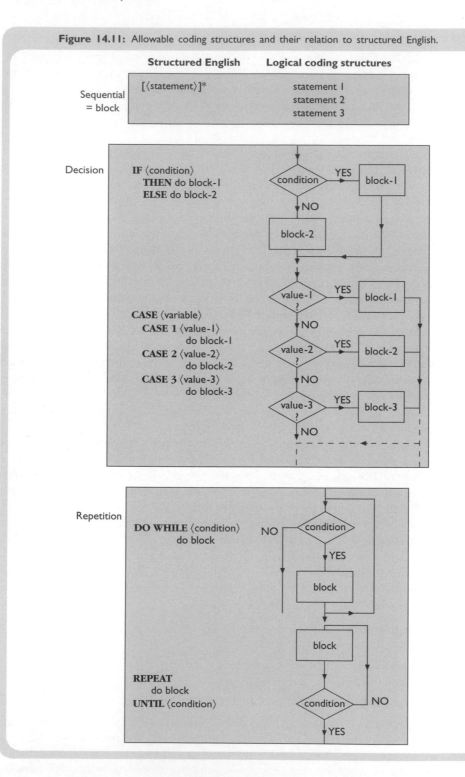

and limitations of this approach were covered in Chapter 3. A decision to adopt a package will have been taken on the basis of an analysis of the organization's requirements and the existence of the appropriate software package. It is unlikely that this software can be just loaded into the system and run. It is usual for the package to require tailoring to meet the needs of the organization. This is not to say that programs must be written. Rather, the package will have routines already available for customization. Examples are the design of reports, the determination of an account coding structure, and the setting of password controls. Alternatively, it may have been decided at an earlier stage to adopt a prototyping approach to software and systems development using a fourth-generation language. Prototyping and the use of fourth-generation languages were covered in Chapter 3 and 5. The application of a prototyping approach to expert systems development is explained in Chapter 17.

14.3.2 Hardware acquisition and installation

The characteristics of the hardware required were included in the systems specification. The analyst may have had certain manufacturers of hardware in mind. This is likely to be true if the organization already has a commitment to an existing manufacturer in its current and ongoing systems. In other cases the hardware specification can be put out to tender and it is up to different suppliers to make contract offers.

Hardware is usually purchased new though there is a second-hand market for computers – particularly microcomputers and minicomputers. An alternative to purchasing is leasing. This is recommended in circumstances where there are tax concessions to be gained. Computer rental is sometimes used when extra hardware is needed for peak periods or where the system has a designated short lifespan.

Installation of hardware is costly. It may require building new rooms that are air-conditioned and dust free. It will almost certainly involve laying data communication and power cables. Physical security such as fire alarms, video monitoring and secure rooms for data file libraries will also be installed.

14.3.3 Training and staff development

Users are the key element in any successful computer system. Their knowledge and understanding will have been tapped during systems investigation and analysis. Models of users will have influenced the user–machine interface design. But unless staff are adequately prepared for the new system it will have little chance of being effectively used. This requires staff training and education.

Education is to be distinguished from training in that the former involves providing staff with a general understanding of the system, the way it functions, its scope and its limitations. They will be informed of how the system can be used to provide information for their needs or carry out processing tasks for them. Training, in contrast, involves the familiarization of staff with the skills necessary to operate the computer system to perform tasks. In either case there are several approaches:

- Lectures and seminars can be used for instructive overviews. Their advantage is that a large number of staff are reached using one instructor.
- Simulation of the work environment is used for training. This is a costly, though effective, training technique.

- On-the-job training involves supervision of personnel as skills that are progressively more complex are gradually mastered. This is a popular way of training new staff on an existing system.

- Software packages are used for training personnel in applications software. For example, there are tutorial programs for most of the major word processing packages.

- The information centre should devise training courses for staff involving some, if not all, of these techniques.

Staff training and education need to take account of the abilities of the trainees as well as the tasks for which training is provided. Staff will have different requirements and expectations of training. Insufficient attention to staff development is one certain way of ensuring that an information system will fail.

14.3.4   Data store conversion

The file or database structure will have already been designed. In the case of a database the conceptual, internal and external schemas were defined using the data definition language of the database management system. An organization will have historic data that must be entered into the files or database of the new computer system before it can be used for the organization's needs.

In the case of computer-held data this generally involves writing programs that accept data from the old files or database and convert it to the format required for the new system. This data is then written.

With manual files the task is more time-consuming. Decisions are made as to what data to transfer. This data is unlikely to be in the format required for input into the new system. It is common for data to be transcribed onto intermediate documentation prior to data entry. Though costly, this minimizes errors in transcription. Careful attention must be paid to control during this conversion. Batch and hash totals can be used in the transfer of accounting data. Balances should be agreed with clients of the system whether such clients are internal or external to the organization. Listings of input are produced and maintained for later queries and visual inspection.

During data store conversion the organization is continuing to function as near normal as possible. The old data store itself will be changing rather than remaining static. This adds further problems.

14.4   Systems changeover

At some stage the new computerized system will be brought into operation. How and when this is done will depend on the confidence that management have in its reliability. All systems will have undergone a **systems test** involving the use of the installed software and hardware. This however is very different from the situation that the system is likely to encounter in practice – peak loading, many users and many users committing errors in interacting with the system.

Four changeover strategies are considered here (see Figure 14.12). They are not mutually exclusive. Each has its benefits and limitations. They have varying degrees of safeguards against the effects of system malfunctions on the organization.

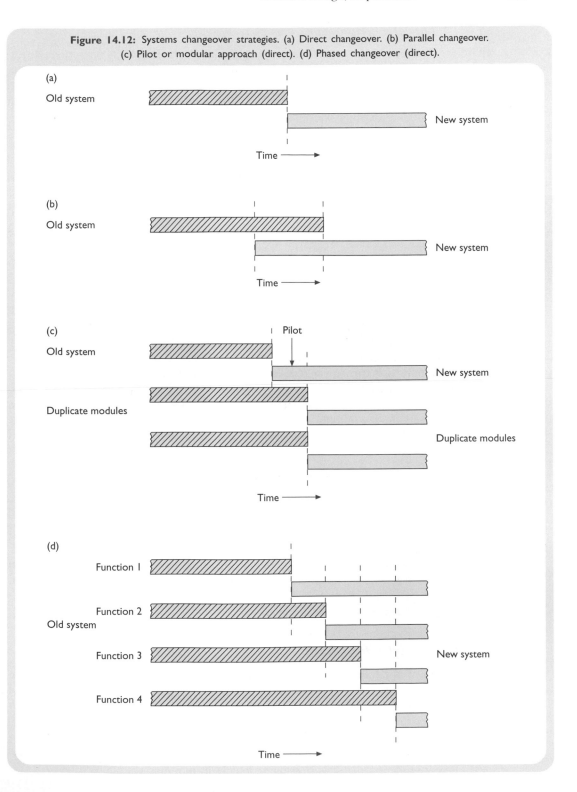

Figure 14.12: Systems changeover strategies. (a) Direct changeover. (b) Parallel changeover. (c) Pilot or modular approach (direct). (d) Phased changeover (direct).

14.4.1 Direct changeover

With direct changeover the new system is brought into operation in its entirety on a designated date. This has the advantage of being quick but relies heavily on the reliability of the systems design, implementation and testing, and on how the staff were trained. It is not generally recommended, though it may be unavoidable in cases where the system does not replace an existing one.

14.4.2 Parallel approach

The parallel approach, or some version of it, is very common in practice. It can be used when there is a great deal of similarity between the old and the new systems. This similarity needs to exist between inputs and outputs. Both systems are run in parallel until there is enough confidence in the new system to dispense with the old. Parallel running can take weeks or months. An advantage is that if the new system malfunctions then there is a backup system on which to rely. The output of the old and the new systems can also be compared. If there is any discrepancy then this can be investigated.

It is easy to stress the advantages of the parallel approach while ignoring its limitations. Staff will be put under enormous pressure if they have to use not only the old system but must repeat the same operations with an unfamiliar new system. If staff were working near to capacity prior to the introduction of the new system it is doubtful whether they will be able to handle the extra load. Overtime working and temporary staff are possible solutions, though each carries dangers. In the former case staff will not be performing at peak efficiency – not a desirable situation in which to run a new system. In the latter, the temporary staff will need to be trained. Should they be trained to use the old or the new system or both? These difficulties cannot be brushed away glibly, particularly if it is desired to reap the benefits of parallel changeover in terms of its safety and reliability.

14.4.3 Pilot or modular approach

Some systems can be broken down into several identical and duplicate modules. For instance, an automated point of sales and stock updating system for a supermarket chain will be repeated in many branches. A stock control system for handling 10,000 types of item performs identical functions on each type of item, independent of its type. Changeover to these systems can be effected by first changing over to one module either in parallel or directly. If this proves satisfactory then changeover to the entire system can be made. This is a way of minimizing the risks. The pilot system can also be used for on-the-job training of staff.

14.4.4 Phased changeover

Where a system is composed of different self-contained modules performing different functions it may be possible to phase in the new system while gradually phasing out the old. For example, a system involving nominal, sales and purchase ledger accounts, stock control, financial planning, sales forecasting and payroll can be phased in gradually, one function at a time. Although in the final integrated system there will be data flows between these various modules, each is sufficiently self-contained and directed towards a recognized business function that it is possible to phase in modules gradually.

This creeping commitment to computerization need not be restricted to changeover but can involve the whole development process. Its advantage is that cash flow outlay can be spread over time, analysts and programmers are employed consistently, resources are generally distributed more evenly over time, and the gradual commitment to the computerized system ensures that any difficulties in changeover are more easily handled. The drawback is that interfacing modules will need to have continuously changing modes of interface. For example, between a financial planning and sales ledger system there will initially be a manual–manual interface. If the ledger system is computerized then a computer–manual interface will need to be developed. Finally, a computer–computer interface is required. The continuous changeover process experienced by users, while distributing resources over time, can also give the feeling that computerization is a never-ending process. This is bad for morale.

14.4.5 Changeover in Kismet

The central purposes for developing a computerized information system for Kismet were to:

1. process customer orders quickly;
2. be able to satisfy customer enquiries in such areas as the status of orders, prices of goods, and delivery availability;
3. provide management with a greater variety of relevant up-to-date information on company performance.

Kismet is a firm that is beginning to embark on computerized systems. It does not currently have the experience or confidence gained by organizations that have a continuing systems development policy, possibly over 20 years or more. Kismet therefore wishes to embark on a changeover strategy as risk free as possible. Much of the new system, such as the part dealing with transaction processing, is very similar to the old system. A parallel changeover will allow the necessary processing checks to be carried out and at the same time will allow a manual system to be provided as backup. There will be difficulties performing these checks as the computerized system works almost instantaneously whereas the manual system took many days to process orders – that was one of its faults. With respect to order enquiry it has been decided to rely entirely on the new system, though sample checks are to be recorded and verified later. Similarly, the management reports as generated by the new system will be used. Sample checks against reports from the old system are to be made, but given the limited number of types of report that were generated this part of the system will rely heavily on the adequacy of systems testing prior to changeover.

The parallel run is to be initially for a period of one month. There will then be a formal review of the system prior to its final acceptance and the discarding of the old manual system.

14.5 Evaluation and maintenance

No computerized system once implemented remains unaltered through the rest of its working life. Changes are made, and maintenance is undertaken. Hardware maintenance is usually carried out under a maintenance contract with the equipment suppliers. Hardware maintenance involves technical tasks often requiring circuitry and other specialized parts.

Software maintenance is also carried out. In time, bugs may be discovered in the programs. It is necessary to correct these. Modular program design, structured code and the documentation techniques of structured systems analysis and design ensure that this task can be effected efficiently. Software maintenance is no longer the complex and costly contribution to the entire systems project that it used to be.

User needs also evolve over time to respond to the changing business environment. Software is amended to serve these. New applications programs must be written. It is the responsibility of the computer centre or information centre to ensure that the system is kept up to date.

Some time after the system has settled down it is customary to carry out a **post-implementation audit**. The purpose of this audit is to compare the new system as it actually is with what was intended in its specification. To ensure independence this audit will be carried out by an analyst or team not involved in the original systems project.

The audit will consider a number of areas:

- The adequacy of the systems documentation that governs manual procedures and computer programs will be checked.
- The training of personnel involved in the use of the new system will be assessed.
- Attempts will be made to establish the reliability of systems output.
- Comparison of the actual costs incurred during implementation is made against the estimated costs, and significant variances investigated.
- Response times will be determined and compared with those specified.

The original purposes of the systems project will once again be considered. Does the system as delivered meet these objectives? The post-implementation audit will yield a report that will assess the system. Suggestions for improvements will be made. These may be minor and can be accommodated within the ongoing development of the project. If they are major they will be shelved until a major overhaul or replacement of the system is due.

During the course of the useful life of the system, several audits will be made. Some of these will be required by external bodies. Examples are financial audits required by the accountancy profession for accounting transaction processing systems. Other audits are internal. They will deal with matters such as efficiency, effectiveness, security and reliability. The topic of auditing of computers systems was covered in Chapter 8 on control.

Summary

Having selected the overall systems design, detailed design of the system then commences. Programs are defined by the use of structure charts and individual module specifications. These ensure that the programming task can be carried out in a controlled and reliable way. The datastore is designed. In the case of file-based systems this involves the specification of file and record layouts. For databases, schema design is required. An important aspect of input/output design is that of the user interface. This is determined not only by the types of task for which input or output is used but also by a model of the user. There are various categories of user. In all these areas hardware requirements must be established, given ▷

the data processing and information provision requirements of the organization as identified during analysis.

The systems specification is an important landmark between detailed design and implementation. This is a report covering all aspects of the systems design in detail. As well as giving cost estimates it will also provide a schedule for the implementation stage of the project. Once the specification is agreed with management implementation can then commence.

During implementation large sums of money are allocated and spent. Hardware as specified is acquired and installed. Programs are coded and tested. The structured hierarchical input/process/output design facilitates the use of structured programming. Targeted training and education are provided for staff. Historical data is loaded into the system. The systems test is a major step in the implementation stage prior to changeover to the new system.

Systems changeover can be effected in a number of ways, each of which has certain benefits, drawbacks and areas of application. After the system has been running for some time a post-implementation audit compares the system as delivered with that as specified. Suggestions for further improvements are made. As the information needs of the organization evolve so the system is amended, programs adapted and new applications software written to take account of this.

Great achievements can be made using structured systems analysis and design. Information systems can now be produced that:

- involve integrated redesign rather than piecemeal copying of old manual systems;
- are based on the logical information requirements of the organization rather than the physical dictates of old processing patterns;
- are more likely to be delivered on time and on budget because of the added control that modular development confers on the project;
- contain software that is reliable, well documented and easily amendable.

There are some though who point to limitations in structured analysis and design. They comment on its lack of suitability in all cases. These reservations are founded on three implicit assumptions. These are:

1. A technical solution to an organization's information problems is always desirable and possible.

2. The experts in systems analysis and design are the analysts and programmers. Users come in only to provide information about the existing system during investigation and as a consideration in interface design. They themselves do not design and develop the system.

3. The correct approach to development is to progress in a linear fashion through a number of clearly definable stages with exit criteria.

Chapter 15, 6, and 17 consider how these assumptions have been challenged by soft systems analysis and design, user participation in socio-technical analysis and design, and prototyping as an approach to systems development.

Exercises

1. Outline the areas to be covered in the detailed design of a system.

2. What benefits accrue when software has been developed as a result of modular design?

3. Explain the terms *module decoupling* and *module cohesion*. Why are they desirable characteristics in modular software design?

4. Using the data flow diagrams developed for the library example (Chapter 11, Problem 1) derive a hierarchical structure chart for the system.

5. How do structured techniques in systems analysis and design aid systems development at later stages?

6. What is the difference between a *conceptual data model* and a *conceptual schema*?

7. What features of interface design affect the acceptance of computer systems by users?

8. How could each of the following be analyzed according to the categories of systems users covered in the text:
   (a) customer order data input personnel?
   (b) customer cashpoint users?
   (c) flight booking and reservation enquiry personnel?
   (d) spreadsheet model developers?
   (e) programmers?
   (f) middle-management users of summary accounting decision support information?

9. What is the role of a systems specification?

10. Distinguish between the various types of test carried out during implementation.

11. What security features must be present in the conversion of historic accounting data for entry into a new system?

12. Which of the following should be incorporated in a systems test: hardware, software, data storage, manual procedures, backup facilities, computer operations staff, users, data communications, security and control?

13. Explain **four** different changeover strategies. Are they mutually exclusive?
    In each of the following cases suggest a changeover strategy. Explain its merits and drawbacks. Justify your choice by giving reasons why other strategies are not appropriate.
    (a) A computerized inventory control system to replace antiquated manual methods. It is to be installed in eight warehouses and deals with 10,000 types of item.
    (b) A major high street bank has commissioned an automated cheque and cash deposit system for its branches. It is to be operated by the bank's counter personnel and will allow instant account updating for deposits.
    (c) A new company has developed a computerized lottery system to be installed in lottery ticket offices throughout the country. ▷

14. What are the purposes of a post-implementation audit?

15. Why is software maintenance, as distinct from software creation, traditionally regarded as an arduous unpopular task?

16. Why is software maintenance necessary?

Recommended reading

● Budgen D. (1994). *Software Design.* Addison-Wesley
  This is a clear comprehensive text suitable for final-level undergraduates in systems analysis and design. Part 1 explores the nature of the design process and the various roles played in software development. Part 2 gives a detailed examination of well-established structured approaches – JSP, SSADM and JSD.

● Monk. A., ed. (1988). *Fundamentals of Human Computer Interaction.* Academic Press
  This consists of an interesting collection of articles on the psychological aspects of human perceptual appreciation of information input, together with practical advice on interface design.

● Norton H. (1988). *Computing Procurement: Guidelines and Procedures.* Oxford University Press
  As well as giving a basic introduction to the need for correct systems identification, this text provides a procurement methodology involving contractual and negotiating issues for computer systems development.

● Simpson H. and Casey S.M. (1988). *Developing Effective User Documentation: A Human Factors Approach.* McGraw Hill
  This book covers the development of user documentation from the analysis of requirements, through design, implementation and evaluation. This is a valuable text for those involved at any stage in document design.

Chapter 15

Systems Analysis and Design: Alternative Approaches

15.1 'Hard' approaches to systems analysis and design
15.2 'Soft' approaches to systems analysis and design
15.3 CASE and object-oriented approaches to analysis and design
15.4 Rapid Applications Development

Up to now a particular approach to the analysis and design of computerized information systems has been taken. This is not the only approach. Nor is it *the* correct approach in all circumstances. Different approaches have differing strengths and weaknesses, differing areas of applicability and differing objectives. It is the purpose of this chapter to outline some alternatives and highlight their points of difference. Two 'soft' approaches will be chosen: the first is due to Peter Checkland and generally known by his name, the second is a socio-technical approach stressing the participation of users in analysis and design. Here, both of these will be termed 'soft' approaches as compared to the 'hard' approaches of which the structured methodologies considered so far are exemplars.

This chapter will also provide a general comparison between hard and soft methodologies. The underlying philosophies of each will be explained and contrasted. It is not intended to treat any additional approaches in detail but rather to give the reader a flavour of the debate that occurs between the proponents of hard and soft methodologies. This is a fruitful topic for discussion. It not only reveals deep and important divergences in attitudes to the analysis and design of information systems, particularly those in which persons as social beings are heavily involved, but also sets the framework for a debate that is likely to persist for several years and may mark an important turning-point in the development of attitudes to systems analysis and design.

As well as outlining these 'hard' and 'soft' approaches other trends will be examined. In particular the emergence of object-oriented approaches will be explained. This links with the increasingly important use of computers themselves in the process of analysis and design – computer aided software engineering (CASE). Although end-user computing and prototyping are covered elsewhere in the book their importance is highlighted in this chapter with the consideration of Rapid Applications Development.

15.1 'Hard' approaches to systems analysis and design

Several approaches to the analysis and design of information systems have been termed 'hard' approaches. What do they have in common? In answering this it is useful to have a look at three central examples of hard systems approaches as applied to the analysis and design of computerized information systems. The common features of these will then be more apparent. The three examples chosen here are structured functional/process analysis and design, data analysis, and what is often called the 'traditional approach' to the development of computer systems. The first two of these have been covered extensively in Chapters 11 and 12. There though, the emphasis was on an explanation of the tools and techniques and how these are applied through the systems life cycle. The focus of this chapter is different, in concentrating on the underlying assumptions, philosophies and typical areas of application of each approach. The aim is to compare and assess them rather than explain how to undertake practical projects.

15.1.1 Structured functional/process analysis and design

This has spawned many commercial methodologies. These are highly detailed, giving precise instructions as to the tools to be used at each stage and the documentation to be completed. Although each of these methodologies will differ they all share most of the following characteristics:

- **Function/process orientated:** The attention of the analyst is concentrated on analyzing and designing what are seen as the most important elements in systems analysis and design. These are the functions and processes that are carried out in the existing system and are designed to be present in the new system. Once these are clearly specified the remainder of analysis and design is seen to follow naturally.

- **Top-down:** In analysis and design the approach taken is to concentrate on the most general processes and functions in the initial stages. Only then are these decomposed again and again until a fine-grain representation of the systems processes is obtained.

- **Logical has priority over physical:** Compatible with a top-down approach is the emphasis on a logical analysis of the functions/processes of the existing system and on the design of a logical model of the desired system. Physical aspects of design – file, program and hardware specifications – are postponed for as long as possible. This lack of early commitment to the physical aspects of design is seen as preventing premature physical decisions that would constrain design alternatives. In the early stages physical analysis is seen as a necessary stepping-stone to deriving a logical model of what the existing system does. It then plays little role in the remainder of the project.

- **Stages and exit criteria:** In common with other hard approaches to systems analysis and design the process is seen as a linear development from the initial systems investigation and feasibility study, through analysis and design, to implementation and review. Each of these has its own exit criteria. For instance, the feasibility study is completed by the production and agreement of a feasibility report. This staged approach with objective deliverables is a characteristic of approaches that place a high emphasis on project control.

● **Tools and techniques:** Structured tools and techniques emphasize the general philosophy of the approach. Processes, top-down analysis and design, and the development of logical models are encouraged by use of the techniques. Data flow diagrams illustrate the logical flow of information and data between processes, structured English represents the logic of a process, and data dictionaries specify the logical content of data flows and data stores. The emphasis is always on the logical rather than the physical aspects of information systems, so these paper representations are clear communication devices between users, analysts and programmers. Repeated use of these structured tools ensures a program specification suitable for structured programming techniques and the use of structured programming languages. Hierarchical input/process/output charts ensure that complete modular specifications are developed. Different programmers can work independently on different parts of the system.

The movement to develop structured methods arose from severe problems arising in software engineering. It was not uncommon for computer projects to run considerably over budget on both time and costs. This often arose out of the difficulty of coordinating large teams of programmers. By concentrating on a top-down approach leading to modular specifications, structured approaches make possible a more accurate estimation of costs and schedules.

Another area in which structured approaches attempt to overcome difficulties is in the design of complex, highly integrated systems. Traditional methods are unsuitable for these. By concentrating on the overall logic of an information system it is possible for the analyst to transcend the barriers imposed by physical departmental divisions.

Structured techniques in analysis and design, backed up by structured programming, ensure that the final software is modular in nature. This means that not only individual programs but parts of programs are separately testable and can be easily amended. The modular nature of the program specifications also allows more adequate project control. The scope of the programmer for ingenuity and creativity is significantly reduced. 'Quality control' techniques are more easily applicable to the programmer's end product. This changes the nature of the programmer's task. The 'art' of programming has been de-skilled to meet the needs of 'scientific' management.

15.1.2   Data analysis

All approaches to systems analysis and design require attention to be paid at some stage to the data store aspects of the information system. What distinguishes approaches that are said to be based on data analysis is the importance and priority attached to the analysis and design of a logical *data* model of the organization in the design of an information system.

Up to now an entity–relationship approach to data modelling has been taken. This is the most common, though there are now alternatives that attempt to overcome some of the limitations imposed by the over simplicity of the entity–relationship structure. The various methodologies based around data analysis share the following features:

● **Data model orientated:** The emphasis is on deriving a data model of the entities and relationships within the organization rather than attempting to analyze or model the functions and processes. The thinking behind this is that the overall structure of an organization changes little over time. Once an accurate data model of this is established and incorporated in a computer-based data store it will be the foundation on which applications programs can be written. These programs will carry out the various data processes required by the organization. Applications change over time. It is therefore sensible to analyze and design around a common database rather than on the shifting sands of changing functions.

● **Logical has priority over physical:** The emphasis is placed on building a logical data model of the organization prior to taking any physical decisions on how this is to be incorporated in a physical database, how many records there are, what file sizes will be and so on. The logical model is later translated into a form suitable for implementation, using one of the commercial database systems.

● **Top-down:** Data analysis approaches stress the need to concentrate on an overall analysis prior to detail. For example, in entity–relationship modelling the important entities and their relationships are first identified. The structure of the model is then specified. Only at a later stage will attention be directed to attributes. This is to be contrasted with a bottom-up strategy in which the concentration would be on the attributes at an earlier stage.

● **Documentation:** All approaches based on data analysis emphasize the importance of structure. The clearest way of revealing structure is pictorially. Diagrammatic representations play an important role in data analysis at the early stages.

The impetus to develop methodologies based around data analysis came from a number of areas. Modern commercial databases allow the sharing of common data by different applications and users within the organization. They also allow for considerable complexity in storage structures and retrieval. It is crucial to ensure that the best use is made of these facilities. Entity–relationship modelling and other data analysis modelling approaches assist the design of the complex models suitable for modern database management systems.

Another reason for the emphasis on data analysis is the recognition that data structures, if they are to be enduring, should mirror the real world of the organization. Organizations have complex structures. It requires more than a piecemeal approach to deal adequately with the modelling task.

15.1.3 Traditional approaches

What is often called the 'traditional approach' to systems analysis and design has played a major historical part in the development of early computerized data-processing systems. Methodologies based on this approach (such as the National Computing Centre (NCC) methodology) in the UK have been successful in developing many systems. They are still in widespread use today. These methodologies arose out of the need to systematize the process of analysis and design. Characteristics of these traditional approaches are:

● **Emphasis on detailed analysis and design:** Little attempt is made to establish an overall analysis or evaluation of the existing system prior to the development of a computerized replacement. The traditional approach is associated with the computerization of an existing system rather than the development of a new one that is more likely to meet user information requirements.

find it difficult to get off the ground. They assume that there is no difficulty in defining the existing and desired states of the system. When this assumption fails they provide no help in further analysis.

2. Hard systems approaches are mathematically/logically based. This limits the range of problems that can be tackled. Moreover, they assume that factors and models to be used in remedying problems also have this orientation. Decision tables, entity–relationship models and logic flowcharts are all cases in point from the area of systems analysis and design. However, it goes further than this. As one might expect from their antecedents in engineering, operational research techniques play an important part in suggested aids to decision making. Linear programming, queuing theory, Monte Carlo simulation and statistical sampling theory are used. These all pre-suppose that a mathematical model is useful in the decision process. However, problems in an organization may not be amenable to this type of approach. For example, a failure to coordinate production schedules may not be the result of poor information flows and scheduling, which can be solved by the use of a comput-erized system with computer-based operational research scheduling techniques. It may be caused by disagreement about the role of production and sales within the organiza-tion, personality conflicts, individual interests not coinciding with company objectives or any number of things. To use a hard approach is already to straightjacket the problem as one soluble by mathematical/logical techniques when it may not be.

3. The emphasis on mathematics and logic presupposes the importance of quantitat-ive information as compared to qualitative or vague information, intuitions, and psychological models of decision making. This may be acceptable when there is clear agreement on problems and solutions and the task is seen as one of moving from the given undesirable state to a new desired state. In other cases, though, the range of useful types of information is broader. Closely connected to this is the assumption that quantitative information equals objectivity whereas qualitative in-formation equals subjectivity. From the scientific outlook the latter is to be avoided. Whether subjectivity is to be avoided is a moot point. However, the proponents of a hard approach often ignore the fact that the requirement to provide quantitative information where none is accurately known often leads to unjustified assumptions being made. Claims to objectivity can then be seen to be spurious.

4. Closely allied to the previous points is the lack of recognition given to the organ-izational context in which a problem lies. Hard approaches tend to concentrate on data, processes, functions, tasks, decisions, data stores, flows, entities and relation-ships. They do not pay any attention to the social or organizational aspects of the system.

5. The emphasis is always on linear problem solving: there is a problem, it is solved, the next problem arises, it is solved and so on. This leads to a reactive approach to management. An alternative is an ongoing developmental approach that stresses proactive attitudes.

6. The dichotomy between the client and the expert can act as a barrier to successful systems analysis and development. This may happen in a number of ways. There may be communication problems. The client is an expert in the area for which systems analysis is being carried out. The expert is probably from a technical background, so they do not share the same language. Tools used in structured approaches help

to overcome this limitation. By stressing the logical aspects of the system and using diagrammatic tools that illustrate this, technicalities that may confuse the clients are removed. There is though a more subtle effect of this dichotomy. The expert is seen to be outside the problem area. He or she observes it objectively. Not so. Once involved, the analyst interacts with the system – particularly the people operating within it. The analyst brings his or her own set of experiences, knowledge, prejudices and background to bear on the problem area.

These comments on hard approaches to systems analysis and design are not meant to be damning. Rather, they illustrate the need for caution before adopting a hard methodology. In particular, the applicability of the chosen methodology should first be established. Areas that are unstructured, with a lack of agreement on problems and what would count as a solution, are just those areas that are not suited to a technical approach to systems analysis and design.

15.2 'Soft' approaches to systems analysis and design

Hard approaches to systems analysis and design have been very successful at developing computer systems that, viewed from a technical perspective, are efficient and effective information providers. However, there have been cases when new information systems have not had user acceptance or seem to be misplaced as a solution to a spurious problem. These difficulties have led to developments that challenge the assumptions made by approaches deriving from a 'hard' view of systems.

Two approaches are outlined in this chapter. Each perceives different weaknesses in the approaches considered so far and so each has a different remedy. They both identify the presence of people in a system as leading to complications not acknowledged by proponents of hard approaches.

Checkland's approach recognizes that different people have different perceptions of problems and of the systems within which they lie. It is therefore a mistake to assume automatically that there is agreement on 'where we are now' or even on 'where we want to go'. Rather, problems are much less structured, much fuzzier than supporters of hard approaches would have us believe.

The socio-technical approach stresses the recognition that computerized information systems are part of interacting social and technical systems. If one part is changed, for example the technical system, by means of computerization, then the other will be affected. It is important to realize that the social and technical systems (the socio-technical system) cannot be designed independently of each another. One way to ensure that sufficient weight is given to the social aspects of the system is to involve users in the process of analysis and design. This undercuts the assumption of 'hard' approaches that the end product of design is a purely technical system. It also challenges the assumption of the necessity or desirability of the expert/user division.

15.2.1 Checkland's approach

In order to understand the rationale for Checkland's approach it is helpful to look at some of the underlying philosophical assumptions made.

First, the assumption is that problems are not regarded as being 'out there' in a realist sense. There are no objectively given problems. Different people may see different problems in the 'same' situation.

It is, perhaps, misleading to talk of the 'situation' as though it were objectively given. A situation is a combination of the external world together with the way that it seems to the observer. This will be influenced by the background and beliefs of that observer. For example, an experienced doctor will unconsciously interpret an X-ray photograph and see shapes of importance within it. However, to the untrained observer there is very little of substance. Or again, different cultural backgrounds interpret voice inflections in different ways. So the same sentence uttered by two different people may be variously interpreted as being hostile or friendly.

Not only will different people disagree over the 'neutral' description of a situation but they will also disagree as to its problematic nature. For example, the student may regard end-of-course failure rates in professional exams as a problem – another hurdle to cross on the way to a career. A qualified professional, however, may regard them as a non-problematic essential for the maintenance of small numbers of qualified professionals. This guarantees high incomes for those who are qualified. The professional institute setting the exams has a third view – the failure rates are taken as evidence that standards are being maintained.

It should be clear that not only may different people see the same situation as problematic in different ways but some may not see any problem at all. One man's meat is another man's poison. What determines an individual's view of a situation is the nexus of beliefs, desires and interests that the individual has. It is the combination of beliefs about 'what is' and 'what ought to be' that is so important on determining a situation as 'problematic' for an individual.

Second, just as problems are intellectual constructs so are solutions. Two people may agree on a problem and yet disagree as to what constitutes a solution. Take an examination for example. Very high failure rates on a course may be regarded as problematic by both students and the course director. Students see the solution in terms of easier examinations and more effective teaching. The course director sees the need to raise entry qualifications.

The third assumption states that problems very rarely come singly, neatly packaged and ready for a solution. It is more likely that there are several interlocking problems. Moreover, if one problem is solved this may generate a problem elsewhere. Problems are often messy and not amenable to simple solutions such as the installation of a computerized information system. This is another reason why the term 'problem situation' rather than 'problem' is used to describe what confronts the analyst.

Fourth, it is obvious from these points that it is important that the problem area is investigated and analyzed prior to any decisions on the desirability of computer systems. The role of the systems analyst is seen, at least initially, as much more akin to a therapist than a technical computer expert. The analyst encourages participants in the existing system to examine their own perceptions of the system and its interconnections with others, its objectives, their role within it and the role of others. This learning process is an essential prerequisite for development. It is recognized at the outset that a computer system may not be suitable for the organization or, at least, not a total solution.

The final assumption implies that the analyst cannot be divorced from the system and the participants involved in it owing to the early therapeutic role of the analyst.

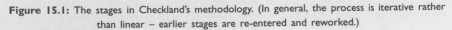

Figure 15.1: The stages in Checkland's methodology. (In general, the process is iterative rather than linear – earlier stages are re-entered and reworked.)

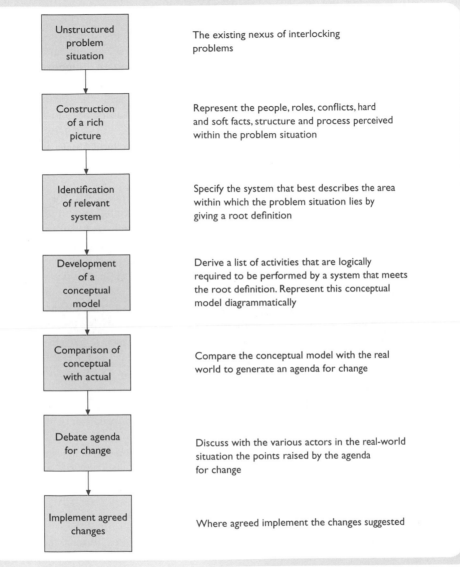

Unstructured problem situation	The existing nexus of interlocking problems
Construction of a rich picture	Represent the people, roles, conflicts, hard and soft facts, structure and process perceived within the problem situation
Identification of relevant system	Specify the system that best describes the area within which the problem situation lies by giving a root definition
Development of a conceptual model	Derive a list of activities that are logically required to be performed by a system that meets the root definition. Represent this conceptual model diagrammatically
Comparison of conceptual with actual	Compare the conceptual model with the real world to generate an agenda for change
Debate agenda for change	Discuss with the various actors in the real-world situation the points raised by the agenda for change
Implement agreed changes	Where agreed implement the changes suggested

The methodology

Checkland's methodology (Figure 15.1) evolved out of the area of management consultancy. The analyst is not an expert in any particular area, so is therefore not employed to give technical advice. Rather, the analyst should be thought of as a change agent or therapist who is able to stimulate others to new perceptions of the problem situation. The approach is particularly effective compared with other methodologies in cases where there are messy problems. The stages are now outlined. Although progression is from one stage to the next there is not the same rigidity and control over stage exits as in the structured life-cycle approach. Stages may be re-entered once left. The process is iterative rather than linear.

Stage 1. The development of rich pictures: The first task of the analyst is to become acquainted with the problem situation, and an attempt is made to build up a **rich picture** of the problem situation. This is a cartoon of the important influences and constituents of the problem situation. The analyst collects information to incorporate within this picture. Not only is hard information collected, such as facts and other quantitative data, but also soft information is obtained. Here are included the participants in the problem situation, any worries, fears and aspirations they have that are thought by the analyst to be relevant, conflicts and alliances between departments or individuals, and hunches and guesses. In particular the analyst is looking for structure, key processes, and the interaction between process and structure.

It is important that the analyst does not impose a systems structure on the problem situation at this stage. The analyst will be interested in determining meaningful roles that individuals fulfil, such as boss or counsellor. In drawing the rich picture the analyst will identify primary tasks and issues and will attempt to see varying perspectives. At this stage the analyst should take particular care not to pigeon-hole the problem, say as a marketing problem or a communications problem. This will limit the types of change that may ultimately be suggested.

Three important roles in the problem situation are identified. The **client** is the individual who is paying the analyst. The **problem owner** will be the individual who is responsible, or the area within which the problem situation arises. It may not be initially clear who the owner is. Different perceptions of the situation will assume different problem owners (we are all familiar with the conversation 'that's your problem', 'no it's yours'). The analyst may need to experiment with several individuals in order to establish a realistic problem owner. The **problem solver** is normally the analyst. These three roles may be held by three different people or they may coincide in two individuals. It is common for the client and problem owner to be the same person.

An example of a rich picture is shown in Figure 15.2. It corresponds to the Kismet case study covered in Chapter 10. There have been a few added details in order to make the problem area more unstructured, and the picture therefore richer, as the original case as presented was fairly 'cut and dried'.

The purpose of a rich picture is:

- To help visualize a complex mess of interacting people, roles, threats, facts, observations and so on. Its purpose is to facilitate understanding of the problem situation.

- To avoid imposing a rigid structure on the appreciation of the problem situation. A systems perspective is to be avoided at this early stage. It would tend to force perception of the problem through systems concepts such as inputs/outputs, systems objectives, feedback and the like. This may not be appropriate for the situation.

- To aid an investigative approach by the analyst towards the problem situation.

- To act as a communication tool between participants. This will aid a consensus perception of the problem situation. It is all to easy for the fact that different participants have importantly divergent views of the situation to go unnoticed.

Figure 15.2: A rich picture of Kismet.

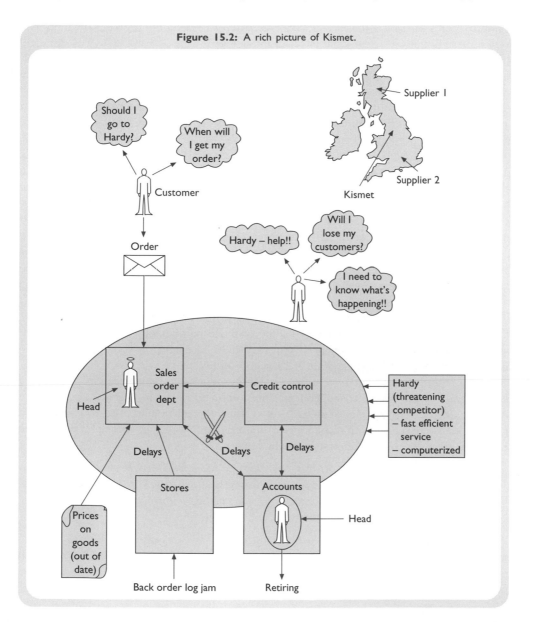

It should be clear, already, that there is considerable divergence between this approach and the structured approach taken in Chapters 9–14. There, the initial stages were restricted to the identification of key functions and processes, key entities in the organization and their formal relationships.

Stage 2. Identification of the relevant system and the root definition: The rich picture is a pictorial representation of the problem situation. In order to progress it is necessary to view the problem from a systemic point of view. This is where the idea of a **relevant**

system comes in. This is the most appropriate way of viewing the problem situation as a system. It is not always clear what the relevant system is. The relevant system is extracted from the rich picture. There is no one correct answer to the question 'what is the relevant system?' Several suggestions may be made. The one that is accepted is agreed by negotiation, often between the problem owner and the problem solver. This relevant system should be the one that provides most insight into the problem situation and is most appropriate for stimulating understanding and change in the organization – the ultimate goal of the methodology.

In the case of Kismet the task is probably straightforward. It is a system for effectively and efficiently processing orders. Other cases where things are less structured may require consideration of several 'relevant' systems before one that fits becomes apparent. For instance, a local technical college might be regarded alternatively as 'a system for educating pupils in order to meet the labour need of the local area' or 'a system for removing local unemployed adolescents at their potentially most disruptive and destructive age from the streets'. Or again the owner/manager of a small business may regard it as 'a system for maintaining a stable financial income', 'a system for maintaining a stable and interesting employment for himself and his employees', or 'a system for providing a valued community service'.

Generally, relevant systems are issue-based or primary-task-based. When agreed on, they may come as quite a revelation to some of those participating in the problem situation. Identification of the relevant system may help cast light on the otherwise seemingly non-understandable behaviour of their colleagues.

Just to name the relevant system gives a highly generalized specification of the area associated with the problem situation. It is important to be more precise. This is done by means of developing a **root definition** of the relevant system. The root definition gives a precise description of the *essence* of the relevant system. A root definition of the Kismet sales order processing system might be:

> *A business function within Kismet operated by sales and credit control staff to accept and process orders provided by customers, transforming them into validated requests to stock and notifications into accounts, within speed and cost constraints set by Kismet management.*

Producing a root definition is not a mechanical task. It can only be achieved through trial and error. However, there is a checklist, called by its mnemonic CATWOE, which every adequate root definition should satisfy. All the CATWOE components should be present (or at least their absence needs to be justified and acknowledged).

1. **Customers:** These are the group of people or body who are served by or who benefit from the system. In the Kismet case it is not only the customers of Kismet but also the stores and accounts functions.

2. **Actors:** These are the people, or rather types of people, who carry out the essential activities within the relevant system.

3. **Transformation process:** This is what the system does – that is, the process that converts inputs into outputs.

4. **Weltanschauung:** The Weltanschauung or 'world view' that is relevant to the system is specified somewhere in the root definition. In the case of Kismet this is indicated by the assumption of performance according to cost and time constraints.

5. **Owners:** The owners of the system are those to whom the system is answerable. They have power to change the system or make it cease to exist. In the case of Kismet this will probably be the management of the company.

6. **Environment:** This is the environment in which the relevant system is located.

The purpose of identifying the relevant system and deriving a root definition is to concentrate on the *essence* of the system covering the problem situation. It is then easier to proceed to develop a logical model of a system that meets this description.

Stage 3. Building a conceptual model: Given that the relevant system has been identified and a root definition has been provided the next stage of the methodology is to develop a conceptual model. This is a logical model of the key activities or processes that must be carried out in order to satisfy the root definition of the system. It is not a model of the real world. It may bear no resemblance to what occurs in the problem situation and is not derived by observing it. Rather, it consists of what is logically required by the root definition. The distinction between what *must* be done in order to satisfy the root definition and what *is* actually done in the system is of fundamental importance. Its recognition is at the heart of the usefulness of the methodology in stimulating organizational learning and change.

The key activities are shown in the conceptual model in Figure 15.3. Each of these key activities themselves represent a subsystem that would carry the activity out – for example, the subsystem to monitor and control performance. These high-level activities give rise to second-level activities that must be performed in order that the high-level activities can be executed. For instance, monitoring and control requires collection of the standard, collection of the sensed data, comparison between the two, and taking the necessary action. This gives rise to second-level conceptual models that can replace the relevant part of the first-level model.

When completed, the conceptual model is tested against the formal requirement of a general systems model (a systems model was covered in Chapter 1). Examples of typical questions that need to be asked are:

- Does the model illustrate an activity that has a continuous purpose?
- Is there a measure of performance?
- Is there some kind of decision-making process or role?
- Are there subsystems that are connected?
- Is there a boundary?
- Is there some guarantee of long-term stability?

Stage 4. Compare the conceptual model with the real world: The previous two stages have attempted to build up some ideal model of what should happen in a system that carries out the essential activities required by the agreed root decision of the relevant system. Now is the time to see what actually happens.

The rich picture provides a good representation of the real situation and it is against this that the conceptual model must be compared. Alternatively, the conceptual model may be compared directly with the problem situation. Differences should be highlighted as possible points for discussion. Typical of the questions considered by the analyst at

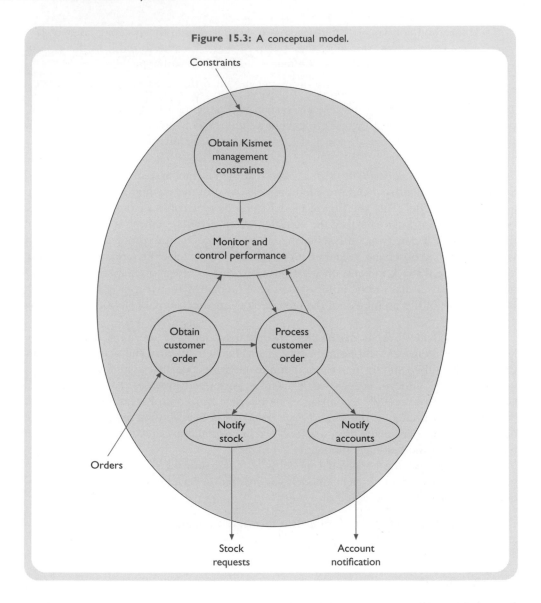

Figure 15.3: A conceptual model.

this stage are 'Why is there a discrepancy between the conceptual model and the real world at this point?', 'Does this activity in the conceptual model really occur?' The point of this investigation is not to criticize the way that things are actually done, but rather to derive a list of topics – an **agenda for change** – that can be discussed with the actors in the problem situation.

Stage 5. Debate the agenda: This stage involves a structured discussion of the points raised on the agenda with the participants in the problem situation. It is important to realize that this is a consciousness-raising exercise as much as anything. The analyst should restrict discussion to changes that are systemically desirable and culturally feasible. That is, the changes should not run counter to the thinking that has gone into the selection of the relevant system and the root definition. Nor should they ignore the particular organizational culture within which the participants have lived and worked. The aim is to obtain agreement on a list of changes to be implemented.

Stage 6. Implementing agreed changes: Checkland is not very specific on how this stage is to be carried out. This is understandable in that a large range of changes might be agreed as feasible and desirable. It may be the case that a need for a computerized information system that will serve specific functions has been identified. In this case it is probable that formal information modelling and structured analysis and design techniques will take over. However, the necessity of other types of change may be agreed. For instance, it may be thought necessary to change aspects of the organizational structure such as departmental responsibilities, the degree of centralization, or even the physical layout. Changes in overall policies, strategies or procedures may be agreed. The process of analysis may have revealed divergent attitudes concerning the problem situation. The outcome of the debate on the agenda may be an agreement to foster changed attitudes within the problem situation.

The stages in Checkland's methodology are not necessarily carried out in a linear fashion. It is often necessary to re-enter an earlier stage for revision. For instance, when comparing the conceptual model with the real world it may become apparent that the relevant system has not been identified correctly. This will require backtracking. There is another important way in which Checkland's methodology is not linear. It would be a mistake to assume that once the stages have been executed the problem in the problem situation has been resolved. It is not a problem-solving methodology, but rather it aims at *improvement* of situations through organizational understanding, learning and change.

15.2.2   Participation in socio-technical analysis and design

The socio-technical approach grew out of work started in the Tavistock Institute for Behavioural Research in the 1950s. This derived from the introduction of new technology in the coalmines. The approach recognized that successful introduction of new technology required the identification of social needs and goals as well as technical/economic objectives. The underlying assumption was that a system will only function effectively if human needs such as job satisfaction are acknowledged.

In the 1970s the socio-technical approach began to be adopted in various guises for the development of computer systems within organizational environments. The common element in these approaches is the recognition of the interdependence of four factors – technology, tasks, people and the organization (Figure 15.4). If one of these is altered, for example the introduction of new computerized technology, it will have an impact on all the others. It therefore makes sense to take account of all aspects of the socio-technical system in computerization so that harmony may be maintained.

One socio-technical approach, due to Mumford (and colleagues) (Land and Hirscheim, 1983) sees the best way of obtaining this harmony as involving users participatively in the process of analysis and design. This idea meshes neatly with the general trend towards industrial democracy experienced over the last 20 years, together with the increasing acceptance of humanistic values as applied to the workplace.

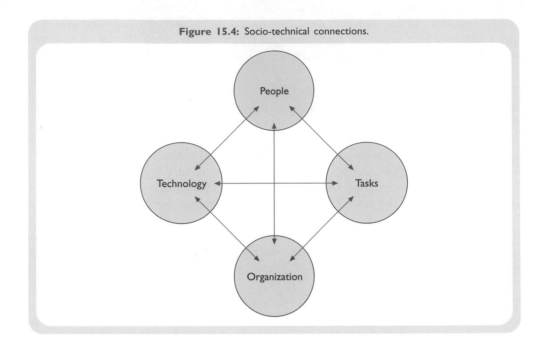

Figure 15.4: Socio-technical connections.

Benefits of participation

From the management point of view, participation in analysis and design enables valuable knowledge and skills of the workforce to be incorporated in the final system. The analyst may be a technical expert in the area of computers but is unlikely to be familiar with the organization, tasks and people within which the final system must fit. Participation is seen as a more effective way of obtaining this experience than the 'classic' approaches such as the formal interview or questionnaire.

Also, from the management perspective, it is more likely that users will show commitment to and confidence in the final installed system if they have had a hand in its development. This stems from two sources. First, it is difficult for an individual to participate in the design of a system and not establish a psychological investment in and therefore commitment to it. Second, the continued presence of the participants in the process of analysis and design educates them in an appreciation of the final system and also allays their fears of its likely effects. Users may fear job de-skilling, removal of job satisfaction or their ability to cope with the new system. Even if groundless, these fears lead to resistance to the implementation of the new system and ultimately to its ineffective use or failure. Participation allays these fears by providing information as the system is developed.

From a 'worker' point of view participation can be seen as a way of maintaining control over the introduction of new technology. By being involved at all stages of the process participants can ensure that jobs and job satisfaction are maintained. It also serves as a public recognition of the importance of participants' knowledge and skills in the workplace.

Issues involved in participation

Several issues are involved in participation:

1. What role do participants play in the design process?
2. At which stage in the life cycle are participants involved?
3. Which groups should participate in the design process?
4. How are participants to be selected?

These questions are dealt with below:

1. *What role do participants play in the design process?* Three different levels of involvement can be identified for participants. These correspond to deepening degrees of commitment to the participative approach.

   (a) *Consultative*: The participants are consulted for their views and understanding by an expert. The expert analysts note these responses and take account of them at their discretion. This is little different from the 'traditional' approach towards interview as a source of information about the system. Where this differs in a socio-technical approach is that the analyst will not only be interested in the technical aspects of analysis and design but also in a complete socio-technical design.

   (b) *Representative*: Selected users from relevant interest groups join the design teams. Their views are taken into account though it is still recognized that the analysts are the 'experts' and ultimately they are responsible for design.

   (c) *Consensus*: With consensus participation the interest groups take over responsibility for the analysis and design. Analysts are now regarded as just another interest group whose responsibility it is to provide technical knowledge and ensure that the design is technically sound.

2. *At which stage in the life cycle are participants involved?* This may happen at any or all stages of the project. Major stages are as follows:

   (a) Project initiation – it is unlikely that management will allow participation at this stage. It is traditionally regarded as the province of strategic decision making.
   (b) Definition of systems objectives.
   (c) Description and analysis of the existing system.
   (d) Identification of problem areas within the existing system.
   (e) Suggestion, design and evaluation of alternative solutions to the problems identified in (d).
   (f) Detailed design of the human work (social) and computer (technical) systems.
   (g) Preparation of systems specification.
   (h) Implementation of the human work and computer systems.
   (i) Evaluation and monitoring of the working system.

3. *Which groups should participate in the design process?* The answer to this is 'any group that will be significantly affected by the computer system'. This may include outside groups in the early stages (such as watchdog committees for the nationalized industries) as well as groups from within the organization. Examples of the latter are trade unions, clerical and shopfloor workers, middle management and programmers and analysts.

4. *How are participants to be selected?* Interest groups may elect their own members or participants may be chosen by management. Both approaches may be politically sensitive. With the former method it may be the case that only those with the most strongly militant anti-technology views are put forward whereas with the latter, management's buddies may be chosen.

The presupposition so far has been that participation is to be thought of as being limited to analysis and design. There is no reason why participants should not be involved in the decision-making process. This though is unlikely to be agreed by management at the major decision points – when global terms of reference are being established for the project or when stop/go decisions are needed. At other points – fixing of local terms of reference or choice amongst alternative solutions – the decision-making process is almost invariably interwoven with analysis and design. Then participation in decision making goes hand in hand with analysis and design.

Methodology

In order to gain the benefits promised by participation it is necessary to have an effective methodology. Without this those involved in participation will be directionless. The methodology outlined here is due to Enid Mumford. It involves various procedures such as variance analysis, job satisfaction analysis and future analysis to aid the participative approach: these procedures are briefly described. However, it does not preclude the use of other tools or techniques, such as data flow diagrams or entity–relationship modelling, particularly in the latter stages of systems design.

The important components in the methodology advocated by Mumford are now discussed.

(A) The diagnosis of needs and problems: Three diagnostic tools are used here. They are variance analysis, job satisfaction analysis and future analysis.

1. **Variance analysis:** This involves identifying weak parts of the existing system that produce operational problems. The design group will identify key operations within a department and note those areas where there is a systematic deviation of the results of those operations from the standards set. This may often occur on the boundaries of a system where there are coordination problems. Variances may affect one another; therefore it is important to reveal connections and dependencies. A variance matrix may be of assistance here. In systems design the aim is to control these variances where they originate rather than by control at a later stage.

2. **Job satisfaction analysis:** The amount of job satisfaction obtained in a work situation may be explained in terms of the fit between what the participants expect from their jobs and what they are obtaining. Three important needs should be considered. These are connected with the personality of the individual, the personal values held by that individual and the need for competence and efficiency. If systems are designed with these in mind job satisfaction will be improved. This is a necessary condition to ensure that the socio-technical system will function effectively.

3. **Future analysis:** Large systems take a long time to design. If a large project is undertaken it may be three or four years or even longer from initiation to the start of the successful operation of the new system. The life of the new system will need

to be more than three or four years in order to recover the costs of the project. This implies that in analysis and design the time horizon with which the project is concerned is many years. In order to achieve a system that will meet the needs of the future then the future has to be predicted. This becomes more difficult and uncertain the greater the forecasting period. Future changes may not be just in volumes of transactions processed or types of information required of the information system. Changes in the economic climate, new technology and changes in organizational structure such as decentralization or merging of companies will all have a significant impact on the satisfaction of future needs by the system currently being designed.

Many traditional approaches do not take the need to design for the future seriously and have consequently produced systems suffering from the 'dinosaur syndrome'. The requirement of a system to meet future demands can be achieved by:

(a) Predicting the future by modelling and simulation. The predictions are then catered for in current design.

(b) Designing a system that is robust. This means that the system has inbuilt redundancy and flexibility to deal with uncertain future requirements. The system is also designed to be modular for easy adaptation.

(c) A structured approach to future analysis. This involves the design team(s) drawing up a list of factors of relevance to the system that may be the subject of change. The likelihood of each of the factors changing over the lifetime of the system is then evaluated. The impact of these changes on the system is then assessed. The components of the system that are subject to these effects should be identified so that the stage of design can take account of them.

(B) The consideration of the groups affected by the system: The groups that will be affected by the system are identified. The goals of these are then established by consultation with company policy and the diagnosis of user needs and job satisfaction analysis. An attempt is made to establish the weightings to be associated with each goal. Ideally, this would be by consensus between the various groups as a result of negotiation.

(C) Socio-technical approach to the analysis and design of the system: The purpose of socio-technical analysis and design is to produce an end system consisting of social and technical structures that satisfies both technical and social goals. This proceeds by using a general stage that is followed by a detailed one.

Initially, alternative systems strategies are suggested. The effects of each of these are forecasted for the period of the planning horizon. The impact of each strategy is then compared against both the goals of the system and the predicted performance of the existing socio-technical system up to the planning horizon. Optimistic and pessimistic estimations are made for each strategy by changing the values of uncertain parameters. The strategy with the best fit to the social and technical goals is selected.

Detailed design progresses through social and technical analysis. In technical analysis logically integrated sets of tasks, called **unit operations**, are identified. These unit operations consist of tasks that are logically cohesive in transforming an input into an output in preparation for the next unit operation or stage. For example, a unit operation would be the batching, error checking and input of sales data into a daybook preparatory to updating the sales ledger. Each design group receives one or more operations within its scope. In the analysis of the social aspects of the work system the relationships between individuals and the roles they play are investigated. The results of job satisfaction analysis would be used at this point. Each workgroup has the responsibility for eliminating variances that have been discovered in variance analysis. Within the workgroup the existing and future users of the system are of particular importance in the development of the social system and the earlier stages of technical analysis. The impact of the computer analysts is felt most during the latter stages of technical design.

(D) Implementation: Once designed the system may be implemented. This may occur as a linear process or may take the form of prototyping. In prototyping an experimental smaller version of the system is built. This will not have the full functionality of the final system and will probably not be technically efficient in a computing sense. It does however enable an evaluation to be made of the extent to which it meets some of the social and technical goals of the design. This will provide a direction for improvement of the final system before any major expenditure has gone into its weaknesses. Indeed, several prototypes may be built before a satisfactory version on which the final design can be based is reached.

(E) Post-implementation evaluation: After the system has been installed and running some assessment of its performance in the light of its social and technical goals is made. This allows correction as part of normal ongoing maintenance or provides valuable knowledge that is relevant in the design of a future system.

In summary the participative approach differs from 'hard' approaches in a number of ways:

1. There is a recognition that technical systems cannot be treated independently of the social systems with which they interact.

2. Following from point 1, in the design of computer-based information systems the social system within which the work occurs must be the subject of analysis and design as much as the technical system itself. Without this harmonious design any resultant technical system is subject to a high risk of failure on the grounds of its inadequacy from a social point of view.

3. The current and the future users of the system possess a knowledge of existing work practices and deficiencies that makes their experience valuable in the process of analysis and design. In order to utilize this experience it is necessary to use a set of diagnostic procedures (job satisfaction analysis, variance analysis, and so on). The traditional role of the expert systems analyst is restricted to technical aspects of analysis and design.

4. Participation in analysis and design is a prerequisite for a successful implementation of technical systems as it reduces users' fears over the introduction of new technology.

5. There is an ethical commitment to the belief that users of technology and those affected by it have a right to express some say over the design and operation of these systems.

15.2.3 Checkland's methodology and the participative approach: reservations

Both Checkland's methodology and the participative socio-technical approach offer alternatives to the 'hard' approaches covered in previous chapters. How realistic are they? Although they both have their supporters there are serious questions that need to be addressed.

Checkland

The main criticism levelled at Checkland's methodology is directed at its lack of comprehensiveness, particularly at the later stages of analysis and design. This has led critics to argue that it is not a methodology that takes the analyst through the life cycle. The idea of a 'life cycle' is not one that fits well with Checkland's approach, though it is undeniable that the methodology is strongest in the early stages of problem identification and analysis. At the very least, proponents would argue that it explores possibilities for organizational learning and progress in problem situations that are neglected by 'hard' approaches. The methodology from this viewpoint is regarded more as a front-end approach to carry out the necessary problem analysis prior to the technical analysis that would imply a computerized system.

Another comment made on the methodology is that the analyst is not only in the position of attempting to understand an existing system, but is also required by the methodology, via root definitions and conceptual models, to be an originator of systems. Although this remark has some foundation it is not clear that it does not also apply to structured methods if properly carried out. In these, during the transition from analysis to systems design, there is always an element of assessing what needs to be done logically in order to perform a function, as well as analyzing what actually is done.

Although Checkland's methodology has been used commercially it does not have the same extensive track record as is associated with the structured methods covered in Chapters 9–14. This is not to say that there have been significant failures using the methodology but, rather, that the number of times on which it has been employed provide an insufficiently large sample from which to draw conclusions. It remains to be seen whether the methodology will have a lasting impact on approaches to analysis and design.

Participative socio-technical approaches

The participative element of this has been criticized from the point of view of its heavy cost. To involve users participatively in analysis and design places a great burden on the personnel within an organization. Proponents of the approach would not argue with this but would point out that the extra cost is more than justified by the production of systems that are accepted by and meet user needs – it produces effective and not merely technically efficient systems.

The emphasis on participation and the omission of specific tools is seen as a shortcoming by critics. However, the approach should be seen as setting a framework within which successful analysis and design can be carried out. It does not preclude the use of data flow diagrams, entity modelling or any other technique that aids analysis and design. Participation is seen as a recognition of the importance of implementing a system that meets socio-technical as well as purely technical goals.

There may be resistance to the use of participation in its fullest forms. From one quarter, management can see it as a way of losing managerial control; from another, analysts can view it as diminishing the importance of their status and roles. This is not an objection to the approach, but resistance to its use will weaken its effectiveness. So it is important that a commitment to participation is obtained from all parties involved.

Finally, in common with Checkland's methodology, there are too few cases in which the approach has been applied to judge its success from an empirical standpoint.

Both Checkland and those who have developed the participative approach have undoubtedly identified weaknesses in the universal applicability of 'hard' approaches. It remains to be seen whether their solutions will fulfil the promises they intend to keep.

15.3 CASE and object-oriented approaches to analysis and design

Systems analysis and design is not a static discipline. New approaches and methodologies are being produced regularly. Many of these are variations on old themes – the themes covered in the earlier parts of this chapter. Some, though, are different in nature. This section examines, amongst others, computer-aided software engineering and object-oriented analysis and design. **Computer-aided software engineering** (CASE) provides new tools for the speedy development of reliable computer systems. It is not uncommon for these to be based around object-oriented approaches to analysis and design. Object-oriented methods are having a large impact because they mesh with developments in other areas – particularly with object-oriented programming languages, object-oriented databases and, not least, CASE. Although prototyping has been covered earlier in connection with end-user computing and decision support systems its influence can be felt in other areas. In particular it may be used with the design of systems using CASE. While object-oriented methods currently have little in common with end-user computing there is a thread running through CASE and prototyping, which is likely to be emphasized in the coming years.

15.3.1 CASE (computer-aided software engineering)

The traditional cost curve for the design and development of a business information system locates most of the cost as falling within the area of implementation, particularly coding. Fourth-generation languages (4GLs) and other applications generation tools are an attempt to cut the cost in this area by enabling speedy development of systems through the automation of the production of code.

The success of this can be measured by the fact that it is now possible to build a system and, if it fails to meet user needs, to redevelop it quickly and cheaply. This, in essence, is the philosophy behind prototyping. A problem with the approach is that it diminishes the role of formal requirements specification and systems design. This may be acceptable or even desirable for small systems, particularly for decision support, but the approach cannot cope with larger projects unless considerable design effort has been undertaken.

Structured methodologies, developed in the late 1970s and early 1980s, and covered elsewhere in this book, were a significant improvement in approaches to systems analysis

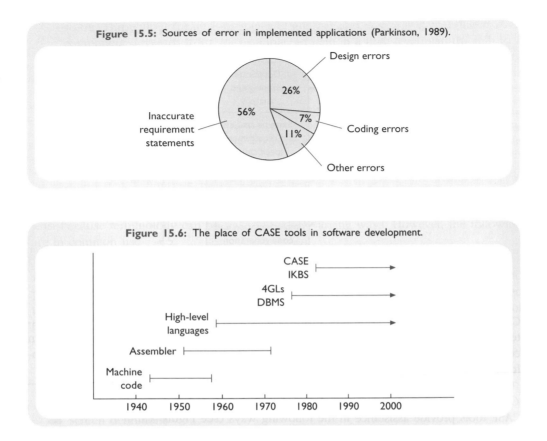

Figure 15.5: Sources of error in implemented applications (Parkinson, 1989).

Figure 15.6: The place of CASE tools in software development.

and design as compared with traditional methods. By clearly identifying stages, tools and techniques, and documentation standards, consistency and quality control were maintained for systems design projects. Design errors were significantly reduced.

However, as emphasized earlier in this chapter, requirements analysis, especially if linked to strategic requirements, is not readily accessible to structured techniques. Errors still occur as a result of inaccurate requirements analysis and specifications (see Figure 15.5). Changes in requirements mean lengthy redesign. But just as the computer itself has been utilized to assist the coding process (4GLs and application generators) the next step was to use the computer in the requirements specification, analysis and design process itself. This is the place of computer-aided software (systems) engineering (CASE) (Figure 15.6).

CASE automates various stages of the analysis and design process with the assistance of software tools. The CASE philosophy involves the use of these software tools working together with a methodology of systems analysis and design to:

- develop models that describe the business;
- aid in corporate planning;
- provide support for systems specification, documentation and design;
- aid in the implementation process.

Reverse engineering/re-engineering: Reverse engineering is the opposite of the standard implementation process for the production of code. Reverse engineering takes existing unstructured code as input (often COBOL programs) and produces restructured code as output. In particular the reverse engineering process produces output where:

- Common subroutines and modules are identified.
- Conditional branches and loops are simplified in structure.
- Blocks of code are collapsed into single-line statements for ease of reference and use.
- Subroutines are called in hierarchies.
- New source code is generated fitting the above conditions.

The need for reverse engineering is generated by the recognition that most software used within an organization needs enhancement from time to time. Unless this was produced using a rigorous methodology (and many systems still in use based on COBOL code were not) the task facing the programmer is immense. Complex spaghetti logic structures are impossible or, at best, time-consuming to disentangle and alter. If the software has undergone amendment the side-effects of code alteration are not easily identifiable. The software tends to be bug-ridden and difficult to validate. Reverse engineering creates code that is structured and easily amendable. It thus enables existing software to be enhanced rather than abandoned when update is necessary.

CASE benefits

CASE has grown in use over the last decade and is predicted to continue to increase in importance over the next decade. Some of the benefits of CASE are as follows:

1. *Enhancement of existing applications*: This can occur in two ways. First, systems produced using CASE tools can be rejuvenated when required by altering the systems specifications, already incorporated in the previous use of CASE, to take account of new needs. These can then be fed into back-end CASE tools to produce new code. The process is considerably quicker than attempting alterations via manually held systems specifications. Second, by the use of reverse engineering tools existing applications can be recast in a way that makes them suitable for amendment.

2. *Complete, accurate and consistent design specifications*: Most errors in the development of a new system occur in the systems specification stage. Most of these are not picked up until acceptance testing by users has taken place. CASE, by the use of computer specification tools and a central information repository, forces certain aspects of consistency and completeness on the design process.

3. *Reducing human effort*: CASE tools reduce human effort in analysis and design by offloading development work onto computers.

    Diagramming and charting tools cut the development time, especially when it is considered that each diagram may have to undergo several versions before completion.

    By keeping track of the development process CASE tools can relieve the human of considerable project management burdens. These tools keep note of authors, versions of models and a calendar. CASE tools also provide for consistency and completeness checking across various stages of the development process. They do this by tracking entities, process, data definitions, diagrams and other things that would otherwise take up much human effort.

Back-end CASE tools significantly reduce the human programming requirement by generating source and object code, and database definitions.

4. *Integration of development*: CASE tools, particularly I-CASE tools, encourage integration of the development process from the early stages of corporate analysis through information systems specification to code implementation. This is a trend that has been emerging in paper-based methodologies and it is now mirrored in CASE tools and methodologies. It is based on a recognition that the design of an information system is not merely technical issue deriving from a clear understanding of where we are now and where we want to go, but rather an activity that has to link and translate corporate information systems requirements into deliverable systems.

5. *Speed*: CASE tools speed the development process for a project. The tools also allow considerable interactive input from systems developers during the process. This is compatible with a prototyping approach to systems development.

6. *Links to object-oriented analysis*: Object-oriented analysis and design is fast becoming the dominant design approach of the 1990s. Object-oriented methods are particularly suited to incorporation in CASE tools. Central to any CASE approach is a central information repository, which can be viewed as information on objects.

15.3.2   Object-oriented analysis and design

Data analysis and structured process analysis have been highly influential in generating commercial methodologies centred around one or both approaches. However, some of the difficulties experienced in analysis and design using these perspectives are rooted in the assumption that an organization can be understood separately in terms of processes that manipulate data and in terms of objects on which data is stored. This separation between processes and objects, as practitioners of object-oriented analysis and design would claim, is ill founded.

It is suggested that our understanding of the world is based on objects that have properties, stand in relationships to other objects, and take part in operations. For example, we understand a motor car in terms not just of its static properties and relationships (is a Ford, has four wheels) but also in terms of the operations in which it takes part (acceleration, transportation of people). In a business context an order is not merely an object that has an order number, date, an item number ordered, a quantity ordered, but also takes part in operations – is placed by a customer, generates a stock requisition. This notion of object is central to an understanding of object-oriented analysis.

From the perspective of programming rather than analysis, objects and object types were a natural development out of the need to define types of things together with permissible operations performable on them. In early programming languages there were only a few types of object (data types). Examples were integer and string. Certain operations were permissible on integers, such as addition, but not on strings. Other operations were defined for strings, such as concatenation, but not for integers. Later the ability to define many different data types, together with their permissible operations, became incorporated in languages. This meshed with an object-oriented approach to analysis.

Essential concepts

Object: An **object** is any thing on which we store data together with the operations that are used to alter that data. An **object type** is a category of object. For instance an object might be Bill Smith, which is an instance of the object type *employee*. Another object is order#1234, which is an instance of the object type *order*.

A **method** specifies the way in which an object's data is manipulated – the way in which an **operation** is carried out. For instance, the sales tax on an invoice might be produced from a method that takes the sales amount and calculates a percentage of this. The important point is that the object consists not only of the data but also of the operations that manipulate it. This is one of the important features that distinguishes an object from an entity as used in entity–relationship modelling.

Encapsulation: The data held on an object is hidden from the user of that object. How then is data retrieved? All data operations and access to data are handled through methods. Packaging the data so that the data is hidden from users is known as **encapsulation**. The data is also hidden from other objects.

In implementation the methods are not considered to be packaged with the object but rather with the object type, as the same method for handling a certain type of data applies to all objects of that type. This corresponds well with object-oriented languages, which store the method as program code with the object type (or **object class** as it is known). See Figure 15.8.

Message: In order to retrieve data, or indeed carry out any operation on an object, it is necessary to send a **message** to the object. This message will contain the name of the object, the object type, the name of the operation and any other relevant parameters – for example, data values in the case of an update operation. When an operation is invoked by a message, that message may have come from another object or, more strictly, from an operation associated with that object. The first object is said to send a **request** to the second object. The request may result in a response if that is part of the purpose of the operation. This is the way objects communicate. See Figure 15.9.

Inheritance: Object types may have subtypes and supertypes. The types *dog* has as sub-types *Alsatian* and *poodle*, and as supertypes *carnivore* and *mammal*. All Alsatians are dogs. All dogs are mammals and all dogs are carnivores. Rover has certain properties by virtue of being an Alsatian; Fifi by virtue of being a poodle. Alsatians are said to **inherit** their dog characteristics by virtue of those properties being had by their supertype – *dog*. Similarly for poodles. Dogs inherit their mammalian characteristics, such as suckling young, from their supertype – *mammal*.

An object type will have some operations and methods specific to it. Others it will inherit from its supertype. This makes sense from the point of view of implementation, as it is only necessary to store a method at its highest level of applicability avoiding unnecessary duplication. *Manager* and *clerical staff* are two object types with the common supertype *employee*. An operation for employee might be *hire*. This would be inherited by both *manager* and *clerical staff*. The idea of inheritance is also covered in Chapter 16 on expert systems as it plays an important role in representing knowledge for the purposes of artificial intelligence. See Figure 15.10.

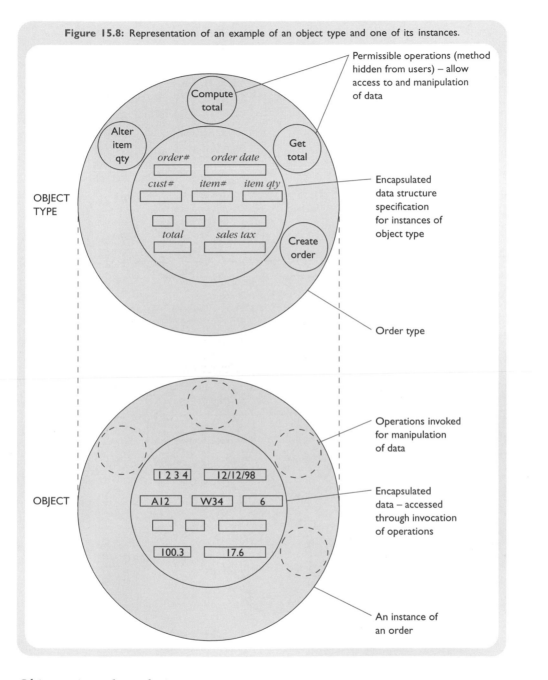

Figure 15.8: Representation of an example of an object type and one of its instances.

Object-oriented analysis

Modelling using object-oriented analysis differs from the approach adopted earlier in this book. Instead of the key components being entities and processes, the model built is composed of object types and what happens to them. The two key aspects of the analysis phase are the analysis of the structure of the object types (object structure analysis) and an analysis of their behaviour (object behaviour analysis).

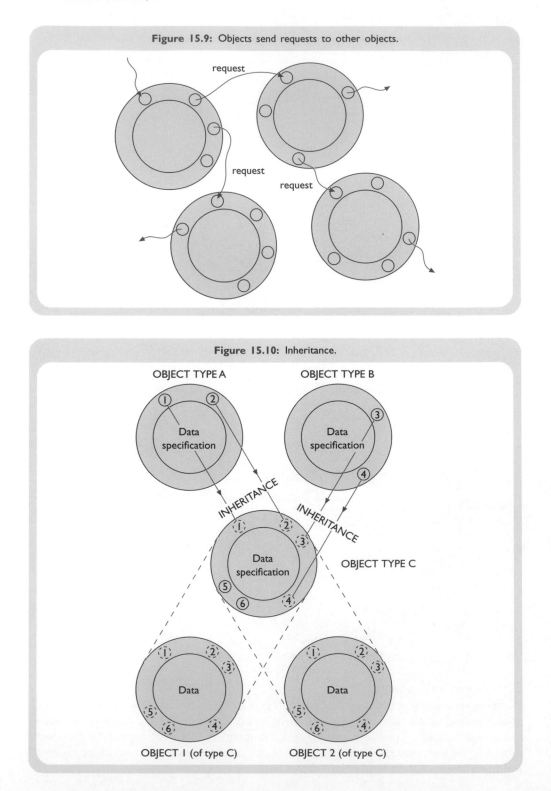

Figure 15.9: Objects send requests to other objects.

request

request

request

Figure 15.10: Inheritance.

OBJECT TYPE A

OBJECT TYPE B

Data specification

Data specification

INHERITANCE

INHERITANCE

OBJECT TYPE C

Data specification

Data

Data

OBJECT 1 (of type C)

OBJECT 2 (of type C)

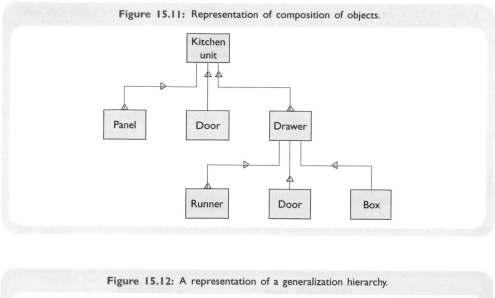

Figure 15.11: Representation of composition of objects.

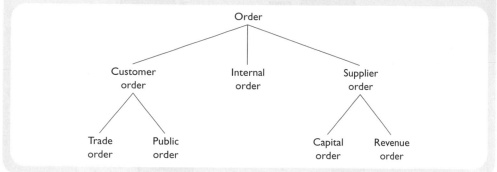

Figure 15.12: A representation of a generalization hierarchy.

Object structure analysis: The following tasks are undertaken:

● The object types and their relationships are identified. This is very similar to the process of establishing entities and their relationships. The diagrammatic conventions are similar. Two special types of relationship, described below, are separately identified – composition and generalization.

● Some types of object are complex, as they are composed of others. These compositions are identified. Each complex object can be manipulated as a single object composed of other objects. A typical representation is shown in Figure 15.11.

● Generalization hierarchies, used to indicate inheritance, are established and represented by diagrams as in Figure 15.12.

Object behaviour analysis: In object behaviour analysis event schemas are designed. These show the sequence of events that occur and how they affect the states of objects. When a customer places an order an event has occurred. This triggers off a series of events. The placing of the order leads to the creation of a company order. This is then checked.

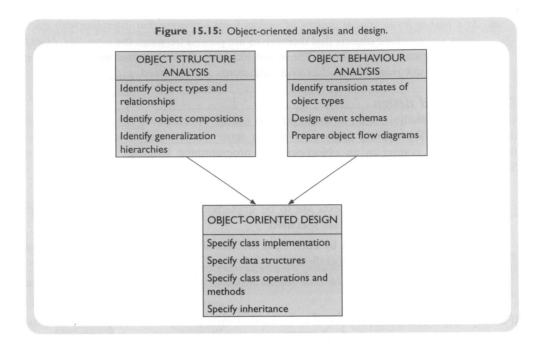

Figure 15.15: Object-oriented analysis and design.

of computer systems as proceeding through a number of iterative loops. At each stage some version of the system is prepared for assessment and alteration at a later stage.

Prototyping is treated extensively in Chapter 5 on decision support and end-user computing. Its application is further extended in Chapter 17 on the development of expert systems through prototyping. The reader is requested to refer to these sources for an explanation and assessment of prototyping. It is sufficient to note that prototyping methods are beginning to pervade the specification and development of systems through the use of 4GLs and CASE tools.

15.4   Rapid Applications Development

Rapid Applications Development (RAD) grew out of the recognition that businesses need to respond quickly to changing, often uncertain, environments in the development of their information systems. RAD is directly opposed to the traditional life-cycle approach with its emphasis on complete linear development of a system and concentration on technical perspectives. RAD borrows from other approaches and uses prototyping, participation, and CASE tools as well as other formal techniques. It recognizes the importance of gaining user, particularly senior management, involvement in its evolutionary approach to information systems development. RAD was first separately identified and introduced by James Martin (1991). His exposition set the methodology clearly within his Information Engineering approach to the development of business information systems. Now, though, the term Rapid Applications Development is used much more loosely to encompass any approach which emphasizes fast development of systems. Within the UK a consortium of systems developers are attempting to define a framework of standards for RAD called the Dynamic Systems Development Method (DSDM).

Central to the concept of RAD is the role of clearly defined workshops. These should:

- involve business and information systems personnel;
- be of a defined length of time (typically between one and five days);
- be in 'clean rooms' – i.e. rooms set aside for the purpose, removed from everyday operations, provided with technical support, and without interruption;
- involve a facilitator who will be independent, control the meeting, set agendas, and be responsible for steering the meeting to deliverables;
- involve a scribe to record.

RAD has four phases:

1. *Requirements planning*: The role of Joint Requirements Planning (JRP) is to establish high level management and strategic objectives for the organization. The workshop will contain senior mangers often cooperating in a cross-functional way. They will have the authority to take decisions over the strategic direction of the business. The assumption behind RAD is that JRP will drive the process from a high level business perspective rather than a technical one.

2. *Applications development*: Joint Applications Development (JAD) follows JRP and involves users in participation in the workshops. JAD follows a top-down approach and may use prototyping tools. Any techniques that can aid user design, especially data flow diagrams and entity modelling will be employed. I-CASE (see Section 15.3.1) will be used at this stage. The important feature of applications development is that the JAD workshops short-circuit the traditional life-cycle approach which involves lengthy interviews with users and the collection of documentation often over considerable time periods. In JAD the momentum is not lost and several focused workshops may be called quite quickly.

3. *Systems construction*: The designs specifications output by JAD are used to develop detailed designs and generate code. In this phase graphical user interface building tools, database management system development tools, 4GLs, and back-end CASE tools are used (see Section 15.3.1). A series of prototypes are created which are then assessed by end users which may result in further iterations and modifications. The various parts of the systems are developed by small teams, known as SWAT teams (Skilled With Advanced Tools). The central system can be built quickly using this approach. The focus of RAD is on the development of core functionality, rather than the 'whistles and bells' of the system – it is often claimed that 80% (the core) of the system can be built in 20% of the time.

4. *Cutover*: During cutover the users are trained and the system is tested comprehensively. The objective is to have the core functioning effectively. The remainder of the system can be built later. By concentration on the core and the need to develop systems rapidly within a 'timebox' the development process can concentrate on the most important aspects of the information system from a business perspective. If the process looks as though it is slipping behind schedule, out of its timebox, it is likely that the requirements will be reduced rather than the deadline extended.

Rapid Applications Developments makes the assumption that:

- businesses face continual change and uncertainty;
- information requirements and therefore information systems must change to meet this challenge;
- information systems development should be driven by business requirements;
- it is important that information systems are developed quickly;
- prototyping and development tools are necessary to ensure quick responses;
- users should participate in development;
- the 'final system' does not exist.

RAD also assumes, unlike Checkland, that consensus on aims and objectives can be reached and that problems are not 'messy'.

Summary

Approaches to systems analysis and design have been divided into two categories – 'hard' and 'soft'. Although this is a useful division it must always be remembered that there are many differences in the underlying assumptions and practices between different methodologies within each category.

'Hard' approaches seek to develop a technical solution to problems through the implementation of a computer system (Table 15.1 – traditional, structured, data analysis). They assume the possibility of a clear and agreed statement both of the current situation and its problems and of the desired state of affairs to be achieved. The problem for systems analysis and design is then seen as designing a solution that will take us from where we are now to where we want to go. The assumptions underlying this approach are akin to those in engineering. Users of the existing system are seen as providers of useful information about it. Users of the proposed system are seen in terms of their information requirements and as devices for input of data. The role of the analyst is as *the* expert brought in on a client–consultant basis to design the system.

Traditional methodologies concentrate on the automation of existing business processes. They do this by recommending procedures and documentation to describe the current system and turn this into a set of program and file specifications. Structured process analysis and design grew out of the failure of traditional methods when designing complex integrated systems or when providing systems that involve substantial redesign of functions or procedures. The emphasis is on transcending the physical limitations of the current system by developing a logical model of data flows, functions and processes prior to design. The perspective of approaches based around data analysis acknowledges that databases are a corporate resource and consequently need careful design. This is achieved by deriving a logical data model of the organization from which a database structure can be defined.

'Soft' approaches recognize the impact of human beings within the area of systems analysis and design (Table 15.1 – Checkland, socio-technical participation). First, these methodologies deny the premise that it is easy to specify current ▷

Table 15.1: Comparison of methodologies.

Methodology	Reasons for development	Aim	Area	Method	Key words/concepts examples
Traditional	The need to systematize analysis and design	To develop a technically efficient (data processing) system	Functions, subsystems	Accurate representation of systems functions via the breakdown and optimization of subfunctions	Program logic flowcharts, input output matrix, document description forms
Structured	Failures at developing large integrated systems and inability to coordinate programmer teams	To develop a technically efficient, modular, integrated system	Functions, total systems	Development of a logical model of a system emphasizing functions, data processes and data flows	Data flow diagrams, data dictionaries, structured HIPO charts
Data analysis	Development and increasing importance of database technology	To develop a database structure suitable for supporting the organization's changing applications	Organizational data structures	Development of a logical data model of an organization emphasizing entities, relationships and structures	Entity–relationships models
Object-oriented analysis	An increasing use of abstract data types in programming languages	To develop a modular system based on objects, which integrates functions and data	Total technical system	Development of a logical model emphasizing objects that incorporate data and processes	Object, message, event schema, inheritance
Checkland	Failure to take account of fuzzy problems in organizational contexts	To achieve user understanding of organizational problem situations thereby leading to learning and improvement	Fuzzy systems, problem situations	Development of a conceptual model of an ideal system through which participants can identify weaknesses and stimulate change	Rich pictures, conceptual models, root definitions, CATWOE, agenda for change
Socio-technical participation	Failures of systems as a result of user non-acceptance	To develop a fit between social and technical systems by participation thereby ensuring systems acceptance	Socio-technical system	Involvement of the user in the process of analysis and design	Participation, consensus, job satisfaction, variance analysis, autonomous workgroups
Rapid Applications Development	The need to develop systems quickly to respond to changing business needs	To develop an effective core system quickly to meet user needs	Functions, end user needs	Involvement of management and users in an iterative development process which may involve a variety of tools, including CASE	Joint requirements planning, workshops, joint applications development

and desired systems – problem situations are messy and the solutions are intellectual constructs as perceived by actors within the system (Checkland). Second, the role of the analyst is not one of an expert to give definitive knowledge on systems analysis and design but rather that of a therapist (Checkland) or as just one of a design team involving users (participative approach). Third, the role of participants in the existing system is integral to successful system development. Checkland's approach concentrates on enriching the systems participants' perceptions of the current system. This is aimed at stimulation of change and improvement of the problem situation in the fuzzy system within which it occurs. The participative approach emphasizes the need to obtain a harmonious design of interacting social and technical systems by involving users in the process of analysis and design. Both deny that a computer system is *the* only solution – the former by recognizing that not all problems require computer-based solutions, the latter by asserting that designing a technical computer system independently of people's needs will lead to failure.

Approaches to development are not static. The influence of CASE tools on the process of analysis and design is becoming increasingly significant. These are likely to be centred around object-oriented approaches, which concentrate on a perspective of the world as being composed of objects, relationships between objects and operations using those objects. CASE may cover the entire spectrum of systems analysis and design from the strategic planning of information systems to the automatic generation of executable code.

The recent development of Rapid Applications Development (RAD) has emphasized the need for fast core systems development to meet rapidly changing business need. RAD uses a combination of 4GLs and CASE tools to build prototypes.

Exercises

1. Explain the difference in the meanings of the terms *hard* and *soft* as applied to approaches to systems analysis.

2. State **four** main features of:
   (a) structured process analysis and design
   (b) structured data analysis and design
   (c) traditional systems analysis and design.

3. What are the limitations of 'hard' approaches to systems analysis and design?

4. Outline the stages in Checkland's methodology.

5. What is the purpose of drawing rich pictures?

6. By using examples of your own choice explain the terms *root definition, relevant system* and *conceptual model*.

7. What is CATWOE and why is it important?

8. What is meant by 'a participative approach to socio-technical design'? ▷

9. Explain and distinguish the different possible levels of involvement of participants in the analysis and design stages of a project.

10. What benefits are claimed for user participation in analysis and design?

11. What roles do variance analysis, job satisfaction analysis, and future analysis play in socio-technical analysis and design?

12. The hard approaches to analysis and design are often criticized for assuming that by using a technical solution it is possible to solve, or at least alleviate, problems within the organization. But if a technical solution is what the organization wants why should this be a criticism?

13. 'In much of Checkland's approach there is no clear-cut or objective way of settling differences in perceptions between participants – for example over root definitions, relevant systems or conceptual models. The approach is hopelessly subjective, non-scientific and therefore useless.' To what extent is this a valid criticism?

14. 'User participation is an advantage in analysis and design but the real benefits for the workforce and ultimately management would occur if users also participated in the decision process involving new technology and information systems.' Do you agree?

15. Could there be a socio-technical approach to systems analysis and design without a participative approach (and vice versa)?

16. This chapter, in common with many texts, uses the term *methodology* frequently. What is a methodology?

Recommended reading

● Avgerou C. and Cornford T. (1993). *Developing Information Systems: Concepts, Issues and Practice.* Basingstoke: Macmillan
This provides an interesting introduction to approaches and issues in information systems development. The book adopts a conceptual and critical perspective. It is suitable as a supplementary to a detailed explanatory text.

● Avison D.E. and Fitzgerald G. (1995). *Information Systems Development: Methodologies, Techniques and Tools* 2nd edn. Oxford: Blackwell Scientific Publications
As well as covering techniques and tools this text makes a comparison between different commercial methodologies and their underlying philosophies.

● Avison D.E. and Wood-Harper A.T. (1997). *Multiview: An Exploration in Information Systems Development* 2nd edn. Oxford: Blackwell Scientific Publications
Through six case studies the text explores the human and technical aspects of information systems development. This is achieved by way of an introduction to the Multiview methodology. The book is suitable for both computing and business studies students.

● Brown D. (1997). *An Introduction to Object-Oriented Analysis: Objects in Plain English.* Wiley
This book is aimed at students doing Information Systems and Business Information Systems courses on business degrees or MBAs. It presents object-oriented analysis and object oriented-concepts in a straightforward way using 'plain English' and business related

examples. Each chapter has self-test questions and other exercises along with explanations of key concepts.

● Checkland P.B. (1981). *Systems Thinking, Systems Practice*. Chichester: Wiley
This book develops the thinking behind the Checkland methodology.

● Coad P. and Yourdon E. (1991). *Object-oriented Analysis* 2nd edn. Englewood Cliffs NJ: Prentice-Hall
A straightforward introductory text covering the major tasks associated with object-oriented analysis.

● De Marco T. (1978). *Structured Analysis and Systems Specifications*. New York: Yourdon Press

● Dixon R.L. (1992). *Winning with CASE: Managing Modern Software Development*. New York: McGraw-Hill
A comprehensive text in a readable style, which covers the main components of CASE and its position within information systems planning and development.

● Fisher A.S. (1991). *CASE: Using Software Development Tools* 2nd edn. Wiley
This is an excellent comprehensive introduction to CASE tools suitable for both the manager and student. It is clearly written and covers extensively the methodologies as well as the tools involved. It also provides a good introduction to structured methods of analysis and design.

● Gane C. and Sarson T. (1979). *Structured Systems Analysis: Tools and Techniques*. Englewood Cliffs NJ: Prentice-Hall
Both De Marco and Gane and Sarson provide readable practical accounts of structured techniques in systems analysis and design.

● HMSO (1993). *Applying Soft Systems Methodology to an SSADM Feasibility Study*. London: HMSO Publications
This is an interesting explanation of the soft systems methodology and its application to the feasibility study module in the SSADM approach. The aim is to produce by soft systems method an SSADM feasibility study output.

● Holloway S. and Bidgood T. (1993). *CASE Strategies Guide for Information Managers*. Aldershot: Ashgate
This is most suitable for those wishing a higher-level guide to the strategies of vendors of CASE tools. The text examines the factors determining the future of CASE and provides strategies of seven major CASE vendors.

● Land F. and Hirscheim R. (1983). Participative systems design: rationale, tools and techniques. *Journal of Applied Systems Analysis*, **10**

● Martin J. (1991). *Rapid Applications Development*. Englewood Cliffs NJ: Prentice-Hall
This is an important text as the first identifiable approach with the underlying theme of Rapid Applications Development. Other texts on RAD have diverged from Martin's original approach and the term RAD is now more loosely defined.

● Martin J. (1989). *Information Engineering*. Englewood Cliffs NJ: Prentice-Hall
A clear and comprehensive statement of the main ideas behind the influential methodology of Information Engineering.

● Martin J. and Odell J. (1992). *Object Oriented Analysis and Design*. Englewood Cliffs NJ: Prentice-Hall
This is an excellent and readable introduction to all aspects of object-oriented methods. As well as object-oriented analysis and design, the relations with CASE tools and object-oriented databases are investigated.

● Martin J. and Odell J. (1991). *The Object Oriented Revolution*. Carnforth: Savant Institute
  Similar to the previous reference this book gives a highly readable introduction to all aspects of object-oriented analysis, design, programming languages and databases. It is suitable for those wishing an extended but not highly technical treatment of object-oriented issues. This book stresses the importance of the relationship between object-oriented approaches and the use of CASE tools in systems design.

● Newman W.M. and Lamming M.J. (1995). *Interactive Systems Design*. Harlow: Addison-Wesley
  This text provides a coherent framework for user-oriented design covering all stages of analysis, design, implementation and evaluation. It illustrates points with examples from air traffic control, police detective work and medical practice. Prototyping and evaluation play a major role in this approach and this is fully explained.

● Olle W.T. *et al.* (1991). *Information Systems Methodologies: A Framework for Understanding* 2nd edn. IFIP
  This is an updated version of an earlier text with the addition of CASE. The book has a valuable appendix identifying many methodologies with a short synopsis of each.

● Open University (1984). *Technology: A Third Level Course: Complexity Management and Change: Applying a Systems Approach Block IV: The Soft Systems Approach*. Milton Keynes: Open University

● Open University (1984). *Technology: A Third Level Course: Complexity Management and Change: Applying a Systems Approach Block III: The Hard Systems Approach*. Milton Keynes: Open University
  These two books provide an understandable and stimulating introduction to some of the underlying issues involved in 'hard' and 'soft' approaches to systems analysis. Their scope extends beyond analysis for computerized information systems to considering general systems approaches to organizational problems. However, the scope is limited to analysis and not design.

● Parkinson J.P. (1989). *CASE: An Introduction*. IBC Financial Books.
  This is a straightforward introduction to CASE. It is useful for those who do not need a technical perspective but wish to understand the basic concepts, developments and benefits of CASE.

● Wood-Harper A.T. and Fitgerald G. (1982). A taxonomy of current approaches to systems analysis. *Computer Journal*, **25** (1)
  This short article summarizes major approaches to systems analysis and sets them in the context of different (Kuhnian) paradigms.

Chapter 16

Expert Systems and Knowledge Bases

In Chapters 6 and 7 various ways to store and retrieve information were considered. Important though data and information handling are to an organization's information system they are only one component. Modern developments allow the storage and use of expert knowledge as well. These are known as expert systems. It is the purpose of this chapter to explain the nature of expert systems and knowledge bases together with features of these systems that distinguish them from traditional information processing using file-based and database structures. It is important to treat (in some depth) the internal working of expert systems and the way that knowledge is stored within them. Unlike traditional information systems, where the business person or accountant will need a broad understanding of aspects of analysis and design but is little concerned with the technical implementation of the system, it is increasingly common for the expert to take a major role in the detailed aspects of the development of an expert system.

The chapter begins with an introduction to the role of an expert and the nature of expertise. This allows a definition of the basic ideas lying behind expert systems. More detailed coverage involves explanation of the important distinction between procedural and declarative knowledge. This is used as an introduction to the idea of the representation of knowledge in the form of rules and leads to an explanation of the basic components or architecture of an expert system. Various forms of knowledge representation are described and their particular applications and limitations are highlighted. Reasoning with certain knowledge is dealt with by providing classical rules and methods of inference. The representation of uncertainty and its use in reasoning is also covered. The chapter as a whole acts as an introduction to the ideas behind expert systems. The characteristics of application areas that make them suitable for expert systems development, the likely benefits of these systems, and the process of developing an expert system are covered in Chapter 17.

16.1 Expert systems architecture

The next ten years will witness a spectacular growth in artificial intelligence (AI) in business, as projects currently under development come to fruition. One of the greatest limitations of current information processing systems is that their scope has been restricted to the fast and accurate processing of numeric and text data. Broadly speaking, this processing has involved numeric and algebraic functions on numbers, or various forms of insertion, deletion and retrieval of text. The processing is controlled by a program working on the numeric and text data. This mimics many tasks that were performed manually in the past. The accountant added debits and credits to arrive at balances, the scientist performed statistical tests on survey data, or the office clerk inserted or deleted data in files in cabinets. Other sorts of tasks, though, cannot be regarded as falling into these categories.

The doctor having a knowledge of diseases comes to a diagnosis of an illness by reasoning from information given by the patient's symptoms and then prescribes medication on the basis of known characteristics of available drugs together with the patient's history. The solicitor advises the client on the likely outcome of litigation based on the facts of the particular case, an expert understanding of the law and a knowledge of the way courts work and interpret this law in practice. The accountant looks at various characteristics of a company's performance and makes a judgement as to the likely state of health of that company. All of these tasks involve some of the features for which computers traditionally have been noted – performing text and numeric processing quickly and efficiently – but they also involve one more ability – reasoning. Reasoning is the movement from details of a particular case and knowledge of the general subject area surrounding that case to the derivation of conclusions. Expert systems incorporate this reasoning by applying general rules in a knowledge base to aspects of a particular case under consideration.

What is an expert system? The short answer is that it is a computerized system that performs the role of an expert or carries out a task that requires expertise. In order to understand what an expert system is, then, it is worth paying some attention to the role of an expert and the nature of expertise. It is then important to ascertain what types of experts and expertise there are in business and what benefits will accrue to an organization when it develops an expert system.

An expert typically has a body of knowledge and handles that knowledge in its application to problems in a way not possessed by the layman. An expert:

- has a body of knowledge in a particular subject area;
- can apply this knowledge to problem situations, often in conditions of uncertain or incomplete information;
- can deliver effective and efficient solutions, such as the diagnosis of a problem, an assessment of a situation, advice, planning or recommended courses of action and decisions;
- is able to provide explanations and justifications for these solutions;
- can provide information on the subject area of expertise;
- is able to identify his or her limitations in this subject area and know where to obtain further advice;

- can interact with a person requiring the expert's assistance;
- can improve their knowledge and expertise by learning.

For example, corporate tax specialists:

- will have a body of tax knowledge on tax legislation and principles, together with the way that government taxation boards apply;
- will be able to apply this expertise in particular situations given corporate facts to, for instance, recommend ways of classifying corporate assets to minimize tax liability;
- will be able to justify and explain their recommendations to government tax authorities and internal management within the organization for which the expert is acting as tax specialist;
- will be able to answer specific tax enquiries;
- will be aware of the limitations of their own tax expertise;
- will be able to interact with those requiring tax advice at a level that takes account of the enquirer's level of knowledge and interests;
- will be able to update their expertise in the light of new tax legislation or precedent.

Organizations have experts in many areas. A business organization will probably probably have general expertise in such areas as tax, accounts, marketing, production and personnel as well as specific expertise in the narrow area of its activity – for example, the design, production and retail of motor cars. As well as 'high-level' expertise there will be 'low-level' expertise. An example of this might be the knowledge possessed by a clerk of the way that an organization stores its records with cross-referencing and the handling of exceptions.

In order to justify the cost of an expert system an organization will want to realize benefits. Amongst many possible benefits of an expert system are:

- A cost-effective consultant system to aid or replace existing expertise within the organization. Being computer based, expert systems perform consistently unlike human experts, who may have 'off days'.
- An archive of specific skills that the organization possesses and on which it is dependent for its successful functioning – experts may leave or retire.
- A training aid for 'future experts'.
- A standard for expertise against which human experts can be compared.

A detailed coverage of the benefits of expert systems is given in Chapter 17 of this book on the development of expert systems. Also treated there in detail are the characteristics of an area of expertise that make it suitable for the design of an expert system. Amongst the important points for this chapter are:

- The area of expertise should involve the analysis of a complex set of conditions, and the application of these to a specifiable area of knowledge that is amenable to computerized representation (see Sections 16.1 and 16.2).
- The area of expertise is narrow, clear cut and can be made explicit. It does not for instance involve the expert in using general knowledge or 'common sense'.

- The expert's task typically takes between a few minutes and, say, three hours. Less than this and the use of computer input will slow the task; more than this and the task is likely to be too complex.

What is an expert system? We can return to this original question. Although a detailed answer is provided by the rest of the chapter a brief answer follows from the previous considerations of the role of an expert and the nature of expertise. An expert system typically:

- incorporates expert knowledge in a particular subject area, usually by storing and representing this as rules or other representation forms (**knowledge base**);
- separates the general knowledge from the details of a particular case under consideration to which the knowledge base is applied (**particular context**);
- clearly distinguishes the knowledge from the mechanism of reasoning (**inference engine**);
- possesses an interactive user interface for providing explanations, justifications and questions to the user;
- Provides, as its output, advice or decisions in the area of expertise.

In addition, an expert system may be able to handle uncertain or incomplete information. It may also be able to learn – that is, modify its knowledge base or inference engine.

Expert systems have been developed and are currently being developed for a wide variety of areas of expertise in business. A few examples are:

- a system that provides advice to employers on the dismissal of employees;
- a system that provides advice on registration under the Data Protection Act in the UK;
- a system that develops investment plans for personal clients tailored to their needs;
- a system that aids auditors in providing an effective and complete audit of a company's accounts;
- a system that provides an assessment of a company's health from various perspectives such as the auditor, the trade creditor, and the financier of loans.

Before embarking on the remainder of the chapter a word of warning is appropriate. Expert systems in business are 'the flavour of the month'. Therefore sellers of software and systems may tend to describe their products as 'expert systems' for marketing reasons. The reader should be wary. As one software vendor of a major mainframe package explained, 'Our software has gone through various upgradings over the last ten years, but it is still essentially the same product. Ten years ago we called it a "management information system", five years ago a "decision support system" and now we sell it as an "expert system"'.

Expert systems are sometimes known as 'knowledge-based systems' or 'intelligent knowledge-based systems'. The architecture of a typical expert system is shown in Figure 16.1. Each of the parts is considered separately in the following sections in order to give an overview of the way an expert system works. Knowledge representation in the domain-specific knowledge base and the ways that inferences are drawn are also considered in more detail in Sections 16.2 and 16.3.

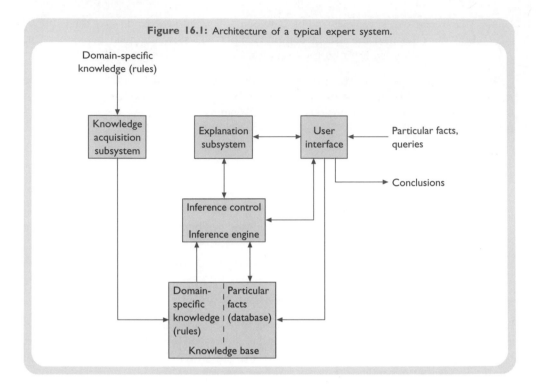

Figure 16.1: Architecture of a typical expert system.

16.1.1   Domain-specific knowledge base

This is one of the two logically distinct components of the knowledge base. The domain-specific knowledge is the representation of the static expertise of the experts. As most experts are knowledgeable in limited areas this is reflected in the term 'domain specific'. An example of expertise might be how to interpret a complex tax law in such a way that it is most advantageous to a client. This is to be distinguished from general or common-sense knowledge that we all have. The latter is often mundane. The fact that all objects fall to the ground when released, except if they are lighter than air or are fairly light and there is a strong wind blowing, is an instance of common-sense knowledge. Another example is that one might bring a bottle of wine, flowers or a box of chocolates to a friend's supper party but not a plate of cold, uncooked liver. This latter sort of common-sense knowledge although widespread amongst people is most difficult to represent and use in reasoning in expert systems. This is because common-sense knowledge often involves a mixture of pictorial and verbal, general and specific, and uncertain and vague knowledge from many areas. It is linked to an understanding of the meanings of natural-language terms that surpasses that of any computer of today. Common-sense knowledge may be inextricably interwoven with moral beliefs, complex social attitudes and individual interests. All of this makes it difficult to represent such knowledge in a way that is accessible to automated reasoning. Common sense is widespread but not simple.

Declarative and procedural knowledge

Fundamental to any expert system is the assumption that much knowledge is declarative rather than procedural. To see the difference it is illustrative to consider an example. The following is from a recipe for making moussaka:

> First slice the aubergines, pack into a colander and then sprinkle with salt. Place a plate on top and a large weight on the plate and leave for half an hour. Meanwhile, fry the garlic and onions in olive oil for about 5 minutes before adding the minced meat. In a basin, mix together the tomato puree, parsley and wine, season it with salt and pepper and when the meat has browned pour the mixture over it.

The knowledge contained in the above is largely procedural. With procedural knowledge it is common to see statements such as '**do** ⟨this⟩. . . . **then do** ⟨that⟩. . . .' or 'meanwhile **do** ⟨this⟩. **. . . until** ⟨that⟩ occurs'. The knowledge consists of actions or activities linked by temporal connections. Procedural knowledge can be easily incorporated in conventional programs, which execute code (activities) in the order in which they appear in the program. Cooking knowledge may still be beyond the computer of today but numeric computation is procedural. In order to find the average of a set of numbers the following recipe can be followed:

> Set a running total and a count to zero. Take the first number and add it to the total and add one to the count. **Do** this with each successive number **until** there are no more numbers. **Then** divide the running total by the count. The result is the average.

A computer program could provide a coded version of this requested set of actions. In contrast, declarative knowledge, illustrated in the following example, is rather different:

> **If** the student has successfully completed Level 1 of the examination **or** has been exempted from Level 1 by virtue of satisfying **any** of the conditions laid out in paragraphs 3 (a) to 3 (f) below, **then** the student is entitled to register for Level 2 of the examination. A student registered for Level 2 is exempt from examination papers 2.3 **and** 2.4 **if** he/she has obtained exemption from Level 1 by virtue of satisfying the conditions 3(a) **or** 3(b) below, **or** satisfying 3(d) **and** being in possession of an honours degree awarded by a British University **or** accredited by the Council for National Academic Awards.

Here, the knowledge consists of propositions linked together by logical relationships. It is common to find expressions of the form '**if** ⟨such-and-such⟩ **then** ⟨so-and-so⟩ is the case' or '⟨so-and-so⟩ **unless** ⟨this⟩ **or** ⟨that⟩'. There is no sense in which one activity is performed before another. Rather, there is a set of conditions or area of knowledge that is declared.

Rules

It is often possible to represent this declarative knowledge in the form of rules. Figure 16.2 is an example of a set of rules representing declarative knowledge in the area of the assessment of a company's financial health. It is this set of rules that forms the domain-specific knowledge in the knowledge base.

> **Figure 16.2:** Rules from a knowledge base dealing with a company's financial health.
>
> Rule 1   **IF** the quick ratio is higher than the industry average quick ratio
>   **AND** the inventory turnover ratio is higher than the industry average turnover ratio
>   **THEN** short-term liquidity is good
>
> Rule 2   **IF** the debt to equity ratio is low
>   **AND** the dividend cover is high
>   **THEN** the medium-term insolvency risk is low
>
> Rule 3   **IF** the short-term liquidity is good
>   **AND** the medium-term insolvency risk is low
>   **AND EITHER** the market is likely to expand
>   **OR** the market is stable
>   **AND** the company has a majority market share
>   **THEN** the company is financially stable

The rules given in Figure 16.2 are often known as **if–then** rules. They have the form:

If ⟨antecedent condition⟩ **then** ⟨consequent⟩

where the antecedent condition is any sentence or set of sentences connected with '**and**', '**or**', or '**not**'. These are known as **Boolean operators**. This gives the structure of the rule. The simplest expert systems will treat expressions such as 'short-term liquidity is good' as simple and unanalyzable atomic units. Their sole function is to be assigned a truth value (True or False). More complex systems might be capable of treating this expression as saying of the attribute 'short-term liquidity' it has the value 'good' – it might have had the value 'poor' or 'average'. The presence of attribute–value pairs allows more complex reasoning to be undertaken by the system. This will be seen later in Section 16.2.1.

Of course not all knowledge can be represented in the form of **if–then** rules. It has already been seen that some knowledge is procedural; also much declarative knowledge cannot easily be cast into the **if–then** mould either. Any knowledge that relies on pictorial representation, such as the relative positioning of streets as shown on a street map, cannot appropriately be represented as propositional knowledge and therefore not as **if–then** rules. Some declarative knowledge is best understood as knowing that certain entities have attributes; they inherit these attributes by virtue of being instances of other entities. It is unnatural to attempt to encode this in the form of rules. For example, salmon have fins by virtue of being fish, as do trout. Rather than represent this as **if–then** rules about salmon and trout separately, this knowledge can be represented as being facts about fish which salmon and trout then inherit. Other suitable forms of representation such as semantic networks and frames are treated later in the chapter in Sections 16.2.3 and 16.2.4. However, for the explanation of the architecture of the expert system a rule-based representation will be assumed.

The knowledge base may consist of several hundreds or even thousands of rules for complex areas of expertise. As a rough guide it is convenient to class expert systems as small if they have between 50 and 200 rules and as large if over 1000 rules. With much less than 50 rules the area covered is becoming so small that it will hardly qualify as expertise.

16.1.2 Knowledge acquisition subsystem

The domain-specific knowledge in the form of rules, or some other chosen representation form, needs to be entered into the system. This is achieved by the knowledge acquisition subsystem. In the simplest case rules are entered at the keyboard. The rules are required to follow a specified syntax called the **knowledge representation language** (KRL). As well as rules, other information can be added. For instance, in Figure 16.2, Rule 1 requires that the quick ratio, a measure used in accounting, is higher than the industry average as a necessary condition that liquidity is good. When this rule is considered by the expert system in a later consultation the system will attempt to determine the truth of that antecedent condition. It may be the case that whether the quick ratio is higher than the industry average or not is determined by further rules. Alternatively, the expert system may need a basic piece of evidence in order to establish the company's financial health and the only way of finding this is to ask the user of the expert system a question. The exact text of the question can be specified when the rule is first input into the knowledge base. This may lead to the following representation in the KRL:

> The quick ratio is higher than the industry average: **ASK TEXT** 'Is the quick ratio for the company higher than the average quick ratio for the industry as a whole?'

The user might require further explanation in order to be able to answer the question. The KRL can provide the facility for this. It is also clear that the condition is Boolean – TRUE or FALSE (or possibly UNKNOWN) should be assigned to the value of the proposition. All this can be incorporated, leading to the following full specification in the KRL:

> The quick ratio is higher than the industry average: **ASK TEXT** 'Is the quick ratio for the company higher than the average quick ratio for the industry as a whole', **YES/NO**, **EXPLANATION** 'The quick ratio may be determined from the company's financial accounts and is given by the following formula:
>
> quick ratio = ⟨current assets less inventory⟩/current assets'.

These rules and other details can be entered via a standard word processing package. The text file is created and then compiled, the syntax is checked and the rules and other information are converted into a form suitable for storage in the knowledge base. Alternatively, the rules may be entered interactively during a rule-building consultation with the expert system. Each rule is checked for correct syntax as it is entered and checks are made immediately to ensure that the rule is consistent with the existing rules. The process is analogous to the interpreting of a program in a high-level language as compared with compiling, although this analogy should not be taken too far.

The methods of entry mentioned in the previous paragraph are typical of knowledge acquisition subsystems associated with expert systems built from application packages called **expert system shells**. These are expert systems that initially contain no knowledge in their knowledge base. The knowledge is entered by the builders of the expert system. Shells and their role and suitability for the development of expert systems are considered in Chapter 17 on building expert systems.

The kind of knowledge acquisition just described is similar to rote learning. Just as scientific progress does not occur through rote learning of new rules (where do they come from?) so expert systems imbued with greater power may obtain knowledge in additional ways. Perhaps the most common is by deriving rules from a large number of cases. Given, for example, many cases of plant disease symptoms and other environmental conditions, together with the diagnosed disease in each case, a pattern connecting certain symptoms and environmental conditions with particular disease can be established. The knowledge acquisition subsystem scans details of these cases, often held on a conventional database, and derives this pattern in the form of rules, which are automatically generated and entered in the knowledge base. The process is called **rule induction** and is considered in more detail in Chapter 17. Although automated machine learning is gradually being developed there are still technical and theoretical difficulties that restrict its usage to very specialized applications.

By far the most common method of acquisition is direct rule entry via the keyboard. To do this requires overcoming one of the major problems involved in building an expert system. That problem is to obtain the knowledge and represent it in the required form (for example, as a set of rules) when the knowledge originally resides in the mind of an expert and, as any psychologist will confirm, the way knowledge is represented to the human in the mind is still a mystery. The process of extracting the knowledge in the required form is called **knowledge elicitation** and is covered in a separate section in Chapter 17.

16.1.3 Case-specific knowledge base (database)

The other component of the knowledge base contains details relevant to a particular consultation of the expert system. An expert system used to diagnose a company's financial health will have permanently within it rules governing the factors that affect company financial health in general (domain-specific knowledge) but during use will have factual detail on the company under consideration (the XYZ company). Details on XYZ will be stored in the case-specific knowledge base. The facts are either directly input by the user, for instance in response to a question, or taken directly from an external conventional database holding company data, or derived from the content of the factual knowledge base by reasoning with the rules.

The term 'database' is sometimes used to refer to the case-specific knowledge base. It must be realized that this is not the same use of 'database' as in Chapter 7 but refers merely to the store of case-specific data.

16.1.4 Inference engine

Given details of a particular case and general domain-specific rules, what conclusions can be drawn? The process of drawing conclusions is not a static one. It involves the application of sound methods of reasoning to evidence as it currently stands in the knowledge base.

The inference engine (or interpreter) applies the domain-specific knowledge base to the particular facts of the case under consideration to derive these new conclusions. Principles govern the work of the inference engine. Some of these concern the allowable types of inference that can be performed. The strictest inference principles are logically sound. That is, if we are given initial data as true, then the inferences drawn with the use of the principle must also be true. Some principles of inference, particularly those concerned with probabilistic or uncertain reasoning, do not meet this requirement.

Figure 16.3: Some inference principles for Boolean algebra. (a) *Modus ponens.* (b) *Modus tollens.* (c) Conjunction introduction. (d) Disjunction introduction. (e) Resolution. (f) Disjunction elimination.

		Principle	Example
(a)	Rule	if A then B	If the creature has feathers **then** it is a bird
	Fact	A	the creature has feathers
	New fact	B	it is a bird
(b)	Rule	If A then B	If the creature has feathers **then** it is a bird
	Fact	not B	it is **not** a bird
	New fact	not A	the creature does **not** have feathers
(c)	Fact	A	it is a fish
	Fact	B	it weights 10 kilograms
	New fact	A **and** B	it is a fish **and** weighs 10 kilograms
(d)	Fact	A	it is raining
	New fact	A **or** B	it is raining **or** snowing
(e)	Fact	(**not** A) **or** B	either it does **not** have gills **or** it is a fish
	Fact	(**not** B) **or** C	either it it is **not** fish **or** it lives in water
	New fact	**not** A **or** C	either it does **not** have gills **or** it lives in water
(f)	Fact	(**not** A) **or** B	either it does **not** have gills **or** it is a fish
	Fact	A	it does have gills
	New fact	B	it is a fish

In a rule-based system the most common example of a sound inference principle is logical derivation by *modus ponendo ponens* (usually shortened to *modus ponens*). This is an obvious inference principle known to the ancients. A simple example of *modus ponens* is:

Given rule	**If** it is raining **then** the ground is wet
Given fact	It is raining
Derived new fact	The ground is wet

A similar though perhaps slightly less obvious inference is *modus tollendo tollens* (usually shortened to *modus tollens*). Using a weather example again:

Given rule	**If** it is raining **then** the ground is wet
Given fact	The ground is not wet
Derived new fact	It is not raining

In most formal systems these can be shown to be logically equivalent forms of reasoning (specifically those systems in which we are entitled to assume the negation of an assumption if that assumption leads to a contradiction – another intuitively sound move known as *reductio ad absurdum*). However, some expert systems make use of *modus ponens* without *modus tollens*. This implies that they are unable to derive certain obvious and particularly useful conclusions from a given set of rules and particular facts.

Common inference principles for Boolean algebra are given in Figure 16.3. (a) and (b) have already been considered, (c) and (d) are trivial but important for those systems that allow antecedents of rules to contain conjunctions and disjunctions (as in Rule 1 concerning short-term liquidity in Figure 16.2). They generate complex propositions from simple ones. (e) is known as the resolution principle and can be used for reducing a set of complex propositions to simpler ones and (f) can be used to eliminate a disjunction. All expert systems will use some or all of these or their equivalents in the inferencing process.

These abstract inference principles need to be applied selectively in order to achieve a useful derivation of new facts during the consultation. At any given point of time there may be many ways of proceeding from the set of rules and particular facts in the knowledge base. There must not only be principles for deriving new facts but also a way of choosing which principle is to be used at any moment. And given that, for example, *modus ponens* is chosen then which rules and existing facts should be used if there is more than one possible use? In short, there must not only be sound inference principles but also an inference control strategy for selecting which principles are to be applied to which rules in the knowledge base at a given time. ('Inference principles' has been used in the text to mean any method of inference. It is common elsewhere to refer to these also as 'inference rules'. This has been avoided as it may lead to confusion with rules held in the knowledge base that are domain specific and provide empirical knowledge or definitions such as in Figure 16.2. The matter is further complicated by the inclusion of inference rules within the rule base of some expert systems.)

An example of inference control is shown in Figure 16.4. This is a model of a very simple expert system illustrating the way that the inference engine dynamically interacts with the rule base and the fact base (database) to derive new facts. The inference engine is a set of activities that is incorporated in a computer program. The inference engine is procedural – the rules and facts are declarative.

The expert system attempts the identification of creatures based on certain characteristics such as whether they live in the sea, have stripes, eat meat and so on. (No claim is made for the sophistication of the system!) The inference engine works by executing instructions (1) to (4). As (4) is a **GOTO** instruction the engine just loops until the exit condition is met in line (3).

Initial data is supplied on the beast to be identified. This is held in the database. In the example the facts given are that the subject:

- is warm blooded
- suckles young
- lives in the sea
- has flippers.

During **Pass 1** Line (1) is executed and matches the data in the database with each rule in turn to establish whether the antecedent is satisfied. This results in rule 2 and rule 9 being selected. A check is made to ignore the rules that add nothing to the database, line (2). This leaves both rules still operative, so some method of resolving which rule to operate (or **fire**, as it is sometimes called) must be used. In the example the simple expedient of executing the lowest-numbered rule is chosen – line (3). This is rule 2, which allows the inference engine to derive the conclusion of the rule, 'mammal' and add it to the database. Line (4) is executed returning control to line (1).

In **Pass 2** both rule 2 and rule 9 have their antecedents satisfied but as 'mammal' is already in the database rule 9 is fired (line (3)) and 'pinniped' is added to the database.

In **Pass 3** rules 2, 8 and 9 have their antecedents satisfied (line (1)). Only rule 8 adds new facts to the database (line (2)). So rule 8 is fired (line (3)) and control is returned to line (1) (line (4)).

Figure 16.4: Model of a simple expert system for classifying creatures.

RULE BASE

(1) **IF** eats meat **THEN** carnivore
(2) **IF** suckles young **AND** warmblooded **THEN** mammal
(3) **IF** **NOT** warmblooded **AND** lives in sea **THEN** fish
(4) **IF** **NOT** carnivore **AND** striped **AND** mammal **THEN** zebra
(5) **IF** carnivore **AND** striped **AND** mammal **THEN** tiger
(6) **IF** mammal **AND** lives in sea **AND** **NOT** pinniped **THEN** whale
(7) **IF** fish **AND** striped **THEN** tiger fish
(8) **IF** pinniped **AND** mammal **THEN** seal
(9) **IF** hind flippers **THEN** pinniped

INFERENCE ENGINE

(1) Find all rules whose antecedents are satisfied by the database
(2) Ignore rules found in (1) whose consequents are in the database
(3) Execute lowest numbered rule remaining, **if** no rule **then** quit
(4) **Go to** (1)

DATABASE

Initial: suckles young, warmblooded, lives in sea, hind flippers

	Pass 1	Pass 2	Pass 3	Pass 4
Rules relevant	2, 9	2, 9	2, 8, 9	2, 8, 9
Rule fired	2	9	8	
Database at end of pass	suckles young warmblooded lives in sea hind flippers mammal	suckles young warmblooded lives in sea hind flippers mammal pinniped	suckles young warmblooded lives in sea hind flippers mammal pinniped seal	suckles young warmblooded lives in sea hind flippers mammal pinniped seal QUIT

In **Pass 4**, rules 2, 8 and 9 have their antecedents satisfied. But as their consequents are in the database no operative rules remain and line (3) ensures that the process quits.

The rule base can be given an alternative representation as in Figure 16.5. This representation highlights the logical connectives **and**, **not**, and **or**. It also serves to establish a hierarchy of rules based on dependence. For instance, rule 8 can be seen to be dependent on rules 2 and 9. This kind of representation may be used when developing the knowledge base. Some people prefer it as they find it easier to work with a picture than the linguistic statement of rules.

A number of features are worth noting about the model in Figure 16.4:

1. The order of rules in the rule base is irrelevant to the final outcome. Reordering the rules might lead to facts being derived in a different sequence during the inferencing, but on completion the same set remains in the database. This is characteristic of some, though not all, expert systems and corresponds to the fact that rules do not appear to be ordered in the human brain (except possibly by dependence).

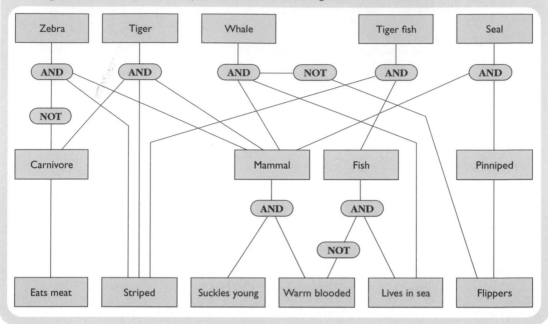

Figure 16.5: An intermediate representation of the knowledge base for the classification of creatures.

2. The inference engine contains no domain-specific knowledge but only procedural rules for generating inferences. The rule base contains only domain-specific knowledge. Put another way, the inference engine could be used on a set of rules diagnosing a company's financial health – the strategy is the same. This feature explains why it is possible to have expert system shells.

3. Rules can be added to the rule base as more knowledge is incorporated. For instance the following can be added:

> Rule 10 **if** warm blooded **and** feathers **then** bird.

This does not require any other change in the rule base or in the inference engine. In the latter case the inference strategy works for 9 or 900 rules. The knowledge base can grow. This would not be so easy if rules in the knowledge base were not purely declarative.

4. The expert system in Figure 16.4 is very primitive. This is not just because the rules are naive and cover only a fraction of the taxonomy of the animal kingdom. Rather the inference control strategy (using *modus ponens*) is simple: given the antecedents of conditionals then derive the consequents. This strategy when applied repetitively is called **forward chaining**. Looked at from the point of view of Figure 16.5 it can be seen that given baseline facts, such as 'eats meat' and 'suckles young', the strategy amounts to moving forwards (upwards) through the chart until no more progress can be made. This may be unwieldy if there are a large number of rules and facts to be handled, and it is often better to adopt a different inference control strategy.

An alternative is to take a conclusion as a working hypothesis. In the case of Figure 16.5 this might be to take as the initial assumption that the creature is a tiger. The inference strategy is to look for rules that 'prove' that it is a tiger. If one of the rules is found (rule 5) the next step is to attempt to prove the antecedent – in this case that the creature is a carnivore, it is striped and it is a mammal. The inference control strategy will attempt to prove each of these in turn. To prove it is a carnivore it is sufficient to show it eats meat; this does not depend on a further rule as a basic element. If the fact is not in the database then the creature is not a carnivore and not a tiger. The inference strategy then selects another goal – for example, it is a whale – and repeats the entire backtracking process.

However, if 'eats meat' is in the database then it can be proved that the creature is a carnivore. This is the first step to proving it is a tiger. The inference control strategy then attempts to show that the creature is striped and then that it is a mammal. If either of these fails the strategy is to move on to another goal as before. This involves backtracking from conclusions to attempt to establish the facts that would prove them, and so the inference strategy is known as **backward chaining**.

5. There is no facility for adding data from the user once the system has started its processing. The typical expert will, in the course of a consultation, ask for further information to back up a line of reasoning that he or she is pursuing. Here, the system just proves all it can from the initial data using forward chaining. It might be argued that there is nothing wrong with this provided that all the relevant facts are given at the beginning. This is inappropriate because the relevant facts may only be established as relevant in the course of a consultation. For example, in a medical expert system it is not of much relevance to know if a patient is a rock musician, accountant or shop assistant in diagnosing the cause of spots, a high temperature and a sore throat. Matters change though if the symptoms are deafness. To say that all the facts should be given initially if they are relevant to the proof of some conclusion (relevant to the diagnosis of some disease) is just not practical – there are often too many and only the expert knows which facts are relevant. In any case the aim of an expert system is to simulate the behaviour and knowledge of experts and they proceed by selective questioning having been given an initial set of facts. The vast majority of expert systems follow this approach. It is generally associated with inference strategies other than forward chaining.

16.1.5 Explanation subsystem

The explanation subsystem typically provides the following features.

HOW questions

An important feature of experts is that they are able to justify their conclusions. Indeed, it is this ability that leads us to have confidence in their advice. If a doctor concludes that a patient, X, has say, appendicitis, this conclusion may be justified by saying that 'X's appendix has not been removed. The patient has a high temperature, vomiting and the abdomen is sensitive to touch on the lower-right-hand side. Under these conditions a patient probably has appendicitis. This probability is further increased by the fact that none of the following range of foods has been eaten in the last 24 hours, shellfish, mushrooms . . .' The doctor is providing an explanation of **HOW** these conclusions were reached. It is important that doctors can do this. If they could not we would regard them as merely successful clairvoyants – that is assuming they were right most of the time in their diagnoses.

Expert systems incorporate the possibility of **HOW** explanations in their explanation subsystem. The user of the system may at any stage interrupt the workings of the expert system to establish how a conclusion or intermediate derived fact has been derived. In the model system in Figure 16.4 after the consultation, the user might query the expert system with the keyboard input '**HOW** seal'. The expert system would respond:

> The conclusion 'seal' was reached because rule 8 applied '**if** pinniped **and** mammal **then** seal'. Rule 8 applied because 'pinniped' was derived using rule 9 '**if** flippers **then** pinniped'. Rule 9 applied because 'flippers' was given initially. Rule 8 also applied because 'mammal' was derived using rule 2 '**if** suckles its young **and** warm-blooded **then** mammal'. Rule 2 applied because 'suckles young' and 'warm-blooded' was given initially.

The output given is typical of a response to a **HOW** question provided by an expert system. The proposition for which an explanation is being sought is treated by citing the rules in a backward line of reasoning, together with intermediate conclusions provided by these rules, until 'basic' facts are established – that is, those facts given initially or given in response to questions. The explanatory subsystem inserts expressions such as:

> The conclusion '. . .' was reached because rule. . . . applied

in order to make the explanation more readable.

In a large expert system the line of reasoning to a conclusions may be long and complex. It is usually possible to restrict the explanation facility to a shortened version.

WHY questions

Another form of question that is asked of the expert is a **WHY** question. The doctor may ask the patient X whether X had eaten shellfish recently. The patient may wish to know why the doctor is interested. The doctor responds (perhaps rather insensitively), 'I am trying to establish whether you have appendicitis. I have already established that you have a high temperature, vomiting and sensitivity to pressure in the lower-right-abdomen. This makes appendicitis possible. This possibility is increased if I can rule out the possibility of food poisoning. I can do this if you have not had one of a range of foods recently. Shellfish is one of this range.'

Here the doctor is citing a possible diagnosis (conclusion) and explains how the answer to the question will impact on the proof of this diagnosis. It is important that expert systems provide this possibility. It is achieved by means of a **WHY** question. The system in Figure 16.4 does not ask questions of the user during a consultation. Imagine though that it had this facility – no initial facts were given and it derived its conclusions by attempting to prove that the creature in question was each of the possibilities in turn. (This means that the inference engine cannot be identical to that in Figure 16.4.) Suppose further that the system is trying to prove that the creature under investigation is a whale. The expert system needs to establish, if it has not already done so, whether the creature is warm-blooded. The system will generate a suitable question to ask the user. In response the user may type '**WHY** warm-blooded' at the keyboard. The **WHY** explanation facility provides the following on the screen:

I am trying to establish 'whale'.
'Mammal' is a necessary condition for a creature to be a 'whale', rule 6, and
'warm blooded' is a necessary condition for a creature to be a 'mammal', rule 2.

Once again, text is inserted by the expert system to make the explanation more readable.

It is important to see that the explanation follows a template and the rule numbers and the facts or potential facts are added in a standard way to the template. This means that the explanation facility would be of the same form even if the knowledge base were more complex or had a different subject matter.

Requests for further explanation

A third form of explanatory facility has been covered in Section 16.1.2. This is when the system is attempting to establish a fact by means of questioning the user. The question itself may need further explanation (what does the term 'quick ratio' mean in the question 'Is the quick ratio higher for the company than the quick ratio for the industry as a whole?'). This is provided by explanatory text added to the original text of the question. The explanation is optional as it would be irritating and confusing to the experienced user to see large amounts of unnecessary additional text.

Consultation traces

A final explanation facility that may be provided generates a record of the inference paths taken by the system during a consultation. This is generally not so important to the user but may be of considerable help to the person building or testing the expert system. This trace is often graphical, showing the rules executed and the facts established in the chronological order of the consultation. For example, part of the graph of Figure 16.5 traversed during a consultation may be traced on the screen.

In summary, four forms of explanatory facility are generally provided:

1. **HOW** – how has a conclusion been established? What facts and rules were used in deriving it?
2. **WHY** – why is a particular question being asked? What is the impact of the answer to the question on a proof to a conclusion?
3. **FURTHER EXPLANATION** – provide more text accompanying the question as a further explanation.
4. **TRACE** – provide a 'picture' of the consultation. Display the rules fired and the conclusions established in the order in which these events occurred.

16.2   Representation of knowledge

The ways that people represent their knowledge are rich and varied. There are pictorial representations as in maps and diagrams, there are graphical representations showing relationships, and most common and most powerful of all there are representations in natural language. This book is written in a natural language, English, and can be regarded as representing knowledge on various aspects of business information systems – their analysis, design and use. The only limits imposed in the representation are those governed by the rules of English and the amount of existing knowledge that is assumed to be possessed by the reader. English is a comprehensive natural language in terms of

Figure 16.6: Some rules governing entitlement to credit cards.

Rule 1: If income > £30,000 **then** credit type = gold card
Rule 2: If income ≤ £30,000 **and** credit status = OK **then** credit type = normal
Rule 3: If income > £10,000 **then** credit status = OK

its vocabulary and its structure (the structure of a language is the set of its semantic categories together with rules for assembling complex wholes, such as sentences out of simpler parts – nouns, verbs and so on). English is so rich that its rules have never been completely formalized. Attempts are being made, and success in this area is a prerequisite for the development of computers with genuine natural language interfaces. Large subsets of English have been formalized, though computers still have difficulty in treating idiomatic expressions. Few English representations adequately distinguish the fact that 'the whisky is good but the meat is bad' is not an example of 'the spirit is willing but the flesh is weak' (or so the joke goes).

The representation of knowledge used in Figures 16.2 and 16.4 has been very simple. **If–then** rules have been employed together with the limitations that the constituents of these rules be simple sentences (bearers of truth and falsity and sentences made out of these by the logical connectives **AND**, **OR** and **NOT**). Although knowledge representation in expert systems has not approached the power of expression of the English language it has advanced beyond these simple structures.

The next sections consider some of the limitations of these simple structures and the ways that they may be overcome using alternative knowledge representation techniques.

16.2.1 Attribute–value pairs

Imagine that the three rules in Figure 16.6 occur in an expert system that has been set up to deal with applications for credit cards. Part of the system determines whether the applicant's credit status is acceptable, while another part analyzes the income to determine the type of credit card to which the applicant is entitled. The rules are simplified for the sake of the example.

If the representation is taken as being composed of complete propositions with no internal structure then the fact that an applicant's income is £15,000 would not be applicable to these rules 'Income = £15,000' does not occur as the antecedent to any of them. To ensure that rule 3 fires the information 'income > £10,000' must be entered as a unit in the database. But still neither rule 1 nor rule 2 has its antecedents satisfied. It is necessary also to add the fact 'income < £30,000' to ensure that rule 2 fires after 'credit status = OK' has been proved by rule 3.

The simple representation has the following disadvantages:

● It is necessary to translate the details of the applicant, namely that the income = £15,000, into the two facts 'income > £10,000' and 'income < £30,000' in order to ensure that the knowledge base works with the particular facts of the applicant who is the subject of the consultation. Then the level of income may be used in many other rules as well. It is then necessary to make sure that the income is rendered in the correct form to satisfy each.

- The value of the attribute 'income' for the applicant is £15,000. Intuitively speaking this is what should be entered. It should then be possible for the expert system to derive implied income statements such as 'income < £30,000' from this.

- If the thresholds in the rules change, for example the critical income level in rule 3 is increased to £12,000, then the income fact as entered for an individual would need to be altered to take account of this.

These considerations lead to the attribute–value (A–V) pair as a common method of expressing knowledge in expert systems.

Applied to the rules in Figure 16.6 the A–V construction can be expressed as follows. There are three attributes – 'income', 'credit status' and 'credit type'. The values of 'credit status' can be 'OK' or 'not OK', the values of 'credit type' can be 'normal', 'gold card' and 'platinum card' (not shown), and the value of 'income' can be any number greater than zero. The user of the expert system inputs the value for the attribute 'income', which is £15,000 in this particular case. The expert system tests this value of income against the rules and assigns the value 'OK' to the attribute 'credit status' (rule 3) and 'normal' to the attribute 'credit type' (rule 2). The rationale behind the A–V representation is that much expert knowledge and reasoning concerns treatment of an example of an object type and its associated attributes where these attributes can have values. The credit card system is concerned with one type of object, a card applicant, and, for each consultation, one example of the applicant, say John Smith. There are a range of attributes of John Smith. Some have values that are entered into the system, whereas the values of others are derived by the rules.

Many common expert system shells work by using A–V pairs within an **if–then** rule format. It is uncommon, except in the simplest systems, to restrict the representation form to **if–then** rules containing conditions that are not capable of being further decomposed into constituents such as A–V pairs.

16.2.2 Object–attribute–value triples

Frequently it is important to depict more than one object in an expert system. The attribute–value representation is then inadequate as all attributes are assumed to be of one object. This limitation may be overcome by using the object–attribute–value (O–A–V) model of representing knowledge. For example, the expert system that assesses a company's financial health may need to encode and work with information on each of the company's outstanding loans. Each loan will be treated as an object and will have attributes such as 'rate of interest', 'call in date', 'amount', 'creditors' and 'redeemable' with values such as: '10%', '1 Jan 2000', '£1m', 'Federated Bank' and 'True'.

One of the earliest expert systems was MYCIN. This system was developed to aid doctors in the diagnosis and treatment of meningitis and bacterial infections of the blood. MYCIN is an example of a system that represents its knowledge as O–A–V triples within rules. Rule 85 is given in Figure 16.7(a) and its analysis using the O–A–V framework is given in Figure 16.7(b).

Object–attribute–values may be represented in diagrams. Figure 16.8 is the O–A–V triplet representation for two loans to a company. As a company may have many loans, both may be present during a current consultation in Figure 16.9. The blanks indicate

Figure 16.7: (a) A rule from MYCIN. (b) The representation of the rule as an object–attribute–value triplet.

(a) RULE 85

If The site of the culture is blood, and
The morphology of the organism is rod, and
The Gram stain of the organism is Gram-neg, and
The patient is a compromised host

Then there is suggestive evidence (0.6) that the identity of the organism is
Pseudomonas aeruginosas

(b)

	Object	**Attribute**	**Value**
If	Culture	Site	Blood
	Organism	Morphology	Rod
	Organism	Gram stain	Gram-neg
	Patient	Compromised host	True
Then	Organism	Identity	*Pseudomonas aeruginosas*

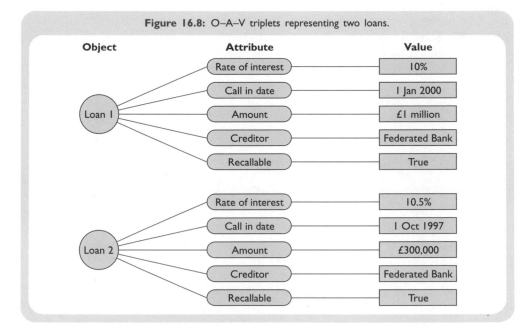

Figure 16.8: O–A–V triplets representing two loans.

where the values of attributes will be added in order to depict an instance of the loan type. Figure 16.9 is the static representation of a generic loan. Figure 16.8 is the dynamic representation of instances of loans during a consultation. The working expert system can be thought of as filling these value slots during the consultation. Some will be filled by the user entering values, others will be entered as a result of the inference process.

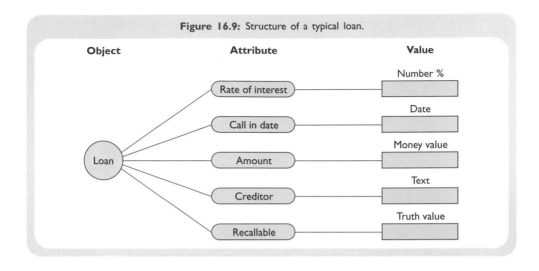

Figure 16.9: Structure of a typical loan.

16.2.3   Semantic networks

The O–A–V triplets go some way towards representing the complexity of knowledge with which experts deal but they are a long way from the flexibility needed to build models for all knowledge domains. O–A–V triplets are a special and well-defined limitation of the more general semantic network. If the subjects of objects, attributes and values are left and attention is focused on the network representation of Figure 16.8 then Figure 16.10 is arrived at. Here there is no distinction made between the nodes (unlike Figure 16.8 where the different types of node have different semantic roles). There are, however, directed links between nodes. '**Has-a**', '**is-a**', and '**is-a-value-of**' are names of these directed links.

Figure 16.11 is an example of a general semantic network. Its formal composition is a network of nodes connected by directed links or arcs. There are well-known methods of representing this kind of structure at the physical level. Virtually no limitation is placed on what can be the content of a node or link but it is usual to restrict the representation to the following:

Nodes
Nodes can be classified into the following categories:

1. Objects are generally represented as nodes. In the example in Figure 16.11, Anita Patel, John Smith, and Jack Jones are all physical objects. Abstract objects are also placed in nodes. 40 is an abstract object. Some objects seem to fall between the two. 'Accounts department' names an object that is more abstract than Jack Jones but less abstract than the number 40. It is also represented as a node.

2. General terms such as 'employee' or 'accountant' are placed at nodes. These terms correspond to classes of individual objects. (In the terminology of data analysis and the development of the entity model covered in Chapter 12, these classes can be regarded as entity types, while the objects themselves will be entities, perhaps as some occurrence of an entity type shown in the figure.)

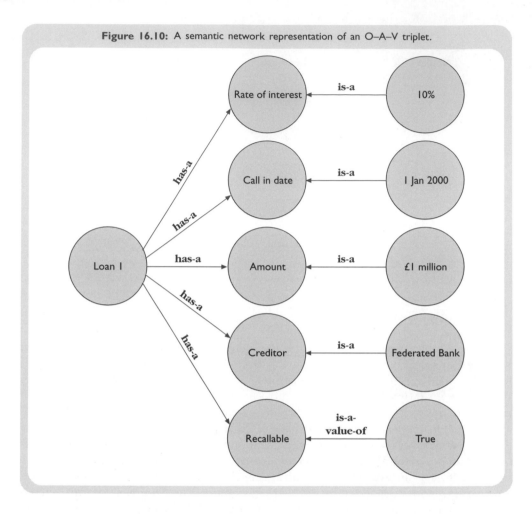

Figure 16.10: A semantic network representation of an O–A–V triplet.

3. Attributes can be considered to be of two types. There are attributes that require values and there are those that do not. 'Age' is an example of the former in that it needs a numeric value. 'Accounting qualification' or 'office' are respectively attributes of 'accountant' and 'employee' that do not require values in the illustrated semantic network. The distinction between attributes and objects is not always clear.

Generally speaking, those attributes that do not require values will rise to the highest possible level of abstraction associated with general terms. In the figure it is a property of each employee that he or she has a company file. Therefore it is also a property of each accountant that he or she has a company file (because they are employees) and of both Anita Patel and John Smith that they each have a company file (because they are accountants). It would be possible to associate the property individually with each object employee of the company – that is, with Anita Patel and John Smith – but this would waste space and miss the generality of the association of the property of having a company file with being an employee.

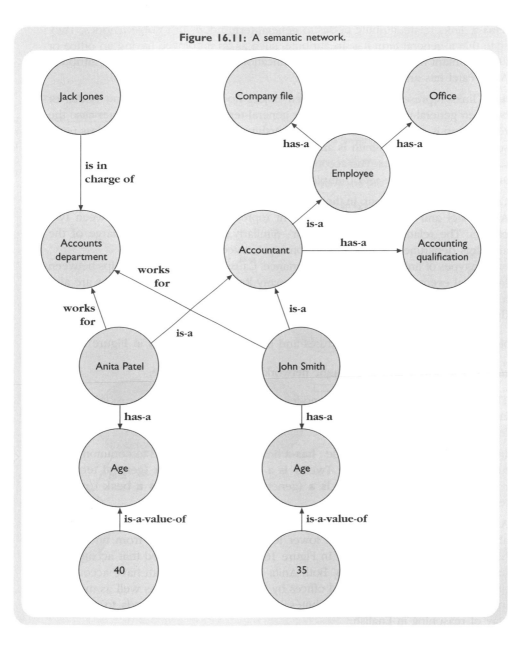

Figure 16.11: A semantic network.

On the other hand 'age' cannot rise up through the hierarchy because it requires a value. Although each employee has an age it is not the same age. Age is really a function from the class of employees to the class of numbers.

Links

Links are one-way directed connections between nodes. These generally fall into one of a number of categories:

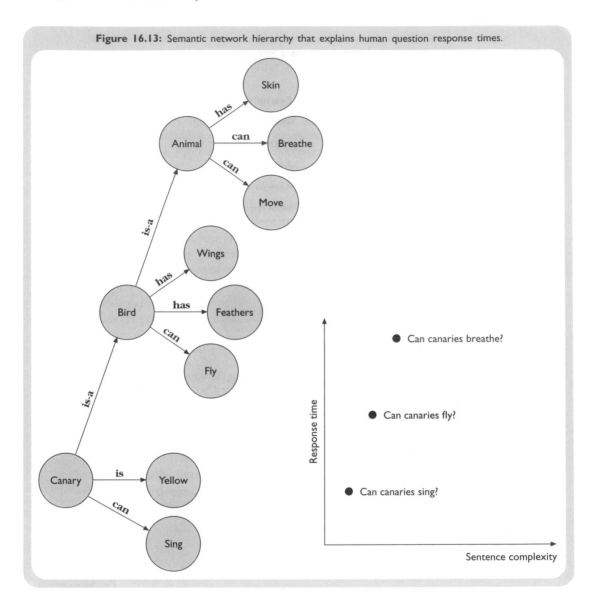

Figure 16.13: Semantic network hierarchy that explains human question response times.

Disadvantages: The disadvantages of them are:

1. The flexibility and simplicity of the structural constituents (links and nodes) as well as being an asset also implies that it is difficult to represent the difference between different semantic categories. For example, the structure ⟨⟨object⟩ **is a** ⟨general term⟩⟩ is represented in exactly the same way as ⟨⟨general term⟩ **is a** ⟨general term⟩⟩ by means of a ⟨node:link:node⟩ structure. This conflates the differences between the two structures. The difference is revealed in the way they can be used to carry out inferences or simply in the difference between '∈' and '⊆' of set theory. One of the aims of linguistic philosophy has been to analyze the semantic

components of propositions into their constituent categories in order to represent meaning and facilitate inferencing. Simple semantic networks obliterate these distinctions.

2. They are particularly efficient as storage media for inheritance hierarchies but as soon as exceptions occur semantic networks can become overly complex. In Figure 16.11 the '**has-a**' link connecting 'office' and 'employee' is a particularly convenient and efficient way of storing information that Anita Patel, John Smith . . . , all of whom are employees (as illustrated by the **is-a** link hierarchy), have offices. However, if there are exceptions then these have to be encoded separately. Suppose, for instance, that John Smith is one of the few employees that does not have an office. This needs to be stored as a special property of John Smith with a '**has-a**' link so that the inheritance by John Smith of the 'office' property through the hierarchy is blocked. As long as there are a few exceptions then a semantic network may be an advantageous storage representation but once exceptions become common it becomes unwieldy.

16.2.4   Frames

Frames are an alternative way of representing knowledge. They use the basic idea of the object–attribute–value representation but build in refinements that overcome some of the limitations of the O–A–V form. The rationale behind frames is that experts represent their knowledge as various concepts (frames), which are interconnected. For instance, 'employee' is a concept that has various attributes and 'storekeeper' is a connected concept, a type of employee, which will have more specific attributes than those of employee.

The use of frames can be understood by using the example in Figure 16.14. This is a frame for a long-term loan. The frame consists of slots in which entries are made for a particular occurrence of the frame type. The frame type can be thought of as an object type, the slots as attributes and the entries as attribute values. The frame is more developed than the O–A–V triplet in the following ways:

1. The frame may have pointers to other frames. These pointers may indicate hierarchies of the '**is-a**' link sort typical of semantic networks or they may indicate other frames that have some bearing on the frame under consideration. In Figure 16.14 the 'long-term loan' is a kind of 'loan'. This corresponds to an '**is-a**' link.

2. It is common for experts to have incomplete knowledge of the facts of a particular case. What does the expert do? In many cases the expert will assume that the missing information is typical for the kind of object under consideration – a 'best guess' philosophy. Frames allow this to be built into the description. In Figure 16.14 the 'rate of interest' of the loan needs to be specified. If it is not then a default is inserted – the current rate of interest. This may be a defined variable or may itself be another frame. Frames may point to other frames elsewhere. At any later stage the default value may be overridden by known complete information being added. The 'type of repayment' also has a default value. In the case of particular long-term loans it is unlikely that the default values will be used, but in many other business examples they will be an integral part of the representation.

3. The difference between declarative and procedural knowledge was explained earlier in Section 16.1.1. Although it is true that expert systems emphasize declarative aspects of knowledge, experts themselves will sometimes use procedures. When

Figure 16.14: A frame for a long-term loan.

ENTRIES

Frame type	long-term loan
Is-a-kind-of	loan

SLOTS		DESCRIPTION
Loan number	1348	Range: numeric
Amount	£300,000	Range: money value
Date acquired	12/12/97	Range: date
Date repayable	12/12/07	Range: date
Creditor	State Shire Bank	Text
Rate of interest	14%	Range: percentage
		Default: current rate of interest
Redeemable	Yes	Range: 'Yes', 'No'
		Default: 'Yes'
Type of repayment	Interest only	Range: 1 = 'interest only', 2 = 'interest plus principal'
		Default: 'interest plus principal'
Amount outstanding	£240,000	Range: money value
Repayment	£40,000	Range: money value
		If type of repayment = 1 **do** procedure *calc repayment 1*
		If type of repayment = 2 **do** procedure *calc repayment 2*

reasoning about a company's long-term loan structure an expert may be required to calculate a future repayment against a loan. This is essentially a procedural task unless the repayment is found by simply looking up tables containing dates, rates of interest and loan amounts. Frames allow slot entries to be filled by the output of procedures as in the 'repayment' slot in Figure 16.14. The frame contains within its specification the procedures to be called and under what circumstances. These procedures are defined in the knowledge base.

Generally speaking, it is best to speak of knowledge not as either procedural or declarative absolutely but as being represented as procedural (or declarative) for a particular purpose. Frames allow this flexibility in a way that O–A–V triplets do

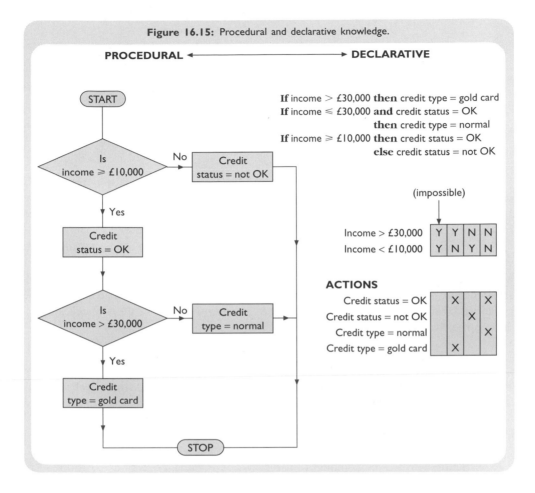

Figure 16.15: Procedural and declarative knowledge.

not. Figure 16.15 gives one procedural and two declarative representations of the same piece of knowledge. It uses a slightly extended version of the rules in Figure 16.6 covering the granting of credit cards.

16.2.5 Logic

Knowledge may also be represented in the form of logic. Philosophers since Aristotle have been interested in correct and incorrect forms of reasoning and have found that valid reasoning conforms to various patterns of argument. In order to reveal these patterns formal logics have been developed as powerful symbolic representation tools. As expert systems are concerned with reasoning correctly using knowledge, it is not surprising that formal logic has been an influence on the representation of knowledge. The influence of formal propositional logic has already been looked at. **If–then** rule representation using the Boolean logical connectives **and**, **or** and **not** is an example of this. The decomposition of the structure of the individual sentences involved in the rule may also be achieved using predicate logic.

Figure 16.16: Representation of grandparent relations.

Grandparent (x,y):-child (x,z) & child (z,y)

Child (George, Sarah)
Child (Sandra, Mary)
Child (George, Sandra)
Child (Sandra, James)
Child (Sarah, Ian)

An example of this is shown in Figure 16.16. The property of being a grandparent is defined in terms of being a child of a child. Individual facts are added to the database as illustrated. This form of representation facilitates drawing inferences according to the canons of classical logic. Each entry is either a rule defining a term or is a fact.

The artificial intelligence language PROLOG is based on the predicate calculus. The expressions in Figure 16.16 are in a PROLOG-like form. The language contains within it its own inferencing procedures. If 'grandparent (George,x)' were entered, a list of names satisfying the individual fact together with the rule definition of grandparent would be produced by the PROLOG system. PROLOG is forming the basis of the artificial intelligence kernel language of the Japanese fifth-generation computers.

16.2.6 Knowledge representation – conclusion

The main forms of knowledge representation have been covered. Many expert systems allow a mixture of techniques, recognizing that each has its own area of suitability and limitations. The most general technique is the semantic network, of which frames, O–A–V triplets and A–V pairs are specializations. Most expert systems to date have employed O–A–V triplets together with production rules for the general knowledge base although it is becoming increasingly common to use frames as well (especially as more low-cost expert system shells using frames are released onto the market). The influence of logic techniques has not yet been fully realized though developments in this area are likely with the advent of the Japanese fifth-generation computers.

16.3 Drawing inferences

The knowledge base contains domain-specific knowledge and particular facts. As can be seen from Section 16.2 these may be represented as production rules, object–attribute–value triplets, semantic networks, frames or statements in logic. The aim of an expert system is to apply the domain-specific knowledge to the particular facts to draw conclusions or give advice. It is the purpose of this section to sketch the ways in which this may be carried out. Principles of inference are considered together with inference control strategies that apply these principles systematically so ensuring that, wherever they exist, the expert system will arrive at proper conclusions.

16.3.1 Principles and methods of inference

There are several principles and methods of reasoning used in expert systems. Two of the most common are *modus ponens* and the resolution principle. These are now explained.

Figure 16.17: Truth tables. (a) A truth table for the logical connectives. (b) A truth table for *modus ponens*. (c) A truth table for the resolution principle.

(a)

A	B	if A then B	A and B	A or B	not A	not A or B
T	T	T	T	T	F	T
T	F	F	F	T	F	F
F	T	T	F	T	T	T
F	F	T	F	F	T	T

(b)

	A	B	if A then B,	A	∴ B
*	T	T	T	T	T
	T	F	F	T	F
	F	T	T	F	T
	F	F	T	F	F

(c)

	A	B	C	not A or B,	not B or C	∴ not A or C
*	T	T	T	T	T	T
	T	T	F	T	F	F
	T	F	T	F	T	T
	T	F	F	F	T	F
*	F	T	T	T	T	T
	F	T	F	T	F	T
*	F	F	T	T	T	T
*	F	F	F	T	T	T

Modus ponens

The principle of *modus ponens* and the closely connected principle of *modus tollens* have been considered in Section 16.1.4. They are basic to the understanding of most expert systems, as some reasoning in virtually any area of expertise is best captured using these principles with **if–then** rules. *Modus ponens* also reflects an obvious form of human reasoning (unlike *modus tollens*). It is so basic that even to question its validity has often been taken as evidence of a failure to understand the **if–then** construction and the words contained within it.

The strictest requirement on principles of reasoning is that these principles must lead to true conclusions when applied to true premises. Some principles dealing with reasoning and propositions were given in Figure 16.3. How do we know that these will meet this strict requirement? In other words, does proof from truth always lead to truth in these cases? To answer this it is necessary to give meanings to the logical connectives.

The use of Truth (T) and Falsity (F) are employed for this task in Figure 16.17(a). The table can be read by looking at a combination of T and F for A and B together and then determining the given value for A and B joined by the logical connective. For instance, **if** 'A' is True **and** 'B' is False then 'A **or** B' is True. The table defines the meanings of '**if–then**', '**and**', '**or**' and '**not**'. Put another way, if a Martian had the concept of truth and falsity then it would be able to understand the meaning of our words '**if–then**', '**and**', '**or**' and '**not**' purely from these tables.

Figure 16.17(b) illustrates why *modus ponens* is a valid principle of reasoning. Here truth tables are used to assign True or False to each premise and to the conclusion in an inference. All possible combinations of Truth and Falsity are assigned to A and B. The truth value is then calculated for each premise and each conclusion. The requirement on a sound reasoning principle is that true premises lead to true conclusions. The starred line (*) is the only case where all the premises are True. Here the conclusion is True.

Resolution

In Figure 16.3(e) the resolution principle is given. This is shown to be a sound principle of reasoning in Figure 16.17(c). Once again the starred lines (*) represent cases where the premises are True. In each of these lines the conclusion is True.

The resolution method is a systematic way of establishing whether a proposition can be proved from a set of **if–then** rules and other facts. Central to the resolution method is the resolution principle. Here is a simple example of the method in practice. The following is assumed:

(1) **If** it is raining **then** the road is slippery   **If** A **then** B
(2) **If** the road is slippery **then** motor accidents increase   **If** B **then** C
(3) It is raining   A

and we wish to establish whether the following can be proved:

(4) Motor accidents increase   C

The resolution method involves four steps.

First, rewrite all **if–then** statements as **or** statements. The equivalence 'if A **then** B' and '(**not** A) **or** B' is shown in Figure 16.17(a). (1) and (2) become (5) and (6):

(5) Either it is **not** raining **or** the road is slippery   **not** A **or** B
(6) Either the road is **not** slippery **or** motor accidents increase   **not** B **or** C

Second, assert the negation of the proposition under test – that is, assume the negation of (4) is true:

(7) Motor accidents do **not** increase   **not** C

Third, use the resolution principle (see Figure 16.3(c)) on (5) and (6) to derive (8):

(5) Either it is **not** raining **or** the road is slippery   **not** A **or** B
(6) Either the road is **not** slippery **or** motor accidents increase   **not** B **or** C
(8) Either it is **not** raining **or** motor accidents increase   **not** A **or** C

Now use the disjunction elimination principle (see Figure 16.3(f)) on (3) and (8) to prove that motor accidents increase (9):

(8) Either it is **not** raining **or** motor accidents increase   **not** A **or** C
(3) It is raining   A
(9) Motor accidents increase   C

Fourth, show that a contradiction has been reached between (9) and (7):

Motor accidents increase **and** motor accidents do **not**   C **and not** C
increase

so that the supposition in (7) must be false, that is

Motor accidents increase   C

has been proved.

The resolution method always follows this four-step strategy. The resolutions in step (3) can be many and complex. The method is very important in expert systems because

(a) it can be automated easily and (b) those expert systems that attempt to prove goals from sets of rules and facts (referred to earlier in Section 16.1.4 as 'backward-chaining systems') can do so easily by asserting the negation of the goal to be proved and using the method to derive a contradiction.

The resolution method can equally well handle expressions in the predicate calculus, although it becomes more complex. This is important, as predicate logic is one of the standard representation techniques for the knowledge base.

16.3.2 Uncertain reasoning

So far, the principles and methods of inference that have been considered all deal with cases that involve certain Truth or certain Falsity and the principles always lead from Truth to Truth. However, much human expertise is concerned with reasoning where propositions are not known with certainty, and conclusions cannot be derived with certainty, or with rules that are themselves perhaps not certain. Indeed, the presence of uncertainty in a real-life situation is for many people the chief reason for using an expert. As was mentioned at the beginning of this chapter there are some who regard the handling of uncertain reasoning as an essential feature of an expert system.

1. An example of the first case of uncertainty mentioned might occur when a doctor attempts to diagnose the cause of fever-like symptoms. Neither the doctor nor the patient knows with certainty whether the patient has been in contact with a Lassa fever carrier from Nigeria. Probably not, but it is still a possibility and one of the factors that needs to be considered if the patient is suffering from some of the symptoms of Lassa fever.

2. An example of the second type of uncertainty concerns credit card applications. If the credit card applicant has an income of more than £30,000 per annum and has a mortgage then the credit status is probably 'OK'. If it is known that the applicant has not defaulted on any other loans or credit card payments in the past then credit status increases to almost certainly 'OK'.

3. An example of the third case can happen on the frontiers of a discipline where heuristic reasoning is carried out by experts using several rules, each of which may be doubted. This may happen where events are supposed, but not known, to be linked as cause and effect.

The implied format for each of these cases is:

(1) Probably A
(2) **If** A **then** probably B
(3) Probably (**if** A **then** B)

Of course some mixture of these may be present in the same case.

Reasoning with uncertainty is a treacherous area. Many plausible reasoning principles turn out to be ill-founded. A student thought that the following was an acceptable reasoning method (note its similarity with the example used to explain resolution):

If it is raining **then** probably the road is slippery	**If** A **then** probably B
If the road is slippery **then** probably accidents increase	**If** B **then** probably C
It is raining	A

therefore

| Probably accidents increase | probably C |

The student thought again when the following instance of the reasoning method was provided:

If there is shortly to be an avalanche **then** probably it has been snowing recently	**If** A **then** probably B
If it has been snowing recently **then** probably I will go skiing	**If** B **then** probably C
There is shortly to be an avalanche	A

therefore

| Probably I will go skiing | Probably C |

There are two major areas to be looked at with respect to uncertainty in expert systems. First, how is uncertain knowledge represented? Second, how is uncertainty handled in reasoning? The way that uncertainty is represented will impact on the way it is handled in reasoning.

Certainty factors

This is the method used in MYCIN and several other expert systems. Each proposition (or value associated with an attribute of an object) is assigned a certainty factor in the real number range -1 to $+1$. -1 indicates certainty that the proposition does not hold, $+1$ certainty that it does and 0 indicates ignorance.

There are different ways that reasoning using certainty factors may be carried out. One method is to regard the certainty factor of a pair of propositions to be the minimum of the two factors if they are connected by **and**, and to be the maximum if connected by **or**, and to regard the certainty of the conclusion of an **if–then** rule to be the certainty of the antecedent multiplied by the certainty of the consequent. The rule normally has some threshold certainty associated with the antecedent. Below this the rule will not fire. 0.20 is a typical threshold that is used in MYCIN.

Consider the following example. Given:

A (certainty = 0.6)
B (certainty = 0.4)
If A **and** B **then** C (certainty = 0.9)

therefore

A **and** B (certainty = min (0.6, 0.4) = 0.4)
C (certainty = 0.9 × 0.4 = 0.36)

Necessity and sufficiency factors

The certainty factors in MYCIN's rules indicate how sufficient the evidence (antecedent) is for a conclusion (consequent). In many areas of expertise the absence of evidence for a conclusion is often taken as indicating that the conclusion does not hold. The evidence is therefore necessary for the conclusion. So, as well as sufficiency factors there are necessity factors. PROSPECTOR is an expert system that contains rules with both of these factors. From PROSPECTOR:

If there is hornblende pervasively altered to biotite **then** there is strong evidence (320, 0.001) for potassic zone alteration.

Without going into the exact meaning of these dual factors the value of 320 indicates that the altered hornblende is highly sufficient for potassic zone alteration but 0.001 indicates that the absence of this evidence does little to rule out the possibility. Necessity and sufficiency factors are particularly important where a condition may be associated with one of a range of circumstances.

Fuzzy sets

The use of fuzzy sets is a formal approach to inexact reasoning that diverges from the basic assumptions of classical logic. In traditional set theory predicates such as 'is red' or 'is a bad debtor' are assumed to denote sets – the set of red things and the set of bad debtors. Each object in the world is either in the set or it is not. Thus Jones is in the set of bad debtors, whereas Smith and the Eiffel Tower are not. Fuzzy set theory, in contrast, interprets predicates as denoting fuzzy sets. A fuzzy set is a set of objects. Some objects are definitely in the set. Some are definitely not and some are only probably or possibly within the set.

Uncertain reasoning – conclusion

Three forms of representing uncertainty and reasoning with uncertainty have been covered. This coverage is only superficial. The treatment that each gives to handling uncertainty is too complex for the scope of this book. References are given at the end of the chapter for the interested reader. There are a number of features that must be highlighted:

1. There is no one agreed method of handling uncertainty. This is not because of technical disagreement but rather reflects deep and theoretical differences of opinion. Moreover, there seems to be little basis for adjudicating between the competing views as criteria for comparison are not agreed.

2. The strict requirement that sound principles of reasoning must lead from truth to truth cannot apply in cases of uncertain reasoning.

3. There may be no one (or even several) correct model of uncertain reasoning to be applied *in vacuo*. It may be the case that the way uncertainty is handled is domain dependent. That is, although accountants, doctors and car mechanics use terms like 'probable', 'unlikely' and 'possible' these are used in different ways in different areas of expertise (domains).

4. Empirical research in each domain of expertise may indicate the models of inexact reasoning that are used there. These models can then be built into an expert system. Nowadays even expert system shells may not impose predefined methods of handling uncertainty upon the expert systems builder. They allow the architect to design control over the way in which uncertainty is handled in the final expert system.

5. Some expert systems provide 'friendly' user interfaces that use terms like 'probable' and 'likely'. These will be working with some numerical model of inexact reasoning behind the friendly and uncomplicated facade presented to the user. In understanding how an expert system arrives at its conclusions it is important to penetrate this mask.

6. Reasoning under uncertainty is, and will remain, one of the most important and controversial theoretical and practical areas in expert systems.

16.3.3 Inference control strategies

Using a principle to draw an inference will yield a new fact or probabilistic conclusion. In order to carry out a consultation, however, an expert system needs to draw many inferences. These cannot be made randomly or else the inference system will 'wander' logically around the knowledge area. Preferably, there needs to be some pattern or strategy to decide which inferences to draw at which time. The purpose of an inference control strategy is to determine this. The strategy used will obviously determine the performance characteristics of the expert system.

Forward chaining

This strategy takes the established current facts and attempts to use the rules (or whatever representation form the domain-specific knowledge base takes) to derive new facts. The new facts are then added to the set of established facts and the strategy attempts to derive further new facts to add to this set. The system is said to be data driven. This is most obvious in the application of *modus ponens*, where the antecedent conditions are amongst the set of established facts and the conclusions when drawn are added to this set. At any one time it may be possible to use more than one rule to derive more than one conclusion. In order to resolve the conflict, the inference control strategy must decide between the competing rules. A simple way of doing this is to number the rules and fire the lowest-numbered rule that has its antecedent satisfied. More complex conflict-resolving techniques are used in larger systems. An example of a forward-chaining system has been given in Figure 16.4, the model expert system dealing with creature classification.

Forward chaining is a useful strategy if there are a large number of possible outcomes given a small number of values for the initial data. This characteristic of an application is typical of expert systems dealing with planning where a relatively few basic constraints are given.

Backward chaining

By far the most common inference control strategy is backward chaining. This is used in MYCIN and all the major systems. In backward chaining a goal is selected and the system establishes the facts that are needed to prove the goal. Each of the needed facts becomes a subgoal and the system establishes the facts that are needed to prove these which, in their turn, become sub-subgoals, and so on. Eventually a basic proposition is reached. A basic proposition is a sub-sub . . . goal that does not depend on other facts.

There are now three possibilities. The proposition required is in the database, in which case the system will go on to establish, if it can, the other facts needed to prove the initial goal; the negation of the proposition is in the database, in which case the system will need to prove the initial goal, if it can, by a different route; neither the proposition nor its negation has been established. In this last situation it is normal for the expert system to interrogate the user. The answer provided can then be used in the reasoning.

In a consultation with an expert, say a doctor, it is usual for the patient to volunteer information at the start of the session ('I have been feeling tired for a week with loss of appetite and a sore throat. I also have a bad headache, which comes in the evening . . .'.) The doctor will use this initial information to select a most likely goal (diagnosis) and then seek to establish this by backward reasoning – performing laboratory tests, asking the patient particular questions, checking reflexes and so on. This form of approach is quite common. Suppose that a client consults an investment adviser when seeking a planned portfolio. The client will start by proffering information such as the amount of money involved, why the client wishes to invest, what special requirements are needed (for example, lump sum capitalization in 15 years to pay for a university education), constraints (such as no wish to invest in companies involved in military hardware) and so on. The investment adviser will use this to select likely strategies, which will require further elicitation of facts from the client.

Both of these examples can be characterized by initial forward chaining followed by backward chaining. It is common for modern expert systems to allow this mix of inference control strategies.

There is much research work yet to be done on inference control strategies. These strategies become particularly important when dealing with large expert systems. The hundreds or even thousands of rules involved may use large chunks of computer processing during searching unless efficient control strategies are adopted. This is crucial with the current trend towards large multi-user expert systems in the areas of finance and insurance.

Summary

Expert systems are a rapidly expanding area in the application of artificial intelligence in business. It is estimated that the increase in investment in expert systems will continue throughout the 1990s. Expert systems incorporate the expertise or competent skills of one or many experts. They do this in a way that separates the general knowledge of the expert from the particular details of a case under consideration. The expert system then applies this knowledge to the case and uses reasoning to come to conclusions, gives advice, makes planning decisions, or suggests analyses and diagnoses.

The main components of an expert system are the knowledge base, the inference engine, the explanation subsystem and the knowledge acquisition subsystem. The knowledge base stores the domain-specific knowledge of the expert together with particular data obtained during a consultation. The inference engine is responsible for dynamically applying the domain-specific knowledge to the particular case during use of the system. The explanation subsystem allows users to interrogate the expert system with requests as to **HOW** a specific conclusion has been derived or **WHY** a question is being asked. The knowledge acquisition subsystem enables the entry of knowledge by the expert or generates general rules from a database of past cases by automated induction. The major problems in knowledge acquisition occur in the earlier stages of knowledge elicitation from the expert and the representation of this in a suitable form for the system.

The choice for the representation form is an important one. Different forms have different areas of suitability. Rule-based representations are common in many expert systems, particularly small systems. This structure may be combined with the representation of attributes and values of objects (A–V pairs) within the rules themselves. If many objects are used within a system it may be convenient to use an object–attribute–value representation strategy. Semantic networks provide a ▷

general way of representing the connections between various objects and concepts. Frame-based representations, in which concepts are modelled as frames with slots for attributes, are now becoming widely used. The ability for default values to fill the slots, references to procedures and the way that frames can be linked together, and in so doing model the interconnections between concepts, enables knowledge to be represented in a powerful way.

Different principles of inference can be used in different systems. Where the reasoning is only concerned with certainty there is some agreement about the constraints that inferences should meet. Matters become more complex though when, as is common with many areas of expertise, the luxury of a certain world disappears. The way that uncertain knowledge is represented interacts with the techniques of reasoning with uncertainty. Various approaches are common. Certainty factors, necessity and suf-ficiency measures and fuzzy sets have all been used. There is still a large area of disagreement about the representation and patterns of reasoning to be used with uncertain knowledge. It may be the case that what counts for adequate uncertain reasoning cannot be based on analytical or mathematical investigation but will rely on empirical research, which may deliver different results for different areas of expertise.

Inference control strategies ensure that the inference engine carries out reasoning in an exhaustive and efficient manner. Systems that attempt to prove selected goals by establishing propositions needed to prove these goals, which in themselves become secondary goals, are backward-chaining or goal-driven systems. This is in contrast to forward-chaining systems, which attempt to derive conclusions from existing established fact.

It is important for the business person involved with the development (and use) of expert systems to have an understanding of their components, the way that knowledge is represented within them and the forms of reasoning used. This is because it is likely that in the development of such systems they (the experts) will be more intimately involved than they would in the development of traditional information systems.

Exercises

1. Briefly explain the following terms:

knowledge base	**HOW** question	**has-a** link
inference engine	backward chaining	inheritance hierarchy
inference principle	declarative knowledge	forward chaining
inference strategy	procedural knowledge	uncertain reasoning
if–then rule	object–attribute–value triple	confidence factor
knowledge acquisition	frame	expert system shell
subsystem	semantic network	artificial intelligence
explanatory subsystem	**is-a** link	**WHY** question ▷

2. 'There is little difference between an expert system interrogating a knowledge base and a database management system accessing a database.' Do you agree?

3. Using an example explain the difference between *declarative* and *procedural* knowledge.

4. Select a familiar task that requires the use of knowledge to be carried out successfully.

Specify the central knowledge areas involved in performing the task and represent these as **if–then** rules. A partial example is now given:

Task: Decision on the purchase of a second-hand car.

Areas (1) Is a car needed?

       (2) Is the car that is being considered sound?

       (3) Is the car that is being considered priced reasonably?

       (4) Can I finance purchase of the car?

if–then rules (Area 2)

(2.1) **If** the bodywork is sound

    and the engine is sound

    and the suspension is sound

    and the steering is sound

    and the general condition is satisfactory

    then the car is considered sound.

(2.1.2) If there is not knocking from the engine when idling

    and there is not blue smoke from the exhaust

    and . . .

    and . . .

    then the engine is sound.

5. (a) Explain what it is for a pattern of reasoning to be sound.

   (b) Consider the following argument forms:

     (1) No As are Bs

       Some Bs are Cs

       ∴ No As are Cs

     (2) All As are Bs

       Some Bs are not Cs

       ∴ Some As are not Cs

     (3) Some As are Bs

       No As are Cs

       ∴ Some Bs are not Cs

     (4) Not all As are Bs

       Some Bs are not Cs

       ∴ Some As are Cs

     (5) Some As are Bs and some are not

       Some Bs are Cs and some are not

       ∴ Some As are Cs

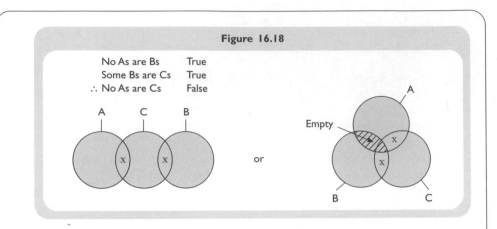

Figure 16.18

No As are Bs   True
Some Bs are Cs   True
∴ No As are Cs   False

(6) All As are Bs
    No Bs are Cs
    ∴ No As are Cs

(i) In each of these cases decide whether the pattern of reasoning is sound. [Hint: Represent each predicate by a set drawn on a Venn diagram constructed to reveal the argument form. Attempt to produce a Venn diagram where all the premises are true yet the conclusion is false. If this can be done the argument form is unsound. Why? See Figure 16.18]

(ii) For unsound patterns of reasoning suggest an English example where the premises are true and the conclusion false.
[Example for (1)
No women are men TRUE
Some men are doctors TRUE
No women are doctors FALSE]

6. Explain the difference between a system that uses attribute–value pairs and a system that uses object–attribute–value triplets for representing knowledge. Give an example when it is necessary to use O–A–V representation rather than A–V representation.

7. Draw a semantic network representation of:
(a) your family, illustrating important relations
(b) a motor car and its parts.

8. Explain, using a simple example, what is meant by a *frame-based representation*. In what ways does a frame-based representation differ from a semantic network? Explain the advantages and disadvantages of a frame-based representation over:
(a) O–A–V triplets
(b) a rule-based representation.

9. Develop a frame for:
(a) a dinner party
(b) a customer for the products of a company.

10. Explain the resolution method of proof. Why is it particularly applicable to backward-chaining strategies?

11. The resolution principle may be stated as:

> A **or** B
> **not** B **or** C
> ∴ A **or** C

Show that this is a sound principle by using a truth table.

12. What is meant by *reasoning with uncertainty* in the context of knowledge systems?

13. Represent the following paragraph (taken from the main text of the chapter) as:
(a) Boolean **if–then** rules
(b) O–A–V triplets within rules.

If the student has successfully completed Level 1 of the examination, **or** has been exempted from Level 1 by virtue of satisfying **any** of the conditions laid out in paragraphs 3(a) to 3(f) below, **then** the student is entitled to register for Level 2 of the examination. A student registered for Level 2 is exempt from examination papers 2.3 **and** 2.4 **if** he/she has obtained exemption from Level 1 by virtue of satisfying the conditions 3(a) **or** 3(b) below, **or** satisfying 3(d) **and** being in possession of an honours degree awarded by a British University or accredited by the Council for National Academic Awards.

14. Are intelligent knowledge-based systems (expert systems) really intelligent in the sense that we use the word 'intelligent' to apply to human beings? If so, by virtue of what characteristics are they to be regarded as intelligent? If not, could a computer-based system be regarded as intelligent and what would constitute the justification for applying the term?

15. 'Backward chaining is an efficient reasoning strategy when the number of goals is small relative to the number of rules to be considered. As technology advances though, the increase in the speed of inferencing using facts and knowledge within the knowledge base will blur the importance of the distinction between forward and backward chaining as far as the user of the expert system is concerned.' Is this true?

16. 'Correct methods for handling probability and uncertainty have been known since the days of Pascal. Indeed, statistical analysis, the offering of odds on the likelihood of poker hands arising and actuarial estimates of risks all testify to a solid, mature, mathematical foundation to the estimation and manipulation of probability. The only problem with the representation of uncertainty in expert systems is that experts do not follow the proven cannons of probability theory. Expert systems would be easier to build and experts would be more accurate in their advice and judgements if they ensured that they reasoned within known probability theory.' What misconceptions are involved in this view?

17. An accounts bookkeeping package incorporates accounting expertise, so is a bookkeeping package an expert system?

18. Is there a mapping between the concepts used in entity–relationship data modelling and the concepts and structures used in a semantic network representation of knowledge? To what extent is the mapping, if it exists, complete?

References and recommended reading

● Arnold M. and Rush D. (1987). An expert system approach to the appraisal of accounting software. *Management Accounting*, January
An introductory article illustrating an application of expert systems in appraisal. This can be read with no prior knowledge of expert systems.

● Beerel A. (1993). *Expert Systems in Business: Real World Applications*. Chichester: Ellis Horwood
This is a readable text that combines an introduction to theoretical aspects of expert systems with the practical knowledge and experience of an expert systems builder. The book also has case studies. Included is material on the relationship between corporate culture and expert systems, project management of expert systems and investment decisions on expert systems development.

● Barr A., Cohen P.R. and Feigenbaum E.A., eds *The Handbook of Artificial Intelligence*, Vols 1 and 2, Los Altos CA: William Kaufmann Inc.

● Cohen P.R. and Feigenbaum E.A., eds (1990). *The Handbook of Artificial Intelligence*, Vol. 3, Los Altos CA: William Kaufmann Inc.
These are invaluable reference books on all aspects of artificial intelligence.

● Collins A. and Quillan M.R. (1969). Retrieval time from semantic memory. *Journal of Verbal Learning and Verbal Behaviour*, **8**, 240–47

● Choforas D.N. *Applying Expert Systems in Business*. McGraw-Hill
This is a readable text that sets expert systems within the context of management perspectives, decision support systems and the information centre. With chapter titles such as 'Expert systems and the industrialization of knowledge' this text provides a broader perspective within the organization to locate expert systems.

● Harmon P. and King D. (1988). *Expert Systems*. New York: Wiley
An excellent introduction to all aspects of expert systems and their development. It is aimed at the intelligent reader from business rather than the computer specialist.

● Newell A. and Simon H. (1972). *Human Problem Solving*. Englewood Cliffs NJ: Prentice-Hall

● Parsaye K. and Chignell M. (1988). *Expert Systems for Experts*. Wiley
A comprehensive readable exposition of the basic concepts used in expert systems. Although not specifically orientated to business applications this book provides one of the best introductions to the central ideas behind business expert systems.

● Silverman B.G., ed. (1987). *Expert Systems for Business*. Reading MA: Addison-Wesley
This provides a series of articles organized around such themes as expert support systems and integrating expert systems into a business environment. It is not an introductory text though basic concepts in expert systems are introduced and explained early in the text.

● Turban E. (1995). *Decision Support and Expert Systems* 4d edn. New York: Macmillan.
This is a comprehensive textbook covering all aspects of DSS and expert systems from the perspective of a manager wishing to know about management support technologies. It has several case studies and chapter-end questions.

● Turban E. (1992). *Expert Systems and Applied Artificial Intelligence*. New York: Macmillan
This student text is a clear comprehensive treatment devoted to applied expert systems. It also contains sections on natural language processing, computer vision, speech understanding and robotics.

Chapter 17

Expert Systems: Development Through Prototyping

17.1   Features of expert systems development
17.2   The need for a methodology
17.3   The stages
17.4   Large and small systems
17.5   A case study – the Bank of America

This chapter considers the stages in the development of an expert system. Initially, the differences between the development of an expert system and a traditional information system are highlighted. The need for an expert systems development methodology is stressed. Prototyping is adopted and explained as a useful approach to expert systems development. The development stages are covered in detail. Properties of a problem or area that make it suitable for the development of an expert system are first discussed. The likely costs and benefits resulting from the expert system are then assessed. An important choice has to be made between using artificial intelligence languages, expert system tools and shells in building a system, and so the characteristics of these are explained. The designer of an expert system is the knowledge engineer. This role is described, together with various methods that may be used by the engineer to elicit knowledge from the expert in a form suitable for representation in an expert system. Having constructed and assessed the prototype the final system is designed and then evaluated. Special problems that are associated with the evaluation of expert systems are discussed. After drawing a distinction between large and small systems the final part of the chapter consists of a case study concerning the development of a small expert system.

17.1   Features of expert systems development

Although it is easy to understand that large expert systems require significant time, effort and planning to develop, it is tempting to regard the building of a small expert system as being a task of the same level of difficulty as that of building a spreadsheet model. It is often assumed that rules are keyed in together with text associated with the questions and that expertise is present at the touch of the microcomputer keyboard controls. At least this is the view often conveyed by reading the advertising literature surrounding expert system shells. The fact is very different from this myth. Design of an expert system, even a small one, is a task that will involve careful thought, planning and several man-weeks, months or even years of development, testing and fine tuning.

Does the analysis and design necessary for building an expert system differ from a traditional data processing or information system? There are three major points of distinction that prevent expert systems development being subsumed under the general framework of analysis and design covered in Chapters 9–15.

1. *The subject matter is knowledge and reasoning as contrasted with data and processing.* Knowledge has both form and content, which need investigation. 'Form' is connected with the mode of representation chosen – for instance, rules, semantic networks or logic. 'Content' needs careful attention as once the form is selected it is still a difficult task to translate the knowledge into the chosen representation form. In the traditional information systems project the analysis of data will lead to entity models where, in essence, the form of a data structure is considered. The specific content is ignored until the final database is loaded. In building expert systems the specific content cannot be ignored. This reflects the fact that knowledge systems reason 'intelligently' with the knowledge whereas database and file-based systems process data in a different way.

2. *Expert systems are expert/expertise orientated whereas information systems are decision/function/organization directed.* The expert system encapsulates the abilities of an expert or expertise and the aim is to provide a computerized replica of these facilities. There may be additions or improvements to the way that the expert system performs a task – after all, experts are not perfect! In contrast, the focus of an information system is to provide information from an organizational database that meets the operational, tactical and strategic decision requirements of the workforce at the relevant levels. It is the needs of the various decisions and functions in the organization that should drive the analysis and design process as compared with the knowledge of a single expert (or group of experts).

3. *Obtaining information for expert systems design presents different problems from those in traditional information systems design.* Many expert systems rely, partly at least, on incorporating expertise obtained from an expert. Few rely solely on the representation of textbook or rule book knowledge. It is difficult generally to elicit this knowledge from an expert. In contrast, in designing an information system the analyst relies heavily on existing documentation as a guide to the amount, type and content of formal information being passed around the system. Much of the interviewing of personnel concerns establishing what information they need (rather than that already possessed) or what they do with information. In summary, it can be said that in the development of an expert system the experts are regarded as repositories of knowledge whereas in information systems development people are regarded as the processors of information or the clients for receiving it.

17.2 The need for a methodology

In the early days of the business use of computers in the 1950s, analysis and design of data processing systems was a haphazard process with a heavy concentration on technical considerations at the expense of human and information aspects. This resulted in the underperformance and underutilization of the systems that were produced together with problems involved in costing and scheduling the project development itself. Out of these deficiencies evolved different types of methodologies of analysis and design – the differences being a product of:

1. what specific weaknesses the methodology was designed to avoid;
2. the areas of application to which the methodology was applicable;
3. the orientation, experience and interests of those developing the methodology.

The major evolutionary strands have been treated in Chapters 8–15 and now there are several proprietary methodologies for information systems analysis and design. These methodologies have detailed explanations of the procedures to be followed and of the documentation to be provided at each stage of the project. However, none of these applies to expert systems development. The three major distinctions considered imply that no tinkering with them will make them instantly applicable.

There is a deep need for an expert systems methodology. It is not surprising though that one is not available. Information systems methodologies have developed to their present maturity over a number of years from failures in past projects. Owing to their recent arrival expert systems, both successes and failures, are only just beginning to emerge. It is too early for distinct methodologies to have developed.

The expert systems development process explained in this chapter involves prototyping.

17.2.1 Prototyping

Prototyping is an approach towards the development of systems that is increasingly used. Although it is applied here to expert systems projects, prototyping is appropriate for other areas of mainstream information and decision support systems development. The idea of prototyping is not new. In engineering the building of a prototype is often regarded as an essential early part of a project's development. With regard to computerized systems prototyping has the following characteristics:

- **User driven:** End users of the system and, in the case of expert systems, those with knowledge or expertise, are intimately involved in the development process. Their view of the task, information and knowledge area is taken as the basis from which the prototype is developed. This is to be compared with traditional life-cycle approaches, which translate the user view into a computer-orientated set of design and program specifications.

- **Computer assisted:** The analysis, design and development of the prototype is assisted and implemented through computer-based aids and tools. This is achieved using interactive software often providing a visual (graphics) interface for users. These aids then generate program code for the prototype system. Fourth-generation languages (4GLs) and spreadsheet modelling packages are examples of aids to prototyping which were covered in Chapter 6.

- **High speed:** One of the advantages of prototyping is the speedy production of a working system that can be assessed and improved.

- **User requirements:** The emphasis in prototyping is on the production of a system that meets user requirements in terms of the functions it provides and the way it provides these via the user interface. There is little attention to optimization of the generated computer code. Consequently, prototypes are usually inefficient in their run-time use of computer hardware (as measured from a technical point of view).

● **Easily adaptable:** Owing to their speedy production using interactive computer-based tools, prototypes can be easily adapted to meet changing user requirements or existing user needs if these are not met by the prototype.

● **Differs from the linear life-cycle approach:** Many approaches to systems analysis and design, including the structured approach covered in the middle chapters (Chapters 9–14) of this book, assume formal stages of analysis, design, specification (detailed design) and then implementation. The intention is that these stages be passed through only once and that each stage is 'properly' carried out so that it need not be re-entered. In the development of the prototype the analysis, design and implementation phases are less distinct. It is recognized that the prototype is itself part of the development process and may need amendment.

Expert systems can be developed using a linear life-cycle approach, though the tools and techniques of most methodologies, such as data flow diagrams, structured English or flowcharts, are more appropriate for information systems development. This is hardly surprising – it is for this area that they have been developed.

In contrast to the linear life-cycle approach expert systems development is more suited to a prototyping approach. There are a number of factors determining this:

1. Representation structures in which knowledge is encoded and strategies are used in reasoning fall into a number of generic types – for example, frames and rules for knowledge representation, and backward chaining for an inference strategy. These have been covered in Chapter 16. To produce the computer code each time from 'scratch' for these structures and inference strategies would be time-consuming and costly. Consequently, expert systems tools and shells have been developed. This facilitates prototyping.

2. It is often only with a working expert system that an expert can obtain a 'feel' for the effectiveness of the system.

3. Expert systems must be easily adaptable to accommodate changes in knowledge and for amendment in the light of evaluation by experts.

4. It is impossible to dissociate the expert from the process of development of the expert system as much of the intended knowledge for the system resides within the expert. The user-driven interactive nature of prototyping provides useful fast feedback in development. In contrast, it is possible (though seldom desirable) to keep users at 'arm's length' in the development of a traditional information system.

17.3   The stages

The stages in development are shown in Figure 17.1. They are contrasted with a traditional life-cycle approach in two main ways. First, there is a heavy emphasis on knowledge elicitation. This illustrates the dissimilarity from traditional analysis and design where (the equivalent) information gathering is a comparatively straightforward process. Second, systems prototyping is a commonplace method that is made possible by the existence of

Figure 17.1: The stages in the development of an expert system.

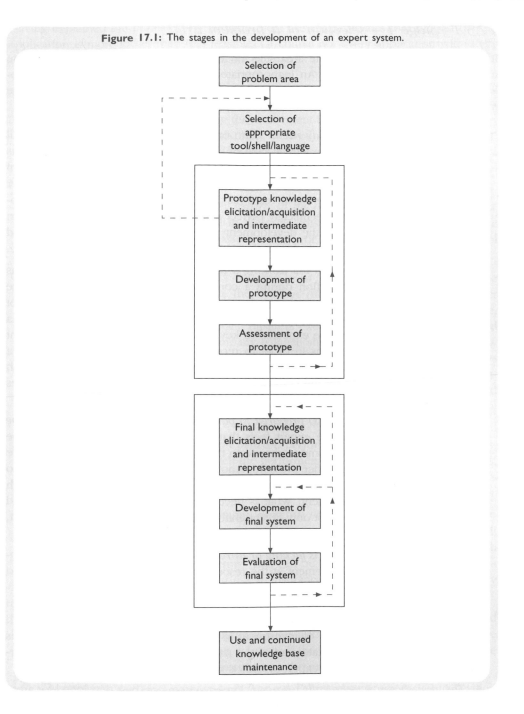

sophisticated development shells and tools. Although the development of the prototype is shown as the task prior to the development of the final system, in some cases the prototypes themselves, after several modifications and extensions, come to be accepted as the final system.

Table 17.1: A classification of expert systems.

Category	Example
Diagnosis/classification	Disease diagnosis, mechanical fault diagnosis
Advice	Data protection registration advice, advice on a company's financial health
Prediction	Prediction of corporate failure
Planning/design/repair	Investment plan adviser, office allocation adviser
Training	Training in handling letters of credit for import/export

Figure 17.2: Examples of expert systems applications in business.

System description

Provides advice to employers on dismissal of employees

Provides welfare benefits advice

Advises on statutory sick pay and entitlements

Interprets tax legislation with respect to minimization of tax liability

Filters CVs for personnel selection

Provides an assessment of the financial health of a company from different perspectives

Advises on the requirement and procedures for registration under the Data Protection Act of the UK

Advises on the selection of a portfolio of stocks and securities

Advises on the categorization of property for the purposes of tax assessment

Develops an investment plan for customers

Assists with the allocation of offices

Assists in the recruitment of employees (job design to final selection of applicants)

Aids auditors in assessing the effectiveness of controls

Provides assessment of risk for insurance underwriters

Provides for in-house assessment of staff loans

These guidelines for the selection of an appropriate area allow expert systems to be applicable to a wide range of business, industrial and commercial activities. A selection of these systems is given in Figure 17.2. A brief description of the system is provided. All of these systems have been developed recently or are currently in the process of being built. Expert systems can be classified, not only by the subject area, but also by the type of service they provide (see Table 17.1).

Costs and benefits of expert systems

Generally, a company, government department or any organization will not attempt involvement in expert systems development without some assessment of the costs and likely benefits (though there have been some notable exceptions).

Expert systems are new and the art of assessment of costs is still at the level of educated guesswork. These costs may be broken down into four main areas: hardware costs, software costs, development costs and maintenance costs.

Hardware costs: Expert systems may be developed and used on an organization's existing mainframe (or even microcomputers for small systems). It is also possible for dedicated machines and workstations (for example, SUN and APOLLO) to be employed, at least in the development stage. These have central processors designed especially for handling the processing requirements of artificial intelligence languages such as LISP.

Software costs: These depend on the extent to which the expert system program is to be coded from programming languages of a conventional nature, such as C++ or Pascal, which may already be used by the organization, through to the use of high-level expert system tools or shells. In the former case the cost of the software language will be low but the program development costs high, whereas in the latter the development time may be short, and therefore costs will be low, but there will be a large 'up front' cost for the purchase of the shell or other tools that are used. The selection of the appropriate language, tools, or shells is discussed in Section 17.3.3 of this chapter.

Development costs: Apart from using the programmer's time, there are two other main types of personnel involved in the development of the system. The experts will need to be released from their normal area of practice in order to allow the transfer of knowledge from them to the system. They must be costed if possible at their normal working value to the organization. The release time will usually run into man-weeks, months or even years. This may be on the basis of a set number of hours per day rather than a block release. There also needs to be a 'knowledge engineer' who is responsible for eliciting the knowledge from the expert and recasting it in a form suitable for the programmers or expert system tool/shell that is being used. This person fulfils a role akin to a systems or data analyst in a traditional information systems project. The major difficulty in deriving the costs of developing an expert system surround the problems involved in estimating the time commitment and cost for the experts and knowledge engineers.

Maintenance costs: Once developed, an expert system may need its knowledge base updated. This is particularly true for systems that give advice on the interpretation of legislation where that legislation changes periodically. Tax systems are an example. Good expert system design should allow for straightforward modular alteration, otherwise complete redesign of large sections of the knowledge base may be necessary.

There are problems with cost estimation but these are minor compared with the difficulty of assessing benefits. The range of types of benefit are now covered and it is obvious that many are intangible. This leads to the usual problems in making an economic cost–benefit comparison. Most of the benefits will refer to one or more of the desirable characteristics of the area for which the expert system is selected.

Skills archive benefits: Organizations are particularly vulnerable if single individuals possess organization-specific skills in areas that are essential for the smooth functioning of business activities. In this case if the person leaves no replacement is possible. Examples in this area may be quite mundane but important. Mrs Jones may be the only person who understands the idiosyncrasies of tracing enquiries through the manual filing system. Mr Black may be the only person who can estimate the cost to a textile company associated with setting up the looms for and production of a complex cloth pattern. These two people have skills that should be archived.

Standardization of procedures: It is common for a company to attempt to standardize procedures governing its business activities for control and comparison purposes. This is difficult when the procedure is one carried out separately by a number of experts. An expert system that incorporates standards to be followed in the majority of the experts' problem cases may ensure that the overall quality of the expert task is improved and standardized while releasing the experts for the more unusual and demanding problems.

Cost-effective trainers: Owing to their capacity to reason, provide explanations and to carry out what-if functions, expert systems are often suitable for use as a training or tutoring medium. They can also be used by trainees as a check on their own performance prior to mastering a particular complex task. To be effective tutoring systems they need to be specially designed with educational objectives in mind.

Cost-effective consultant (expert replacer): Replacing the rare skills of the expert by a machine performing the role of consultant was, in the early days, seen to be one of the main benefits of an expert system. Machines are cheap, work 24 hours a day, do not take holidays or become sick, and always perform at a consistent standard. It is now becoming clear though that the expert system as an expert replacer is generally not possible. There are a number of reasons for this:

1. It is difficult to design a system that interacts in a sufficiently flexible way with non-expert users and provides questions that can be understood and answered. Experts can easily translate their questions into the most understandable form compatible with the intelligence, knowledge, cultural background and interests of the person requiring the expert opinion. Expert systems cannot handle this at their present stage of development.

2. An expert uses non-verbal clues in a consultation. Hesitation, facial expressions and intonation are all guides that experts use in assessing responses to questions.

3. People often feel happier consulting with humans than with computerized experts.

4. There are still problems concerning the legal liability involved surrounding the advice given by expert systems. Experts make mistakes and so will expert systems. In each country there will be legislation governing the liability of experts but at present the liability of expert systems is not clear.

5. Most experts use more general knowledge in their day-to-day practice than was originally recognized in the early years of expert systems. To understand how general knowledge impinges, choose an area of expertise and then select an event in an unrelated area that clearly affects the first area but would not be incorporated in any expert system on it. For example, the investment analyst reads that the President of the USA has been assassinated. Would this affect the advice given by the investment analyst to clients over the following few days? It is hard to see how expert systems can be expected to deal with all eventualities. The point really is that the human expert, as well as possessing knowledge in the narrow area of expertise, can integrate this with a vast base of general knowledge. The expert system does not possess this.

6. If experts realize that their area of expertise is to be replaced with a computerized system they may refuse to cooperate in the imparting of their knowledge. In these cases expert systems cannot be developed.

7. Expert systems use natural language in both questions asked of users and in responses and explanations given. With non-expert users the natural language representations of these statements will use non-technical terms. These are often gradually changing in meaning and connotation over time and unless this semantic shift is taken into account in the maintenance of expert systems they will become outdated in their application.

Expert-augmentor: Though expert systems may not be used for replacing experts, aiding experts is quite another matter. Experts may welcome a system that can act as an independent second opinion on their decision. Again, experts may need prompting when considering unusual paths of reasoning. The comprehensive searches of an expert system will not miss these. It is also much easier to design an effective expert system for use by experts, as technical jargon with precise meaning can be used in questions and explanations.

A cost-effective front-end adviser: A small company approaching a bank for a business loan may not have a clear idea of what sorts of information the bank will require in order to assess the acceptability of the loan. It would save a journey to the bank (and therefore company cost and bank cost) if an expert system provided advice on the kinds of information that needed to be submitted. This is one type of front-end advice that expert systems can be used for – the provision of advice on how or whether to approach an expert. There may also be scope for an expert system as a front-end adviser on a computerized information system. Information retrieval from large text databases may be made more efficient and successful in hitting the search targets if intelligent advice for non-specialists is given on how best to frame the search queries. This may be provided by a front-end expert system.

Marginal improvement on volume or large transactions: This is a measurable, though not easily predictable benefit that will occur when a small increase in performance yields large absolute financial returns. For example, there is a large and costly commercial expert system (the cost to purchase is around $1m) for assessing freight and marine underwriting risk. A marginal improvement in this area quickly compensates for the expensive purchase price of the system, because the sums of money involved in underwriting are so large.

As with most investments in computerized systems it is impossible to estimate costs and benefits accurately but this should not prevent serious consideration of the outlays and returns at the start of a project – a rough and ready sketch is better than no idea at all.

17.3.2   Stage 2 – selection of an appropriate tool, shell or language

The expert system will need to be developed using standard languages, tools or shells. Just as with a conventional information system where there is the possibility of using an assembly language, a traditional programming language (such as C++), a fourth-generation language tool (such as FOCUS) or an application package, there is scope for choice in building an expert system. The main parameters of choice are:

- the amount of computing expertise needed by the system builders;
- the flexibility of the approach adopted;
- the special requirements of the area under consideration;
- the cost and time-scale involved;
- the size of the final system.

The choice lies between using a general-purpose programming language, an artificial intelligence language or environment, an expert system building tool, or an expert system shell. A combination of these may be used. For example, special procedures may be written in an artificial intelligence language though the major part of the system is designed using tools.

Conventional programming languages: Expert systems may be developed using conventional programming languages. Pascal, C++ and BASIC have all been used for this purpose. The advantages of coding an expert system from one of these languages are:

- Little limitation is imposed on the type of knowledge representation or inference control strategies used.
- There are many trained programmers for the language.
- The languages themselves are highly standardized.
- They run efficiently on existing hardware.

However, it is a time-consuming task. It is also difficult to adopt a prototyping approach as the use of conventional languages is based on the assumption that adequate analysis and design has been carried out to ensure that major rewriting of code is not necessary. With the continued development of specialized language tools and shells it is less likely that this path will be followed in the future.

Artificial intelligence programming languages and environments: A more popular route if maximum flexibility in systems design is required is to develop the expert system using an artificial intelligence language or environment.

LISP and its variants have been developed specifically to meet the structures encountered in AI programming. Processing lists and list structures are an important feature of this language. All data structures are represented as lists of one form or another.

PROLOG is a language based around the first-order predicate calculus. Developed in London and Marseilles it has come into prominence with its adoption as the AI language of the Japanese fifth-generation computers. It is more than a programming language in the conventional sense. It not only enables specification of facts in a predicate-based language but also contains within it backtracking inference procedures that establish whether further facts may be derived from a given set. The important variation, PARLOG, allows parallel processing in a PROLOG-type language.

POPLOG combines features of LISP, PROLOG and another language, POP-II. It is a further movement along the spectrum away from languages towards environments.

The advantages of using an AI language over a conventional language such as PASCAL or C++ are:

- The constructs in the language are particularly applicable to AI and therefore expert systems.
- Project development time is reduced.
- Maximum flexibility in the type of systems developed is retained.

However, the expense of specialized hardware and a lack of qualified programmers have held back the use of these languages. This is likely to change as artificial intelligence in business becomes commonplace in the first decade of the 21st century.

Expert system tools: Developing an expert system using an AI language is a costly and lengthy project. Expert systems generally follow the knowledge representation techniques, inference principles and control strategies explained in Chapter 16, so it is possible to use software tools that speed up and simplify the process of design. Flexibility may be sacrificed as the particular tool chosen may commit the expert systems developer to a narrow range of representation forms. The advantage is that it may be simple enough for use by personnel whose basic training does not lie in the area of programming. Other tools may be more flexible and consequently require more training to use. These tools will provide sophisticated graphics facilities to aid in the development process. The following discussion gives some idea of the facilities offered by a more flexible tool.

Knowledge Engineering Environment (KEE) is a sophisticated tool that allows maximum flexibility in design. It incorporates the use of frames with **if–then** rules and allows multiple objects and extensive inheritance (these terms are explained in Chapter 16). The builder has a high degree of management over the inference and control used by the end-product system. Extensive graphics and window facilities are used to aid the system builder. The cost of the tool is around $60,000 and it is suitable for building large systems.

The larger, more sophisticated tools are best used with expensive, dedicated hardware such as that marketed by XEROX or SYMBOLICS. This imposes a cost constraint on the final use of the system and it is now not uncommon, after having developed a system on one of the machines, to recast it in an expert system shell to run on a different target machine, for instance on a DEC VAX or a PC. The use of expert system tools is likely to increase during the next few years.

Expert system shells: Shells are effectively expert systems without their knowledge base. They are restrictive in that only limited control is available to the builder over inference strategies and knowledge representation forms. Shells are designed so that expert systems can be built quickly and cheaply (once the shell has been purchased). Shells often contain very friendly builder interfaces that allow interactive entry of rules in quasi-English with key words such as 'if' and 'not' being picked up by syntax checkers, which then impose the correct logical structure on the rules. The use of microcomputer-based shells has led to the proliferation of small expert systems in the UK. In the USA and Europe the trend has been towards larger shells or tools, leading to the development of larger expert systems. Shells may cost from as little as £50 to many thousands of pounds. Shells allow the quick development of limited systems. Some shells (for example CRYSTAL) are specifically designed to be used by personnel with no formal training or extensive experience in computing. It is intended that the expert or someone familiar with the necessary expertise be the builder of the system. This cuts out the 'middleman' – the knowledge engineer. It is likely that the use of shells will continue as an important aid to building

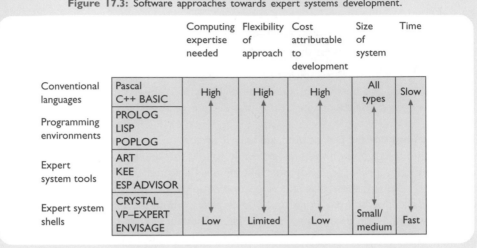

Figure 17.3: Software approaches towards expert systems development.

		Computing expertise needed	Flexibility of approach	Cost attributable to development	Size of system	Time
Conventional languages	Pascal C++ BASIC	High	High	High	All types	Slow
Programming environments	PROLOG LISP POPLOG					
Expert system tools	ART KEE ESP ADVISOR					
Expert system shells	CRYSTAL VP–EXPERT ENVISAGE	Low	Limited	Low	Small/ medium	Fast

small expert systems though because of the limitations imposed by the structure of the shell it is unlikely that they will be used to develop large systems in the future.

Commercial expert systems

One solution to acquiring an expert system is to buy it rather than build it. At present this market is underdeveloped. Two types of strategy are possible. A software house may market a low-price high-volume turnover expert system for personal computers. An example is the DATA PROTECTION ADVISER. The potential market for this was the hundreds of thousands of users of personal computers in the UK that needed to consider registration under the Data Protection Act 1984. This is a complicated Act and procedures for registration are not easy to understand. It was therefore a suitable area for an expert system. Alternatively, a company may build a highly specialized system of great power with an investment of hundreds of thousands or even millions of dollars. These systems are intended to be sold to a handful of customers at an expensive purchase price. Palladian Inc. is an American company involved in this strategy. It is unlikely that this approach to acquiring expert systems will dominate the future markets because, generally, knowledge-based systems are either too specialized to have widespread appeal or they involve specific and closely guarded corporation expertise from which competitors may benefit.

The choice of approach is crucial and will determine the success or otherwise of the project. Figure 17.3 shows, in a simplified form, the ways that the criteria map onto the spectrum from conventional languages to expert system shells.

The role of the knowledge engineer in analysis and design

In the development of large expert systems the knowledge engineer plays a major role. Who is this person and what role does he or she play?

The knowledge engineer will generally, though not necessarily, be a computer professional such as a systems analyst. He or she will be acquainted with the range of expert systems tools, shells and languages available commercially, their particular strength and weaknesses, and with areas for which each is most suitable. In reality, the knowledge engineer will be most familiar with a small selection of tools or shells and will tend to restrict his or her view of knowledge engineering to these.

It is the responsibility of the knowledge engineer to assess and identify the areas of knowledge and tasks that are suitable for an expert systems project. He or she will also recommend the most appropriate tool or shell.

The least technical and most difficult task for the knowledge engineer is 'extracting' or 'eliciting' the knowledge and patterns of reasoning from the expert. It may be helpful to adopt one of the knowledge elicitation techniques explained in Section 17.3.6.

Prior to finally encoding the area of expertise in a system it is usual for the knowledge engineer to produce an intermediate representation of the knowledge. One of the advantages of structured tools, such as data flow diagrams, in traditional information systems analysis and design is that the diagram can be used as a focal point for discussion between participants; it is clear, unambiguous and at the right level of detail to emphasize the important features of the data flows between processes. An intermediate representation of knowledge performs much the same function. Often diagrammatic, it conveys an external representation of knowledge that can be considered, discussed and altered by the engineer or expert. With large projects, several engineers and experts may be involved. The role of intermediate representation is then even more crucial to the successful development of the expert system. Unfortunately, this is one area where more research needs to be carried out. Too often intermediate representations are little more than the result of *ad hoc* additions to the kind of hierarchy diagram shown in Figure 16.5 in Chapter 16. Until standard techniques are designed this will be a continuing weakness in expert systems analysis and design.

The next stage for the knowledge engineer is to build a prototype for part of the knowledge domain. Here, shells and tools can act to aid quick provision of a rough-and-ready system. The purpose of the prototype is to give the expert, user and management some idea as to how the final system will look. It is common for those who are unfamiliar with artificial intelligence in business to have unrealistically high expectations of what can be achieved. The prototype provides the knowledge engineer with important feedback on any weaknesses involved in the approach and indicates how technical performance may be improved in the final system.

The final system is developed by the knowledge engineer and, in conjunction with the expert, the system is evaluated against previously agreed performance criteria. The role of the knowledge engineer is summarized in Figure 17.4.

17.3.3 Stage 3 – building a prototype

A prototype is a small working version of the final system. It will model only some of the knowledge domain. It is used for:

1. checking and testing assumptions about the way knowledge and inference are to be represented;
2. establishing an adequate knowledge elicitation strategy between the knowledge engineer and the expert;
3. provision of a demonstration model that can be assessed and commented on by all those who are involved in the project.

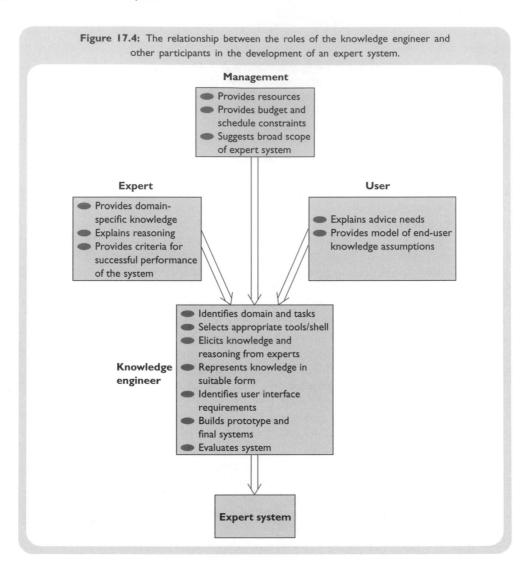

Figure 17.4: The relationship between the roles of the knowledge engineer and other participants in the development of an expert system.

Knowledge elicitation

Although some expert systems are derived from source documentation, such as legislation, the vast majority of expert systems rely, partly at least, on expertise that is resident in the mind of an expert(s). It shows itself in behavioural terms only when required to perform a task. This expertise needs to be extracted and displayed in a form suitable for incorporating into a computerized system. The process is known as **knowledge elicitation**.

The systems analyst relies heavily on interviewing personnel within an existing system in order to identify key tasks, information flows, data stores and so on. This interview model has formed the basis of initial attempts at knowledge elicitation. However, even if the expert is willing to spend the considerable time and effort with the knowledge engineer in order to part with the expertise there are major obstacles to a smooth, orderly and exhaustive elicitation stage.

1. Many areas of expertise are highly technical, and unless the knowledge engineer is familiar with the area, he or she will have great difficulty in understanding and representing it correctly.

2. A knowledge engineer may attempt to become familiar with the domain by text-book research. Unfortunately, it is often the non-textbook heuristic approaches taken by experts, based on experience, that make their expertise so valuable. A little learning on the part of the knowledge engineer may be a dangerous thing. It can force the expert into the position of providing 'textbook' answers to questions asked from a textbook background.

3. An expert's time is precious and knowledge elicitation is a lengthy task.

4. The expert may be a competent practitioner but may not be used to verbal discussion of the domain area in the manner required for knowledge engineering.

5. The chosen tool may affect the way that the engineer attempts to elicit the expertise. The expert, though, may not represent the knowledge internally in the form that the engineer is attempting to extract it. This provides difficulty and the expert may need to rethink the domain. This can, though, be an instructive educational process for the expert. It forces valuable systematization and the adoption of new perspectives on the domain.

6. There is a temptation on the part of the expert to wish to discuss the more unusual and difficult areas that he or she deals with, whereas the primary purpose of the knowledge engineer is to concentrate on the central and often more mundane cases.

These problems have prompted the development of a number of knowledge elicitation techniques that go beyond the traditional interview.

Forward scenario simulation: This is rather like a structured interview in which the expert is given a series of hypothetical case-study problems and asked how to solve them. The expert is required to explain what facts are being considered and how they are being treated, as the problem is solved. The major advantage of this approach is that by a judicious selection of problems by, for example, another expert or even the expert subject of the elicitation process, the engineer can ensure a comprehensive coverage of the central types of problem in the domain area.

It is usual to conduct the interview on each problem in two stages:

1. Ask the interviewee to outline the task to be accomplished in solving the problem, including a description of the possible outcomes, variables and rules used.

2. Establish how general and how specific each of the discovered rules are.

Typical questions from the knowledge engineer might be:

- When do you do (such-and-such)?
- Why do you do (such-and-such)?
- Under what circumstances would this rule apply?
- Under what circumstances would this rule not apply?
- How did you establish (such-and-such)?

Protocol analysis: In protocol analysis the knowledge engineer observes and probably audio/video tapes the expert in the course of performing tasks. These records are searched for key variables, rules and the order of approach taken during problem solving. This has one advantage over the structured interview in that the expert is not required to give explanations and justifications for every decision. The pressure that is present during the interview may generate spurious responses – experts do not like to say 'I just don't know why I did that' or 'It was no more than a guess'. However, unless all major types of case come up, protocol analysis techniques will not lead to a complete knowledge elicitation.

Goal decomposition: This is a set of techniques most suitable where the knowledge domain is structured in a hierarchy. The techniques derive from use in psychology. 'Laddered Grid' and '20 Questions' are two examples of goal decomposition. In the latter, the expert is confronted with an interviewer who has a set of hypothetical problems. The expert is provided with no initial information, and by a series of questions attempts to establish as much as possible about the problem. The types of question asked and the order in which they are put gives the knowledge engineer valuable insights into the way that the expert perceives the structure of the knowledge domain. This technique can only be used by an engineer with some familiarity with the domain.

Multi-dimensional techniques: These techniques provide some kind of map as to how the elements in a knowledge domain are put together where there are complex interactions. Many of these techniques also derive from the discipline of psychology, where they are used to build a model of the way that a person perceives the world. The techniques often involve determining ways in which two things are alike and different from a third. If this is repeated many times with different objects a set of differentiating concepts that are important to the expert is established. Techniques such as repertory grid, factor analysis and multidimensional scaling fall into this category. Details of these may be obtained from the references at the end of this chapter.

Automated elicitation and acquisition: In the future, expert systems may be able to abstract general principles and rules applicable to knowledge domains directly from sets of given examples. The current state of the art is many years behind such developments. However, primitive **induction** techniques are already used for inferring straightforward rules governing a domain. Some expert system shells may have this induction facility, the aim being to bypass much of the work of the knowledge engineer and rapidly produce working expert systems. These shells typically work by requiring the expert (or some person) to select key attributes that are applicable to a task and then input a large number of instances of the task while giving the associated values of attributes and outcomes. The automated induction module of the shell is called up and a set of rules is inferred. There are standard algorithms for this. An example is given in Figure 17.5. Here it is intended to determine the rules governing the selection of candidates for a post. Nine previous cases and their decisions lead to the four rules shown in the figure being inferred.

These systems will only be useful when theoretical issues surrounding induction have found algorithmic solutions. In particular:

Figure 17.5: An automatic induction to provide a set of rules governing job selection.

CASE	ATTRIBUTES			DECISION
	DEGREE CLASS	*QUALIFICATION*	*EXPERIENCE*	
1	1	YES	1 YEAR	OFFER
2	3	YES	2 YEAR	REJECT
3	2	YES	2 YEAR	OFFER
4	1	YES	*	OFFER
5	2	YES	2 YEAR	OFFER
6	*	NO	*	REJECT
7	2	YES	3 YEAR	OFFER
8	3	NO	3 YEAR	REJECT
9	3	*	*	REJECT

(Note * = Unknown)

Rules

IF *DEGREE CLASS* = 1 **AND** *QUALIFIED*
  THEN *OFFER*

IF *DEGREE CLASS* = 2 **AND** *QUALIFIED*
    AND (*EXPERIENCE* = '3 YEAR' **OR** *EXPERIENCE* = '2 YEAR')
  THEN *OFFER*

IF *DEGREE CLASS* = 3 **THEN** *REJECT*

IF NOT *QUALIFIED* **THEN** *REJECT*

● How can an automated system decide upon the relevant attributes that are to be used in the induction, having been given a number of cases?

● How can the system derive probabilistic rules governing attributes that take real-number values?

● How can the system identify and ignore freak cases without upsetting the existing system of rules?

Prototype construction

It would be an inaccurate oversimplification to suggest that the knowledge necessary for the prototype is obtained by the knowledge engineer and then the prototype is built. Rather, prototype construction and knowledge elicitation proceed hand in hand. Of course some elicitation is necessary prior to starting the construction of the prototype but development is interleaved from that stage onwards.

Interviews, forward scenario simulation and protocol analysis are the most popular initial techniques, and once the knowledge engineer has gained an understanding of the way that the expert handles a case-study problem the prototype construction soon begins.

It is better to start the prototype construction early and resist the temptation to postpone building until more knowledge on a greater number of cases has been collected. This latter approach soon escalates into an attempt to capture the entire knowledge area on paper prior to expert systems design on the computer.

It is important that the engineer identifies the major aspects of the problem early on as this will greatly influence the design of the prototype. During the prototyping stage the knowledge engineer should restrict the sphere of interest to a small number of core-case problems that are representative of the expert's work. These cases should be different enough to reveal different perspectives on the expert's practice.

As well as clearly distinguishing knowledge from inferencing, the knowledge engineer should pay particular attention to knowledge brought by the expert to the task area that is not domain specific. These are aspects of outside or general knowledge that are necessary to carry out the task. These aspects can and often must be assumed of the end user of the system. It is therefore important that the knowledge engineer has a clear model of the end user at the outset. It is not just a question of tailoring the user interface at a later stage. Unless the target user has the necessary knowledge to complement that provided by the expert system the system will not be effective in meeting its aims. Different types of end user will have different levels of knowledge. If the system is being built for an expert as an end user (expert system as expert augmentor) then clearly less extra general knowledge needs to be built into the expert system than if the target user is a lay person.

The knowledge engineer pays little attention at this stage to matters of memory, space and efficiency. If this is a key constraint, and often it is not, then the restructuring or possibly recoding of the system in another language can be achieved later.

Prototype assessment

The prototype can be checked by using it on a number of new core cases or problems. The knowledge engineer and expert assess the way that the prototype handles these. They determine whether the general strategy taken towards representation of the knowledge area and the inference control is adequate. If not, then a second prototype is built using an adjusted representation. It may be necessary at this stage to reconsider the development tool or shell chosen for the project. The engineer is also concerned that the knowledge is structured in a manner suitable for the task area. Prototype iteration can occur several times, though major changes should not occur in each iteration.

The prototype also fulfils another function. It may be the first time that the expert has seen and used a knowledge-based system. At a later stage the final system will need fine tuning by the expert and this introduction to a prototype provides an invaluable early warning of what is to be expected.

The prototype also serves the purpose of ensuring commitment by all those involved – the potential of the final system can be seen in the prototype. A working model, though rough and ready, is worth a thousand glib promises of what is to come.

A successful prototype will also act as the basis on which the engineer can put forward a development plan for the final system. As well as a schedule for the times at which various stages of the development will be completed a more detailed budget plan can be provided at this stage. The target knowledge area and task are also more precisely defined. Sometimes it becomes clear that the initial intentions were over-enthusiastic and that the aims of the final system need to be tailored or narrowed in some way.

Any system needs to be evaluated and at the end of the prototype stage a set of performance criteria are set.

17.3.4 Stage 4 – development of the final system

A decision has to be made immediately this stage is entered. One school of thought argues that the prototype should be thrown away – the lessons have been learned and the prototype was never intended to be perfect anyway. The new system is developed from the beginning using the experience gained from prototyping. The second school of thought sees the prototype as an initial development of part of the system; to discard it is to waste valuable time.

Whichever approach is taken the process of knowledge elicitation and acquisition continues. The system is developed in breadth (knowledge areas outside the prototype are brought in) and depth (existing rules are extended). Development tools and shells assist in these tasks.

From the earliest stages of the project a clear model of the intended users and their interests is employed. This is one of the determinants of the scope of the knowledge base. Although considered in Section 17.3.7 it is during this stage that emphasis is given to detailed design of the user interface. This is not just a matter of ensuring that inappropriate technical jargon does not appear on the screen nor is it merely determining that questions asked are at the right level of ignorance. As already mentioned, in performing a task an expert will be conscious of using explicit knowledge or at least knowledge that can be made explicit. Also, there will be much implicit knowledge used. The able knowledge engineer will be skilled in realizing at what points implicit knowledge is employed and will render this explicit. Some of this will be domain-specific and needs to be incorporated in the final system. The remainder can be assumed to be brought to the consultation with the final expert system by the end user. It is crucial that the knowledge engineer constantly maintains a picture of the knowledge that can be assumed of the end user so that decisions can be made as to what knowledge must be built into the system and what can be left out. This is shown diagrammatically in Figure 17.6. Figure (a) is an illustration of an incorrect and naive approach to the process. Figure (b) stresses the need for the engineer to be aware of the end user as much as the expert when building the system.

There is a related difficulty. Knowledge engineers can become expert in the domain area during the development process. They themselves can fall foul of the tacit knowledge trap.

During the building of the final system the expert will be involved in fine tuning of the knowledge base. The skills gained in considering the prototype will be of valuable use to the expert at this point. Particular rules may be refined and exception clauses added. The knowledge base can be tested against new cases and necessary adjustments made.

Systems evaluation

The attempted evaluation of an expert system leads to problems over and above those normally associated with the evaluation of a traditional information system. Certain technical features can be easily assessed, such as response rates and main-memory usage, but the success of the system as an expert system is more difficult to measure.

Part of the problem lies with the fact that the area of human expert evaluation is fraught with difficulties and these are transferred to the systems for which they are models. Certain approaches have been adopted:

1. The system is evaluated by a series of test cases (either structured or random). The performance of the system may then be compared with a control set consisting of responses to these cases provided by specialists. The problem here is that experts often genuinely differ (if they did not, much civil litigation would be carried out under false pretences!). It is therefore no automatic adverse reflection on the system if it, too, differs.

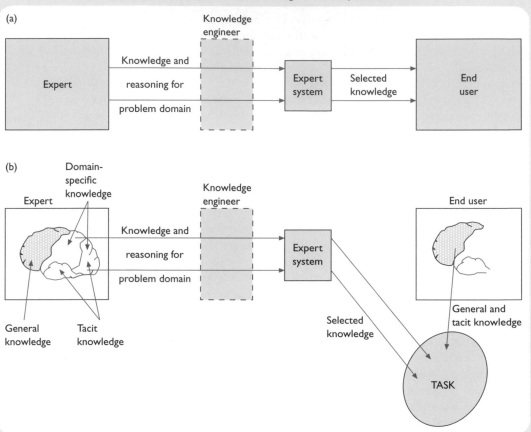

Figure 17.6: (a) A naive representation of knowledge transfer. (b) A less naive version of the knowledge transferred and the knowledge added to perform a task.

2. The evaluation of the system is carried out as a test against reality. Real problems for which there are known analyses are put into the system. If it comes up with the right answers it succeeds, otherwise it fails. Difficulties occur if the system involves giving probabilistic recommendations. The system's success rate may also be compared with human rates.

3. More informal tests involve a human expert (not the person involved in building the system) interrogating the knowledge base and assessing the responses. This is more subjective and can be looked down upon because of its 'non-scientific' nature. This may be a valid point but it also tells against methods used to assess human expertise – the job interview and the college viva or written examination. Although these are not 'scientific' in the limited sense of the word they do provide insights of value into assessment and there is no reason why the same attitude should not be adopted towards the evaluation of expert systems.

One of the main problems associated with evaluation is the large number of logical paths that may be taken by the system. Only a fraction of these can be tested. The position is further complicated if the system uses reasoning under uncertainty. Ultimately, this limitation can only be overcome by following sound development techniques during expert systems construction. Paying particular attention to hierarchical and modular development is helpful.

The areas to which attention is drawn by the evaluation are these:

- Is the system delivering the right advice for the right reasons?
- Is the system attuned to the knowledge level of the end users in terms of both the level of knowledge required of the user and the advice given?
- Is it designed in such a way that individual changes may be made to the system without unpredictable side-effects?
- Is it easy for users to operate?
- Are specific performance criteria achieved?

With respect to the last point, as an example, an advice system might be developed for assisting students in choosing the most suitable course on entry into higher education. A domain-specific performance criterion might be that the numbers involved in course changes in the first six months should drop by 25% as compared with a sample group not using the system. Lessons will be learned from the evaluation, which will assist in the next phase of ongoing use and maintenance.

It is not uncommon once a system has been built and successfully evaluated to transfer it to another programming language or shell for actual use. No improvements are intended except those concerned with technical performance. For instance, a system written in LISP may be recoded in C++ or Pascal to meet efficient processing requirements on conventional computing hardware, or an expert system developed using a tool such as ART on dedicated hardware may be slotted into a simple shell for distribution to company PCs.

17.3.5 Stage 5 – ongoing use and maintenance

No expert should be content with his or her level of expertise. Indeed, it is considered to be one of the important characteristics of an expert that they should be able to develop their band of expertise by changing their implicit, resident knowledge and the rules for applying this in a changing environment. Examples are lawyers who change their understanding of the law in the light of new legislation or auditors who change their approach as a result of experience.

Similarly, knowledge systems are refined. This may take a number of forms:

- The knowledge base may be extended to bring in areas not previously covered by the system.
- The existing knowledge may be in need of change as a result of perceived errors.
- The knowledge base may need to change because the human expert's heuristic rules change.
- Changes in formal rules such as the alteration in a company's procedures, tax legislation or professional requirements lead to knowledge-base changes.

These forms of expanding – correcting errors, developing with external change – must always be accompanied by consideration of the effects of changes of the system on end users.

Systems only tend to be maintained if they are of proven value from the outset. For instance, DEC's XCON for configuring VAX computers has a full-time team of knowledge engineers and programmers associated with it.

17.4 Large and small systems

The development of a large expert system differs from that of a small system in a number of ways. As well as the number and complexity of rules being greater in a larger system, the modes of knowledge representation used are likely to be more varied and sophisticated and will include a range of the techniques covered in Chapter 16. Similarly, small systems will commonly use straightforward control strategies involving forward and backward chaining and the use of demons (devices to pass control in unusual situations from execution of one part of the knowledge base to the execution of some other section), whereas large systems may have more complex strategies for searching (and reducing the area of search) in order to cope with the large number of rules.

Another area of difference is in the amount of graphics presented to the user. It is common for many systems to allow users to open windows (view different parts of the system on the screen at the same time) but it is only in larger systems that intricate high-resolution diagrams can be provided with selections by pointers controlled by a mouse or some other device.

Nowadays many systems also have features that allow the expert system to interact with a conventional database or spreadsheet model. These are now so common that the major microcomputer-based expert system shells have facilities to interact with Excel worksheets and database package databases or any files stored in standard formats (such as SYLK, WKS, XLS or DIF).

Larger systems may be mainframe based with multiaccess facilities. The levels of monetary investment in larger systems would often be unjustifiable unless the facility for multiuser access was present.

The area in which most difference between large and small systems is noticeable is their development. Typically, a small system may be built by a single knowledge engineer in union with an expert. It is almost certain that an expert system shell will be used. Modern shells vary in the amount of understanding required of the expert system builder, and in some areas the domain may be so clear cut and the facilities provided by the shell so straightforward to use that the services of the knowledge engineer may be dispensed with altogether. It is unlikely that a clear distinction will be drawn between the prototyping stage and the development of the final system. Often the area is so small that to develop a prototype for a section of it is not feasible. Rather, what happens is that a system is built through an iterative process of refinement, with the user interface being attended to at the latter stages. The close interaction of the expert and the engineer makes this relatively unplanned approach possible.

With larger systems the situation is different. There may be several experts involved with different areas of expertise. For example, a large expert system might be concerned with the analysis of the financial health of a company. This may be undertaken from several perspectives depending on the interests of the advice seeker. For instance, auditors, potential creditors, bankers, or potential investors may all be seeking differing points of view. Several experts will be sought to cover these areas as no one individual can be expected to have an overall knowledge of the entire domain. There will also be a number of knowledge engineers to cope with the elicitation and design. Already it should be clear that problems arising from lack of communication and integration can arise unless adequate planning and channels for information interchange are arranged. It is probable that an expert system shell will not solely be used and it is quite likely that expert system building tools will be employed and/or special routines written in either AI programming languages or conventional third-generation languages. In this case programmers will be involved and specifications designed and testing established. The need for an adequate intermediate representation of the knowledge (for example, a paper-based diagrammatic approach) becomes more pressing. The point being made here is that large systems require more staff, which in its turn leads to greater communication and planning problems. The prototyping stage will be much more clearly defined than in the development of a smaller system. An area(s) will be selected and formal assessment of the prototype carried out according to agreed criteria. The final systems development will be planned in detail and responsibilities, deadlines and 'deliverables' will be clearly specified. It is also probable that a clearer idea of the end-user requirements will be modelled. The assessment of the final system is likely to be along more formal lines than with a smaller system.

17.5   A case study – the Bank of America

The application selected for the case study (based on an article in *Expert Systems User* October 1986 Vol. 2 Number 7) bears many of the hallmarks of the development of a smaller system. Banking and finance are prime areas for investment in expert systems projects although many of these have not, as yet, come to fruition and the area is one naturally associated with secrecy and confidentiality.

The UK branch of the Bank of America acts as a 'wholesale' bank dealing only with other banks and companies. It has developed a small expert system dealing with the treatment of letters of credit. When a UK company makes an agreement to export or import goods from another country certain documents must be prepared and checked. These documents pass between the UK company, its bank, the overseas company, its bank and sometimes other intermediary banks and agencies as well. This documentation is often quite extensive and may occupy a file more than one inch thick. The letters of credit contained need to be checked for completeness, accuracy, authenticity, correct cross-referencing and so on. It is estimated that Britain loses in excess of £50 million per year through refused payments as a result of incorrect paperwork in this area. The checking of the letters, although mechanical, requires a great deal of obscure knowledge. The Bank of America requires that its employees have at least ten years' experience before allowing them to authorize payments of substantial sums of money involved in overseas trade. It takes up to two years to train junior clerks.

This seemed suitable as an expert system domain as the task was clear cut, the expertise was at least worth archiving if not developing as a system for expert assistance, and there was a commitment from those involved, including the Bank's head of marketing and development, for cash management and electronic banking services in the UK. Originally it was intended that the domain would cover the entire set of documents relevant to granting letters of credit and it was hoped that a system could be designed that would detect all the shortcomings in the supporting documentation. It soon became clear that this area was too large, at least for the Bank's first attempt to build an expert system, and so the domain was pruned by restricting the system to the seven most important documents. These included the invoice, certificate of origin, insurance certificate, drafts and the transport documents.

It was decided to use an expert systems shell (Expert Edge) together with an experienced knowledge engineer and one expert – the head of documentary services at the bank. Expert Edge is a backward-chaining PC shell written in C. It took about six weeks of knowledge elicitation and six weeks of testing to arrive at a working system. There were 270 rules, perhaps a large number to count as a small system.

The knowledge elicitation began by developing a structure similar to a semantic network though in the form of a tree (called a **name tree**). This had a root called 'discrepancy' with branches for each of the documents such as the transport document, invoice and so on. Each of these also had branches. For instance, 'transport document' had branches called 'signature', 'endorsement', and 'quantities' and others. The name tree is part of the knowledge base and is referred to during a consultation. The rules are either added via standard word processed text in the knowledge representation language of the shell or are added through a facility of Expert Edge that prompts users for the various parts of a rule. This is simpler for 'uneducated' users as it avoids the necessity to master the syntax of the knowledge representation language.

A number of problems were encountered in development. First, there was a shortage of expert time available. This was particularly noticeable in the testing stage of the system and it was difficult to choose a comprehensive set of test examples. Second, there was a trade-off concerned with the use of technical terms. These terms are preferable as they have a precise meaning and they often aid conciseness in the final system. Unfortunately, however, their use makes the system less comprehensible to experienced users.

This is also connected with a third problem area. It was initially intended that the system should be used as a training medium for the Bank's personnel and that it should be sold to outside import/export companies. Both of these aims required the use of different questions and recommendations depending on the nature of the end user. For instance, a particular discrepancy should lead to a recommendation that the Bank should refuse payment if the bank was using the system, but lead to the recommendation that the export/import company should correct the inaccurate documentation if it is using the system. Much of the knowledge would be most naturally represented in tabular form but the particular expert system shell had no facility for this although interfacing with dBASE was possible.

A consultation with the system typically takes about 20 minutes and involves the system interrogating the user to obtain answers to yes/no, numeric, or menu selection questions. There are no questions that require a text response. Complex calculations may be performed by the system during a consultation. Whenever a rule governing the correct use of documentation is found to be infringed an error message is displayed on the screen, normally detailing the type of error found and a recommended course of action. The system allows for **WHY** questions and answers them by proceeding up the rule trees of dependent rules as far as the user wishes. Most trees are broad and shallow reflecting the nature of the task – carrying out checks over a wide range of areas where each check does not exhibit much depth. As was explained earlier the system only covers the seven most important documents. What happens if other documentation is involved? This is handled by the system asking the question as to whether the letters of credit require other documents. If the answer is 'yes' then the user is directed to a senior officer.

The system is now used for training purposes and it is estimated that the previous training period of one and a half to two years can be reduced to about two weeks with the system – a substantial saving. The system always performs reliably and makes the user think about the task in a systematic way. It is simple to use; even the typist is using it. However, it is not being used as a live system. There are two reasons. First, the system is slower than the human being. The need to input data at the keyboard means that the time taken in a consultation is (slightly) longer than the average time taken for a manual check of the documentation. Second, and more importantly, the system has not, as yet, passed the test of confidence. Whether it does so subsequently depends on its performance in continued future usage. The Bank has been favourably impressed by its first expert system development and intends to continue with other developments if suitable domains are found. The main lessons learned by the participants in the process seem to be that it is necessary to establish that the chosen area is representable as a set rules prior to the start of the project, that time should be made clearly available by the expert, and that the project should proceed with an interactive prototyping approach combined with clear checkpoints along the development trail.

Summary

In common with other computer projects, well-planned and well-executed development stages will lead to expert systems that perform to the standards required of them. Unlike traditional data processing and information systems though, there has been little time to evolve the clearly documented and reliable methodologies that characterize the development of traditional systems projects. There is general, though by no means universal, agreement that prototyping offers a useful approach.

One of the key factors leading to a successful expert system is the choice of problem domain within which to work. An area that is rule-based and clearly defined, together with the presence of experts willing to aid in the development process, offers the opportunity to benefit from the production of an expert system. These benefits depend on the type of system but might include cost savings for consultation, improvements in and standardization of specialists' performances, the archiving of rare skills, the development of a consistent and effective training tool for employees and the possibility of marginal improvements on high-volume or large-value transactions.

The building of the prototype is facilitated by the choice of an appropriate expert system tool, shell or possibly AI language. Knowledge is elicited by the engineer using a combination of techniques. Examples are structured interviewing, protocol analysis, goal decomposition and multi-dimensional scaling. In some cases automated induction on a set of examples may generate appropriate rules. The evaluation of the prototype provides a guide to the knowledge engineer of the success of the representation and inference strategies chosen.

Development of the main system may involve expanding the prototype in both breadth and depth, though often the prototype is forgotten and the final system is built anew using the lessons learnt in prototyping. As well as ▷

concentrating on the problem area and the relevant representation, the knowledge engineer needs a model of the level and types of knowledge assumed of the target user in order to define the scope and content of the knowledge base and the system's user interface. Fine tuning of the developed system is necessary at the final stages of the development.

The evaluation of an expert system leads to problems not encountered in the assessment of traditional information systems. This results from the large number of logical paths generated by the total space of possible cases to which the system may be applied. Further exacerbation is caused by the presence of uncertainty and the recognition that the expert system need not always be right (unless it is going to outperform the human experts from which it was built).

Over the next few years it is likely that expert system methodologies will be developed as AI in business becomes increasingly important.

Exercises

1. What criteria are useful in deciding on the suitability of a problem area for expert systems development and what initial pitfalls should be avoided?

2. Outline the major benefits that can be expected from the representation of an expert's knowledge in an expert system and the use of that system in business.

3. What problems are encountered in performing a cost–benefit estimation for a feasibility study on an expert system?

4. An organization intent on using an expert system has a number of options open to it:
   (a) developing, designing and building the system using a conventional third-generation language such as Pascal or C++;
   (b) developing, designing and building the system using an artificial intelligence programming language such as LISP or PROLOG;
   (c) designing the system with the aid of sophisticated expert system tools;
   (d) using a proprietary expert system shell for the development:
   (e) purchasing an expert system that has already been developed;
   (f) developing a system by some combination of the above approaches.
   Outline factors that will influence the choice between these for the organization.

5. Distinguish between *knowledge elicitation* and *knowledge acquisition.*

6. What problems are involved in extracting knowledge from experts in a form suitable for representation in a rule-based expert system?

7. What is an *intermediate knowledge representation* and why is it important in building expert systems?

8. What is the difference between forward scenario simulation and interviewing an expert in order to elicit knowledge?

9. Why is a prototyping approach recommended for the development of expert systems?

10. What problems are involved in the evaluation of an expert system?

11. In what respects does building a large expert system differ from the development of a small system?

12. Complex knowledge domains require large expert systems. What criteria should be used to decide on the complexity of a knowledge domain?

13. From your college or company work experience select a task that requires knowledge for its successful performance. Assess its suitability in the light of criteria discussed in this chapter for the development of an expert system.

14. How does the analysis and design of expert systems differ from that of traditional information systems?

15. Are the following areas suitable for expert systems development? Justify your answers.
(a) selection of personnel for promotion from middle to upper management
(b) provision of careers guidance to graduates
(c) production scheduling for a firm producing many products
(d) provision of advice on entitlement to State benefits
(e) calculation of employee tax payable by an employer.

16. What areas in business, accounting or finance are suitable for expert systems development? Justify your answer and outline the major benefits that would be expected for each area.

17. Many expert systems are developed by the use of an expert system shell. Explain the advantages and disadvantages of this method.

18. What is *knowledge*?

19. It has been argued that only those expert and experienced in knowledge engineering can reliably build expert systems. Is it possible that this expertise may itself become the subject of an expert system?

20. Is it, in principle, possible for an expert system to develop or alter its own rules? If so, in principle how could this be achieved?

Recommended reading

● Choforas D.N. (1987). *Applying Expert Systems in Business.* McGraw-Hill
This is a readable text that sets expert systems within the context of management perspectives, decision support systems and the information centre. The latter half of the book is concerned with expert systems projects.
● Harmon P. and King D. (1988). *Expert Systems.* New York: Wiley
An excellent introduction to all aspects of expert systems and their development. It is aimed at the intelligent reader from business rather than the computer specialist.

- Hart A. (1989). *Knowledge Acquisition for Expert Systems*. London: Kogan Page
  This is one of the few introductory texts that provides the reader with a coverage of knowledge elicitation techniques. Other aspects of expert systems and their development are also tackled. The book is an easily accessible read.
- Midsker L. and Liebwitz J. (1994). *Design and Development of Expert Systems and Neural Networks*. New York: Macmillan
  This text is aimed at those wishing to understand the basics of expert systems and neural networks as well as existing knowledge engineers. The book has a practical perspective to enable simple systems to be developed.

Index